JOURNAL FOR THE STUDY OF THE OLD TESTAMENT SUPPLEMENT SERIES

363

Editors
David J.A. Clines
Philip R. Davies

Executive Editor
Andrew Mein

Editorial Board
Richard J. Coggins, Alan Cooper, J. Cheryl Exum, John Goldingay,
Robert P. Gordon, Norman K. Gottwald, John Jarick,
Andrew D.H. Mayes, Carol Meyers, Patrick D. Miller

EUROPEAN SEMINAR IN HISTORICAL METHODOLOGY

4

Editor
Lester L. Grabbe

Sheffield Academic Press
A Continuum imprint

'Like a Bird in a Cage'

The Invasion of
Sennacherib in 701 BCE

edited by
Lester L. Grabbe

Journal for the Study of the Old Testament
Supplement Series 363

European Seminar in Historical Methodology 4

Published by Sheffield Academic Press Ltd
The Tower Building, 11 York Road, London SE1 7NX
370 Lexington Avenue, New York NY 10017-6550

www.continuumbooks.com

British Library Cataloguing-in-Publication Data

A catalogue record for this book is available from the British Library

Typeset by Sheffield Academic Press
Printed on acid-free paper in Great Britain by Bookcraft Ltd, Midsomer Norton, Bath

ISBN 0-8264-6215-4

CONTENTS

Abbreviations   vii
List of Contributors   xiii

Part I
INTRODUCTION

LESTER L. GRABBE
Introduction   2
    Preliminary Remarks   2
    Archaeology and Sennacherib   3
    Two Centuries of Sennacherib Study: A Survey   20
    Summary of Papers in this Volume   36

Part II
ARTICLES

BOB BECKING
Chronology: A Skeleton without Flesh? Sennacherib's Campaign
as a Case-Study   46

EHUD BEN ZVI
Malleability and its Limits: Sennacherib's Campaign against Judah
as a Case-Study   73

PHILIP R. DAVIES
This Is What Happens...   106

LESTER L. GRABBE
Of Mice and Dead Men: Herodotus 2.141 and Sennacherib's
Campaign in 701 BCE   119

ERNST AXEL KNAUF
701: Sennacherib at the Berezina   141

NIELS PETER LEMCHE
On the Problems of Reconstructing Pre-Hellenistic Israelite
(Palestinian) History   150

WALTER MAYER
Sennacherib's Campaign of 701 BCE: The Assyrian View   168

NADAV NA'AMAN
Updating the Messages: Hezekiah's Second Prophetic Story
(2 Kings 19.9b-35) and the Community of Babylonian Deportees   201

CHRISTOPH UEHLINGER
Clio in a World of Pictures—Another Look at the Lachish
Reliefs from Sennacherib's Southwest Palace at Nineveh   221

Part III
CONCLUSIONS

LESTER L. GRABBE
Reflections on the Discussion   308

Bibliography   324
Index of References   347
Index of Authors   350

ABBREVIATIONS

ÄAT	Ägypten und Altes Testament
AB	Anchor Bible
ABD	David Noel Freedman (ed.), *The Anchor Bible Dictionary* (New York: Doubleday, 1992)
AbrN	*Abr-Nahrain*
ABS	Archaeology and Biblical Studies
AfO	*Archiv für Orientforschung*
AGJU	Arbeiten zur Geschichte des antiken Judentums und des Urchristentums
AHw	Wolfram von Soden, *Akkadisches Handwörterbuch* (Wiesbaden: Harrassowitz, 1959–81)
ALASPM	Abhandlungen zur Literatur Alt-Syrien-Palästinas und Mesopotamiens
ALGHJ	Arbeiten zur Literatur und Geschichte des hellenistischen Judentums
AMI	*Archäologische Mitteilungen aus Iran*
AnBib	Analecta biblica
ANET	James B. Pritchard (ed.), *Ancient Near Eastern Texts Relating to the Old Testament* (Princeton: Princeton University Press, 1950)
AnOr	Analecta orientalia
AOAT	Alter Orient und Altes Testament
AOS	American Oriental Series
ARAB	Daniel David Luckenbill, *Ancient Records of Assyria and Babylonia* (2 vols.; 1926–1927)
ASOR	American Schools of Oriental Research
Ash.	R. Borger, *Die Inschriften Asarhaddons* (AfO Beiheft 9; Osnabrück: Biblio Verlag, 1956)
ATD	Das Alte Testament Deutsch
ATD, E	Das Alte Testament Deutsch, Ergänzungsband
AUSS	*Andrews University Seminary Studies*
BA	*Biblical Archaeologist*
BAIAS	*Bulletin of Anglo-Israel Archaeological Society*
BAL²	R. Borger, *Babylonisch-Assyrische Lesestücke* (Analecta Orientalia, 54; Rome: Pontificium Institutum Biblicum, 2nd edn, 1979)

BARev	*Biblical Archaeology Review*
BASOR	*Bulletin of the American Schools of Oriental Research*
BETL	Bibliotheca ephemeridum theologicarum lovaniensium
BHS	*Biblia hebraica stuttgartensia*
Bib	*Biblica*
BibInt	*Biblical Interpretation: A Journal of Contemporary Approaches*
BibOr	Biblica et orientalia
BIWA	R. Borger, *Beiträge zum Inschriftenwerk Assurbanipals: Die Prismenklassen A, B, C = K, D, E, F, G, H, J und T sowie andere Inschrifen* (Wiesbaden: Harrassowitz, 1966)
BJRL	*Bulletin of the John Rylands University Library of Manchester*
BN	*Biblische Notizen*
BO	*Bibliotheca orientalis*
BWANT	Beiträge zur Wissenschaft vom Alten und Neuen Testament
BZ	*Biblische Zeitschrift*
BZAW	Beihefte zur *ZAW*
CAD	Ignace I. Gelb *et al.* (eds.), *The Assyrian Dictionary of the Oriental Institute of the University of Chicago* (Chicago: Oriental Institute, 1964–)
CAH	Cambridge Ancient History
CBC	Century Bible Commentary
CBQ	*Catholic Biblical Quarterly*
CBQMS	*Catholic Biblical Quarterly*, Monograph Series
CHANE	Culture and History of the Ancient Near East
ConBOT	Coniectanea biblica, Old Testament
CRBS	*Currents in Research: Biblical Studies*
DDD	K. van der Toorn, B. Becking and P.W. van der Horst (eds.), *Dictionary of Deities and Demons in the Bible* (Leiden: E.J. Brill, 2nd edn, 1999)
EA	J.A. Knudtzon, *Die El-Amarna Tafeln* (2 vols.; VAB, 2 Berlin: Hinrichs, 1908–15)
EBib	Etudes bibliques
EHAT	Exegetisches Handbuch zum Alten Testament
EI	*Eretz-Israel*
ESHM	European Seminar in Historical Methodology
ET	English translation
FAT	Forschungen zum Alten Testament
FOTL	The Forms of the Old Testament Literature
FRLANT	Forschungen zur Religion und Literatur des Alten und Neuen Testaments
FS	Festschrift
GM	*Göttinger Miszellen*
HAT	Handbuch zum Alten Testament
HBT	*Horizons in Biblical Theology*

HSM	Harvard Semitic Monographs
HdA	Handbuch der Archäologie
HdO	Handbuch der Orientalistik
HSS	Harvard Semitic Studies
HTR	*Harvard Theological Review*
HUCA	*Hebrew Union College Annual*
ICC	International Critical Commentary
ICC (Layard)	A. Layard, *The Inscriptions in the Cuneiform Character from Assyrian Monuments* (London: J. Murray, 1851)
IDB	George Arthur Buttrick (ed.), *The Interpreter's Dictionary of the Bible* (4 vols.; Nashville: Abingdon Press, 1962)
IDBSup	*IDB*, Supplementary Volume
IEJ	*Israel Exploration Journal*
JANESCU	*Journal of the Ancient Near Eastern Society of Columbia University*
JAOS	*Journal of the American Oriental Society*
JARCE	*Journal of the American Research Center in Egypt*
JBL	*Journal of Biblical Literature*
JCS	*Journal of Cuneiform Studies*
JDDS	Jian Dao Dissertation Series
JNES	*Journal of Near Eastern Studies*
JNSL	*Journal of Northwest Semitic Languages*
JQR	*Jewish Quarterly Review*
JSOT	*Journal for the Study of the Old Testament*
JSOTSup	*Journal for the Study of the Old Testament*, Supplement Series
JSS	*Journal of Semitic Studies*
JTS	*Journal of Theological Studies*
KAI	H. Donner and W. Röllig, *Kanaanäische und aramäische Inschriften* (3 vols.; Wiesbaden: Harrassowitz, 1962–64)
MDOG	Mitteilungen der deutschen Orient-Gesellschaft
KAT	Kommentar zum Alten Testament
MT	Masoretic text
NABU	*Notes Assyriologiques brèves et utiles*
NCB	New Century Bible
NEAEHL	Ephraim Stern (ed.), *New Encyclopedia of Archaeological Excavations in the Holy Land* (1992)
NEASB	*Near Eastern Archaeological Society Bulletin*
NJPS	New Jewish Publication Society translation of the Hebrew Bible.
OAC	Orientis Antiqui Collectio
OBO	Orbis biblicus et orientalis
OIP	D.D. Luckenbill, *The Annals of Sennacherib* (OIP, 2; Chicago: University of Chicago Press, 1924)
Or	*Orientalia*

OTL	Old Testament Library
OTS	*Oudtestamentische Studiën*
PAPS	Proceedings of the American Philosophical Society
PEQ	*Palestine Exploration Quarterly*
PIASH	Proceedings of the Israel Academy of Sciences and Humanities
R	H. Rawlinson, *The Cuneiform Inscriptions of Western Asia* (London: J. Murray, 1861–1909)
RA	*Revue d'assyriologie et d'archéologie orientale*
RB	*Revue biblique*
RlA	*Reallexikon der Assyrologie*
RIMA	Royal Inscriptions of Mesopotamia, Assyrian Periods
SAAB	*State Archives of Assyria Bulletin*
SAAS	State Archives of Assyria Studies
SANE	Studies on the Ancient Near East
SBL	Society of Biblical Literature
SBLASP	SBL Abstracts and Seminar Papers
SBLBMI	SBL Bible and its Modern Interpreters
SBLDS	SBL Dissertation Series
SBLMS	SBL Monograph Series
SBLSBS	SBL Sources for Biblical Study
SBLSCS	SBL Septuagint and Cognate Studies
SBLTT	SBL Texts and Translations
SBT	Studies in Biblical Theology
ScrH	*Scripta Hierosolymata*
Sg. 8	F. Thureau Dangin, *Une relation de la huitième campagne de Sargon* (TCL, 3; Paris, 1912); additional fragments: *Keilschrift-texte aus Assur* (1922), II, 141; AfO 12 (1937–38), pp. 141-48; W. Mayer, MDOG 115, pp. 65-132
SHANE	Studies in the History of the Ancient Near East
SHCANE	Studies in the History and Culture of the Ancient Near East
SJOT	*Scandinavian Journal of the Old Testament*
TA	*Tel Aviv*
TCS	Text from Cuneiform Studies
ThW	Theologische Wissenschaft
TT	Texts and Translations
TUAT	*Texte aus der Umwelt des Alten Testaments*
TZ	*Theologische Zeitschrift*
UF	*Ugarit-Forschungen*
VAB	Vorderasiatische Bibliothek
VT	*Vetus Testamentum*
VTSup	*Vetus Testamentum*, Supplements
WMANT	Wissenschaftliche Monographien zum Alten und Neuen Testament
WO	*Die Welt des Orients*

WZKM	*Wiener Zeitschrift für die Kunde des Morgenlandes*
YNER	Yale Near Eastern Researches
ZA	*Zeitschrift für Assyriologie*
ZAW	*Zeitschrift für die alttestamentliche Wissenschaft*
ZDPV	*Zeitschrift des deutschen Palästina-Vereins*
ZKT	*Zeitschrift für katholische Theologie*
ZTK	*Zeitschrift für Theologie und Kirche*

LIST OF CONTRIBUTORS

Bob Becking is Professor of Old Testament Studies at the University of Utrecht.

Ehud Ben Zvi is Professor of Religious Studies at the University of Alberta.

Philip R. Davies is Professor of Biblical Studies at the University of Sheffield.

Lester L. Grabbe is Professor of Hebrew Bible and Early Judaism at the University of Hull.

Ernst Axel Knauf is Professor of Hebrew Bible and Biblical Archaeology at the University of Bern.

Niels Peter Lemche is Professor of Theology at the University of Copenhagen.

Walter Mayer is Professor of Assyriology at the Westfälische Wilhelms-Universität in Münster.

Nadav Na'aman is Professor of Biblical History in the Department of Jewish History at the University of Tel Aviv.

Christoph Uehlinger is Senior Lecturer in the Department of Biblical Studies, University of Fribourg, Switzerland.

Part I
INTRODUCTION

INTRODUCTION

Lester L. Grabbe

Preliminary Remarks

The 2000 meeting of the European Seminar on Methodology in Israel's History was held in conjunction with the first European Association of Biblical Studies meeting in Utrecht, 6–9 August. Previous meetings of the Seminar had considered a number of broader questions.[1] Although these had produced some useful discussions and had helped clear both the ground and the air, it was nevertheless rightly felt that there was a lot of talking past one another and a lack of close engagement with the various arguments and positions advanced by Seminar members. It was therefore decided to pick a quite specific topic: the invasion of Sennacherib in 701 BCE. It had a number of advantages: there were a variety of sources, both biblical and extra-biblical sources were extant, and the topic included a number of issues of disagreement among scholars. Several scholars outside the discipline of biblical studies were invited to participate, though in the event only one was in a position to accept the invitation. We were also pleased to have a guest paper from a biblical scholar based in Canada.

The purpose of the papers in this volume is to carry on a debate about historical methodology. The papers are those that busy scholars thought would be useful in the debate about how to do history and how to evaluate sources, historical reconstruction, and the like. The editor did not assign subjects to contributors or parcel out aspects of the subject to participants.

---

1.   For the papers of these, see Lester L. Grabbe (ed.), *Can a 'History of Israel' Be Written?* (JSOTSup, 245; ESHM, 1; Sheffield Academic Press, 1997); *Leading Captivity Captive: 'The Exile' as History and Ideology* (JSOTSup, 278; ESHM, 2; Sheffield Academic Press, 1998); *Did Moses Speak Attic? Jewish Historiography and Scripture in the Hellenistic Period* (JSOTSup, 317; ESHM, 3; Sheffield Academic Press, 2001). The aims and membership of the Seminar will not be discussed here. They were listed in *Can a 'History of Israel' Be Written?* (pp. 11-14) and *Did Moses Speak Attic?* (pp. 16-20), which should be consulted by those not already familiar with them.

Each contributor was free to contribute the paper that he thought appropriate. There is, therefore, no attempt to be comprehensive in the treatment of the subject nor are there any claims that this volume will be a primary reservoir for those wanting the latest information relating to Sennacherib. The volume has gaps from the point of view of a systematic treatment of the subject, particularly in view of the fact that no one addressed the question of archaeology. In order to fill out the context and background, I have included two additional sections in this 'Introduction', one on the archaeology and one a survey of scholarship for the nineteenth and twentieth centuries. (David Ussishkin was invited to write a paper on the question of archaeology, but he was prevented by the need to complete his study of the Lachish excavations.)

Archaeology and Sennacherib[2]

A number of recent general treatments of the archaeology of ancient Palestine include a discussion of what archaeological data might be associated with Sennacherib.[3] The *New Encyclopedia of Archaeological Excavations in the Holy Land* is the most comprehensive general source of information on the different sites that may be relevant to the question.[4] Beyond these

---

2. My thanks to Professors Na'aman, Knauf, and Ben Zvi for their suggestions for additional bibliographical items and other improvements.

3. Recent introductions to archaeology include Ze'ev Herzog, *Archaeology of the City: Urban Planning in Ancient Israel and its Social Implications* (Tel Aviv University Monograph Series, 13; Tel Aviv: Tel Aviv University, 1997), and Israel Finkelstein and Neil Asher Silberman, *The Bible Unearthed: Archaeology's New Vision of Ancient Israel and the Origin of the Sacred Texts* (New York: Free Press, 2001). Other studies include Amnon Ben-Tor (ed.), *The Archaeology of Ancient Israel* (trans. R. Greenberg; New Haven, CT: Yale University Press, 1992); Helga Weippert, *Palästina in vorhellenistischer Zeit* (HdA, Vorderasien 2, Band 1; Munich: Beck, 1988); Amihai Mazar, *Archaeology of the Land of the Bible 10,000–586 B.C.E.* (New York: Doubleday; Cambridge: Lutterworth Press, 1993); Ephraim Stern, *Archaeology of the Land of the Bible. II. The Assyrian, Babylonian, and Persian Periods (732–332 B.C.E.)* (The Anchor Bible Reference Library; New York: Doubleday, 2001).

4. Ephraim Stern (ed.), *The New Encyclopedia of Archaeological Excavations in the Holy Land* (4 vols.; New York: Simon & Schuster; Jerusalem: Israel Exploration Society, 1992), cited below as *NEAEHL*; cf. also Eric M. Meyers (editor-in-chief), *The Oxford Encyclopedia of Archaeology in the Near East* (5 vols.; Oxford: Oxford University Press, 1997).

general treatments there are also specialized studies of the archaeology that will be cited below.

Unfortunately, at the moment there is no agreed terminology among archaeologists for the period from about 1000 BCE to the fall of Jerusalem in 587/586 BCE. Some schemes are based on supposed 'historical' periods, which can be question begging, but most schemes tend to associate certain artifacts with particular historical periods. After the Hazor excavations of the 1950s, Aharoni and Amiran proposed Iron II (1000–840 BCE) and Iron III (840–586 BCE), but the *Encyclopedia of Archaeological Excavations in the Holy Land* when first published in Hebrew in 1970 had the following scheme: Iron IIA (1000–900), IIB (900–800), IIC (800–586).[5] W.G. Dever notes that American archaeologists tend to begin Iron II about 920 BCE, whereas Israeli archaeologists usually begin it about 1000 BCE.[6] His treatment ends Iron IIA at 722 and Iron IIB with 586 BCE. However, the editor of the volume to which Dever contributes divides as follows: IIA (1000–900); IIB (900–700); IIC (700–586).[7] But even among Israeli writers the Iron II is differently divided. Barkay divided as follows: Iron IIa (10th–9th centuries BCE), Iron IIb (8th), IIIa (7th and early 6th), IIIb 6th (586 to the late 6th BCE). The *NEAEHL* used the terminology Iron IIA (1000–900 BCE), IIB (900–700), IIC (700–586), Babylonian and Persian periods (586–332). However, A. Mazar divided slightly differently, as follows: Iron IIA (1000–925 BCE), IIB (925–720), IIC (720–586). H. Weippert differed from them all, with Iron IIA (1000–900 BCE), IIB (925/900–850), IIC (850–587).

This should warn the reader to make no assumptions about what period of time is meant to be covered by a particular designation in the Iron II period but ascertain what the individual scholar has in mind in each case. In the past, there has also been the difficulty of finding agreement on which particular levels should be specifically associated with Sennacherib's

5.   See Gabriel Barkay, 'The Iron Age II–III', in Ben-Tor (ed.), *The Archaeology of Ancient Israel*, pp. 302-73 (305); this scheme was also maintained in the English translation: Michael Avi-Yonah and Ephraim Stern (eds.), *Encyclopedia of Archaeological Excavations in the Holy Land* (Oxford: Oxford University Press, 1975–78), IV, p. 1226.

6.   William G. Dever, 'Social Structure in Palestine in the Iron II Period on the Eve of Destruction', in Thomas E. Levy (ed.), *The Archaeology of Society in the Holy Land* (New Approaches in Anthropological Archaeology; London: Leicester University Press, 2nd edn, 1998), pp. 416-31 (416).

7.   Thomas E. Levy, 'Preface', in Levy (ed.), *The Archaeology of Society in the Holy Land*: x-xvi (xvi).

invasion. After a considerable debate, however, some consensus seems to have been reached about most of the sites that show a destruction layer associated with Sennacherib's invasion. The main sites to be considered are Jerusalem and Lachish, but other sites may also relate to the Assyrian attack and are discussed in a further section.

Central to determining Sennacherib's destruction have been two factors: (1) the stratigraphy of Lachish and (2) the 1200+ *lmlk* seal impressions found on storage jars in Jerusalem, Lachish, and elsewhere. The *lmlk* seal impressions[8] were discovered in some of the earliest excavations in Palestine in the late nineteenth century. They tended to be found on a particular type of jar, the four-handled jars with certain physical characteristics in common, and to occur associated with two particular emblems: a four-winged type (in two varieties) and a two-winged type. In some cases, 'private seals' are found on jars which also have the *lmlk* seal impressions. On various of the *lmlk* seal impressions are found names, four in total, which seem to be place-names: Hebron, *mmšt*, Socoh, and Ziph.

Studies up to about 1970 suggested that the jars contained the produce of particular estates, and that the four-winged and two-winged stamps were chronologically separated, the latter near the end of the Judaean kingdom and the former perhaps in the reign of Hezekiah and/or Manasseh.[9] However, subsequent studies found that the jars all seem to have a remarkably homogeneous origin, being produced in a single pottery centre,[10] and examples of the four-winged seal impressions have been found in the same

---

8.   See especially David Ussishkin, 'The Destruction of Lachish by Sennacherib and the Dating of the Royal Judean Storage Jars', *TA* 4 (1977), pp. 28-60; Nadav Na'aman, 'Sennacherib's Campaign to Judah and the Date of the *LMLK* Stamps', *VT* 29 (1979), pp. 60-86; *idem*, 'Hezekiah's Fortified Cities and the *LMLK* Stamps', *BASOR* 261 (1986), pp. 5-21; A.D. Tushingham, 'New Evidence Bearing on the Two-Winged *LMLK* Stamp', *BASOR* 287 (1992), pp. 61-65; Gabriel Barkay and Andrew G. Vaughn, '*Lmlk* and Official Seal Impressions from Tel Lachish', *TA* 23 (1996), pp. 61-74; Andrew G. Vaughn, *Theology, History, and Archaeology in the Chronicler's Account of Hezekiah* (Archaeology and Biblical Studies 4; Atlanta: Scholars Press, 1999).

9.   See, e.g., Frank M. Cross, Jr, 'Judean Stamps', *EI* 9 (1969), pp. 20-27; Peter Welten, *Die Königs-Stempel: Ein Beitrag zum Militärpolitik Judas unter Hiskia und Josia* (Abhandlungen der Deutschen Pälastina-Vereins; Wiesbaden: Harrassowitz, 1969).

10.   H. Mommsen, I. Perlman, and J. Yellin, 'The Provenience of the *lmlk* Jars', *IEJ* 34 (1984), pp. 89-113; Na'aman, 'Hezekiah's Fortified Cities', pp. 16-17.

sealed destruction layer as the two-winged.[11] The conclusion is that the jars were produced by Hezekiah as a storage unit important in trade and his economic developments; however, as soon as he contemplated rebellion they were ideal for stockpiling liquid foodstuffs (especially wine) in anticipation of invasion and even siege.[12] Their use was likely to have been over a rather short period of time because of the seal impressions of named officials on them, which would not have been used for more than a few decades, and because *lmlk* jars were found in some sites (e.g. in Philistia) that did not come under Judah's control until Hezekiah's reign. If their production and use was thus over a very narrow timeframe, they can be used to date particular events in the context of Hezekiah's rebellion and subsequent Assyrian attack.

Lachish
The location of Lachish is now almost universally accepted as Tell ed-Duweir.[13] The Wellcome-Marston Archaeological Research Expedition led by J.L. Starkey excavated the site from 1932 to 1938.[14] Level II, which had been destroyed by a major conflagration, was interpreted as representing the end of the Judaean monarchy by the Babylonian conquest. The

11. Yohanan Aharoni (*The Land of the Bible, A Historical Geography* [trans. Anson F. Rainey; London: Burns & Oates, 1967], pp. 340-46; [2nd edn, 1979], pp. 394-400) seems to have been the first to keep the seals together; cf. also his *The Archaeology of the Land of Israel* (trans. Anson F. Rainey; Philadelphia: Westminster, 1982), pp. 254-64. H.D. Lance ('The Royal Stamps and the Kingdom of Judah', *HTR* 64 [1971], pp. 315-32) also argued that they belong together, though he spends much of his time arguing for a Josianic date for both sorts of seal impressions. Ussishkin's renewed excavations settled the matter by finding both sorts together in situ ('The Destruction of Lachish', pp. 54-57). Cf. also Na'aman, 'Sennacherib's Campaign to Judah', pp. 70-71.
12. Cf. the discussion in Vaughn, *Theology, History, and Archaeology*, pp. 152-57.
13. In spite of other views by some prominent scholars in the past, Gösta W. Ahlström ('Is Tell ed-Duweir Ancient Lachish?' *PEQ* 112 [1980], pp. 7-9) was one of the few in recent years who continued to maintain that the site of Lachish had been misidentified, but see the response by G.I. Davies, 'Tell ed-Duweir = Ancient Lachish: A Response to G.W. Ahlström', *PEQ* 114 (1982), pp. 25-28. Cf. also Ahlström, *The History of Ancient Palestine* (ed. D. Edelman; Minneapolis: Fortress Press; Sheffield: Sheffield Academic Press, 1993), pp. 709-12.
14. The relevant archaeology for the Iron Age was published after Starkey's death in a series of volumes: Olga Tufnell *et al.* (eds.), *Lachish III: The Iron Age* (Oxford: Oxford University Press, 1953); Y. Aharoni, *Investigations at Lachish: The Sanctuary and the Residency (Lachish V)* (Tel Aviv: Tel Aviv University, 1975).

question was, then, when to date the layer immediately below (Level III) which had also been destroyed by an intense fire. Starkey argued that Level III had also been destroyed by the Babylonians, but not long before 587 BCE, in the invasion of 597 BCE following which King Jehoiachin and his family had been deported.[15] However, when O. Tufnell published the volume with the Iron Age material from Starkey's excavation, she argued that Level III was brought to an end by the siege of Sennacherib in 701 BCE.[16] A number of prominent scholars attacked her interpretation and continued to support Starkey.[17] Even as late as 1976 it was asserted, 'Henceforth the burden of proof is on anyone who wants to argue an earlier date and the demonstration will have to assume as its first order of business the carrying back of the entire series of royal stamped jar handles into the eighth century'.[18] Despite this the matter now seems to be settled by the new excavations of Aharoni (1966, 1968) and, especially, Ussishkin (1973–1987).[19]

The recent excavations have not only established a good deal about the history of Lachish but, together with the remarkable reliefs from Sennacherib's palace, provide a unique insight into an ancient historical event.[20]

15. J.L. Starkey, 'Lachish as Illustrating Bible History', *PEQ* 69 (1937), pp 171-79 (175-77); *idem*, 'Excavations at Tell ed Duweir', *PEQ* 69 (1937), pp. 228-41 (235-36).

16. Tufnell (ed.), *Lachish III*, pp. 45, 48, 55-56; cf. Tufnell and Ussishkin, 'Lachish', in Avi-Yonah and Stern (eds.), *Encyclopedia of Archaeological Excavations in the Holy Land*: III, pp. 735-53, especially 744-45.

17. E.g., William F. Albright, 'Recent Progress in Palestinian Archaeology: Samaria-Sebaste III and Hazor I', *BASOR* 150 (1958), pp. 21-25, especially p. 24; G. Ernest Wright, review of *Lachish III*, *JNES* 14 (1955), pp. 188-89; *idem*, review of *Lachish III*, *VT* 5 (1955), pp. 97-105; Kathleen M. Kenyon, 'The Date of the Destruction of Iron Age Beer-Sheba', *PEQ* 108 (1976), pp. 63-64.

18. J.S. Holladay, Jr, 'Of Sherds and Strata: Contributions toward an Understanding of the Archaeology of the Divided Monarchy', in Frank M. Cross, Werner E. Lemke, and Patrick D. Miller (eds.), *Magnalia Dei, The Mighty Acts of God: Essays on the Bible and Archaeology in Memory of G. Ernest Wright* (Garden City, NY: Doubleday, 1976), pp. 253-93, quote from p. 267.

19. David Ussishkin, 'The Destruction of Lachish'.

20. David Ussishkin, 'The Excavations at Tel Lachish—1973–1977, Preliminary Report', *TA* 5 (1978), pp. 1-97; *idem*, 'The "Lachish Reliefs" and the City of Lachish', *IEJ* 30 (1980), pp. 174-95; *idem*, *The Conquest of Lachish by Sennacherib* (Tel Aviv, Publications of the Institute of Archaeology; Tel Aviv University, 1982); *idem*, 'Excavations at Tel Lachish—1978-1983, Second Preliminary Report', *TA* 10 (1983), pp. 97-175; *idem*, 'Lachish', *ABD* IV, pp. 114-26; *idem*, 'Lachish', *NEAEHL* III, pp. 897-911; *idem*, 'The Assyrian Attack on Lachish: The Archaeological Evidence from the

The pictorial depiction of the siege and conquest of Lachish is found in Sennacherib's palace in the new capital of Assyria at Nineveh. These wall reliefs were already found and described in the early days of Assyriology.[21] Combined with the original and the new excavations a good deal of interest has emerged. The savage attack on and destruction of Lachish (hinted at in 2 Kings) are confirmed by the remains. The massive defences of the city suggest that just such an attack was anticipated. The most vulnerable part of the city was in the region of the city gate where the hill on which Lachish stood was not so steeply separated from its neighbours. Here the Assyrians built a siege ramp, so far the only one surviving in the ancient Near East, to bring up their rams against the wall. The defenders built a counter ramp inside the wall opposite to where the Assyrians were attacking, but in the end the city fell. The remains show that the houses had been ransacked before being deliberately burnt. Some old tombs seem to have been reused to contain about 1500 bodies, bodies that had apparently first been burnt in the fire. Curiously, the siege and fall of Lachish are not mentioned in Sennacherib's inscriptions.

Jerusalem
One of the central questions has been the way in which Sennacherib shut up Hezekiah 'like a bird in a cage'. Was this by the standard siege methods of surrounding the city by a siege mound? This used to be the general view. The difficulty has been excavation work in Jerusalem that found evidence of this period. Some recent studies seem to be relevant to the question, though. D. Ussishkin proposed that the 'camp of the Assyrians' mentioned by Josephus (*War* 5.7.3 §303; 5.12.2 §504) was to be identified with the similar expression in 2 Kgs 19.35 and localized on the northwest hill of Jerusalem.[22] In his view the Assyrians had camped outside the walls of Jerusalem, although the city itself had not fallen to the besieging army.

Southwest Corner of the Site', *TA* 17 (1990), pp. 53-86; *idem*, 'Excavations and Restoration Work at Tel Lachish 1985–1994: Third Preliminary Report', *TA* 23 (1996), pp. 3-60.
    21. Austen Henry Layard, *Discoveries among the Ruins of Nineveh and Babylon* (New York: G.P. Putnam, 1853); *A Second Series of the Monuments of Nineveh* (London: J. Murray, 1853). Some of the most interesting pictorial material has been conveniently collected in Ussishkin, *The Conquest of Lachish*. See also Christoph Uehlinger's study, pp. 221-305 below.
    22. David Ussishkin, 'The "Camp of the Assyrians" in Jerusalem', *IEJ* 29 (1979), pp. 137-42.

This interpretation was attacked by A. van der Kooij, however.[23] The problem revolves around two issues: (1) whether the Assyrian statements imply a siege and (b) whether there is any evidence for such a siege. Not strictly based on the archaeology, van der Kooij's argument involved the question of how to interpret the statements in the Assyrian inscriptions. He concluded that the wording of the Assyrian inscriptions did not envisage an actual siege. H. Tadmor also argued that Jerusalem did not come under siege; indeed, the Assyrian text also implies that it did not.[24] More recently W. Mayer has similarly argued that the Assyrian army did not in fact set up siege works around Jerusalem directly.[25]

Some sites not far from Jerusalem are thought to show evidence of an Assyrian siege at this time. One of the most important of these is Ramat Raḥel (Ḥirbet Ṣāliḥ) which lies only about 4 km southwest of Jerusalem. It was excavated for five seasons during 1954–62 by Y. Aharoni,[26] and in 1984 by G. Barkay.[27] The site was identified as Beth-haccherem by Aharoni, but Barkay and A.D. Tushingham both suggest that it is the hitherto-unknown *mmšt* found on some of the *lmlk* seal impressions.[28] The earliest remains so far found are from Iron II. Level VB shows evidence of an eighth-century palace, with the hilltop surrounded by a massive defensive wall on the west, south, east, and partially on the north. Very little remains of this layer, but its destruction has been interpreted as due to the efforts of Sennacherib's army. This conclusion is based in part on the remains of 170 *lmlk* jar handles that seem to have originated in stratum VB, as well as on some other private seal impressions that match those found in Lachish and elsewhere.[29] The next phase, Level VA, seems to

23. Arie van der Kooij, 'Das assyrische Heer vor den Mauern Jerusalems im Jahr 701 v. Chr', *ZDPV* 102 (1986), pp. 93-109.

24. Hayim Tadmor, 'Sennacherib's Campaign to Judah: Historical and Historiographical Considerations', *Zion* 50 (Jubilee volume) (1985), pp. 65-80 (Heb.).

25. Walter Mayer, *Politik und Kriegskunst der Assyrer* (ALASPM, 9; Münster: Ugarit-Verlag, 1995); see also his article below, pp. 168-200.

26. See the summary of Yohanan Aharoni, 'Ramat Raḥel', *NEAEHL*, IV, pp. 1261-67.

27. Gabriel Barkay's excavations remain unpublished, though a brief summary paragraph is given in *NEAEHL*, IV, p. 1267; see also Vaughn, *Theology, History, and Archaeology*, pp. 39-40.

28. Randall W. Younker, 'Ramat Rahel', *ABD*, V, pp. 615-16.

29. J.P. Dessel, 'Ramat Raḥel', in Meyers (ed.), *The Oxford Encyclopedia of Archaeology in the Near East*, pp. 402-404; Vaughn, *Theology, History, and Archaeology*, pp. 102-105.

have been built shortly after the destruction of VB and itself ends in de-struction, usually associated with the Babyonian conquest of 587/586 BCE.

One site has become controversial in recent years. 2 Kgs 20.20 states that Hezekiah made the 'pool' (*habbĕārēkāh*) and the 'conduit' (*hattĕ'ālāh*) and brought water into the city. The Siloam tunnel has long been thought to provide the evidence for the truth of this verse. Recently, however, J. Rogerson and P.R. Davies sought to redate the tunnel and its inscription to the time of the Maccabees.[30] A set of responses organized for the *Biblical Archaeology Review* appeared to border on a hatchet job.[31] More sober and balanced replies were given by R.S. Hendel[32] and S. Norin,[33] but they both remained unconvinced. Although not mentioning specifically the Rogerson and Davies article, S. Rosenberg noted that the engineering methods used did not show the sophistication one might expect of later times: 'From a technical point of view, this would seem to demonstrate that the tunnel was cut well before the Hellenistic (Hasmonean) period'.[34] More recently E.A. Knauf has argued for the reign of Manasseh as the time of its building.[35] Thus, the question of whether the Siloam tunnel belongs to Hezekiah's time is far from settled.

30. John Rogerson and Philip R. Davies, 'Was the Siloam Tunnel Built by Hezekiah?', *BA* 59 (1996), pp. 138-49.

31. See Jo Ann Hackett *et al.*, 'Defusing Pseudo-Scholarship: The Siloam Inscription Ain't Hasmonean', *BARev* 23/2 (March/April 1997), pp. 41-50, 68. Neither the tendentious and unjustified use of the term 'pseudo-scholarship' in the title of the article nor the condescending and smug tone of some of the comments suggest that the authors have always made a dispassionate analysis of the arguments presented by Rogerson and Davies; however, the different authors vary in the extent to which they respond with proper rebutting arguments, as opposed to sarcasm, and there are some important data and arguments for consideration even here.

32. Ronald S. Hendel, 'The Date of the Siloam Inscription: A Rejoinder to Rogerson and Davies', *BA* 59 (1996), pp. 233-47.

33. Stig Norin, 'The Age of the Siloam Inscription and Hezekiah's Tunnel', *VT* 48 (1998), pp. 37-48.

34. Stephen Rosenberg, 'The Siloam Tunnel Revisited', *TA* 25 (1998), pp. 116-30, quotation from p. 129. The recent article of Avraham Faust ('A Note on Hezekiah's Tunnel and the Siloam Inscription', *JSOT* 90 [2000], pp. 3-11) seems not to have anything on this particular issue. Cf. also Dan Gill, 'How They Met: Geology Solves Mystery of Hezekiah's Tunnelers', *BARev* 20/4 (July/August 1994), pp. 20-33, 64.

35. E. Axel Knauf, 'Hezekiah or Manasseh? A Reconsideration of the Siloam Tunnel and Inscription', *TA* 28 (2001), pp. 281-87. Cf. also Israel Finkelstein, 'The Archaeology of the Days of Manasseh', in Michael D. Coogan, Cheryl J. Exum, and Lawrence E. Stager (eds), *Scripture and Other Artifacts: Essays on the Bible and*

Other Sites

For understandable reasons, Jerusalem and Lachish have been the focus of interest for what happened during the Assyrian attack. A number of other sites in Judah were destroyed at this time, however, according to conventional interpretation,[36] as confirmed by a survey undertaken by Y. Dagan. Of 354 Judaean settlements in existence in the late eighth century and destroyed, only 39 are presently known to have been rebuilt in the seventh century.[37]

Tell en-Naṣbeh: This is widely, though not universally, identifed with ancient Mizpah. It was excavated during 1926–35 by W.F. Badé, but the original excavation reports have recently been re-assessed by J.R. Zorn.[38] Unfortunately, the excavation methods used at the time, combined with severe erosion of the site, have made it difficult to determine the stratigraphy. The Iron II stratum (stratum 3) seems to have three levels, but there was little major change over four centuries because the city was not destroyed during this time. Among the finds were 87 *lmlk* seal impressions, but there does not seem to be any evidence of a conquest by Sennacherib.

Gezer (Tell Jezer): Excavated off and on throughout the twentieth century (the latest season in 1990),[39] Gezer's early finds were confusingly reported. W.G. Dever mentions that stratum VI ended in a violent conflagration, which he assigned to Tiglath-pileser III's invasion of 733 BCE,[40] while he associated the end of stratum V with the Babylonians. However, there are

---

Archaeology in Honor of Philip J. King (Louisville, KY: Westminster/John Knox Press, 1994), pp. 169-87.

36. Stern, *Archaeology*, pp. 130-65.

37. Stern, *Archaeology*, p. 142; see also the survey in Finkelstein, 'The Archaeology of the Days of Manasseh'.

38. Jeffrey R. Zorn's principal study, his 1993 PhD thesis, remains unpublished, but several of his articles summarize the data: 'Naṣbeh, Tell en-', *NEAEHL*, III, pp. 1098-1102; 'Naṣbeh, Tell en-', in Meyers (ed.), *The Oxford Encyclopedia of Archaeology in the Near East*, IV, pp. 101-103; 'William Frederic Badè', *BA* 51 (1988), pp. 28-35; 'The Badè Institute of Biblical Archaeology', *BA* (1988), pp. 36-45; 'Estimating the Population Size of Ancient Settlements: Methods, Problems, Solutions, and a Case Study', *BASOR* 295 (1994), pp. 31-48.

39. William G. Dever, 'Gezer', *NEAEHL*, II, pp. 496-506; *idem*, 'Gezer', in Meyers (ed.), *The Oxford Encyclopedia of Archaeology in the Near East*, pp. 396-400.

40. In a palace of Tiglath-pileser III's at Nimrud, a relief of a city being besieged has the caption, *ga-az-ru*.

still some significant disagreements between archaeologists in interpreting the data from this site. For example, the outer wall is dated to the Late Bronze by Dever but to the Iron II by Finkelstein.[41] Na'aman argues that the city was an Israelite one annexed by the Assyrians, though it could have been taken and held for a time by Hezekiah.[42] Macalister apparently found at least 31 *lmlk* handles at Gezer.[43] This suggests that stratum V might be the best candidate for the period associated with the reign of Hezekiah.[44] In the seventh century, it was an Assyrian administrative centre, suggesting that stratum V may have covered the period from the late eighth to the late seventh century and was not destroyed by Sennacherib.

Tel Batash: This site was excavated between 1977 and 1989 by G.L. Kelm and A. Mazar. The identification with Timnah made in the 1950s is still widely accepted. Stratum III represents a fortification built perhaps in the eighth century, including a large public building (in area H) that may have been an administrative centre. This ended in a partial destruction of the city (including the building in area H), now generally taken to have been by the Assyrians in 701 BCE. A large number of *lmlk* jars were found, as well as a seal impressions apparently with the name of an individual, which has parallels with seals found in Azekah and Jerusalem.[45]

41. Israel Finkelstein, 'Penelope's Shroud Unravelled: Iron II Date of Gezer's Outer Wall Established', *TA* 21 (1994), pp. 276-82. But cf. Eli Yanai, 'A Late Bronze Age Gate at Gezer?', *TA* 21 (1994), pp. 283-87, who thinks the outer gate is Late Bronze, thus supporting Dever.

42. Na'aman, 'The Date of 2 Chronicles 11.5-10—A Reply to Y. Garfinkel', *BASOR* 271 (1988), pp. 74-77 (74).

43. Lance, 'The Royal Stamps', p. 330 n. 70; cf. also Hanan Eshel, 'A *lmlk* Stamp from Beth-El', *IEJ* 39 (1989), pp. 60-62 (62 n. 12).

44. Ronny Reich and Baruch Brandl, 'Gezer under Assyrian Rule', *PEQ* 117 (January–June 1985), pp. 41-54.

45. Amihai Mazar, 'Batash, Tel', in Meyers (ed.), *The Oxford Encyclopedia of Archaeology in the Near East*, I, pp. 281-83; Amihai Mazar and George L. Kelm, 'Batash, Tel', *NEAEHL* I, pp. 152-57; *idem*, 'Batashi, Tell el-', *ABD* I, pp. 625-26; George L. Kelm and Amihai Mazar, 'Three Seasons of Excavations at Tel Batash— Biblical Timnah: Preliminary Report', *BASOR* 248 (1982), pp. 1-36; *idem*, 'Tel Batash (Timnah) Excavations: Second Preliminary Report (1981–1983)', *BASORSup* 23 (1985), pp. 93-120; *idem*, 'Tel Batash (Timnah) Excavations: Third Preliminary Report, 1984–1989', *BASORSup* 27 (1991), pp. 47-67; Kelm, 'Timnah—A City of Conflict within the Traditional Buffer Zone of the Shephelah', *BAIAS* (1984-85), pp. 54-61; Kelm and Mazar, *Timnah: A Biblical City in the Sorek Valley* (Winona Lake, IN: Eisenbrauns, 1995).

Beth-Shemesh: The tell had originally been excavated by D. Mackenzie in 1911–12 and E. Grant in 1928–33. Mackenzie had interpreted stratum IIc as having been brought to an end by Sennacherib's invasion. G.E. Wright (who wrote up the results of Grant's expedition) opposed this interpretation and related it to the Babylonian invasion of 587 BCE. Bar-Ilan University launched new excavations in 1990. For stratum IIc many *lmlk* jars were found, while no pottery or other remains from the seventh century were uncovered. The conclusion is that Mackenzie was correct, and Grant and Wright wrong: IIc was ended by Sennacherib's intervention in 701 BCE.[46]

Tell es-Safi (Tell Zafit): Although many archaeologists regard this as the site of ancient Gath,[47] there is considerable dispute.[48] We are still dependent on the excavations conducted in 1899 by Bliss and Macalister who reported their results in four 'periods'. Among the finds from the 'Jewish period' were some *lmlk* seal impressions. New excavations began in 1997, another *lmlk* jar handle being one of the finds.[49] It was originally suggested that the name 'Gath' should be restored in the inscription of Sennacherib newly reconstructed by Na'aman.[50] However, Na'aman has now accepted the arguments of Mittmann that the reading should be 'Ekron' rather than 'Gath'.[51]

Tel Zakariyah: This site has been widely identified as ancient Azekah. It was excavated by F.J. Bliss and R.A.S. Macalister at the end of the

46. Shlomo Bunimovitz and Zvi Lederman, 'Beth-Shemesh', *NEAEHL* I, pp. 249-53; Miriam Aharoni and Yohanan Aharoni, 'The Stratification of Judahite Sites in the 8th and 7th Centuries BCE', *BASOR* 224 (1976), pp. 73-90; William G. Dever, 'Beth-Shemesh', in Meyers (ed.), *The Oxford Encyclopedia of Archaeology in the Near East*, pp. 311-12; G.J. Wightman, 'The Date of Bethshemesh Stratum II', *Abr-Nahrain* 28 (1990), pp. 96-126.

47. Ephraim Stern, 'Zafit, Tel', *NEAEHL*, IV, pp. 1522-24.

48. For example, Lawrence E. Stager thinks Gath is more likely to be Tel Haror: 'The Impact of the Sea Peoples in Canaan (1185–1050 BCE)', in Levy (ed.), *The Archaeology of Society in the Holy Land*, pp. 332-48 (343).

49. Stern, *Archaeology*, pp. 145-46.

50. Nadav Na'aman, 'Sennacherib's "Letter to God" on his Campaign to Judah', *BASOR* 214 (1974), pp. 25-39 (34-35).

51. Nadev Na'aman, 'Hezekiah and the Kings of Assyria', *TA* 21 (1994), pp. 235-54 (245-46), following S. Mittmann, 'Hiskia und die Philister', *JNSL* 16 (1990), pp. 91-106 (98-99).

nineteenth century.[52] Since this was one of the early Palestinian digs, it
is perhaps not surprising that the stratigraphy is somewhat uncertain. Of
the four occupation 'periods' *lmlk* seal impressions were found in both B
and C. The new inscription of Sennacherib's restored by Na'aman was
taken to speak of a siege and conquest of Azekah, but others disagree,
and Na'aman himself has now changed his mind.[53]

Tell Judeideh: This has been identified with Moresheth, the home of the
prophet Micah. Originally excavated by Bliss and Macalister in 1899–
1900,[54] S. Gibson has recently been able to study unpublished data from
those digs and make them available for the first time.[55] In his six 'clear-
ance' pits Bliss found strong evidence from Iron IIB (especially in Pit 4).
The Iron IIB stratum could be divided into upper and lower phases. The
upper phase ended in a major conflagration. At least 37 *lmlk* handles, some
also with private seal impressions, were found in this layer, and the pottery
assemblage in general was late eighth century. It has been argued that
Micah 1.14 pictures Moreshet(-Gath) as one of the cities destroyed by
Sennacherib.[56]

Tel 'Erani (Tell esh-Sheikh Aḥmed el-'Areini): There is no agreed identity
for this site. Excavated in the 1956–61 by S. Yeivin, this location has so
far had only preliminary reports published for it.[57] Yeivin had associated
stratum IV with the Babylonian destruction in the early sixth century BCE,
with stratum VII put in the late eighth/early seventh, and stratum VIII in
the eighth century. Now B. Brandl, who has responsibility for publishing
the final report from Yeivin's dig, has noted that stratum VI should be
redated to the late eighth century because of the presence of *lmlk* jars and

52. For a summary, see Ephraim Stern, 'Azekah', *NEAEHL*, I, pp. 123-24; 'Azekah',
in Meyers (ed.), *The Oxford Encyclopedia of Archaeology in the Near East*, p. 243.

53. See nn. 50-51 above; Knauf has suggested that 'Lachish' might be restored in
this inscription (see p. 144 n. 9 below).

54. Summarized by Magen Broshi, 'Judeideh, Tell', *NEAEHL* III, pp. 837-38.

55. Shimon Gibson, 'The Tell ej-Judeideh (Tel Goded) Excavations: A Re-appraisal
Based on Archival Records in the Palestine Exploration Fund', *TA* 21 (1994), pp. 194-
234.

56. See the discussion in Ehud Ben Zvi (*Micah* [FOTL 21b; Grand Rapids, MI:
Eerdmans, 2000], pp. 17, 35-36) who himself has doubts about this conclusion.

57. Much of the secondary literature focuses on the Chalcolithic and Bronze Ages.
For the Iron Age, see the summary in Shmuel Yeivin, 'Erani, Tel', *NEAEHL*, II, pp.
417-19.

other artifacts. It was most likely this stratum that ended with Sennacherib's destruction.[58]

Tel Maresha (Tell eṣ-Ṣandaḥanna): First excavated by Bliss and Macalister in 1898–1900, and then by A. Kloner in 1989 to 1993, most of the finds relate to the Hellenistic city of Marisa. Evidence of the Persian period and Iron Age were also found, however, with 16 *lmlk* seal impressions uncovered in the 'Israelite layer' of the original excavations.[59]

Tell 'Eton (Tell 'Aitun): Only salvage operations have been carried out on this site, which makes any conclusions only tentative. But the pottery assemblage was very similar to that found in the Lachish III, though there were also vessels characteristic of Lachish IV.[60]

Tell Beit Mirsim: This was originally excavated by Albright who identified the site with ancient Debir and considered that it had ended with the Babylonian destruction of 587 BCE. Subsequent evaluations have disagreed. It is no longer identifed with Debir, but also with no other ancient site. Stratum A2 is now thought to have been brought to an end by the Assyrian invasion of 701 BCE, based on more recent pottery studies by Ussishkin and Aharoni.[61]

Tel Ḥalif (Tell Khuweilifeh): The main excavations were conducted during 1976–89 and found evidence of habitation for most of the period from the Chalcolithic Period to the twentieth century. Although there is no agreed

58. Baruch Brandl, ' 'Erani, Tel', in Meyers (ed.), *The Oxford Encyclopedia of Archaeology in the Near East*, pp. 256-58.

59. Amos Kloner, 'Maresha', in Meyers (ed.), *The Oxford Encyclopedia of Archaeology in the Near East*, III, pp. 412-13; Michael Avi-Yonah and Amos Kloner, 'Mareshah (Marisa)', *NEAEHL*, III, pp. 948-57.

60. Etan Ayalon, 'Trial Excavation of Two Iron Age Strata at Tel 'Eton', *TA* 12 (1985), pp. 54-62; Orna Zimhoni, 'The Iron Age Pottery of Tel 'Eton and its Relation to the Lachish, Tell Beit Mirsim and Arad Assemblages', *TA* 12 (1985), pp. 63-90.

61. William F. Albright, 'Beit Mirsim, Tell', *NEAEHL*, I, pp. 177-80; Raphael Greenberg, 'Beit Mirsim, Tell', *NEAEHL* I, p. 180; *idem*, 'Beit Mirsim, Tell', in Meyers (ed.), *The Oxford Encyclopedia of Archaeology in the Near East* I, pp. 295-97; William G. Dever, 'Beit Mirsim, Tell', *ABD*, I, pp. 648-49; Orna Zimhoni, 'The Iron Age Pottery'; David Ussishkin, 'Royal Judean Storage Jars and Private Seal Impressions', *BASOR* 223 (1976), pp. 6-11; Aharoni and Aharoni, 'The Stratification of Judahite Sites'; Yosef Garfinkel, 'The *Eliakim Na'ar Yokan* Seal Impressions: Sixty Years of Confusion in Biblical Archaeological Research', *BA* 53 (1990), pp. 74-79.

identification for this site, Rimmon[62] and Hormah[63] are two possibilities. In Stratum VIB a fortification complex begun perhaps as early as the ninth century was brought to an end by a violent destruction. The pottery assemblage suggests that this was the Assyrian invasion of 701 BCE. The burials of Tomb 20 (on a hill opposite) contain a large number of iron arrow heads and may also relate to this invasion.[64]

Tel Sheva (Tell es-Saba'): Excavations begun in 1969 by Aharoni have been carried on intermittently by Z. Herzog.[65] Iron II Beersheba had four strata: V-II. There is an indication that a horned altar had stood somewhere on the site, but in stratum II it had apparently been incorporated into a wall. Some have connected the dismantling of the altar with Hezekiah's reform,[66] but one can only say that there is much uncertainty. The pottery assemblage associated with stratum II is very similar to that of Lachish III (though, surprisingly, no *lmlk* pots), and Herzog and others believe that Sennacherib's invasion ended stratum II. After its destruction, the site was abandoned for nearly a century before some attempts at rebuilding. It was then abandoned for three centuries.[67] However, Knauf has now argued against a destruction by Sennacherib.[68]

Khirbet Rabud: Although denied by Albright, this site is widely assumed to be ancient Debir/ Kiriath-Sepher. It was excavated in 1968 and 1969 by

---

62. Oded Borowski, 'The Biblical Identity of Tel Halif', *BA* (1988), pp. 21-27.

63. Nadav Na'aman, 'The Inheritance of the Sons of Simeon', *ZDPV* 96 (1980), pp. 136-52.

64. Joe E. Seger and Oded Borowski, 'Ḥalif, Tel', *NEAEHL*, II, pp. 553-60.

65. Summarized by Ze'ev Herzog, 'Beersheba', *NEAEHL*, I, pp. 167-73; *idem*, 'Beersheba', in Meyers (ed.), *The Oxford Encyclopedia of Archaeology in the Near East*, I, pp. 287-91.

66. E.g., Anson F. Rainey, 'Hezekiah's Reform and the Altars at Beer-sheba and Arad', in Michael D. Coogan, Cheryl J. Exum, and Lawrence E. Stager (eds.), *Scripture and Other Artifacts: Essays on the Bible and Archaeology in Honor of Philip J. King* (Louisville, KY: Westminster/John Knox Press, 1994), pp. 333-54.

67. Nadav Na'aman: 'The site is a remarkable example of the disasterous results of Sennacherib's campaign for cities located on Judah's southern border' (private communication).

68. E. Axel Knauf, 'Who Destroyed Beersheba II?', in Ulrich Hübner and E.A. Knauf (eds.), *Kein Land für sich allein: Studien zum Kulturkontak in Kanaan, Israel/ Palästine und Ebirnâri für Manfred Weippert zum 65. Geburtstag* (OBD, 186; Freiburg: Universitätsverlag, 2002), pp. 181-95.

M. Kochavi.[69] Unfortunately, many of the ancient remains had eroded away, but two trenches found evidence of habitation from the Early Bronze I to Roman times. A massive wall from about the ninth century had enclosed much of the mound. The original preliminary report mentions only that in trench B, stratum II contained many *lmlk* jar handles and ended in a major destruction associated with Sennacherib.[70] However, in a later report the excavator claimed that evidence for Sennnacherib's destruction was found in both trenches A and B.[71]

Arad: This is an important site but also one about which prominent archaeologists have come to some significantly different conclusions.[72] Seven strata have been associated with the Iron Age at Arad: XII-VI. According to the most recent interpretation of one of the excavators,[73] the unfortified site of stratum XII was followed by a walled fortress (stratum XI) which was destroyed by fire. The rebuilt fortress (X) included a shrine consisting of a courtyard with a large altar, a broadroom, and a small inner room apparently with a stela (*maṣṣevah*) and two incense altars. Stratum IX consisted of some alterations to the building of stratum X, but in stratum VIII some significant changes were made in the temple area: it was dismantled and much of it covered in a metre-thick layer of earth. This activity has been associated with the cult reforms of Hezekiah. Strata VII and VI both had ostraca and inscriptional material relating to an Eliashib who seems to have been a commander of the fortress. What most seem to agree on is that the fortress of stratum VI was brought to an end by the Babylonians at the time of Jerusalem's final siege, but the archaeology, the dating of the previous Iron Age strata, and the possible historical events with which they are to be associated are all disputed. Ussishkin, for example, came to some significantly different conclusions (though depending on the preliminary publications and interviews with some of the excavators). He notes (with

69. Moshe Kochavi, 'Khirbet Rabûd = Debir', *TA* 1 (1974), pp. 2-33; *idem*, 'Rabud, Khirbet', in Meyers (ed.), *The Oxford Encyclopedia of Archaeology in the Near East*, IV, p. 401; *idem*, 'Rabud, Khirbet', *NEAEHL*, IV, p. 1252.

70. Kochavi, 'Khirbet Rabûd = Debir', pp. 16, 18.

71. *The Oxford Encyclopedia of Archaeology in the Near East*, IV, p. 401.

72. See especially the summary in Dale W. Manor and Gary A. Herion, 'Arad', *ABD* I, pp. 331-36.

73. Ze'ev Herzog, 'Arad: Iron Age Period', in Meyers (ed.), *The Oxford Encyclopedia of Archaeology in the Near East*, I, pp. 174-76.

others, such as Zimhoni[74]) that the homogeneity of the pottery from strata X–VIII suggests a relatively short period of time, and these layers may represent only different stages of a single building phase. The shrine, which some had dated even as early as stratum XI, was in fact not built until stratum VII. Strata VII and VI may be only two phases of the same stratum, with the shrine destroyed at the end of stratum VI. This redating of the temple means that any association with the alleged religious reforms of either Hezekiah or Josiah is problematic. Firm conclusions will have to wait until the publication of the final reports, but what still seems to accord with all interpreters is that the destruction of stratum VIII is to be assigned to Sennacherib's invasion.[75]

Conclusions

This survey, brief as it is, indicates a number of things. We can summarize them as follows:

1. Archaeology is interpretative, and there are differences of opinion among respected archaeologists on a number of points in this survey. We cannot claim a complete consensus, though there is perhaps more of one now than there was thirty years ago. But the archaeology is vital for a proper understanding of the history of this episode—and any other in the history of ancient Palestine.[76]

2. The stratigraphy and dating at Lachish is extremely important, and much of the interpretation of other sites depends on their relation to the finds at Lachish.

3. The *lmlk* seals are also quite important, but there is some difference of opinion on them even now. The question is whether they continued in use after the reign of Hezekiah. The old view was that they continued to be used to the fall of the kingdom of Judah, but more recently interpreters have seen them as confined to the reign of Hezekiah. However, A. Mazar

74. Zimhoni, 'The Iron Age Pottery'.

75. Miriam Aharoni, 'Arad: The Israelite Citadels', *NEAEHL* I, pp. 82-87; Yohanan Aharoni, 'Excavations at Tel Arad: Preliminary Report on the Second Season, 1963', *IEJ* 17 (1967), pp. 233-49; *idem*, 'The Israelite Sanctuary at Arad', in D.N. Freedman and J.C. Greenfield (eds.), *New Directions in Biblical Arachaeology* (Garden City, NY: Doubleday, 1971), pp. 28-44; Ze'ev Herzog, Miriam Aharoni, Anson F. Rainey, and S. Moshkovitz, 'The Israelite Fortress at Arad', *BASOR* 254 (1984), pp. 1-34.

76. See the recent evaluation of the relationship between archaeology and the history of ancient Israel by Ernst Axel Knauf, 'History, Archaeology, and the Bible', *TZ* 57 (2001), pp. 262-68.

and more recently Stern have argued that a few continued to be used for some decades after Hezekiah's death.[77] Mazar seems to be suggesting not that more jars were manufactured but that jars already in use continued to be around and utilized until their working life came to an end; Stern, however, puts forward the view that the jars continued to be manufactured, with only the seal types changing (to the rosette and concentric circle), though at least one *lmlk* seal was used as late as Josiah's reign. It seems to be widely accepted that the rosette seal and the concentric circles are developed stylized forms of the four-winged and two-winged seal impressions.[78] However, the idea that *lmlk* jars continued to be produced has been strongly challenged by Vaughn.[79] He accepts that because Jerusalem would have had many such jars but was not conquered, it is inevitable that some would have been used after Hezekiah's time. But of the other sites adduced (including Arad) only Khirbet Shilḥah has a case of a *lmlk* jar handle from a clear seventh-century context (and the jar itself was not restorable).

4. The area of Judah where the *lmlk* seals are found and where destruction seems to have taken place in relation to the events of 701 BCE is a fairly well-defined area.[80] The main cities of defence were those in the Judaean hill country and the Shephelah, with Hebron as the main hub. Most of them show evidence both of the stamped jar handles and attack by the Assyrians. The distribution of finds also has interesting affinities with the list of fortified cities in 2 Chron. 11.5-10, though the exact relationship has been much debated.[81]

5. There is so far no archaeological or other evidence that Jerusalem was invested by the Assyrian army in the sense of being surrounded by a siege

77. Mazar, *Archaeology of the Land of the Bible*, pp. 455-58; Stern, *Archaeology of the Land of the Bible, II*, pp. 174-78.

78. Stern, *Archaeology of the Land of the Bible*, pp. 176-78; Na'aman, 'The Kingdom of Judah under Josiah', *TA* 18 (1991), pp. 3-71 (31-33).

79. Vaughn, *Theology, History, and Archaeology*, pp. 106-109.

80. See especially Na'aman, 'Hezekiah's Fortified Cities'.

81. This was pointed out by Na'aman, 'Hezekiah's Fortified Cities' This led to the response by Yosef Garfinkel ('2 Chronicles 11.5-10 Fortified Cities List and the *lmlk* Stamps—Reply to Nadav Na'aman', *BASOR* 271 [1988], pp. 69-73), which was answered by Na'aman ('The Date of 2 Chronicles 11.5-10—A Reply to Y. Garfinkel'). See also T.R. Hobbs, 'The "Fortresses of Rehoboam" Another Look', in Lewis M. Hopfe (ed.), *Uncovering Ancient Stones: Essays in Memory of H. Neil Richardson* (Winona Lake, IN: Eisenbrauns, 1994), pp. 41-64; Ehud Ben Zvi, 'The Chronicler as a Historian: Building Texts', in Patrick M. Graham, Kenneth G. Hoglund and Steven L. McKenzie (eds.), *The Chronicler as Historian* (JSOTSup, 238; Sheffield: Sheffield Academic Press, 1997).

mound and having an Assyrian army camped outside its wall. It was 'shut up' by having the various communication routes blocked, but the nearest evidence of the Assyrian army is presently at Ramat Raḥel, four kilometres from Jerusalem.

Two Centuries of Sennacherib Study: A Survey[82]

Before the decipherment of cuneiform in the nineteenth century, researchers were almost entirely dependent on the biblical text. As scholars began to take account of Sennacherib's own inscriptions, a number of issues emerged that continue to exercise researchers even to the present. These include the questions of (1) the literary and source analysis of the account in 2 Kgs 18.13–19.37; (2) the relationship of 2 Kgs 18.13-16 to the rest of the account; (3) how many invasions of Palestine were carried out by Sennacherib; (4) the question of the Rabshakeh's mission and speech; (5) the significance of Hezekiah's 'fourteenth year' in 2 Kgs 18.13; and (6) the place of Taharqah (Tirhaka) and the Egyptians in the story.

The Nineteenth Century

At the beginning of the nineteenth century the collective knowledge of events at the end of the eighth century BCE period was no different from that of the previous several centuries. Basically, all scholars had were the biblical text, a strange story in Herodotus 2.141, and a handful of Jewish sources such as Josephus. The first half of the nineteenth century changed all this, with the decipherment of both Egyptian hieroglyphic writing and Mesopotamian cuneiform. The effect was a knowledge explosion that we too often forget because of long acquaintance with these additional sources.

What soon emerges in a study of earlier scholarship is to what extent most of the problems that have exercised scholars to the present were already issues before 1900. One of the first to write on the subject after Sennacherib's inscriptions became known was George Rawlinson, brother of the Sir Henry Rawlinson who had so much to do with deciphering cuneiform and making available some of the early inscriptions. George Rawlinson's study of Assyria in his work, *The Five Great Monarchies of the Ancient Eastern World*, attempted to interpret the events of Sennacherib's invasion in the light of all that was known in the mid-nineteenth

82. My thanks to Professors Knauf, Na'aman, and Ben Zvi for their suggestions for amendments and additional bibliography in this section.

century.[83] Rawlinson had available several sources that contained inscriptions of Sennacherib.[84] His chronology was slightly off that now known, with a dating of the attack on Judah to 700 BCE.[85] As Rawlinson saw it, when Jerusalem was invested, Hezekiah saw the error of his ways and sought to surrender; for his part Sennacherib was glad to be saved a long and perhaps inconclusive siege. He therefore limited his punishment to the collection of a large tribute and returned to Nineveh. However, about two years later in 698 BCE he invaded Judah for a second time. This conclusion was not made on the basis of the Assyrian inscriptions but the requirements of the biblical text.[86] It is to this second invasion that the events of 2 Kgs 18.17–19.37 refer.

Thus, the idea of reconciling the two sets of texts by postulating more than one invasion was already present not long after the Assyrian inscriptions had begun to give new understanding to the events of Sennacherib's reign.[87] The main object of this second campaign, according to Rawlinson, was really the Egyptians who were encouraging Hezekiah's stance. Rawlinson recognizes that Taharqa did not become king until '690, *eight* years after this; but he may have been already—as he is called in Scripture— "king of Ethiopia"', a strange statement not further clarified.[88] He dealt

---

83. George Rawlinson, *The Five Great Monarchies of the Ancient Eastern World: The Second Monarchy: Assyria* (4 vols.; London: John Murray, 1864), II, pp. 430-46.

84. E.g., Henry C. Rawlinson, *A Commentary on the Cuneiform Inscriptions of Babylonia and Assyria* (London: J.W. Parker, 1850).

85. This was already corrected to 701 BCE in the 2nd edition a few years later in 1870.

86. 'There is nothing in the Assyrian records to fix, or even to suggest, this date. It is required in consequence of the length of Hezekiah's reign' (Rawlinson, *Assyria*, p. 439 n. 4).

87. This interpretation apparently first appeared in Rawlinson's edition of Herodotus: *The History of Herodotus: A New English Edition* (London: J. Murray, 1858–60) (not available to me). Since Henry Rawlinson wrote several of these supplementary essays, the creation of this thesis has been ascribed to him (e.g., Eberhard Schrader, *The Cuneiform Inscriptions and the Old Testament* [trans. O.C. Whitehouse; 2 vols.; London: Williams & Norgate, 1885–88], I, pp. 305-306 n. *; ET of *Die Keilinschriften und das Alte Testament* (Giessen: J. Ricker, 2nd edn, 1883). However, as noted by Robert William Rogers ('Sennacherib and Judah', in Karl Marti [ed.], *Studien zur semitischen Philologie und Religionsgeschichte: Julius Wellhausen zum siebzigsten Geburtstag* [BZAW, 27; Giessen: Alfred Töpelmann, 1914], pp. 317-28), only those essays directly signed by Henry Rawlinson are to be credited to him. George Rawlinson seems to be the author of this interpretation.

88. Rawlinson, *Five Great Monarchies*, II, p. 442 n. 2, italics his.

with the problem of the 'fourteenth year' of Hezekiah's reign by suggesting a textual emendation, without giving any justification for this change.[89]

Wellhausen wrote at a time when Assyriology had already made rapid strides; for example, he correctly dates Sennacherib's campaign against Judah to 701 BCE.[90] His brief account of the invasion follows the biblical account more closely than some modern critics.[91] He states (giving no citation of passages) that when Hezekiah rebelled against Assyrian rule following the death of Sargon in 705, Isaiah was bitterly opposed to the action. When Sennacherib re-asserted his control of Philistia, defeated an Egyptian/Ethiopian army at Eltekeh, and devasted various towns in Judah, Hezekiah made haste to come to terms, which were accepted by Sennacherib. However, as the Assyrian pushed toward Egypt Sennacherib began to have second thoughts about the unconquered citadel of Jerusalem in his rear. When he sent his officer to demand Jerusalem's surrender, Isaiah responded by encouraging Hezekiah not to give in. The Assyrian army was devasted by 'a still unexplained catastrophe' (an Egyptian tradition of which is given by Herodotus), and Jerusalem was saved. Wellhausen noted that 2 Kgs 18.14-16 is closer to the Assyrian accounts and based on a source different from the rest of the narrative.

Wellhausen does not appear to have been aware of Rawlinson's thesis of two invasions; however, E. Schrader, although discussing Rawlinson's theory at some length, held a similar view to Wellhausen's, concluding, 'There is absolutely no space in the Biblical record for this subsequent campaign'.[92] Unlike Wellhausen and many subsequent interpreters, Schrader placed a good deal of weight on the battle between the Assyrians and Egyptians. He argued that it was a 'a Pyrrhus-victory' which left the Assyrians severely weakened and in no position either to advance further against Egypt or even to take Jerusalem. This interpretation was supported by the fact that the Assyrian inscriptions had no list of prisoners taken or spoils of battle acquired.[93]

89. Rawlinson, *Five Great Monarchies*, II, 434 n. 12: 'The Hebrew and Assyrian numbers are here irreconcilable. I should propose to read in 2 Kings xviii.13 "twenty-seventh" for "fourteenth".'

90. Julius Wellhausen, *Prolegomena to the History of Israel* (trans. J.S. Black and A. Menzies, with a preface by W. Robertson Smith; Edinburgh: A. & C. Black, 1885); ET of *Prolegomena zur Geschichte Israels* (2 vols.; Berlin: G. Reimer, 1878).

91. Wellhausen, *Prolegomena*, pp. 481-84.

92. Schrader, *The Cuneiform Inscriptions*, I, pp. 305-306.

93. Schrader, *The Cuneiform Inscriptions*, I, pp. 299-301.

In 1886 B. Stade produced a basic analysis of the narrative in 2 Kgs 18.13–19.37 that has continued to dominate the literary discussion.[94] He noted that 18.14-16 has already been recognized as an insertion from a good sources that was early.[95] He then argued that 18.13, 17 to 19.9a was parallel to 19.9b-37. Neither of these narratives could be considered trustworthy historical sources but were both 'legendary', even if here and there they contained a correct historical datum.

The Twentieth Century to 1970
Almost half a century after Rawlinson but when Assyriology was still a new science, A. Jeremias attempted to bring together the latest information from textual and other discoveries that might illuminate the Old Testament.[96] He put forward a variant of Rawlinson's hypothesis that there were three campaigns by Sennacherib against Jerusalem: one in 701 BCE (found in 2 Kgs 18.13-16) in which Lachish was held as a threat against Jerusalem (necessary since many of Sennacherib's troops had to be dispatched home because of a rebellion in Babylon[97]); one as an episode in the same siege in which the Rabshakeh came to Jerusalem (2 Kgs 18.17–19.8); and one after 691 BCE in which Tirhakah (who came to the throne in that year) played a role (2 Kgs 19.9-37).[98] One of the main factors in his postulating two invasions seems to be the name of Taharqa (Tirhakah) who was not king until 691 BCE, suggesting that the name in 2 Kgs 19.9 is either an error or an indication of a later incident after Taharqa had become king.[99] This interpretation of two campaigns was also accepted by R.W. Rogers.[100]

Through the early decades of the twentieth century, various attempts were made to reconstruct the sequence of events in Sennacherib's campaign.

94. Bernhard Stade, 'Anmerkungen zu 2 Kö. 15-21', *ZAW* 6 (1886), pp. 156-89 (173-83).
95. Some of the earlier views, such as those of P. Kleinert, W. Nowack and Victor Floigl are summarized by Schrader (*The Cuneiform Inscriptions*, I, pp. 303-305).
96. Alfred Jeremias, *The Old Testament in the Light of the Ancient East: Manual of Biblical Archaeology* (2 vols; Theological Translation Library; London: Williams & Norgate, 1911); revised edition of *Das Alte Testament im Lichte des Alten Orients: Handbuch zur biblisch-orientalischen Altertumskunde* (Leipzig: J.C. Hinrichs, 2nd edn, 1906).
97. This interpretation is now known to be erroneous.
98. Jeremias, *The Old Testament*, II, pp. 222-28; *Das Alte Testament*, pp. 526-31.
99. Jeremias, *The Old Testament*, II, p. 226 // (German edition) pp. 529-30.
100. Robert William Rogers, *Cuneiform Parallels to the Old Testament* (New York: Eaton and Mains, 1912); *idem*, 'Sennacherib and Judah', pp. 317-28.

L.L. Honor's PhD thesis, later published, laid out six different reconstructions before concluding that the available data made it impossible to reconstruct the sequence of events.[101] R.P. Dougherty pointed out how closely the account in 2 Kgs 18.13-16 is supported by both the Assyrian inscriptions and archaeology (as then available).[102] Although not giving any detailed discussed, he indicated his acceptance of the view that the two accounts in 2 Kgs 18.17–19.37 refer to a second invasion of Palestine by Sennacherib. A. Ungnad argued that the figure of 200,150 taken captive by Sennacherib, was the result of a textual misreading, and the text should be understood as 2150.[103]

A good summary of the situation to the Second World War is given in the posthumous commentary by J.A. Montgomery.[104] He emended the 'fourteenth year' of Hezekiah (2 Kgs 18.13) to 'twenty-fourth year', but he was not alone in doing so.[105] Broadly following Stade he divided 2 Kgs 18–20 into five sections. He considered section B (18.17–19.7) and section C (19.8-37) as 'variant traditions of Isaiah's part in the historical drama'. This conclusion is important because it led to a rejection of the two-invasion hypothesis. Noting that a number of scholars had accepted this explanation, he sided with several important scholars (such as J. Meinhold, A. Alt, A.T. Olmstead, and E. Meyer) who had rejected it.[106] Montgomery did not happen to mention W.F. Albright, but it was probably the opinion of W.F. Albright, expressed in a number of publications, that made the two-invasion hypothesis widely accepted.[107] Albright stated, 'The writer still believes in the "two campaign" theory of Sennach-

101. Leo Lazarus Honor, *Sennacherib's Invasion of Palestine: A Critical Source Study* (Contributions to Orienal History and Philology, 12; New York: Columbia, 1926).

102. Raymond P. Dougherty, 'Sennacherib and the Walled Cities of Judah', *JBL* 49 (1930), pp. 160-71.

103. A. Ungnad, 'Die Zahl der von Sanherib deportierten Judäer', *ZAW* 59 (1943), pp. 199-202. On this, cf. Marco De Odorico, *The Use of Numbers and Quantifications in the Assyrian Royal Inscriptions* (SAAS, 3; Helsinki: The Neo-Assyrian Text Corpus Project, 1995), pp. 173-74, 114-15.

104. James A. Montgomery, *A Critical and Exegetical Commentary on the Books of Kings* (ed. H.S. Gehman; ICC; Edinburgh: T. & T. Clark, 1951), pp. 480-518 (513-18).

105. Montgomery, *Books of Kings*, p. 483. See also below, pp. 29-30.

106. Montgomery, *Books of Kings*, pp. 516-17.

107. E.g. Albright, 'The History of Palestine and Syria', *JQR* 24 (1934), pp. 363-76, especially pp. 370-71; *idem*, 'New Light from Egypt on the Chronology and the History of Israel and Judah', *BASOR* 130 (1953), pp. 4-11, especially pp. 8-11.

erib's invasion of Judah'.[108] Part of his argument was that Taharqa was only nine years old in 701 BCE. A. Parrot cited Albright's position, though he himself followed the view that a single campaign was in question.[109]

In the middle of the twentieth century, the options for interpreting Sennacherib's invasion could be gleaned—as so often in the history of ancient Israel—by comparing the histories of Noth and Bright. Noth gave an interpretation that depended almost entirely on 2 Kgs 18.16-19 (along with the Assyrian inscriptions); the rest of the biblical account was essentially ignored.[110] Bright, on the other hand, followed the well-known Albrightian convention of reconciling the biblical account as far as possible with other sources and, like Albright, postulated two invasions of Sennacherib.[111] He admitted that this was a minority opinion,[112] but he was able to refer to a recent Egyptological study that considered Taharqa to be only about ten years old in 701 BCE.[113]

Despite the number who opted for the two-invasion thesis, John Gray (who had also accepted it in the first edition of his commentary) summed up the situation by noting:

> If from a literary point of view 18.17–19.37 were a historical passage, then there would be a serious doubt of its reference to the same episode and certainly to the historical situation of 701 noted in the historical passage in 18.13-16. But 18.17–19.37, despite the proportion of prose narrative, is not of the literary genre of history, but belongs rather to popular anecdotal tradition centring on the prophet Isaiah and 'the good king Hezekiah' and the general theological theme of God's vindication of his honour and the

108. Albright, *From the Stone Age to Christianity: Monotheism and the Historical Process* (Garden City, NY: Doubleday, 2nd edn, 1957), p. 314 n. 53.

109. André Parrot, *Nineveh and the Old Testament* (Studies in Biblical Archaeology 3; London: SCM, 1955), p. 55; (ET of *Ninive et l'Ancien Testament* [Neuchâtel: Delachaux et Niestlé, 2nd edn, 1955]).

110. Martin Noth, *The History of Israel* (London: A. & C. Black; New York: Harper and Row, rev. trans, 1960), pp. 266-69; (ET of *Geschichte Israels* [Göttingen: Vandenhoeck & Ruprecht, 1950]).

111. John Bright, *A History of Israel* (Philadelphia: Westminster Press, 1959), pp. 267-69, 282-87.

112. Bright, *A History of Israel*, p. 282.

113. Reference was made to Miles Frederick Laming Macadam, *The Temples of Kawa: Oxford University Excavations in Nubia* (2 vols.; Oxford University Press, 1949), especially I, pp. 18-20. See also J.M.A. Janssen, 'Que sait-on actuellement du Pharaon Taharqa?', *Biblica* 34 (1953), pp. 23-43. According to this argument the Kawa inscriptions indicated that Taharqa was only 20 years old when taking the throne in 690 BCE.

inviolability of Zion, the place of his throne, a theme familiar in cult-liturgy and re-echoed on occasion by the prophets, especially Isaiah of Jerusalem.[114]

Another who rejected the two-invasion hypothesis was H.H. Rowley.[115]

This period of study was brought to a climax by the seminal monograph of the biblical tradition by B.S. Childs.[116] His form-critical study of the passages in 2 Kings and Isaiah refined the analysis originally carried out by Stade. He dismissed the Herodotus passage in a brief footnote.[117] One of his main contributions to the debate was the comparison of the Rab-shakeh's speech with that of an Assyrian document in which a persuasive case not to side with rebels was put by an Assyrian official, leading Childs to argue that the B_2 biblical account reflected historical reality.[118] His overall conclusion was that it was not possible to reconcile the Assyrian and biblical accounts without further information.

The Past Three Decades

The past 30 years have seen an enormous amount of activity relevant to the question of Sennacherib's invasion. Particularly important in this development has been the archaeological work. This is not to say that much important archaeological work had not already been done before 1970, but the past three decades have seen not only the re-interpretation of digs earlier in the century but also a the series of new excavations in important sites such as Tel Lachish. These have been summarized above (pp. 3-20) and will be mentioned only in passing here.

Ronald Clements picked up where Childs left off and attempted to find an overall solution to the problem. His was that the 'inviolability of Zion' belief was not that of Isaiah; on the contrary, Isaiah had opposed

114. John Gray, *I and II Kings* (OTL; Philadelphia: Westminster, 2nd edn, 1970), pp. 657-704.

115. H.H. Rowley, 'Hezekiah's Reform and Rebellion', in *Men of God: Studies in Old Testament History and Prophecy* (London: Thomas Nelson & Sons, 1963), pp. 98-132 (earlier published in *BJRL* 44 [1961–62], pp. 395-461).

116. Brevard S. Childs, *Isaiah and the Assyrian Crisis* (SBT, Second Series 3; London: SCM Press, 1967).

117. Childs, *Isaiah and the Assyrian Crisis*, p. 101 n. 70.

118. Childs, *Isaiah and the Assyrian Crisis*, pp. 78-93. For the comparative material he draws on H.W.F. Saggs, 'The Nimrud Letters, 1952—Part I', *Iraq* 17 (1955), pp. 21-56; 'The Nimrud Letters, 1952—Part II', *Iraq* 17 (1955), pp. 126-60; 'The Nimrud Letters, 1952—Part III', *Iraq* 18 (1956), pp. 40-56 + plates 9-12. See also the discussion below (pp. 27-29).

Hezekiah's nationalistic expansion.[119] The reception of Clement's solution was mixed, with one reviewer accepting that he 'clarifies and (I think) solves the problem of Sennacherib's invasion(s) of Judah'[120] but another avering that 'Clement's historical arguments are simply not cogent, and his theological arguments are even more suspect... It can be recommended only with the gravest reservations.'[121]

Some years later I.W. Provan investigated the Hezekiah narrative in the context of investigating the composition of the Deuteronomistic History.[122] He argued that a version of the Dtr-H up to and including the reign of Hezekiah was composed in the reign of Josiah. More recently he returned to the topic in a discussion of principles in historiography.[123] Here he seems to put all the accounts on the same level. Although he does not say so explicitly, the view seems to be that the biblical accounts were all written fairly near in time to the actual events. Account A is seen only as an episode in a sequence of events in which B_1 and B_2 are not parallel accounts (to Account A and to each other) but further episodes in a linear narrative. Few are likely to be willing to follow him in what seems to be a naive harmonistic reading of the text as a straightforward account of the events at the time.

Christoph Hardmeier also took up Childs's challenge.[124] His solution

119. Ronald E. Clements, *Isaiah and the Deliverance of Jerusalem: A Study of the Interpretation of Prophecy in the Old Testament* (JSOTSup, 13; Sheffield: Sheffield Academic Press, 1980); cf. also his study, 'The Politics of Blasphemy: Zion's God and the Threat of Imperialism', in Ingo Kottsieper, Jürgen van Oorschot, Diethard Römheld, and Harald Martin Wahl (eds.), *'Wer ist wie du, HERR, unter den Göttern?' Studien zur Theologie und Religionsgeschichte Israels für Otto Kaiser zum 70. Geburtstag* (Göttingen: Vandenhoeck & Ruprecht, 1994), pp. 231-46. For the analysis of the Isaiah tradition that disassociated all pro-Zion views from Isaiah, Clements depended on Hermann Barth, *Die Jesaja-Worte in der Josiazeit* (WMANT 48; Neukirchen-Vluyn: Neukirchen Verlag, 1977).

120. Carroll Stuhlmueller, review of Clements, *Isaiah and the Deliverance of Jerusalem* in *CBQ* 43 (1981), pp. 273-75, quote from p. 274.

121. J.J.M. Roberts, review of Clements, *Isaiah and the Deliverance of Jerusalem* in *JBL* 101 (1982), pp. 442-44, quotes from p. 444.

122. Iain W. Provan, *Hezekiah and the Books of Kings: A Contribution to the Debate about the Composition of the Deuteronomistic History* (BZAW, 172; Berlin: W. de Gruyter, 1988).

123. Provan, 'In the Stable with the Dwarves: Testimony, Interpretation, Faith and the History of Israel', in André Lemaire and Magne Saebø (ed.), *Congress Volume: Oslo 1998* (VTSup, 80; Leiden: E.J. Brill, 2000), pp. 281-319 (309-18).

124. Christoph Hardmeier, *Prophetie im Streit vor dem Untergang Judas: Erzähl-*

was to dismiss any association of 2 Kgs 18–19 with Sennacherib but to connect it with events shortly before the fall of Jerusalem. Instead of describing the siege of Jerusalem by Sennacherib, these chapters are a fictional creation to support those nationalists who wanted to resist the Babylonians. Written in 588 BCE, with the same background as described in Jer. 37–40 (but from the opposite perspective), they held up Sennacherib's invasion as an exemplar of how God would intervene to save his people. When this did not happen, the narratives were re-interpreted as an actual description of events in the time of Hezekiah. He thus rejects the consensus that the A narrative is an actual report of what happened. Hardmeier's is a major challenge to much previous thinking. Although others are willing to argue that parts of the Hezekiah narrative (particularly the B narrative) are even later than Hardmeier proposes,[125] his argument that the entire narrative is a fictive creation goes further than most are willing to go.

    F.J. Gonçalves's comprehensive study covers all aspects of the Sennacherib episode, including a lengthy analysis of the relevant biblical texts of 2 Kings, Isaiah, 2 Chronicles, and Micah. He accepts Childs's basic analysis into accounts A, B_1, and B_2 and, like many before him, thinks account A is the most trustworthy (based on a Judaean annal), with B_1 from about the middle of the seventh century and B_2 a rewriting of B_1 during the exilic period. However, like Clements he thinks that the historical Isaiah was opposed to Hezekiah's rebellion and alliances against Assyria; the present text represents a radical re-interpretation of Isaiah's message at a later time (though not as late as the time of Josiah).[126]

    As noted, a number of researchers had accepted that the Rabshakeh's speech came out of an authentic historical context close to the time of Hezekiah. This had been argued by M. Weinfeld,[127] and Childs had advanced the argument.[128] This view seems to have gone unchallenged until 1990

---

kommunikative Studien zur Entstehungssituation der Jesaja- und Jeremiaerzählungen in II Reg 18–20 und Jer 37–40 (BZAW, 187; Berlin: W. de Gruyter, 1989).

    125. See Nadav Na'aman's study below (pp. 201-20).

    126. Francolino J. Gonçalves, *L'expédition de Sennachérib en Palestine dans la littérature hebraïque ancienne* (Ebib, 7; Paris: Galbalda, 1986).

    127. Moshe Weinfeld, 'Cult Centralization in Israel in the Light of a Neo-Babylonian Analogy', *JNES* 23 (1964), pp. 202-12. He based his argument on the Assyrian material published by A.L. Oppenheim, '"Siege-Documents" from Nippur', *Iraq* 17 (1955), pp. 69-89.

    128. See above, n. 118.

when an article by Ehud Ben Zvi undermined the whole basis of the argument by showing that the alleged parallels were made up of common biblical language, and the reference to Hezekiah's reform shows Deuteronomic features.[129] Following on this are studies by Klaas Smelik,[130] who considers the speeches free compositions by the author, and D. Rudman,[131] who points out the resemblance of the Rabshekeh's speech to biblical prophetic language. However, W.R. Gallagher has recently argued that both this passage and Isa. 10.5-19 were written close to the time of the alleged speech and are summaries of it.[132]

In an important study S. Parpola showed that the name of Sennacherib's assassin had been wrongly interpreted for many years.[133] It should be read as Arda-Mulišši of which the biblical Adrammelech (2 Kgs 19.37) is a corrupt but recognizable form. Berossus is even closer with Adramelos. This was the older son of Sennacherib who was passed over as heir to the throne in favour of the younger son Esarhaddon. Thus, Arda-Mulišši killed his father to gain what he thought was rightfully his; however, Sennacherib had taken the precaution of sending Esarhaddon away from the capital. The latter was therefore able to lead the attack against the assassin and his followers in their attempt to replace him.

The question of Hezekiah's fourteenth year (2 Kgs 18.13) has been a problem since the Assyrian inscriptions showed that Sennacherib's invasion was in 701 BCE. According to 18.1 Hezekiah became king in Hoshea's third year, while Samaria fell in Hezekiah's fourth year. If so, the events of 701 would have taken place about Hezekiah's twentieth year. What is one to do, then, with the fourteenth year of 18.13? A simple—and possibly simplistic—solution is to assume a textual error, already found as early as

129. Ehud Ben Zvi, 'Who Wrote the Speech of Rabshakeh and When?' *JBL* 109 (1990), pp. 79-92.

130. Klaas A.D. Smelik, 'King Hezekiah Advocates True Prophecy: Remarks on Isaiah xxxvi and xxxvii//II Kings xviii and xix', in K.A.D. Smelik (ed.), *Converting the Past: Studies in Ancient Israelite and Moabite Historiography* (OTS, 28; Leiden: E.J. Brill, 1992), pp. 93-128.

131. Dominic Rudman, 'Is the Rabshakeh also among the Prophets? A Rhetorical Study of 2 Kings xviii 17-35', *VT* 50 (2000), pp. 100-10.

132. See pp. 33-34 below.

133. Simo Parpola, 'The Murderer of Sennacherib', in B. Alster (ed.), *Death in Mesopotamia: Papers Read at the XXVIᵉ Rencontre assyriologique international* (Mesopotamia: Copenhagen Studies in Assyriology, 8; Copenhagen: Akademisk Forlag, 1980), pp. 161-70.

30 *'Like a Bird in a Cage'*

Rawlinson.[134] Emendation of 'fourteenth year' to '24th year' has often been done, though another view was that the synchronism with Hoshea's reign was the error.[135] Several other solutions have been advanced in the past few decades. One was by A.K. Jenkins who argued that the 'fourteenth year' refers to the invasion under Sargon II about 713–711 (Isa. 20). According to this explanation the original account had an anonymous Assyrian king, but this king was later identified with Sennacherib. This interpretation depends on the 'high chronology' which makes Hezekiah's reign about 727–698 BCE.[136] Very recently a similar explanation was given by J. Goldberg who argued for a 'limited invasion' of Palestine by Sargon II in 712 BCE, referred to in 18.13-16 and later confused with the 701 invasion.[137] Hayim Tadmor and Michael Cogan put forward the case that the '14th year' was a reference to Hezekiah's illness, an incident that originally preceded the account of Sennacherib's invasion. Since Hezekiah's life was extended for 15 years after his illness, this gave the 29-year total of his reign.[138] In 1994 Na'aman surveyed the arguments on both sides (citing earlier studies) and argued that, though not conclusive, the balance of evidence favoured taking the fourteenth year as correct and dating Hezekiah's reign c. 715–686.[139] Sennacherib's inscriptions continued to be revised at least until 691, yet Hezekiah's death is not mentioned, making it unlikely that he died in 698 as some have thought. The problem created with regard to Manasseh's reign by this dating is resolved by assuming a ten-year co-regency between Hezekiah and his son.

The issue of chronology was more recently discussed by B. Becking.[140]

134. See p. 22 n. 89 above.

135. See above, n. 105. On the earlier attempts to resolve the problem, see H.H. Rowley, 'Hezekiah's Reform and Rebellion', pp. 111-15. Also, John Gray, *I and II Kings*, p. 673.

136. A.K. Jenkins, 'Hezekiah's Fourteenth Year: A New Interpretation of 2 Kings xviii 13-xix 37', *VT* 26 (1976), pp. 284-98.

137. Jeremy Goldberg, 'Two Assyrian Campaigns against Hezekiah and Later Eighth Century Biblical Chronology', *Biblica* 80 (1999), pp. 360-90.

138. H. Tadmor and M. Cogan, מאירועי שנת ארבע־עשרה לחזקיהו : מחלת המלך וביקור המשלחת הבבלית ('Hezekiah's Fourteenth Year: The King's Illness and the Babylonian Embassy'), *EI* 16 (1982), pp. 198-201 (Eng. abstract 258*-59*).

139. Na'aman, 'Hezekiah and the Kings of Assyria', pp. 236-39.

140. Bob Becking, *The Fall of Samaria: An Historical and Archaeological Study* (Studies in the History of the Ancient Near East, 2; Leiden: E.J. Brill, 1992), pp. 51-56; ET and updating of ch. 2 of the doctoral thesis, *De ondergang van Samaria: Historische, exegetischee en theologische opmerkingen bij II Koningen 17* (ThD, Utrecht

He has argued for the dating of the fall of Samaria to 723 BCE, a year earlier than the conventional 722. He accepts that the synchronism made by the Dtr editor between the reigns of Hoshea and Hezekiah (2 Kgs 18.9-10) is based on Judaean archives. This means that the fourteenth year of Hezekiah has to be either spring 715 to spring 714 or autumn 716 to autumn 715. At that time Sargon II dispatched an expedition to Palestine that was relatively peaceful. This may have been led by the crown prince Sennacherib. This was the 'first campaign' of Sennacherib, dated to the summer of 715 BCE. Becking thus hypothesizes two campaigns of Sennacherib, but his schema differs from the conventional one in that the 701 invasion was his second campaign.

Although developed early in the modern study of the episode, the standard 'two invasion' hypothesis (701 and after 689 BCE) has tended to be supported by conservative scholars. Siegfried Horn wrote on the subject not long after Bright's history appeared,[141] but it was his colleague William Shea whose main contribution advanced well beyond Bright with a lengthy circumstantial argument that Sennacherib had conducted a second invasion after 689 BCE.[142] However, Shea's argument was refuted point by point by Frank Yurco.[143] The Egyptian data were crucial to the question: when did Taharqa take the throne and what was his age in 701 BCE? K.A. Kitchen, who could hardly be accused of wanting to refute the biblical account, argued strongly that the Egyptian inscriptions allowed only one invasion.[144] A. Rainey and Yurco had also written on the question.[145]

Fakulteit de Godgeleerheit, 1985). His most recent treatment is in this volume, pp. 46-72 below.

141. Siegfried H. Horn, 'Did Sennacherib Campaign Once or Twice against Hezekiah?' *AUSS* 4 (1966), pp. 1-28.

142. William H. Shea, 'Sennacherib's Second Palestinian Campaign', *JBL* 104 (1985), pp. 410-18.

143. Frank J. Yurco, 'The Shabaka-Shebitku Coregency and the Supposed Second Campaign of Sennacherib against Judah: A Critical Assessment', *JBL* 110 (1991), pp. 35-45.

144. Kenneth A. Kitchen, 'Egypt, the Levant and Assyria in 701 BC', in Manfred Görg (ed.), *Fontes atque Pontes: Eine Festgabe für Hellmut Brunner* (Ägypten und Altes Testament, 5; Wiesbaden: Harrassowitz, 1983), pp. 243-253; also *The Third Intermediate Period in Egypt (1100–650 BC)* (Warminster, Wilts.: Aris & Philips, 2nd edn, 1986), pp. 154-61, 552-59. Cf. also P. E. Dion, 'Sennacherib's Expedition to Palestine', *Bulletin of the Canadian Society of Biblical Literature* 48 (1988), pp. 3-25.

145. Anson F. Rainey, 'Taharqa and Syntax', *TA* 3 (1976), pp. 38-41; Yurco, 'Sennacherib's Third Campaign and the Coregency of Shabaka and Shebitku', *Serapis* 6 (1980), pp. 221-40.

They asserted that new grammatical studies of the relevant inscriptions had led to improved readings of the text and new interpretations, and it was now clear that Taharqa was at least twenty years old in 701 BCE and fully capable of leading a military campaign as crown prince.[146] However, it should be noted that not all Egyptologists agree on this interpretation. D. Redford[147] still read the relevant inscription as saying that Taharqa was only 20 when he came from Nubia to Egypt in 690, while J. von Beckerath argued that Taharqa came to Egypt in 700 BCE at the earliest and probably later.[148]

Most recently, though, a new inscription has been assigned to the reign of Taharqa,[149] and Shea has argued that this inscription is to be connected to an invasion of Sennacherib, though not the one in 701 BCE but a postulated 'second invasion'.[150] M. Cogan, however, has dismissed this argument, pointing out that those deported by the Egyptians could not have been the Assyrian army and that subsequent Assyrian rule has no place for such a defeat of the Assyrian army.[151]

We can sum up the situation by noting that as long as detailed information on Sennacherib's reign after 689 BCE remains undiscovered, we cannot absolutely rule out a second Assyrian invasion of Judah. However, all the available evidence presently known is against this scenario. For better or for worse, we have to consider the biblical narrative as referring to the 701 invasion alone and proceed from there.

Going against the consensus, C. R. Seitz[152] doubts whether the Annals

146. Kitchen, *The Third Intermediate Period*: pp. 164-70; Anson F. Rainey, 'Taharqa and Syntax'; Yurco, 'Sennacherib's Third Campaign and the Coregency of Shabaka and Shebitku': pp. 222-23 plus notes.

147. Donald B. Redford, *Egypt, Canaan, and Israel in Ancient Times* (Princeton, NJ: Princeton University Press, 1992), pp. 351-53, especially n. 163.

148. J. von Beckerath, 'Ägypten und der Feldzug Sanheribs im Jahre 701 v.Chr'., *UF* 24 (1992), pp. 3-8, especially p. 7. Although von Beckerath cites Kitchen, *Third Intermediate Period*, he does not seem to know Yurco, 'Sennacherib's Third Campaign'.

149. Donald B. Redford, 'Taharqa in Western Asia and Libya', *EI* 24 [1993], pp. 188*-91*.

150. William H. Shea, 'The New Tirhakah Text and Sennacherib's Second Palestinian Campaign', *AUSS* 35 (1997), pp. 181-87; *idem*, 'Jerusalem under Siege', *BAR* 26/6 (Nov/Dec 1999), pp. 36-44, 64. For a more recent study on the chronology of the 25th Dynasty, see Donald R. Redford, 'A Note on the Chronology Dynasty 25 and the Inscription of Sargon II at Tang-i Var', *Or* 68 (1999), pp. 58-60.

151. Mordechai Cogan, 'Sennacherib's Siege of Jerusalem', *BAR* 27/1 (January/February 2001), pp. 40-45, 69.

152. Christopher R. Seitz, 'Account A and the Annals of Sennacherib: A Reassessment', *JSOT* 58 (1993), pp. 47-57.

of Sennacherib can be said to confirm 2 Kgs 18.14-16. He concludes that whatever its basis in fact account A must still be interpreted in the larger redactional context of 2 Kings; it may even be intended to tone down the otherwise positive account of Hezekiah. One cannot assume a unilateral development from real facts to theological idealization, that is, that the development of the text was of increasing idealization of Hezekiah. Further, these verses have not been deleted from the parallel passage in Isaiah 36; they simply had no purpose in that different context. Klaas Smelik examined the question of how much history there might be in the biblical account.[153] Historical reconstruction must be based on 18.13-16 and Assyrian sources, which can be reconciled 'in all essentials'. The narratives were written as a reaction to the destruction of the Jerusalem temple, retrojecting current problems into the past; thus, they cannot be used for historical reconstruction of 701 but rather of 586.

Antti Laato pointed out the propagandistic nature of the Assyrian inscriptions.[154] They have much reliable data but also attempt to censure and suppress inconvenient facts (much of the article is devoted to this question). He concludes that the supposed second attack of the Egyptian army is incorrect and draws on the Herodotus story to suggest that the Assyrian army withdrew because of a plague, but Hezekiah sent tribute to prevent a further invasion. B. Oded responded to Laato, arguing that in Sennacherib's relief the artist could have carved a siege of Jerusalem which he then labeled 'Lachish' when Jerusalem did not fall[155]. He also suggests that the figure of those alleged to be deported by Sennacherib was actually the total of the population of Judah at the time. The recent study by M. De Odorico on numbers in the Assyrian texts also has information of relevance to the numbers in Sennacherib's inscriptions.[156] De Odorico shows that all sorts of factors affect the preservation of numbers in texts; although they usually cannot be taken as trustworthy statistical information, they are not normally the gross exaggerations sometimes alleged by modern scholars.

W.R. Gallagher's study 'most closely adheres' to the approach that uses

---

153. Smelik, 'King Hezekiah'.

154. Antti Laato, 'Assyrian Propaganda and the Falsification of History in the Royal Inscriptions of Sennacherib', *VT* 45 (1995), pp. 198-226.

155. Bustenay Oded, 'History vis-à-vis Propaganda in the Assyrian Royal Inscriptions', *VT* 48 (1998), pp. 423-25.

156. Marco De Odorico, *The Use of Numbers*.

all sources and assumes that they are largely reliable.[157] The first part (chs. 1–2) looks at Isaiah 21.1–22.14 (written in 704 or 703, before Sennacherib's campaign), Isaiah 10.5-19 (a contemporary summary of the Rabshekeh's speech), and 14.4b-21 (a taunt song of Isaiah's written on the death of Sargon II). The second part (chs. 3–9) looks at the various sources in an attempt to reconstruct Sennacherib's third campaign; however, about half this section is devoted to 2 Kgs 18.13–19.37//Isaiah 36–39. This indicates that Gallagher's interest is primarily in the biblical material. He also comes to some quite conservative conclusions about it. He accepts that account A is from a separate source but rejects the division of account B into two separate sources and the idea that they form two accounts of the same events. The two speeches by the Rabshakeh are genuine, based on authentic Assyrian speeches and close to his actual words if not actual quotation. The B account as a whole is by and large reliable. He would excise the name 'Tirhakah' from 19.9 but accept an Egyptian-Cushite force of some sort. The interpretation of 19.35 as referring to a plague is looked at sympathetically but seen as uncertain. His reconstruction of events is thus heavily influenced by the biblical account B read as a sequential narrative (account A is seen essentially as an overall summary). With major reviews still to come, it remains to be seen how many (apart from conservative evangelicals) will find his arguments convincing.

Sennacherib's Inscriptions and Reliefs
Scholarly work on the Sennacherib inscriptions has made an important contribution to progress in historical understanding.[158] The various inscriptions were collected in an edition and English translation by D.D. Luckenbill.[159] Translations of the texts alone over the next few decades made access to them available to biblical scholars without Akkadian.[160] The next

---

157. W. R. Gallagher, *Sennacherib's Campaign to Judah* (SHCANE, 18; Leiden: E.J. Brill, 1999).

158. For a discussion of the subject, see Louis D. Levine, 'Preliminary Remarks on the Historical Inscriptions of Sennacherib', in H. Tadmor and M. Weinfeld (eds.), *History, Historiography and Interpretation: Studies in Biblical and Cuneiform Literatures* (The Hebrew University of Jerusalem, The Institute for Advanced Studies; Jerusalem: Magnes Press; Leiden: E.J. Brill, 1983), pp. 58-75.

159. D.D. Luckenbill, *The Annals of Sennacherib* (Oriental Institute Publications, 2; University of Chicago, 1924).

160. James B. Pritchard (ed.), *Ancient Near Eastern Texts relating to the Old Testament* (with Supplement; Princeton: Princeton University Press, 3rd edn, 1969); *idem*, *Ancient Near East in Pictures* (Princeton: Princeton University Press, 1954); William

work on the text was undertaken by Rykele Borger.[161] One of the significant recent additions to the textual repertory was made by Nadav Na'aman,
who demonstrated that fragments already known actually belonged together.[162] The most recent study is that of E. Frahm.[163] However, W. Mayer
has now rechecked the inscriptions and includes an edition and English
translation in this volume (pp. 168-200 below).

The most recent study of the reliefs, with impressive drawings by Judith
Dekel, was given by Ussishkin.[164] A critique of Ussishkin and others, with
an extensive new interpretation of the reliefs is now given by C. Uehlinger
in this volume.[165]

Summary

This brief survey has demonstrated that the issues in the first part of the
nineteenth century remain, by and large, those that are still with us. Once
the Assyrian inscriptions (and to a lesser extent the Egyptian) had become
available, much labour was expended in trying to reconcile the biblical
text to them. Despite some objections, it is still widely felt that 2 Kgs 18.13-
16 agrees remarkably with Sennacherib's own statements, but this has left
the question of what to do with the rest of the narrative (18.17–19.37).
One of the main insights (Stade's) has been to recognize that 18.17–19.9a,
36-37 and 19.9b-35 are parallel accounts. Two basic positions have been
taken over the years: to consider 18.17–19.37 as referring to a second invasion of Sennacherib after 689 BCE or to reject this passage as mainly legendary (even if a few authentic data may be found in it). The question of
Tirhakah (Taharqa) in 19.9 has been a major issue in arguing for one or
the other of these alternatives. Only a few have argued for one invasion
but substantial historicity in the 18.17–19.37 narrative.

The present situation can be stated succinctly as follows. The 'two-
invasion' hypothesis, although once widely accepted, looks now to be in
tatters. The main extra-biblical support has collapsed. Although Sennach-

W. Hallo (ed.), *The Context of Scripture: Volume II Monumental Inscriptions from the
Biblical World* (Leiden: E.J. Brill, 2000), pp. 300-305 (texts 2.119).

161. R. Borger, *Babylonisch-assyrische Lesestücke* (Rome: Pontifium Institutum
Biblicum; 2nd edn, 1979).

162. Na'aman, 'Sennacherib's "Letter to God"; 'Sennacherib's Campaign to Judah'.

163. E. Frahm, *Einleitung in die Sanherib-Inschriften* (AfO Beiheft, 26; Horn:
F. Berger & Söhne, 1997).

164. Ussishkin, *The Conquest of Lachish*.

165. See pp. 221-305 below.

erib's reign is poorly documented after 689 BCE, there does not seem to be any room for another campaign to Palestine. Although still debated, the weight of opinion seems to be that Taharqa was capable of leading a military expedition against the Assyrians in 701 BCE. Whether he did or not is naturally still a matter of debate, but the reason for his mention in 2 Kgs 19.9 probably derives from his later image as the great Egyptian (Nubian) king who stood up to Assyria.[166] However, the chronology of Hezekiah's reign remains disputed, and the way in which Jerusalem avoided a siege is considerably debated. For a continuation of the debate, see the last chapter of the present volume (pp. 308-23 below).

Summary of Papers in this Volume

Note that a number of the following papers survey the original sources. In such cases, only interpretative comments are mentioned.

Bob Becking, 'Chronology: A Skeleton without Flesh? Sennacherib's Campaign as a Case-Study', is concerned with the question of where chronology fits in the concept of 'objective' history (if there is such a thing). This investigation involves examining the various Assyrian sources relating to Sennacherib, their dating, and the dating of the events described within them. A combination of the Assyrian and biblical accounts indicates two main invasions. The old two-invasion hypothesis (of invasions in 701 and 688 BCE) is rejected, but a new hypothesis with invasions in 715 (by Sargon II) and 701 BCE (by Sennacherib) is put forward. In the light of this interpretation, the accounts of 2 Kgs 18.14-16 and the Assyrian sources can be easily reconciled. 2 Kgs 18.17–19.37 is much more complicated, because of its tradition history, but the core of the narrative can be explained from the 715 BCE invasion. On the methodological question, a chronological framework may be considered objective in the sense of being a matter of fact (or not), but it does not equal history. Writing history means supplying meaning to the chronological statements. There is objectivity in history writing, but only in the narrow area of chronological data which supplies the skeleton of any history that we write. A plea is made for a moderate position between a 'correspondence theory' and a 'coherence theory' of historical truth, a position taken by many other historians.

Ehud Ben Zvi, 'Malleability and its Limits: Sennacherib's Campaign against Judah as a Case-Study', uses the episode to investigate historical

166. Cf. Dion, 'Sennacherib's Expedition to Palestine', pp. 12-13.

method. His detailed survey of the sources argues that the 2 Kings account was written to be read by Jews in the postexilic period, who would notice the parallels between the events in the time of Hezekiah with those a century later in the time of Zedekiah, but would also notice the contrasting fates. Hezekiah (unlike Zedekiah) tried to submit, but Sennacherib invaded anyway; hence, it was an attack on Yhwh himself, putting Sennacherib in a different category from Nebuchadnezzar. The account in 2 Chronicles is quite different, being only a small unit within a literary complex lionizing Hezekiah for his piety. Together with Josephus's version, these illustrate how malleable the tradition was in the various sources, depending on the interests and ideology of the composer, the context in which it was composed, and the intended message for a particular audience. Yet there are limits to this malleability, for we do not find unrestrained creativity. One constraint is what the intended audience already believes and is prepared to believe. It is not stated anywhere, for example, that Hezekiah was deposed. Being closer to the event does not mean that the sources are less interpretative or found in a more accurate form, as modern accounts of recent military campaigns show; their historical accuracy still has to be tested. One test is whether diametrically separate groups share perceptions or representations; if so, this may point to something outside their representation, that is, a 'historical event'.

Philip Davies, 'This Is What Happens...', begins with a quotation from Morton Smith (for more on this interesting quotation, you must read his article) that the big guy almost always wins and you cannot beat the odds. History tells us what we already know, that is, what we know tells us what is history. Objectivity in history writing is impossible because history can only exist as narrative, and every narrative has to have a narrator. 'Biblical historians' are not above ideology critique, and the ideology still lying behind much study of 'biblical history' can be seen in the splentic reaction to challenges concerning, for example, the historicity of David—the historical study of Priam or Charlemagne hardly arouses such passions. However, we must go beyond Smith and ultimately disagree with him. Historians do not study 'what happens'; they study the way in which humans discourse about the past. There is no objective 'history' because what constitutes the abstract concept of 'history' is our experience and our perception and our memory. Historians are primarily exegetes, exegetes of the ancient discourse of the sources. Yet we cannot carry out the task of analysing human discourse about the past unless we have a notion of truth or reality as a criterion. To separate distortion from invention in any story is an important exegetical task. It matters to the modern historian, in a way that it did not matter to the Assyrian or Judaean writer, that we do justice to all stories and their tellers by seeking to understand what their stories meant and what the events they witnessed and recorded meant.

Lester Grabbe, 'Of Mice and Dead Men: Herodotus 2.141 and Sennacherib's Campaign in 701 BCE', considers the report of Herodotus on how the Egyptians confronted Sennacherib's army but were delivered because mice rendered useless the weapons and armour of the Assyrian army. Some have suggested that the mice tie in with 2 Kgs 19.35//Isa. 37.36 in indicating the destruction of the Assyrian army by a plague. Greek knowledge of the ancient Near East was often partial and distorted. A good example is the Ninus-Semiramus legend of Ctesias and later writers. Yet there is a (small) historical core to even that legend, and different writers were more careful than others. Herodotus is one of the more believable writers, though he was at the mercy of his sources. We know from some examples that his sources were often quite good (e.g., the accession of Darius I to the throne). He reports the Sesostris legend, but this was probably already extensively developed among the Egyptians (who were his likely source) and does have a historical core. Herodotus probably also obtained his Sennacherib story from the Egyptians. It looks like an independent Egyptian version of the invasion of 701 in which the Assyrian attack on the Egyptians was thwarted by some unusual happening. However, there is no indication of a connection between his account and the story in 2 Kgs 18–19//Isa. 36–37 (the mice in Herodotus's story do *not* suggest a plague). Several points of historical methodology arise from this example, including the principle that each source must be read and analysed in its own right before being combined with others for purposes of reconstruction. No potential source should be dismissed without careful analysis; on the other hand, no potential source should be accepted without similar scrutiny. Scholars of classical history have wrestled with some of the same problems of source material and problematic data as biblical scholars, and there is much that the latter can learn from the former. On the other hand, historians of the ancient Near East also have things to teach to both; especially relevant is the work of those who combine expertise in both classical and ancient Near Eastern history.

Axel Knauf ('701: Sennacherib at the Berezina') seeks to reconstruct the events of Sennacherib's campaign in Palestine through a critical use of all available sources. The Assyrian inscriptions do not usually lie, but they often intentionally exaggerate the achievements of the Assyrian king. Sennacherib's account is arranged roughly according to geography rather than chronologically. Hezekiah capitulated not because of any miraculous event but because his economic base was destroyed. Jerusalem was not itself besieged (as the archaeology shows; 2 Kgs 18.17–19.37 relates to Nebuchadnezzar's siege and is thus of no value as a source), but once the Shephelah was removed from Hezekiah's control, Judah was no longer self-sufficient in food. Hezekiah's Arab allies deserted, and he had no choice but to submit. In the first part of the campaign Ekron had been temporarily bypassed as a relatively unimportant site, but this allowed the Egyptian army to move up and outflank the Assyrians. The battle of Eltekeh came toward the end of the campaign, when the Assyrian army was exhausted by campaigning all summer and besieging nearly 50 towns. Eltekeh was not the splendid victory for Sennacherib that the inscriptions portray. This is indicated in part by the fact that Sennacherib himself had to join the fight. The Assyrians, Egyptians, and Philistines then negotiated a peace settlement. Hezekiah got the short end of the stick because part of his territory was taken away and given to several of the Philistine cities. But Sennacherib had fought to a standstill and campaigned no more in Palestine the rest of his reign. Thus, Judah was now useful to the Assyrians because it flanked Philistia where Egypt maintained a foothold. Hezekiah began the politics of appeasing the Assyrians that Manasseh continued. Jerusalem expanded in the seventh century because of Assyrian aid.

Niels Peter Lemche's contribution ('On the Problems of Reconstructing Pre-Hellenistic Israelite [Palestinian] History') has already been published in the electronic *Journal of Hebrew Scriptures*. He addresses directly the question of historical method, using two main examples: the invasion of Sennacherib and the actions of Mesha king of Moab. The 'historical-critical' method developed two centuries ago distinguished between *Bericht* ('story, interpetation') and *Überreste* ('remains of historical data') on the assumption that it could differentiate between the two. Because of the information from the Assyrian annals, it is not so difficult to draw a line between *Überreste* and *Bericht* in 2 Kgs 18–19 since the main outlines of what happened are clear. The speech and letter of the Rabshakeh are invented (though some would wish to defend their genuineness), but much of the story reflects an actual campaign of Sennacherib. The picture of king Mesha in 2 Kgs 3 is rather different. Although the Moabite inscription shows a king Mesha of Moab who lived close to the time of Omri, there is little in 2 Kgs 3 that is confirmed by the inscription. Contrary to expectations, Ahab is not mentioned by name, and Omri could be the eponymous figure of *Bit Ḥumri* 'house of Omri' of the Assyrian inscriptions. The piece of assured data is the name Mesha plus a bit on Moab of the time. The problem is historical reconstruction because most of ancient Israel's history is based on the biblical text alone and forms a 'hermeneutical circle', that is, a logical circle. We have some external data, and the history of Israel and Judah as told by biblical historians is not totally devoid of historical information. There are historical remains in the biblical text, as well as an approximate chronological framework. The problem is how to determine what is *Überreste* without use of circular reasoning. The first step is to establish the genres of historiography in the ancient Near East. The biblical writers were not trying to write history in the modern sense; the past was of interest mainly for examples of good and bad behaviour. Thus, Omri's achievements are suppressed because the writer was not interested in giving a comprehensive account of the past as we might expect of a modern historian. There is history in the narrative, but it is mainly short notes. Recent study has shown that the patriarchal narratives are not history, that the exodus and conquest are a fiction, that the 'judges period' is a series of hero tales, and that the empires of David and Solomon and the 'united monarchy' are a fictional representation. There were certainly the two kingdoms of Israel and Judah, but the other 'actors' of the region are mostly ignored or their part distorted. During the so-called exile, most of the population remained in the land. The Persian period is mainly a dark spot, while Ezra is probably a late invention. We should give up hope of reconstructing pre-Hellenistic history on the basis of the Old Testament; it is simply an invented history with only a few referents to things that really happened.

Walter Mayer's contribution is a translation and revision of a chapter in his book, *The Art of Warfare and Politics of the Assyrians.*[167] Its aim is to give full discussion of the data and current scholarship relating to Sennacherib's third campaign. 2 Kings 18.13-16 appears to have a source from the palace or temple archives; important for its worth is the admission by Hezekiah that he has 'sinned'. It was normal to station troops on the border when preparing for an invasion. The natural route for Sennacherib's army brought him to the coast at Sidon, where the hill country of Judah could be bypassed. The various vassals who send representatives to show submission to Sennacherib also sent troop contingents. Sennacherib would not have kept his entire army together, first taking one city and then moving to the next; on the contrary, it was split up and many different cities besieged simultaneously. The Egyptian army did not come because of an urgent

167. Walter Mayer, *Politik und Kriegskunst der Assyrer* (ALASPM, 9; Münster: Ugarit-Verlag, 1995).

message for help from Eqron or Judah, because there would not have been enough time. Help must already have been requested sometime before the Assyrian invasion. This fact is also indicated by the place of engagement near Beersheba: a newly arrived Egyptian army coming by the quickest route would have been engaged by the Assyrians on the coastal route. The image of a siege of Jerusalem, with catapults and other siege engines and a siege mound surrounding the city, comes from the classical world but does not represent the state of the poliorcetic skills in Assyrian times. Sennacherib shut up Hezekiah 'like a bird in a cage' by guarding the routes out of Judah to the neighbouring peoples—which would not have taken major troop resources. The Assyrians did not find Jerusalem of major interest; Hezekiah's territory was left in ruins, with much of it removed out of his control, a state of things continuing under subsequent kings. As far as the Assyrians were concerned, it was a victory over a rebel, as the amount of booty described shows. Assyrian booty was enumerated in two different ways, even in the same text. One is an exact count; the other is to give totals which may look inflated or even incredible. In the latter case, they may represent not booty but the grand total of all requisitioned supplies from the region during the campaign.

Nadav Na'aman's article ('Updating the Messages: Hezekiah's Second Prophetic Story [2 Kings 19.9b-35] and the Community of Babylonian Deportees') is a revised version of his recent article in *Biblica*. His aim is to re-examine 'Account B$_2$' (2 Kgs 19.9b-35) in order to shed more light on the date and place of composition. This passage is notable for its reference to unusual toponyms, either conquered by the Assyrians in the ninth century BCE or being rather remote and out of the way (19.12-13: Gozan, Haran, Rezeph, the Edenites in Telassar, Lair, Sepharvaim, Hena, Ivvah). However, a careful study shows that these names reflect the late seventh-century Babylonian campaigns of Nabopolassar and Nebuchadnezzar. The writer also shows ignorance of Assyrian policy (e.g. the claim that the Assyrians destroyed the gods of those they conquered, though it is possible that the Babylonians destroyed Assyrian cult statues, which is perhaps reflected in vv. 17-18). The knowledge of areas in the eastern Babylonian area suggests that the author of the Account B$_2$ was probably a descendant of a Judaean deportee who lived in eastern Babyonia in the second half of the sixth century BCE. The reference to 'my ancestors' is probably to Nabopolassar and Nebuchadnezzar, which would puts the time of composition after 562 BCE, either in the late Neo-Babylonian or early Persian period. He has elaborated the story of Sennacherib's campaign from his knowledge of a new physical location and more recent historical events in

order to convey a theological message. It thus differs from 'Account B₁'
(2 Kgs 18.17–19.9a, 36) which drew on the conquests of Sargon II and
was written before the destruction of Jerusalem (since it contrasts the fate
of Jerusalem with that of Samaria). Account B₁ also shows greater aware-
ness of Assyrian military strength. The memory of Sennacherib's assassination, the accession of Esarhaddon, and knowledge of the Egyptian king
Taharqa's battles with Assyria suggest an early date of composition,
probably in the late years of Manasseh. It looks like a pre-Deuteronomic
prophetic story which the Deuteronomist combined with 'Account A'
(2 Kgs 18.13-16) into a continuous history which he then integrated into
his composition of the history of Israel; however, the editor omitted any
reference to the subjugation of Judah by Assyria to give the impression of
Judah freed from Assyrian rule. Thus, even though the sources were cited
almost verbatim and very little was added, the Deuteronomist has shaped
the history of Judah decisively according to his ideological and theological
considerations. Account B₂ is a revised theological version of Account B₁
which the author has updated and adapted to the new experience of the
Jewish community in Babylonia.

Christoph Uehlinger ('Clio in a World of Pictures—Another Look at the
Lachish Reliefs from Sennacherib's Southwest Palace of Nineveh') contributes a fresh study of the reliefs picturing the siege of Lachish. Although
these have often been appealed to in discussing the historical campaign of
Sennacherib, little new was said about their interpretation between Layard
and Ussishkin. Appreciation is expressed for the important contribution
made by Ussishkin, but the latter's interpretation is challenged that Lachish
is depicted in quasi-perspective, as if seen from Sennacherib's position in
front of the Assyrian attack. The reliefs are not a 'photographic' depiction
of the siege but draw on the conventional, stereotypical tradition of Assyrian iconography. On the other hand, they are not just a stereotypical creation of the artist but show actual knowledge of the historical siege, though
this knowledge probably came from written (and possibly oral) accounts
of the siege, not drawings by a 'field artist'. Sennacherib's sculptures
should not be given precedence over the textual data, as if they were a
neutral attempt to record his campaigns, but they should be understood in
their own right as another Assyrian interpretation of the events. Considering
texts and sculptures as partly independent, and complementary sources,
Uelinger insists on the necessity for the modern historian to take into
account the rules and constraints of actual data processing inherent in the
work of both ancient scribes and sculptors. A good deal of the article is
devoted to discussing how the central slabs of the Lachish series relate to

one another, how the scene they contain should be reconstructed, and what might have been in the damaged areas. It is argued that the missing citadel of Lachish was probably shown in the damaged area toward the top of slab 7. The study concludes by asking why Sennacherib's sculptures give such prominence to the conquest of Lachish, which is not even mentioned in Sennacherib's annals, while they seem to ignore Jerusalem. It is suggested, with due caution, that Jerusalem may actually be shown on slab I-28 in Sennacherib's throne room. In any case, it cannot be concluded that Jerusalem was absent when Sennacherib's sculptures were originally carved, and scholars should thus refrain from putting too much stress on this apparent contradiction between texts and images.

Part II
ARTICLES

CHRONOLOGY: A SKELETON WITHOUT FLESH?
SENNACHERIB'S CAMPAIGN AS A CASE-STUDY*

Bob Becking

But there is a hitch. As we put meat and muscles on the bare bones of the
happening-truth, we can be caught up—captured, if you will—within our
own stories. We become confused about where the happening-truth leaves
us off and the story-truth begins, because the story-truth, which is so much
more vivid, detailed and *real* than the happening-truth, becomes our reality.
Elizabeth Loftus[1]

Introduction

When queuing for the reception in the city hall of Oslo during the IOSOT
meeting of 1998, I had an interesting discussion with Axel Knauf. He was
responding to my paper in which, among other things, I had expressed my
view that any history is a reconstructed representation of the past. In this
reconstruction the symbol-system of the historian plays an important part
in the selection and the arrangement of the material. By implication, any
history is a subjective picture of the past.[2] Knauf challenged my view by
stating that objective information on the past is nevertheless possible.[3] We

---

* The abundance of studies on the topic is so overwhelming, that I had to make a
choice in the literature referred to in the footnotes. I hope to have made the right choice
and apologize for not having quoted everybody. The dissertation of P.K. Hooker, *The
Kingdom of Hezekiah: Judah in the Geo-Political Context of the Late Eighth Century
BCE* (Ann Arbor, MI: University Microfilm, 1993), unfortunately was not at my
disposal.

1.   E.R. Loftus and K. Ketcham, *The Myth of Repressed Memory* (New York: St.
Martin's Griffin, 1994), p. 39.

2.   B. Becking, 'No More Grapes from the Vineyard?: A Plea for a historical-
critical Approach in the Study of the Old Testament', in A. Lemaire and M. Sæbø,
Congress Volume: Oslo, 1998 (VTSup, 80; Leiden: E.J. Brill, 2000), pp. 123-41.

3.   Without, however, giving any connotation to the adjective 'objective'. See also
his remarks in E.A. Knauf, 'From History to Interpretation', in D.V. Edelman (ed.),

soon agreed that chronological data supply trustworthy information on the past and that this information is more than helpful in constructing the skeleton for a history. They are the 'bare bones of the happening-truth'. A skeleton does not equal the body, however. Bare bones need muscles on them in order to function. The methodological question to be discussed in this paper therefore would be: How helpful are the chronological data for a historical reconstruction of Sennacherib's campaign to Judah? A first step would be to display the available evidence.

Calendars, Chronicles and King-Lists

Long ago, Finkelstein has argued that a group of lists and list-like texts are the only Mesopotamian inscriptions that are not 'motivated by purposes other than the desire to know what really happened'.[4] In search of 'objective history', it would be of great importance to analyse these inscriptions.

The Eponym calendars are a primary source for the reconstruction of the chronological framework of the history of ancient Mesopotamia. The lists are a by-product of the Assyrian (and Babylonian) administration. Years were named after an important official, hence the expression: eponyms. The lists were a useful tool in dating events, legal decisions, business documents etc. Scribes throughout the empire were able to check information. In some of the lists additional information is supplied in mentioning important events from a specific year. This additional information is related to such features as royal building projects, military campaigns and celestial events. The eponymate of Bur-Sagillê during the reign of Ashur-Dan III mentions a solar eclipse. Modern astrological calculations arrive at an eclipse in June 763 BCE. This date perfectly matches the reign of the Assyrian king mentioned. This and other synchronisms make the Eponym calendars a trustworthy source.[5]

The Fabric of History: Text, Artifact and Israel's Past (JSOTSup, 127; Sheffield: Sheffield Academic Press, 1991), pp. 26-64.

4. J.J. Finkelstein, 'Mesopotamian Historiography', *PAPS* 107 (1963), pp. 461-72; see also J. van Seters, *In Search of History: Historiography in the Ancient World and the Origins of Biblical History* (New Haven/London: Yale University Press, 1983), pp. 55-99.

5. A recent presentation and discussion of the material can be found in A.R. Millard, *The Eponyms of the Assyrian Empire 910–612 BC* (SAAS, 2; Helsinki: Neo-Assyrian Text Corpus Project, 1994), esp. pp. 1-14; see also J.K. Kuan, *Neo-Assyrian Historical Inscriptions and Syria-Palestine* (JDDS, 1; Hong Kong: Alliance Bible Seminary, 1995), pp. 7-18.

Unfortunately, not much specific evidence for the reign of Sennacherib is given. The eponym for the year 701 BCE has been Hanânu.[6] The eponym calendar C^{B}6 supplies some interesting information:

> 705   On the twelfth Ab, Sennacherib [became] king,
> 704   t[o] Larak, Sarrabanu, [   ]; the palace of Kilizi was made ; in
>   [ ]; the nobles against...[   ].[7]

The eponym calendar C^{B}7 has the entry for 701:

> 701   [f]rom the land of Halzi[8]

This does not supply much information, however.

A second group of cuneiform texts that are useful for reconstructing the chronology of the period under consideration are the Assyrian and Babylonian Chronicles. These texts narrate greater periods of ancient Mesopotamian history. Their information is based on astrological diaries, which make them trustworthy to some degree.[9] As for Sennacherib and his campaign to Jerusalem, they, unfortunately, do not supply much evidence. In Babylonian Chronicle I a large section is dedicated to the reign of Sennacherib.[10] The information in this section is, however, confined to Sennacherib's quarrels and clashes with Elam in the east and with Babylon. No mention is made of a campaign to the west. This absence of evidence, however, cannot be assessed as the evidence for the absence or non-existence of a campaign to Judah in 701 BCE for the perspective of this chronicle is very much Babylon-centered. The same holds for the other reference to Sennacherib in the chronicles. In a section, transmitted in two different chronicles we read:

6.   See Millard, *Eponyms*, p. 49.
7.   B^6 Rev.11-15; see Millard, *Eponyms*, p. 48.
8.   B^7.1'; see Millard, *Eponyms*, p. 49.
9.   See A.K. Grayson, *Assyrian and Babylonian Chronicles* (TCS, 5; Locust Valley: J.J. Augustin Publisher, 1975); A.K. Grayson, 'Königslisten und Chroniken', in *RlA* 6, pp. 86-89; Van Seters, *In Search of History*, pp. 79-92; J.A. Brinkman, 'The Babylonian Chronicle Revisited', in T. Abush *et al.* (eds.), *Lingering over Words: Studies in Ancient Near Eastern Literature in Honor of William L. Moran* (HSS, 37; Atlanta: Scholars Press, 1990), pp.73-104.
10. *Bab. Chron.* I ii.19–iii.36; see Grayson, *Chronicles*, pp. 76-81; A. Laato, 'Assyrian Propaganda and the Falsification of History in the Royal Inscriptions of Sennacherib', *VT* 45 (1995), pp. 198-226 (203-209).

For eight years during the reign of Sennacherib, for twelve years during the reign of Esarhaddon—twenty years in sum–Bel stayed in Baltil[11] and the Akitu-festival did not take place.[12]

This piece of evidence stresses the fact that during a period of Assyrian overlordship over Babylon the important New Year festival could not be executed in view of the fact that the statue of Marduk[13] was in exile in Assyria.[14]

The Mesopotamian King-lists supply data as to the sequence and the duration of the reigns of the respective kings.[15] Sennacherib is referred to in the following lists:

Babylonian King List A IV: 8-20[16]

8	2 (years)	Pulu[17]
9	5 (years)	Ululaya,[18] dynasty of Ashur
10	12 (years)	Marduk-apla-iddina,[19] dynasty of the Sealand
11	5 (years)	Sargon
12	2 (years)	Sennacherib, dynasty of Habigal[20]

11. Baltil is the indication in neo-Babylonian for the city of Ashur.

12. Esarhaddon Chronicle (Grayson, *Chronicles*, p. 127), pp. 31-32 and Akitu Chronicle (Grayson, *Chronicles*, p. 131), pp. 1-4.

13. As in DtIsa. Bel is a name for Marduk; see T. Abush, 'Marduk', in *DDD* second edition, pp. 543-49.

14. On the Akitu-festival see, e.g., J. Black, 'The New Year Ceremonies in Ancient Babylon "Taking Bel by the Hand" and a Cultic Picnic", *Religion* 11 (1981), pp. 39-59; K. van der Toorn, 'The Babylonian New Year Festival: New Insights from the Cuneiform Texts and their Bearing on Old Testament Study', in J.A. Emerton (ed.), *Congress Volume: Leuven 1989* (VTSup, 43; Leiden: E.J. Brill, 1991), pp. 331-39.

15. For an outline see W. Röllig, 'Zur Typologie und Entstehung der babylonischen und assyrischen Königslisten', in M. Dietrich und W. Röllig (eds.), *lišan mithurti* (Festschrift W. von Soden; AOAT, 1; Neukirchen–Vluyn: Neukirchener Verlag, 1969), pp. 265-77; Grayson, 'Königslisten und Chroniken', pp. 89-125; Van Seters, *In Search of History*, pp. 68-76.

16. See A.L. Oppenheim, in *ANET*, p. 272; Grayson, 'Königslisten und Chroniken', pp. 90-96; A.R. Millard, 'Babylonian King Lists', in W.W. Hallo (ed.), *The Context of Scripture*, I (Leiden: E.J. Brill, 1997), p. 462. The Ptolemaic Canon seems to have used the tradition present in Babylonian King-List A, although it has replaced Sennacherib twice by αβασιλευτα; cf. Grayson, 'Königslisten und Chroniken', p. 101.

17. = Tiglathpileser III.

18. = Shalmaneser V.

19. = Merdodakhbaladan II.

20. Most probably a form of Hanigalbat, a traditional term for Upper Mesopotamia, see Millard, 'Babylonian King Lists', p. 462.

13	1 months	Marduk-zākir-šumi, son of Ardu
14	9 months	Marduk-apla-iddina, soldier of Habi
15	3 (years)	Bel-Ibni, dynasty of Babylon
16	6 (years)	Aššur-nadin-šumi, dynasty of Habigal
17	1 (year)	Nergal-ušezib
18	4 (?; years)	Mušezib-Marduk, dynasty of Babylon
19	8 (?; years)	Sennacherib
20	x (years)	Esarha[ddon]

This text lists the rulers over Babylon. It indicates that after the death of Sargon II, Sennacherib took over the Babylonian throne for two years and that at the end of his reign he had full control over Babylon. In the intermediate period, there was a constant interchange of rulers over Babylonia some local rulers and some puppet kings under Assyrian control. This evidence concurs with the remarks in the Annals of Sennacherib that he had to establish his power over Babylon several times after rebellions of local rulers against his rule or against his *locum tenens*.

Synchronistic King List IV:1-10[21]

1	[Senn]acherib, king of Assyria	[...]
2	Nabu-apla-iddina, his master	[...]
3		[...] × [...][22]
4		king of Babylon, after the people of [Babylonia]
5		broke the treaty
6		[Aš]šur-nadin-šumi was placed on the throne
7	Sennacherib	Nergal-šezib, son of Ga[h]ul
8		Mušezib-Marduk, son of Dakuri
9		kings of Babylonia
10	Sennacherib, king of Ashur	and Babel

This list is less informative on dates, but concurs with the evidence of the Babylonian King-List A.

Synchronistic King List Fragment IV:4[23]

4	Sennach[erib]	king of Babylon, after the people of [Babylonia]
5	Esar[haddon]	broke the treaty
6	Ashur[banipal]	

21. See *ARAB* II, §1188; A.L. Oppenheim, in *ANET*, pp. 272-74; Grayson, 'Königslisten und Chroniken', pp. 116-21.

22. *ARAB* II, §1188 reads Bêl-[ibni]; according to Grayson, 'Königslisten und Chroniken', p. 120, no traces of this name are left.

23. Grayson, 'Königslisten und Chroniken', pp. 121-22.

This list only confirms the order of the Assyrian Kings.

The name Sennacherib might be restored in a fragment of another Syn-chronistic King List.[24] The Assyrian King Lists end with Ashur-Nerari V and Shalmaneser V respectively, not supplying evidence on Sennacherib.[25]

In what does this exercise result? From the evidence it can be inferred that Sennacherib was king over Assyria from 705–681 BCE. A campaign against Judah is not attested in these inscriptions that, however, do not falsify the assumption that the king besieged Jerusalem in 701 BCE. The base for an 'objective' history is, however, rather small. This implies that other texts should be taken into consideration.

Dates from Assyrian Royal Inscriptions

The deeds and doings of Sennacherib are recorded in a great variety of texts. Thanks to the careful and detailed research of Eckart Frahm, we now have a better understanding of the available evidence.[26] It should be noted that the Annals and many of the other inscriptions have a narrative charac-ter and that they cannot be assessed as objective reports on past events.[27] The texts are biased and drenched in royal ideology. Although the colo-phons of these texts make clear that most of them have been composed during the reign of Sennacherib and by implication are based on 'eye-witness reports', they still are good examples of narrative history in which the selection and the arrangement of the available material is steered by the symbol system of its composers.[28]

This implies that the elements in the story should be interpreted before using them in a historical reconstruction. A history based on this interpre-

24. Grayson, 'Königslisten und Chroniken', pp. 125, 135.

25. The 'Khorsabad King List' and the 'SDAS King List', edited by I.J. Gelb, 'Two Assyrian King Lists', *JNES* 13 (1954), pp. 209-30; see also Grayson, 'Königslisten und Chroniken', pp. 101-15.

26. E. Frahm, *Einleitung in die Sanherib-Inschriften* (AfO Beiheft, 26; Horn: F. Berger und Söhne, 1997).

27. See, e.g., Van Seters, *In Search of History*, pp. 60-68; H. Tadmor, 'History and Ideology in the Assyrian Royal Inscriptions', in F.M. Fales (ed.), *Assyrian Royal Inscriptions: New Horizons* (OAC, 17; Roma: Institutu per l'Oriente, 1981), pp. 13-33; Laato, 'Assyrian Propaganda'.

28. For a methodical background to this approach of history writing see my paper 'Ezra's Reenactment of the Exile', in L.L. Grabbe (ed.), *Leading Captivity Captive: 'The Exile' as History and Ideology* (JSOT Sup, 278; ESHM, 2; Sheffield: Sheffield Academic Press, 1998), pp. 40-61.

tation is by implication not an objective history, but a tentative proposal. Nevertheless, the Annals and other inscriptions of Sennacherib supply us with some 'hard facts' as to the chronology of his reign and his campaigns which are summarized in the following outline.[29]

Year	Campaign/gerru	Main activity
705		Sennacherib succeeds his father Sargon II on the throne
704	1	Marduk-zākir-šumi II usurps the throne in Babylon
		After a month he is relieved by Marduk-aplu-iddina II
		Sennacherib reacts with a punitive campaign late in the year
703	1	Continuation of the campaign Pacification of Babylonia
702	1 + 2	On return from Babylonia in the beginning of 702 the Assyrians subdued the cities of Hirimmu and Hararatu in the eastern Tigirs-area
		The second campaign as such is directed against inhabitants of the Zagros-mountains
701	3	Campaign against the West:
		Sidon, Philistia and Jerusalem
700	4	Consolidation of the relations in Babylonia
699		Building activities in Nineveh
698		Building activities in Nineveh
697	5	Campaigns against the North and the Northwest

Later Sennacherib was mainly occupied in Elam and Babylonia. This outline indicates that Sennacherib in the beginning of his reign was occupied with settling peace in Babylonia, 'Persia' and the Levant. A campaign against Jerusalem is part of this picture.

Hezekiah's Fourteenth Year

Within the discussion on the chronology of the Assyrian threat to Judah, the interpretation of the phrase 'the fourteenth year of Hezekiah' plays an important role. In 2 Kgs 18.13 a campaign by Sennacherib against Judah is dated in this year. When was this 'fourteenth year'? When 701 BCE is construed as Hezekiah's fourteenth year, then a chronological oddity is implied. That date would imply that Hezekiah became king in 715/714 BCE. According to the Book of Kings, Hezekiah already was king over Judah at the time of the fall of Samaria. Regardless of the date of this

---

29. For evidence and secondary literature, see Frahm, *Sanherib-Inschriften*, pp. 4-19.

event in 723, 722/21 or 720 BCE[30] this date cannot easily be reconciled with Hezekiah ascending the throne in 715/714 BCE.[31] Before making further remarks on this point, it should be noted that my basic assumption is that the numbers for the reigns of the kings of Israel and Judah in the Book of Kings are not to be assessed as a deliberate and meaningful 'invention' by the redactors of the Book. Until they are falsified by contemporaneous evidence I take them as historically trustworthy.[32] This does not imply that I share the 'maximalistic' view that data in the Hebrew Bible are *always* reliable unless proven otherwise. Such a view is an indication of (1) dogmatic prejudice and (2) too positivistic an approach in the field of historical science.[33] The observation that the dating-formula is phrased in a different way in 2 Kgs 18.3 does not supply a falsification of my theses.[34]

As a starting point for my chronological argument, I take the rebellion that broke out in Samaria and Ashkelon during or after the campaign of Tiglath-Pileser III in 732 BCE against the West. As a result of this campaign Damascus was conquered by the Assyrians and the Northern Kingdom of Israel was reduced in territory to the area surrounding Samaria. But then Pekah, king of Israel, and Mitinti, ruler over Ashkelon, were driven from the throne by Hoshea and Rukibti.[35] A new reading of the Tiglath-Pileser III Summary Inscription 9: Rev. 11 made clear that the new king of Israel, Hoshea, paid tribute to his Assyrian overlord in... *Sa]rrabanu*.[36] This collation is of great

30. For a discussion, see B. Becking, *The Fall of Samaria: An Historical and Archaeological Study* (SHANE, 2; Leiden: E.J. Brill, 1992).

31. See also the remarks by G. Galil, *The Chronology of the Kings of Israel and Judah* (SHCANE, 9; Leiden: E.J. Brill, 1996), pp. 100-101; D. Edelman, 'What If We Had No Accounts of Sennacherib's Third Campaign or the Palace Reliefs Depicting His Capture of Lachish?', in J.C. Exum (ed.), *Virtual History and the Bible* (Leiden: E.J. Brill, 2000), pp. 88-103.

32. They might be based on an Israelite King List, the existence of which has been proposed by S.B. Parker, 'Did the Authors of the Book of Kings Make Use of Royal Inscriptions?', *VT* 50 (2000), pp. 374-76, or on the data from an Israelite Chronicle.

33. See, e.g., Knauf, 'From History to Interpretation', pp. 27-34; Becking, 'No More Grapes'; E.A. Knauf, 'The "Low Chronology" and How Not to Deal with It', *BN* 101 (2000), p. 59.

34. *Pace* L. Camp, *Hiskija und Hiskijabild: Analyse und Interpretation von 2 Kön 18–20* (MTA, 9; Altenberge: Telos Verlag, 1990), pp. 96-97.

35. See Becking, *Fall of Samaria*, pp. 19-20.

36. Collation of P. Hulin in, R. Borger and H. Tadmor, 'Zwei Beiträge zur alttestamentliche Wissenschaft aufgrund der Inschriften Tiglathpileser III', *ZAW* 94 (1984), p. 246; see also H. Tadmor, *The Inscriptions of Tiglath-Pileser III King of Assyria*

chronological importance. From other sources it is known, that the Assyrian king besieged Sarrabanu during his campaign in Babylonia in 731 BCE.[37] Relating these two pieces of evidence it becomes very probable that Hoshea paid this tribute in 731 BCE to secure the formal recognition of his reign.[38] This leads to the synchronism that the first full regnal year of Hoshea must have been autumn 732—autumn 731 BCE.[39]

These observations are relevant for the chronology of Hoshea. The years of Hoshea 7 and 9 are then to be dated in 725 and 723 BCE; which means that the fall of Samaria took place in 723 BCE, that is in the reign of Shalmaneser V, but not in his final year.

The synchronism mentioned above, however, is also relevant to the chronology of Hezekiah since this date for the conquest of Samaria fits the

(Jerusalem: Israel Academy of Sciences and Humanities, 1994), pp. 189, 277. The reading has been adopted by G.W. Jones, *1 and 2 Kings* (NCB; Grand Rapids: Eerdmans, 1984), p. 545; N. Na'aman, 'Historical and Chronological Notes on the Kingdoms of Israel and Judah in the Eighth Century B.C.', *VT* 36 (1986), pp. 71-74; S.A. Irvine, *Isaiah, Ahaz and the Syro-Ephraimite Crisis* (SBLDS, 123; Atlanta: Scholars Press, 1990), p. 57 n. 141; H. Cazelles, 'La guerre Syro-Ephraïmite dans le contexte de la politique internationale', in D. Gatrone and F. Israel (eds.), *Storia e Tradizione di Israeli* (FS J.A. Soggin; Brescia: Paideia Editrice, 1991), p. 44; Becking, *Fall of Samaria*, p. 19.53; G.W. Ahlström, *The History of Ancient Palestine from the Paleolithic Period to Alexander's Conquest* (JSOTSup, 146; Sheffield: Sheffield Academic Press, 1993), p. 636; Kuan, *Neo-Assyrian Historical Inscriptions*, p. 183; K.L. Younger, 'The Deportations of the Israelites', *JBL* 117 (1998), p. 210.

37. On this campaign see: H. Tadmor, *Introductory Remarks to a New Edition of the Annals of Tiglath-Pileser III* (PIASH, 2,9; Jerusalem: Israel Academy of Sciences and Humanities, 1969), pp. 15, 18; W. Schramm, *Einleitung in die assyrischen Königsinschriften* (HdO, I,V,I/2; Leiden: E.J. Brill, 1973), p. 131; Borger and Tadmor, 'Zwei Beiträge', pp. 247-248.

38. See Borger and Tadmor, 'Zwei Beiträge', p. 249; Na'aman, 'Historical and Chronological Notes', pp. 73-74.

39. Thus Borger and Tadmor, 'Zwei Beiträge', p. 249; Na'aman, 'Historical and Chronological Notes', pp. 73-74; Tadmor, *Tiglath-Pileser III*, pp. 277-78; Galil, *Chronology*, p. 70; Kuan, *Neo-Assyrian Historical Inscriptions*, p. 185; M. Dijkstra, 'Chronological Problems of the Eighth Century BCE: A New Proposal for Dating the Samaria Ostraca', in J.C. de Moor and H.F. van Rooy (eds.), *Past, Present, Future: The Deuteronomistic History and the Prophets* (OTS, 45; Leiden: E.J. Brill, 2000), p. 78. The view has been unconvincingly challenged by J. Goldberg, 'Two Assyrian Campaigns against Hezekiah and Later Eight Century Biblical Chronology', *Bib* 80 (1999), pp. 378-80. Goldberg assumes 729 BCE to be the first regnal year of Hoshea and he makes this year the starting point of his calculations that, however, are very problematical for the regnal years of Pekah, king of Israel.

data of his reign. According to 2 Kgs 17.1 Hoshea became king in the twelfth year of Ahaz. Supposing that Hoshea ascended the throne after the revolt in the summer of 732, the twelfth year of Ahaz must have been spring 732–spring 731 (or autumn 733–autumn 732). The regnal years of Ahaz were probably reckoned from the moment of his co-regency with Jotham and not from the moment of his undivided rule after the death of Jotham. Ahaz reigned for 16 years. His 16th year, the year of his death, is consequently spring 728–spring 727 BCE (or autumn 729–autumn 728 BCE).

It is important to note that the accession-year of Hezekiah is not the same as the year of Ahaz's death. This can be inferred from 2 Kgs 18.1. Hezekiah ascended the throne in the third year of Hoshea, that is autumn 730—autumn 729 BCE. This calculation suggests that Hezekiah became co-regent in Ahaz's 15th year.

This implies that the fourth year of Hezekiah must have been the period spring 725–spring 724 BCE (or autumn 726–autumn 725). The fall of Samaria, dated in 2 Kgs 18.10 in Hezekiah's sixth year, therefore took place in the period spring 723–spring 722 BCE (or autumn 724–autumn 723): probably in the summer of 723 BCE. This date fits the above mentioned chronology of Hoshea and has some interesting implications for the other chronological data in 2 Kings 18. I disagree with Galil who dates Hezekiah's fourth year in 722/21 BCE and does not account for the synchronisms mentioned in 2 Kgs 18.10.[40]

2 Kgs 18.13 mentions an Assyrian military campaign against Jerusalem which took place in the 'fourteenth year of Hezekiah'. A traditional view takes the textual fragment 2 Kgs 18.13-16 to be a trustworthy primary source.[41] The textual unit is taken as a starting point for complicated chronological reasoning leading to the conclusion that this source (2 Kgs 18.13-16) takes 715 or 714 BCE to be the first year of Hezekiah. The fourteenth year of Hezekiah must then have been 701 BCE, in which year the expedition of Sennacherib mentioned in the Assyrian sources took place. This traditional

40. Galil, *Chronology*, pp. 83-97.

41. Cf., e.g., Van Seters, *In Search of History*, p. 301; E. Vogt, *Der Aufstand Hiskias und der Belagerung Jerusalems 701 v. Chr.* (AnBib, 106; Roma: Biblical Institute Press, 1986), p. 24; K.A.D. Smelik, *Converting the Past: Studies in Ancient Israelite and Moabite Historiography* (OTS, 28; Leiden: E.J. Brill, 1992), p. 124; J.A. Soggin, *An Introduction to the History of Israel and Judah: Second, Completely Revised and Updated Edition* (London: SCM Press, 1993), p. 250; Gallagher, *Sennacherib's Campaign*, pp. 160-62.

view, however, would imply two different systems of dating events from the reign of Hezekiah within the one chapter 2 Kings 18.

In my chronological proposal, the fourteenth year of Hezekiah was the period between spring 715 and spring 714 BCE (or autumn 716–autumn 715).[42] It would be interesting to know what evidence for this year is provided by the Mesopotamian inscriptions. Sargon II's main activity for the year 715 BCE was a campaign against Ursa, king of Urartu.[43] Some scholars have suggested a relatively peaceful campaign against southern Palestine in 715 BCE.[44] There is, however, no direct evidence for such a campaign. This does not imply that a campaign as suggested could not have taken place. Some details are known that might argue for the campaign. In 716 BCE the Egyptian king Pir'u paid tribute to Sargon II.[45] In the same year, Sargon II settled Arabs in the newly established Assyrian province of Samerina.[46] In my view the so-called Azekah-fragment should be construed as referring to events in 715 BCE.[47] The text relates the military revenge of an unknown

42. See also Dijkstra, 'Chronological Problems'.

43. See, e.g.,
- Sg II Annals from Khorsabad (A. Fuchs, *Die Inschriften Sargons II. Aus Khorsabad* [Göttingen: Cuvillier Verlag, 1994], pp. 105-110), :ll. 101-120
- Sg II Annals 711 (A. Fuchs, *Die Annalen des Jahres 711 v. Chr.* [SAAS, 8; Helsinki: Neo-Assyrian Text Corpus Project, p. 29], III.e.12'-25'.

See also H. Donner, *Israel unter den Völkern* (VT Sup, 11; Leiden: E.J. Brill, 1964), p. 108; E. Noort, *Die Seevölker in Palästina* (Palaestina Antiqua, 8; Kampen: Kok Pharos, 1994), pp. 27-28; Fuchs, *Inschriften*, pp. 381-82.

44. E.g., Becking, *Fall of Samaria*, p. 54.

45. Sg II Annals from Khorsabad (Fuchs, *Inschriften*, p. 110), ll. 123-25.

46. Sg II Annals from Khorsabad (Fuchs, *Inschriften*, p. 110), ll. 120-23; see Becking, *Fall of Samaria*, pp. 102-04.

47. Sg II Azekah-fragment (K. 6205 + BM 82-3-23,131; joined by N. Na'aman, 'Sennacherib's "Letter to God" on his Campaign to Judah', *BASOR* 214 [1974], pp. 25-39; recent collations in G. Galil, 'Judah and Assyria in the Sargonic Period', *Zion* 57 [1992], pp. 111-33 [Hebr.]; Frahm, *Sanherib-Inschriften*, pp. 229-232; M. Cogan, 'Sennacherib', in W.W. Hallo (ed.), *The Context of Scripture. II. Monumental Inscriptions from the Biblical World* [Leiden: E.J. Brill, 2000], pp. 304-05); note that this fragment has been related to
- events in 720 BCE (Fuchs, *Sargon*, pp. 314-15; Frahm, *Sanherib-Inschriften*, p. 231);
- in 712 BCE (A. Spalinger, 'The Year 712 B.C. and its Implications for Egyptian History', *JARCE* 10 [1973], pp. 95-101; Vogt, *Aufstand*, pp. 21-23; M. Cogan and H. Tadmor, *II Kings* (AB, 11; New York: Doubleday, 1988), pp. 261-62; S. Timm, *Moab zwischen den Mächten: Studien zu historischen Denkmälern und*

Assyrian ruler to Hezekiah, king of Judah. The aim of the campaign seems to have been the strengthening of the border with Egypt. Since Sargon II was occupied with Urartian affairs, it might be possible that a high officer or the crown-prince Sennacherib, who held a high military rank by that time[48], went to Jerusalem to secure the paying of tribute. In my opinion this action was later claimed as a deed of Sargon II when he says in a Summary inscription that it was:

  mu-šak-niš ^{kur}*Ja-ú-da*[49]

  'He who subjected Judah'

The Š-stem of the verb *kanāšu*, 'to make subject', need not refer to a military campaign at all. Na'aman proposed that this inscription should be dated to late 717 or early 716 BCE. This view would make it impossible that the inscription would refer to an event that allegedly took place in 715 BCE.[50] Against Na'aman it should, however, be noted that the inscription under consideration is not dated by a colophon. This implies that the in-

---

Texten (ÄAT, 17; Wiesbaden: Harrosowitz, 1989), pp. 337 n. 19, 356 n. 50; Galil, 'Judah and Assyria'; G. Galil, 'Conflicts between Assyrian Vassals', *SAAB* 6 [1992], pp. 61-63; Galil, *Chronology*, pp. 98.104; Goldberg, 'Two Assyrian Campaigns', p. 363), and

• in 701 BCE (Na'aman, 'Sennacherib's "Letter to God"'; Irvine, *Isaiah, Ahaz and the Syro-Ephraimite Crisis*, pp. 101-102; Ahlström, *History of Ancient Palestine*, p. 625; N. Na'aman, 'Hezekiah and the Kings of Assyria', *TA* 21 [1994], pp. 235, 245-47; W. Mayer, *Politik und Kriegskunst der Assyrer* [ALASPM, 9; Münster: Ugarit Verlag, 1995], pp. 350-51; Laato, 'Assyrian Propaganda', p. 214; W.R. Gallagher, *Sennacherib's Campaign to Judah: New Studies* [SHCANE, 18; Leiden: E.J. Brill, 1999], pp. 110-12).

Tadmor, *Inscriptions*; Noort, *Seevölker*, p. 28; Cogan, 'Sennacherib', p. 304, leave the question of dating this fragment open.

48. H. Tadmor, 'The Campaigns of Sargon II', p. 78; A.K. Jenkins, 'Hezekiah's Fourteenth Year', *VT* 26 (1976), p. 296.

49. Sg II Nimrud Inscription (ed. H. Winckler, *Die Keilschrifttexte Sargons nach dem Papierabklatsche und Originalen neu herausgegeben* [Leipzig: Verlag von E. Pfeiffer], Band II, t 48 = A.H. Layard, *The Inscriptions in the Cuneiform Character from Assyrian Monuments* [London, 1851], No. 33-34), l. 8. Translation: Winckler, *Sargon*, I, p. 168; *ARAB* II, §137; K.L. Younger, 'Sargon II', in W.W. Hallo (ed.), *The Context of Scripture*. II. *Monumental Inscriptions from the Biblical World* (Leiden: E.J. Brill, 2000), pp. 298-99.

50. N. Na'aman, 'The Historical Portion of Sargon II's Nimrud Inscription', *SAAB* 8 (1994), pp. 17-20; see also Tadmor, 'Campaigns of Sargon II', p. 36.

scription would not refer to an event in 720 BCE as suggested by Na'aman on the basis of his dating of the inscription under consideration.[51] The view elaborated by Winckler and adopted by Vogt, that the Assyrian scribes have simply exchanged the 'Bruderreiche Israel und Juda' and that the reference should be construed as another piece of evidence for the conquest of Samaria by Sargon II, is ingenious but not convincing.[52] In 720 BCE Sargon II aimed at the destruction of the coalition under Jaubi'di of Hamath. Nowhere in the inscriptions of Sargon II referring to that campaign is a military encounter with Judah mentioned.[53]

This implies that in the complex chronological problems of Sennacherib's campaign or campaigns against Jerusalem, Jenkins basically seems to be right.[54] In my opinion there were 'two campaigns': one in 715 BCE and one in 701 BCE, the second one being well documented in the inscriptions of Sennacherib. Jenkins, however, dates Hezekiah's fourteenth year in 714 BCE and relates the campaign mentioned in 2 Kgs 18.13 with the expedition of an Assyrian commander-in-chief against rebellious Ashdod, which, however, took place in 712 BCE.[55] In my opinion the 'first' campaign, which took

51. Na'aman, 'Hezekiah and the Kings of Assyria', p. 235; Na'aman, 'Historical Portion', pp. 17-20; see also K.L. Younger, 'Sargon's Campaign against Jerusalem—A Further Note', *Bib* 77 (1996), pp. 108-110.

52. Winckler, *Sargon*, p. VI; Vogt, *Aufstand*, pp. 31-32.

53. See Becking, *Fall of Samaria*.

54. Jenkins, 'Hezekiah's Fourteenth Year'.

55. The campaign against Ashdod is referred to in:

•   Sg II Annals (Fuchs, *Sargon*, pp. 123-35.362), ll. 241-54;

•   Sg II Display-Inscription (Fuchs, *Sargon*, p. 219), ll. 90-97;

•   Sg II Display Inscription Room XIV (Fuchs, *Sargon*, p. 76), ll. 9-13;

•   Sg II Inscriptions on the Palace doors (Fuchs, *Sargon*, p. 262), IV l. 33

•   Sg II Bull Inscription (Fuchs, *Sargon*, p. 63), l. 18;

•   Sg II Annals of 711 (Fuchs, *Annalen* = Sm. 2022 II.14-16; k. 1668b + DT 6, I II.1-48; cf. Tadmor, 'Campaigns of Sargon II', p. 91), VII.b ll. 1-33.

•   Sg II Tang-i Var inscription (ed. G. Frame, 'The Inscription of Sargon II at Tang-i Var', *Or* 68 [1999], pp. 31-57 + Plates i-xviii; cf. Younger, 'Sargon II', pp. 199-300), ll. 19-21.

See Wäfler, *Nicht-Assyrer*, pp. 28-32; Z. Kapera, *The Rebellion of Yamani in Ashdod* (Kraków: Enigma Press, 1978); N. Na'aman and R. Zadok, 'Sargon II's Deportations to Israel and Philistea (716–708 B.C.)', *JCS* 40 (1988), pp. 43-44; Timm, *Moab zwischen den Mächten*, pp. 334-37: G.W. Ahlström, *The History of Ancient Palestine from the Paleolithic Period to Alexander's Conquest* (JSOTSup, 146; Sheffield: Sheffield Academic Press, 1993), pp. 691-94; Na'aman, 'Hezekiah and the Kings of Assyria', pp. 239-40.

place in Hezekiah's fourteenth year, has to be dated in the summer of 715 BCE. If this is correct all the chronological data from 2 Kgs 18 fall into place.

It should be noted that another two-campaign theory has been promoted. Defenders of this historical reconstruction suppose (1) a campaign by Sennacherib in 701 BCE as a result of which Hezekiah paid a tribute to the Assyrian king and (2) an otherwise unrecorded campaign in about 688 BCE in which the deliverance of Jerusalem took place.[56] This proposal might be an elegant solution for two problems in the account in the Book of Kings:

1. A literary tension: how could the payment of a tribute be reconciled with a divine deliverance?
2. The mention of Tirhaqa, king of Egypt, in 2 Kgs 19.9 who according to the available evidence would only have been nine years old in 701 BCE.

This supposed second campaign, however, has no base in the available historical evidence. A second campaign to the west by Sennacherib is not attested in the written documentation.[57] All in all, this proposal seems very unlikely.[58]

Note that Fuchs, *Sargon*, pp. 381-82; Fuchs, *Annalen*, pp. 82-124-131, dates this campaign to Ashdod in 711. In case he is correct a connection between 'Hezekiah's fourteenth year' and the campaign against Ashdod is even more problematic.

56. The idea goes back to H. Rawlinson in 1864, see L.L. Honor, *Sennacherib's Invasion in Palestine* (New York: Dissertation Columbia University, 1926; New York: AMS Press, 1966) p. 24, and has recently been defended by, e.g., J. Bright, *The History of Israel* (London: SCM Press, 2nd edn, 1972), pp. 296-308; C. van Leeuwen, 'Sanchérib devant Jérusalem', *OTS* 14 (1965), pp. 245-72; W.H. Shea, 'Sennacherib's Second Palestinian Campaign', *JBL* 104 (1985), pp. 401-18; W.H. Shea, 'Jerusalem under Siege: Did Sennacherib Attack Twice?', *BARev* 25/5 (1999), pp. 36-44, 64.

57. A campaign against Arabia is mentioned in a Summary Inscription of Sennacherib from Nineveh: Frahm, *Sanherib-Inschriften*, T 62.53'-59'. Both Esarhaddon and Ashurbanipal refer to this conquest by Sennacherib of the Arabian stronghold Adumutu; Esarh. Nin F. (R. Borger, *Die Inschriften Esarhaddons Königs von Assyrien* [AfO Beiheft, 9; Osnabrück: Biblio Verlag, 2nd edn, 1967, p. 53], IV.1-5; Ashurbanipal (R. Borger, *Beiträge zur Inschriften werk Assurbanipals: Die Prismenklassen A, B, C = K, D, E, F, G, H, J und T sowie andere Inschriften* [Wiesbaden: Otto Harrassowitz, 1996], pp. 69-70). The supposed campaign is dated tentatively in 690 BCE by Frahm, *Sanherib-Inschriften*, p. 7, see also 135. There are no indications whatsoever that this campaign would imply a detour over Jerusalem.

58. See also the criticism by Jenkins, 'Hezekiah's Fourteenth Year'; C.D. Evans, 'Judah's Foreign Policy from Hezekiah to Josiah', in *Scripture in Context: Essays on*

The same holds for the traditional 'one campaign-theory'. According to this view, Hezekiah ascended the throne in Judah in 715/14 BCE. His fourteenth year then has been 701 BCE.[59] This view does not account for the fact that Hezekiah was already in power when the Samaria fell into the hands of the Assyrians.

My chronological calculations lead to a clarification as to the dates of the two campaigns. It should be noted that the outcome cannot be classified as 'objective history'. It is a tentative proposal based on a set of assumptions.[60]

A Chronological Framework

The outcome of these considerations is that:

- Most probably an Assyrian king besieged Jerusalem in 715 BCE;
- Sennacherib conducted a campaign against Jerusalem in 701 BCE.

Is this an objective history? Are these propositions true? An answer to these questions depends on one's theory of (historical) truth. It should be

the Comparative Method (PThMS, 34; Pittsburgh: The Pickwick Press, 1980), pp. 165-66; K.A. Kitchen, The Third Intermediate Period in Egypt, Supplement (Warminster: Aris & Philips, 1986), p. 550; Chr. Hardmeier, Prophetie im Streit vor dem Untergang Judas: Erzählkommunikative Studien zur Entstehungssituation der Jesaja- und Jeremiaerzählungen in II Reg 18–20 und Jer 37–40 (BZAW, 187; Berlin/New York: W. de Gruyter, 1990), p. 164; D.B. Redford, Egypt, Canaan and Israel in Ancient Times (Princeton: Princeton University Press, 1992), p. 354 n. 165; Frahm, Sanherib-Inschriften, p. 10.

59. Strong advocates for this view are, e.g., R.E. Clements, Isaiah and the Deliverance of Jerusalem: A Study of the Interpretation of Prophecy in the Old Testament (JSOT Sup, 13; Sheffield: Sheffield Academic Press, 1980), pp. 9-27; Vogt, Aufstand, pp. 6-77; Cogan and Tadmor, II Kings, pp. 246-51; Smelik, Converting the Past, pp. 93-128; Na'aman, 'Hezekiah and the Kings of Assyria', pp. 236-39; Gallagher, Sennacherib's Campaign. W.G. Dever, 'Archaeology, Material Culture and the Early Monarchical Period in Israel', in D.V. Edelman, The Fabric of History: Text, Artifact and Israel's Past (JSOT Sup, 127; Sheffield: Sheffield Academic Press, 1991), p. 107, interprets the Biblical evidence as if one campaign took place in 714 BCE.

60. Criticism of this view has been uttered, without argument however, by Evans, 'Judah's Foreign Policy', p. 165; H. Spieckermann, Juda unter Assur in der Sargonidenzeit (FRLANT, 129; Göttingen: Vandenhoeck & Ruprecht, 1982), p. 347; H.J. Tertel, Text and Transmission: An Empirical Model for the Literary Development of Old Testament Narratives (BZAW, 221; Berlin/New York: W. de Gruyter, 1994), p. 157.

noted that the testing model used in various sciences to verify or—better—
falsify hypotheses and propositions by putting a test-implication to the test
is in principle inapplicable. Since time is irreversible, historical propositions and hypotheses cannot be tested this way. Like many historians, I
would plead for a moderate position between a 'correspondence theory'
and a 'coherence theory' of historical truth.[61] The propositions just mentioned are 'true' since they correspond with authentic evidence and are
coherent with the general picture I have of the Assyrian expansion in the
late eighth century BCE.

From Chronology to History

Chronology, however, does not equal history. Bare bones need muscles on
them in order to function. Chronology is a, coherent, set of propositions on
dates of events that took place in the past. History is a narrative on the
events of the past in which as many pieces of evidence as possible are
digested. How do we leap from chronology to history, from source to
discourse? It should be noted that this 'leap' runs in a way parallel to the
distinction between *histoire évenementelle* and *histoire conjoncturelle* as
made by Braudel.[62] Chronological data contain propositions on the level of
the events, but should be interpreted against a wider horizon to acquire
meaning.

Let me first give an example from the recent past. In July 1914 the
Austrian crown prince Ferdinand was shot to death in Sarajevo. This is a
chronological proposition that is generally held to be true, since there is
correspondence and coherence in it. But what does it mean and why is it
important for us to know this proposition? Relations and associations give
the importance. The untimely death of the prince should be related to the
political turmoil of his time and we associate it with the World War I that
is generally seen as the result of this incident. Or was this shooting only
the last straw in a situation that was heading for war already? In other

61. See, e.g., N. Rescher, *The Coherence Theory of Truth* (Oxford: Clarendon Press,
1973); O. Handlin, *Truth in History* (Cambridge, MA: London: Belknap Press, 1979);
W.J. Abraham, *Divine Revelation and the Limits of Historical Criticism* (Oxford:
Oxford University Press, 1982); F.R. Ankersmit, *Narrative Logic: A Semantical Analysis of the Historian's Language* (Den Haag: Mouton, 1983); Knauf, 'From History to
Interpretation'; R.J. Evans, *In Defence of History* (London: Granta Books, 1997), esp.
pp. 75-102. 224-53.

62. F. Braudel, *La Méditerranée et le monde méditerranéen à l'époque de Philippe
II* (Paris: Collin, 1949) ; see also Knauf, 'From History to Interpretation', pp. 42-43.

words the chronological proposition on July 1914 receives significance when seen in a greater framework. This framework is supplied by an evaluation of the available, often biased evidence: German newspapers, diaries of soldiers written in the trenches, minutes from staff-meetings etc.[63]

To supply meaning to the chronological statements on 715 and 701 BCE and by doing so to construct an historical narrative, an evaluation of the associations and the evidence related to the statements must be made. Therefore, I will now turn to the Hebrew Bible and the cuneiform texts.

The Book of Kings as an Explanatory History

In 2 Kgs 18–20, with a parallel in Isa. 36–39,[64] the siege of Jerusalem by Sennacherib is related. Old Testament scholars have assessed the historiographic value of these texts differently.[65] We do not possess objective

63. See, e.g., K. Kautsky, *Die deutschen Dokumente zum Kriegsausbruch: Vom Attentat in Serajevo bis zum Eintreffen der serbischen Antwortnote in Berlin* (Berlin: Deutsche Verlagsgesellschaft für Politik und Geschichte, 1927); L. Albertini, *The Origins of the War of 1914* (3 vols.; London: Oxford University Press, 1965–67).

64. For the relationship with 2 Chron. 32, see, e.g., Tertel, *Text and Transmission*, pp. 156-71; G.N. Knoppers, 'History and Historiography: The Royal Reforms', in M.P. Graham *et al.* (eds.), *The Chronicler as Historian* (JSOTSup, 238; Sheffield: Sheffield Academic Press, 1997), pp. 178-203; A.G. Vaughn, *Theology, History and Archaeology in the Chronicler's Account of Hezekiah* (ABS, 4; Atalanta: Scholars Press, 1999), and the paper by Ehud Ben Zvi in this volume (pp. 73-105 below).

65. See, e.g., Van Leeuwen, 'Sanchérib devant Jérusalem'; Childs, *Assyrian Crisis*; Clements, *Deliverance*, pp. 9-27; Wäfler, *Nicht-Assyrer*, pp. 42-53; S. Stohlmann, 'The Judaean Exile after 701 B.C.E'., in W.W. Hallo *et al.* (eds.), *Scripture in Context II* (Winona Lake: Eisenbrauns, 1983), pp. 147-175; Shea, 'Sennacherib's Second Palestinian Campaign', pp. 410-418; A. van der Kooij, 'Das assyrische Heer vor den Mauern Jerusalems im Jahr 701 v. Chr'., *ZDPV* 102 (1986), pp. 93-109; Vogt, *Aufstand*; A. Laato, 'Hezekiah and the Assyrian Crisis in 701 B.C.', *SJOT* 2 (1987), pp. 49-68; I.W. Provan, *Hezekiah and the Book of Kings: A Contribution to the Debate of the deuteronomistic History* (BZAW, 172; Berlin New York: W. de Gruyter, 1988); Cogan and Tadmor, *II Kings*, pp. 223-52; Hardmeier, *Prophetie im Streit*; E. Ruprecht, 'Die ursprüngliche Komposition der Hiskia-Jesaja Erzählungen und ihre Umstrukturierung durch den Verfasser des deuteronomistischen Geschichtswerk', *ZTK* 87 (1990), pp. 33-66; S.L. McKenzie, *The Trouble with Kings: The Composition of the Book of Kings in the Deuteronomistic History* (VTSup, 42; Leiden: E.J. Brill, 1991), pp. 101-109; N. Na'aman, 'Forced Participation in Alliances in the Course of Assyrian Campaigns to the West', in M. Cogan and I. Eph'al (eds.), *Ah Assyria! Studies in Assyrian History and Ancient Near Eastern Historiography Presented to Hayim Tadmor* (ScrH, 33;

knowledge on the emergence or on the date of the final composition of these texts. I don't have space here to present a full discussion on these themes. I confine myself to my personal view which, I assume, is shared, at least at some points, by some colleagues but challenged by others.

With Williamson I suppose that the account in the book of Isaiah has been taken over at some point in history from the traditions that lead to the book of Kings.[66]

The account in 2 Kgs 18–20 in its final form is part of the so-called deuteronomistic history. I am, still, of the opinion that this composition should be dated in the early years of the 'exilic' period[67] and should be seen as an explanatory history.[68] The aim of DtrH is not to satisfy modern historians with eyewitness reports of events from Iron Age Judah and Israel, but to help a distressed people to cope with the reality of exile, lost independence and a torn-down temple. Reading 2 Kgs 18–20 against this 'exilic' background, with its antagonism, for example, between the faith of Hezekiah and the transgressions of the inhabitants of the Northern Kingdom; the death of Sennacherib and the recovery of Hezekiah from a deadly illness, is a hermeneutical enterprise and supplies 'historical' information only at the level of *Ideengeschichte*.[69]

The authors, or composers, of DtrH have used older material. With Christof Hardmeier, I assume that they have incorporated material from the 'Erzählung von der Assyrischen Bedrohung und der Befreiung Jeru-

---

Jerusalem: Magnes Press, 1991), pp. 94-96; Smelik, *Converting the Past*, pp. 123-28; Laato, 'Assyrian Propaganda'; Gallagher, *Sennacherib*.

66. H.G.M. Williamson, *The Book Called Isaiah: Deutero-Isaiah's Role in Composition and Redaction* (Oxford: Oxford University Press, 1995), pp. 189-209.

67. On the 'exilic' period see B. Becking, 'Babylonisches Exil', in H.D. Betz *et al.* (eds.), *Religion in Geschichte und Gegenwart: Handwörterbuch für Theologie und Religionswissenschaft* Band 1 A-B (4. völlig neu bearbeitete Auflage; Tübingen: J.C.B. Mohr [Paul Siebeck] Verlag, 1998), kk. 1044-1045; and the essays in L.L. Grabbe (ed.), *Leading Captivity Captive: The 'Exile' as History and Tradition* (JSOTSup, 278; ESHM, 2; Sheffield: Sheffield Academic Press, 1998).

68. See, e.g., Van Seters, *In Search of History*, pp. 292-321. The reader is supposed to easily find a way to the abundance of literature on the 'deuteronomistic' problem and its perplexity.

69. A commendable effort to read 2 Kgs 18–19 has been proposed by A. van der Kooij, 'The Story of Hezekiah and Sennacherib (2 Kings 18–19): A Sample of Ancient Historiography', in J.C. De Moor and H.F. van Rooy (eds.), *Past, Present, Future: The Deuteronomistic History and the Prophets* (OTS, 44; Leiden: E.J. Brill, 2000), pp. 107-19.

salems'.[70] This ABBJ (*Assyriche Bedrohung und Befreiung Jerusalems*; 'Assyrian Threat and Liberation of Jerusalem') is also a literary and explanatory composition. Its author does not suggest two Assyrian campaigns against Judah. He is telling a story, using and reworking older material, to his contemporaries. A literary analysis of ABBJ yields the picture that the narrator has built in an element of complication: After Hezekiah's payment of tribute an Assyrian withdrawal is expected but it does not take place immediately; other things have to happen first. Hardmeier argues that the final years before the fall of Jerusalem to the Babylonians should be seen as the historical context of the ABBJ-narrative. On the level of historical reconstruction it should be noted that a temporary withdrawal by the Babylonian forces in 588 BCE was provoked by a march of Egyptian troops to relieve the beleaguered Judaean capital.[71] This implies that the historical propositions present in ABBJ cannot simply be transported to a situation at the end of the eighth century BCE. The mention of Tirhaqa, King of Egypt, in 2 Kgs 19.9 is a good example. The name was known from the oral or written traditions that were at the disposal of the author of ABBJ. Within the composition this name functions as a cipher for Pharaoh Apries who ruled over Egypt in the early sixth century BCE.[72] This implies that the ABBJ-narrative too supplies 'historical' information only at the level of *Ideengeschichte*.

Is ABBJ based on sources and can they eventually be reconstructed? This is a simple question that is, however, not easily answered. It is very plausible that the composer of ABBJ had various sources at his disposal. It is, however, impossible to reconstruct them. This implies that I do not agree with the solution of Brevard Childs who construes three sources behind 2 Kgs 18–20: A, B$_1$ and B$_2$.[73]

But even if it turns out that Childs is correct, it should be noted that his sources in fact are discourses. They are later perceptions of the event(s) and do not equal 'what really happened'.[74]

It can be observed that 2 Kgs 18–20 does not explicitly state that Jerusalem has been besieged twice. This observation is not to be assessed as an

70. 'Account of the Assyrian Siege and of the Deliverance of Jerusalem'.

71. Hardmeier, *Prophetie im Streit*.

72. Hardmeier, *Prophetie im Streit*, p. 327.

73. B.S. Childs, *Isaiah and the Assyrian Crisis* (SBT, 3; London: SCM Press, 1967); adopted by many scholars. See the criticism in Smelik, *Converting the Past*, pp. 93-128, esp. p. 124.

74. See, e.g., Clements, *Deliverance*; Smelik, *Converting the Past*, pp. 93-128.

argument against the view that two military operations have been conducted. As with the two campaigns against Samaria, the two campaigns against Jerusalem have been telescoped by tradition into one narrative.[75] It is apparent that two traditions are present in 2 Kgs 18–20. 2 Kgs 18.14-16 narrates a buying off of a siege by presenting a tribute, while 2 Kgs 19.35-36 states that the angel of YHWH caused the death of 185, 000 Assyrians overnight which compelled the Asyrian king to retreat. It is an almost defiant challenge to distribute these two causes of the Assyrian retreat over the two hypothesized campaigns assumed.[76] This, however, is impossible on the basis of the Hebrew Bible alone.

Finally, at all the stages of its supposed development the story or stories in 2 Kgs 18–20 should be construed as explanatory history. The text(s) explains how things that were observable to its readership have come into being. The explanation(s) given is related to the symbol system of the authors. It is in a way the muscles to the bare bones, that could have been shaped in other forms.

Annals as Royal Glorification

The inscriptions of Sennacherib mentioning the siege of Jerusalem should also be assessed not as sources but as discourses. In several inscriptions the siege of Jerusalem is mentioned.[77]

Rassam-cylinder	T 4[78]	700 BCE	.32-58
K 2627[+]	T 171[79]	?	Obv.15-Rev.21
Heidel/King-prism	T 12[80]	694 BCE	II.60-IV.9
Chicago or Taylor-prism	T 16[81]	691-89 BCE	II.37-III.49

75. See also Younger, 'Deportations of the Israelites'; Dijkstra, 'Chronological problems'.

76. Jenkins, 'Hezekiah's Fourteenth Year', relates 2 Kgs 18.17–19.37 (sources B_1 and B_2) with the 'first' campaign, while 2 Kgs 18.14-16 would refer to 701 BCE, while Goldberg, 'Two Assyrian Campaigns', takes the opposite view: 2 Kgs 18.14-16 would refer to events in 712 BCE while behind the traditions in 2 Kgs 18.17–19.37 reminiscences of 701 BCE are to be assumed.

77. See the outline in Frahm, *Sanherib-Inschriften*, p. 6.

78. Frahm, *Sanherib-Inschriften*, pp. 47-61; recent translation by Cogan, 'Sennacherib', pp. 302-303.

79. Frahm, *Sanherib-Inschriften*, pp. 199-201; the inscription is parallel to the Rassam-cylinder.

80. Frahm, *Sanherib-Inschriften*, pp. 87-89.

81. Frahm, *Sanherib-Inschriften*, pp. 102-05.

Although there are differences between these inscriptions, the deviations are not that great as in the various reports on Sennacherib's first campaign.[82] Therefore I will confine my analysis to one text. It should be noted that summarizing accounts are present in the following inscriptions:

Bull 2//3	T 26//27[83]	?	.17-22
Bull 4	T 29[84]	?	.18-32
Nebi-Yunus-inscription	T 61[85]	± 690 BCE	.13-15
BM 134496[+]	T 172[86]	?	.1'-Rev. 8
K 2625[+]	T 173[87]	?	.1'

I will confine myself to one text here. The Rassam Cylinder can be seen as an authentic report on the event. It is, however, also a discourse. Gallagher has collected some cases that make clear that the military report is moulded in literary, or even artistic language. Next to the well-known simile 'like a bird in a cage' for the position of Hezekiah in a city surrounded with armies, he points at the parallel for the expression *šā'alu kakkīšun*, 'to sharpen their weapons', in Enuma Elish IV.92.[88] Meanwhile the text is full of ideology. Several expressions are related to the terminology of treaties and loyalty-oaths. Other elements function as a glorification of the Assyrian king in his role as defender and maintainer of the cosmic order on earth. The king is represented as instrumental for the *Schreckenglanz* of Ashur. These features imply that the text should be analysed carefully when inferring references to events from it. The following information can be detracted:

- After military operations against Sidon,[89] Ashkelon[90] and Ekron,[91] Sennacherib is heading for Jerusalem.
- Sennacherib attacks Jerusalem since Hezekiah had taken over Padi, the former king of Ekron and a vassal of Assyria who had been thrown in chains by the people and the rulers of Ekron.[92] Sennacherib obviously wanted to liberate his former vassal.

82. See Tertel, *Text and Transmission*, pp. 67-96.
83. Frahm, *Sanherib-Inschriften*, pp. 115-16.
84. Frahm, *Sanherib-Inschriften*, pp. 116-18.
85. Frahm, *Sanherib-Inschriften*, pp. 128-29.
86. Frahm, *Sanherib-Inschriften*, pp. 201-02.
87. Frahm, *Sanherib-Inschriften*, pp. 202-06.
88. Gallagher, *Sennacherib's Campaign*, pp. 121, 133.
89. Rassam.32-35; see Gallagher, *Sennacherib's Campaign*, pp. 91-104.
90. Rassam.39-41; see Gallagher, *Sennacherib's Campaign*, pp. 117-19.
91. Rassam.42-48; see Gallagher, *Sennacherib's Campaign*, pp. 120-27.
92. Rassam.42.

- Sennacherib captured a great number of cities and strongholds. He distributes the territory among his loyal vassals Mitinti of Ashkelon, Padi of Ekron and Silbel of Gaza. In a counterbalance, he raises the amount of their yearly payment.
- Sennacherib besieged Jerusalem. Hezekiah is locked 'like a bird in a cage'.
- A capture of Jerusalem is not narrated. With the glorification-language of the annals as a background, this can be interpreted as a sign that Sennacherib for one reason or another did not defeat Hezekiah.
- Sennacherib received a heavy tribute from Hezekiah that is sent to Nineveh after the campaign.[93]
- A reason for this tribute is not narrated except for the fact that Hezekiah was overwhelmed by the radiant splendour of Sennacherib's lordship. The political outcome of the tribute also is not mentioned.

The picture arising from the report in the Annals is that Sennacherib attacked Hezekiah with the purpose of releasing his former vassal Padi of Ekron.

Something Happened in Jerusalem

It is the task of the historian not only to analyse the evidence but also to present a picture of his reconstruction of the past. Therefore, the next step in this paper will be a preliminary proposal.

In my view the evidence from the Annals of Sennacherib can easily be reconciled with the narrative in 2 Kgs 18.13b-16.[94]

- Both texts relate a Judaean tribute. The extent of the tribute is basically the same in the two pieces of evidence. Both texts relate the payment of 30 talents of gold. The amount of silver seems to be contradictory. Sennacherib mentions 800 talents, while 2 Kgs 18.14 relates that 300 talents were paid. Several explanations for the diverging numbers have been given: (a) the Assyrian talent of

93. Rassam.55-58.
94. *Pace* Dever, 'Archaeology, Material Culture and the Early Monarchical Period in Israel'; C.R. Seitz, 'Account A and the Annals of Sennacherib: A Reassessment', *JSOT* 58 (1993), pp. 50-52; Goldberg, 'Two Assyrian Campaigns'.

silver would have been ⅜ as large as the Judaean;[95] (b) the Assyrian quantity would include silver stripped from the doors of the temple, the biblical quantity would not.[96] I would prefer the interpretation of Mayer who argues that the number 800 in the Rassam–Cylinder does not refer to the weight of silver alone, but should be taken as in indication of the total amount of goods enumerated in the inscription (silver, choice antimony, large blocks of carnelian, beds [inlaid] with ivory and so on), while the number 300 in 2 Kgs 18.14 would only refer to the amount of silver in the tribute.[97]

• Both texts mention the conquest of many Judaean cities.[98]
• Both texts imply the retreat of the Assyrian king.

According to Van Seters, 2 Kgs 18.(13)14-16 should be assessed as deriving from official records. By implication the evidence is trustworthy.[99] By relating it to the chronological evidence inferred from the Mesopotamian inscriptions, I would like to date this event in 701 BCE. Hezekiah has often been presented as the leader of the anti-Assyrian coalition.[100] For this view no argument is given. There is no evidence in written sources that Hezekiah took the lead in a coalition. This view must be abandoned as based on scholarly prejudice. Although Sennacherib apparently did not conquer Jerusalem, Hezekiah presented him a heavy tribute. As a result of that the Assyrian king withdrew. I am of the opinion that the tribute not only was meant to buy off the siege of the city, but also to regain control over the areas occupied by Sennacherib and distributed

95. H.H. Rowley, 'Hezekiah's Reform and Rebellion', *BJRL* 44 (1961–62), p. 432; Cogan & Tadmor, *II Kings*, p. 229.

96. Cogan and Tadmor, *II Kings*, p. 229.

97. Mayer, *Politik und Kriegskunst*, pp. 360-63.

98. 2 Kgs 18.13b; Rassam.56.

99. Childs, *Assyrian Crisis*, pp. 68-73; Van Seters, *In Search of History*, p. 301; Vogt, *Aufstand*, pp. 24-33; Clements, *Deliverance*, pp. 9-27; see even Smelik, *Converting the Past*, p. 124. Camp, *Hiskija und Hiskijabild*, p. 105, nevertheless assumes a complex redaction historical process of the textual unit under consideration.

100. E.g., by Redford, *Egypt, Canaan and Israel*, p. 351; Vogt, *Aufstand*, pp. 6-9; Na'aman, 'Forced Participation', p. 94; Na'aman, 'Hezekiah and the Kings of Assyria', p. 248; Soggin, *History*, p. 249; Ahlström, *History of Ancient Palestine*, pp. 695-96; R. Lamprichs, *Die Westexpansion des neuassyrischen Reiches: Eine Strukturanalyse* (AOAT, 239; Neukirchen–Vluyn: Neukirchener Verlag, 1995), pp. 147-49; Noort, *Seevölker*, p. 28; Gallagher, *Sennacherib's Campaign*, esp. pp. 110-12, 263-74.

among the Philistine kings. In the seventh century BCE there are no indications that the territory of Judah was confined to Jerusalem and its immediate surroundings. The archaeological evidence hints at a continuation of Jerusalemite control over the Judaean countryside.[101] The evidence of the palaeo-Hebrew inscriptions excavated at various Judaean sites (e.g. Tel Arad, Khirbet Beit Lei, Khirbet el-Qom, Mesad Hashabjahu) stands contrary to the idea that the area was Philistine territory.

As regards 2 Kgs 18.13a,17-19.37, things are more complicated. I assume a complex history of tradition, which implies that many details in the present story are not original and cannot be used as historical evidence. I further assume that the core of the narrative should be related to events 'in the fourteenth year of Hezekiah', in my view 715 BCE. I do not think that it is possible to reconstruct the text of the original report. Important elements in this report might have been:

- The campaign against Jerusalem was conducted not by the king of Assyria, but by an officer of high military rank.
- The king of Assyria was in the meantime waging war against Egypt.
- The representative of the Assyrian king did not succeed in conquering Jerusalem.
- The representative of the Assyrian king did not succeed in causing Jerusalem to surrender by negotiations.
- The Assyrian army had to withdraw due to unexpected massive dying of soldiers. In 2 Kgs 19.35 this feature is interpreted as a result of divine intervention.

The Assyrian inscriptions mentioned above relate to a relatively peaceful campaign against southern Palestine with the strengthening of the border with Egypt as its goal. In the so-called Azeka-fragment the following remark is made:

11' [the city of ?[102]] a royal [city] of the Philistines that H[ezek]iah had captured and strengthened for himself [...

101. See basically H. Weippert, *Palästina in vorhellenistischer Zeit* (Handbuch der Archäologie, II, 1; München: C.H. Beck, 1988), pp. 559-681; Ahlström, *History of Ancient Palestine*, pp. 716-40, and the relevant entries in E. Stern (ed.), *The New Encyclopedia of Archaeological Excavations in the Holy Land* (New York: Simon & Schuster; Jerusalem: Israel Exploration Society, 1992).

102. Na'aman, 'Sennacherib's "Letter to God"', p. 27, originally read Gath; see also Vogt, *Aufstand*, pp. 21-23; Laato, 'Assyrian Propaganda', p. 214. S. Mittmann, 'Hiskia

This remark might be seen as coinciding with a note in 2 Kgs 18.8

> He [= Hezekiah] defeated the Philistines as far as Gaza and its border areas, from watchtower to fortified city.[103]

This brings to mind the idea that the military action against Jerusalem in Hezekiah's fourteenth year was intended to punish the Judaean king for an act of violence against a Philistine city that had been an Assyrian vassal for several years. Assyrian kings had the obligation to defend their vassals against foreign powers. Since an action against Jerusalem was not the main goal of the campaign in 715 BCE, it is probable that this 'side campaign' was conducted by an officer of high rank, if not by the crown prince himself.

In his explanation of 2 Kgs 19.35, Gallagher has elaborated the traditional idea that the theological language of this verse masks the reminiscence of a historical event: an epidemic plague that took the life of many Assyrian soldiers.[104] Gallagher supposes the event took place in 701 BCE. A plague is known to have occurred in Mesopotamia in 707 BCE.[105] Neither for 715 nor for 701 a plague is attested. The absence of evidence is, however, not the evidence of absence. A suddenly spreading lethal disease could explain the tradition.

The Wider Framework

Is objective history writing possible? How helpful is chronology? At the end of my exercise, I would like to say that there is (some) objectivity in

und die Philister', *JNSL* 16 (1990), pp. 89-99; Na'aman, 'Hezekiah and the Kings of Assyria', p. 245; Galil, 'Judah and Assyria', prefer Ekron. Noort, *Seevölker*, p. 28; Frahm, *Sanherib-Inschriften*, p. 230; Cogan, 'Sennacherib', p. 304, are undecided.

103. *Pace* Cogan and Tadmor, *II Kings*, pp. 217, 220-21; Soggin, *History*, p. 250; Laato, 'Assyrian Propaganda', p. 214; Lamprichs, *Westexpansion*, p. 148, who relate this remark to exploits by Hezekiah in the years before 701 BCE. A.H.J. Gunneweg, *Geschichte Israels bis Bar Kochba* (ThW, 2; Stuttgart/Berlin/Köln: W. Kohlhammer, 3rd edn, 1979), p. 118; Camp, *Hiskija und Hiskijabild*, pp. 90-91, offered the view that 2 Kgs 18.8 would refer to events after the third campaign when Hezekiah was recapturing the territory handed over by Sennacherib to some Philistine kings. On the basis of the Assyrian evidence it can be concluded that Judah has been a faithful and loyal vassal. A military exploit as suggested by Gunneweg and Camp stands contrary to this view.

104. Gallagher, *Sennacherib's Campaign*, pp. 241-52.

105. Babylonian Chronicle I ii.5; Grayson, *Chronicles*, p. 76. The disease probably reached as far west as Damascus and Ribla, see the letters *SAA* I 171.14; 180.e11'; with Gallagher, *Sennacherib's Campaign*, p. 267.

history-writing, but only on the small and well-defined scale of chronological data. They form the backbone of our reconstruction of the past. But
as such, they are quite meaningless. Just as a word outside a phrase has no
meaning, a historical 'datum'—how true and objective it may be—makes
no sense. The albeit superficial analysis of the Assyrian and Biblical narratives has provided some flesh on the skeleton. Two things, however, should
be kept in mind.

1. The flesh on the bones is tentative. It has been put there with the
   help of the imagination of the historian. This also implies that on
   the same skeleton different arrangements can be made.
2. A wider framework is needed. As in the case of the assassination
   of the Austrian crown prince Ferdinand in Sarajevo, the data on
   715 and 701 BCE and the narrative(s) related to them only make
   sense when they are related to a broader historical framework. To
   say the same in Braudelian terminology: the intermediate *histoire
   évenementelle* can only be understood when seen as part of a
   histoire conjoncturelle. This framework would consist in an analysis of the political, military and economic movements in the
   ancient Near East during the Sargonid Empire. The monograph
   by Lamprichs supplies good material and should be seen as a
   starting point for writing such a wider framework.[106]

The Subjective Historian

Reconstructing history is an ambivalent form of art, since it is both scholarly and subjective. The person of the historian is always involved. Reread-
ing the remarks above, I have been asking myself in which parts my
personal view was too dominant. Where did I pass the limits of objectivity? Where did I leave the dimension of the 'happening' truth and enter
the field of the 'story-truth'? This question should not be misunderstood,
since two different forms of subjectivity are involved that should not be
confused:

1. Subjectivity at the level of values and ideology;
2. Subjectivity at the level of perception. *Esse est percipi*.[107] I can
   only talk about the reality outside as I perceive it in my mind.[108]

---

106. Lamprichs, *Westexpansion*.
107. George Berkeley, 'A Treatise Concerning the Principles of Human Knowledge',

As to the first form, I have tried to avoid a biased position, for instance by not making Hezekiah the pivotal point in all the events as has so often been done by biblical scholars. But did I succeed? It is, I assume, up to the reader of this paper to determine how much of my personal views on war and peace can be detected.

As to the second form, the scarcity of evidence implies that my perception is limited as well as guided by the narratives of the ancients, subjective in the first sense of the idea as they are. By looking at the evidence from various angles and by weighing as carefully as possible the information supplied, I have tried to overcome subjectivity and to reach a discourse that is open to inter-subjectivity. In the end, history writing—and not only of the 'Biblical period'—will remain an art, although based on science.[109]

§3 (1710), in A.A. Luce and T.E. Jessop (eds.), *The Works of George Berkeley, Bishop of Cloyne* (Oxford: Clarendon Press, 1948–1957), II, p. 42.

108. See, e.g., K. Mannheim, *Wissenssoziologie: Auswahl aus dem Werk* (Neuwied: Luchterhand, 1970).

109. See, e.g., Evans, *Defence of History*, esp. pp. 45-74.

Malleability and its Limits: Sennacherib's Campaign against Judah as a Case-Study[*]

Ehud Ben Zvi

Introduction

As per its title, the purpose of this paper is to deal with the campaign of Sennacherib against Judah as a case study for the more general issue of malleability *and* its limits in ancient historical reporting and particularly Israelite historiographical writings. This issue raises important questions for the study of ancient historical writing in general, and in particular for the study of its dependence on outside-the-narrative referents and on the question of representation.[1]

Several of the features of this campaign contribute to its being a good case study for this purpose. First, one has to deal with a single, clearly

---

[*]   May this paper serve as a token of appreciation for Professor John Van Seters. I have learned much from John, and enjoyed greatly our talks and meals together. It is with a deep sense of gratitude that I dedicate this paper to him.

1.   To be sure, conclusions based on a particular case should not be assumed to hold true for the general case, but still they raise good heuristic issues and concerns for its study.

Discussions on the question of representation, external referentiality and the like are becoming more common, and increasingly 'passionate' in theoretical discussions about history and history writing. See, for instance, the following exchange of articles, Perez Zagorin, 'History, the Referent, and the Narrative: Reflections on Postmodernism Now', *History and Theory* 38 (1999), pp. 1-24; K. Jenkins, 'A Postmodern Reply to Perez Zagorin', *History and Theory* 39 (2000), pp. 181-200; Perez Zagorin, 'Rejoinder to a Postmodernist', *History and Theory* 39 (2000), pp. 201-209.

Unlike these works on the theory of history, however, the present one discusses the inferences that may be reasonably gleaned from a study of different constructions of a particular historical event, and focuses particularly on these that contribute to our understanding of the work and limitations of ancient historians. As such, this article does not attempt at all to be a contribution to meta-history, but to the study of ancient Israelite historiography.

defined campaign[2] whose historical outcome was a stable situation that lasted for a relatively long period. This being the case, there is no room for telescoping of subsequent military campaigns and military outcomes.[3]

2. Two-campaign models have been advocated for more than a century. But there is no clear evidence that either Sargon or Sennacherib much later in his reign (e.g., 688–687 BCE) campaigned against Judah. Moreover, all the accounts of Sennacherib's campaign—in their present form at least—describe only one campaign, and as usual, one should not multiply hypothesis without necessity. These issues have been debated at length many times. Regarding the proposal of two campaigns by Sennacherib, see, for instance, W.H. Shea, 'Senacherib's Second Palestinian Campaign', *JBL* 104 (1985), pp. 401-18 but see also the response to his proposals in F.J. Yurco, 'The Shabaka-Shebiktu Coregency and the Supposed Second Campaign of Sennacherib against Judah: A Critical Assessment', *JBL* 110 (1991), pp. 35-45. On the proposal of an early campaign by Sargon and second one by Sennacherib, see A.K. Jenkins, 'Hezekiah's Fourteenth Year: A New Interpretation of 2 Kings xviii 13-xix 37', *VT* 26 (1976), pp. 284-98; Bob Becking, *The Fall of Samaria: An Historical & Archaeological Study* (SHANE, 2, Leiden: E.J. Brill, 1992), pp. 54-55. But see also N. Na'aman, 'Hezekiah and the Kings of Assyria', *TA* 21 (1994), pp. 235-54, esp. 235-47. A detailed analysis of the arguments involved is beyond the scope of this paper. However, it is perhaps worth mentioning that recent contributions to the study of the 25th dynasty and its chronology in no way require or support a double campaign model. As for these contributions, see D.B. Redford, 'Taharqa in Western Asia and Libya', *Eretz Yisrael* 24 (1993), pp. 188-91, A. Fuchs, *Die Annalen des Jahres 711 v. Chr.* (SAAS 8; Helsinki: The Neo-Assyrian Text Corpus Project, 1998), pp. 124-31; G. Frame, 'The Inscription of Sargon II at Tang-i Var', *Or* 68 (1999), pp. 31-57; D.B. Redford, 'A Note on the Chronology of Dynasty 25 and the Inscription of Sargon II at Tang-i Var, *Or* 68 (1999), pp. 58-60.

For the purpose of this study, it will suffice to state that the account of the third campaign in the annalistic sources, those in Kings and Chronicles—at least in their present form—the reports in Josephus and the archaeological evidence pointing to massive destruction in Judah either reflect or attempt to represent the events of 701 BCE (see also n. 4).

3. This is certainly an issue for the study of Sennacherib's southern campaigns. See L.D. Levine, 'Sennacherib's Southern Front: 704–689 B.C.', JCS 34 (1982), pp. 28-55. It is worth stressing that because the past is always becoming past, reports of events may reflect and vary according to changes later than the described events. These variations are at times very large; see, for instance, the accounts of the fate of Merodach Baladan at the hands of Sennacherib or the issue of the appointment of Bel-Ibni as King of Babylon. On these matters, see M. Liverani, 'Critique of Variants and the Titulary of Sennacherib', in F.M. Fales (ed.), *Assyrian Royal Inscriptions: New Horizons in Literary, Ideological, and Historical Analysis: Papers of a Symposium Held in Cetona (Siena), June 26–28, 1980* (Orientis antiqui collectio, 17; Rome: Istituto per l'Oriente, Centro per le antichita e la storia dell'arte del vicino Oriente, 1981), pp. 253-57.

Second, archaeological data—and other information from the area—allows a good historical-critical reconstruction of the political (and demographic) outcome of the campaign. This reconstruction is, at least in its main lines, not dependent on either the neo-Assyrian or any biblical description of the events. [4] This being the case, one can compare the actual historical outcome with the ideological outcomes of Sennacherib's campaign to Judah in diverse literary constructions of the event.[5] Such comparisons may

---

4.   D. Edelman recently claimed that 'in spite of the important information contained in the various accounts of Sennacherib's campaign and the reliefs of his conquest of Lachish that were on the palace wall at Nineveh, their absence would have little effect upon the recreation of the events in the reign of Hezekiah by historians of Judah'. See D. Edelman, 'What If We Had No Accounts of Sennacherib's Third Campaign or the Palace Reliefs Depicting the Capture of Lachish?', in J. Cheryl Exum (ed.), *Virtual History and the Bible* (Leiden: E.J. Brill, 2000), pp. 88-103, quotation from p. 102 (= D. Edelman, 'What If We Had No Accounts of Sennacherib's Third Campaign or the Palace Reliefs Depicting the Capture of Lachish?', *Bib Int* 8 [2000], pp. 88-103).

5.   It might be argued from some corners that this or similar critical reconstructions are nothing more than another 'narrative' created by a certain group (i.e., critical historians) at a particular time, and as such essentially not different in value from the account in Kings, or some paraphrases of it.

It seems to me that the 'nothing more' in this type of claims is highly misleading. This and similar reconstructions are the best approximation that present historians have now to what may called 'temporary historical truth'. The latter term requires some explanation. This and similar reconstructions account better for the facts that are agreed upon by critical historians at this time than any other possible reconstructions. Given that the facts agreed upon by critical historians at a particular time are the best possible approximation for their time to the historical facts and if by 'historical truth' one means correspondence with facts, then reconstructions like the one mentioned above are the best approximation to truth that exists at this moment, and as such they can be considered a 'temporary historical truth'.

The alternative to an approach that evaluates the claims of different reconstructions against the best possible approximations to historical fact, has to be based either on a denial of factual reality or of any possibility to refer to it. Very few historians seem willing to follow that path. After all, most historians (and not only professional historians) would maintain that there is a difference between the following statements: (a) During WWII Nazis murdered numerous Jews (and people from other target groups) in Auschwitz as part of a general policy of extermination against them, and (b) during WWII Jews murdered numerous Nazis in Auschwitz as part of a general policy of extermination against them. To be sure, the obvious difference between the statements is that the first one is true, but the other is blatantly false. How do we know that? Because whereas statement (a) corresponds to historical facts, (b) does not. These historical facts are surely not dependent on whatever narrative/text/discourse the references to the events in Auschwitz may be embedded in. If so, they have to stand outside (or

contribute to study of the nature and extent of malleability in historical reports. Third, it is possible to compare two accounts of the campaign written from substantially different perspectives and social locations. One can compare (a) the account in Kings, within its own ideological and literary context, with (b) the account of the campaign against Judah in Sennacherib's annals within its own ideological and literary context. Such comparison may contribute to assess how ideological backgrounds and literary contexts enable and further malleability in ancient historical writings, but it may also point to some of the limitations for malleability that they also create. Fourth, the construction of this event in Kings led to subsequent constructions in later pieces of Israelite/Judean historical writing, namely Chronicles and Josephus.[6] What kind of malleability does appear in successive, partially dependent constructions of the event?[7]

Given the genre limitations of an academic paper, the scope of the discussion has to be narrowed from the outset. First, it is consistent with the

---

beyond) purely narrative or textual worlds. For a theory of history approach to some of the issues raised here and on the implied notion of progress in historical research that they advance, cf. R. Martin, 'Progress in Historical Studies', *History and Theory* 38 (1998), pp. 14-39. Cf. Perez Zagorin, 'History, the Referent, and the Narrative'.

One may also approach the difference between the mentioned reconstructions of the Assyrian campaign and alternative ancient reconstructions from the perspective of whether they qualify as a 'scientific theory'. By the latter I mean here a well-substantiated explanation of a particular set of related events (including particular actions and outcomes) that incorporates known/agreed-upon facts, historical 'laws' (i.e., usual relations between causes and effects within a particular society/ies), inferences and tested hypotheses better than any of its proposed alternatives and that has not yet been falsified. (This definition is a substantial adaptation of the definition of theory advanced by the National Academy of Sciences.) If this terminology is accepted, then the reconstruction mentioned above is not only 'another narrative', but the current 'theory of Sennacherib's campaign'. To be sure, theories may be falsified later, but until they are, they represent the best approximation to 'methodological truth' that is possible under the circumstances in which they are tested. The narratives in Kings, Chronicles, Josephus and the annalistic account cannot be considered as 'theories' because they contradict known (or agreed-upon) facts, and are therefore falsified to some extent or another.

On the possibility of testing hypotheses in relation to this particular matter see D. Edelman, 'What If'.

6. See 2 Chron. 32.1-23; *Ant* 10.1-23 and cf. *War* 5.386-88, 404-408.

7. It goes without saying that there are very substantial differences among these constructions of the campaign, as one may expect from writings written from very different perspectives, for diverse purposes, in more than one language or sociolect and with different public in mind. Yet there are also similarities. The issue is whether similarities and differences may be clustered and explained in general terms.

focus of this paper—namely questions of ancient historiography—to focus mainly on narrative accounts of the campaign as they appear in works that shape and reconstruct a larger image of the past,[8] rather than all possible sources for the study of Sennacherib's campaign against Judah. Second, despite the fact that neo-Assyrian material is and must be discussed—and that occasionally some observations will be made—the focus is on Israelite historiography.[9] Third, the basic aim of this paper is neither to advance the most likely historical reconstruction of the events nor to provide a full analysis of its representation in historical writings (e.g. the book of Kings, Chronicles), nor to study the potential sources that could be reflected in the account in 2 Kings.[10] The goal of the paper is to explore the issue of malleability and its limits in a particular set of accounts all of which (a) claim to refer to a single historical event and (b) are an integral part of larger historical narratives. This being the case, the paper will explore the relation between ideologically oriented narratives and referents that stand outside the world created by each narrative. Numerous matters that are directly pertinent to the study of the campaign itself but not necessary to achieve the purposed mentioned above will not be covered.[11]

Malleability in Historical Writing: Shape and Purpose of Reports of the Campaign within their Own Contexts. Meaning/Significance in Historical Narratives

Survey of Evidence: The Annalistic Account
The neo-Assyrian account of the campaign against Judah that suits the purpose of this study is the one present in the annalistic tradition.[12] Its

8. There is no need to enter here into the question of how to define 'historical writings'. If would suffice to say that the Book of Kings and the Book of Chronicles, but not the Book of Isaiah, qualify as works of ancient historiography.

9. Although this is simply a study case, it may be advisable to take note of the danger of 'universal' explanations. Conventions found in Israelite historiography may or may not work in neo-Assyrian historiography. It is worth noting that different conventions about what can and cannot be changed, and accordingly on malleability and its limitations seem to appear within the Mesopotamian tradition itself (cf. the Synchronistic History and Chronicle P).

10. Possible but hypothetical pieces of ancient historiography, such as proposed editions of the Book of Kings prior to the present form are also not considered given the uncertain character of these hypothetical texts.

11. I am confident that other contributions will more than make up for what is not, and cannot be discussed here.

12. The account of the third campaign itself is basically stable in the different

literary context is clear. It is part and parcel of the account of Sennacherib's third campaign, namely the one against the land of Hatti. In other
words, the third campaign is one among others, and the campaign against
Judah is a subset of this third campaign. Thus, the geographical horizon
of the campaigns in the annals as a whole is imperial. [13] The particular
horizon of the third campaign is clearly regional; it focuses on the land of
Hatti rather than on Judah. Further, both the annals in general and each of
the reported campaigns in particular construct time as imperial, sequential
time based on successive royal campaigns carried out by a particular

versions of the annals of Sennacherib since the Rassam Cylinder (700). The main
difference is that the Rassam Cylinder shows a longer description of the booty. For the
'traditional' edition of the annals in the Oriental Institute Inscription (the Chicago
Prism), see D.D. Luckenbill, *The Annals of Sennacherib* (The University of Chicago
Oriental Institute Publications, 2; Chicago: University of Chicago Press, 1924), pp. 23-
47. The account of the third campaign is in OIP II, 37-III, 49 (Luckenbill, *Annals*, pp.
29-34). The text in the Rassam Cylinder that is omitted in the later editions can be found
in Luckenbill, *Annals*, pp. 60-61. For a comparison of the relevant texts, one may con-
sult R. Borger, *Babylonisch-Assyrische Lesestücke* (Rome: Pontificium Institutum Biblicum, 2nd edn, 1979), I, pp. 73-77. The Rassam Cylinder has been published recently,
see E. Frahm, *Einleitung in die Sanherib-Inschriften* (AfO Beiheft, 26; Horn: Selbstverlag des Instituts für Orientalistik der Universität Wien, Druk F. Berger & Söhne, 1997),
pp. 47-61. In this work, it is referred to as T4. The relevant sections of the text of the
Rassam Cylinder are discussed at some length in W.R. Gallagher, *Sennacherib's
Campaign to Judah* (SHCANE, 18; Leiden: E.J. Brill, 1999). The 'annalistic' tradition
includes also a generally shortened, but at points slightly different version in Bull IV.
See, for instance, Gallagher, *Sennacherib's Campaign*, pp. 12, 99-101, 105-10, 135.

The mentioned, basic textual stability is due in part to the tendency of the authors of
these texts to use previous versions when dealing with the same subject matter and to
the lack of major differences in ideological or rhetorical requirements (contrast with,
for instance, Nabonidus' inscriptions concerning the building of the temple of Sin at
Harran). On these matters, see J. Van Seters, *In Search of History* (New Haven: Yale
University Press, 1983), esp. pp. 62-64

13. This is true, despite the weight of the reports about Sennacherib's actions in the
Southern front—six out of the eight campaigns described in the annals deal with this
area. Here, beyond-the-narrative events pre-shape the possible ways in which the
narrative may evolve. In other words the historical emphasis on the 'southern problem'
in Sennacherib's day results in an annalistic narrative that has no alternative but to
reflect such emphasis in a literary manner. On Sennacherib's southern front, see, for
instance, L.D. Levine, 'Sennacherib's Southern Front: 704–689 B.C.', *JCS* 34 (1982),
pp. 28-55.

Further, the imperial approach is true already in the first appearance of this account,
in the Rassam Cylinder (700 BCE).

Assyrian (/world) king.[14] The account of the campaign against Judah and its literary context are fully embedded in the discourse of, and convey the ideology of the Assyrian center of power.

The account of the third campaign carried numerous messages, but one that is surely central can be summarized as follows: The Assyrian king succeeded—as expected—to return the land of Hatti to its normative, 'godly' order.[15] Because of his actions, rebellion is no more in the area.[16] In a nutshell, he defeated and punished those who did not submit, and accepted homage and tribute from those who submitted. Those who opposed him suffered the expected and well-deserved defeat, and severe punishment. Hezekiah, who is described as one of the main enemies of the victorious Assyrian king, is portrayed as a pathetic anti-hero who is unable to defend his country, his people and even his own household and palace before the proper ruler, Sennacherib. The latter destroys forty-six cities, numerous villages, exiles a multitude, and takes a large booty. He later receives Hezekiah's tribute, which includes not only his army but his daughters and the women of the palace.[17] As for Hezekiah, he was terrified by the radiant splendor of Sennacherib's lordship, so accepted servitude and sent him his extraordinary 'gift'. True, he was left as king over Judah, but those who were exiled did not return after his servitude, and his kingdom did not return to its former border. Sennacherib diminished his land and raised his tribute. Hezekiah was left as king because he became a servant of the Assyrian king, but he did not go unpunished, nor his land, nor his people.

In sum, the account of the third campaign is presented as 'empiric proof' supporting the ideology of the Assyrian center of power (including the persona of the reigning king) in a multitude of ways.

14. The way (or usually ways) in which an historiographical work constructs time communicates much of the (often implied) worldview advanced and reflected by the work. Cf. E. Ben Zvi, 'About Time: Observations about the Construction of Time in the Book of Chronicles', *HBT* 22 (2000), pp. 17-31.

15. For a detailed study of the account see, among others, H. Tadmor, 'Sennacherib's Campaign to Judah: Historical and Historiographical Considerations', *Zion* 50 (1985), pp. 65-80 (71-78) (in Hebrew).

16. This includes agents of rebellion beyond-the-region forces. The Egyptian-Nubian expedition is rooted out the area, and its allies are no more.

17. Needless to say, the text communicates not only a transfer of 'goods', but also a clear 'transfer' of honor and markers of honor from Hezekiah to Sennacherib.

80   'Like a Bird in a Cage'

Survey of Evidence: The Account in Kings

The account in 2 Kgs 18.13–19.37 is an integral part of the book of Kings and of what may be called the deuteronomistic collection of historical books (as opposed to the 'chronistic' collection of historical books).[18] The account in Kings is not only an extended one, but it is also far from simple. Numerous studies have focused on its possible sources, its redactional history, and its relation to Isa. 36–37. For the purpose of this study it would suffice to point to some of the main lines of this account.[19]

---

18. The account is paralleled, in the main, in Isa. 36.1–37.38. It bears note, however, that the literary context of the account is clearly not the same. The book of Isaiah is not a historiographical work; the book of Kings is.

19. There are numerous studies on this account. It is usually divided in accounts A (2 Kgs 18.13-16) and B (2 Kgs 18.17–19.37). Account B is often divided in B₁ (2 Kgs 18.17–19.9a+36-37 and B₂ (2 Kgs 19b–35), with vv. 19a+36-37 usually, but not always, considered to be the fulfillment of the promise in v. 7. The extent and the relations between these proposed sources or traditions, the editorial processes that led to the present form in Kings, their degree of 'historicity', as well as its relation to the parallel account in the Book of Isaiah have been discussed extensively, though no full agreement is in sight. See, among many others, B.S. Childs, *Isaiah and the Assyrian Crisis* (SBT, Second Series 3; London: SCM Press, 1967), pp. 69-103; R.E. Clements, *Isaiah and the Deliverance of Jerusalem* (JSOTSup, 13; Sheffield: JSOT Press, 1980); P.E. Dion, 'Sennacherib's Expedition to Palestine', *Bulletin of the Canadian Society of Biblical Studies* (presidential address; 1989), pp. 3-25; F.J. Gonçalves, *L'expédition de Sennachérib en Palestine dans la littérature hébraïque ancienne* (EB NS 7; Paris: Gabalda, 1986), esp. pp. 331-487; and more recently, idem, 'Senaquerib na Palestina et a tradiçao bíblica. Da grande derrota de Judá à maravilhosa salvaçao de Jerusalén', *Didaskalia* 20 (1990), pp. 5-32; C. Hardmeier, *Prophetie in Streit vor dem Untergang Judas* (BZAW, 187, Berlin: W. de Gruyter, 1990); Antti Laato, 'Hezekiah and the Assyrian Crisis in 701 B.C.', *SJOT* 2 (1987), pp. 49-68; I. Provan, *Hezekiah and the Books of Kings: A Contribution to the Debate About the Composition of the Deuteronomistic History* (BZAW, 172, Berlin: W. de Gruyter, 1988), pp. 118-30; C.R. Seitz, *Zion's Final Destiny. The Developments of the Book of Isaiah, A Reassessment of Isaiah 36–38* (Philadelphia: Fortress Press, 1991); idem, 'Account A and the Annals of Sennacherib: A Reassessment', *JSOT* 58 (1993), pp. 47-57; M.A. Sweeney, *Isaiah 1–39 with an Introduction to Prophetic Literature* (FOTL XVI; Grand Rapids, MI: Eerdmans, 1996), pp. 454-88; J. Vermeylen, 'Hypothèses sur l'origine d'Isaïe 36–39', J. Van Ruiten and M. Vervenne (eds.) *Studies in the Book of Isaiah. Festschrift Willem A.M. Beuken* (BETL, 132; Leuven: Leuven University Press, 1997), pp. 95-118.

There are also numerous contributions to the study of particular portions or aspects of these accounts. See, for instance, H. Tadmor, 'Rab-saris and Rab-shakeh in 2 Kings 18', C.L. Meyers and M. O'Connor (eds.) *The Word of the Lord Shall Go Forth; Essays in Honor of David Noel Freedman in Celebration of his Sixtieth Birthday* (Winona

First, the narrative in Kings moves straight from the fall of the Northern kingdom at the hands of the Assyrians (2 Kgs 18.9-12) to Sennacherib's campaign against Judah. Further, the latter is presented as fully successful at first,[20] as the text reports that all fortified cities of Judah were conquered (2 Kgs 18.13). The narrative was clearly written so as to convey a sense that what remained of Judah (Jerusalem?[21]) was about to fall just as the Northern kingdom.[22] At this moment, the text brings forward what, on the surface, seems to be the turning point of the narrative, namely Hezekiah proclaims his 'sin' (compare and contrast with 2 Sam. 24.17),[23] and decides to pay tribute to Sennacherib. The latter accepts the tribute given by Hezekiah, but contrary to all expectations this extreme anti-hero decides

---

Lake, IN: Eisenbrauns, 1983), pp. 279-86; E. Ben Zvi, 'Who Wrote the Speech of Rabshakeh and When?', *JBL* 109 (1990), pp. 79-92; D. Rudman, 'Is the Rabshakeh Also Among the Prophets? A Rhetorical Study of 2 Kings XVIII 17-35', *VT* 50 (2000), pp. 100-110.

20. Of course, none of this is holds true for Isa. 36–37, but this is another book with a different story to tell.

21. It is worth noting that the language of text already communicates a strong Jerusalem-centered ideology. Jerusalem is not among all the fortified cities of Judah; it stands in a category of its own.

22. To be sure, the intended readership knew well that this was not to be. They knew well the end of the story before reading it. The purpose of the text was never to inform the literati able to read the Book of Kings that Jerusalem was not destroyed by Sennacherib, but rather to explain the why and how lessons relevant to them may be learned. For that purpose the narrative had to be read as such. People could approach and recreate the ideological and theological messages conveyed by the text by closely following the narrative, its plot and the characterization of the main protagonists.

23. The precise language of the text bears note. Hezekiah is not described as saying חטאתי לך (cf. Judg 10.10). The text as it stands allows a multiplicity of meanings. To be sure, in the narrative Sennacherib is supposed to understand that Hezekiah sinned against him, but the character Hezekiah and above all the intended readers may have understood that the king thought he has sinned against YHWH by rebelling against Sennacherib (cf. 2 Kgs 18.7, 24.20; Jer 52.3 and see Ezek 17.16). This impression is supported by the fact that his actions directly led to the removal of all the silver treasures of the temple and to its physical downgrading (2 Kgs 18.15-16) which are acts that convey dishonor of the temple (contrast with Hag. 2.7-9). It is worth noting that the book of Chronicles, which has a very different version of the events and omits completely any report about this matter, in a subtle way turns the entire issue upside down (2 Chron. 32.23). Alternatively, the reader may think that Hezekiah's confession of 'sin' is not reliable. But if this were the case, then Sennacherib's fault will be lessened. This reading is less likely, see below.

to continue the campaign, to exile the people and destroy Jerusalem.[24] In other words, the text creates a literary (and ideological) scenario that leads to clear anticipations and then frustrates them to negatively characterize Sennacherib. To be sure, this is not the worst that the implied author ascribes to Sennacherib. Much of the rest of the account serves now to characterize Sennacherib as a blasphemer who confronted YHWH. This characterization is carried out through (reported) citations from his words, and it is explicitly reinforced by the evaluation placed twice in the mouth of Hezekiah (see 2 Kgs 19.4; 16) and four times in YHWH's (see 2 Kgs 19.6, 22, 23, 28).[25] The extremely negative characterization of Sennacherib stands in sharp contrast to those of Hezekiah, Isaiah and a number of minor Jerusalemite characters, including the people in general (see, for instance, 2 Kgs 18.36).

Once all these characterizations are well-established, the text moves to describe the (by now anticipated) salvation for Jerusalem, the dramatic destruction of the army of the sinful anti-hero—involving a nocturnal attack carried out by מלאך יהוה—and his shameful death.[26] Further, since the Assyrians are never mentioned again in Kings, the implication is that the yoke of Assyria was removed from Israel forever.[27]

The perspective of the account—and of the book of Kings as a whole as well as the mentioned collection of historical books—is clearly Judah- and Jerusalem-centered, and to be sure, it is YHWH-centric. It also communicates support for centralization, Hezekiah's reform, for stressing the futility of relying on mighty worldly powers (e.g. Egypt) rather than YHWH, and, for other central biblical messages.[28]

The account does exist within the book of Kings. The events that it creates are part and parcel of the world created by the book of Kings. Thus particular contextual meanings deserve much attention. The introduction

---

24. Cf. Josephus, *War* 5.405. It is worth noting that Josephus faced a situation comparable to that of the intended readership of the book of Kings. He had to explain why Jerusalem was saved in Hezekiah's days but not in his, why the correct response to the crisis in his time would have been submission to Rome rather than confrontation whereas Hezekiah was right in standing against Assyria (2 Kgs 18.17–19.37). In this regard, Josephus, in whose writing the destruction of Jerusalem looms large, can be considered close to the intended readers of the book of Kings. See below.

25. Both of whom are reliable and authoritative characters in the narrative.

26. 2 Kgs 19.35, 37.

27. This implication influenced some constructions of the past in rabbinic times. See b. Pesahim 119a. It is worth noting that Chronicles contradicts Kings at this point.

28. I discussed some of these issues in Ben Zvi, 'Who Wrote the Speech'.

to the report on this campaign (i.e. the account in 2 Kgs 18.9-12) serves, on the surface, to compare and contrast the fate of the Northern Kingdom and Judah. But, as with similar references to the Northern Kingdom in the context of either destruction or threatened destruction against Judah in other works in the Hebrew Bible (e.g. Mic. 1), the goal is to sharpen the focus on the ensuing description of the fate of Judah in the text, and—from the postmonarchic perspective of the readership of the book of Kings—the actual destruction of Jerusalem and the underlying reasons that led to it.[29]

From the perspective of this postmonarchic readership, the report about the Assyrian campaign against Judah and Jerusalem could not have been read but in a way that was strongly informed by their knowledge of the outcome of the Babylonian campaign against Judah and Jerusalem in the days of Zedekiah.[30] In fact, it is highly plausible that the obvious contrast between the two campaigns is one of the reasons for the unusually extended coverage of Sennacherib's campaign in Kings. (No military or political crisis of the divided monarchy received so much narrative space in the book, including the story of the fall of Jerusalem.)

This being so, a most salient issue is the acute dissimilarity in the outcomes of these campaigns. To be sure this book provides, directly and indirectly, several explanations for the fall of monarchic Jerusalem. These explanations, which on the surface may contradict each other, in fact inform each other and contribute to the creation of a more sophisticated multivocal approach to this ideologically central issue.[31]

---

29. The destruction of monarchic Judah and of Jerusalem looms heavily on the book of Kings as a whole, and on its intended readership

30. Cf. Seitz, 'Account A'.

31. If all the difference had been that Hezekiah lived before Manasseh (cf. 2 Kgs 24.3) there would be no need for the expanded narrative about Sennacherib nor the description of the sins of Northern Israel in 2 Kgs 17. If Jerusalem was saved because YHWH will never let YHWH's city to fall into the hands of its enemies, as a non-contingent understanding of 2 Kgs 19.34 may suggest, then there is a priori no explanation for the destruction of Jerusalem. Clearly such a reading is falsified in the context of the book of Kings.

The presence of networks of positions on some ideologically (or theologically) significant matter in which each position interacts and intermingles with others, and all shed light on each other and as whole provide and reflect a more comprehensive and balanced response is clearly attested in other books (e.g. Micah, Chronicles, Jonah). I wrote on these issues elsewhere. See, for instance, E. Ben Zvi, *Micah* (FOTL XXIB, Grand Rapids, MI: Eerdmans, 2000), passim; *idem*, 'A Sense of Proportion: An Aspect of the Theology of the Chronicler', *SJOT* 9 (1995), pp. 37-51.

The account of Sennacherib's campaign in Kings contributes to this set of ideological responses, among others, by explicitly pointing to the difference between the situation in Hezekiah's days and that in Zedekiah's. According to the book, the Jerusalemites are pious in the former but not the latter period. But piety alone does not cover all the differences between the two cases.

From the perspective of the mentioned readers, it is obvious that Zedekiah should not have rebelled against the Babylonian king in the first place, and once he has rebelled, he should have tried to come to terms with the Babylonian king, just as Jehoiachin did (2 Kgs 24.12).[32] On the surface, the same holds true for Hezekiah.[33] He did rebel, but here is the first pointed difference, as a good king, and unlike Zedekiah, he was willing to submit, and pay even a very high tribute to the foreign king when the fate of Jerusalem was at stake, and he actually did so.[34] However, Hezekiah's actions did not produce the expected result, because Sennacherib was not any other king, not even Nebuchadnezzar. Hezekiah states, 'Withdraw from

32. Of course, they were well aware of the consequences of that rebellion, but see also Jer. 38.17-23; Ezek. 17.11-21. One may also compare the ending of the story of Jehoiachin (2 Kgs 25.27-30) and that of Zedekiah in the light of the (perceived and actual) fact that Jerusalem was saved by Jehoiachin's surrender (cf. Jer. 38.17-23) and destroyed by Zedekiah's defiance.

It is true that the book of Kings characterizes negatively those who willingly submit to a foreign power (see N. Na'aman, 'The Deuteronomist and Voluntary Servitude to Foreign Powers', *JSOT*, 65 [1995], pp. 37-53), but from this observation it does not follow at all that the book characterizes positively those who rebelled against a suzerain king.

33. To be sure, according to Kings, when Sennacherib decided to continue his campaign and mock YHWH, then Hezekiah was right to stand firm against the Assyrian king, but his actions at that point do not necessarily express retroactive approval for his decision to rebel against Assyria in the first place, nor an evaluation that he was right to rebel before he knew the actual goals and character of Sennacherib.

(One may argue that, because of its context, the reference in 2 Kgs 18.7 is positive, although it is not necessarily the case. In any event, the note stands within a general summary of his reign and it performs a double duty. On the one hand, as an evaluative note in a general summary it looks at the entire enterprise from a holistic perspective that was influenced by 'the end of the story'. On the other hand, it provides the reader with information needed to understand the reasons for Sennacherib's arrival.)

34. Of course, it would have been better if he had not rebelled at all. Neither of the cities would have been destroyed nor the tribute taken from temple and palace, which is not considered a positive result. But Hezekiah's rebellion was already a given. What was left open was how to deal/describe Hezekiah and his rebellion.

me, whatever you impose on me I will bear'. Sennacherib makes clear what it is he wants, and Hezekiah pays. Despite the fact that Sennacherib took the large tribute (2 Kgs 18.14-15), he still continued to attack Jerusalem—unlike the Babylonian king, or any other king, in Kings, for that matter. The reason for this unexpected behavior according to the text is that Sennacherib's real target is not Hezekiah—nor the tribute he may pay—but YHWH, whom he mocks.[35] The lengthy account in 2 Kings 18–19 strongly communicates that Nebuchadnezzar, certainly not a beloved character in the book, was still far from being Sennacherib. The 'demonization' of Sennacherib is *not* a peripheral element in the account of the Assyrian campaign against Judah in Kings, rather it strongly contributes to an understanding of the difference between the events in Hezekiah's and Zedekiah's days, and as such contributes to an understanding of the destruction of Jerusalem.[36]

In addition, the account contributes to the understanding of the dissimilarity between the two events from a second perspective. It stresses and elaborates at some length the (proper) relation between a true prophet and a king in monarchic Judah. The contrast between the relation between Hezekiah and Isaiah, on the one hand, and that between Jehoiakim/Zedekiah and Jeremiah is obvious. Significantly, just as the 'demonization' of Sennacherib is allocated substantial narrative space in the account in Kings, so does the prophet-king interaction.

Survey of Evidence: The Account in Chronicles

The account of Sennacherib's campaign against Judah in the book of Chronicles (2 Chron. 32.1-23) is dependent on the one in Kings. To some extent it is a streamlined version of the latter. Minor characters are erased

---

35. On this matter see also D. Rudman, 'Is the Rabshakeh Also Among the Prophets?'.

36. Nebuchadnezzar is not 'demonized' in Kings. He is, however, in later literature. Sennacherib, however, was very negatively characterized particularly in Babylonian circles because of his destruction of Babylon, a sacrilege. See Nabonidus' stela, *ANET* 309a; and the implicit, but strong negative characterization in Chronicle 1, iii 1. 28 (see A.K. Grayson, *Assyrian and Babylonian Chronicles* [Locust Valley, NY: J.J. Augustin, 1975], pp. 81, 240). It bears note that unlike other cases involving Assyrian kings (e.g. Sargon), the biblical rendition of the name Sennacherib seems to be influenced by Babylonian—rather than Assyrian—phonology. See A.R. Millard, 'Assyrian Royal Names in Biblical Hebrew', *JSS* 21 (1976), pp. 1-14.

It is worth noting that the same double argument that the foreign king is not Sennacherib-like and that the Jerusalemites are not pious are used by Josephus in *War* 5.404-8. On Josephus, see below.

and so are even main narrative detours.[37] While doing so, the (implied) author of Chronicles shows a high degree of reading competence, if by this one means a reading position close to that of the intended reader. This author does not miss the strong message in support of the centralization of the cult, nor the main issue that Sennacherib's speech brought up, namely his mocking of YHWH. The basic plot of both stories is also similar, namely Sennacherib comes, commits a sacrilege with his derisive comments about YHWH, and is miraculously defeated.

All this said, the account in Chronicles is not, and cannot be considered an abbreviated and simplified version of that in Kings. It is a different account, and it stands on its own. Although as a whole it is much shorter than its source in Kings, it expands on certain issues and raises others that are not mentioned at all. It is set in an ideological and literary context that is unlike that of its predecessor, and serves different ideological and rhetorical purposes.

To begin with, the account is not preceded by the report of the fall of the Northern kingdom, but by an unusually extended description of Hezekiah's pious deeds (2 Chron. 29–31). Even the language of the text strongly suggests to the (intended) readership that they should read this description and the campaign as two associated events.[38] In fact, the account of the campaign of Sennacherib is only a subunit of the general account of Hezekiah in Chronicles (2 Chron. 29–32). In fact, it is not even the most elaborated of the subunits that together constitute this account.

A closer reading of the report of the campaign shows a number of differences between Chronicles and Kings. For instance, in Chronicles there was a siege of Jerusalem (2 Chron. 32.10), and the number of casualties in the Assyrian army goes unmentioned.[39] More importantly, there is no

37. See H.J. Tertel, *Text and Transmission. An Empirical Model for the Literary Development of Old Testament Narratives* (Berlin: W. de Gruyter, 1994), pp. 156-71.

38. One may notice that the campaign is not dated to the fourteenth year of Hezekiah but 'after these things and these acts of faithfulness' (2 Chron. 32.1) which explicitly link this unit to the preceding, and see the language of 2 Chron. 31.20. On this matter see, for instance, S. Japhet, *I and II Chronicles. A Commentary* (OTL, Louisville, KY: Westminster/John Knox Press, 1993), pp. 980-81.

39. The former attempts to strengthen the sense of peril for Jerusalem, which is diminished by the lack of reference to the conquered cities and by the certitude about the character of the king expressed in Chronicles. The latter may be due to a sense that the great miracle mentioned there is diminished by a reference to 185,000 people (2 Kgs 19.35). Chronicles prefers 'all mighty warriors, and commanders and officers' (2 Chron. 32.21).

reference to Hezekiah's revolt, no reason is given or suggested for Sennacherib's invasion: Hezekiah never rebelled,[40] nor are his cities conquered (see 2 Chron. 32.1), nor is there any reference to his submission to Assyria, and his 'sin' is nowhere mentioned.[41] As a result the ideological and literary links that bind this unit in Kings to the report about the fate of the Northern Kingdom are fully removed.[42] Moreover, some significant aspects of the comparability between the events in Hezekiah's and Zedekiah's days are either minimized or removed altogether.

Sennacherib remains a strongly negative character, but whereas the narrative space allocated to his characterization is much larger in 2 Kings than in Chronicles, the opposite holds true for the *positive* characterization of Hezekiah. Hezekiah is characterized as the best king of Judah since Solomon. His characterization takes most of the literary space not only in 2 Chron. 29–32 as a whole, but also in 2 Chron. 32.1-23. Hezekiah is described as trusting in YHWH, busy organizing the defense of Jerusalem, encouraging people, giving excellent theological speeches, serving in this capacity as an *ad hoc* prophet and working together with Isaiah.[43] In other words, Hezekiah is doing what an ideal Chronicler's king[44] would have done in such circumstances. Significantly, the narrative space allocated to the interaction between prophet and king in Kings is removed, since the distance between the two is minimized (see 2 Chron. 32.20; and note also the quasi-prophetic speech of Hezekiah in 32.7-8; cf. 2 Chron. 15.1-7). As a result, the relation between this unit and the Zedekiah/Jehoiakim-Jeremiah story loses salience.

Hezekiah is not only, or even mainly, a positive counterpart to either Sennacherib or to Zedekiah but rather a peerless example. The choice of

40. This absence of a report about Hezekiah's revolt may suggest that the Chronicler too was troubled about this characterization of Hezekiah.

41. The image of Hezekiah as a rebel is problematic for Kings—see above. Significantly, it disappears completely in Chronicles—a text in which Hezekiah is lionized. It is problematic again in Josephus (see below). Most likely at least some of the reasons for this tendency are related to the social and political circumstances at the time of the writing and first reception of these historiographical works. It is worth noting that whereas Hezekiah does not rebel, Zedekiah does in Chronicles (see 2 Chron. 32.13).

42. This is consistent with the ideology of the Chronicler on this matter. Note the omission of a parallel account to 2 Kgs 17 in Chronicles.

43. Y. Amit, 'The Role of Prophecy and the Prophets in the Teaching of Chronicles', *Beth Mikra* 28 (1982/83), pp. 113-33 (117, 121-22) (in Hebrew).

44. By Chronicler, I mean here and elsewhere in this paper, the implied author of the book of Chronicles.

words at the beginning of the account not only suggests a comparison with Josiah—the best king of the divided monarchy according to Kings—but also Hezekiah's superiority (see 2 Chron. 32.1 and cf. 35.20).[45] The extended description of Hezekiah's Passover in Chronicles (not present in Kings) is consistent with this tendency (and cf. with the extent of the 'coverage' of Josiah's Passover in Chronicles; also cf. 2 Kgs 23.22 with 2 Chron 35.18).[46]

One may attempt to reconstruct the thought of the Chronicler at this point. Since YHWH defeated the Assyrians in the days of Hezekiah according to the world of knowledge shared by authorship and primary readership, the Chronicler most likely assumed that such a great event must have been associated with Hezekiah's approach to YHWH. [47] The greater the deliverance, and this was a great deliverance, the greater the piety of Hezekiah.

But the greater the piety of Hezekiah, the less suitable he is for a meaningful comparison with Zedekiah. His account may easily evoke now meaningful comparisons between him and Solomon[48] or Josiah, but not with Zedekiah or Jehoiakim. Moreover, the greater his figure is, the more the account of his actions (2 Chron. 29–32) as a whole may serve to communicate the Chronicler's understanding of the role of a worthy king in monarchic Judah to the readership of the book.

As a final comment, in Kings the account of Sennacherib's campaign serves several rhetorical purposes. One of the most important of them is to contribute to its readership's understanding of the fall of Jerusalem. But explanations of that particular event are less important in Chronicles. This book focuses less on the (traumatic) experience of the temporary fall of

---

45. Cf. I. Kalimi, *The Book of Chronicles. Historical Writing and Literary Devices* (Jerusalem, Mosad Bialik, 2000), pp. 28, 50 (in Hebrew).

46. All in all this is the beginning of a tendency to lionize Hezekiah that leads eventually to the traditions reflected in b. Sanh. 94a. One has to take into account also that the characterization of Hezekiah in Chronicles is strongly associated through opposition with that of Ahaz. See P.R. Ackroyd, 'The Biblical Interpretation of the reigns of Ahaz and Zedekiah', in W.B. Barrick and J.R. Spencer (eds.), *In the Shelter of Elyon. Essays on Ancient Palestinian Life and Literature in Honor of G.W. Ahlström* (JSOTSup, 31, Sheffield: JSOT Press, 1984), pp. 247-59.

47. This assumption is fully consistent with the theology/ideology expressed in the book of Chronicles.

48. See H.G.M. Williamson, *Israel in the Books of Chronicles* (Cambridge: Cambridge University Press, 1977), pp. 119-25.

Jerusalem and, in any case looks (a) for general explanatory rules of the divine economy and (b) beyond the destruction of 586 BCE and the 'exile'.[49]

Survey of Evidence: Josephus

For the purpose of this paper, a few words about Josephus's construction of Sennacherib's campaign will suffice. His main sources were biblical. The reference to Berossus and Herodotus in *Ant.* 10.18-23 serve in the main to authenticate his reconstruction of the events to the intended readership of *Antiquities*. Except for the reference to Herodotus the plot follows the basic biblical story and particularly its Kings' version.[50]

Josephus's rhetorical situation was closer to that of the readership (and authorship) of Kings than Chronicles. His focus was, however, not on the Babylonian destruction of Jerusalem, but rather the Roman. As mentioned above, within his opus in general but particularly and explicitly in *War*, his dealing with Sennacherib's campaign allows him to dwell on why Jerusalem was saved in Hezekiah's days but not in his. Why was the correct response to the crisis in his time submission to Rome rather than confrontation, whereas Hezekiah was right to stand against Assyria? Following the lead of Kings, Josephus stresses the difference between the Romans (who stand now instead of the Babylonians of Kings) and the Assyrians.[51] Although a positive characterization of Hezekiah is pre-shaped by the traditions he inherited, he is also worried about being a rebel and subtly attempts to tarnish somewhat Hezekiah's image.[52]

Malleability, Meaning/Significance, Narratives, and Ideological Constraints
The preceding considerations are positive proof that ancient constructions of Sennacherib's campaign against Judah were highly malleable. In other words, ancient writers could mould their account of the campaign to serve particular theological, ideological, literary and rhetorical purposes, as required by their own situation.

It should be stressed that their actions should not be constructed as hypocritical or cynical, that is the work of a group of literati who knowingly *lied* to helpless readers to pursue their own good and the good of those

---

49. Cf. J. Dyck, *The Theocratic Ideology of the Chronicler* (Leiden: E.J. Brill, 1998), esp. pp. 80-81.

50. The citation from Berossus serves to communicate the report in 2 Kgs 19.35-37.

51. See Josephus, *War* 5.404-8; *Ant.* 10.1-23. See also *War* 5.386-88.

52. See L.H. Feldman, 'Josephus's Portrait of Hezekiah', *JBL* 111 (1992), pp. 597-610.

who supported them. For ideology to be successful—and those represented in the neo-Assyrian account, and in Kings' and Chronicles' ideologies were successful—not only the 'consumers' of the ideology but also those constructing and propagating it should be believers.[53] In fact, it is much better to place the entire issue *not* under heuristic questions such as who deviated from the truth, when and why, but rather to view it in terms of the particular significance of certain historical events for particular groups.[54]

The significance of an historical event—be it ancient or modern—can be discerned only in terms of a particular historical narrative.[55] This significance is deeply dependent on expectations or consequences associated with the event. To use examples of recent events, one may think of 'the meaning' of disparate events such as the fall of the Berlin Wall, the election of Franklin D. Roosevelt or Ronald Reagan, the Oslo agreements between Israel and the PLO, the use of an atomic bomb on Hiroshima, or WWI; or one may think of earlier historical events such as the one in 1492 CE referred to as either 'the discovery of America' or 'the First Encounter'. Whatever significance a historian—or any person for that matter— would ascribe to these events depends on the set of consequences (and at times expectations) that such a historian associates with them. Needless to say, these sets reflect (and indirectly communicate) information about events, or construction of events later—and at times much later—than the event being discussed. Thus these sets and the significance ascribed to events in the past are influenced by ideological frames and considerations.[56]

53. Cf. M. Liverani, 'The Ideology of the Assyrian Empire', in Mogens Trolle Larsen (ed.), *Power and Propaganda. A Symposium on Ancient Empires* (Mesopotamia, 7; Copenhagen: Akademisk Forlag, 1979), pp. 297-317 (299).

54. To be sure there was much inventiveness and literary creativity among the literati—a group that includes ancient historians—but the outcome of their works was pre-shaped to some degree by their understanding of the particular significance of the event they are writing (and reading) about. This holds true whether they were aware or unaware that such is the case. On creativity and particularly creative imitation in the Hebrew Bible, see J. Van Seters, 'Creative Imitation in the Hebrew Bible', SR 29 (2000), pp. 395-409.

55. 'Narrative' is here understood in a broad sense.

56. This type of issues has been discussed, in one way or another, numerous times in articles on *History and Theory*. See, for instance, L. Hölscher, 'The New Annalistic: A Sketch of a Theory of History', *History and Theory* 36 (1997), pp. 317-35; R. Martin, 'Progress in Historical Studies'. To be sure, from the mentioned observations it certainly does *not* follow that 'anything goes'. See, for instance, the mentioned bibliography and the results of the present examination of this case study.

This being so, differences of viewpoints on consequences (and at times, expectations) lead to different meanings ascribed to events, and to different narratives of them. For instance, an account of the *'third* campaign' already connotes and reflects a viewpoint that construes this campaign as one in a set of successive successful campaigns, and carries an expectation of further victorious campaigns against any possible group that may defy the king and the gods.[57]

Since the meaning of the event is expressed by means of an historical narrative, and both are dependent on the discourse and potential repertoire of the writers and readers ('producers' and 'consumers') of this literature, it is only to be expected that the narrative construction of the account will be strongly influenced by the significance ascribed to the event. The present discussion has shown that differences in the narratives that result from these considerations affect not only 'the lesson to be learned' but also involve very basic issues such as how the event came about and how it ended, as well as narrative details. These conclusions hold true for Kings and the Annals and their inversions of the story. They also hold true even when a clear line of dependence and of pre-shaping traditions links separate works (see Kings, Chronicles and Josephus).

One final observation, the mentioned malleability is strongly contingent on the general discourse of the producers and intended consumers of these historical narratives. Malleability here does not mean that 'everything

57. The only scenario that would allow a rejection of that expectation is one in which there will be no 'sinners' ever, so there will be no need for the heroic military actions of the king, but this was not a likely scenario, either historically nor ideologically. The king is expected to demonstrate his heroism, his outstanding prowess as a warrior. See B. Oded, *War, Peace and Empire. Justification for War in Assyrian Royal Inscriptions* (Wiesbaden: Dr Ludwig Reichert Verlag, 1992), pp. 145-62. Moreover, there is the ideological construction that the king is supposed to enlarge the borders of Assyria. As expected, this construction created some difficulties to the authors of Sennacherib's inscriptions, because one of their constraints was that he—unlike his predecessors and successors—did not expand the territory of Assyria, i.e., there was tension between the expected characterization of the king and facts that were agreed upon by the society within which these texts were composed and displayed. On these ideological characterizations of the king and on how Sennacherib's scribes actually coped with this issue, see H. Tadmor, 'World Dominion: The Expansion Horizon of the Assyrian Empire', in L. Martino, S. de Martino, F.M. Fales and G.B. Lanfranchi (eds.), *Landscapes. Territories, Frontiers and Horizons in the Ancient Near East* (Part I, History of the Ancient Near East/Monographs-III/1, Padova: Sargon srl, 1999), pp. 54-62. On the general issue of constraints on (historical) writing due to facts agreed upon by the producers and consumers of texts, see discussion below.

goes', or that inner demands of the world of the narrative are the only factors to be taken into account. There is a social reality 'out there' in the
world of the producers and consumers that includes their respective ideologies, expectations, ranges of potentially acceptable meanings and significances, as well as worlds of knowledge. The following section will
approach the issue of the potential extent of malleability from a somewhat
different perspective.

*Possible Extent of Malleability: Some Considerations Based on
Historical Events as Reconstructed Today and Ideological Quests for
Meaning/Significance.*
The accounts differ not only among themselves, but also from what 'most
likely happened' according to contemporaneous, historical-critical analysis. This is true also of the two that were the closest to the events, among
those studied here.

There is no doubt from a historical-critical approach that Sennacherib's
campaign to the West in 701 BCE was a great strategic success. First, without having to expend the enormous resources that would have been
required to conquer Tyre, Sennacherib brought the entire Phoenician
coastland under his control and begun a process that led to the steady
decline of Tyre and its replacement as the main city of the area by Sidon.[58]
The Philistines were under clear control after the campaign and did not
rebel again. The southern commercial routes remained open to Assyria,
and Ekron developed into a major industrial/commercial city. Judah, the
ringleader of the rebellion, was so weakened that it became a 'faithful'
vassal to the end of the Assyrian dominion and was never again to be any
kind of threat to the imperial suzerain. As for the Egyptians, they did not
send armies to the area until much later, under very different circumstances. In fact, Sennacherib created a new and stable regional balance of
power that allowed Assyria to control the area (except Phoenicia) success-
fully for more than century—in fact, till the downfall of Assyria—with
minimal costs.[59]

It is obvious that this description of the events is substantially different

58. See J. Elayi, 'Les relations entre les cites phéniciennes et l'empire assyrien sous
le règne de Sennachérib', *Semitica* 35 (1985), pp. 19-26. One may notice that—all
things equal—a regional center of power around Sidon (as opposed to Tyre) was strategically preferable from an Assyrian perspective. It was far easier to subdue Sidon—if
the need arose—than to subdue Tyre.

59. It is noteworthy that this successful combination of strategic achievements was

from the one in Kings and later writings in that tradition, but it is also different from the story in the Assyrian annals too. Strategic wisdom and careful use of (large, but always limited) military resources was not something to be glorified in Assyrian royal ideology. The latter emphasized the king as a successful military leader, as a mighty hero and builder. So, for instance, although one may conclude that Sennacherib's decision not to invest his military and logistic resources in an attack on Tyre itself or its Cypriot territories, and consequently to allow Luli to remain as its king was correct in strategic terms, the annals do not report about it. In the annalistic narrative, Luli is referred to as the king of Sidon—rather than Tyre[60]—so he can be replaced with a 'proper king'.[61] Further, the strate-

the result of one campaign and did not require significant direct administrative involvement on Assyria's part, but rather an effective use of local leaders. This is consistent with Sennacherib's policy, not to annex territories.

For a similar historical reconstruction and for an evaluation of Sennacherib's campaign to the West as an overwhelming success, see, among others, N. Na'aman, 'Hezekiah and the Kings of Assyria;' *idem*, 'Forced Participation in Alliances in the Course of the Assyrian Campaigns to the West', in M. Cogan and I. Eph'al (eds.), *Ah, Assyria! Studies in Assyrian History and Ancient Near Eastern Historiography Presented to Hayim Tadmor* (ScrH, 33; Jerusalem: Magnes Press, 1991), pp. 80-98 (94-97).

To be sure, it might be argued from some corners that this reconstruction is nothing more than another 'narrative' created and adopted by a certain group/s of scholars at a particular time, for their own reasons, and according to their own perspectives and expectations, and that this being the case, their narrative is not *essentially* different from, for instance, the account in Kings, or paraphrases of it. But there is a difference between this, or substantially similar reconstructions of the events on the one hand, and non-critical—by present historiographical standards—reconstructions on the other. See n. 5.

60. N. Na'aman who maintains that Luli was indeed the king of Sidon, and not the king of Tyre, has recently questioned the consensus on this matter. See N. Na'aman, 'Sargon II and the Rebellion of the Cypriote Kings against Shilta of Tyre', *Or* 67 (1998), pp. 239-47 (245-47). But a number of considerations suggest that the consensus position is still preferable. Thus, for instance, Luli is explicitly associated with Tyre in the inscriptions in Bulls 2, 3 and 4 inscription that mention that he fled to Cyprus—which was Tyrian territory; this is the first reference to Cyprus in Assyrian material since the days of Sargon; see Gallagher, *Sennacherib's Campaign*, p. 99). Moreover, Tyre was the regional center of power, rather than Sidon at the time of the campaign. Although one may question the tactical wisdom of Luli's decision to move from Tyre to his Cypriot territories in 701 BCE, good reasons for that move may be envisioned too, particularly given the Tyre's control of the sea, the importance of supplies, and the previous rebellion of Cypriote kings against Tyre, a few years earlier, when Shilta reigned over Tyre. On these matters, see Elayi, 'Les relations', and Gallagher, *Sennacherib's Campaign*, pp. 91-104. On Bulls 2, 3, 4 (T 26, 27, 29) see Frahm, *Einleitung*, pp. 115-18.

gically irrelevant fact that Luli died a few years after the campaign becomes an important ideological fact in later versions of the annalistic narrative/s of Sennacherib's campaign to Phoenicia, because it brings a superior (ideological) closure to the story of Luli.[62] Similarly, although the decision to leave Hezekiah on the throne of a substantially weakened Judah and not to conquer Jerusalem was proven to serve well Assyrian interests, the narrative had to allocate a relatively substantial space to the defeat of Hezekiah,[63] not only because of his political importance in the anti-Assyrian coalition, but also to compensate for the lack of reference to the

61. This observation raises already an interesting issue regarding factual constraints on the narrative. Luli could be, and was, characterized as the king of Sidon since his dominion included the city, but his replacement, Tuba'lu could not and was not characterized as king of Tyre because the city was not under his control. See below.

62. He probably died only a few years after 700 BCE. See Gallagher, *Sennacherib's Campaign*, pp. 93-96; Elayi, 'Les relations', pp. 22-23. References to his death appear in T10 (697 BCE; Frahm, *Einleitung*, p. 66); T12 (BM 103.000; 694 BCE; Frahm, *Einleitung*, pp. 87-89), the inscriptions in Bulls 2, 3 and 4 (694 BCE), and later versions of the annals (e.g. OIP). A comparable reference to the (late) death of a king within a narrative that suggests immediacy and some correlation between sinful behavior and death occurs in 2 Kgs 19.37. The villain there is, however, Sennacherib.

(It seems that by 694 BCE some kind of compromise between Assyria and Tyre—including the Cypriot territories—was worked out. Such arrangement would have included vassal status for Tyre.)

These observations imply again some factual constraints on the narrative. It seems that Luli could not be described as dead in the annalistic narratives until he actually was. On this matter, see below. This being so, the lack of reference to Hezekiah's death in this literature may suggest that he was alive by the time it was composed.

63. This claim has to be set also in some general proportion. Despite the fact that within the ideological constrains of the annals, the submission of Hezekiah was likely the greatest deed Sennacherib could boast in the Western front, the account itself is relatively minor in terms of the full version of the annals.

Yet, the conquest of Lachish still stood as a significant symbol of Assyria's power—and of its rhetoric of terror at Sennacherib's palace, in a room that had some architectural prominence, room XXXVI. It bears notice that the 'story' told by the reliefs there is clearly not identical with that of the annalistic sources (where Lachish is not even mentioned), and that the latter could not have been the source for the reliefs, nor do these sources and the reliefs share—in the main—a common audience. Reliefs that may be associated with the third campaign were likely present in other rooms in the palace (e.g. I, X, XII, XXIV). On these matters, see J.M. Russell, *Sennacherib's Palace without Rival at Nineveh* (Chicago: University of Chicago Press, 1991), pp. 28-31, 64, 160-64, 200-209, 245-57, and passim; D. Ussishkin, *The Conquest of Lachish by Sennacherib* (Tel Aviv: The Institute of Archaeology, 1982), pp. 59-126.

conquest of Jerusalem and for his being left sitting on his throne.[64] This problem was developed by the logic of the narrative and the ideological construction of the character of the king, as the successful, powerful military leader. The text implies a tripartite division of the Judahite cities: (a) main cities (and they were numbered, 46) (b) minor (and they go unnumbered) cities that surround the main cities, and (c) a capital city. Since Sennacherib is described as one who conquered the first two categories of cities, the text has to avoid any potential implication that the lack of completion of the series might suggest that he was unable to conquer the capital city and, accordingly, tarnish his characterization.

Thus, the differences that do exist between the account and the events as reconstructed today by critical historians involve much more than some form of frame that conveys meaning to the events themselves. It directly affects and shapes details in the narrative, such as the basic material concerning the Luli-Tyre episode, the number of Judahite exiles, which is obviously an exaggeration,[65] the ideological characterization of Hezekiah, and how much narrative space will be allocated to each episode. (One may also note that the narrative omits any reference to events such as the likely takeover [conquest?] of Gaza by the enemies of Assyria.[66])

There is nothing surprising about these conclusions. A plethora of examples of military, political and social crises in recent years show that very soon after the events—or even at the time they actually occur—clearly different descriptions of them do arise. These descriptions vary according

---

64. Cf. H. Tadmor, 'Senacherib's Campaign', esp. p. 77; J.M. Russell, *Sennacherib's Palace*, p. 256. On the tripartite division, here and in other texts, see M. de Odorico, *The Use of Numbers and Quantifications in the Assyrian Royal Inscriptions* (SAAS III; Helsinki: The Neo-Assyrian Text Corpus Project, 1995), p. 15.

65. The number of Judahite exiles—i.e. 200,150—is impossible. On the use of this 'very high+exact' number see M. de Odorico, *Use of Numbers and Quantifications*, pp. 114-16 and 171-74. These numbers 'represent the attempt to associate the sense of emphasis given by the "high round number"…with the (appearance) of truthfulness given by their "exact" form' (p. 172)

66. The Egyptian army reached as far north as Eltekeh, so it is unlikely that Gaza remained a pro-Assyrian island in the area till the final victory of Sennacherib. In addition, there is also the strong tendency towards force participation in regional alliances. Significantly, there is no reference to the king of Gaza among the faithful kings of the Amurru who 'willingly' brought their tribute to Sennacherib (Rassam, pp. 36-38; OIP, II, 50-60). A similar event, the takeover of Ekron is mentioned, however, but within a context that glorifies the Assyrian king as the restorer of the proper order and as the one who overwhelmed Hezekiah, the agent of 'chaos'.

to the expectations, rhetorical and ideological perspectives and needs of the opposing sides. They describe and construe (or wish to others to construe) the events and their consequences in a way that reflects their 'true' significance or meaning, from their own viewpoint. The Gulf War, numerous events and clashes in the Palestinian–Israeli conflict, and even the case of one Cuban child rescued from the sea in the USA (Elian Gonzalez) to mention only a few examples, provide positive proof that such is the case.

To be sure, these considerations strongly undermine the principle that the closer to the events, the higher the historical accuracy of a document. Each document reflects the worldview, expectation and goals of those who write them and those for whom they are intended, if the writer is proficient. Its level of historical accuracy has to be tested rather than privileged 'by default'.[67] Although close-to-the event reports tend to show more details, these do not necessarily contribute to the larger historical picture and may well serve rhetorical needs for verisimilitude than 'factual' observations. Needless to say, this conclusion cannot be construed in any way or manner as a veiled preference for later documents.[68]

All this said, it is worth noting that the account of the third campaign does not claim that Sennacherib conquered Jerusalem, or that he deposed Hezekiah, or that Luli—or the city of Tyre for that matter—was captured, or that Tub'alu was made king of Tyre, or that the Hezekiah—rather than Luli—passed away, implicitly because of his sins, nor does the account contain any reports of Luli's death prior to the event itself. In other words, despite the fact that such claims would have been supportive of the ideology and genre of the report, they were not made. There seems to be a grammar of writing that does not allow unrestrained creativity with some matters.[69] These considerations lead us directly to the discussion of limits to malleability.

67. One may note that whereas Kings implies that the Assyrian domination came to an end with Sennacherib's defeat, Chronicles suggests that this is not the case, as the story of Manasseh demonstrates. In this particular instance, Chronicles' picture is more consistent with our knowledge of the period than the one offered in Kings.

68. At times, some 'historical perspective' is gained and some telescoping might be useful, but there are numerous examples that show how reports in later narratives may share little with the actual events.

69. To be sure, there is much ideologically-oriented creativity in other matters. Some battles in which the Assyrians, at least, did not achieve complete victory were described as unequivocal successes (e.g. Der, Halulei; see A.K. Grayson, 'Problematic Battles in Mesopotamian History', in H.G. Güttersbock and Th. Jacobsen (eds.), *Studies in Honor of Benno Landsberger on his Seventy-Fifth Birthday, April 25, 1965*

Limits to Malleability Questions of Representation and Historical Referents

The preceding considerations have also hinted at some limitations imposed on these narratives, of some pre-shaped elements that condition the narratives. These pre-shaped elements are of a variety of kinds. The ideological and literary constraints discussed above certainly constrain and control the potential malleability of the narrative.

There is a second type of constraints: What the authorship/intended readership group may consider acceptable in a historiographical work. To be sure, the standard by which something is or is not considered to be acceptable cannot be a feature of the narrative itself. It is a standard by which different historical narratives created in the world of various works are evaluated. As such, it stands outside the world created by any particular book or historical narrative embedded in it. The existence of the standard creates a situation in which certain accounts do pass the test and become plausible narratives from this perspective, whereas others fail and accordingly, become potential but implausible historical narratives. As such they are unlikely to be written, and if they are written at all, the 'consumers' will reject them.

Given that these narratives shape history, it stands to reason that at least some of these standards are directly related to the question of the plausibility of historical representation. In other words, on whether the narrative's description/construction of an event, as a whole, may be considered a plausible representation of what the authorship and intended readership of the work assumed is being represented, that is, the historical event as they construe it.[70]

This construction of the historical event may be based directly or indirectly on some witnesses of the event, or on narratives that are directly

(Oriental Institute, Assyriological Studies, 16; Chicago: Chicago University Press, 1965), pp. 337-42; A. Laato, Assyrian Propaganda and the Falsification of History in the Royal Inscriptions of Sennacherib', *VT* 45 (1995), pp. 198-226 (199-213). Even if this or that example may be debatable, the fact that no neo-Assyrian king reported a defeat in his annals is positive proof of a strong principle of selection. It is disputable, however, whether the highly loaded, evaluative term 'falsification of history' is appropriate for these and similar cases (e.g. the account of Sennacherib's campaign in Kings and Chronicles).

70. In other words, the description should correspond to at least some degree with what the authorship and readership think that the historical facts were.

related to these witnesses, or on accepted narratives that may be quite remote from the event itself and are only vaguely related to any direct or indirect witness. Thus, for instance, it is clear that the Assyrian narrative of the third campaign was written close to the events—it existed in 700 BCE—and it is reasonable to assume that the mentioned standard of representation had to do, at least to some extent, with Assyrian recollections of the events of the campaign.[71] If this is so, then the question is what was required to qualify as plausible by this representation standard? And given the focus of this paper on the extent of malleability, what could the account *not* claim about the campaign against Judah lest it becomes implausible to its readership, from the perspective of this particular standard[72]?

One has to admit that there is no sure answer to these questions. But in light of the considerations advanced above and given that the account was considered plausible by an Assyrian readership that had some knowledge of the historical events, the range of answers to these question seems to consist of a subset of the set created by the overlap between the Assyrian account and the most likely reconstruction of the events. In the case of the campaign against Judah this set includes: (a) the names of the two kings involved in the Assyrian campaign against Judah, and, of course, the existence of such a campaign; (b) some basic elements of the order imposed by Assyria on the area, namely the removal of lands from Judah's domain, the 'transformation' of Hezekiah into a loyal vassal king, the payment of tribute; (c) the destruction of the main cities of Judah along with the lack of conquest of its capital; and (d) the failure of the Egyptian expedition. In all these cases, the world of the narrative points to referents outside this narrative and represents them in what was considered to be a plausible manner.

To be sure, reference to all these elements was not necessary to maintain the general plausibility of a reference to the campaign as a representation of the historical events, for the Assyrian readership.[73] But, significantly, there is no account of this campaign in Assyrian sources in which the names

71. Cf. J.M. Russell, *Sennacherib's Palace*, pp. 28-31.

72. To be sure, there are other standards too, such as consistency with the accepted ideology, meaning conveyed, genre considerations, and the like. For instance, a reference to the king's defeat would have rendered the account as an implausible representation of the events. On these issues, see above.

73. See the Nebi Yunus Inscription (Frahm's T 61; Luckenbill's H4), l. 15; Luckenbill, *Annals*, p. 86. The minimal reference there includes the name of the king of Judah, his submission to Sennacherib and the substantial damage that the latter inflicted on Judah.

of the kings are changed, nor one in which Jerusalem was conquered, or in which Hezekiah did not become (eventually) a vassal king who submitted to Assyria,[74] or for that matter one in which Hezekiah passed away, when he was still alive.

These considerations raise an important point, to omit references to the agreed-upon facts of the time is possible, and at times may be desirable for different reasons (e.g. genre, ideological bent, rhetorical needs), but to contradict them openly and maintain plausibility is a much more difficult task. Moreover, this task becomes impossible if the agreed-upon facts that are contradicted by the potential account were considered not peripheral but 'core' facts for the understanding of the historical event (e.g. the name of Hezekiah, his being a Judahite king, etc.)

If a similar analysis is carried out for the account of Sennacherib's campaign in the book of Kings, which is an account much later than the events themselves and much later than the annalistic account, then the set created by the overlap between this account *as a whole*—that is when the full outcome of the campaign is taken into consideration[75]—and the most likely reconstruction of the events includes: (a) the names of the two kings involved in the Assyrian campaign against Judah, and, of course, the existence of such a campaign; (b) the conquest of the main cities of Judah—including Lachish—along with the lack of conquest of Jerusalem; and (c) the murder of Sennacherib.[76] It is difficult to see the references to the conquest of the main cities of Judah and to the death of Sennacherib as a *sine qua non* component for the plausibility of the representation for the producers and consumers of the book of Kings in its present form. In fact, they seem to be present in the text mainly for narrative purposes. If this is the case then the plausibility of the account—from the perspective of these standards—required only that there was a campaign and that it involved

74. To be sure, the latter would also be implausible for ideological reasons, if Hezekiah is left on the throne.

75. The narrative reference to Hezekiah's paying tribute does not show a good overlap with the historical reconstruction of the events, because in Kings it did not lead to a stable position of servitude. Similarly, the narrative reference to the Tirhakah does not qualify because it does not directly point to the failure of the Egyptian expedition. In fact, if 2 Kgs 19.9a is to be read in a way informed by 2 Kgs 19.36, then Tirhakah's expedition cannot be considered a failure. The connection between the two verses is, however, debated, see n. 19.

76. Perhaps one may add also the presence of Sennacherib at Lachish, but this is somewhat implied in item (b).

kings Sennacherib and Hezekiah. One may reach similar conclusions if the accounts in Chronicles and in Josephus are examined in this way.[77]

It must be stressed that this conclusion is true only within the limits of the frame from which it emerges, that is, comparisons between the different account of the event in the mentioned texts and the most likely reconstruction of the events, as agreed by the majority of critical historians of the ancient Near East. But this conclusion shows an inherent and severe limitation: Referents do not have to point to the historical events, but to what the producers and intended consumers of the reports thought happened, in other words, to the system of agreed-upon facts held by a particular social group. For instance, Josephus did not and *could not* have advanced a case for the plausibility of his narrative on the basis of a correspondence between the historical events as known to critical historians today and his representation of them in the narrative. For him, the limitation raised by the demand for plausibility involved the correspondence between his knowledge of the events (i.e. the facts agreed upon by him and his peers) and his narrative. His knowledge of the Assyrian period in Judah was based on Kings and Chronicles. For Josephus (and his intended readership), a plausible representation of the events is one that can be judged favorably by some basic standards set by the accounts in Chronicles and Kings.[78]

Chronicles, as it is well-known, departs from Kings and Samuel on numerous occasions. But the presence of these departures does *not* mean, 'anything goes'. The study of the limitations on malleability that strongly influenced the work of the Chronicler deserves a separate study.[79] It will

77. The difference between the account in Kings and the annalistic account may be associated with their temporal distance from the events they are narrating, and with the actual outcome of the events that was at the time of the events more suitable for direct Assyrian than Judahite ideological appropriation.

78. On Josephus and his use of Kings and Chronicles, see I. Kalimi, 'History of Interpretation. The Book of Chronicles in Jewish Tradition. From Daniel to Spinoza', *RB* 105 (1998), pp. 5-51 (17-19).

79. See my 'Shifting the Gaze: Historiographic Constraints in Chronicles and their Implications', in J.A. Dearman and M.P. Graham (eds.), *The Land that I Will Show You: Essays on the History and Archaeology of the Ancient Near East in Honor of J. Maxwell Miller* (JSOTSup, 343; Sheffield: Sheffield Academic Press, 2001), pp. 38-60. A substantial outline of Israel's story of its past was already fixed, 'canonical' one may say, by the time of the composition of Chronicles. Although there was never a 'true' canonical history (i.e. a single, authoritative version) the authority of the book of Kings—and narratives about the past in other authoritative books—reflected and

suffice here to state that its historical plausibility was contingent on the acceptance of a core construction of the past (e.g. David could not have been described as the actual builder of the Temple, since the authorship and readership of the book were well aware that Solomon, and only Solomon, built it—again an issue of main,—or core,—facts agreed upon by the community and the necessity of correspondence).[80] Turning to our particular case, the question is what aspects of this core construction of the past had the Chronicler to abide by in the account of Sennacherib's campaign?

Given the considerations mentioned above, and assuming that the main source of Chronicles is the account in Kings, the range of answers to these questions consists of a subset of the set of claims created by the overlap between the account in Kings and that in Chronicles. The set includes: (a) the names of the two kings involved in the Assyrian campaign against Judah; (b) the salvation of Jerusalem; (c) the piety of Hezekiah; (d) the collaboration between a pious king and the prophet Isaiah; and (e) the blasphemy of Sennacherib and his punishment. To be sure, Kings and Chronicles shape different meanings in their respective accounts and each deal with the issues in the set in (slightly) different ways. But for the narrative in Chronicles to be considered a plausible representation of the events and outcomes of Sennacherib's campaign against Judah, all these basic elements had to be present in some way and be incorporated in the narrative, due to the social reality and world of knowledge within which (and for which) Chronicles was composed

shaped a kind of communally agreed basic history of the past. This history served to create a sense of (mythical) unity with the past, and contributed to social solidarity and identity in the present.

80. To put it simply, had the Chronicler claimed that David actually built the temple and not Solomon, the book would not have been accepted by the intended readership. Of course, this fact does not mean that the Chronicler could not shape the story in very particular, and inventive ways. Thus, for instance, David is described as responsible for the planning of the temple and of its construction, for preliminary actions towards its building, and even for aspects of its work when it was built. Yet he cannot actually build it. Since, as it is well-known, Chronicles did not maintain a full correspondence with all facts that could have been agreed upon by the community on the basis of Kings, the question is one of a hierarchy of facts. Some facts can be challenged, but others—e.g. that Solomon built the temple—are so central that challenge is impossible. The latter may be considered 'core facts' within the world of the writers and intended and primary readers of the book. These issues stand beyond the scope of this paper and are discussed in the article mentioned in the preceeding note.

To be sure, the plausibility of the account of the campaign in the book of Kings was also contingent on its acceptance of a traditional reconstruction of the past. It is unlikely that the authors of the present form of the book in the postmonarchic period invented, out of nothing, a full tradition about the miraculous salvation of Jerusalem or the related tradition on Sennacherib's sinfulness, or even the link between prophet and king. It is much more likely that they reflected what was believed by Judahites at the time of the composition of the book to be core elements of a plausible representation of the campaign.

This observation may lead to a move towards the study of hypothetical written sources of the account in Kings and to attempts to analyze their dependence on the degree of plausibility of their own representation of the events within the discourse of their time and social-ideological group, and so on. But a study of hypothetical sources stands beyond the intent of this paper. Still, there is an important point here. The significant lack of correspondence between the historical facts and the facts agreed upon by the social group within which one finds the authorship and first readership of the book of Kings demands an explanation.[81] A process in which the significance or meaning of the event begins to shape the communal understanding of the event, and along with it the facts that are agreed upon by the community, seems to bridge the gap between these two sets of facts. To illustrate, an emphasis on the 'salvation of Jerusalem' possibly led to a construction of accepted facts such as the destruction of the Assyrian army, and eventually the implied full independence of Judah from Assyria.

These are a few final considerations. The discussion has shown that narratives as separate as the accounts of the campaign in Kings and in Sennacherib's annals share a few claims: there was a campaign, it involved Hezekiah and Sennacherib, Jerusalem was not conquered—though the main cities of Judah were, Hezekiah remained in power, and there was an Egyptian expedition. In other words, both texts, despite all their differences, point to similar referents, however they may be represented (and evaluated). A referent that belongs to more than one narrative *cannot* exist only in the world of any one of its narratives, and so it has to be present in a world that exists beyond any of them individually.[82] This world is the general discourse—including the world of knowledge—shared by the

---

81. If this were not the case, then the book would not have been accepted as a plausible representation of the past.

82. Cf. L. Hölscher, 'New Annalistic', esp. pp. 318-20.

writers and readers of this type of literature; it certainly includes their own understanding/s of the past, and along with it a set of facts they agree upon. This discourse is an integral part of the social reality within which ancient historical works were written and read.

Both the Chronicler and Josephus lived within their own social reality and accordingly they wrote within the limits created by shared core facts derived from the report of Sennacherib's campaign in Kings. In sum, they were not constrained by the historical facts themselves—or as known to us—but by the facts agreed upon by their respective groups, and the expectations that were raised in these discourses by these particular facts.

But what about Kings and the annalistic traditions? There are very few shared elements and traditions that could have strongly informed both the discourse of the writers and readers of Kings and those of the Assyrian Annals. The authors of the Annals certainly did not have the book of Kings, nor any of the possible sources of this book. It is very unlikely that the authors of Kings—or any of the mentioned sources for that matter—based their account of the campaign on the Annals, or certainly they did not assume that their readers will have any reason to accept the annalistic version of the events as a norm from which deviation is possible but certainly limited. If so, how to explain claims shared by the two accounts? Shared claims between these two independent discursive constructions most likely reflect shared core attributes ascribed to the events themselves as they were perceived or represented by those involved at the time they happened and immediately after. In turn, shared perceptions or representations by diametrically separate groups must point to something that stands beyond or outside their own perceptions or representations, although these perceptions or representations surely point at it. If these perceptions or representations are independent, this 'something' is likely to be what we usually call the historical event.[83]

---

83. Which, of course, is immediately appropriated and given significance in a way that is consistent with particular discourses, ideologies, worlds of knowledge, expectations and the like.

It is to be stressed that the independence of the representations is a *sine qua non* condition. If the representations are not independent they point to a shared discourse or a shared world knowledge. For instance, Manetho and biblical tradition (and later Jewish traditions influenced by the latter; e.g., Jewish-Hellenistic writers, Josephus, etc.) refer to a clash between the ancestors of the Jewish settlers in Judea and Jerusalem and the ('true') Egyptians that took place in Egypt and that led to the exit of the former from Egypt. The presence of the motif in two clearly different discursive worlds points to a shared referent, namely a 'core fact' agreed upon by both discursive

Summary

The different accounts of Sennacherib's campaign against Judah serve as a good case study for the extent and limitations of malleability in ancient Israelite historiography. The significance of the event as communicated (and shaped) by different accounts varies significantly. This variation in turn strongly influences the accounts since their narratives are the means by which this significance is shaped and communicated, and since there was ample—but not limitless—room for innovation and creation. These significances directly relate to and are contingent on social and ideological expectations, worlds of knowledge—including constructions of the past—and the like. Moreover, they lead to a process in which the sets of facts that are agreed upon about the past may change. The creation of new facts agreed upon by the relevant community/ies leads in turn to future pre-shaped accounts.

There are also limitations on the malleability of the narratives. These limitations are associated with the contingencies mentioned above, but also with the conditions for plausibility of historical representations that exist among different groups. These conditions may depend on an accepted, pre-shaped understanding of the past or on perceptions of historical events. The latter are to some extent pre-shaped directly or indirectly by the his-

communities, namely that there was such a clash. Needless to say, this 'core fact' is given very different significance in these two cases and is embedded in different general metanarratives. This 'core fact' does go back to an historical event, but to a point in which constructions of the past share a particular element. One cannot learn from the dual attestation of this 'core fact' that it points to an historical exodus from Egypt, because either Manetho or the sources behind Manetho's knowledge of this particular clash are not totally independent from biblical or related traditions. Manetho's knowledge does not go back to a series of referents and representations that eventually reaches representations emerging out the experiences of those involved in the events, nor is it 'untouched' by biblical or related traditions on these matters.

On Manetho and the texts relevant to the discussion here, see M. Stern, *Greek and Latin Authors on Jews and Judaism* (Jerusalem: The Israel Academy of Sciences and Humanities, 1976), pp. 62-86; cf. P.R. Davies, 'Judaeans in Egypt: Hebrew and Greek Stories', in L.L. Grabbe (ed.), *Did Moses Speak Attic? Jewish Historiography and Scripture in the Hellenistic Period* (JSOTSup, 317, Sheffield: Sheffield Academic Press, 2001), pp. 108-28.

On general matters discussed in these final considerations, cf. Hölscher, 'The New Annalistic'.

torical events,[84] and by whatever facts are agreed by the community/ies within which the authorship and readership of the work were situated. Historical events and historical facts agreed upon by communities stand outside and beyond the particular narrative in which a representation of the historical event is embedded. Some of the mentioned agreed facts are less changeable than others; they represent a 'core' of facts strongly ascribed to the understanding of the event in the relevant community/ies.

This line of analysis has the potential to contribute to the understanding of the texts themselves as social productions that involve writers and intended readers who live within particular social realities and because of that had to deal, and in most cases follow, a certain socio-cultural grammar of historical writing.[85] This grammar deserves much attention.

84. Insofar as it influences the communal set of agreed facts about the past.

85. To some extent compare with several of the 'grammatical' claims advanced in D.H. Akenson, *Surpassing Wonder: The Invention of the Bible and the Talmuds* (New York: Harcourt, Brace & Company; Montreal/Kingston: McGill-Queen's University Press, 1998).

This Is What Happens…

Philip R. Davies

The Assyrian came down like a wolf on the fold
And his cohorts were gleaming in purple and gold

> Matthew Arnold, *Sohrab and Rustam*

This is what happens when little kings get too ambitious. The big men may stumble now and then but in the end might is right. You can't beat the odds very often.

As usual, both sides in this case claim some kind of victory, but we all know who was calling the shots. If you want to know what really happened, just ask Manasseh. His opinion of Hezekiah is unprintable.

> Morton Smith (attrib.)

Smithism

No, the second quotation above isn't really from Morton Smith (the first *is* Matthew Arnold!), but it might have been, and since he is dead and thus history, I can make him say what I think he would have wanted to say, in the manner of, say, Thucydides with Pericles. Morton Smith was not much interested in theory or in the philosophy of history, as I am, and he would surely have resented being included in a methodological, or philosophical, reflection in this volume. So be it. As far as I am concerned, history is ultimately what a historian says it is. The past is our patch, and people can't expect to make their own history.

Morton Smith's verdict illustrates better than pages of argument what I want to contribute to this collection of analyses and reflections: that objectivity in history writing is impossible because *history can only exist as narrative and every narrative has to have a narrator*. The question 'what happened?' is a request for a story and the answer has to begin 'once upon a time'. Morton Smith's imputed words constitute, in fact, a *meta*-narrative: 'this is what happens when…', 'as usual', 'we all know who...' And the appeal to Manasseh—well, there is a classic narratorial ploy: 'if you don't believe me, ask *him*!'

Still, Smithism might well appear to the average reader of this book as the kind of common-sense observation that cuts through ideology and propaganda and exposes a basic truth, which the reader will instantly acknowledge, about human affairs. What makes his verdicts seem objective is that they cohere with the reader's own understanding of how the world works. People who reject Smithian stories do so because they reject his view of human nature, not because they know something he doesn't. Our construction of history is inevitably a story about the past of a world that we know and it generally implies that the rules governing human behaviour are constant. It is a constant that in historical narratives, taken together, the little guy wins only once in a while, whereas very often in fiction (which is why it is fiction) the reverse is true. Why so? The simple answer is that history is supposed to be about what happens and fiction about what does not: what we would either like to happen, or not like to happen, or what happens to unreal people. This distinction between historiography and fiction, however, is sustained by our own categorization, which could certainly be changed. In the classical world, indeed, the distinction was not usually thus: the imagined worlds of fiction and the past worlds of historiographers were not so neatly separated, partly because the world of the past consisted largely of other people's stories about it and partly because historiography was not an academic pursuit. But this discussion, which could go on at some length, is not really the topic of this paper, or this volume.

To resume my thread: I have to confess that I always enjoyed reading Morton Smith because of his exploitation of a wide knowledge in the service of what I once felt (and can still recall) as a 'realistic', slightly cynical, view of human nature and its dealings. It was when I met Morton Smith personally that I realized how much this *Weltanschauung* reflected his own particular brand of misanthropy, but I still resound to his caustic reflections and subscribe to his broad understanding of human political behaviour as a catalogue of cunning, treachery and feebleness. But the basic Smithian proposition that in history the big guy nearly always wins is thoroughly endorsed by the biblical narrative. After all, the big guy is Yahweh, and if you are on his side, you will win, too. So, in the narration of Kings, Sennacherib's man claims he will win because Yahweh is on his side, while the biblical narrator wants to show that the Assyrians will not win, because Yahweh is on Hezekiah's side. Smithism certainly has biblical roots.

The laughter that greeted my recitation of the above quote at the Seminar seemed to confirm my suspicion that Smithian analysis strikes a modern chord. Equally interesting was that this moment occurred at the end of six hours of detailed and often technical discussion, and if my perception was correct, it was with some relief that the participants saw, however briefly and imperfectly, a complicated analysis of various pieces of ancient propaganda perverted into a lucidly simple statement of what really matters, which is how the world works. Morton's Law is both experimentally verifiable and aesthetically elegant.

Underneath all the ancient rhetoric and modern scholarship that comprise the writing of histories, then, the members of the Seminar were briefly invited to see merely another illustration of a common truth about human history; not so much a *reductio ad absurdum* but a *reductio ab absurdo*. Morton Smith's quote provided something that previously had been lacking: a succinct statement of what it was all about. History tells what we already know. That is how we can see what is history and what is not. And, like any true equation, it can be expressed in reverse: what we know tells us what is history.

The simplicity of Morton's Law is a powerful tool in the cause of exegeting biblical historiography. Smith had a temperament prone to react against the tendency (still rampant in his day) of biblical scholarship to exempt biblical writers from the sort of ideological critique that in more recent times has become more pronounced. The solid wall of 'salvation history' was dismantled in favour of a force-field, which buttressed the privileges of the biblical narratives both as more plausible and as enjoying the unique protection: anyone wishing to question its authority was immediately suspect of having an Ulterior Motive, which could be anything up to and including anti-semitism. Tweaking that history is allowed, so long as the result can still work in Biblical History 101 in your average seminary. It has to deliver a history with an assured minimum salvation quotient. This protection can be concealed by arguing that since there is no other ancient story of such detail or scope, there is effectively no basis on which to challenge it anyway. It's either the bible story or no story at all; biblically based history or no history.

And thus when the historian of ancient Israel seeks to identify and describe the ideologies of the ancient narratives that are the primary source, she or he finds what biblical scholars call the 'theology of the Old Testament'. What the historian seeks to discount is precisely what for others really counts. The bias of the story is exactly what matters for most bible readers. Or, as von Rad would have put it, it's the *tradition* or the *witness* that matters, not the (real or imagined) event. What the ancient Israelites or Judaeans believed had happened was what mattered, not what really happened or didn't happen. Here was, briefly, a golden opportunity. The theologians and the historians could still identify the biases of biblical historiography; the theologian could effectively discard the 'facts' because they contained no theological truth, and thus, it followed, the historian could discard the 'theology' because it contained no history. Smithism declares that the historian is interested in the facts, because history is made up of facts, and that a historian has no business messing with theology. Or, indeed, that the theologian has no business messing with history. Both are equally appealing propositions, and would have served the modernist world very well. Unfortunately, we have all moved on, and some of us, especially in Europe, I have to say, *know* we have moved on. The French have produced the best twentieth century historians; it is a real pity that the country produces so few good biblical scholars.

For intelligent historians know that there is no electrolysis to separate fact and value so neatly. Merely selecting some facts and omitting others already injects value. But, at a somewhat cruder and more ignorant level, a large body of biblical scholars (and other interest groups) was not prepared to let the *facts* of biblical history get submerged under 'kerygma'. The American 'biblical theology' movement, entirely uninterested in theology but most anxious about 'the facts' (an attitude wonderfully parodied in the Dragnet catchphrase 'Just the facts, m'am; I just wanna know the facts') insisted that the core of biblical theology lay in historical events. Even if the biblical writers did not tell it exactly like it was, it nevertheless was and that was what the Bible was all about, including the many lives and *floruits* of Father Abraham.

The Bible as kerygma or as history? The two bequests have not yet been spent. Why do modern biblical historians have such a stake in the historicity of 2 Kings (for that is the issue)? Exempting my colleagues in the Seminar, I would observe that among those in the affirmative camp, some maintain an interest in proving the biblical account of Sennacherib versus Hezekiah as historically reliable, while others are concerned rather to endorse the biblical understanding of Yahweh as one who keeps promises and defends his chosen people. Within and beyond these inclinations, the propaganda of the biblical historical narratives exerts a gravitational pull on our own cultural narratives of history, notably in our not-so-distant colonial enterprises, in the belief of some people that history conforms to a divine script, or that it illustrates divine reward and punishments for human behaviour. In the countries involved in the war of 1939–45 millions of people thought God was on their side, and indeed this was the reason why their side would win. In pre-Christian cultures the gods were more numerous and considered to be less reliable. And the USA is, like biblical Israel, a 'country under God'; though some would say by a considerable distance.

This biblical pull on modern interpretation of history is perhaps little evident in the discourse of most intelligent modern historians of ancient Israel and Judah (i.e. most members of this Seminar). But no-one can deny that it is tugging very hard elsewhere. Why, one might ask by way of illustration, is there so much anger and abuse encountered by those who cast doubt on the existence of 'King David'? Such splenetic reactions are not generally to be encountered in debates about king Priam or Charlemagne, for example. Our modern Western world still has a peculiarly valuable stake in biblical history and historicity. For even among the Bible-ignorant public media, the kind of TV programmes one sees on the subject of the Bible are nearly all about the Bible and history. The public perception is: the Old Testament, the Hebrew Bible, is a history book, and full of ancient learning. The ark of Noah, the ruins of Sodom and Gomorrah, the ark of the covenant—all remain to be recovered. Those who disdain such nonsense go away thinking that the Bible is a load of superstitious nonsense, myths about the past and no more. Don't blame Smithism for this. Blame those who say 'the Bible is history or it is nothing!'

Morton Smith certainly enjoyed exposing and countering the traces of biblical propaganda in modern historiography. And it remains a task for historians working within the confines of the discipline of theology or biblical studies (where all histories of ancient Israel and Judah come from). But the historian of ancient Israel and Judah should really not have to expend great energy on this task, and, rightly, the Seminar did not devote much time or effort to it. There are deeper methodological and philosophical issues, where I would find myself in disagreement with Morton Smith. To these I now want to turn.

Beyond Smithism

There are three sets of narrators participating in this Seminar. Two have submitted written texts ages ago, but are unable to attend in person; the third set have mostly submitted written texts and are also present in person.

The position broadly taken up by the absentees is analysed by the members of the Seminar. The Assyrian accounts, it emerges, served different immediate purposes: lists of booty ensured that soldiers were not tempted to plunder (the treatment of Achan in Josh. 7 is probably the best-known illustration of this principle of military discipline); figures in such sources are thus likely to be reliable. (Thus it follows that if a biblical source gives the same figures, that source had access to Assyrian data.) In the case of royal annals, the purpose is less clear. Who, after all, read these, especially when they were festooning the walls of the king's throne room (and were in part hidden from sight anyway)? Could even the king read them? But presumably people who looked at them were supposed to know what they said, more or less. If not, then there were the pictures of Lachish. Sources of this kind are not interested in factual accuracy so much as in the sustenance of imperial ideology, even of cultivating a sense of 'Assyrian-ness' of which the human servants of the Great King could be proud and those others subject to Assyria respectful and prompt with their payments of tribute.

These matters are best left to the papers of my more learned colleagues. All that needs to be said here is that no ancient sources were composed for the simple purpose of conveying information impartially or disinterestedly. A thesis on the role of information and data in ancient societies would be a useful addition to the scholarly corpus. In this particular instances, I will not focus in detail on the various Assyrian sources, real or reconstructed, but suggest that they all in some way reflect the discourse of a victorious imperial state, by which I mean one that is not only usually victorious but which also *represents itself as victorious*. The development of military discipline in an army of sometimes uncertain loyalty and instincts is instanced in booty lists, while the requirement of the monarch to represent himself and his kingdom as victorious is evident in the annals (though the practice of documenting reminds me gruesomely of the Nazi practice of individually documenting the exterminated Jews and other 'inferior' humans, as if this somehow legitimated the barbarism); here we see the necessary display of invincibility deployed to terrorize or at least frighten potential enemies and warn potential usurpers—not to mention as well the need of the king to justify his occupancy of the throne, ostensibly to the Assyrian gods, more importantly to would-be usurpers or rivals.

Here, then, we find a certain kind of imperial world-view, one that we can in fact easily compare to some highly organized modern totalitarian states. And invariably, we shall have to bear modern parallels in mind, since we cannot interpret ancient totalitarian regimes without the aid of those we know better. Hence, the important lesson that our explanation of the Assyrian world-view, which the relevant sources serve, is coloured by our knowledge of our own times. We can only understand if we recognize.

Once we appreciate the imperial world-view, we can put into proper context the Assyrian versions of the siege of Jerusalem. Whatever the details, for the Assyrians Jerusalem was not particularly important (not as important as Lachish, for instance), but it was important that Hezekiah had been taught a severe lesson. What happened to Jerusalem simply illustrated what happened to Assyria's rebellious vassals. For the Assyrians there was no other history, and the defeat of Hezekiah was part of it. (Whether the kings, or generals, or soldiers had any other private view of the episode is unlikely but does not matter, since such views never made it into an ancient narrative, and we have little hope of plausibly recreating them).

On the Judaean side there are of course different sources: Kings, Isaiah, Chronicles, canonized writings each with their own spin. But the wider picture they share can still be drawn: a society whose god had shown his allegiance to his chosen city. He had not spared Lachish, or anywhere else, but he had left *Jerusalem* intact (indeed, Sennacherib did more for Deuteronomic-style cult centralization than any Judaean king by leaving it the only sanctuary available!). The military superiority of the Assyrians is not disputed by these Judaean sources, not even disguised. But these mighty forces are not totally in charge of history. The punishment they inflict is not theirs, but that of Judah's god. And Judah's god can frustrate the logic of their superiority when it suits his purposes, which are ultimately pro-Judaean, or (as in Isaiah) pro-Jerusalem.

Now, the conflict between Assyrian and Judaean accounts is not really significant at the level of detail. I suggest, then, that if we are trying to find out what is in common between the various accounts, and make this the basis of a reconstruction, our task will not be too difficult. The departure of the Assyrian army with the city intact does not need an angel of death (the Seminar does not, after all, even discuss this as a possible historical event). This embellishment in the canonized Judaean version of events simply ensures that the message of the story is not lost on the simple: there are divine forces on the side of Jerusalem. The exaggeration of numbers in such cases is a standard procedure hardly worth mentioning in the comparison of ancient (or indeed modern) war propaganda. Numbers, to paraphrase the saying, are the first casualty of war. So, one or two campaigns, then? Here I doubt whether we can establish any reliable conclusions. Becking's thesis I find ingenious, and plausible; but these qualifications at best get on only as far as the shortlist. And it is not an explanation that is necessary in order to explain the character of the biblical texts.

Certainly, at the level of details such as these little can be resolved about the 'reliability' of either set of accounts, since reliability is a slippery term. Ancient narrators, I suspect, understood 'reliability' to mean *ideological* reliability: was this the right way to present the story? Was it sound? We might nowadays argue in a similar vein for a politically correct formulation of a statement or even a description rather than one that is more accurate but unacceptable to fashionable taste. For the modern historian, 'reliability' is something that reflects the degree to which an ancient story is internally consistent, and consistent with other data; and also to the extent that it corresponds with our own notions of *what we are inclined to accept,* for whatever reasons. Relying on something is in the end a subjective reaction; it is not an intrinsic value of whatever we place our reliance upon. The 'reliability' we accord to an ancient source has everything to do with our will to trust, since we can rarely know whether or not in actuality it deserves that trust. The world 'reliability' usually points you to what the historian's preferences or prejudices are.

In truth, I am of the opinion that issues of detail are in cases such as this pedantry, if not a positive distraction. This pedantry often has to do with proving the Bible technically correct (or technically wrong), as if technical accuracy was ever a factor in the construction of ancient historiographical narratives. In this meeting of the Seminar, we seem to be concerned rather with establishing 'what happened'. The attempt has been useful, even if only to reinforce (for me) the opinion that 'what happened' cannot be represented objectively, but only narratively. Is it possible that 'what happened' belongs to a neutral space in which events transpire independently of perception or interpretation? And that we can create a narrative of our own that preserves this neutrality? I doubt this. All stories carry a worldview in their genes. The ancient accounts certainly tell us 'what happened', but according to their norms of what did happen, what should have happened, and what this happening meant. If we moderns are to write a history, we have to follow this law: we can't claim to tell the truth of 'what happened' (Ehud Ben Zvi commented rightly in the Seminar that we should not use the word 'truth').

There are perhaps two major motivations (let us put aside the occasional desire simply to make the scriptural account as authentic as possible) in writing a modern history of the Hezekiah and Sennacherib episode. One is to establish 'what really happened'; the other to write a new and more intellectually or emotionally satisfying narrative, one that reflects the worldview of the modern historian and her/his reader onto the past, uniting then and now in a single reality. Now, I am suggesting, and I want to insist further, that these two goals amount to the same thing. 'What really happened' is after all, indistinguishable from 'the narrative that should be generated by a modern historian'. What happened is what we *understand* to have happened (since we can't actually *know* it). There are, nevertheless, persons who do believe in a 'what happened' that can be accurately and objectively described, and therefore in a way free from any cultural influence and true for all time in whatever context.

Let us try such a neutral, objective account of Sennacherib's invasion. We must first get rid of the term 'invasion' since 'invasion' is not a datum, but an interpretation. It implies that Judah was a foreign country over which its king had no jurisdiction save by permission of the Assyrian monarch. 'Invasion' implies that the Assyrians were doing something wrong, entering a country illegally. But Sennacherib and Hezekiah probably had a treaty (one of those famous Assyrian vassal treaties?), which would make Hezekiah's withholding of tribute a breach of contract. From the Assyrian point of view, campaigns against other kingdoms in their sphere of influence were thus probably not really understood as 'invasions'. Rather like 'exile', we have a term that goes beyond description and implies evaluation. (If you find this claim difficult to believe, ask a Briton about the 'invasion' of the Falklands, or an Israeli about Israel's 'invasion' of Palestine). If we are to be on no-one's side, we have to be careful how we describe the situation. And thus, how we choose to understand it.

One must therefore also refrain from the language of 'submitting' or 'being defeated'. Whether Hezekiah 'submitted' and whether Sennacherib 'succeeded' depends on how you count success or defeat. Both terms mean different things in different discourses, from different perspectives. The essential point about the Assyrian understanding of the episode is that Hezekiah did submit; the essential point in the biblical account is that he did not, even though he did pay up. The facts themselves do not include either victory or defeat: these are verdicts. I suppose that one can nevertheless remove all elements that are not strictly descriptive and verifiable on the grounds that both ancient accounts agree. But one would end up with a list of data, not history. And the data, of course, are only those that all the ancient sources wished to record, for their own reasons. We are obliged, in our task of creating an objective account, to chronicle only the data they wanted to record, not the data we would like to—we are doomed at the outset! So what sort of story shall we be left with? What are we really aiming to achieve and what can we do with it once we have it?

What can we do?

If we want in some sense to be objective and neutral, we can do so by *refusing to tell a story*. We can instead identify the relevant 'sources' and expound them as ancient cultural explanations of what really happened. A modern account of the confrontation of Sennacherib and Hezekiah could thus evaluate the Assyrians as a civilizing and perhaps a necessary force, not to be criticized merely on the grounds that they were more powerful. We need not doubt that Judah would have behaved in much the same way in a reversed position (read about the Hasmoneans). Global power and global reality is something we moderns well understand. Modern American politicians have interfered violently in neighbouring states (Cuba, Chile, Panama, Colombia) in order to protect their own interests. We can not only understand, but even recognize the Assyrian world view in our own times. Nineteenth century historians would as happily have defended the activities of empires, seeing in the Romans the ancient counterparts of the British empire. Dammit, our Western culture *believes* in empires! Imperializing is, or has been, our favourite game, all over the world. Sennacherib is part of our history. What we surely find more difficult to understand is the desire of a small land or people to run their own affairs. Especially in the vicinity of the big boys.

But we can simultaneously see the alternative story that the Judaean version represents, even without recourse to the continuing faith that some moderns have in Yahweh. For we moderns (all of us sometimes, some of us always) also have a dislike of bullies, a distrust of big business, and we are at the very least morally dubious about the benefits of even the Roman and British empires. We tend to believe in the right of self-determination and constantly celebrate in our entertainment industry the victory of the small over the great. Just as we celebrate the defeat of crime by forces of justice (both myths shielding us against the realities of life).

Thus, the modern historian in us can maybe fulfil the demand of objectivity to some extent by refusing to interpose, by refusing, in fact, to be 'objective' regarding the 'facts' but being objective about the ancient accounts, not taking sides, expressing, like Picasso, several dimensions at once. I would have some sympathy with this agenda. It promotes that pluralism and that ambiguity which are characteristic of our contemporary culture. Why, after all, *should* we take sides? Why should one story ever be enough? If we can't see the whole picture (assuming there is one) we can at least show different sides of it, demonstrating the multi-dimensionality of all 'historical events'. We need not endorse any ancient worldview, but we can, in an inevitable transgression of accuracy, permit ourselves to represent the ancient ideologies in our own world, to keep the battle going rather than resolve it.

The moral dimension, however, makes the task very hard. The ancient accounts imply (or even express) a morality. The pious Hezekiah lives, the impious Sennacherib dies (having provoked Yahweh perhaps by claiming to have his support?). On the Assyrian side, too, there is a morality. Rebellion is wrong and should be punished. Might has rights. Or (I thank Lester Grabbe for this alternative) they believed that they were fulfilling the demands of their god Asshur, who commanded them to conquer in his name and prove his superiority among the hordes of heaven. Lest we dismiss this view too readily, we should remember that it is entirely in accord with the practice of the time: kings (notionally) protected subjects and extorted taxes, punishing rebellion. Warfare was necessary to justify the existence (and pay the expenses) of monarchy. Even more so: the Judaean scriptures themselves hold treaties in very high esteem, for according to a very prominent strand, their religion was actually a treaty, which they had to observe. Why not, then, observe a treaty with the Assyrians? Underneath the positions of both monarchs there was probably a degree of shared morality about how the world works. Perhaps ultimately the moral issue was about the reputation of the monarch or the reputation of the national god. Not a great difference between the two, and not much morality, either, we might think. Our leanings to one side, one story, are triggered by our own biasses, not that of the ancient narrators or their heroes.

So much for the postmodern version of objectivity: preserving plurality, the art of the fugue. History once upon a time claimed to have something to teach. But we are more wary of grand lessons than we used to be. Yet 'history' requires a grand narrative, and only grand narratives can permit us to learn. What can a juxtaposition of partial, subjective stories, orphaned of their parent, the Master Narrative, tell us? My argument that 'history' subsists now only in narratives that ultimately cannot and should not be reconciled actually rids us of an assured past, a firm base on which to build our present and future. It becomes a game, played with differently-coloured counters of experience, memory, observation and imagination.

Why I Don't Like Smithism

Morton Smith would have rejected my analysis and my proposal in characteristic terms. But he was a very fine historian and his invented quote has been useful. I have made him reveal a moral: 'this is what happens'. The defeat of Hezekiah is true because it conforms to a universal truth. The statement 'you can't beat the odds' is also revealing: can we historians calculate odds except after the event? In my own upbringing, we are supposed to study history in order to learn from it. Now I wonder whether Smithism believes there is anything to learn; history is nothing more than the repeated exemplification of probabilities. And how do we calculate the improbabilities? When do we stop extrapolating from individual cases to general laws and reverse the process? This whole question poses the discipline of history in positivistic terms: observation leads to formulation of laws that can then be applied. To say that history repeats itself is to endorse this view.

But I doubt that historians work this way, even when they think they do. Among many of my colleagues (including those in the Seminar) are individuals who respect above all the uniqueness of each event, and who rightly say that laws of probability cannot determine the outcome of a single case. Then there are those like myself (and the late Robert Carroll) who think that historians do not study 'what happens', at least, not directly. They study (and participate in) the way in which human beings discourse about the past.

There is no objective 'history' because what constitutes the abstract 'history' is our experience and our perception and our memory. What happens in the world is what we see happening, and what history we write is the story we want to tell. As historians of an ancient world we have as sources nothing but ancient discourse, plus our own perceptions of what might or might not happen. We are primarily exegetes here, and no amount of archaeology or sociology is going to help us in deciding the facts. The facts we can establish will be limited to those that the ancient sources choose to mention, and will divide into cases where the stories independently agree (and so we can be reasonably assured of a fact), and where they do not, in which case we have no facts, only different possibilities.

And yet. We cannot carry out the task I am recommending, of analysing human discourse about the past, unless we can have the notion of truth or reality as a criterion. To detect ideological bias, as opposed to imputing or assuming it, means to discover where and how a story deviates from 'what happened'. And thus I think that to separate in any story what is distortion from what is invention is an important exegetical task. Notionally, at any rate, we have to posit 'facts' as a means of measuring different stories. But the more I reflect upon it, the more I see facts as analogous to subatomic particles: they mostly cannot be directly observed (at least not their mass and their position at the same time), but their existence can be detected by the effect they have. History can be detected in the way humans react to it, especially in the way they witness, interpret and remember it.

It is possible for us, then, to evaluate human discourse in terms of how far it conveys recognizable images of reality, is 'reliable'. For some reason this matters to us, as it did not matter to the Assyrians or the Judaeans. In the end, I do think that it matters that we do justice to all stories, to all ancient storytellers, by seeking to understand what their stories meant, and what the events they witnessed and recorded meant. We cannot in the end understand 'history', but we should try and understand ourselves, for all of us are wrapped in stories about the past, and perhaps sometimes too tightly for our own good. Stories, sacred stories, about the past are certainly a major contributing factor at this moment to conflict in the area where the Assyrians and Judaeans once confronted each other. Here, as everywhere, 'history' is not negotiable, but peace, if it ever comes, will bring its own story and history will accordingly have to be rewritten.

OF MICE AND DEAD MEN:
HERODOTUS 2.141 AND SENNACHERIB'S CAMPAIGN IN 701 BCE

Lester L. Grabbe

One of the seminal studies of Sennacherib's invasion in relation to the biblical text is Brevard Childs' *Isaiah and the Assyrian Crisis*.[1] Childs carefully considered all the biblical texts that might have related to Sennacherib. Although mentioning Herodotus 2.141, Childs did so only briefly, mainly in a footnote, and he dismissed the story as of no real value in resolving the question of what happened in Syro-Palestine in 701 BCE.[2] This has not prevented subsequent scholars from making suggestions of how Herodotus may have supplied vital information for reconciling the biblical accounts and Assyrian records.[3]

My purpose is not primarily to determine 'what actually happened' (though that question cannot be ignored); it is, rather, to compare selected accounts of Oriental history in Herodotus with what is known from the Near Eastern records. The idea is not only to investigate the extent which Herodotus is reliable when he relates ancient Near Eastern history but also to consider the wider implications of using his history. Herodotus as a historical source is not too dissimilar to some of the biblical texts in that he incorporated diverse material of varying ages, origins, and historical value into his work; this suggests that principles for using his account may be applicable to using the biblical text. After considering Herodotus's history writing in general, I shall make some observations about the Sennacherib

---

1. Brevard S. Childs, *Isaiah and the Assyrian Crisis* (SBT, Second Series 3; London: SCM Press; Naperville, IL: Alec R. Allenson, 1967).
2. 'The Herodotus account continues to be used by some American scholars to defend an "historical kernal" theory… In the light of the tremendous problems associated with this legend, this procedure appears to me unjustified' (Childs, p. 101 n. 70).
3. E.g. Antti Laato, 'Hezekiah and the Assyrian Crisis in 701 B.C.', *SJOT* 2 (1987), pp. 49-68 (60-61); 'Assyrian Propaganda and the Falsification of History in the Royal Inscriptions of Sennacherib', *VT* 45 (1995), pp. 198-226, especially pp. 220-23.

story and, finally, in the light of these investigations, some methodological points about using such 'secondary' texts will be explored.

The Greeks and the Ancient Near East

The connections between the Aegean world and the ancient Near East have a long history, attested both in hieroglyphic and cuneiform records and by Greek stories, myths, and legends of various sorts. Despite some shifts in position in recent years, the belief that the Sea Peoples originated in the Aegean is still generally held.[4] Yet the Homeric epic poems probably also embody in somewhat legendary form interaction between Mycenaean Greeks and Asia Minor.[5]

The Greeks were infamous for their distortion of the culture and history of Near Eastern peoples. Although this was not necessarily a habit peculiar to the Greeks—how many peoples in history have given a fair description of alien cultures?—we have it firmly described because the Greeks were conquerors. Berossus complained that the Greeks told false stories about the history of the Babylonians (as reported by Josephus [*Ag. Apion* 1.20 §142-44]).[6]

---

4.   A recent study on the question is Othniel Margalith, 'Where Did the Philistines Come From?' *ZAW* 107 (1995), pp. 101-109.

5.   Studies on the relationship between the Homeric poems and history include Michael Wood, *In Search of the Trojan War* (London: Guild Publishing, 1985); Martin P. Nilsson, *Homer and Mycenae* (repr. Philadelphia: University of Pennsylvania, 1972); Denys L. Page, *History and the Homeric Iliad* (Berkeley: University of California, 1959); C.M. Bowra, *Homer* (Classical Life and Letters; New York: Charles Scribner's Sons; London: Routledge, 1972). For more general connections between the ancient Near East and the Greek world, see Peter Walcot, 'The Comparative Study of Ugaritic and Greek Literatures', *UF* 1 (1969), pp. 111-18; 2 (1970), pp. 273-75; 4 (1972), pp. 129-32; A.F. Campbell, 'Homer and Ugaritic Literature', *Abr-Nahrain* 5 (1964-65), pp. 29-56; M.L. West, *Early Greek Philosophy and the Orient* (Oxford: Clarendon Press, 1971) and *The East Face of Helicon: West Asiatic Elements in Greek Poetry and Myth* (Oxford: Clarendon Press, 1997).

6.   Interestingly, Berossus himself seems to have attempted to create a hero legend around Nebuchadnezzar II: see the previous paragraphs in Josephus (*Ag. Apion* 1.19 §§128-41), as well as the one quoted here. On Berossus in general, see Stanley Mayer Burstein, *The Babyloniaca of Berossus* (Sources and Monographs on the Ancient Near East: Sources from the Ancient Near East 1.5; Malibu, CA: Undena Publications, 1978); Amélie Kuhrt, 'Berossus *Babyloniaka* and Seleucid Rule in Babylonia', in Amélie Kuhrt and Susan Sherwin-White (eds.), *Hellenism in the East* (London: Gerald Duckworth, 1987), pp. 32-56. The Greek text can be found in Felix Jacoby, *Fragmente*

Such is the account given by Berosus of this king [Nebuchadnezzar II], besides much more in the third book of his *History of Chaldaea*, where he censures the Greek historians for their deluded belief that Babylon was founded by the Assyrian Semiramis and their erroneous statement that its marvellous buildings were her creation. On these matters the Chaldaean account must surely be accepted. Moreover, statements in accordance with those of Berosus are found in the Phoenician archives, which relate how the king of Babylon subdued Syria and the whole of Phoenicia. To the same effect writes Philostratus in his *History*, where he mentions the siege of Tyre, and Megasthenes in the fourth book of his *History of India*, where he attempts to prove that this king of Babylon, who according to this writer subdued the greater part of Libya and Iberia, was in courage and in the grandeur of his exploits more than a match for Heracles.

Berossus's contemporary in Egypt Manetho similarly complained about Herodotus (also reported by Josephus [*Ag. Apion* 1.14 §§73-92]:

I will begin with Egyptian documents. These I cannot indeed set before you in their ancient form; but in Manetho we have a native Egyptian who was manifestly imbued with Greek culture. He wrote in Greek the history of his nation, translated, as he himself tells us, from sacred tablets; and on many points of Egyptian history he convicts Herodotus of having erred through ignorance.

Manetho is alleged specifically to have written 'criticisms of Herodotus', perhaps even a separate work; if so, it unfortunately has not survived.[7]

One of the most notorious writers among the Greeks was Ctesias of Cnidus. He was court physician to Artaxerxes II, for 17 years according to his own statement, which would mean that he must have begun his duties under Darius II since he left Persian in 398 BCE.[8] Whether such a position should have given him access to historical information is doubtful, despite his claim to have read 'the royal records, in which the Persians in accordance with a certain law of theirs kept an account of their ancient affairs'

der griechischen Historiker: Dritter Teil Geschichte von Städten und Völkern (Horographie und Ethnographie), C Autoren über Einzelne Länder Nr. 608a–856 (Leiden: E.J. Brill, 1958), no. 680 (pp. 364-97), and in the classic study by Paul Schnabel, *Berossos und die babylonisch-hellenistische Literatur* (Leipzig: Teubner, 1923).

7. W.G. Waddell, *Manetho* (LCL; London: Heinemann; Cambridge, MA: Harvard, 1940), pp. 204-7.

8. For a good general introduction to Ctesias, see Truesdell S. Brown, *The Greek Historians* (Civilization and Society; Lexington, MA: D.C. Heath, 1973), pp. 77-86; see also Friedrich Wilhelm König, *Die Persika des Ktesias von Knidos* (Archiv für Orientforschung Beiheft, 18; Graz: Archiv für Orientforschung, 1972).

(Diodorus Siculus 2.32.4). In any case, his history appears to have been mainly a collection of court gossip, fairy tales, and legend. Ctesias seems to be the origin of a number of stories about Oriental heroes and heroines, such as Ninus and Semiramis, that circulated widely in later literature.

The Ninus/Semiramis legend was widespread in the Hellenistic Near East but is best attested in the version of Diodorus of Sicily writing in the first century BCE. Whatever Diodorus's source (which is generally thought to be Ctesias of Cnidus[9]), the story has the following elements (2.1-20):

- Ninus, king of the Assyrians, the first to achieve great deeds.
- Collected an army and allied with Ariaeus king of the Arabs.
- Campaigned against the Babylonians (though Babylon not yet founded) and placed tribute on them.
- Campaigned against Armenia but spared the ruler Barzanes.
- Campaigned against Media and crucified the ruler Pharnus.
- Conquered all Asia except the Bactrians and Indians in 17 years, including Egypt, Phoenicia, Syria, Asia Minor, Persia, as far as the Caspian Gates.
- Founded the city Ninus (Nineveh) on the Euphrates (*sic!*).
- Semiramis born in Ashcalon and raised by doves until found by shepherds.
- Semiramis seen by Oannes a minister of Ninus who marries her.
- Ninus assembles an army of almost two million men and attacks Bactriana and its king Oxyartes, taking all but the city Bactra.
- Oannes brings to the camp Semiramis who observes Bactra's weakness and takes with her soldiers who capture the acropolis.
- Ninus falls in love with her, takes her from Oannes, and marries her.
- They have a son Ninyas, Ninus dies, and Semiramis is left as ruler.
- Semiramis founds the city of Babylon and many other cities on the Tigris and Euphrates.
- Sets up an inscription on the Bagistanus mountain (Behistun).
- Builds a road through the Zarcaeus (Zagreb) mountains.

9.   Ctesias is cited as a source a number of times (2.2.2; 2.7.1; 2.7.3-4; 2.15.2; 2.17.1; 2.20.3) but, as noted below, Diodorus's version has probably assimilated the story to the Alexander legend, in which case he must have had an additional source. One suggestion is Cleitarchus of Alexandria who is cited at 2.7.3 (Samuel K. Eddy, *The King Is Dead: Studies in the Near Eastern Resistance to Hellenism 334–31 B.C.* [Lincoln, NB: University of Nebraska, 1961], p. 123).

- Builds a palace at Ecbatana.
- Visits Persis and every other country in the Asian empire.
- Goes to Egypt, subdues Libya, and visits the oracle at Ammon.
- Visits Ethiopia.
- After extensive preparation, Semiramis makes an unprovoked attack on the Indian king Stabrobates but is defeated by him, with even Semiramis herself wounded.
- Her son Ninyas conspires against her; she turns the kingdom over to him and disappears.

As will immediately be clear, a number of the deeds performed by Semiramis have a close parallel in events in Alexander's conquests.[10]

Herodotus's information on pre-Persian Mesopotamia is not very extensive. He states the intention of writing a history of Assyria (1.184), but we have no evidence that he ever got around to this project. He mentions a few Mesopotamian figures (e.g. the ubiquitous and infamous final Assyrian king Sardanapallus[11]) but gives nothing like the list of Egyptian rulers, brief as the latter is. He mentions Semiramis in a short paragraph but without presenting her as exceptional. He says that she was a ruler of Babylon and built the dykes to prevent flooding (1.184), but the main work of building the city was done five generations later by Nitocris (1.185). It appears that Herodotus does not know the Semiramis legend or, if he did know it, he has given it no credence, while he does not even mention Ninus. On the other hand, the 'Nitocris' mentioned by him may have a historical basis in a later queen, showing that Herodotus's information was better than sometimes recognized.[12]

---

10. Cf. Eddy, *The King Is Dead*, pp. 122-23.

11. 2.150. This is all that Herodotus says, but Ctesias apparently gave a more elaborate account of him (Diodorus Siculus 2.24-28). Sardanapallus is a composite of several Assyrian kings. The Greek name Sardanapal(l)os (Latin Sardanapal[l]us) is obviously a reflex of Ashurbanipal (*Aššur-bāni-apli*), and Berossus clearly considers Sardanapallus to be the same as Ashurbanipal (see below). Ashurbanipal was not the last king of Assyria, but the persona of the weak final ruler Sin-shar-ishkun has been transferred to Ashurbanipal whose name was the one remembered. The Mesopotamian sources do not tell us what happened to Sin-shar-ishkun, but according to Berossus he (Greek Sarakos) burned his palace down with himself in it, the exact fate ascribed to Sardanapallus in the Greek tradition. On this, see Burstein, *The Babyloniaca of Berossus*, p. 25 n. 95. See also F.H. Weissbach, 'Sardanapal', in Georg Wissowa and Wilhelm Kroll (eds.), *Paulys Real-Encyclopädie der classischen Altertumswissenschaft* (Stuttgart: J.B. Metzlersche Verlagbuchhandlung, 1920), 2ter Reihe (R-Z), I, cols. 2436-75.

12. Contra Walter Baumgartner ('Herodots babylonische und assyrische Nachrich-

C.F. Lehmann-Haupt was one of the first to recognize that at the basis of the Semiramis legend was a historical Assyrian queen, Sammuramat the wife of Shamshi-adad V (823–811 BCE).[13] Sammuramat seems to have been an unusual person. It was once thought that she was co-regent with her son Adad-nirari III (810–783 BCE), but this now seems not to have been the case. Nevertheless, she is mentioned alongside her son in several inscriptions, which is rather unusual. Although the precise reason for her being remembered is not clear, we have some indications that she was not a run-of-the-mill Assyrian queen.

The situation is different with Ninus, on the other hand, because it is often stated that no clear historical figure lies behind him. Shamshi-adad V, the husband of Sammuramat, was not a particularly distinguished ruler, with only a short rule, and little that one can see of his person in Ninus. Ninus is of course the name of the capital of Assyria, and it has often been assumed that Ninus is only an eponymous founder of that city. If so, the figure of Ninus in the legend is made up more or less of whole cloth. His deeds look stereotyped, with considerable similarities to those of Sesostris

ten', *Zum Alten Testament und seiner Umwelt: Ausgewählte Aufsätze* [Leiden: E.J. Brill, 1959], pp. 282-331, originally published in *Archiv Orientalní* 18 [1950], pp. 69-106) who dimisses Nitocris as merely a reflection of Nebuchadnezzar. Other scholars have argued that she is to be identified with one or the other of well-known queens. Hildegard Lewy ('Nitokris-Naqî'a', *JNES* 11 [1952], pp. 264-86) thought she fits well the activities of Naqia-Zakutu, one of the wives of Sennacherib and the mother of Esarhaddon. She was indeed a remarkable woman about whom we would like to know more, though some of Lewy's arguments are somewhat speculative (see A.K. Grayson in *CAH²* III/2, pp. 138-40). Wolfgang Röllig ('Nitokris von Babylon', in Ruth Stiehl and Hans Erich Stier [eds.], *Beiträge zur alten Geschichte und deren Nachleben: Festschrift für Franz Altheim* [Berlin: W. de Gruyter, 1969], I, pp. 127-35) dismisses this identification (though not citing Lewy) but argues that Adad-guppi, the well-attested mother of Nabonidus, fits the Nitocris of Herodotus well. Professor Becking kindly drew to my attention the recent study of Sarah C. Melville, *The Role of Naqia/Zakutu in Sargonid Politics* (SAAS, 9; Helsinki: The Neo-Assyrian Text Corpus Project, 1999).

13. C.F. Lehmann-Haupt, 'Semiramis', in W.H. Roscher (ed.), *Ausführliches Lexikon der griechischen und römischen Mythologie* (Leipzig: Teubner, 1909–1915), IV, cols. 678-702. See also König, *Ktesias von Knidos*, pp. 37-40; Wilhelm Eilers, *Semiramis: Entstehung und Nachhall einer altorientalischen Sage* (Sitzungsberichte der Österreichische Akademie der Wissenschaften, Phil.-hist. Klasse, 274; 2. Abhandlung; Vienna: Kommissionsverlag der Österreichischen Akademie der Wissenschaften, 1971); Wolfgang Schramm, 'War Semiramis assyrische Regentin?' *Historia* 21 (1972), pp. 513-21.

and other hero figures, even of Semiramis. It would not be difficult to write a hero tale by following the standard features of other such tales. Nevertheless, it has been argued that an actual figure lies behind this Ninus: none other than Sennacherib.[14]

The Near Eastern origin of the hero tales is in part confirmed by what happened to their development. As time went on, the original hero stories were expanded and elaborated on in their Greek context, as described above. However, in their Greek milieu something else happened as well: they became romances.[15] The Ninus/Semiramis legend became a love story between a young prince Ninus and a young princess Semiramis.[16] When the 13-year-old Semiramis wanted to approach Ninus's mother to marry her 17-year-old son, she became completely tongue-tied. Ninus is indeed a brave and worthy young prince, but the mighty queen of the Semiramis story has become the fragile heroine of the romance. Sesostris (see below) similarly became the subject of a romance.[17] There is a very interesting parallel to this in the Moses story. Among Hellenistic Jewish writers, Moses becomes a warrior hero figure like Sesostris, Ninus, and Alexander by defeating the Ethiopians in battle. Elements of romance are also included in that he marries the daughter of the Ethiopian king.[18]

---

14. Hildegard Lewy, 'Nitokris-Naqî'a', pp. 266-70. This ties in with her argument that Nitocris was his consort, in the person of the historical Naqia-Zakutu.

15. On the romances, see Ben Edwin Perry, *The Ancient Romances: A Literary-Historical Account of their Origins* (Berkeley: University of California, 1967); Tomas Hägg, *The Novel in Antiquity* (Oxford: Basil Blackwell, 1983); ET of *Den Antika Romanen* (1980); Graham Anderson, *Ancient Fiction: The Novel in the Graeco-Roman World* (London/Sydney: Croom Helm; Totowa, NJ: Barnes & Noble, 1984).

16. Three main fragments of the romance are presently extant (A, B, C). The text and translation of two of these fragments (A and B) are found in George Thornley (trans.), revised and augmented by J.M. Edmonds, *Daphnis and Chloe by Longus* and S. Gaselee (trans.), *The Love Romances of Partenius and Other Fragments* (LCL; Cambridge, MA: Harvard; London: Heinemann, 1916), pp. 381-99. The text and a translation of Fragment C is given by Perry, *The Ancient Romances*, pp. 161-63.

17. Fragments of this have been found among the Oxyrhynchus papyri: E.G. Turner, *et al.* (eds.), *The Oxyrhynchus Papyri, Part XXVII* (London: Egypt Exploration Society, 1962), n. 2466 (pp. 134-36); R.A. Coles and M.W. Haslam (eds.), *The Oxyrhynchus Papyri, Part XLVII* (London: Egypt Exploration Society, 1980), n. 3319 (pp. 11-19).

18. See the account of Artapanus, as preserved in Eusebius, *Praep. evang.* 9.27.1-37. For an edition and commentary, see Carl Holladay, *Fragments from Hellenistic Jewish Authors, Volume I: Historians* (SBLTT, 20, Pseudepigrapha Series, 10; Atlanta: Scholars Press, 1983), pp. 189-243.

Herodotus and Ancient Near Eastern History

This section examines some examples of where Herodotus's account can now be analyzed in the light of substantial finds of contemporary original documents. It is important to have some perspective on Herodotus's general trustworthiness as a historian in the area of the ancient Near East. Classical historians have long discussed the question of Herodotus's reliability, and I shall draw on these insights with gratitude. It is not possible to rehearse the history of Herodotean scholarship here, but the following examples will help to illustrate the problems involved.[19]

The Beginning of Darius I's Reign[20]

Herodotus's work revolves around the Persian empire. Although he gives information on Egypt and a bit on the earlier history of Mesopotamia, much of his text relates to recent or past Persian history. He has a good deal of information on the Persians. In the absence of Near Eastern sources, Herodotus has been an important source for Persian history; however, we now have some native Persian sources for the reign of Darius I which allow us to evaluate the classical accounts of at least that time in Persian history. It is specifically Darius I's rise to power that we want to look at here. According to Herodotus (Book 3), Darius came to the throne through the following steps:

- Cambyses secretly assassinates his own brother Smerdis out of jealousy and because of a dream (3.30).
- A Magus left in charge of Cambyses's houshold in Susa revolts and appoints his brother to pretend to be Smerdis and sit on the throne (3.61).
- Cambyses hears the news, eventually hits on the truth of what has happened (3.62-63).
- He starts back to Susa but wounds himself with a sword by accident (3.64).

---

19. Much of the bibliography to 1987 is given by Balcer (next note). To that may be added especially John Gould, *Herodotus* (London: Weidenfeld & Nicolson, 1989) and Donald Lateiner, *The Historical Method of Herodotus* (Phoenix Supplement, 23; University of Toronto Press, 1989).

20. An important study used throughout this section is that of Jack Martin Balcer, *Herodotus and Bisitun: Problems in Ancient Persian Historiography* (Historia Einzelschriften, 49; Stuttgart: Steiner, 1987).

- He confesses to Smerdis's death to the Persian nobles and dies in Ecbatana (3.65-66).
- The Pseudo-Smerdis is believed by many to be genuine and benefits his subjects greatly (3.67).
- A Persian noble Otanes manages to obtain evidence that the man on the throne is not the real Smerdis (3.68-69).
- Otanes gathers six noble Persians around him (including Darius son of Hystaspes) in a conspiracy to get rid of the false Smerdis (3.70-75).
- Darius takes the lead in leading an attack on the two Magi and killing them, after which many of the Magi are slaughtered (3.76-79).
- After debate among the seven, Darius is chosen as king (3.80-88).
- The revolt of Babylon against Darius and a long story of how it was taken by the strategem of one Persian noble is described, though the impression is that this was long after Darius's accession to the throne (3.150-59).

The Behistun (or Bisitun) inscription occurs in four versions, each in a different language (Elamite, Neo-Babylonian, Old Persian, Aramaic).[21] Although the Elamite version is probably the earliest, there is some question as to whether one is to be considered 'more original' than the others; rather, each represents a particular oral tradition.[22] Darius first gives his genealogy, being the son of Vishtaspahya and grandson of Arshamahya. He then states that Cambyses had assassinated his brother Bardiya but kept it quiet from all the people, and then had gone to Egypt (§10.1.28-35). A

---

21. For the different versions, see the following editions: Elamite: F.H. Weissbach, *Die Keilinschriften der Achämeniden* (VAB, 3; Leipzig: Hinrichs, 1911; reprinted Leipzig: Zentral-Antiquariat der DDR, 1968); Old Persian: Roland G. Kent, *Old Persian* (AOS, 33; New Haven: American Oriental Society, 2nd edn, 1953); Neo-Babylonian: Elisabeth N. von Voigtlander, *The Behistun Inscription of Darius the Great. Babylonian Version* (Corpus Inscriptionum Iranicarum, Part I: Inscriptions of Ancient Iran. II. The Babylonian Versions of the Achaemenian Inscriptions, Texts I; London: Humphries, 1978); Aramaic: J.C. Greenfield and B. Porten, *The Bisitun Inscription of Darius the Great: Aramaic Version* (Corpus Inscriptionum Iranicarum, Part I: Inscriptions of Ancient Iran. V. The Aramaic Versions of the Achaemenian Inscriptions, Texts I; London: Humphries, 1982). The inscription is cited according to the paragraph divisions of Kent, *Old Persian*.

22. Balcer, *Herodotus and Bisitun*, pp. 67-66.

magus by the name of Gautama had then pretended to be Bardiya, had raised a rebellion and taken over the kingdom, after which Cambyses had committed suicide (§11.1.35-43). The people were afraid to say that the man on the throne was not Bardiya in case he should kill them. No one did anything until Darius, with the help of Ahura Mazda and a few others, killed him (§§12-13.1.43-71). A number of rebellions broke out, and it took Darius a good part of a year to put them down; much of the inscription is given over to describing these (§14.1.72–§57.4.45).

A great deal of Herodotus's account is taken up with anecdotal material, often about minor incidents or individuals. It is unlikely that we shall find evidence for most of these in the various finds from the Persian period, nor do we. However, the Behistun inscription has given startling confirmation of the main outlines of Herodotus's story of Darius's rise to power: the name of Darius's father, Cambyses's assassination of his brother, this assassination kept secret, the magus who pretends to be the brother and raises a revolt against Cambyses, the death of Cambyses, the plot of Darius and a few others, their killing of the deceiver, and Darius's ascension to the throne.

Some details need further consideration. The Greek name Hystaspes (Darius's father) is clearly the Persian Vishtaspahya, the Persian *v* normally appearing in Greek as a rough breathing. Perhaps less immediately recognizable the Greek name Smerdis is actually a good reflection of the Persian Bardiya. Herodotus's version says nothing of the many revolts that arose after Darius had killed the 'pseudo-Smerdis', though the revolt of Babylon is mentioned somewhat later.

We must keep in mind that the coincidence of Herodotus's story of Darius's rise with the Behistun inscription does not prove the one or the other correct; on the contrary, it shows that Herodotus was acquainted with the official version and reported it. He is reliable in the outlines of the version, though the details cannot be confirmed and may in many cases be the result of embellishment. When the historian asks what actually happened, though, the answer is probably different. If recent analysis is correct, Darius was probably a usurper.[23] Following years of successful campaigning by Cyrus and Cambyses, the Persian army had suffered a major disaster against the Nubians. Cambyses was responsible for this. His brother Bardiya took the opportunity to capitalize on building dissatisfaction in the Persian heartlands and set himself up as king with quite a large following. Cambyses set out from Egypt to crush the rebellion but died on the way.

23. See Balcer, *Herodotus and Bisitun*, pp. 150-66.

Darius, who was with Cambyses, went on to assassinate Bardiya, with the aid of a few loyal nobles. Revolts broke out all over because his usurpation of the throne was not immediately accepted in many parts of the empire. However, his leadership was compelling, his loyal troops were successful, and he brought the Persian empire under his own control. At this point, the story of the false Bardiya—the pseudo-Smerdis, the magus Gautama—was invented to explain how an act of regicide was instead the deeds of a loyal noble Persian who stepped in to combat the great Lie that had overcome so many.

Sesōstris[24]

We have a longish section in Herodotus describing the deeds of an Egyptian king called *Sesōstris* (2.102-11). As with most of the pharaohs Herodotus's chronology is vague, but the king is said to have done the following things:

- Sailed with a fleet from the Arabian gulf and subdued all those who dwelled by the Red Sea.
- Took an army overland and subdued all peoples through Asia as far as Europe, including the Scythians and Thracians.
- Set up pillars describing his exploits (one of which Herodotus claims to have seen in Palestine).
- Left some of his army at Phasis (Colchis).
- His brother attempted to murder him and his family by setting fire to a house, but Sesostris escaped by sacrificing two children.
- Made captives of his campaigns drag blocks of stone to build the temple at Hephaestus and dig canals.
- Divided the land and gave an equal parcel to each Egyptian.
- Established a yearly tax on the land.
- Only Egyptian king who also ruled Ethiopia, setting up statues of himself and his family before the temple of Hephaestus to commemorate this.

24. Probably the best overview of the subject is Alan B. Lloyd, *Herodotus Book II: Commentary 99-182* (Etudes préliminaires aux religions orientales dan l'Empire romain, 43; Leiden: E.J. Brill, 1988), pp. 16-37; see also Kurt Lange, *Sesostris: ein ägyptische König in Mythos, Geschichte und Kunst* (Munich: Hirmer Verlag, 1954); H. Kees, 'Sesostris', in Georg Wissowa and Wilhelm Kroll (eds.), *Paulys Real-Encyclopädie der classischen Altertumswissenschaft* (Stuttgart: J.B. Metzlersche Verlagbuchhandlung, 1923), 2ter Reihe (R-Z), II, cols. 1862–76; and the older work of Kurt Sethe, *Sesostris* (Untersuchungen zur Geschichte und Altertumskunde Aegyptens 2/1; Leipzig: Hinrichs, 1900).

In Egyptian history there are three kings named Senwosret or Senusret (*S-n-wsr.t*), the Egyptian form of which the Greek Sesostris seems to reflect. They were kings of the 12th Dynasty in the Middle Kingdom early in the second millennium BCE. Do any of these match the Sesostris of Herodotus? The most straightforward answer is no; however, there is some coincidence between several of the activities of the various Sesostris kings, as follows.[25]

Senwosret I ruled for ten years as co-ruler with his father Amenemhet I and ascended the throne when his father was assassinated. He proved to be an effective and exceptional ruler. His main military exploits were to subdue Lower Nubia as far as the second cataract of the Nile and establish the Egyptian border there (or possibly even further south). He also took action against the Libyans in the west. A cult to his divinity began already during his reign and continued long after. Two important writings were produced during his reign, the *Tale of Sinuhe* and the *Instructions of Amenemhet I*,[26] the latter of which tells of his father's murder.

Neither his son Amenemhet II nor his grandson Senwosret II seem to have done anything memorable but had fairly quiet reigns, without major military expeditions. Despite this—or perhaps because of it—Egyptian culture, trade, and influence reached widely into Syria and Asia Minor, and Mesopotamia. One of Senwosret II's accomplishments was to begin a large project on flood control and land reclamation in the Fayum region, a task carried on by his successors.

Senwosret III was the most vigorous of the three rulers. He centralized administration, removing the power of the local nomarchs. Like his great-grandfather he campaigned in Nubia, where the Egyptian hold had become loosened over the intervening century, and set the border at Semna. Subsequently, he was worshipped as a god by the Nubians. Senwosret also had a short campaign in Palestine, apparently to the region of Shechem, but this was no great feat. However, some of the main Execration Texts are to be dated to his reign.

Can one of these kings explain the Sesostris of Herodotus? None of the three Senwosrets is likely to be Herodotus's legendary ruler by himself,

25. For a convenient summary of the what Senwosret I, II, and III accomplished, see William C. Hayes, 'Chapter XX: The Middle Kingdom in Egypt', *CAH*², I, Part 2, pp. 499-509.

26. For an introduction to these writings, with an English translation, see Miriam Lichtheim, *Ancient Egyptian Literature* (Berkeley: University of California, 1973), I, pp. 135-39, 222-35.

but the activities of the three together give a number of the main features found in the Herodotus account:

- Conquest and rule over Nubia (Ethiopia) (I and III).
- Water projects and land reclamation (II).
- Temple building (I, II, III).
- Administrative re-organization (III).

The first point is fairly clear and needs little elaboration. Herodotus has exaggerated by saying that no other rulers controlled Ethiopia, but Senwosret I and III would have been remembered for their domination of that region. The alleged dividing up of the land and the tax system is not historical, as far as is presently known, but Senwosret III's far-reaching administrative changes might be remembered even if the details were distorted. Temple building is not unusual since all Egyptian kings aimed to be remembered as temple builders; indeed, only the Pharaoh was allowed to initiate a new temple foundation. This still leaves some features unaccounted for, such as the use of captives to carry out major public works. However, the main problematic point is Sesostris's military campaign into Asia as far as the Thracians and Scythians, which will be discussed below.

Interestingly, the *Aegyptiaca* of the native Egyptian priest Manetho[27] also describes a campaign of Sesostris as far as Thrace:

> Sesôstris, for 48 years: he is said to have been 4 cubits 3 palms 2 fingers' breadth in stature. In nine years he subdued the whole of Asia, and Europe as far as Thrace. Everywhere he set up memorials of his subjugation of each tribe: among valiant races he engraved upon pillars a man's secret parts, among unwarlike races a woman's, as a sign of disgrace. Wherefore he was honoured by the Egyptians next to Osiris.[28]

Manetho is still a valuable source for certain periods of Egyptian history.[29] He provided the original dynastic framework which was quite important in

27. A useful edition and translation with introduction to the manuscript tradition is found in the Loeb Classical Library: W.G. Waddell, *Manetho* (LCL; London: Heinemann; Cambridge, MA: Harvard University Press, 1940). For the text, see also Felix Jacoby, *Fragmente der griechischen Historiker*, n. 609 (pp. 5-112).

28. Waddell, *Manetho*, pp. 71, 73.

29. See Donald B. Redford, *Pharaonic King-Lists, Annals and Day-Books: A Contribution to the Study of the Egyptian Sense of History* (Society for the Study of Egyptian Antiquities Publication 4; Mississauga, Ontario: Benben Publications, 1986), especially ch. 6. A classic study is R. Laqueur, 'Manethon', in Georg Wissowa and Wilhelm Kroll (eds.), *Paulys Real-Encyclopädie der classischen Altertumswissenschaft* (Neue Bearbeitung; Stuttgart: J.B. Metzlersche Verlagbuchhandlung, 1930), XIV, cols. 1060–1101.

the early days of modern Egyptology. Native Egyptian records have now given better information for much of Egyptian history; however, after the time of Ramesses II Manetho is still the primary source for the framework of reigning kings. As might be expected, there are several complications with using Manetho's account. There is, first of all, the fact that the only fragments of his work are preserved through quotations in the Christian writers Eusebius and Julius Africanus. Even then the versions of these two writers come to us in Greek only as they are quoted by the fifth-century Byzantine writer Syncellus.[30] A second problem is that Manetho apparently included a diversity of material in his study, including not only the bare dynastic lists and also historical details but even oral traditions which were more in the category of folklore.[31]

The question, then, is whether the account of Sesostris quoted in Manetho's name is actually from his pen or whether it might have been contaminated by information from Herodotus or even Diodorus Siculus in its transmission. Manetho is not infallible, and his text contains material that a modern Egyptologist finds unacceptable. Therefore, it might not be unlikely that Manetho had reason to perpetuate the Sesostris myth. Nevertheless, it has been argued that this paragraph was not in the original Manetho because Josephus does not seem to have got his information on Sesostris from Manetho.[32] The statements about Sesostris, brief as they are, certainly agree with Herodotus, and some scholars have argued that they are unlikely to be from Manetho's original work.[33] The reference to monuments with the display of male and female genitals, depending on the resistence of the natives to Egyptian rule, looks unlikely from the pen of a native priest who could read the hieroglyphs. Yet Manetho, who is writing 150 years after Herodotus, might have drawn on a Greek tradition here because it would support Egyptian nationalistic purposes. This possibility must be weighed in the light of Manetho's attempts to refute Herodotus (discussed above). On balance, though, it looks as if the statements about

30. E.g. Syncellus quotes Africanus as speaking in the first person when quoting Manetho on king Suphis of Dynasty 4 (Waddell, *Manetho*, pp. 46-47).

31. Cf. Redford, *Pharaonic King-Lists*, pp. 211-12.

32. M. Braun, *History and Romance in Greco-Oriental Literature* (Oxford: Basil Blackwell, 1938), pp. 14-15. Josephus states that Herodotus has described the invasion of Shishak but mistakenly assigned it to Sesostris (*Ant.* 8.10.3 §260). He was unlikely to have made such a statement if he knew that Manetho had described Sesostris in these terms.

33. Redford, *Pharaonic King-Lists*, p. 212 n. 35.

Sesostris, apart from the bare reference to his rule, are probably a contamination and not a part of Manetho's original work.

Since the campaign through Asia is not likely to have come from the deeds of any of the historical Sesostrises, where has it come from? It is customary to explain this as an importation of Ramesses II's deeds into the story. This is probably an over-simplification, for two reasons. First, Ramesses did not take Egypt's northern border—or even campaign—as far as Thrace or Scythia. A number of the kings of the 18th and 19th dynasties (e.g. Tutmosis III and IV, Ramesses II) took military expeditions into northern Syria, even as far as the Euphrates. Thus, there could be a memory here, not necessarily of Ramesses II specifically but of the activities of a number of Pharaohs at this time. Although this is a plausible explanation, a more convincing scenario is at hand, which is my second point. Herodotus states that Sesostris exceeded the deeds of Darius I: for Sesostris 'had subdued the Scythians, besides as many other nations as Darius had conquered, and Darius had not been able to overthrow the Scythians' (1.110). What is clearly of major concern here is rivalry with the hated Persians who had conquered Egypt. The Persians had conquered many peoples but not the Scythians, whereas the Egyptian king Sesostris had not only overcome as many peoples as the Persians but had even done better by conquering the Scythians. This is not historical record but nationalist invention.

Nevertheless, Herodotus's version is simpler and more believable than the story as it developed in Greek tradition. Diodorus Siculus also gives a version but in much more elaborated and legendary form. Yet most features of the story in Diodorus are parallel to those in Herodotus and appear to be capable of explanation as a mere elaboration of Herodotus. The differences in detail do not affect the essential structure of the tale. Diodorus paints a picture of arduous youthful training, arranged by Sesostris's father, but this is a commonplace feature of such hero tales.[34]

There is some evidence that this legendary development was not confined to Sesostris. As noted, the tale may have picked up features of Ramesses the Great, but a Ramesses hero story seems also to have circulated independently. Writing in the second century CE, the Roman historian

---

34. Xenophon has already written such an account of youthful training in his *Cyropaedia*, which served as a model for later writers. A similar focus on rigorous training in the hero's youth is found in Diodorus's story of Ninus, as already discussed above.

Tacitus refers to a tour down the Nile taken by Germanicus in the year 19 CE (*Annals* 2.60):

> On piles of masonry Egyptian letters still remained, embracing the tale of old magnificence, and one of the senior priests, ordered to interpret his native tongue, related that 'once the city contained seven hundred thousand men of military age, and with that army King Rhamses, after conquering Libya and Ethiopia, the Medes and the Persians, the Bactrian and the Scyth, and the lands where the Syrians and Armenians and neighbouring Cappadocians dwell, had ruled over all that lies between the Bithynian Sea on the one hand and the Lycian on the other'. The tribute-lists of the subject nations were still legible: ...revenues no less imposing than those which are now exacted by the might of Parthia or by Roman power.

Tacitus is reporting what the Egyptians themselves stated and, to the best of my knowledge, this tale has no exact parallel elsewhere in Greek or Latin literature. Yet the story told by the priest is blatant propaganda: Ramesses II made no such conquests as outlined here, and certainly none of the other Ramesseses. We clearly have another instance of a legendary hero whose deeds, interestly, exceed even those of Sesostris. But such a hero is necessary if the world-conquering Romans were to be at all impressed. Unless the priest made up the story on the spot (not impossible but unlikely), this is evidence of another hero cycle developed by a native people to keep up their self-respect under the domination of more recent power.

In sum, what can we say about the Sesostris story? Is it history? The answer is that it has a historical core but many of the details are not historical. Without corroborating evidence, it would be hard to say whether some features were historical or not, but we fortunately have enough evidence from the native Egyptian sources to control much of the tradition in Herodotus. Herodotus's story is a legend, though it appears to be a legend of Egyptian origin. It may also be found in Manetho, though this is uncertain. Herodotus's account is closer to the historical figure(s) than the later embellishments found in Diodorus Siculus and the *Sesostris-novelle*. Without being able to cross-check with native sources, it would have been difficult to evalute this story.

Herodotus and Sennacherib

The story given by Herodotus is as follows (2.141):

> The next king was the priest of Hephaestus, whose name was Sethos... So presently came king Sanacharib against Egypt, with a great host of Arabians

and Assyrians; and the warrior Egyptians would not march against him. The priest, in his quandary, went into the temple shrine and there bewailed to the god's image the peril which threatened him. In his lamentation he fell asleep, and dreamt that he saw the god standing over him and bidding him take courage, for he should suffer no ill by encountering the host of Arabia: 'Myself', said the god, 'will send you champions'. So he trusted the vision, and encampled at Pelusium with such Egyptians as would follow him, for here is the road into Egypt; and none of the warriors would go with him, but only hucksters and artificers and traders. Their enemies too came thither, and one night a multitude of fieldmice swarmed over the Assyrian camp and devoured their quivers and their bows and the handles of their shields likewise, insomuch that they fled the next day unarmed and many fell. And at this day a stone statue of the Egyptian king stands in Hephaestus' temple, with a mouse in his hand, and an inscription to this effect: 'Look on me, and fear the gods'.

The first point to notice about this account is that it seems to be independent of any of the other extant accounts about Sennacherib, whether Assyrian or biblical.[35] Unless Herodotus has misled us about the source of this story, it came from the Egyptian priests. They could have passed on a version that had developed in a Greek milieu, but this seems less likely than a story that had developed among the Egyptians. This looks very much like a native Egyptian tradition that Herodotus has heard from the priests and has passed on in his own version. In the process Herodotus has transformed it, whatever its original Egyptian form, but it is not immediately evident what changes he might have made. There are no obviously Grecized features to the story.[36] The statement about a statue in the temple of 'Hephaestus' is likely to be Herodotus's own for what he thought he saw. The king's name Sethos does not fit, but Lloyd has argued that it is a corruption of Shebitku ($S3\text{-}b3\text{-}t3\text{-}k3$).[37] If so, Herodotus has preserved the correct succession Shabaka (Herodotus 2.137-39: *Sabakōs*) followed by Shebitku.

Unfortunately, this passage is often assimilated to the biblical passage, the account of Herodotus being used to help explain the biblical and vice

---

35. The possibility has been raised that Herodotus's account represents a development of the biblical account (Mordechai Cogan and Hayim Tadmor, *II Kings: A New Translation with Introduction and Commentary* [AB, 11; New York: Doubleday, 1988], p. 251, who cite the PhD thesis of Alexander Rofé, *Israelite Belief in Angels in the Pre-exilic Period as Evidenced by Biblical Traditions* [unpublished PhD thesis in Hebrew; Jerusalem: Hebrew University, 1969], p. 217).

36. Baumgartner, 'Herodots babylonische und assyrische Nachrichten', pp. 282-331.

37. Lloyd, *Herodotus Book II* (n. 24 above), p. 100.

versa. This procedure ignores the fact that the two accounts different significantly in certain areas. Proper method says that each must be analyzed in
its own right before any attempt at synthesis is undertaken.

It has often been argued that the fieldmice in the story suggest that the
real devastation to the Assyrians was caused by a plague transmitted by
the rodents. This is not in itself a problematic interpretation since mice
were associated with plagues in antiquity, and the use of surrogate language for a plague is found in a variety of literature.[38] The question is
whether this is how Herodotus intended his story to be understood. This
interpretation in fact looks like a blatant reading of (an interpretation of)
2 Kgs 19.35 into Herodotus, while the argument that Herodotus has
changed an account of a plague to fit Greek views is unjustified[39]: why is
the gnawing of mice more 'Greek' than a plague? I can see no reason
why Herodotus would have changed the story nor any way that a plague
story has been misunderstood by Herodotus; the Greeks were, after all,
quite well acquainted with plagues and their traumatic effects.

It is only because Herodotus has been read in the light of 2 Kgs 19.35//
Isa. 37.36, with the reference to the 'angel of YHWH' interpreted as a reference to the devastations of a plague on the Assyrian army, that the mice
have been turned into symbols of disease. Whether when 'the angel of
YHWH' 'strikes' (the Hebrew verb *nkh*) in 2 Kgs 19.35//Isa. 37.36 is rightly
to be understood as referring to a plague can be debated, but it is not an
unreasonable interpretation. Nevertheless, there is no hint of such an interpetation in Herodotus's account when it is read in its own right. The mice
are not plague carriers in Herodotus, whatever they might symbolize in
other contexts. Herodotus does not say that they caused the death of the
Assyrians but that they rendered their armour and weapons unusable. No
plague acts in such a way. The Assyrian army is not defeated by the death
of the soldiers but by their being rendered unable to fight.

But this is further evidence that the story in Herodotus did not develop
from the biblical story. There is no element in Herodotus's story that could

38. In his review of Clements (p. 27 above), J.J.M. Roberts notes, 'When the
ancient text says "Erra cut down enemies" (VAB, 7, 132-133, viii 17) or "Istar rained
fire on Arabia" (VAB 7, 78-79-81), is it rationalizing to explain this by reference to
plague and Assurbanipal's scorched-earth policy? Certainly not' (*JBL* 101 [1982], pp.
442-44 (443). Many readers will remember that the Iliad opens with Apollo raining his
arrows down on the Greek forces, which is widely understood to mean a plague in the
Greek camp (*Iliad* , book 1).

39. As asserted by Cogan and Tadmor (*II Kings*, p. 251), following Baumgartner,
'Herodots babylonische und assyrische Nachrichten', p. 306.

be said to show remarkable agreement with 2 Kgs 19 or Isa. 37. The only resemblance between the two is that Sennacherib is defeated. Whatever gave rise to the Herodotean story, it was not the biblical version. This can be stated on internal grounds alone. When external considerations are taken into account, any connection is rendered even less likely. Many would argue that 2 Kings was not written down until long after Sennacherib, perhaps as late as the Persian period.[40] How would this version have been transmitted to the Egyptians, or the Greeks for that matter? The Septuagint translation of the story into Greek came long after Herodotus. At that point, it would be possible for a Greek-speaker to gain access to the story (though the Septuagint seems to have been hardly read by any but the Jews themselves). It could have circulated in oral form, of course, but it is even harder to explain how a Jewish oral tradition gained a foothold among the Greeks.

When Herodotus's account is read in its own right, without interpretation in the light of the biblical, it tells us of an Egyptian defeat of Sennacherib. The defeat was not by normal force of arms but entailed some unusual happening. The Assyrian army was not destroyed but was rendered ineffectual in fighting so that many were killed. Unless we accept the literal statement about the fieldmice, which few of us would, we would have to think of some extraordinary event in which the Egyptian army was unexpectedly victorious. Although we cannot confirm the Egyptian story, it appears to be independent of other accounts and yet fits well into what we know from the Assyrian records. According to some, there were two Egyptian encounters. Since the Egyptian army was apparently defeated or driven off in its first encounter with the Assyrians, this would mean that any later success would have been more likely to be unexpected.[41]

40. E.g. Laato ('Hezekiah and the Assyrian Crisis' [n. 3 above], p. 119) argues that 2 Kgs 18–19 have been redacted to fit the pattern of the siege of Jerusalem as recounted in Jer. 37–39. See also Nadav Na'aman ('The Debated Historicity of Hezekiah's Reform in the Light of Historical and Archaeological Research', *ZAW* 107 [1995], pp. 179-95) who argues that 2 Kgs 18.4, 22 are redactions of the deuteronomistic historian no earlier than the seventh century BCE. See also his study in this volume, pp. 201-220 below.

41. Oriental Institute Prism Inscription of Sennacherib II,73—III,17; text and translation in D.D. Luckenbill, *The Annals of Sennacherib* (OIP 2; Chicago: University of Chicago, 1924), pp. 31-32; English translation in *ANET* 287-88. Sennacherib mentions only the 'kings of Egypt' and the 'king of Ethiopia'. Taharqa the Nubian prince and future king is often thought to be in mind because of 2 Kgs 19.9, but Taharqa did not become king until a decade later. This may not be a major problem; see, e.g., Kenneth

This explanation is entirely consistent with the reconstructions of several Egyptologists and others. K.A. Kitchen has posited a second Egyptian attack (led by Taharqa, the brother of the king Shebitku, as commander) after the initial defeat at Eltekeh.[42] The Egypto-Kushite force had been repulsed but not routed. The second Egyptian action came after Sennacherib had divided his forces between Libnah, Lachish, Maresha, and Jerusalem. Kitchen thinks the Egyptians retreated without a major engagement when Sennacherib regrouped, but another interpretation is possible. For example, D.B. Redford states that Shabaka led a substantial expeditionary force to attack the Assyrians at Eltekeh.[43] He goes on to say,

> Even though our sources for Eltekeh are confined to the Assyria records—Egyptian relief and textual material employ stereotyped images of uncertain application—there can be no doubt that it was an unexpected and serious reverse for Assyria arms, and contributed significantly to Sennacherib's permanent withdrawal from the Levant.

F.J. Yurco also takes the interpretation of an Egyptian defeat of the Assyrians seriously.[44] Additionally, see also the comments and reconstruction of Axel Knauf in this volume (pp. 141-49 below) where it is suggested that the engagement at Eltekeh might have come later in the campaign and was at least difficult enough for the Assyrians to come to terms with the Egyptians.

The Assyrians do not mention a defeat by the Egyptians, but they are not likely to have done so.[45] What is clear is that Sennacherib returned to

A. Kitchen, *The Third Intermediate Period in Egypt (1100–650 BC)* (Warminster, Wilts.: Aris & Philips, 2nd edn, 1986), pp. 154-61, 552-59. A recently found inscription has been assigned to the reign of Taharqa (Donald B. Redford, 'Taharqa in Western Asia and Libya', *EI* 24 [1993], pp. 188*-91*). It has now been argued that this inscription is to be connected to an invasion of Sennacherib, though not the one in 701 BCE but a postulated 'second invasion': William H. Shea, 'The New Tirhakah Text and Sennacherib's Second Palestinian Campaign', *AUSS* 35 (1997), pp. 181-87. But see the objections of Mordechai Cogan, 'Sennacherib's Siege of Jerusalem', *BAR* 27/1 (January/ February 2001), pp. 40-45, 69. On the whole question, see the discussion above, pp. 31-33.

42. Kenneth A. Kitchen, *The Third Intermediate Period*, pp. 383-86, 584.

43. Donald B. Redford, *Egypt, Canaan, and Israel in Ancient Times* (Princeton, NJ: Princeton University Press, 1992), pp. 351-54.

44. Frank J. Yurco, 'Sennacherib's Third Campaign and the Coregency of Shabaka and Shebitku', *Serapis* 6 (1980), pp. 221-40 (233-37). In this case, Herodotus is cited, among other sources.

45. It has been argued that the Assyrian inscriptions omit defeats or attempt to turn

Nineveh without defeating Hezekiah, and his listing of the destruction wrought on Judah and the resultant tribute by Hezekiah only confirms the peculiarity in Hezekiah's being allowed to remain on the throne and the strange silence about the taking of Jerusalem. An unexpected defeat or serious setback by the Egyptians could be one of the reasons for his withdrawal without taking Jerusalem. Herodotus's account is a useful piece in the puzzle and must be recognized as such; however, it must not be shaped by biblical scissors before fitting it into place.

Conclusions about Herodotus and Historical Method

The work of the historian of ancient history is a fraught one. Historians of more recent times take the abundance of primary sources for granted, while their fellows in ancient history can only be envious of what can be written with proper records. But this is one of the hazards of the trade. If we want to say anything about the ancient Near East, we have to make do with what we have, not what we would like to have. This should not cause us to take over any potentially useful bit of data uncritically; on the contrary, the state of the sources should make us recognize the limits of our knowledge and the need to scrutinize all sources carefully. On the other hand, the paucity of information means that no potential source should be dismissed without careful analysis. This leads to the following methodological points:

1. No source should be used without careful and critical analysis.
2. Likewise, no source should be dismissed without careful and critical analysis.
3. Sources should first be understood in their own right before attempting to combine them. Herodotus's story of fieldmice needs initially to be analyzed for what it says, not for how it seems to confirm or fit with other potential sources.
4. It is not illegitimate to combine the data from different sorts of sources; indeed, all history writing involves use of all the reliable data available, whatever the origin, but the combining must be done only after each source is scrutinized and understood in its own environment and milieu. Sources may eventually throw

defeats or standoffs into victories. See Laato, 'Assyrian Propaganda and the Falsification of History' (n. 3 above); also the response by B. Oded, 'History vis-à-vis Propaganda in the Assyrian Royal Inscriptions', *VT* 48 (1998), pp. 423-25.

light on one another, but independent corroboration is always preferable to assimilated data. To use Herodotus to confirm a plague destroying the Egyptian army is nothing but circular reasoning, because Herodotus has already been assimilated to the biblical account.

5.   The examples looked at in this paper confirm what has often been stated by classical scholars: Herodotus is a useful source and has a good deal of important data. His statements must be treated critically like any other, but overall he is a much better historian than many of his successors. None of his data should be dismissed out of hand, though analysis does sometimes show it to be false or misleading.

6.   In the present search for methodological guidance to the history of ancient Israel and Judah, the experience and practice of classical historians has much to tell us. They face much the same problems as historians of ancient Palestine and Syria, and historical methodology has long been debated by our fellow historians in the classical tradition.

7.   Historians of the ancient Near East have some tricks to teach to the classicists, however, and some of the best work is being done by those who have been able to combine expertise in both areas.[46] Biblical scholars and historians have much to learn from both camps. The wheel has been invented; fire was discovered long ago. We should spend our time building on the solid foundations already laid for us. Of course, that does not exempt us from testing those foundations to see where the builders might have used too much sand or too little cement.

---

46.   Two major examples are found in Amélie Kuhrt and Susan Sherwin-White (eds.), *Hellenism in the East* (n. 6 above); Susan Sherwin-White and Amélie Kuhrt, *From Samarkhand to Sardis: A New Approach to the Seleucid Empire* (London: Gerald Duckworth, 1993).

SENNACHERIB AT THE BEREZINA

Ernst Axel Knauf

This is my reconstruction. It depends on the input of notions, ideas, interests and questions I received from teachers, colleagues and friends in the course of time. It also depends on the amount of sources I became familiar with; and these sources—*l'histoire étant une et indivisible*—are by no means restricted to written, or written and iconographic, or written, iconographic and archaeological material, or to material from the Near East and the first millennium BCE. Military historians always try to become as familiar as possible with the terrain on which their battles were fought; and althought not as well acquainted with the Shephelah and the Judaean mountains as with other parts of the Holy Land, I do have a reasoned vision of what the country looked like in 701. Colleagues who had and have other teachers, colleagues and friends, and who inhabited another (or even a slightly different) universe of sources, will construe differently.

Assyrian royal inscriptions (nearly) never lie, at least not in so many words. As B. Halpern ingeniously pointed out under the term of the 'Tiglathpileser principle' (which, as the critical tool it deserves to become, might as well be labelled the 'Halpern theorem'), they just make the reader attribute more glorious deeds (or nefarious misdeeds) to the Assyrian king than he ever committed, and intentionally so.[1] In the case of Sennacherib's 'third campaign' (Chic. II 37–III 49),[2] even modern scholars credit the king with achievements he never claimed, like the conquest of Ashkelon or the siege of Jerusalem. To separate historical record (which is there) from intended propaganda (which is also there) necessitates a most scru-

---

1. B. Halpern, *David's Secret Demons: Messiah, Murderer, Traitor, King* (Grand Rapids, MI: Eerdmans, 2001), pp. 107-32 (126): 'The technique is that of putting extreme spin on real events.'
2. Translations following D.D. Luckenbill, *The Annals of Sennacherib* (OIP, 2; Chicago: University of Chicago Press, 1924) if not otherwise stated.

tinizing look at what is actually said, and, of rather more importance, at what is not said at all,[3] in addition, some regard for the events and political constellations which result from the actions narrated might also prove helpful.[4]

The first observation: Sennacherib's account of 701 is not completely chronological in nature, but rather geographically arranged, from north to south; insofar as the Assyrian army basically moved in this direction, chronological and geographical progress do correlate, but only to a certain degree. Sidon is occupied without a fight, and everybody around who depends on Phoenician trade makes haste to pay their respects, and in cash (II 37–60). The exception is Ṣidqā of Ashkelon, who is slow to deliver, and therefore replaced by his predecessor (II 60–68). According to the narrative sequence, it sounds as if this action was taken at the 'Sidonian congress of Syrian princes'. The following episode covering a campaign against Ṣidqā fought in the region of Beth-Dagon, Yafo, Bene-Baraq and Asor (II 68–72) suggests another chain of events: Ṣidqā had not shown up at Sidon, and Sennacherib attacked a stretch of the coast which Ashkelon had brought into its possession (Ashkelon was by that time the largest and probably most powerful Philistine kingdom).[5] The loss of its northern possessions was enough for the Ashkelonites to depose their anti-Assyrian ruler, hand him over, and re-appoint his pro-Assyrian predecessor. The closest the Assyrian siege-machines ever came to Ashkelon was up to the walls of Beth Dagon, as Sennacherib clearly states.[6] For superior effect,

3.   Might I suggest the term 'Napoleon principle' to this particular aspect of lying with the truth? When, in his last communication from his Russian campaign, Napoleon stated that 'The health of His Majesty has never been better', by not commenting on the health of the army he actually said a lot.

4.   Lützen 1632 was tactically a draw. Vienna celebrated a victory when Gustavus Adolphus got killed, but it was the Swedish, not the Imperial army which wintered in Saxony as a result of the battle.

5.   After Gath had been reduced by Hazael, and Ashdod by Sargon II in 711. Ekron, in 701, had probably not yet expanded from its 4 ha in the 8th century to the 24 ha it covered again (as it did previously in the 11th and 10th centuries) in the 7th century. Ashkelon might have covered c. 40 ha by this time.

6.   By not talking about any march to Ashkelon, any siege operations, any conquest achieved—he only deported the royal family who fell into his hands without Sennacherib moving his little finger (had he moved the aforementioned body-part, the text would indulge in another deed of his mighty arm). Sennacherib's 'conquest of Ashkelon', ubiquitous in contemporary historiography (cf. R. Lamprichs, *Die Westexpansion des neuassyrischen Reiches: Eine Strukturanalyse* [AOAT, 239; Neukirchen–Vluyn: Neukirchener Verlag; Kevelaer: Butzon & Bercker, 1995], pp. 149-50; B.U.

the result of the action (Ṣidqā's extradition) is narrated before the action which caused it.

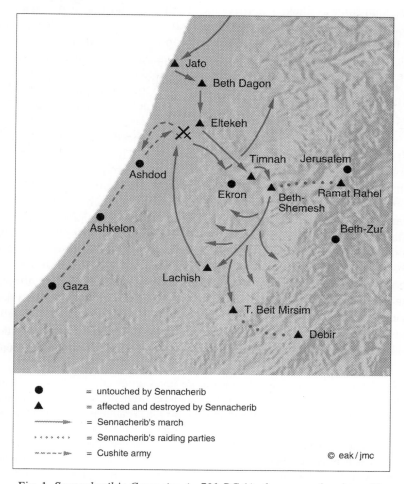

Fig. 1. *Sennacherib's Campaign in 701 BC* (Authors own drawing with graphics by Julia Mueller-Clemm, Berne).

Schipper, *Israel und Ägypten in der Königszeit: Die kulturellen Kontakte von Salomo bis zum Fall Jerusalems* [OBO, 170; Freiburg: Universitätsverlag; Göttingen: Vandenhoeck & Ruprecht, 1999], p. 210: 'im Sturm genommen'), is just an indication of what good 'spin-doctors' the Assyrian scribes were; note, however, that Ashkelon is corrrectly missing on the map of M. Cogan and H. Tadmor, *II Kings: A New Translation with Introduction and Commentary* (AB, 11; New York: Doubleday, 1988), p. 245, where there still is one conquest of Ekron too many (Sennacherib's march led from Eltekeh via Timnah to Lachish, and from there back to Eltekeh).

In geographical sequence, Ekron is next (II 73–III 17). The Ekronites having secured Egyptian support, the Assyrians blast the Egyptian army to kingdom come at Eltekeh, north of Ekron. Eltekeh and Timna are besieged, Ekron capitulates and its former king, Padi, is re-established, released just in time by Hezekiah who had held him captive at Jerusalem, and against whom Sennacherib now turns. Here, chronology is in serious trouble. If there was a Cushite-Egyptian army in the field powerful enough to face the Assyrians in ranged battle, why then did Ashkelon capitulate already? If Hezekiah was to be attacked next—and he knew it, given his provisioning activities[7]—why did he release his most valuable hostage prematurely? It is safe to assume that, when Sennacherib advanced from Beth-Dagon to Eltekeh, an Egyptian army was nowhere in sight. That he attacked Timnah next indicates that he bypassed Ekron on his march south, being content to cut off the rebels from their Judaean ally for the moment (probably not covering more than 4 ha at that time, Ekron was not much of a threat to his rear anyway, or so it seemed). Re-installing Padi at Ekron (and settling the affairs of southern Syria for the next 20 years) must belong to the very end of the campaign, and the battle of Eltekeh with it[8]. Admittedly, its present finale, the submission of Hezekiah, makes better reading and bestows on Sennacherib more glory, praise and honor to take back with him to Assyria than the 'Peace Conference of Ekron' would have left him in case it had been reported.

Of the '46 cities' he took from Hezekiah (III 19), only two are mentioned by name: Lachish and Azekah, and in the 'annals', neither.[9] Timnah,

---

7.   Hezekiah's preparations for the war are amply documented by the distribution of the *lmlk*-jars. In all the Shephelah they are found in 701 destruction debris, wherever the published reports allow for the identification of the stratigraphical context. In the Judaean mountains, some sites provisioned by Hezekiah were destroyed (Ramat Raḥel, Ḥirbet Rabūd), others were not (Beth-Zur). North of Jerusalem (Mizpah, Gibeon, Tell el-Fūl) and in the Negev (Beersheba II, Aroer III, Arad VIII) all stratified *lmlk*-handles derive from 7th-century strata, i.e. Sennacherib did not campaign there at all. I will discuss the archaeological evidence in more detail in another article.

8.   D.B. Redford, *Egypt, Canaan, and Israel in Ancient Times* (Princeton, NJ: Princeton University Press, 1992), pp. 351-53 proposes the same chain of events, in all probability overrating the Egyptian success just slightly.

9.   For Lachish, cf. Luckenbill, *Annals*, p. 156; E. Frahm, *Einleitung in die Sanherib-Inschriften* (AfO Beiheft, 26; Horn: Berger & Söhne, 1997), p. 127 (T 50); for Azekah: 'Letter to God' K 6205+, 5. 10 (ed. N. Na'aman; 'Sennacherib's "Letter to God" on his Campaign to Judah', in *BASOR*, 214 [1974], pp. 25-39); it is still unclear in which royal Philistine city's name is to be restored K 6205, 11. The description 12-13 would fit the position of Tell eṣ-Ṣāfī on top of its hill, but Gath ceased to be a royal city, or any kind of city, more than a century before. Could Sennacherib refer to Lachish

having been garrisoned by Hezekiah as well (without Sennacherib explicitly paying attention to the fact), had been mentioned before under the heading of 'Ekron'. After the fall of Lachish, Hezekiah had no choice but to send his envoys into Sennacherib's camp (at Lachish, *nota bene*) and to capitulate (2 Kgs 18.13-16); with the Shephelah devastated and lost, there was nothing left with which to fight a war, or run a state. It was not exactly Sennacherib's splendour that turned Hezekiah's Arab allies away from him (III 37-41), but rather a lack of further funds and means. Judah proper, tree-growing and herding territory, has never been able to sustain a full-blown state on its own. Judaean statehood, or attempts thereof, was always dependent on the acquisition of areas capable of producing cereal surplus: the plateau of Benjamin (under David and Solomon, and then from Josiah onwards) or the Shephelah (from the middle of the ninth century to 701, and again under Josiah) or the Negev (under Manasseh).[10] There never was a siege of Jerusalem—all Sennacherib's verbiage implies no more than that he had picketed the, or some, gates of Jerusalem with one or more cavalry troops, one of which might have dug itself in:

> Himself, like a caged bird (28) I shut up in Jerusalem, his royal city. (29) Earthworks I threw up against him—(30) the one coming out of the city-gate, I turned back to his misery.

(III 27-30; and note that Sennacherib does not provide information about the distance between his 'turning-back' pickets and the gate—100 m, 1 km or 10 km? In addition, the verbal forms employed in this section are all indicating individual, not repetitive or prolonged action; i.e. every deed reported happened at least once, but not necessarily twice.[11]) For 'siege language', on the contrary, cf. III 6f; 19-23:

by this term? In the slightly more recent past, a king of Judah had been killed there (2 Kgs 14.19), and re-attributing Lachish to Philistia after its conquest could indicate that Sennacherib thought that it rightfully belonged there in the first place.—Frahm's attempt (*Einleitung*, pp. 229-32) to re-attribute the text to Sargon II and to the year 720 requests one Assyrian confrontation with Hezekiah too many (within the universe of sources as it stands at the time).

10. Cf. for the 10th century, E.A. Knauf, 'Who Destroyed Megiddo VIA?', in *BN* 103 (2000), pp. 30-35 (p. 35); for the 9th and 8th centuries, I. Finkelstein, 'The Rise of Jerusalem and Judah: the Missing Link', in *Levant* 32 (2001), pp. 105-15; for the 7th century, I. Finkelstein, 'The Archaeology of the Days of Manasseh', in M.D. Coogan, J.C. Exum and L.E. Stager (eds.), *Scripture and Other Artifacts. Essays in Bible and Archaeology in Honor of Philip J. King* (Louisville, KY: Westminster/John Knox Press, 1994), pp. 169-87 (175-79).

11. Nor does the 'I' of the text imply that Sennacherib went to Jerusalem in person.

46 of his strong, walled cities, as well as (20) the small cities in their neighborhood (21) which were without number–by levelling with battering-rams (22) and by bringing up siege-engines, by attacking and by storming on foot (23) by mines, tunnels and breaches, I besieged and took.

Archaeology attests to raids, burning and pillage south of Jerusalem[12], but to no damage north of Jerusalem where, simply for the fact that it had to be fed, any sizeable Assyrian army would have been quartered (with the ensuing collateral damage to habitations and their inhabitants).

To make the final victory (in the narrative sequence) look better, the booty of the whole campaign with its 200,105 captives is registered under 'Jerusalem'.[13] This is nearly twice as many as the whole kingdom of Judah had inhabitants; the Shephelah had had some 60,000–65,000.[14] Hezekiah gets off lightly, for the moment, because his economic backbone was broken, and nobody wanted Jerusalem—not yet. But finally, Hezekiah did not get off lightly at all.

Now the Egyptian army moves in.[15] Having left Ekron unconquered in

Cf. for the non-siege of Jerusalem in 701 W. Mayer, *Politik und Kriegskunst der Assyrer* (ALASPM 9; Munich: Ugarit, 1995), pp. 359-61. When will the last biblical and/or ancient Near Eastern scholar have recognized that Isa. 36–39 (<=> 2 Kgs 18.17–20.19) is not a source at all for the events of 701, but a piece of propaganda from the second siege of Jerusalem by Nebuchadnezzar, incidentally, also the second siege in the history of Jerusalem of which I know? Cf. Ch. Hardmeier, *Prophetie im Streit vor dem Untergang Judas. Erzählkommunikative Studien zur Entstehungssitua-tion der Jesaja- und Jeremiaerzählungen in II Reg 18–20 und Jer 37–40* (BZAW, 187; Berlin: W. de Gruyter, 1990); U. Becker, *Jesaja—von der Botschaft zum Buch* (FRLANT, 178; Göttingen: Vandenhoeck & Ruprecht, 1997), pp. 220-22; and also J. Blenkinsopp, *Isaiah 1–39. A New Translation with Introduction and Commentary* (AB, 19; New York: Doubleday, 2000), p. 102.

12. Cf. n. 7.

13. To be precise, under 'Hezekiah' between the paragraphs 'Devastation of the Shephelah' and 'Harrassment of Jerusalem'.

14. Finkelstein, 'Days of Manasseh', p. 176. On the enormous number of Sennach-erib's captives, at least two oceans of ink have been spilt by now. The figure is credible if it includes the total of his opponents' losses in 701. Most recently, W. Mayer sug-gested (in this volume, p. 182 that 205,150 is the total number of heads, bipeds and quadrupeds included.

15. The Isaiah-legend might contain a piece of historical memory by letting the Egyptians appear on the scene when Jerusalem is already threatened (Isa 37.9 = 2 Kgs 19.9); Tirhakah, of course, is a blatant anachronism (Schipper, *Israel und Ägypten*, pp. 215-16). My reconstruction of the 701 campaign does not depend on the historicity of Isa. 37.9—it helps to establish the partial historicity of this verse.

his rear, the Egyptians took the chance to outflank the Assyrian army and to threaten its lines of communication. In addition, after 50 sieges, a summer of fighting, looting and burning, the Assyrian army's fighting power must have been severely diminished by now—no angel of the Lord was needed, nor an invasion of mice.[16] That Eltekeh was far from a glorious victory for the Assyrians and much more of a close run thing is indicated by Sennacherib's phraseology, once more (II 82–III 5):

> In the neighborhood of Eltekeh (83) their ranks being drawn up before me (1) they offered battle. (Trusting) in the aid of Assur (2) my lord, I fought with them and (3) brought about their defeat. The Egyptian charioteers and princes (4) together with the charioteers of the Ethiopian king (5) my hands took alive in the midst of the battle.

An army has to be in dire straits indeed if the commander-in-chief sees himself forced to join the mêlée.[17] If the battle of Eltekeh was a draw, or not fought at all, the outcome would have been the same:[18] Sennacherib,

16. Siege warfare has always been more costly for the attacker due to the better protection of the defender. In addition, no military camp in the pre-modern world was free from camp-diseases, and the less so the longer they stayed at the same place. And, as any student of the Thirty Years War, the Peninsular War of 1808–14, and Napoleon's retreat from Moscow can tell, nothing destroys an army more quickly and more thoroughly than a systematically devastated region supposed to feed it. In addition, the human mind is attracted by spectacular catastrophes, but very slow, if not wholly unable, to regard the consequences of slow processes. Napoleon's army of 1812 was destroyed by 'General Winter'? Far from that; the 'Grande Armée' had crossed the Njemen 450,000 strong, of which 100,000 reached Moscow; no more than 50,000 had been bloody casualties (11.1 per cent); 300,000 had died, or were dying, of typhoid fever (66.7 per cent), of which the contemporary memoirs, left by nearly every survivor from the Duc des Vincence, Grand-Ecuyer Impérial, down to Serjeant-Major Peter (who, being illiterate, dictated them to his daughter), took no account at all. 25,000 crossed the Njemen again; this means, the army lost during the retreat no more than 16.7 per cent of its original strength (but 75 per cent of those who had reported for duty when they left Moscow). It should also be noted that in most of the fighting during the retreat, the French and their allies were still victorious, and that the pursuing Russian army was in no better state than their enemy when reaching western Poland. Cf. for this and other well-documented disasters, G. Regan, *Geoffrey Regan's Book of Military Blunders* (London: Deutsch, 2001).

17. One might adduce the examples of Ramses II at Qadesh, Ney at Waterloo, Bazaine at Rezonville, Wimpffen at Sedan, Liman von Sanders at Nazareth (cases of hare-brained 'chivalry' or of GOCs Cavalry discounted).

18. That it was not a resounding Egyptian victory either (*pace* Redford, *Egypt*, p. 353) results from the status of Southern Syria between Assyria and Egypt during the following 20 years: stalemate, or a cold truce in a frozen war.

the Egyptians and the Philistines all saved their necks (and their faces), and Hezekiah was left out in the cold to foot the bill. The settlement reached at the 'Ekron Peace Conference'[19] was that Ekron returned to the Assyrian fold; Gaza, popping up from nowhere, gets the same compensation as Ekron and Ashdod did.[20] Is it too bold to assume that at least Gaza was in fact an Egyptian pied-à-terre? This might be inferred from the fact that Ashdod, having been reduced to the status of province in 711, was re-established as a vassal-kingdom.[21] If there were no frictions to be covered over, what need was there for a buffer-state? Sennacherib's retreat to Ekron after the battle of Eltekeh could mean that the Egyptians blocked his retreat to Assyria, and remained in the North. But this is rather unlikely, because at Ekron, Sennacherib was free to dispose of his vassal kingdom to his liking. Had the Egyptian position been more advantageous, they might have tried to oust the Assyrians from Philistia completely. So the Egyptian army probably concentrated around Ashdod and resuscitated this Philistine kingdom from its involuntary sleep. Being silent about the usual awful things the Assyrians used to inflict on captured 'rebels' in the case of the Egyptian 'princes' (or officers) captured at Eltekeh, Sennacherib probably put them to the same use as Napoleon did with the Austrian general Meerveldt after the Battle of Dresden, and sent them back as intermediaries.

All three Philistine kingdoms were compensated with parts of the Shephelah taken from Judah (III 31-34).[22] Now it becomes intelligible why Hezekiah sent his harem (amongst other treasures) off to Nineveh even after Sennacherib had departed (III 41-49). The Assyrians might have

19. Note that Sennacherib does not state that he besieged and/or conquered Ekron, or set foot in the city. All he says is 'I drew near to Ekron' (III 8). This reads as if the peace was negotiated between Egypt and Assyria in the Assyrian camp.

20. According to the 'Bull Inscription', pp. 29-30 (Luckenbill, *Annals*, p. 70; Frahm, *Einleitung*, p. 117), Ashkelon also benefitted from the partitioning of the Shephelah, but the fourth city is missing from the Rassam Cylinder composed in 700. The 'Bull Inscription' dates to 694/3 (Frahm, *Einleitung*, p. 118). Was Ashkelon regarded as unworthy of compensation by both Egyptians and Assyrians in 701, but had made up to Sennacherib by 694, only to fall from grace again before 689?

21. H. Donner, *Geschichte des Volkes Israel und seiner Nachbarn in Grundzügen* (ATD.E 8/2; Göttingen: Vandenhoeck & Ruprecht, 1995), p. 358 pays attention to the problem. The solution can be construed from the fact that in 669, i.e. after the first conquest of Egypt, Ashdod was a province again.

22. Sennacherib is explicit in stating that he redistributed only the part of Hezekiah's kingdom which he had conquered (III 31).

wanted some counterweight against their own Philistine vassals, not having been able to oust Egypt completely from the southern Palestinian scene; Hezekiah needed somebody to back him—after the Egyptians and their proxies had so liberally partaken of the booty taken from him[23]. From now on, Jerusalem would be important as a position flanking Philistia, and it looks as if the politics of Manasseh were inaugurated by Hezekiah at the end of his rule; and, that the growth of Jerusalem in the seventh century (up to 50-60 ha) was more due to Assyrian interests and 'aid in development' than to untraceable fugitives from the North.[24]

After what had happened to the Shephelah, nobody involved wanted to see the Assyrians back again; the *pax Assyriaca* had become the uneasy peace of a graveyard, and would remain so for the next 20 years. The Assyrian–Egyptian conflict ended in stalemate, not to be settled until 671. As for Sennacherib, after his narrow escape at/from Eltekeh he had no intention of returning to southern Canaan either.[25] In 700 the Assyrians fought some indecisive police actions in southern Babylonia, probably with local garrisons. It was not until 697 that the king's army was back in the field again.

23. Sennacherib (III 79-81) is quite clear about the Egyptians coming to the rescue of Ekron, not Hezekiah.

24. Who would in any case have had to find employment at Jerusalem in order to stay there. Archaeology strongly argues against associating Isa. 1.7-9 with 701 and its aftermath.

25. He could well have published a bulletin stating 'The Health of His Majesty has never been better'; as a result of his 701 campaign, the Assyrian standing army needed 20,000 recruits (Rassam-Cylinder of 700 BCE, line 59; Frahm, *Einleitung*, pp. 55, 59).

ON THE PROBLEMS OF RECONSTRUCTING PRE-HELLENISTIC ISRAELITE (PALESTINIAN) HISTORY*

Niels Peter Lemche

The so-called 'historical-critical' school that created a universe of its own, dubbed 'ancient Israel', has dominated the last two hundred years of biblical studies. The texts of the Old Testament—in some circles called 'the Hebrew Bible'—were believed to refer to an 'ancient Israel' thought to be a historical reality. Already at an early stage of the development of historical-critical methodology scholars accepted that the Old Testament was not simply a history book—or textbook—that told the truth and nothing but the truth about ancient Israel. In accordance with developments within the field of general history this was not considered an insurmountable problem to biblical scholars. Historians began in the early nineteenth century to develop methods of source criticism that enabled them—or so they believed —to make a distinction between real information and secondary expansion. In the words of the leading historian of this period, Johann Gustav Droysen (1808–84), the historian had to distinguish between 'Bericht', that is story or interpretation, and 'Überreste', that is, what is left of historical information. In every part of the historical narrative in the Old Testament, it would, according to this view, be possible to make a distinction between information that originates in the past, and additions and commentaries to this information from a later period.[1]

Let me quote as an example of such a source analysis the story about Sennacherib's attack on Jerusalem in 701 BCE:

> Now in the fourteenth year of king Hezekiah did Sennacherib king of Assyria come up against all the fenced cities of Judah, and took them. And Hezekiah king of Judah sent to the king of Assyria to Lachish, saying, I

* Originally published in *Journal of Hebrew Scriptures* 3/1 (2000); available at http://purl.org/jhs and http://www.jhsonline.org
1. More about this in my *The Israelites in History and Tradition* (Library of Ancient Israel; Louisville, KY: Westminster/John Knox, 1998), pp. 1-21, 22-34.

have offended; return from me: that which you puttest on me will I bear. And the king of Assyria appointed unto Hezekiah king of Judah three hundred talents of silver and thirty talents of gold. And Hezekiah gave *him* all the silver that was found in the house of the LORD, and in the treasures of the king's house. At that time did Hezekiah cut off *the gold from* the doors of the temple of the LORD, and *from* the pillars which Hezekiah king of Judah had overlaid, and gave it to the king of Assyria (2 Kgs. 18.13-16; KJV).

This story that can be found in 2 Kgs 18–19 opens with notes about King Hezekiah's reign, how he behaved well in the eyes of the Lord and how he revolted against the Assyrians and smote the Philistines. The narrative about King Hezekiah is broken off by a short interlude explaining how King Shalmanasser of Assyria besieged and conquered the city of Samaria —an event already mentioned in the preceding chapter. After this break, the narrative continues with a description of Sennacherib's attack on Hezekiah's fortified cities. While the Assyrian king rests at Lachish, King Hezekiah gives in and surrenders to the Assyrians and pays a handsome tribute to mollify his overlord, the king of Assur. After this tribute has been paid, the Assyrian king sends his general to Jerusalem. There is the famous Rabshakeh incident, when the Assyrian officer stands in front of the gates of Jerusalem and delivers a harsh speech that intends to scare the inhabitants of Jerusalem and its king that they may surrender to the Assyrians. Hezekiah in great distress turns to the prophet Isaiah who promises the assistance of God against the Assyrians. The Assyrian general returns to his master now with his army at Libnah in order to move against an Egyptian army trying to outflank the Assyrian army. Rabshakeh sends a letter to Hezekiah repeating many of the threats against Judah already delivered in his speech in front of Jerusalem. When he receives this letter, Hezekiah approaches the Lord in order that he might help him against the Assyrian army. As a result the avenging angel of the Lord kills 185,000 Assyrian soldiers during the night, whereupon Sennacherib returns to Assyria in dismay, only to be murdered some time later.

Already a casual reading of these chapters makes it certain that the narrative does not constitute a homogenous description of the events of the fateful year of 701 BCE. The Rabshakeh incident is clearly superfluous as Hezekiah had already surrendered and paid his tribute to the king of Assyria, before Rabshakeh moved to Jerusalem in order to deliver his speech. There was no reason for the Assyrian king not to return home since he already achieved his goal, to stop the rebellion in southwestern Palestine. In the text, however, a letter from Rabshakeh to Hezekiah that includes the same themes as his speech provokes the intervention of Isaiah and leads to God destroying the Assyrian army. It is as if the author of this narrative prefers to present his scenes in pairs. However, from the modern historian's point of view, it should be possible in 2 Kgs 18–19 to distinguish between—in Droysen's words—*Bericht* and *Überreste*. Such a historian would primarily look for historical information in the short description of Sennacherib's campaign at the beginning of the narrative in 2 Kgs 18–19 rather than in the literarily elaborated passages which follow. Most historians would say that after the paying of Hezekiah's tribute, the remaining part is a *Bericht*, i.e. a reflection from a later date of the events of 701 BCE.

Now we actually possess another version of this campaign of Sennacherib, in Sennacherib's royal annalistic report of the campaign.[2] In Sennacherib's version, the campaign opens with a diversion to Phoenicia, to Sidon, in order to clear any obstacles that may arise behind the frontline and to safeguard the route of retreat. The Sidonian king flees before the Assyrians. The main aim of the campaign is, however, to settle matters in Palestine where the Judaean Hezekiah (Sennacherib's wording) has interfered with loyal Assyrian vassals including Padi, the king of Ekron, who is kept as a prisoner by Hezekiah. Hezekiah and his allies had also approached the king of Egypt and an Egyptian army had already arrived and had prepared for a battle at Elteqeh. The Egyptian army was no match for the Assyrians and Sennacherib could, after having dismissed the threat from Egypt, continue to settle matters along the coast of Palestine. Here he conquers the cities of Elteqeh and Timnah and attacks and occupies Ekron. Hezekiah is evidently (Sennacherib does not say how it happened but we may guess why) persuaded to set Padi of Ekron free and return him to his city, where he is reinstalled as an Assyrian vassal. Hezekiah does not yield any further but Sennacherib devastates his country, destroys 46 fortified cities and shuts Hezekiah in his city of Jerusalem, like a bird in a cage. The devastated parts of Hezekiah's kingdom are handed over to the Philistine cities. Hezekiah gives up the hope of fighting the Assyrians and pays a heavy tribute that is delivered by his envoys to the Assyrian king in Nineveh.

There can be no doubt that the biblical narrative and Sennacherib's annalistic report are two reflections of the campaign of Sennacherib that ended when Hezekiah gave in and paid the tribute which the Assyrians demanded including his daughters. There are many differences between

2.   *ANET* 3, pp. 287-88.

the biblical and the Assyrian version, but they also agree on several important points. Hezekiah rebelled against the Assyrians. Sennacherib attacked his country and destroyed many cities. At the end Hezekiah paid a tribute, but Jerusalem remained in his hand unharmed. The astonishing fact claimed by 2 Kings that the Assyrians did not conquer Jerusalem is obviously a historical fact. Otherwise the differences have mostly to do with chronological details and numbers such as when and where did Hezekiah send his tribute and how big was this tribute. These are minor points. Basically the two accounts are in agreement.

When these two versions are compared it is obvious that the Rabshakeh incident may have been invented by the author of 2 Kings in order to create the impression that Sennacherib did not conquer Jerusalem because the holy city was saved by its God.[3] Rabshakeh's actions follow the payment of the tribute. The Assyrians had already closed the case of the rebellion. Although this section includes one piece of historical information: the appearance of an Egyptian army in Palestine, it is a safe guess to conclude that there is nothing historical about the Rabshakeh incident. The biblical narrative that follows the payment of the tribute is invented history or simply fiction.

This example may count as an easy one. Other examples are less obvious. Among them, we may mention the story about the campaign of the kings of Israel and Judah against King Mesha of Moab in 2 Kgs 3. The story opens with a note saying that Mesha paid a heavy tribute to Israel but also that he had revolted against his master after the death of Ahab. The king of Israel accordingly invited his colleague in Jerusalem to join him in a war party against Moab. The party also included the King of Edom. The campaign opens with a seven day-long march but it is halted because of lack of water. The kings turn to the prophet for help, and on the prophet's instructions rites are performed and water made available by a miracle. The prophet also delivers an oracle predicting the fall of all of Moab. The following battle between the Israelites and Moabites ends in disaster for the Moabite army, and Mesha retreats to his city of Kir-hareseth. After an unsuccessful breakout from Kir-hareseth, Mesha sacrifices his son on the wall of his city, 'and there was great indignation against Israel' (KJV) or

3.   For a different look on the Rabshakeh incident as historical cf. among others Brevard S. Childs, *Isaiah and the Assyrian Crisis* (SBTSS, 3; London: SCM Press, 1967), pp. 76-93, and more recently Mordechai Cogan and Hayim Tadmor, *II Kings: A New Translation with Introduction and Commentary* (AB, 11; Garden City, NY: Doubleday, 1988), pp. 240-44.

better 'there was such great consternation among the Israelites' (REB) that the Israelites lifted the siege and returned home.

Now is this a historical report? The central part of the story has to do with the water miracle and the Moabite misinterpretation of it that brings disaster upon their heads. Miracles are certainly out of focus in a historical report of events that really happened, and very impractical for the historical analysis. It is safe to say—from a historian's point of view—that it never happened. Does it mean that this narrative in 2 Kgs 3 is totally devoid of historical information? Hardly, because we are in possession of not only one but also two inscriptions carrying the name of Mesha, king of Moab. One of them is only a short fragment, the second probably the most important royal inscription from the southern Levant ever found.[4]

Also Mesha has a story to tell. In his version, he describes how Omri oppressed Moab for forty years in all of his time and the half of his son's time. Mesha, however, attacked Israel and destroyed it forever. Most of the inscription is devoted to a description of the cities retaken—in Mesha's words—from Israel and the rearrangement prepared for them by Mesha, all of this made possible by Kemosh, the god of Moab.

If we compare the biblical story in 2 Kgs 3 with the inscription of Mesha of Moab, there may be a slight degree of communality between them. Both texts explain how Mesha revolted against Israel and reckon Mesha to be king of Moab. Otherwise it is a hopeless affair to try to unite the information in the biblical text with the information provided by Mesha himself. Although the biblical text includes maybe one or two pieces of information that are historical, it has nothing to do with Mesha's text. Mesha has a totally different story to tell. Mesha's story may constitute a historical report, but it is far from certain. Maybe it is just as much literature as the version in 2 Kgs 3. Mesha is not telling the truth and nothing but the truth. It is clear that his inscription is also to a large degree fictional and propagandistic and includes such elements from popular literature as the proverbial period of oppression of forty years. Mesha somehow makes a show of not knowing the name of any king of Israel

---

4. Cf. John C.L. Gibson, *Textbook of Syrian Semitic Inscriptions*. I. *Hebrew and Moabite Inscriptions* (Oxford: Clarendon Press, 1971), pp. 71-84. For an extensive analysis of the main text, cf. Andrew Dearman (ed.), *Studies in the Mesha Inscription and Moab* (ASOR/SBL Archaeology and Biblical Studies, 2; Atlanta: Scholars Press, 1989). Although the second inscription from Kerak is broken at the beginning where we find Mesha's name, the name of his father (*kmšyt*) has been so well preserved that it is beyond doubt that this is a second inscription by Mesha king of Moab.

except Omri. He 'forgets' to mention Omri's successor, Ahab—after all, a very important king in his time and who is mentioned by the Assyrians —and therefore makes Omri the oppressor of Moab also in his son's time.

By introducing these two texts, 2 Kgs 3 and the Moabite royal inscription of Mesha, we have penetrated further into the problem of studying the history of ancient Israel. There are some general similarities between Mesha's version and the biblical one. Mesha was really the king of Moab and Moab was, before Mesha's revolt, a vassal of Israel. Furthermore, Israel was not able to subdue Moab again. Apart from this, no extra-biblical evidence can substantiate the plot of the narrative in 2 Kgs 3. The text might well be an invented and fictional piece of work that only includes a name and a few other things to act as its historical credentials. We cannot harmonize the information. Not even the chronology fits. According to 2 Kgs 3, Mesha revolts after the death of Ahab, while Mesha speaks about Israelite oppression that lasted for half the reign of Omri's son who only appears without a name in the Moabite text. Although the Mesha inscription is usually dated to c. 850 BCE, the vagueness of the information included here does not preclude that it could be later than that date. The argument in favor of such a position is the mentioning of Omri who oppressed Moab in the time of his son. This indicates that in this text Omri may not be Omri the king of Israel but the eponymous king of *Bet Omri*, the 'house of Omri', which in Assyrian documents of the ninth and eighth century BCE is the usual name of the state otherwise known as Israel.[5] Omri and Israel in the Mesha inscription are synonymous.

To conclude: The Mesha inscription does not make 2 Kgs 3 a reliable historical source, nor changes its basic genre. 2 Kgs 3 remains as miraculous and fictional as ever although it mentions a historical king of Moab and refers to a general political situation that may have some historical nucleus.

It is nevertheless often assumed that 2 Kgs 3 has a historical nucleus that can be reconstructed by modern historians. Such historians may be of the conviction that a distinction can be made also in this text between *Bericht* and *Überreste*. This is a very imprudent position to take. The only piece of *Überreste* in this chapter is a name and some general knowledge of the status of Moab in Mesha's time. It is hardly enough to make a narrative historical. This should not surprise us. Ancient history writing is very different from modern historical reconstruction. When reconstructing the

---

5.   For a recent review of this evidence, cf. my *The Israelites in History and Tradition*, pp. 51-55.

past, the modern historian must reject many sorts of information found in an ancient source. To illustrate my point, I only have to quote from Danish 'national' history as told by Saxo Grammaticus who includes a long tale about the Viking king Regner Lodbrog, who killed a dragon to find a wife.[6] All kinds of legendary material are included in Saxo's version of Regner's life. Such tales can easily be dismissed when we try to write a history of Denmark's beginnings. However, the name of Regner is historical, as this Viking king appears in a Frankish chronicle from the ninth century CE as a contemporary of the writer of this chronicle.[7] It is, alas, hardly evident that this historical Regner ever killed a dragon.

In biblical studies the problem is that it is almost impossible to decide which part of a biblical narrative belongs to the genre of *Bericht*, and which part includes *Überreste* if we have no other information than that which is included in the biblical texts. If we do not possess external evidence, it is the individual scholar who decides what is history and what fiction, and this scholar will only have his or her common sense as a guideline. This is clearly a logical problem that has to do with historical-critical studies at large.

Historical-critical biblical scholarship operates within a hermeneutical circle that is really a logical circle. The source of information is more often than not the biblical text that stands alone. The conversation goes between the scholar who studies the text and the text itself. The scholar presents a theory that is based on the text and the text confirms the theory. It is an amazing fact that in biblical studies this has worked for almost 200 years, since the early days of modern scholarship at the beginning of the nineteenth century. Although every historical-critical scholar explains that there is a problem, it has to a large degree been ignored when it comes to history writing. The standard procedure is—to quote Bernd Jørg Diebner—that although we cannot prove it, it is a fact! We cannot prove that Moses ever existed but as we cannot explain the development of Israelite monotheism without a Moses, he must have existed. Otherwise we would have to invent him…disregarding the possibility that ancient writers did exactly that! When in a bad mood, one may be willing to say that historical-critical

---

6.   Saxo, a monk in the service of the bishop Absalon, the founder of Copenhagen, wrote his *Res gestae danorum* towards the end of the 12th century CE.

7.   The reference dates to 845 CE when Regner's army of Normans at the Seine was destroyed by a plague. He may also be mentioned in other contemporary sources as one of the main figures in the Danish process of conquering England in the second half of the 9th century CE.

scholarship is nothing but a bluff. The procedure—the hermeneutical circle—is from a scientific point of view false, and a false procedure in science will automatically tell you that the results obtained by this method are false and can be discarded without further ado. The conclusion that historical-critical scholarship is based on a false methodology and leads to false conclusions simply means that we can disregard 200 years of biblical scholarship and commit it to the dustbin. It is hardly worth the paper on which it is printed.

It is no excuse to say that this is the only way we may obtain historical information from the Bible. That is only a bad excuse for laziness. It has also to do with greediness: scholars want to say more than they can possibly do. Since the Bible has to do with religion and most scholars have been and still are religious people, there has been a constant pressure on biblical scholars to produce results that concur with results obtained in other fields such as general history. And biblical scholars have readily lived up to such expectations. In my dissertation on 'Early Israel' (1985) I presented a number of maxims, the first of which said that the most important thing is to acknowledge your ignorance. The second added that when you know the extent of your ignorance, you also have an idea about what you really know.[8] These maxims form a kind of Procrustes' bed on which to place all kinds of biblical studies, because the demand is that we start our investigation by accepting that we know almost nothing about the past and that we should begin with the little we know.

Now, some people might object, is it really true that we know so little about ancient Israel that we cannot reconstruct the history and religion of this society? The truth is that from the time that precedes the introduction of the so-called 'Hebrew Monarchy' we only possess one external source mentioning Israel. This Israel is included among a host of vanquished foes placed in Palestine in an Egyptian inscription dating to the time of Pharaoh Merenptah c. 1210 BCE.[9] It is likely that this inscription refers to Israel as a population group of some kind. Apart from this, nothing is known about the circumstances referred to in this inscription, which uses a lot of traditional language and might have less to say about historical events in Palestine at the end of the thirteenth century BCE than often believed.

There is a gap of more than 300 years from the Merenptah inscription to the next references to Israel. One of these has already been mentioned,

8.　*Early Israel: Anthropological and Historical Studies on the Israelite Society before the Monarchy* (VTSup, 37; Leiden: E.J. Brill, 1985), p. 414.

9.　*ANET*[3], pp. 376-78.

namely the Mesha-inscription from Moab. A second inscription contains
an Assyrian reference to a battle in 853 BCE in which Ahab of Sirla'a—it
is definitely a corrupted form of Israel—participated.[10] The third one mentions an anonymous king of Israel who is supposed to have been killed by
the author of the recently found so-called 'Bet David' inscription from Tel
Dan in northern Palestine.[11] From the eighth century BCE a small number
of Assyrian texts refers to Israel either as 'the house of Omri' or simply as
Samaria, i.e. the capital of the kingdom of Israel in northern Palestine until
722 BCE. Most of these inscriptions include rather short references to Israel,
a few can directly be related to information contained in the Old Testament such as Tiglatpileser III's regulations in northern Palestine a few years
before the fall of Samaria.[12]

This Israel of the inscriptions from the 1st millennium BCE is, however,
not ancient Israel but the state of Israel that existed between c. 900 BCE
and 722 BCE. In the Old Testament this state appears as one of the two
successor states to David's and Solomon's empire.

The second successor-state is referred to as Judah. Not before the eighth
century do Assyrian inscriptions refer to this Judah. Again most of the
texts include rather limited information, the most important being without
doubt the already mentioned report of Sennacherib's campaign to Palestine. After the fall of Nineveh a few Babylonian inscriptions include references to Judah or to events that can be related to the fate of Judah in the
sixth century BCE, the most important being the Neo-Babylonian Chronicle
that includes a report of the Babylonian conquest of Jerusalem in 597
BCE.[13]

The ancient Near Eastern inscriptions that refer to Israel and Judah are
limited in number but are nevertheless important evidence. They tell us
that the names of Israel and Judah are not invented—fictitious—names,
but refer to political structures that really existed. They also mention a
selection of kings otherwise known from the Old Testament. They show
that so far as we can control the evidence the succession of these kings as
well as the synchronisms that can be established between the kings of

10. *ANET*[3], p. 279.
11. Avraham Biran and Joseph Naveh, 'An Aramaic Stele Fragment from Tel
Dan,' *IEJ* 43 (1993), pp. 81-98 and 'The Tel Dan Inscription: A New Fragment,' *IEJ*
45 (1995), pp. 1-18. As to this writer's present position on the inscription, cf. his *The
Israelites in History and Tradition*, pp. 38-43.
12. *ANET*[3], pp. 282-84; cf. 2 Kgs. 15.29-30.
13. *ANET*[3], pp. 563-64.

Israel and Judah and Assyrian and Babylonian kings are not totally misleading. Sennacherib really attacked Judah in the days of Hezekiah and Nebuchadnezzar really conquered Jerusalem and installed Zedekiah on the throne of Judah more than a century later.

To conclude this section, it is obvious that the history of Israel and Judah as told by biblical historians is not totally devoid of historical information. The people who wrote the historical narratives of the Old Testament did at least know some facts about Israelite and Judaean history. We might even say that there is a certain number of *Überreste*—i.e. historical remains—included in the texts of the Old Testament. There might even be a kind of coherency that binds this information together and creates a kind of chronological framework for the historical narrative.

All this is rather unproblematic. The problematic part is when we are confronted with the task of deciding what is *Überreste* and what *Bericht* when we read about events in ancient Israel that cannot be compared to external evidence. How do we solve this problem without ending in the famous hermeneutical circle already described?

One way would be to approach ancient near eastern historiography in general in order to perceive how it worked and how far it can be trusted. The first step would be to establish the genres of historiography in the Near East in antiquity. Here two genres dominate the field, on one hand the year-chronicle system that lists for every year its most important events in a kind of shorthand, and on the other, more extensive royal inscriptions such as the Assyrian royal annals claiming another Assyrian conquest of the world.

Sometimes the authors of 1 and 2 Kings refer to the chronicles of Israel or of Judah.[14] If we are to trust these notes as references to something that really existed (we must never forget that it was not uncommon in literature from ancient times to include fictitious references in order to create confidence), these chronicles would most likely be of the shorthand type. Such annals only included short references to past events. They would probably not have contained extensive narrative, not to say long reports. If we turn to the chronicles of Assyrian and Babylonian kings, it might be possible here to gain an impression of exactly what kind of information we should look after in order to reconstruct this source. Again, we should not forget that the biblical author might have invented the reference while at the same time writing in a chronistic style when it suited his purpose.[15]

14. E.g. 2 Kgs. 15.6-11, 21-26, 31-36.
15. Cf. on the possibility of information coming from royal Israelite and Judaean

When it comes to royal literature of the kind found, for example, in Assyrian inscriptions, it is much more difficult to establish the presence of such sources in the Old Testament. A large part of the Assyrian inscriptions contain war reports. Although it cannot be excluded that such literature also existed in Israel and Judah in the Iron Age, we cannot say for sure on the basis of the extant books of Kings that it did. It must be realized that as soon as we approach this genre, we move into literature, into the world of fiction and invention. This is certainly the case in many Assyrian inscriptions where the acts of the king are embellished—defeats hardly acknowledged. Such reports are always written with a purpose and are often composed to make an impression on the gods who were to approve the acts of the king in question. Some might call it propaganda!

Returning to the books of Kings, it is safe to say that although minor sections may have an annalistic background in royal chronicles, most of the literature there neither belongs to this genre nor to that of the royal inscriptions of the Assyrian and later Babylonian type. This is a natural consequence of the aim and scope of the books of Kings, which are not written in order to praise the institution of kingship in Israel and Judah or to establish an exalted position for their kings. On the contrary, the impression gained from reading these biblical books is the opposite, that a human kingdom represented a departure from the just rule of God and that its human exponents were hardly heroes of the Yahwistic faith. Only very few among the kings of Judah are praised for their piety—all of the kings of Israel are condemned. Royal laudatory inscriptions would simply be the wrong type of literature to quote and are hardly present among the narratives of 1 and 2 Kings. Rather than tracing non-existing historical events, we should study the *topoi* of the authors of the books of Kings. It would be the goal of such an investigation to find out whether some kind of a pattern can be found. Already several years ago scholars realized that the biblical books of 1 and 2 Chronicles are dominated by a series of stereotypical *topoi*—each of them having a special purpose, either to recommend a king loved by God or reject a godforsaken king.[16] The very character of the

archives, J.A. Montgomery, 'Archival Data in the Books of Kings', *JBL* 53 (1934), pp. 46-52. The question by Gösta W. Ahlström is, however, very relevant: 'But where have these archives been preserved so that the material could be used by later scribes or historiographers?' See *The History of Ancient Palestine from the Palaeolithic Period to Alexander's Conquest* (ed. D. Edelman; JSOTSup, 146; Sheffield: Sheffield Academic Press, 1993), p. 661 n. 9.

16. Cf. the interesting study by Peter Welten, *Geschichte und Geschichtsdarstellung*

narrative in 1 and 2 Kings speaks against extensive use of royal inscriptions as the base of this narrative. The authors of Kings used some extant annalistic information but only selected what suited their purpose. Their selection was dominated by the wish to create a generally negative impression of the period of the Hebrew kingdom.

When a modern author writes historical fiction, for example books like Robert Graves's *I Claudius*, we do not expect such a writer to be faithful to history. We allow this author the liberty to reformulate history in such a way that it supports the author's intention to make history conform to his intended goal. Although we may be in possession of the interpretation of the past also by professional historians, we can enjoy and appreciate historical fiction. Now, this is quite extraordinary and contrary to the belief of many scholars. Also people of the modern age can be more interested in literature than in historical facts. Hollywood would a long time ago have gone bankrupt without this human ability to disregard historical facts.

If we—having in a scientific way studied history for 200 years—do not always think that historical exactitude is a virtue that cannot be counterbalanced by morally acceptable fiction literature, what about people of ancient times who never shared our sense of history? Would they have paid attention to the historical correctness of a narrative about the past or would they have placed more emphasis on its aesthetical and probably moral values? The answer is provided not by ancient Near Eastern literature—we know very little about the reception of this literature among ordinary people— but by the discussion among classical intellectuals about the value of history. Here Cicero's famous characterization of history as the 'teacher of life' is important, as Cicero on the basis of Hellenistic philosophy regards history not as a literary genre dealing with the past but as a genre that uses the past to educate the present and future generations.[17]

We should not limit our interest in, say, 1 and 2 Kings in order to find historical information. Such information may only be present in short notes. We should pay attention to the purpose of this literature, because it is a safe guess to assume that the literature was composed to impress the present, and not to save recollections from the past for its own sake. It is a long story that exceeds the limits of one short article.[18] However, it is my

in den Chronikbüchern (WMANT, 42; Neukirchen–Vluyn: Neukirchener Verlag, 1973).

17. Cicero, *De oratore*, 2.9.36.

18. Cf. also my forthcoming article, 'Good and Bad in History. The Purpose of historiography', in Steven McKenzie and Thomas Römer (eds.), *Rethinking the Founda-*

thesis that the authors of ancient literature of the kind found in the Old Testament did not care much about the historical exactitude of their description of the past. The past was not very interesting except for the examples of good and bad behaviour it provided for the present and future. The past was interesting because it explained the present—even sometimes made present arrangements seem legitimate or natural. Otherwise let the dead bury the dead!

This is one side of the coin. The other has to do with the claim that we should not expect ancient historical narrative to be precise about the past or even related to it except in a superficial way. How can I prove my case? The easy solution to this problem is to say that it is sometimes possible to point at passages where the authors of Kings directly say that they are not interested in history. The already mentioned references to the chronicles of the kings of Israel and Judah actually tell us this. Thus king Omri is dismissed in a few verses in 1 Kgs 16. We are informed that he assumed power by a *coup d'état*, and that he ruled Israel for twelve years and built Samaria. After this, focus changes and we hear about his sins against Yahweh. The author of 1 Kgs 16, however, knows that Omri was a great king but says, 'Go and look for yourself in the chronicles of the kings of Israel!' (1 Kgs 16.27). The biblical historiographer has no intention of providing his reader with an exact report of Omri's reign. Although he accepts that Omri was a great king—after all, after his death his kingdom carried his name for more than a hundred years—this is from the perspective of the ancient history writer absolutely immaterial. Thus this historiographer does not deny Omri's greatness; he silences it.

A more complicated way to solve the problem presented here will be to establish whether or not the history of ancient Israel as told by biblical writers is exact in any comprehensive way. I mean, this history can be split into several succeeding periods, the period of the patriarchs, the time of the exodus, the Israelites travelling in the desert for forty years, the conquest of Canaan, the heroic exploits of the hero-judges of Israel, the period of national greatness under David and Solomon, impending disaster under the kings of Israel and Judah, and so on. Has this anything to do with the real past of this geographical region otherwise known as the southern Levant or Palestine?

I have no intention of reviewing this history in any detail in this place. I

tions. Historiography in the Ancient World and in the Bible: Essays in Honor of John Van Seters (BZAW, 294; Berlin: W. de Gruyter, 2000), pp. 127-40.

have already presented such reviews in several publications.[19] Other scholars have contributed. The history of Israel as told by the Old Testament begins with the patriarchal age. It continues with the sojourn in Egypt followed by the Exodus and the wanderings in the desert. Then follows in succession the conquest of Canaan, the period of the Judges, the empire of David and Solomon, the era of the Hebrew kings, the exile, and the Persian period. This history officially ends with Ezra's promulgation of the *Torah*, the Law of Moses, in front of the assembled inhabitants of Jerusalem and Judah.

1999 represents the silver anniversary of the final settlement—represented by the contributions by Thomas L. Thompson and John Van Seters —with the idea that there ever was a patriarchal period.[20] This is based on family stories, sagas and legends about the past, and has nothing to do with history. The idea once formulated by Albrecht Alt that there was a special patriarchal religion based on the belief in *der Gott der Väter*, 'the God of the fathers', is simply nonsense as Alt based his argument on Nabataean evidence from the second century BCE through the second century CE.[21]

The exodus has a long time ago passed from history into fiction. It never happened. Neither did the conquest ever happen. Several biblical scholars including myself have made this clear. From an historical point of view, the Israelites could not have conquered Canaan by destroying Canaanite forces, for the simple reason that the Egyptians still ruled Canaan when Joshua is supposed to have arrived, that is shortly before 1200 BCE.[22] Secondly, there is no trace of foreign immigration, and thirdly, even the biblical account about the conquest is contradictory (compare Joshua to Judg. 1).

19. For convenience, *Ancient Israel: A New History of Israelite Society* (The Biblical Seminar, 5; Sheffield: JSOT Press, 1988) (which is after all not so new anymore).

20. Cf. Thomas L. Thompson, *The Historicity of the Patriarchal Narratives: The Quest for the Historical Abraham* (BZAW, 133; Berlin: W. de Gruyter, 1974), and John Van Seters, *Abraham in History and Tradition* (New Haven: Yale, 1975).

21. Albrecht Alt, *Der Gott der Väter. Ein Beitrag zur Vorgeschichte der israelitischen Religion* (BWANT, 48; Stuttgart: W. Kohlhammer, 1929; ET [R.A. Wilson] 'The God of the Fathers', in Albrecht Alt, *Essays on Old Testament History and Religion* [The Biblical Seminar: Sheffield: JSOT Press, 1989], pp. 1-77).

22. For a recent evaluation of the duration of the Egyptian empire in Asia, cf. Donald B. Redford, *Egypt, Canaan, and Israel in Ancient Times* (Princeton, NJ: Princeton University Press, 1992), pp. 283-97. Redford dates the Egyptian withdrawal to c. 1150 BCE.

In my original monograph on the period of the judges that appeared almost thirty years ago, I argued that the narratives in Judges about the heroic exploits of the Israelite judges were coloured by later experience.[23] They were also dominated by the wish, in a paradigmatic meaning, to demonstrate how Israel should fight its enemies, the Canaanites, the Moabites, Ammonites, Philistines, Aramaeans etc. These narratives do not allow us to reconstruct the history of the period between the (non-existing) conquest and the (likewise non-existing) empire of David and Solomon. The stories about the judges of Israel belong among the genre of heroic tales that most civilizations include among their memories of the past.

The empire of David and Solomon believed to have existed in the tenth century BCE is evidently based on a fictional representation of the past. Many things speak in favour of this conclusion. One of them has to do with the status of Jerusalem in the tenth century BCE when Jerusalem was at most a village or a small town.[24]

We have already discussed the period of the Hebrew kings. Although the two kingdoms of Israel and Judah are historical facts, we are in possession of very little in the way of solid knowledge about them. Furthermore, when reviewing the evidence we have in the Old Testament and in other sources, it is evident that the Old Testament has totally distorted our view of ancient Palestinian history. This was far more complicated and included many more actors than just these two kingdoms. Thus the Old Testament never explains why and how this territory got the name of Palestine ('the land of the Philistines'). Foreigners including Assyrian authors of royal annals and Herodotus knew the name of Palestine. Herodotus simply states

23. *Israel i dommertiden: En oversigt over diskussionen om Martin Noths 'Das System der zwölf Stämme Israels'* (Tekst og Tolkning, 4; Copehagen: C.E.G. Gad, 1972), pp. 86-87.

24. I have no intention in this place to go into a detailed discussion about the historicity or non-historicity of David and Solomon. The idea of an united monarchy of Israel/Judah died as terminology changed. Now, it is preferable to see the period from c. 1250 to c. 900 as one long intermediary period, a 'transitionary period', and the way to approach this period has been demonstrated by e.g. Israel Finkelstein, 'The Emergence of Israel: A Phase in the Cyclic History of Canaan in the Third and Second Millennia BCE', in Israel Finkelstein and Nadav Na'aman (eds.), *From Nomadism to Monarchy: Archaeological and Historical Aspects of Early Israel* (Jerusalem: Israel Exploration Society, 1994), pp. 150-78, and Shlomo Bunimowitz, 'Socio-Political Transformations in the Central Hill Country in the Late Bronze-Iron I Transition', in Finkelstein and Na'aman (eds.) *From Nomadism to Monarchy*, pp. 179-203.

that Palestine is the part of Syria that is situated between Lebanon and Egypt.[25]

There is hardly time to discuss the historicity of the exile, which might not have been as important as described by the Old Testament. Recent investigations have shown that the 'land of Israel' was not deserted in the time of the exile and that it only affected very few among the population of Palestine. There was no 'empty land' as postulated by the biblical books of Chronicles and other biblical literature.[26]

The Persian period is, finally, a dark spot on the historical map of Palestine. We know almost nothing about this period. Ezra, the great hero of postexilic Judaism, is probably a late invention (by Pharisaic authors?), probably 200 years old when he arrived (his father was killed by Nebuchadnezzar's general, Nebuzaradan, in 587 BCE—according to the biblical evidence).[27]

Although this review is in some ways 'reductionist', it is nevertheless very much to the point. It is based on a review of all kinds of evidence, not least the results of extensive archaeological excavations in Palestine that have lasted for more than a hundred years. I need not say that archaeology is not an exact science like mathematics and never will be. Any result obtained by an archaeologist will include a number of hypotheses made by this archaeologist based on the material he or she has found. Furthermore the basis on which the archaeologist founded his or her theories can never be revisited. All excavations include—in Kathleen Kenyon's words—destruction. The archaeologist destroys the evidence when it is excavated. The original archaeological situation can never be re-established.

25. Cf. Herodotus, *The Histories*, 1.105; 2.104; 3.5.91; 4.39; 7.89.

26. Cf. Hans M. Barstad, *The Myth of the Empty Land: A Study in the History and Archaeology of Judah during the 'Exilic' Period* (Oslo: Scandinavian University Press, 1996). See, however, also Ehud Ben Zvi, 'Inclusion in and Exclusion from Israel as Conveyed by the Use of the Term "Israel" in Post-Monarchic Biblical Texts,' in Steven W. Holloway and Lowell K. Handy (eds.), *The Pitcher is Broken. Memorial Essays for Gösta W. Ahlström* (JSOTSup, 190; Sheffield: Sheffield Academic Press, 1995), pp. 95-149, and the discussion in Lester L. Grabbe (ed.), *Leading Captivity Captive. The 'Exile' as History and Ideology* (JSOTSup, 278; Sheffield: Sheffield Academic Press, 1998).

27. Cf. Ezra's pedigree, Ezra 7.1: Ezra, son of Seraiah, son of Azariah, son of Hilkiah, son of Shallum, etc. On Seraiah's death, cf. 2 Kgs. 25.18. Hilkiah was high priest in the days of Josiah, 2 Kgs. 22.4. Of course many scholars will maintain that the genealogy is either false or telescoped.

However, archaeologists continually formulate general hypotheses about the development of this geographic area in ancient times that speak against the evidence of a late-written source such as the Old Testament (which according to me and the members of my school hardly predates the Graeco-Roman Period). It is therefore a safe guess to argue that this late source—although written—does not constitute a historical source. It is not—to recall Droysen—*Überreste*, it is definitely *Bericht*, a tale about the past.

The development in Palestine between, say 1250 and 900 BCE is an example of this. Archaeology as well as other non-biblical information about ancient Palestine will tell us that Palestine in the late Bronze Age (roughly the second half of the second millennium BCE) was an Egyptian province ruled by local princes who looked upon themselves as faithful vassals of their patron, the Pharaoh. For most of the time, Palestine was left alone. Only occasionally did the Egyptians interfere directly with the mundane problems of Palestine. The everlasting internecine war-games played by the local chieftains who saw themselves as 'kings' (the Egyptian had other ideas about their importance and called them *hazanu*; i.e. 'mayors') had a devastating effect on the well-being of the country. It was not before the so-called 'Ramesside restoration' of the Egyptian presence in Western Asia after the debacle that ended the 18th dynasty, that matters changed and the Egyptian presence became more dominating. Some could say that Ramesses II created a kind of 'Pax Egyptiaca' in Palestine. Now, the Egyptian masters limited the devastating effects of the 'free-for-all' politics of the local Palestinian chieftains. The Egyptians created a situation of relative peace in the country that might have had a positive demographic effect as people moved from the cities to the countryside to live closer to their fields. The late thirteenth, the twelfth and the early eleventh centuries BCE were witnessing the foundations of scores if not hundreds of insignificant and unprotected village settlements, not least in the mountains of Palestine. Life must have become pretty safe. From at least the eleventh century BCE, a certain reduction of the number of villages took place. This demographic chance was counterbalanced by the rise of certain settlements to the status of sometimes heavily fortified townships. Tel Beersheva with its circular walls and planned layout is a typical example of such a settlement that may look more like a mediaeval fortress than a proper city or town.

This stage may have occurred as a consequence of an at least partial Egyptian withdrawal from Palestine (although it now seems likely that at least in Bet She'an an Egyptian garrison was present as late as the beginning of the tenth century BCE[28]). Life became more dangerous and the socio-political system of the past (local patrons fighting other local patrons) emerged again. I have once described this development as a move from one patronage society to another patronage society, from an old political system to a new system that was an exact copy of the former system.[29] This period lasted until probably the middle of the ninth century when some of the local chieftains were able to create large political structures that exceeded the boundaries of those present in the Late Bronze Age, a time when most Palestinian political systems were extremely small. Such large political structures might have existed before the Iron Age, for example in the Early Bronze Age (third millennium). Here remains of considerable cities are found. The Middle Bronze Age might be another period that included comprehensive political organizations although we know very little about the exact political structure of the Palestinian society before the Late Bronze Age.

The biblical picture of ancient Israel does not fit in but is contrary to any image of ancient Palestinian society that can be established on the basis of ancient sources from Palestine or referring to Palestine. There is no way this image in the Bible can be reconciled with the historical past of the region. And if this is the case, we should give up the hope that we can reconstruct pre-Hellenistic history on the basis of the Old Testament. It is simply an invented history with only a few referents to things that really happened or existed. From an historian's point of view, ancient Israel is a monstrous creature. It is something sprung out of the fantasy of biblical historiographers and their modern paraphrasers, that is, the historical-critical scholars of the last two hundred years.

28. Cf. the short discussion by Patrick E. McGovern, 'Beth-Shean', *ABD* I, pp. 694-95. The LBA phase of occupation continued to about 1000 BCE. Only after that date a new stratum reveals different layouts and culture. The city was hardly Philistine (the author of 1 Sam. 31 got it totally wrong); only a single piece of Philistine pottery has been found at the tell (McGovern, same place).

29. 'From Patronage Society to Patronage Society', in Volkmar Fritz and Philip R. Davies (eds.), *The Origins of the Ancient Israelite States* (JSOTSup, 228; Sheffield: Sheffield Academic Press, 1996), pp. 106-20.

SENNACHERIB'S CAMPAIGN OF 701 BCE: THE ASSYRIAN VIEW

Walter Mayer

Introduction[1]

In the year 701 BCE, Sennacherib (704–681), the king of Assyria, launched a campaign against Palestine. Although the campaign is important to military history, it is perhaps even more valuable as a lesson on the modern making of ancient history. Knowledge of this campaign is derived from two important yet conflicting sources: cuneiform texts called the Royal Annals of Assyria, which were written immediately after the event, and the Bible. Until recently, the biblical account has been the chief influence on modern historical reconstructions. These pages present the view from the opposite camp, Assyria. Before the discovery and translation of cuneiform texts in the mid-nineteenth century, our knowledge of the ancient Near East, unlike that of ancient Egypt and classical antiquity, relied exclusively on biblical writings and a handful of classical sources. Because cuneiform texts promised to elucidate biblical history, or so it first seemed, they excited great interest among Old Testamentarians. Theologians were in a position to apply their knowledge of Semitic languages to cuneiform translation and thereby established the foundations for the study of the older Semitic language of Akkadian in which Sennacherib's texts were written. The account of his campaign in the book of Kings was already widely accepted by the time the tablets and prisms were excavated, which was one reason the biblical version took precedence over the Assyrian version when the texts were analyzed.[2] Another reason was, of course, that the Bible was believed to have been divinely inspired and utterly without error. For the most part, then, early modern historians looked at this event

1. All Assyrian sources are presented in transcription and translation in the appendix. I am deeply indebted to Julia Assante for translating my German manuscript into English.
2. 2 Kgs 18.13–19.37; 2 Chron. 32.1-23; Isa. 36–37.

and ancient Mesopotamia in general through the eyes of its contemporary enemies, the peoples of ancient Israel.

The conflict between the two versions came into the open in 1852, when Henry Rawlinson, 'the father of Assyriology', published Sennacherib's account.[3] The campaign against Palestine did not resemble in the least that described in 2 Kgs 19.35. When his brother George Rawlinson, a well-established theologian, was preparing his manuscript on the history of ancient Mesopotamia, he asked Henry for clarification.[4] The answer he received was simple—the Assyrian account is distorted because Assyrians never admit defeat. This cut-and-dry explanation became the guiding force for all subsequent interpretation of Neo-Assyrian historical writings. Rawlinson's evaluation of Assyrian Royal Inscriptions as wholly unreliable became dogma, despite their consistency with mounting epigraphic material. Rather than exploring them for their historical worth, early modern historians viewed them as works blatantly in the service of royal propaganda and kingly self-glorification.[5]

Since H.C. Rawlinson's article, which events of 701 are the 'real' events continues to be a heated topic of debate. The literature is considerable, and it is therefore not possible to discuss all the reconstructions submitted. The present study returns to Sennacherib's inscriptions as primary sources and examines them in the light of military history.

The Sources

The fullest accounts of the campaign of 701 come from the Chicago and Taylor Prisms,[6] written in the years 689 and 691 respectively.[7] The Rassam Cylinder, dated to the year after the campaign,[8] inventories in more detail the tribute given to Sennacherib by Hezekiah, the defeated king of Judah. The cylinder's final section summarizes the spoils of Sennacherib's first

3.   H.C. Rawlinson 1852.
4.   G. Rawlinson 1864.
5.   For a critical discussion of the Annals, their development and their importance as historical sources see Mayer 1995: 37-60.
6.   See Appendices 1 and 2; cf. Frahm 1997: T 16.
7.   Cf. Millard 1994: 50, 88 and 94. The dating reads as follows:
Chicago VI: [84]ITU.ŠU.NUMUN.NA *li-mu* m.*Ga-ḫi-lu* [85]LÚ.EN.NAM URU.Ḫa-ta-rík-ka
Taylor VI: [74]*ina* ITU.ŠE.KIN.TAR UD.20.KAM *li-mu* m.EN-IGI.LÁ-*a-ni* [75]LÚ.EN.NAM URU.*Gar-ga-miš*
8.   [95]ITU.GUD.SI.SÁ *li-mu* m.*Mi-tu-nu* LÚ.GAR KUR URU.*I-sa-na*; cf. Millard 1994: 49 and 101.

three campaigns, the distribution of booty and the thousands of captives absorbed into his army.[9] The dates of the remaining texts discussed below cannot be established with certainty. Bull 4,[10] one of several Bull Inscriptions, was probably written after the sixth campaign. It defers to the Chicago and Taylor Prisms, although its description of Hezekiah's tribute is more generalized and the names of Sennacherib's Syrian vassals are omitted.

A fragment of the Letter to the God Assur (K 6205), no doubt written at the close of the third campaign, deserves special mention. In its complete form the letter would have contained the most comprehensive report of the campaign.[11] Despite scholarship's oft-voiced doubts, it seems clear that this fragment belongs to the letter-to-the-god genre[12] rather than to a 'Vorlage' for an annal report, as some have proposed. The fragment contains information uncharacteristically detailed for annal reports but consistent with such letters. For example, the text painstakingly portrays the fortress of Azekah and its siege, both of little significance in the overall historical scheme. Furthermore, it seems improbable that a 'Vorlage' would contain substantially more data than the finished report. Other scholars have attributed fragment K 6205 to Sargon II and his campaign of 711 against Ashdod, although Ashdod is not mentioned. During this time, Sargon was preparing for battle against Babylonia, so that the Ashdod rebellion was then of only minor importance. In fact, Hezekiah's acquiescence to Sargon in 720 was maintained with few interruptions until Sargon's death. The fragment, by contrast, describes Hezekiah and Judah as active, primary enemies worthy of an Assyrian king's full attention. Equally significantly, there are unmistakable orthographic and stylistic discrepancies between this fragment and comparable Sargonid texts. These factors, together with the fragment's findspot in Nineveh, Sennacherib's capital, strongly suggest that the text refers to Sennacherib's campaign rather than to Sargon's.[13]

The biblical reports seem to derive from two different traditions, the first represented in 2 Kgs 18.13-16; and the second in the Rabshakeh narration of 2 Kgs 18.17–19.36, Isa. 36-37 and 2 Chron. 32.1-23. The first, 2 Kgs 18.13-16, appears to have come from palace or temple archives. Its con-

9.   The Rassam Cylinder (Appendix 3) was never fully published.

10.   Appendix 8; cf. Frahm 1997: T 29.

11.   For the function of the Letters to the God and their significance to the annals see Mayer 1995: 57-60.

12.   See Appendix 11; cf. Frahm 1997: 229-32.

13.   *Contra* Galil 1992: 61-62.

tents agree with Assyrian accounts; even the specific amount of gold tribute paid is the same in both. The second tradition begins with the passage
relating the mission of Rabshakeh, the Assyrian high court official whom
Sennacherib commanded to force Jersualem's surrender. It anachronisti-
cally introduces the Ethiopian king Taharka (690–644),[14] and culminates
with the siege of Jerusalem in which 185,000 Assyrians are slaughtered
overnight. After this massacre, Sennacherib supposedly fled to Nineveh
only to meet his fate at the hands of his own sons. This second tradition,
which has prevailed in scholarship, finds no support whatsoever in Assyrian sources. It belongs to the body of postexilic legends that arose during
the time of rivalry between Jerusalem and Samaria. This tradition survived
into the Roman period, for Flavius Josephus incorporates it into his *De
Bello Judaico* nearly eight centuries later.[15]

Herodotus's account of Sennacherib's unsuccessful invasion of Egypt
represents an additional 'historical authority'.[16] According to him, mice
rescued Egypt by gnawing away at the leather equipment of the Assyrian
troops. The army thus stripped was forced to return to Assyria. This fanci-
ful story might have derived from a local tradition that confused the fight
between Sennacherib and Egyptian troops at the Judaean city of Eltekeh
with an invasion of Egypt. W. Baumgartner has convincingly shown that
Herodotus's report should be viewed as Greek-style 'Denkmalnovelle' or
'Bildsage'.[17]

14. See von Beckerath 1992.

15. Josephus mentions a place in Jerusalem called the 'Assyrian camp' (*War* 5.303
and 504), from where he supposedly warned the people of Jerusalem not to confuse the
Romans with Jerusalem's ancient enemies—God may have saved the city from the
Assyrians but God will not save it from the Romans (*War* 5.387 and 404-407). Such
designations of locales do not necessarily reflect historical reality. Germany, for
instance, is studded with areas called camps or fieldworks that folk tradition associated
with Roman occupations or Swedish invasions. In all but a few cases, however, the
presence of neither Romans nor Swedes in these areas can be documented.

16. Herodotus, *Histories* 3.141.

17. Baumgartner 1959: 305-309; von Beckerath 1992; but also note Grabbe (pp.
119-40 above) who gives a different interpretation. Herodotus's knowledge about
different regions was quite varied. He had visited Egypt, could still put questions to
veterans of the Greco-Persian wars, and had considerable experience of the Persian
overlords in his own Ionian home. He had only a cloudy knowledge of other regions
that he did not know from personal observation, however, to which belonged Syro-
Palestine and Mesopotamia (the best example being the Babylonian 'marriage mar-
ket'). On Herodotus's knowledge of the ancient Near East, see further discussion in
Grabbe's contribution.

The Events According to 2 Kings 18.13-16.

The biblical passage 2 Kgs 18.13-16, whose concise wording is a further indication of origins in historical archives, allows us to extrapolate political developments between Assyria and Judah. It reads as follows:

> In the fourteenth year of King Hezekiah, King Sennacherib of Assyria came up against all the fortified cities of Judah and captured them. King Hezekiah of Judah sent to the King of Assyria at Lachish, saying, 'I have done wrong; withdraw from me; whatever you impose on me I will bear'. The King of Assyria demanded of King Hezekiah of Judah three hundred talents of silver and thirty talents of gold. Hezekiah gave him all the silver that was found in the house of the LORD and in the treasuries of the king's house. At that time Hezekiah stripped the gold from the doors of the temple of the LORD, and from the doorposts that King Hezekiah of Judah had overlaid and gave it to the king of Assyria.

These lines present a chain of events most familiar to any Assyriologist working with Neo-Assyrian royal inscriptions. The Assyian army campaigns against fortified cities and captures them. The local rulers concede and pay tribute. From Judah's point-of-view, the sequence represents the most benign course that could befall a local vassal king: he can hold the throne as long as he remains loyal and pays tribute.

Sennacherib captured the Judaean cities and villages between the western foothills of Judah and the Philistine city-states on the Mediterranean. Hezekiah then sent deputies authorized to offer his submission to the Assyrian king at his headquarters, the Judaean fortress of Lachish. The submission was accepted at the cost of 810 kg of gold and 8,100 kg of silver. For the Assyrians, 'Operation Judah' was concluded. Unfortunately, the Old Testament account does not speak of the fate of the conquered territory. Was it returned to the king of Judah or was it kept under Assyrian control?

Of special import is Hezekiah's admission 'I have done wrong'. This statement probably refers to Hezekiah's revolt cited in 2 Kgs 18.7-8: 'He (Hezekiah) rebelled against the king of Assyria and would not serve him. He attacked the Philistines as far as Gaza and its territory, from watchtower to fortified city'. What provoked him to attempt a revolt? Certainly Hezekiah was well aware of Assyria's power. In the year 734, his father, King Ahaz of Judah, submitted to the Assyrian king Tiglath-pileser III (745–727). Furthermore, the young Hezekiah witnessed, at least from afar, Assyria's conquest of Samaria in 721, the result of three years of siege, and later as vassal to Sargon II (721–705), Sargon's conquest of Ashdod in 711. I would suggest that Hezekiah's rebellion began when the great Sargon II died on a battlefield in Anatolia in 705. This shocking event was unprecedented and might have thrown Assyria into a brief period of confusion. At the same time, the state was troubled by rebellion in Babylonia. If Hezekiah were going to throw off his yoke, the moment was now. From the above passage one may infer that the Judaean ruler ceased paying tribute. His attacks on Philistine cities loyal to Assyria were no doubt an attempt to form a hegemony and gain control of their sea trade, an act of *imitatio Assyriae* to be sure. Capturing the growing trade initiated by Sargon between Egypt and the Near East may also have been part of his plan.[18] Finally, one might read the passages of 2 Chron. 30.1-12 in which Hezekiah sends agents into Samaria, at that time an Assyrian province, as a calling on the peoples of Israel to confederate with him against a common enemy. These, together with the defensive tactics described in 2 Chron. 32.2-8, suggest a plan that took considerable time, energy and money to implement. As brilliant as his strategy may have been, it was ultimately miscalculated.

Before Hezekiah's rebellion Assyrian advances in or around Palestine were relatively rare.[19] Like Judah, Phoenician and Philistine city-states, and the lands of Edom, Moab and Ammon had already submitted to Assyria before Sennacherib came to the throne. Their vassal status allowed them a degree of independence under indigenous rule. The expectation that Assyria's strong arm would be relied upon for protection against the menace of Judah and even Egypt may have fuelled the willingness of Hezekiah's immediate neighbours to acquiesce. Occasional uprisings were known in the Philistine camp, however. The people of Ekron turned against their king Padî, a loyal Assyrian vassal, and delivered him into Hezekiah's hands. Furthermore, the deportation of the king of Ashkelon mentioned in Assyrian sources is a strong indication of an insurrection, probably in collusion with Hezekiah. Other Philistine cities seemed to have resisted Judaean pressure, such as one (whose name is unfortunately not preserved) that Hezekiah took by force and annexed as his own.[20] Ashdod and Gaza must be numbered among the resistant for Sennacherib had reason to reward their loyalty with Judaean land. In any case, both

18. Mayer 1995: 320.

19. Campaigns beyond Damascus and into Palestine were launched by Tiglath-pileser III in 734, Shalmanesar V around 732–723 and Sargon II in 720 and 711.

20. Appendix 11, l. 11. Na'aman 1974: 34-35 suggests Gath.

biblical and Assyrian scribes viewed Hezekiah's aggression against the treaty-abiding Philistines as treasonous rebellion.[21] It was also the result of political shortsightedness. Ultimately Sargon's death and the transference of the throne did not effect Assyria's ability to crush insurgency whenever and wherever it arose. Submission was the only way Hezekiah could have literally and figuratively saved his skin.

Interpretation of the Events from Assyrian Sources

Although Assyrian sources do not describe military preparations, Sennacherib's campaign to the southwestern periphery of his empire was no doubt carefully planned. Common military practices dictate that gathered troops were positioned at points that were as close as possible to enemy territory, which in this case would have been the old border area between Israel and Judah.[22] Equally important to a successful campaign were logistics: the accumulation of weapons and supplies,[23] of horses, pack animals and cattle, and the materials necessary for assembling siege engines. Furthermore, an intelligence service—essential to developing military strategy—must have been in place, as it was in the border areas of Urartu during Sargon's time.[24] Quite possibly, Sargon's head office in Samaria[25] was still in use for reconnoitering roadways and watering holes, the numbers and movements of enemy troops, as well as the richest locales for plundering.

The first target of assault, according to Sennacherib, was Sidon. The fact that Sidon is singled out and no other town of similar importance, such as Hamat or Damascus, gives us a hint as to the king's route from Assyria to Palestine. He must have travelled from Assyria by chariot, accompanied by his retinue and mounted guards, to join his awaiting army. With Sidon as his destination, the shortest and therefore the most likely course was

21. Thus the prevailing picture of a united front of rulers under Hezekiah against Assyria has little basis in fact.

22. The notion that the army advanced toward Palestine from central Assyria is untenable from a military standpoint. Such a march would take at least two to three months. As campaigns usually began in May and ended in late September, the march would have taken place under typically seering climatic conditions. The troops would then arrive for battle in Palestine already considerably depleted.

23. Accumulation of weapons and supplies is typical of campaign preparations. See for instance Sg. 8 ll. 76-8.

24. The existence of Assyrian intelligence is well known from Neo-Assyrian letters; see, for example, State Archives of Assyria 1.29-32; 43.

25. In the year after 721.

following the Habur River to the Euphrates where he could then take the old caravan route from the Deir ez-Zor area to the oasis of Tadmor /Palmyra and on to Homs. The way from Homs leads through the Biqa between Lebanon and Anti-Lebanon to Sidon on the coast. The specification of Sidon also makes clear that the king intended to bypass the mountains of Judah and aimed instead for the coastal plains.

At Sennacherib's appearance, Lulî, the king of Sidon, fled from Tyre and set out for Cyprus.[26] Sennacherib's accounts do not give reasons for his flight; they may have included anything from missed tribute payments to treasonous sympathies for Hezekiah's cause. The whole area, which seems to have incorporated the coastal cities of Tyre and Acco, submitted and paid homage. The Assyrian king installed Tuba'lu (whose origins are unknown) as Sidon's new ruler and imposed on him annual tribute. In the vicinity of Ushu, an outlying territory of Sidon, Sennacherib received the remaining kings and princes of Byblos, Arwad, Samsimuruna and Ashdod, and likewise those from Transjordan: Ammon, Moab and Edom. On this occasion the vassal rulers not only delivered their tribute and their greeting gifts but also their auxiliary troops. Although this last fact is not mentioned in the annals, it is nevertheless obvious from the fragment of the 'Letter to the God' in which Sennacherib reports that he made troops from all over the land of Amurru, meaning the auxiliaries presented by these kings, carry masses of earth for the building of a siege ramp at Azekah.[27] Here we glimpse the disparate treatment of troops. To the auxiliaries and not to the Assyrians fell the labour made nearly unbearable by intense heat and dust. Three Palestinian rulers were not present at Ushu, Ṣidqa of Ashkelon, Padî of Ekron, who as Hezekiah's prisoner was kept fettered in Jerusalem, and, of course, Hezekiah.

The modern notion that the Assyrian king and his entire army dashed from city to city, cutting them down, is strategically impossible. Such tactics would have created insurmountable logistical problems—supplying an enormous body of soldiers in constant motion with food and water in a land like Palestine is alone nearly impossible—and would have wasted a great deal of precious time. A more likely scenario is that the army was split up into divisions as soon as it crossed the border. Each division would have been assigned specific targets. Otherwise, conquering 46 Judaean sites whether town, fortress or city, and four within the district of Ashkelon within one campaign of a mere half year's duration is unimaginable. For

26. For the relations between Cyprus and Assyria see Mayer 1996.
27. Appendix 11, 1. 18.

the most part, Assyrians may have met with little or no resistance. The presence of seige ramps at the fortresses of Azekah and Lachish in the archaeological and textual records attests to resistance in those cities as well as to significantly long periods of fighting.[28] With divisions, the king could launch a series of seiges in different areas. He could also keep a task force of suitable size under his personal command. Such a unit, whose first line may have included cavalry and charioteers who were of little use in sieges, would enable Sennacherib to operate independently and with great speed between his headquarters at Lachish and various arenas of struggle.

The Assyrian sources say nothing about why Şidqa of Ashkelon failed to pay homage to Sennacherib, and there is no indication that the city itself resisted. We do know that Şidqa, his family and their family gods were deported to Assyria and his cities and villages were occupied and plundered. His replacement on the throne, Šarru-lū-dâri, was a son of Rukibtu, the man whom Tiglath-Pileser III accepted as ruler of Ashkelon a generation before. During that time, Rukibtu sent hostages to Assyria as a security pledge. The name of his son Šarru-lū-dâri, 'May the king last forever', a name typical for Assyrian officials, suggests that his son was among those special hostages who were brought to the royal court at Kalhu for indoctrination and education.

After the 'purge' of Ashkelon, Sennacherib turned his attention to Ekron where his loyal vassal Padî had been removed and delivered 'like an enemy' to Hezekiah, an event possibly referred to in 2 Kgs 18.8 . Padî had sworn an oath of allegiance to Assur, and he may have been determined to keep it for the good of his kingdom. But at least a faction of citizens among the ranks of high officials and nobles thought otherwise, probably seeking to throw off the heavy obligations of tribute that fell to them.[29] Partly for fear of Assyrian retaliation, the people of Ekron asked assistance from the Egyptian princes or petty kings of the Nile Delta. But the question is, Why did Ekron turn to Egypt rather than Judah for aid? Although it is possible that Hezekiah was also asked for help, the sources say nothing and, in any case, the request was clearly not granted. A more likely explanation is that the people of Ekron turned to Egypt to buffer their tight position between expected Assyrian aggression on one side and Judah's mounting onslaughts of Philistine cities on the other. Because Sennacherib mentions Egyptian troops only in connection with Ekron, we are led to

28. For Lachish see Ussishkin 1982.
29. That the people of Ekron were divided seems evident from the reports of Sennacherib's subsequent selective punishment, as described below.

assume that the city leaders, who had already forfeited their king to Hezekiah, appealed to Egypt to avoid surrendering their city to Judah as well.
The Egyptian unit of charioteers and archers engaged in battle with Assyrians at Eltekeh and was annihilated. This is the only recounted field battle
for the campaign of 701.

The Ekron-Eltekeh episode as I see it differs from current reconstructions
in secondary literature. From these, one gets the impression that Egyptian
troops appeared instantly at Ekron, led by a high king. And although they
were unable to save the city, they did manage to thwart Sennacherib's
planned invasion of Egypt at Eltekeh. The reader might recall here that the
story of an invasion of Egypt is anchored in Herodotus and the notion of
an Egyptian pharoah fighting Assyrians on Palestinian soil relies on the
anachronism of King Taharqa in 2 Kgs 19.9. In 701, Egypt was under the
control of Ethiopia's 25th Dynasty. The Egyptian kings called on by Ekron
were local rulers who enjoyed relative independence as a result of Ethiopia's weak and distant hold. The ability of the dynasty itself to exercise
power, especially power abroad, was extremely limited. As *homines novi* in
the pharaonic kingdom Ethiopians were more Egyptian than Egyptians.[30]
The policy Egypt enforced against Syria during the time of the great dynasties in the second millennium would have appealed to Ethiopian kings, but
they lacked the means to reenact it. Nevertheless, Sennacherib's mention
of chariots and cavalry sent by the 'king of Nubia' indicates that an Ethiopian king, as yet unnamed, did contribute, at least to some degree.

The presence of the Egyptian unit at Eltekeh is perhaps of some significance. The Assyrians took and plundered Eltekeh and Timnah, cities
adjacent to the battle sites. Although we cannot be sure of the exact location of these two cities, neither is cited as belonging to the loyal territories
of Gaza or Ashdod, or to the territory of Ekron. Nor could Eltekeh or
Timnah have been contained in the territory of Ashkelon, since they are
not mentioned in connection with the cities Sennacherib listed as having
destroyed in that region. We should probably assume then that Eltekeh and
Timnah were part of the group of 46 Judaean sites Sennacherib conquered.
They may have been located far south of Ekron, as some have suggested
for Timnah. If this hypothesis is correct, the Egyptian unit was avoiding
the usual route from Egypt, the via maris, that went through Philistine
territory loyal to Assyria, and followed instead a more difficult inland

30. One is reminded here of the great respect Ethiopian kings showed for Theban
cults as well as their adoption of classical Middle Egyptian for the writing of their
royal inscriptions.

route. If these Egyptian troops had comprised a true relief army of consid-erable might, the faster coastal route would have been taken. It is possible that the unit was retreating toward Egypt when the Assyrians caught up with it at Eltekeh.

Another mistaken impression to be adressed here has to do with timing. The events at Ekron could not have taken place within the time-frame of Sennacherib's campaign in 701. Many must have occurred before. First, the people of Ekron would have needed to assemble and then to agree on asking Egypt for military support. The Egyptian central authority (if that is what it should be called) was a great distance from Palestine, in Napata, southwest of the Fourth Cataract, so it may have taken more than a few months for a messenger to reach it. Once the petition was delivered, Ekron and Egypt would negotiate the nature of the support, costing additional time. Finally Egypt had to organize an army and march it to Palestine. Even if it had come from the Delta or from Memphis, there was not sufficient time for all the above events to take place in the duration of the campaign. Given the above, Padî's removal probably came about at the latest in 702, well before Sennacherib launched his campaign, and at the earliest in 705, after the death of Sargon. Therefore, the Egyptian auxiliary must have arrived somewhere between 704 and 701.

There is no evidence that the city of Ekron itself offered any resistance to Sennacherib. Assyrian punishment seemed to have been confined to those involved in the conspiracy against Padî. High officials and nobility were executed and their carcasses displayed on city walls. Other co-con-spirators and followers were deported. The rest were spared. With swift acts of retribution such as these as well as the deportation of Ṣidqa of Ashkelon (and later the treatment of Hezekiah), Sennacherib made explicit to Palestinian leaders that he would not tolerate transgressions. At the same time, his release of the innocent and reinstatement of Padî demonstrated his capacity to protect and reward those loyal to him.

Once the situtation at Ekron was brought into line, Sennacherib proba-bly went on to establish headquarters outside what seems to have been one of Judah's most important fortresses, Lachish, situated between the moun-tains and the lowlands. Sparing no effort, Assyrians launched a siege against the fortress, an event that has provided archaeology with the only Assyrian siege ramp ever excavated.[31] Although the name of Lachish is not given in the annals, the fortress must have been of particular impor-tance to Sennacherib for he dedicated an entire room in his palace at

31. See Ussishkin 1982.

Nineveh to wall reliefs that depict its siege and fall.[32] Furthermore, since Hezekiah's notice of submission was later brought to Lachish, it is fairly clear that this site was Sennacherib's main headquarters.

Was There a Siege of Jerusalem?

In order to answer the question of whether or not Jerusalem was besieged, we must look at certain passages from Sennacherib's report concerning Hezekiah. For the moment, I would like to analyze three pertinent statements:

- 'Himself (Hezekiah) I enclosed in Jerusalem, his royal city, like a bird in a cage';[33]
- 'I laid out forts against him;'[34] and
- (He sent his tribute) 'after me to Nineveh'.[35]

The image of a trapped bird appears several times earlier in letters from Rib-Addi of Byblos written in the Amarna period.[36] It is obvious that the prince of Byblos used the image to describe his cornered position in Byblos and not a military siege. Similarly, Tiglath-Pileser III employed the simile for describing his manoeuvers against Damascus.[37] It is clear from his report that the city was blockaded but not besieged, unlike Arpad previously and Samaria later under Shalmaneser V and Sargon II. The verb *esēru*, 'to enclose, confine',[38] in military contexts means to take away an opponent's initiative and deprive him of his freedom of movement, whereas the verb for besieging a city is *lamû*,[39] a term Assyrian sources do not apply to Jerusalem.

---

32. Paterson 1912–15: pl. 68-73; Ussishkin 1982: 77. Apparently, Sennacherib preferred to conduct sieges personally, as he did at Lachish, Kutha and Babylon. His interest in technology is also evidenced in his non-military reliefs, such as those depicting the transportation of colossi. For a comprehensive discussion of the palace and its reliefs see Russell 1991.

33. Appendices 1 III ll. 27-9, 2 III ll. 20-1 and 8 ll. 28-9.

34. Appendices 1 III l. 29 and 2 III ll. 21-2.

35. Appendices 1 III ll. 47-8, 2 III ll. 39-40, 3 l. 58 and 8 l. 32.

36. *Kīma iṣṣūre ša ina libbi ḫuḫāre (:kilūbi) šaknat kišūma anāku ina* URU.*Gubla* 'Like a bird sitting in a snare, so am I in Byblos', EA 74 ll. 45-8; 78 ll. 13-6; 79 ll. 35-8; 81 ll. 34-6; 90 ll. 39-42; 105 ll. 8-10 and 116 ll. 18-20.

37. Tadmor 1994: 78 l. 11'.

38. AHw: 252; CAD E: 334-5.

39. AHw: 541; CAD L: 69-77.

This interpretation not only fits Sennacherib's meaning but is supported by the second statement, 'I laid out forts against him'. What I have translated here as 'forts' is the Akkadogram URU.ḪAL-ṢU.MEŠ,[40] which in Royal Inscriptions is usually translated as 'siege walls' when it appears in war contexts.[41] This is most certainly an anachronism. By definition, siege walls were built by attackers to effectively enclose a city. The benefits of siege walls were manifold. The besieger had the opportunity to amass fire power while remaining well protected. At the same time, siege walls prevented the city population from escaping and from receiving supplies and reinforcements. The general aim was to force the occupants to surrender through starvation and exhaustion. The siege-wall tactic obviously demands great time and labour and is only efficiently implemented with siege artillery—catapults, scorpions and the like—whose ranges and penetration power are greater than those of the composite bow. With all their practical knowledge of siege ramps, towers, rams and mines (all of which survived into classical antiquity), Assyrians knew nothing about siege artillery. The use of catapults is first attested at Dionysius of Syracuse's conquest of Motya in 397.[42] Surrender by starvation as the result of a siege-wall investment is evidenced for the first time in 432–430 at Potidaia, forced by Athenians.[43] Starvation is sure to have been among the greatest devastations at Apad, Samaria and, later on, Tyre, cities that suffered sieges of several years. In general, Syrian and Palestinian fortress cities presented extremely difficult obstacles to their enemies because of their strategic sitings and structural layouts as well as their supply facilities of storage rooms and cisterns.[44] The costs in time, labour and lives to launch a siege against a highly fortified city must be commensurate with the objectives of the campaign. Evidently, Sennacherib (and his successors) did not consider the city of Jerusalem worth the effort, unlike Lachish. Instead he built URU.ḪAL-ṢU.MEŠ. This word means 'fort', 'fortress' or 'fortification' interchangeably. It was used in Sargon's military correspondence in which the presence of 'frontier fortifications', URU.ḪAL-ṢU.MEŠ—to be read as birātu—on Assyria's northern border are reported. In Neo-Assyrian times,

40. AHw: 313-4; CAD H: 51-52.
41. For siege techniques in the first millennium BCE see Lawrence 1979: 3-66.
42. Diodorus 14, 48-52.
43. Thucydides 1, 64, 1.3; 2, 70, 1.
44. For the architecture of Palestinian fortresses in general see Wright 1985: 172-215 and Weippert 1988.

at least since Tiglath-Pileser III, the majority of Assyrian units were stationed in frontier areas where their concentration and reinforcement could proceed quickly. This outpost system had become necessary when the empire's expansion caused the lines of communication as well as reaction time to lengthen. It also eased the problem of feeding and supplying the growing numbers of troops. Sennacherib had a series of such forts built around Hezekiah's territory, as the text unambiguously states. Although they may have been quite simple, patrols operating from them could rattle Judaean territory, control access routes and prevent Jerusalemites 'from going out from the gate'. Ultimately, the effects of building such forts were similar to the effects of full-scale siege but without the costs.

Sennacherib's careful formulation of the third statement that Hezekiah sent his tribute 'after me to Nineveh' is usually cited as verification of the king's hasty retreat to Assyria after his catastrophic failure at Jerusalem, as in 2 Kgs 19.35. But his return must be understood with regard to Assyrian military practices. First of all, the king and his army did not move together. Just as Sennacherib travelled from his capital to Palestine, unencumbered by masses of slow-moving infantry and accompanied only by his mounted retinue and guards, so did he return. He left some of his troops at the frontier while having others marched to the next zone of operation, which in this case was Babylonia. As Neo-Assyrian palace reliefs show, other units typically accompanied the booty garnered from a campaign, together with prisoners and deportees, to Assyria. Such caravans of animals 'beyond counting' and thousands of people including women and children travelling on foot or in carts drawn by oxen were bound to be extremely slow. It is unimaginable that Sennacherib would accompany them at that pace and under what is likely to have been distressing conditions. Instead, he comfortably awaited their arrival at Nineveh and the subsequent public presentation of his newly won treasures, the documents of royal success.

Looking at Assyrian sources in the light of Assyrian military logic, it is clear that our question is answered—Jerusalem was not besieged in 701. There are no wall reliefs such as those portraying the fall of Lachish that testify to a siege and no mention of one in Assyrian reports. This absence of documentation cannot be construed as royal omission of defeat, as Rawlinson proposed. Instead the tactics Sennacherib used to force Hezekiah's surrender are unequivocally communicated in Assyrian reports. Equally evident is Assyria's success. With Hezekiah chastized, Jerusalem returned to its vassal status intact.

Booty and Tribute

From the birth of Assyriology until the present, critics have cited the numerical data in Assyrian Royal Inscriptions as proof of their unreliability as historical documents, especially if the data refer to prisoners or booty.[45] Sennacherib lists his booty from his campaign of 701 as:

> 205,105—people, young (and) old, male and female; horses, mules, donkeys, camels, big and small cattle beyond counting...[46]

It is highly unlikely that Assyrians deported 205,105 people if only because this number represents too large a portion of Palestine's overall population, although the figure does include the deportees from Judah as well as from Ekron. The wording is typical of the way Assyrians counted live booty—by heads, animal and human, without differentiating between the two. The syntax further indicates that 'small cattle' of sheep, goats and possibly even poultry were not included in the total amount but were 'beyond counting'. Certainly small cattle were eaten *en route*.[47] The number of small cattle from Sennacherib's first campaign in 703 to Babylonia was astonishingly high, given at 800,100 or 800,600.

One must also account for the discrepancy between the amount of Hezekiah's tribute in 2 Kgs 18.14 of 30 talents of gold and 300 talents of silver and the Assyrian computation:

> ...30 talents of gold, 800 talents of silver, select antimony in small blocks, large blocks of AN.GUG-stone, couches (inlaid) with ivory, armchairs (inlaid) with ivory, elephant hides, ivory, ebony, boxwood (and) all kinds of valuable treasures...[48]

The last category is subdivided in the Rassam Cylinder as follows:

> ...garments with colorful embroidery, garments of linen, blue-purple wool, red-purple wool, tools of bronze, iron, copper (and) tin, 'iron' chariots,

---

45. See for details Mayer 1995: 39-48; cf. also De Odorico 1995.
46. Appendices 1 III ll. 24-6 and 2 III ll. 17-9.
47. Until modern times armies lived off the bounty of the enemy. 'An army, like a serpent, marches upon its belly' (attributed to Frederick II of Prussia). More specifically, Sun tsï (II 15) says: 'Hence the wise general sees to it that his troops feed on the enemy, for one bushel of the enemy's provisions is equivalent to twenty of his; one hundredweight of enemy fodder to twenty hundredweight of his' (cited after Griffith 1971: 74).
48. Appendices 1 III ll. 41-5, 2 III ll. 34-7 and 3 l. 56.

slings, lances, armor, swords of iron (with their) girdles, bows and arrows, bridles (and) countless implements of war…[49]

Both sides agree on the amount of gold Hezekiah paid. As far as I am aware, Assyrians always list gold in a separate leading category,[50] whereas silver can be grouped together with other materials. The biblical report specifies the exact weight of silver delivered, whereas the Assyrian either added the weight of silver to the weight of other objects or estimated the combined value of both in terms of talents. If the biblical figure is correct, Sennacherib received 300 talents of silver and 500 talents worth of various other precious goods, such as furniture, clothing, weapons and so on. This amount is hardly exorbitant considering that Hezekiah emptied his own treasury as well as the treasury of the temple in Jerusalem in order to satsify Assyria's terms.[51]

Who were the LÚ.urbū?

In the annals Sennacherib reports that Hezekiah's LÚ.*úr-bi* and elite troops mutinied in Jerusalem.[52] The identity of the LÚ.*úr-bi* is much discussed in the literature. The word *urbu* appears only in Sennacherib's annals and once in a text from the reign of Assurbanipal.[53] W. von Soden interpreted it as 'eine Arbeitstruppe?' (AHw: 1428 b), whereas others have considered it to refer to an ethnic group, in particular Arabs. In my view, the term is neither a social class nor an ethnicity. The word in this form is most probably the result of a metathesis of r and b. If this is so, the word then is *wabru(m)/ubru(m)*, meaning 'stranger', or 'foreign resident' (AHw: 1454 b), which is well-attested in texts from Assyria, Boghazköy and Ugarit. The word *ubru(m)* could in the context of Sennacherib's campaign designate refugees from the area of Jerusalem who fled into the city at the approach of the Assyrians. Alternately, the word may allude to the people

49. Appendix 3 ll. 56-7.

50. See for example Sg. 8.352.

51. If the passage about Hezekiah showing off his riches to an embassy of Merodachbaladan of Babylonia in 2 Kgs 20.12-19 is founded in a real event, the visit must have occurred before he emptied his treasuries in 701, contrary to the biblical dating that places it after 701.

52. Appendices 1 III ll. 39-41, 2 III ll. 31-3 and 8 l. 31.

53. For *urbu* in the Middle-Assyrian inscription from the nude female statue made for Assur-bel-kala (1073–1056) see RIMA 2.A.0.89.10 ll. 4-5: *qé-[reb]* NA[M.ME]Š URU.MEŠ *ù ub-ru-te*.MEŠ 'in the provinces, cities and…'

from the former territory of Israel whom Hezekiah's agents sought to enlist (2 Chron. 38.1-12). The strongest possibility, however, is the third: *urbu* could signify 'mercenary', a word not expressly attested in Akkadian. Until Sargonid times, the need for mercenaries was quite limited, when it existed at all, since armies could draw their personnel from Assyria's own provinces and vassal kingdoms.[54] When it was necessary to hire soldiers, they no doubt came from outside the empire. Thus the notion that the well-known term *ubru(m)*, 'stranger' also meant 'mercenary' is far from unreasonable. The importance Assyrians attached to the LÚ.*úr-bi* as a fighting force is evident in the syntax where Hezekiah's LÚ.*úr-bi* take precedence over his elite troops.

Conclusion

Von Clausewitz's framework of aim, purpose and means helps us evaluate the campaign of 701. While Sennacherib's first two campaigns were southeast of the empire, the third was southwest. The fourth was again directed against southern Babylonia, whereas the fifth transpired in Commagene to the northwest. From then on, it was expedient for Sennacherib to concentrate his forces on Babylonia and Elam. Yet at the same time, some of his generals conducted parallel operations in Cilicia. Besides the southeast frontier, nearly all other frontiers of the empire were fairly quiet during his reign.

As far as we know his third campaign was his only operation in Palestine. The mere appearance of the new king of Assyria and his entourage was reason enough for the rulers of Phoenicia, Philistia and Transjordan to pay homage to him. While his troops carried out sieges, Sennacherib cleared away the problems at Ashkelon, Ekron and Eltekeh. From his headquarters at Lachish he conducted assaults on the most important lowland sites of Judah. From the Assyrian point of view, launching a full-scale offensive against the capital of Jerusalem would have been superfluous and even senseless. At Lachish he accepted Hezekiah's belated submission, leaving the Judaean relatively powerless—stripped of most of his land and no doubt bankrupt—while distributing the occupied territory of Judah to

---

54. Mercenaries seem to have come into regular use when Assyria was forced to adapt to a new mode of warfare, battle on horseback, in their clashes with equestrian nomads, the Cimmerians, Scythians and Medes. In order to effect a quick response, Assyrians may have hired foreigners who were already knowledgable in the ways of equestrian warfare as mercenaries.

loyal Philistine rulers. Sennacherib was able to swiftly and clearly demonstrate three important points to the peoples of Palestine:

- Assyria's new king was not to be taken less seriously than his predecessor and father, Sargon. As his movements against Ashkelon, Judah and Ekron showed, he would not tolerate any rebellion or resistance.
- Loyalty to Assyria is rewarded, as the gifts of territory given to Ashdod, Ekron and Gaza witness.
- Whoever was loyal to Assyria and its god Assur can rely on their protection, as the case of Padî of Ekron demonstrated.

Since all these achievements were executed economically with regard to aim, purpose and means—and with considerable diplomatic flair—modern scholarship's image of Sennacherib as a rampaging despot, especially after his 689 campaign in Babylon, should be reconsidered.

The land below the border of Assyria's Palestinian provinces, now a viable glacis, was secured, as were important routes and lines of communication on the coastal plain. This together with the young king's gained experience and new familiarity with the region were valuable preventive measures against future military conflicts, potentially even with Egypt. Hezekiah, on the other hand, was confined to his remote capital and neighbouring, nearly inaccessible, mountain holdings. Surrounded by the Assyrian provinces in the north, in the east by Transjordan and in the west by Philistia, both loyal to Assyria, Hezekiah was indeed enclosed like a bird in a cage.

Little changed in the relationship between Assyria and Judah during the reigns of Sennacherib's successors. Esarhaddon (680–669) mentions King Manasseh of Judah as one of many tributary rulers who contributed to the building of his palace in Nineveh.[55] Assurbanipal (668–627) also mentions Manasseh along with other Syro-Palestinian tributaries who paid homage to him on his first campaign to Egypt.[56] The last reference to Judah in Assyrian sources comes from a legal document from 660 in which two homers of wheat are weighed in Judaic measurements.[57]

55. Ash. 60 l. 55: *Me-na-si-i*/*Mi-in-se-e* LUGAL/MAN URU/KUR *Ia-ú-di*.
56. BIWA: C II l. 39: m.*Mi-in-se-e* LUGAL KUR *Ia-ú-di*.
57. Kwasman 1988: 9 l. 2: *ina* GIŠ .BÁN *ša* KUR *Ia-ú-di*.

Appendices

Prisms and Cylinders

1. *Chicago Prism*

Luckenbill, 1924: 23-47 and 128-31; BAL^2 1: 68-88.
Translation: Borger, TUAT 1: 388-90; ANET: 287-88 (cf. BAL^2 1.65-66;
Frahm 1997: T16).

Col. II

^{37} *i-na šal-ši ger-ri-ia a-na* KUR Ḫat-ti *lu al-lik*

^{38} m. *Lu-li-i* LUGAL URU.Ṣi-du-un-ni *pul-ḫi me-lam-me*

^{39} *be-lu-ti-ia is-ḫu-pu-šu-ma a-na ru-uq-qí*

^{40} *qa-bal tam-tim in-na-bit-ma šad-da-šú e-mid*

^{41} URU.Ṣi-du-un-nu GAL-*ú* URU.Ṣi-du-un-nu TUR

^{42} URU.*Bet-Zi-it-ti* URU.*Ṣa-re-ep-tu* URU.*Ma-ḫal-li-ba*

^{43} URU.*Ú-šu-ú* URU.*Ak-zi-bi* URU.*Ak-ku-ú*

^{44} URU.MEŠ-*šú dan-nu-ti* É BÀD.MEŠ *a-šar ri-i-ti*

^{45} *ù maš-qí-ti* É *tuk-la-te-šú ra-šub-bat* GIŠ.TUKUL d.*Aš+šur*

^{46} EN- *ia is-ḫu-pu-šú-nu-ti-ma ik-nu-šú še-pu-ú-a*

^{47} m.*Tu-ba-aʾ-lum i-na* GIŠ.GU.ZA LUGAL-*ú-ti*

^{48} UGU- *šú-un ú-še-šib-ma* GUN *man-da-tu be-lu-ti-ia*

^{49} *šat-ti-šam la ba-aṭ-lu ú-kin ṣe-ru-uš-šú*

^{50} *ša* m.*Mi-ini-ḫi-im-mu* URU.*Sam-si-mu-ru-na-a-a*

^{51} m.*Tu-ba-aʾ-lum* URU.*Ṣi-du-un-na-a-a*

^{52} m.*Ab-di-li-iʾ-ti* URU.*A-ru-da-a-a*

^{53} m.*Ú-ru-mil-ki* URU.*Gu-ub-la-a-a*

^{54} m.*Mi-ti-in-ti* URU.*As-du-da-a-a*

^{55} m.*Pu-du*-DINGIR KUR.*Bet*-m.*Am-ma-na-a-a*

^{56} m.*Kam-mu-su-na-ad-bi* KUR.*Ma-aʾ-ba-a-a*

^{57} m.*A-a-ram-mu* KUR.*Ú-du-um-ma-a-a*

^{58} LUGAL.MEŠ KUR MAR.TU.KI *ka-li-šú-un* IGI.SÁ-*e šad-lu-ti*

^{59} *ta-mar-ta-šú-nu ka-bit-tu a-di* 4-*šú a-na maḫ-ri-ia*

^{60} *iš-šu-nim-ma iš-ši-qu* GÌR.II-*ia ù* m.*Ṣi-id-qa-a*

^{61} LUGAL URU.*Iš-qa-al-lu-na ša la ik-nu-šú*

^{62} *a-na ni-ri-ia* DINGIR.MEŠ É AD-*šú šá-a-šú* DAM-*su*

^{63} DUMU.MEŠ-*šú* DUMU.MÍ.MEŠ-*šú* ŠEŠ.MEŠ-*šú* NUMUN É AD-*šú*

^{64} *as-su-ḫa-ma a-na* KUR.*Aš +šur*.KI *ú-ra-áš-šú*

^{65} m.LUGAL-*lu-dà-ri* DUMU m.*Ru-kib-ti* LUGAL-*šú-nu maḫ-ru-ú*

^{66} UGU UN.MEŠ URU.*Iš-qa-al-lu-na áš-kun-ma*

^{67} *na-dan* GUN *kàd-re-e be-lu-ti-ia e-mid-su-ma*

^{68} *i-šá-a-aṭ ab-šá-a-ni i-na me-ti-iq ger-ri-ia*

^{69} URU.*Bet-Da-gan-na* URU.*Ia-ap-pu-ú*

^{70} URU.*Ba-na-a-a-bar-qa* URU.*A-zu-ru* URU.MEŠ -*ni*

71 *ša* m.*Ṣi-id-qa-a ša a-na* GÌR.II-*ia ár-ḫiš*

72 *la ik-nu-šú al-me* KUR-*ud áš-lu-la šal-la-su-un*

73 LÚ.GÌR.ARAD.MEŠ LÚ.NUN.MEŠ *ù* UN.MEŠ URU.*Am-qar-ru-na*

74 *ša* m.*Pa-di-i* LUGAL-*šú-nu* EN *a-de-e ù ma-miti*

75 *ša* KUR *Aš+šur*.KI *bi-re-tu* AN.BAR *id-du-ma*

76 *a-na* m.*Ḫa-za-qi-a-ú* KUR *Ia-ú-da-a-a*

77 *id-di-nu-šú nak-riš a-na an-zil-li i-pu-šú*

78 *ip-làḫ lib-ba-šú-un* LUGAL.MEŠ KUR *Mu-ṣu-re*

79 LÚ.ERIM.MEŠ GIŠ.BAN GIŠ.GIGIR.MEŠ ANŠE.KUR.RA.MEŠ

80 *ša* LUGAL KUR *Me-luḫ-ḫe e-mu-qí la ni-bi*

81 *ik-te-ru-nim-ma il-li-ku re-ṣu-su-un*

82 *i-na ta-mir-ti* URU.*Al-ta-qu-ú*

83 *el-la-mu-ú-a šit-ku-nu*

Col. III

1 *ú-šá-ʾi-lu* GIŠ.TUKUL.MEŠ-*šú-un i-na tukul-ti* d.*Aš+šur*

2 EN-*ia it-ti-šú-un am-da-ḫi-iṣ-ma áš-ta-kan*

3 BAD₅.BAD₅-*šú-un* LÚ.EN GIŠ.GIGIR.MEŠ *ù* DUMU.MEŠ LUGAL

4 KUR.*Mu-ṣu-ra-a-a a-di* LÚ.EN GIŠ.GIGIR.MEŠ *ša* LUGAL KUR *Me-luḫ-ḫi*

5 *bal-ṭu-su-un i-na* MURUB₄ *tam-ḫa-ri ik-šu-da*

6 ŠU.II-*a-a* URU.*Al-ta-qu-ú* URU.*Ta-am-na-a*

7 *al-me* KUR-*ud áš-lu-la šal-la-sún a-na* URU.*Am-qar-ru-na*

8 *aq-reb-ma* LÚ.GÌR.ARAD.MEŠ LÚ.NUN.MEŠ *ša ḫi-iṭ-ṭu*

9 *ú-šab-šu-ú a-duk-ma i-na di-ma-a-ti*

10 *si-ḫir-ti* URU *a-lul pag-ri-šú-un* DUMU.MEŠ URU

11 *e-piš an-ni ù gíl-la-ti a-na šal-la-ti am-nu*

12 *si-it-tu-te-šú-nu la ba-bil ḫi-ṭi-ti*

13 *ù gul-lul-ti ša a-ra-an-šú-nu la ib-šu-ú*

14 *uš-šur-šú-un aq-bi* m.*Pa-di-i* LUGAL-*šú-nu*

15 *ul-tu qé-reb* URU.*Ur-sa-li-im-mu ú-še-ša-am-ma*

16 *i-na* GIŠ.GU.ZA *be-lu-ti* UGU-*šú-un ú-še-šib-ma*

17 *man-da-at-tu be-lu-ti-ia ú-kin ṣe-ru-uš-šú*

18 *ù* m.*Ḫa-za-qi-a-ú* KUR.*Ia-ú-da-a-a*

19 *ša la ik-nu-šú a-na ni-ri-ia* 46 URU.MEŠ-*šú dan-nu-ti*

20 É BÀD.MEŠ *ù* URU.MEŠ TUR.MEŠ *ša li-me-ti-šú-nu*

21 *ša ni-ba la i-šu-ú i-na šuk-bu-us a-ram-me*

22 *ù qit-ru-ub šu-pi-i mit-ḫu-uṣ zu-uk* GÌR.II

23 *pil-ši nik-si ù kal-ban-na-te al-me* KUR-*ud*

24 2 ME LIM 1 ME 1 ME 50 UKÙ.MEŠ TUR GAL NITA *ù* MÍ

25 ANŠE.KUR.RA.MEŠ ANŠE.KUNGI.MEŠ ANŠE.MEŠ ANŠE.GAM.MAL.MEŠ

26 GUD.MEŠ *ù ṣe-e-ni ša la ni-bi ul-tu qer-bi-šú-un*

²⁷ *ú-še-ṣa-am-ma šal-la-tiš am-nu šá-a-šú* GIM MUŠEN *qu-up-pi*

²⁸ *qe-reb* URU.*Ur-sa-li-im-mu* URU LUGAL-*ti-šú*

²⁹ *e-sír-šú* URU.ḪAL-ṢU.MEŠ UGU-*šú ú-rak-kis-ma*

³⁰ *a-ṣe-e* KÁ.GAL URU-*šú ú-tir-ra ik-ki-bu-uš* URU.MEŠ-*šú*

³¹ *ša áš-lu-la ul-tu qé-reb* KUR-*šú ab-tuq-ma*

³² *a-na* m.*Mi-ti-in-ti* LUGAL URU *As-du-di*

³³ m. *Pa-di-i* LUGAL URU.*Am-qar-ru-na ù* m.GISSU-d.EN

³⁴ LUGAL URU.*Ḫa-zi-ti ad-din-ma ú-ṣa-aḫ-ḫir* KUR-*su*

³⁵ *e-li* GUN *maḫ-ri-ti na-dan šat-ti-šú-un*

³⁶ *man-da-at-tu kàd-re-e be-lu-ti-ia ú-rad-di-ma*

³⁷ *ú-kin ṣe-ru-uš-šú šu-ú* m.*Ḫa-za-qi-a-ú*

³⁸ *pul-ḫi me-lam-me be-lu-ti-ia is-ḫu-pu-šu-ma*

³⁹ LÚ.*úr-bi ù* LÚ.ERIM.MEŠ-*šú* SIG₅.MEŠ *ša a-na dun-nun*

⁴⁰ URU.*Ur-sa-li-im-mu* URU LUGAL-*ti-šú ú-še-ri-bu-ma*

⁴¹ *ir-šu-ú baṭ-la-a-ti it-ti* 30 GUN GUŠKIN

⁴² 8 ME GUN KÙ.BABBAR *ni-siq-ti gu-uḫ-li*

⁴³ *ták-kàs-si* NA₄.AN.GUG.ME GAL.MEŠ GIŠ.NÁ.MEŠ ZÚ

⁴⁴ GIŠ.GU.ZA.MEŠ *né-me-di* ZÚ KUŠ AM.SI ZÚ AM.SI

⁴⁵ GIŠ.ESI GIŠ.KU *mim-ma šum-šu ni-ṣir-tu ka-bit-tu*

⁴⁶ *ù* DUMU.MÍ.MEŠ -*šú* MÍ.UN.MEŠ.É.GAL-*šú* LÚ.NAR.MEŠ

⁴⁷ MÍ.NAR.MEŠ *a-na qé-reb* NINA.KI URU *be-lu-ti-ia*

⁴⁸ EGIR-*ia ú-še-bi-lam-ma a-na na-dan man-da-at-te*

⁴⁹ *ù e-peš* ÌR-*du-ti iš-pu-ra rak-bu-šú*

'On my third campaign I marched against Syria. Lulî, king of Sidon, whom the fearsome splendour of my rule overwhelmed, fled far overseas and disappeared forever. Great Sidon, Little Sidon, Bēt-Zitti, Ṣareptu, Maḫalliba, Ushu, Akziba (and) Acco—his mighty cities, fortresses, the place of pastures and water—the source of his supply, the terrifying appearance of the Weapon of Assur, my lord, overwhelmed, and they bowed in submission to my feet. Tuba'lu I installed on the throne over them and I imposed upon him tribute (as) duty to my rule (to be paid) annually without interruption.

As to Miniḫimmu of Samsimuruna, Tuba'lu of Sidon, Abdili'ti of Arvad, Urumilki of Byblos, Mitinti of Ashdod, Pudu-ilu of Bēt-Ammon, Kamusu-nadbi of Mo'ab (and) Ayarammu of Edom, all the kings of Amurru brought sumptuous gifts (and) their heavy greeting-presents fourfold before me and kissed my feet. Ṣidqa, however, king of Ashkelon, who did not bow to my yoke—his family gods, himself, his wife, his children, his brothers (and) all the male descendants of his family I deported and sent to Assyria.

Šarru-lū-dâri, son of Rukibtu, their former king, I set over the inhabitants of Ashkelon, and the payment of tribute (and) greeting-gifts for my rule I imposed upon him, so that he will drag the straps (of my yoke).

In the course of my campaign I besieged, conquered (and) plundered Bēt-Dagāna, Joppe, Banai-Barqa (and) Azuru, cities of Ṣidqa, which did not bow to my feet quickly (enough). The high officials, the nobles (and) the people of Ekron—who had thrown into iron fetters Padî, their king, who was loyal to the treaty and oath with Assyria, and had him handed over to Hezekiah, the Judaean, like an enemy—because of the villainous act they had committed, they became afraid. The kings of Egypt, troops, archers, chariots and the cavalry of the king of Nubia, an army beyond counting, they had called, and they (actually) came to their assistance. In the vicinity of Eltekeh their battle lines were drawn up against me, while they sharpened their weapons. Trusting to Assur, my lord, I fought with them and inflicted a heavy defeat upon them. The Egyptian commander of the chariots and the princes (and also) the commander of the chariots of the king of Nubia I personally captured alive in the mêlée of the battle.

Eltekeh (and) Timnah I besieged, conquered and plundered. I assaulted Ekron and executed the high officials and nobles who had committed the crime and hung their bodies on the towers around the city(-wall). The people of the city who were guilty of sin and crime, I considered booty. The rest of them, those who were not guilty of misdeeds and crime, who were without guilt, I released. I made Padî, their king, come out from Jerusalem and restored him on the throne as their lord, imposing upon him the tribute of my rule.

As to Hezekiah, the Judaean, who did not submit to my yoke, I laid siege to 46 of his strong cities, fortresses and countless small villages in their vicinity (and) conquered (them) by means of building siege ramps, drawing battering-rams up close, hand-to-hand combat of infantry, mines, breaches and assault ladders. 205,105—people, young (and) old, male and female; horses, mules, donkeys, camels, big and small cattle beyond counting—I drove out of them and considered (them) booty.

Himself I enclosed in Jerusalem, his royal city, like a bird in a cage. I laid out forts against him in order to repel him from going out of the gate of his city. His towns, which I plundered, I separated from his territory and handed (them) over to Mitinti, king of Ashdod, Padî, king of Ekron, and Ṣillī-bēl, king of Gaza, and thus I reduced (the size of) his country. In addition to the former annual tribute, I imposed on them more gifts owed to my rule. This Hezekiah the fearsome splendour of my rule overwhelmed, and the *mercenaries* and his elite troops that he had brought into

Jerusalem, his royal city, in order to strengthen (it), ceased their services.

Together with 30 talents of gold, 800 talents of silver, select antimony in small blocks, large blocks of AN.GUG-stone, couches (inlaid) with ivory, armchairs (inlaid) with ivory, elephant hides, ivory, ebony, boxwood (and) all kinds of valuable treasures, he also sent his (own) daughters, women of his palace, (and) male and female musicians after me to Nineveh, my lordly city, and in order to deliver the tribute and to do obeisance as a slave, he sent his messenger.'

2. Taylor Prism

I R 37-42; Luckenbill, 1924: 23-47 and 128-31; BAL^2 1: 68-88.
Translation: Borger, TUAT 1: 388-90; ANET: 287-88 (cf. BAL^2 1: 65-66; Frahm 1997: T 16)[58]

Col. II

34 *i-na šal-ši ger-ri-ia a-na* KUR *Ḫa-at-ti lu al-lik*
35 m.*Lu-li-i* LUGAL URU.Ṣi-*du-un-ni pul-ḫi me-lam-me*
36 *be-lu-ti-ia is-ḫu-pu-šu-ma a-na ru-uq-qí*
37 MURUN$_4$ *tam-tim in-na-bit-ma* KUR-*šú e-mid*
38 URU.Ṣi-*du-un-nu* GAL-*ú* URU.Ṣi-*du-un-nu še-eš-ru*
39 URU.*Bet-Zi-it-te* URU.Ṣa-*re-ep-tú* URU.*Ma-šal-li-ba*
40 URU.*Ú-šu-ú* URU.*Ak-zi-bi* URU.*Ak-ku-ú*
41 URU.MEŠ-*šú dan-nu-ti* É BÀD.MEŠ-*ni a-šar ri-i-ti*
42 *ù maš-qí-ti* É *tuk-la-ti-šú ra-šub-bat* GIŠ.TUKUL
43 d.*Aš+šur* EN-*ia is-ḫu-pu-šu-nu-ti-ma ik-nu-šu*
44 *še-pu-ú-a* m.*Tu-ba-aʾ-lu i-na* GIŠ.GU.ZA LUGAL-*ú-ti*
45 UGU-*šú-un ú-še-šib-ma* GUN *man-da-at-tu be-lu-ti-ia*
46 *šat-ti-šam la ba-aṭ-lu ú-kin še-ru-uš-šú*
47 *ša* m.*Mi-ini-ḫi-im-mu*   URU.*Sam-si-mu-ru-na-a-a*
48 m.*Tu-ba-aʾ-lu*   URU.Ṣi-*du-un-na-a-a*
49 m.*Ab-di-li-iʾ-ti*   URU.*A-ru-da-a-a*
50 m.*Ú-ru-mil-ki*   URU.*Gu-ub-la-a-a*
51 m.*Mi-ti-in-ti*   URU.*As-du-da-a-a*
52 m.*Pu-du*-DINGIR   KUR.*Bet*-m.*Am-ma-na-a-a*
53 m.*Kam-mu-su-na-ad-bi*   KUR.[*M*]*a-aʾ-ba-a-a*
54 m.d.*A-a-ram-mu*   KUR.*Ú-du-um-ma-a-a*

58. Beyond occasional variations in orthography and other minor deviations, the text of the Taylor Prism so closely corresponds to the already published Chicago Prism text that no translation is necessary here.

⁵⁵ LUGAL.MEŠ-*ni* KUR MAR.TU.KI *ka-li-šú-un* IGI.SÁ-*e*

⁵⁶ *šad-lu-ti ta-mar-ta-šú-nu ka-bit-tu a-di* 4-*šú*

⁵⁷ *a-na maḫ-ri-ia iš-šu-nim-ma iš-ši-qu* GÌR.II-*ia*

⁵⁸ *ù* m.*Ṣi-id-qa-a* LUGAL URU.*Iš-qa-al-lu-na*

⁵⁹ *ša la ik-nu-šú a-na ni-ri-ia* DINGIR.MEŠ É AD-*šú šá-a-šú*

⁶⁰ DAM-*su* DUMU.MEŠ-*šú* DUMU.MÍ.MEŠ-*šú* ŠEŠ.MEŠ-*šú* NUMUN É AD-*šú*

⁶¹ *as-su-ḫa-am-ma a-na* KUR.*Aš+šur*.KI *ú-ra-áš-šú*

⁶² m.LUGAL-*lu-dà-ri* DUMU m.*Ru-kib-ti* LUGAL-*šú-nu maš-ru-ú*

⁶³ UGU UN.MEŠ URU.*Iš-qa-al-lu-na áš-kun-ma na-dan* GUN

⁶⁴ *kàd-re-e be-lu-ti-ia e-mid-su-ma i-šá-a-aṭ ab-šá-a-ni*

⁶⁵ *i-na me-ti-iq ger-ri-ia* URU.*Bet-Da-gan-na*

⁶⁶ URU.*Ia-ap-pu-ú* URU.*Ba-na-a-a-bar-qa* URU.*A-zu-ru*

⁶⁷ URU.MEŠ-*ni ša* m.*Ṣi-id-qa-a ša a-na* GÌR.II-*ia*

⁶⁸ *ár-ḫiš la ik-nu-šú al-me* KUR-*ud áš-lu-la šal-la-sún*

⁶⁹ LÚ.GÌR.ARAD.MEŠ LÚ.NUN.MEŠ *ù* UN.MEŠ URU.*Am-qar-ru-na*

⁷⁰ *ša* m.*Pa-di-i* LUGAL-*šú-nu* EN *a-de-e ù ma-miti*

⁷¹ *ša* KUR *Aš+šur*.KI *bi-re-tu* AN.BAR *id-du-ma a-na* m.*Ḫa-za-qi-ia-ú*

⁷² KUR *Ia-ú-da-a-a id-di-nu-šú nak-riš a-na an-zil-li e-pu-šú*

⁷³ *ip-làḫ lib-ba-šú-un* LUGAL.MEŠ-*ni* KUR *Mu-ṣu-re*

⁷⁴ LÚ.ERIM.MEŠ GIŠ.BAN GIŠ.GIGIR.MEŠ ANŠE.KUR.RA.MEŠ *ša* LUGAL KUR *Me-luḫ-ḫe*

⁷⁵ *e-mu-qí la ni-bi ik-te-ru-nim-ma il-li-ku*

⁷⁶ *re-ṣu-us-su-un i-na ta-mir-ti* URU.*Al-ta-qu-ú*

⁷⁷ *el-la-mu-ú-a šit-ku-nu ú-šá-ʾi-lu*

⁷⁸ GIŠ.TUKUL.MEŠ-*šú-un i-na tukul-ti* d.*Aš+šur* EN-*ia it-ti-šú-un*

⁷⁹ *am-da-ḫi-iṣ-ma áš-ta-kan* BAD₅.BAD₅-*šú-un*

⁸⁰ LÚ.EN GIŠ.GIGIR.MEŠ *ù* DUMU.MEŠ LUGAL KUR.*Mu-ṣu-ra-a-a*

⁸¹ *a-di* LÚ.EN GIŠ.GIGIR.MEŠ *ša* LUGAL KUR *Me-luḫ-ḫi bal-ṭu-su-un*

⁸² *i-na* MURUB₄ *tam-ḫa-ri ik-šu-da* ŠU.II-*a-a* URU.*Al-ta-qu*

⁸³ URU.*Ta-am-na-a al-me* KUR-*ud áš-lu-la šal-la-sún*

Col. III

¹ *a-na* URU.*Am-qar-ru-na aq-reb-ma* LÚ.GÌR.ARAD.MEŠ

² LÚ.NUN.MEŠ *ša ḫi-iṭ-ṭu ú-šab-šu-ú a-duk-ma*

³ *i-na di-ma-a-ti si-ḫir-ti* URU *a-lul pag-ri-šú-un*

⁴ DUMU.MEŠ URU *e-piš an-ni ù gíl-la-ti*

⁵ *a-na šal-la-ti am-nu si-it-tu-te-šú-nu*

⁶ *la ba-bil ḫi-ṭi-ti ù gul-lul-ti ša a-ra-an-šú-nu*

⁷ *la ib-šu-ú uš-šur-šú-un aq-bi* m.*Pa-di-i*

⁸ LUGAL-*šú-nu ul-tu qé-reb* URU.*Ur-sa-li-im-mu*

⁹ *ú-še-ṣa-am-ma i-na* GIŠ.GU.ZA *be-lu-ti* UGU-*šú-un*

[10] *ú-še-šib-ma man-da-at-tu be-lu-ti-ia*

[11] *ú-kin ṣe-ru-uš-šú ù* m.Ḫa-za-qi-a-ú

[12] KUR.*Ia-ú-da-a-a ša la ik-nu-šú a-na ni-ri-ia*

[13] 46 URU.MEŠ-*šú dan-nu-ti* É BÀD.MEŠ *ù* URU.MEŠ TUR.MEŠ

[14] *ša li-me-ti-šú-nu ša ni-ba la i-šu-ú*

[15] *i-na šuk-bu-us a-ram-me ù qit-ru-ub šu-pi-i*

[16] *mit-ḫu-uṣ zu-uk* GÌR.II *pil-ši nik-si ù kal-ban-na-te*

[17] *al-me* KUR-*ud* 2 ME LIM 1 ME 50 UKÙ.MEŠ TUR GAL NITA *ù* MÍ

[18] ANŠE.KUR.RA.MEŠ ANŠE.KUNGI.MEŠ ANŠE.MEŠ ANŠE.GAM.MAL.MEŠ   GUD.MEŠ

[19] *ù ṣe-e-ni ša la ni-bi ul-tu qer-bi-šú-un ú-še-ṣa-am-ma*

[20] *šal-la-tiš am-nu šá-a-šú* GIM MUŠEN *qu-up-pi qe-reb* URU.*Ur-sa-li-im- mu*

[21] URU LUGAL-*ti-šú e-sír-šú* URU.ḪAL-ṢU.MEŠ UGU-*šú*

[22] *ú-rak-kis-ma a-ṣe-e* KÁ.GAL URU-*šú ú-tir-ra*

[23] *ik-ki-bu-uš* URU.MEŠ-*šú ša áš-lu-la ul-tu qé-reb* KUR-*šú*

[24] *ab-tuq-ma a-na* m.*Mi-ti-in-ti* LUGAL URU *As-du-di*

[25] m.*Pa-di-i* LUGAL URU.*Am-qar-ru-na ù* m.GISSU-d.EN

[26] LUGAL URU.*Ḫa-zi-ti ad-din-ma ú-ṣa-aḫ-ḫir* KUR-*su*

[27] *e-li* GUN *maḫ-ri-ti na-dan šat-ti-šú-un*

[28] *man-da-at-tu kàd-re-e be-lu-ti-ia ú-rad-di-ma*

[29] *ú-kin ṣe-ru-uš-šú-un šu-ú* m.Ḫa-za-qi-a-ú

[30] *pul-ḫi me-lam-me be-lu-ti-ia is-ḫu-pu-šu-ma*

[31] LÚ.*úr-bi ù* LÚ.ERIM.MEŠ -*šú* SIG₅.MEŠ

[32] *ša a-na dun-nu-un* URU.*Ur-sa-li-im-mu* URU LUGAL-*ti-šú*

[33] *ú-še-ri-bu-ma ir-šu-ú baṭ-la-a-ti*

[34] *it-ti* 30 GUN GUŠKIN 8 ME GUN KÙ.BABBAR *ni-siq-ti*

[35] *gu-uḫ-li ták-kàs-si* NA₄.AN.ZA.GUL.ME GAL.MEŠ

[36] GIŠ.NÁ.MEŠ ZÚ GIŠ.GU.ZA.MEŠ *né-me-di* ZÚ KUŠ AM.SI

[37] ZÚ AM.SI GIŠ.ESI GIŠ.TÚG *mim-ma šum-šú ni-ṣir-tú ka-bit-tú*

[38] *ù* DUMU.MÍ.MEŠ-*šú* MÍ.UN.MEŠ.É.GAL-*šú* LÚ.NAR.MEŠ

[39] MÍ.NAR.MEŠ *a-na qé-reb* NINA.KI URU *be-lu-ti-ia*

[40] EGIR-*ia ú-še-bi-lam-ma a-na na-dan man-da-at-ti*

[41] *ù e-peš* ÌR-*du-ti iš-pu-ra rak-bu-šú*

3. Rassam Cylinder

Luckenbill, 1924: 60-61 and 102 (cf. BAL² 1: 64-65; 75 and 76; Frahm 1997: T4)

[56] 30 GUN GUŠKIN 8 ME GUN KÙ.BABBAR *ni-siq-ti gu-uḫ-li ták-kàs-si* NA₄.AN.ZA.GUL.ME GAL.MEŠ GIŠ.NÁ.MEŠ ZÚ GIŠ.GU.ZA.MEŠ *né-me-di* ZÚ KUŠ AM.SI ZÚ AM.SI GIŠ.ESI GIŠ.TÚG *lu-bul-ti bir-me* TÚG.GADA SÍG.*ta-kil-tu* SÍG.*ar-ga-man-nu*

[57] *ú-nu-ut* ZABAR AN.BAR URUDU AN.NA <<AN.BAR>> GIŠ.GIGIR.MEŠ *ga-ba-bi as-ma-re-e si-ri-ia-am* GÍR.MEŠ.AN.BAR *šib-bi til-pa-ni u uṣ-ṣe til-le ú-nu-ut ta-ḫa-zi šá ni-ba la i-šu-ú*

[58] *it-ti* DUMU.MÍ.MEŠ-*šú* MÍ.UN.MEŠ.É.GAL-*šú* LÚ.NAR.MEŠ MÍ.NAR.MEŠ *a-na qé-reb* NINA.KI URU *be-lu-ti-ia* EGIR-*ia ú-še-bi-lam-ma a-na na-dan man-da-at-te ù e-peš* ÌR-*du-ti iš-pu-ra rak-bu-šú*

[59] *i-na šal-la-at* KUR.MEŠ *šá-ti-na ša áš-lu-la* 10 LIM GIŠ.BAN 10 LIM GIŠ.*a-ri-tú ina lìb-bi-šú-nu ak-ṣur-ma* UGU *ki-ṣir* LUGAL-*ti-ia ú-rad-di*

[60] *ši-it-ti šal-la-ti na-ki-re ka-bit-tu a-na gi-mir* KI.ALAD-*ia ù* LÚ.EN.NAM-*ia* UN.MEŠ *ma-ḫa-za-ni-ia* GAL.MEŠ *ki-ma ṣe-e-ni lu ú-za-'i-iz*

'Thirty talents of gold, 800 talents of silver, select antimony in small blocks, large blocks of AN.GUG-stone, couches (inlaid) with ivory, armchairs (inlaid) with ivory, elephant hides, ivory, ebony, boxwood, garments with colorful embroidery, garments of linen, blue-purple wool, red-purple wool, tools of bronze, iron, copper (and) tin, <<iron>> chariots, slings, lances, armour, swords of iron (with their) girdles, bows and arrows, bridles (and) countless implements of war, together with his (own) daughters, women of his palace, male and female musicians he sent after me to Nineveh, my lordly city, and in order to deliver the tribute and to do obeisance as a slave, he sent his messenger.

From the booty of those lands that I plundered, 10,000 archers (and) 10,000 infantrymen ('shields') I collected therefrom and added them to my royal army. The rest of the heavy booty (taken from the) enemy I divided like sheep among my entire camp as well as my governors and the citizens of my great, all-encompassing cities'.

4. *Thompson Prism*

Thompson 1940.94-5, 7 (cf. BAL[2] 1.66-7 and 76; Frahm 1997: T 19).

[13] *ša* m.*Luli-i* LUGAL URU.*Ṣi-du-un-ni e-kim* LUGAL-*ti-[šu]*

[14] m.*Tu-ba-aʾ-lu* [*in*]*a* GIŠ.GU.ZA-*šú ú-še-šib-ma man-da-at-tu* EN-*ti-ia ú-kin ṣe-ru-uš-šú*

[15] *ú-šal-pit rap-šú na-gu-u* KUR *Ia-ú-di* m.*Ḫa-za-qi-a-ú* LUGAL-*šu e-mid ab-šá-nu*

'From Lulî, king of Sidon, I took his kingdom. Tubaʾlu I installed upon his throne and I imposed upon him the tribute for my rule. I laid waste a wide area of Judah (and) upon Hezekiah, its king, I put the straps (of my yoke)'.

Bull Inscriptions

5. *Bull 1*

Layard, ICC: pls. 59-62; Luckenbill, 1924: 76-77 and 117-25.

Translation: Borger, TUAT 1: 390; ANET: 288 (cf. BAL² 1: 66 and 76; Frahm 1997: T 25).

¹⁷ ù m.*Lu-li-i* LUGAL URU.*Ṣi-du-un-ni e-du-ra ta-ḫa-zi a-na* KUR.*Ia-ad-na-na*
¹⁸ *ša qé-reb tam-tim in-na-bit-ma i-ḫu-uz mar-qí-tu i-na šat-tim-ma šá-a-tu*
¹⁹ *i-na ra-šub-bat* GIŠ.TUKUL d.*Aš-šur* EN-*ia e-mid šad-da-šú* m.*Tu-ba-a'-lu i-na* GIŠ.GU.ZA
²⁰ LUGAL-*ti-šú ú-še-šib-ma man-da-at-tu be-lu-ti-ia ú-kin ṣe-ru-uš-šu ú-šal-pit*
²¹ *rap-šu na-gu-ú* KUR.*Ia-ú-di šep-ṣu be-ru* m.*Ḫa-za-qí-a-a-ú* LUGAL-*šu*
²² *še-pu-u-a ú-šak-niš-ma i-šá-ṭa ab-šá-*[*ni*]

'And Lulî, the king of Sidon, was afraid to fight me. He fled to Cyprus, which is in the midst of the sea, and there he sought a refuge. In that year he vanished before the terrifying appearance of the Weapon of Assur, my lord. Tuba'lu I placed on his throne and I imposed upon him the tribute for my rule. I laid waste a wide area of Judah. The notorious rebel Hezekiah, its king, I brought in submission to my feet, so that he will drag the straps (of my yoke)'.

6 and 7. Bulls 2 and 3

Layard, ICC: pls. 61-62; Luckenbill, OIP 2: 76-78.
Translation: Borger, TUAT 1: 390; *ANET*: 288. (cf. BAL² 1: 66 and 76; Frahm 1997: T 26-27).

¹⁷ ù m.*Lu-li-i* LUGAL URU.*Ṣi-du-un-ni e-du-ra ta-ḫa-zi a-na* KUR.*Ia-ad-na-na*
¹⁸ *ša qé-reb tam-tim in-na-bit-ma i-ḫu-uz mar-qí-tu i-na šat-tim-ma šá-a-tu*
¹⁹ *i-na ra-šub-bat* GIŠ.TUKUL d.*Aš-šur* EN-*ia e-mid šad-da-šú* m.*Tu-ba-a'-lu i-na* GIŠ.GU.ZA
²⁰ LUGAL-*ti-šú ú-še-šib-ma man-da-at-tu be-lu-ti-ia ú-kin ṣe-ru-uš-šu ú-šal-pit*
²¹ *rap-šu na-gu-ú* KUR.*Ia-ú-di šep-ṣu be-ru* m.*Ḫa-za-qí-a-a-ú* LUGAL-*šu ú- ak-niš*
²² *še-pu-u-a* .....

'And Lulî, the king of Sidon, was afraid to fight me. He fled to Cyprus, which is in the midst of the sea, and there he sought a refuge. In that year he vanished before the terrifying appearance of the Weapon of Assur, my lord. Tuba'lu I placed on his throne and I imposed upon him the tribute for my rule. I laid waste a wide area of Judah. The notorious rebel Hezekiah, its king, I brought in submission to my feet.'

8. Bull 4

III R: 12/3; Paterson 1912–15: pls. 5-6; Luckenbill, 1924: 66-76 and 117-25. (cf. BAL² 1: 66-67 and 75-76; Frahm 1997: T 29).

¹⁸ *i-na šal-ši ger-ri-ia a-na* KUR *Ḫat-ti*.KI *al-lik* m.*Lu-li-i* LUGAL URU.*Ṣi-du-un-ni* [*pu*]-*luḫ-ti me-*[*lam-me-ia is-ḫup*]-*šu-ma ul-tu qé-reb* URU.*Ṣur-ri a-na* KUR *Ia-ad- na-na* <*ša*>

¹⁹ *qa-bal tam-tim in-na-bit-ma* KUR-*šú e-mid* m.*Tu-ba-aʾ-lu i-na* GIŠ.GU.ZA LUGAL-*ti-šú ú-še-šib-ma* GUN *man-da-at-tu be-lu-ti-ia ú-kin ṣe-ru-uš-šú* LUGAL.MEŠ KUR MAR.TU.KI *ka-li-šú-un* GUN *ka-bit-tú*

²⁰ *i-na ta-mir-ti* URU.*Ú-šu-ú a-di maḫ-ri-ia ú-bi-lu-ni* ù m.*Ṣi-id-qa-a* LUGAL URU.*Iš-qa-al-lu-na ša la ik-nu-šú a-na ni-ri-ia* DINGIR.MEŠ É AD-*šú šá-a-šú a-di ki-im-ti-*[*šu*]

²¹ *as-su-ḫa-am-ma a-na* KUR.*Aš+šur*.KI *ú-raš-šu* m.LUGAL-*lu-dà-a-ri* DUMU m.*Ru-kib-ti* LUGAL-*šú-nu* [*maḫ-ru-ú* UGU UN].MEŠ URU.*Iš-qa-al-lu-na áš-kun-ma man-da-at-tu* [EN]-*ti-ia ú-kin ṣe-ru-uš-šu*

²² *i-na mi-ti-iq ger-ri-ia* URU.MEŠ-*šú ša a-na* GÌR.II-*ia la ik-nu-šu ak-šu-da áš-lu-la šal-la-su-un* LÚ.GÌR. ARAD.MEŠ *ù* UN.MEŠ URU.*Am-qar-ru-na ša* m.*Pa-di-i* LUGAL-*šu-nu*

²³ EN *a-de-e ša* KUR *Aš+š ur*.KI *bi-re-tu* AN.BAR *id-du-ma a-na* m.*Ḫa-za-qi-a-ú* KUR *Ia-ú-da-a-a id-di-nu-šú a-na an-zil-*[*lì*] *e-pu-šú ip-làḫ-šú-nu* LUGAL.MEŠ KUR *Mu- ṣu-re* LÚ.ERIM.MEŠ GIŠ.BAN

²⁴ GIŠ.GIGIR.MEŠ ANŠE.KUR.RA.MEŠ *ša* LUGAL KUR *Me-luḫ-ḫe e-mu-qí la ni-bi ik-te-ru-ni it-ti-šú-un am-daḫiṣ -*[*m*]*a áš-ta-kan* BAD₅.BAD₅-*šú-un* LÚ.[E]N GIŠ.GIGIR.MEŠ

²⁵ *ù* DUMU.MEŠ LUGAL KUR.*Mu-ṣu-ra-a-a a-di* LÚ.EN GIŠ.GIGIR.MEŠ *ša* LUGAL KUR *Me-luḫ-ḫa bal-ṭu-su-*[*un*] *i-na qa-ti aṣ-bat a-na* URU.*Am-qar-ru-na aq-*[*reb-ma*] GÌR.ARAD.MEŠ *ša ḫi-iṭ-ṭu*

²⁶ *ú-šab-šu'-ú i-na* GIŠ.TUKUL.MEŠ *a-duk* DUMU.MEŠ URU *e-piš an-ni a-na šal-la- ti am-nu si-it-tu-te-šú-nu* [*gu-lu*]*l-ta-šú-un la ib-šu-ú* [*uš-šur-šú-un aq-bi*] m.*Pa-di-i* LUGAL-*šú-nu*

²⁷ *ul-tu qé-reb* URU.*Ur-sa-li-im-ma ú-še-ṣa-am-ma i-na* GIŠ.GU.ZA UGU-*šú-un ú-še- šib-ma man-da-at-tu be-lu-ti-ia ú-kin ṣe-ru-uš-šú ša* m.*Ḫa-za-qi-a-ú* KUR.*Ia-ú-da- a-a ša la ik-nu-šú*

²⁸ *a-na ni-ri-ia* 46 URU.MEŠ-*šú* É BÀD.MEŠ *dan-nu-ti ù* URU.MEŠ TUR.MEŠ *ša li-me-ti-šú-nu ša ni-ba la i-šu-ú al-me* KUR-*ud áš-lu-la šal-la-tiš am-nu šá-šú* [GIM MUŠEN *qu-up-pi*] *qe-reb*

²⁹ URU.*Ur-sa-li-im-ma* URU LUGAL-*ti-šú e-sír-šu* URU.*ḪAL-ṢU*.MEŠ UGU-*šu ú-rak-kis* URU.MEŠ-*šú ša áš-lu-la ul-tu qé-reb* KUR-*šú ab-tuq-ma a-na* LUGAL.[MEŠ URU.*As-du*]-*di* URU.*Is-qà-al-lu-na*

³⁰ URU.*Am-qar-ru-na* URU.*Ḫa-zi-ti ad-din-šú ú-ṣa-aḫ-*[*ḫir*] KUR-*su e-li* GUN *maḫ-ri-ti na-dan šat-ti-šú-un man-da-at-tú ú-rad-di-ma ú-kin* [*ṣe-ru-uš-šú-un šu-ú*] m.*Ḫa-za-qi-a-ú pul-ḫi me-lam-me*

³¹ *be-lu-ti-ia is-ḫu-pu-šu-ma* LÚ.*úr-bi ù* LÚ.ERIM.MEŠ-*šú* SIG₅.MEŠ *ša a-na qé-reb* URU.*Ur-sa-li-im-ma* URU LUGAL-*ti-šú ú-še-ri-bu-ma* [*ir-šu-ú baṭ-la-a-ti*] *it-ti* 30 GUN GUŠKIN 8 ME GUN KÙ.BABBAR

[32] *mim-ma šum-šu ni-ṣir-ti* É.GAL-*šú ù* DUMU.MÍ.MEŠ-*šú* MÍ.UN.MEŠ.É.GAL-*šú*
LÚ.NAR.MEŠ MÍ.NAR.MEŠ *a-na qé-reb* NINA.KI *ú-še-bi-lam-ma a-na na-dan man-da-at-te iš -pu-ra rak-bu-šú*

'On my third campaign I marched against Syria. Lulî, king of Sidon, whom the fearsome splendour of my rule had overwhelmed, fled from Tyre to Cyprus, <which is> in the midst of the sea, and vanished forever. Tuba'lu I installed on his throne and I imposed upon him tribute (as) duty to my rule. All the kings of Amurru brought their heavy tribute before me in the vicinity of Ushu. Ṣidqa, however, king of Ashkelon, who did not bow to my yoke, his family gods, himself and his family I deported and sent to Assyria. Šarru-lū-dâri, son of Rukibtu, their former king, I set over the inhabitants of Ashkelon, and a tribute for my rule I imposed upon him.

In the course of my campaign I besieged (and) plundered his cities, which did not bow to my feet quickly (enough). The high officials, the nobles (and) the people of Ekron—who had thrown into iron fetters Padî, their king, who was loyal to the treaty and oath with Assyria, and had him handed over to Hezekiah, the Judaean, like an enemy—because of the villainous act they had committed, they became afraid. The kings of Egypt, troops, archers, chariots and the cavalry of the king of Nubia, an army beyond counting, they had called. I fought with them and inflicted a heavy defeat upon them. The Egyptian commander of the chariots and the princes (and also) the commander of the chariots of the king of Nubia I personally captured alive.

I assaulted Ekron and by means of weapons I executed the high officials and the nobles who had committed the crime. The people of the city who were guilty of sin, I considered booty. The rest of them, those who were not guilty of misdeeds, I released. I made Padî, their king, come out from Jerusalem and restored him on the throne over them, imposing upon him the tribute for my rule.

As to Hezekiah, the Judaean, who did not submit to my yoke, I laid siege to 46 of his strong cities, fortresses and countless small villages in their vicinity, conquered, plundered (and) considered (them) booty. Himself I enclosed in Jerusalem, his royal city, like a bird in a cage. I laid out forts against him. His towns, which I had plundered, I separated from his territory and handed (them) over to the kings of Ashdod, Ekron, and Gaza, and thus I reduced (the size of) his country. In addition to the former annual tribute, I imposed on them more gifts. This Hezekiah, the fearsome splendour of my rule overwhelmed, and the *mercenaries* and his elite troops that he had brought into Jerusalem, his royal city, in order to strengthen (it), ceased their services.

Together with 30 talents of gold, 800 talents of silver (and) all kinds of valuable treasures, he also sent his (own) daughters, women of his palace, (and) male and female musicians after me to Nineveh, my lordly city, and in order to deliver the tribute and to do obeisance as a slave, he sent his messenger.'

Inscriptions on Slabs

9. *'Nebi Yunus Slab'* or *'Sennacherib Konstantinopel'*

> I R: 43/4; Luckenbill, 1924: 85-89 and 131-34.
> Translation: Borger, TUAT 1: 391; ANET: 288. (cf. BAL² 1: 67 and 76; Frahm 1997: T 61).

¹³ *ša* m.*Luli-i* LUGAL URU.*Ṣi-du-ni e-kim* LUGAL-*su*

¹⁴ m.*Tu-ba-a'-lu i-na* GIŠ.GU.ZA-*šú ú-še-šib-ma man-da-at-tu* EN-*ti-ia ú-kin ṣe-ru-uš-šú*

¹⁵ *ú-šal-pit rap-šú na-gu-ú* KUR *Ia-ú-di* m.*Ḫa-za-qi-a-ú* LUGAL-*šu e-mid ab-šá-ni*

'From Lulî, king of Sidon, I took his kingdom. Tuba'lu I installed upon his throne and I imposed upon him the tribute for my lordship. I laid waste a wide area of Judah and upon Hezekiah, its king, I put the straps (of my yoke)'.

10. *Epigraphs*

> I R: 7 I; Paterson 1912–15: pl. 74; Luckenbill, 1924: 156, 25.
> Translation: Borger, TUAT 1: 391; ANET: 288 (cf. BAL² 1: 66-67 and 76; Frahm 1997: T 50).

¹ m.d.XXX-PAB.MEŠ-SU MAN ŠÚ MAN KUR *Aš+šur*

² *ina* GIŠ.GU.ZA *né-me-di ú-šib-ma*

³ *šal-la-at* URU.*La-ki-su*

⁴ *ma-ḫa-ar-šu e-ti-iq*

'Sennacherib, king of the world, king of Assyria, sat in an armchair and the booty of Lachish passed in review in front of him.'

> I R: 7 J; Paterson 1912–15: pl. 75; Luckenbill, 1924: 157, 32.
> Translation: Borger, TUAT 1: 391 (cf. Frahm 1997: T 51).

¹ *za-ra-tum*

² *šá* m.d.XXX-PAB.MEŠ-SU

³ LUGAL KUR *Aš+š ur*

'Tent of Sennacherib, king of Assyria'.

11. *Letter to the God Assur*

Na'aman 1974: 25-39 (cf. Na'aman 1979: 61-64; BAL^2 1: 134-35; Frahm 1997: 229-32)[59]

1 [.....................]

2 [......] ŠID [.........]

3 [... AN.ŠÁR EN *ú-tak-kil-a*]*n-ni-ma a-na* KUR *Ia-*[*u-di lu al-lik ina*] *me-ti-iq* KASKAL.II-*ia man-da-at-tu šá* LU[GAL.MEŠ KUR MAR.TU.KI DÙ-*šú-un am-ḫur*]

4 [..... *ina da-n*]*a-ni šá* AN.ŠÁR EN-*ia na-gu-ú* [*šá* m.*Ḫa-za-qi-i*]*a-a-u* KUR *Ia-u-da-a-a* GIM [*ḫu-ḫa-re as-ḫu-up-ma* .....]

5 [.....] URU.*A-za-qa-a* É *tuk-la-te-šú šá ina bi-*⸢*rit*⸣ [*áš*⸣-*ri-ia u* KUR *Ia-ú-di* [..........]

6 [..... *ana*] *ṣe-er* ŠU.SI KUR-*e šá-kin* GIM *zi-qip* GÍR.AN?.B[AR?.ME]Š? *la ni-bi ana* AN-*e šá-qu-u šur-*[*šu-šá šuk-šud-du qé-reb a-ra-al-li*]

7 [BÀD.MEŠ-*ni-šu*] *dun!-nu-nu-ma šit-nu-nu* KUR-*e zaq-ru-ti a-na ni-*[*til*] IGI.II.MEŠ *ki-i šá ul-tu* AN-*e* [..........]

8 [*šuk-bu-us a-r*]*a-am-me ù qur-ru-bu šu-pe-e da-*<*na*>-*an ši-pir n*[*im?-gal?-l*]*i? mit-ḫu-uṣ zu-uk* GÌR.II *q*[*u-/ú*[*r-*.........]

9 [*ti-bu-ut* ANŠE.KU]R.RA.MEŠ-*ia e-mu-ru-ma ri-gim um-na!-nat* A[N].ŠÁR *gap-šá-te iš-mu-ma ip-láḫ lìb-*[*ba-šú-un* ....]

10 [URU.*A-za-qa-a al-me*] KUR-*ud áš-lu-la šal-lat-su ap-pul aq-qur* [..........]

11 [URU...... URU] ⸢LUGAL-*ti*⸣ *ša* KUR *Pi-liš-ta-a-*⸢*a ša* m.*Ḫa-z*⸣[*a-qi-i*]*a-a-u e-ki-mu ú-dan-ni-nu-šú-ma* [..........]

12 [..........] *ḫa?* x x x [..........] GIM GIŠ.*gap-ni* [..........]

---

59.   This text consists of three joining fragments. It is unclear how long the lines originally were and what the content of text broken off from the left and right sides might have been. My own collations of the original confirmed the results given by R. Borger in BAL^2 1: 134-35. My restorations which are mostly oriented to Sennacherib's annals and Sg. 8 are only suggestions:

  l. 3.   Cf. Bull 4 ll. 19-20.
  l. 4.   Cf. Sg. 8 l. 194.
  l. 6.   Cf. Sg. 8 l. 19.
  l. 8.   *šukbus*…can only be the object of *ēmurūma* in line 9. As it cannot belong to *alme*] *akšud* in line 10, N. Na'amans restoration of *ina* at the beginning of line 8 is erroneous. The siege engine *nimgallu* 'Big Fly' (AHw: 790 a; CAD N$_2$: .234) appears only in Sennacherib's inscriptions.
  l. 9.   Cf. Sg. 8 l. 178.
  l. 17: Cf. Sg. 8 l. 104.

¹³ [.........] [*di*ˡ-ˡ*ma*ˡ-*a-ti* GAL.MEŠ *ḫu-tas*!-*ḫu*!-*u*[*r*!-*m*]*a šum-ru-ṣa-at* [.........]

¹⁴ [.........] X É.GAL GIM KUR-*e pa-nu-uš-šú-u*[*n*] *ed-let-ma šá-qa-at* [.........]

¹⁵ [.........] *e-kil la na-pi-iḫ-šú* d.UTU-*šu* A.MEŠ-*šú ina e-ṭ*[*u*]-*ti šit-ku-nu-ma mu-ṣa-*

¹⁵   [*šú* ....]

¹⁶ [.........]-*i-šá ina qul-mì-i na-kis ḫa-ri-ṣu i-te-*[*ša*] *šá-pil-ma ka-*[.........]

¹⁷ [LÚ.*mun-daḫ-ṣi-šu* ˡ]*e-*ʾ-*u-te* MÈ *ú-še-rib qé-reb-šú* GIŠ.TUKUL.MEŠ-*šú ú-ra-kis a-*

   n[*a* ....]

¹⁸ [......... *u*]*m-ma-na-at* KUR MAR.TU.KI DÙ-*šú-un* SA[ḪAR.Ḫ]I.A *ú-šá-az-bíl-šu-nu-*

   ti-m[*a* ....]

¹⁹ [.........] X *ṣe-ru-uš-šú-un ina* 7-*šu* X [X X]-ˡ*ri*ˡ?-*šú* GAL.MEŠ GIM *kar-p*[*at*

   ....]

²⁰ [..... GUD.MEŠ *ù ṣe*]-*e-ni ul-tu qer-bi-šú* ˡ*ú*ˡ-[*še-ṣa-am-ma*] ˡ*šal*ˡ-[*la-tiš am-nu*

   ....]

²¹ [.........] XXXXX [.........]

¹ [.....................]

² [.....................]

³ [..... Assur, my lord, encouraged] me and [I marched] against Ju[dah. In] the course of my campaign [I received] the tribute [of all] the ki[ngs of Amurru]

⁴ [..... by the po]wer of Assur, my lord, [I overwhelmed] a district [of Hezeki]ah of Judah as [with a bird-snare .....]

⁵ [.....] Azekah, his supply city, which between my territory and Judah [.....]

⁶ [.....] situated [on] a mountaintop like countless sharp blades of i[ro]n reaching the sky (while) [its] founda[tions reach the center of the netherworld].

⁷ [Its walls] were extremely strong and competed with high mountains, at the lo[ok] of the eyes as if from the sky [.........]

⁸ [The building of sie]ge ramps, drawing battering-rams up close, the powerful work of the 'b[ig fl]y' (?), the hand-to-hand combat of infantry [.....]

⁹ They saw [the storming] of my [hors]es, heard the battle cry of the proud hosts of Assur (and) they became afraid [.......]

¹⁰ [Azekah I besieged], conquered (and) plundered, and I destroyed (it) completely [.........]

¹¹ [......], a royal [city] of Palestine, which Hezekiah had taken away and for himself strengthened [.........]

¹² [.........] .... [.........] like a bush [.........]

¹³ [.........] was surrounded on all sides by great [to]wers and extremly difficult was

¹³   [.........]

¹⁴ [.........] in front of them was shut off by a palace like a mountain and high was [.........]

¹⁵ [..........] was dark, no sun shone on it; its waters were permanently put in darkness and [its] exit [was ....]

¹⁶ [.....] its [.....] was cut off by axes, the ditch beside it was deep and ...[..........]

¹⁷ he made [his warriors], strong in fighting, march into it (=city/fortress?), he prepared his weapons fo[r ....]

¹⁸ [..........] I made the auxiliaries from all Amurru carry up ear[th mas]ses an[d ....]

¹⁹ [..........] against them, on the seventh time, I [........] his/its great [.....] like [.....]-pots [..........]

²⁰ [..... big (and) small ca]ttle I [drove out] from it (=city/fortress) [and considered them] boo[ty ....]

²¹ [...................]

UPDATING THE MESSAGES: HEZEKIAH'S SECOND PROPHETIC STORY (2 KINGS 19.9b-35) AND THE COMMUNITY OF BABYLONIAN DEPORTEES*

Nadav Na'aman

The biblical story of Sennacherib's campaign to Judah has been discussed in a great number of books, articles and commentaries. The list of publications is so long that we may well wonder whether it is still possible—on the basis of the extant sources—to significantly advance our understanding of any aspect of the story.

The majority of scholars agree that the text of Isaiah had its original context in Kings.[1] Bernhard Stade suggested that the account of Sennacherib's campaign was built of two sources: a chronistic record (18.13-16) and two prophetic stories (18.17–19.9a, 37; 19.9b-20, 30-37).[2] His arguments were accepted by some early scholars (Albert Šanda is an exception).[3] Brevard S. Childs revised this suggestion and proposed that the first prophetic story (Account B₁) included 18.17–19.9a, 36-37 and the second

---

* This is a slightly expanded and revised version of an article published in *Biblica* 81 (2000), pp. 393-402 under the title 'New Light on Hezekiah's Second Prophetic Story (2 Kgs 19.9b-35)'.

1. See recently, August H. Konkel, 'The Sources of the Story of Hezekiah in the Book of Isaiah', *VT* 43 (1993), pp. 462-482; Hugh G.M. Williamson, 'Hezekiah and the Temple', in M.V. Fox *et al.* (eds.), *Texts, Temples, and Traditions: A Tribute to Menahem Haran* (Winona Lake, IN: Eisenbrauns, 1996), pp. 47-52; Marvin A. Sweeney, *Isaiah 1–39 with an Introduction to Prophetic Literature* (FOTL, 16; Grand Rapids: Eerdmans, 1996), pp. 477-83; Raymond E. Person, *The Kings-Isaiah and Kings-Jeremiah Recensions* (BZAW, 252; Berlin: W. de Gruyter, 1997), pp. 5-79.

2. Bernhard Stade, 'Miscellen. 16. Anmerkungen zu 2 Kö. 15-21', *ZAW* 6 (1886), pp. 156-89 (172-86).

3. For early scholars who discussed Stade's suggestion, see Albert Šanda, *Die Bücher der Könige übersetzt und erklärt* 2 (EHAT, 9; Münster: Aschendorf, 1912), pp. 289-91; Francolino J. Gonçalves, *L'expédition de Sennachérib en Palestine dans la littérature Hébraïqe ancienne* (EBib, 7; Louvain la-Neuve: Institut Orientaliste de l'Université Catholique de Louvain, 1986), pp. 351-54, with earlier literature.

story (Account B$_2$) included 19.9b-35.[4] Most scholars adopted this revision,[5] and scholarly disagreements have been confined largely to the problem of the original scope of the two prophetic stories, and in particular to the scope of Account B$_2$.[6]

Recently, Raymond E. Person reconstructed the *Urtext* of the Kings–Josiah recension, concluded that the critical evidence of the text rejects the hypothesis of three sources, and suggested that 18.13 belongs with 18.17-37 and that 18.14-16 is a later addition.[7] In his words: 'Hence the Stade-Childs hypothesis is rejected'.[8] However, the close similarity of the texts of 2 Kgs 18.17–19.37 and Isa. 36.2–37.38 indicates that the combination of accounts B$_1$ and B$_2$ could have taken place only before the writing of the

---

4.   Brevard S. Childs, *Isaiah and the Assyrian Crisis* (SBT II/3; London: SCM Press, 1967), pp. 69-103; see Gonçalves, *L'expédition de Sennachérib*, pp. 355-63, 376-94, 449-55, with earlier literature.

5.   For the list of literature, see n. 46 below. For criticism of the Stade-Childs hypothesis, see Klaas A.D. Smelik, 'King Hezekiah Advocates True Prophecy', in K.A.D. Smelik, *Converting the Past. Studies in Ancient Israelite and Moabite Historiography* (OTS, 28; Leiden: E.J. Brill, 1992), pp. 70-93; Christopher R. Seitz, *Zion's Final Destiny: The Development of the Book of Isaiah. A Reassessment of Isaiah 36–39* (Philadelphia: Fortress Press, 1991); William R. Gallagher, *Sennacherib's Campaign to Judah: New Studies* (SHCANE, 18; Leiden: E.J. Brill, 1999), pp. 143-59.

6.   See the list of authors cited by Burke O. Long, *2 Kings* (FOTL, 10; Grand Rapids: Eerdmans, 1991), p. 200; Person, *Recensions*, p. 76 n. 8. For recent detailed discussion of Account B$_2$, see Gonçalves, *L'expédition de Sennachérib*, pp. 449-77, with earlier literature.

7.   Person, *Recensions*, pp. 47-74; *idem*, 'II Kings 18–20 and Isaiah 36–39: A Text Critical Case Study in the Redaction History of the Book of Isaiah', *ZAW* 111 (1999), pp. 373-379. This was already suggested by Seitz, *Zion's Final Destiny*, pp. 51-61; *idem*, 'Account A and the Annals of Sennacherib: A Reassessment', *JSOT* 58 (1993), pp. 47-57; Eberhard Ruprecht, 'Die ursprüngliche Komposition der Hiskia-Jesaja-Erzählungen und ihre Umstrukturierung durch die Verfasser des deuteronomistischen Geschichtswerkes', ZTK 87 (1990), pp. 33-66 (33-36, 65). Ronald E. Clements recently abandoned his former suggestion that Account B$_1$ was composed before the events of year 587, and suggested instead that the story was written in the wake of the disastrous events of 587 BCE. See *Isaiah and the Deliverance of Jerusalem* (JSOTSup 13; Sheffield: Sheffield Academic Press, 1980), pp. 90-108; *idem*, 'The Politics of Blasphemy. Zion's God and the Threat of Imperialism', in I. Kottsieper *et al.* (eds.), *'Wer ist wie du, Herr, unter den Göttern?' Studien zur Theologie und Religionsgeschichte Israels für Otto Kaiser zum 70. Geburtstag* (Göttingen: Vandenhoeck & Ruprecht, 1994), pp. 231-46.

8.   Person, *Recensions*, pp. 76-77. Person admits that there may have been numerous redactions behind the reconstructed *Urtext* and that it is not necessary to assume only one redaction of the *Urtext*.

text worked by the editor of the book of Isaiah. In other words, Person's reconstruction of what he called '*Urtext*' could not shed light on the Stade-Childs hypothesis of the two prophetic stories. Moreover, Person avoided analyzing the text of Kings in terms of sources and composition, and never seriously considered the possibility that the difference between Kings and Isaiah is the result of a deliberate omission by the editor of Isaiah. His solution to the origin of 2 Kgs 18.14-16—namely, that it is an addition 'of another narrative about Hezekiah and Sennacherib'—is arbitrary, assuming something that does not exist.[9] Other scholars emphasized the close similarity between 2 Kgs 18.13-16 and other accounts of campaigns directed against Jerusalem by foreign rulers (e.g. 1 Kgs 14.25-26; 2 Kgs 12.18-19; 15.19-20; 16.5, 7-9), thus demonstrating that all these texts were composed by the same author according to a unified literary pattern.[10] The problem of sources and composition in the account of Sennacherib's campaign to Judah, which fully explains the present form of the text in the 2 Kings 18–19, will be discussed in the second part of this article.

As many scholars have noted, the omission of vv. 14-16 from the text of Isaiah is due to the idealization of the figure of Hezekiah in exilic and postexilic periods as a king who trusted Yhwh, and by his piety rescued Jerusalem from the Assyrian threat. His conduct in time of siege and grave danger was contrasted with that of the last kings of Judah, who, in similar situations, brought about the destruction of Jerusalem and the exile. By omitting the verses that relate the success of the Assyrian campaign, Hezekiah's submission and the payment of a heavy tribute to Assyria, the editor of Isaiah obliterated all signs of failure on the part of Hezekiah, thereby re-shaping the king's image.[11] A clear sign of the extensive intervention of the Isaianic editor in the introduction to the story is the omission of Tartan and Rab-saris from the list of Assyrian delegates (Isa. 36.2). We may conclude that the Stade-Childs hypothesis, according to which the biblical account of Sennacherib's campaign to Judah (2 Kgs 18.13–19.37) grew

9.   Person, *Recensions*, p. 54. For an equally unlikely solution, see Seitz, *Zion's Final Destiny*, pp. 51-61.

10.   Gonçalves, *L'expédition de Sennachérib*, pp. 368-70.

11.   For the idealization of Hezekiah in late periods, see Peter R. Ackroyd, *Studies in the Religious Tradition of the Old Testament* (London: SCM Press, 1987), pp. 109-20 (first published in 1982) and pp. 152-71 (first published in 1974); Sweeny, *Isaiah 1– 39*, pp. 482-83; cf. Christoph Hardmeier, *Prophetie im Streit vor dem Untergang Judas. Erzählkommunikative Studien zur Entstehungssituation der Jesaja- und Jere-miaerzählungen in II Reg 18–20 und Jer 37–40* (BZAW, 187; Berlin: W. de Gruyter, 1990), pp. 108-17.

out of three different sources, is the best solution offered so far for the texts of Kings and Isaiah.

It is the purpose of this article to re-examine some elements in Account B₂ which have not been satisfactorily explained by scholars, in an effort to shed more light on the date and place in which it was composed. The results of this re-examination will also be applied to the discussion of Account B₁. I will not discuss the complicated problem of the original scope of the two stories, since it is external to this discussion. I will also try to avoid repetition of what has already been said by other scholars, and concentrate on some new suggestions that I should like to present.

The List of Conquered Places in 2 Kings 19.12-13

The key for dating Account B₂ (2 Kgs 19.9b-35) is the list of cities mentioned in vv. 12-13. The text runs as follows:

> Did the gods of the nations save them whom my ancestors destroyed, Gozan, Harran, Rezeph, and the people of Eden who were in Telassar? Where is the king of Hamath and the king of Arpad and the king of Lair, Sepharvaim, Hena, and Ivvah?

This text may be compared with 2 Kgs 18.33-34, which is part of the second speech of the Rabshakeh in Account B₁:

> Did any of the gods of the nations ever save his land from the king of Assyria? Where are the gods of Hamath and Arpad? Where are the gods of Sepharvaim? » «[12] <Where are the gods of Samaria?>[13] Did they save Samaria from me?

12. Hena and Ivvah are missing from Isa. 36.19 and the LXX of 2 Kgs 18.34, and many scholars suggested that they entered the text from 19.13. See Harry M. Orlinsky, 'The Kings-Isaiah Recensions of the Hezekiah Story', *JQR* 30 (1939), pp. 33-49 (45); Person, *Recensions*, pp. 18, 62, with earlier literature in n. 53. For a different opinion, see Dominique Barthélemy, *Critique textuelle de l'Ancien Testament. 1. Josué, Juges, Ruth, Samuel, Rois, Chroniques, Esdras, Néhémie, Esther* (OBO 50/1; Fribourg: Éditions Universitaires and Göttingen: Vandenhoeck & Ruprecht, 1982), p. 411.

13. The end of the verse requires a preceding question, like the one found in the Lucianic and Vulgate versions. For the restoration, see Charles F. Burney, *Notes on the Hebrew Text of the Books of Kings with an Introduction and Appendix* (Oxford: Clarendon Press, 1903; repr. New York: Ktav, 1970), p. 342; Šanda, *Die Bücher der Könige*, p. 260; Orlinsky, 'Kings-Isaiah Recensions', p. 46; Moshe Anbar, "'*Kai pou eisin oi theoi tēs choras Samareias*', 'et où sont les dieux du pays de Samarie?'", *BN* 51 (1990), pp. 7-8. For a different opinion, see James A. Montgomery, *A Critical and Exegetical Commentary on the Books of Kings* (ICC; Edinburgh: T. & T. Clark, 1951), p. 503; Barthélemy, *Critique textuelle*, p. 411; Person, *Recensions*, p. 63 n. 69.

Hamath, Arpad and Samaria participated in the anti-Assyrian rebellion that broke out in Syria-Palestine upon the death of Shalmaneser V, when Sargon II ascended the throne in 722 BCE.[14] After he crushed the rebellion in 720 BCE, Sargon annexed Hamath and Samaria to the Assyrian territory. Arpad was an Assyrian province since 738 BCE and after the rebellion was probably re-organized.[15] Sepharvaim appears in 2 Kgs 17.24 as the origin of settlers whom Sargon deported to the province of Samerina in his late years,[16] and is identified in the area of eastern Babylonia.[17] It is mentioned before Samaria, the region where the deportees were settled. The text of 2 Kgs. 18.33-34 refers to three cities that participated in the rebellion against Sargon in 720 BCE, and to a place in eastern Babylonia that was conquered by Sargon during his campaigns against Babylonia in the years 710–709 BCE.[18] It is evident that the four toponyms mentioned in Account B$_1$ are drawn from the western and eastern campaigns of Sargon II, Sennacherib's father.

14. Hayim Tadmor, 'The Campaigns of Sargon II of Assur: A Chronological-Historical Study', *JCS* 12 (1958), pp. 22-40, 77-100 (33-39); Henry W.F. Saggs, 'Historical Texts and Fragments of Sargon II of Assyria', *Iraq* 37 (1975), pp. 11-20 (14, line 20); Andreas Fuchs, *Die Inschriften Sargons II. aus Khorsabad* (Göttingen: Cuvillier Verlag, 1994), pp. 89, line 25, 200-201, line 33.

15. It should be noted that among the six places mentioned in Isa. 10.9, four participated in the anti-Assyrian alliance that fought Sargon in 720 BCE (Hamath, Arpad, Damascus and Samaria). Carchemish was annexed by Sargon three years later, in 717 BCE. Only Calno/Calneh (Assyrian Kullani), the capital of the former kingdom of Unqi/Patina that was annexed by Tiglath-Pileser III in 738 BCE, is not mentioned in Sargon's inscriptions. However, Sargon's annals for the year 720 are broken and details of the anti-Assyrian rebellion in the west in this year are incomplete. Thus it is possible that Kullani/Calneh participated in the anti-Assyrian coalition that fought Sargon in 720 BCE, but is missing from the extent corpus of Sargon's inscriptions. Isaiah could have deliberately selected six central cities conquered and annexed (or re-annexed) by Sargon II in his early years, and that his audience/readers had heard of the conquest of the cities not long before the prophecy was said/written.

16. For the date of the Assyrian deportation to the province of Samerina, see Nadav Na'aman and Ran Zadok, 'Assyrian Deportations to the Province of Samerina in the Light of Two Cuneiform Tablets from Tel Hadid', *Tel Aviv* 27 (2000), pp. 159-88 (177-79).

17. For the identification of places mentioned in 2 Kgs 17.24, see Ran Zadok, 'Geographical and Onomastic Notes', *JANES* 8 (1976), pp. 113-26 (115-16).

18. For the Babylonian campaigns of Sargon II, see John A. Brinkman, 'Merodach-Baladan II', in R.D. Biggs and J.A. Brinkman (eds.), *Studies Presented to A. Leo Oppenheim* (Chicago: The Oriental Institute of the University of Chicago, 1964), pp. 6-53 (12-27); Fuchs, *Die Inschriften Sargons II*, pp. 309-405.

The list of cities in 2 Kgs 19.12-13 is almost entirely different from the list in 2 Kgs 18.33-34, and from the list of peoples settled by Sargon II in Samaria according to 2 Kgs 17.24. Most scholars agree on the identification of the places mentioned in vv. 12-13.[19] Some of these places (Gozan, Harran, Rezeph-Raṣappu and Eden–Bīt Adini) are located in northern Mesopotamia, and were conquered and annexed by Assyria in the time of Ashurnasirpal II (883–859) and the early years of Shalmaneser III (858–824). Why did the author of Account B₂ select places which were conquered and annexed hundreds of years before his time to exemplify the Assyrian conquests? Another group of places (Telassar, Lair, Sepharvaim, Hena and Ivvah) is probably located in eastern Babylonia. Again, why did the author include these remote and unimportant eastern places in his list of conquered towns? Hamath and Arpad are located in Syria, and their location and history differ from the other places in this list. The selection of these places requires an explanation, and we shall first examine the suggestions offered so far by scholars for this enigmatic list.

Hans Wildberger doubted whether the narrator had any clear idea about the time and circumstances in which these places fell to the hands of Assyria. 'Presumably he wanted simply to expand the list in 36.19 and added place-names that were known to him personally, without really knowing either their location or their condition. This tendency to expand such references is indicated by the fact that in the K-text parallel to 36.19 Hena and Iwa have been added.'.[20]

Francolino J. Gonçalves suggested that some cities are connected with the deportation to Samaria (Hamath, Sepharvaim, Ivvah), whereas Gozan is one of the places to which inhabitants of the Northern Kingdom were deported. Being unable to explain the list of towns, he suggested that 'Its

19. For the identification of the list of towns, see Šanda, *Die Bücher der Könige*, pp. 260, 272-73; Godfrey R. Driver, 'Geographical Problems', *Eretz Israel* 5 (1958), pp. 16*-20*; John Gray, *I and II Kings* (OTL; Philadelphia: Westminster, 2nd rev. edn, 1970), pp. 687-88; Zadok, 'Notes', pp. 113-24; Gonçalves, *L'expédition de Sennachérib*, pp. 458-61; Mordechai Cogan and Hayim Tadmor, *II Kings. A New Translation with Introduction and Commentary* (AB, 11; Garden City: Doubleday, 1988), p. 235.

20. 'Vermutlich wollte er einfach die Liste von 36,19 erweitern und hat Ortsnamen hinzugefügt, die ihm gerade bekannt waren, ohne über deren Lage und Schicksal wirklich orientiert zu sein. Für diese Tendenz zur Erweiterung solcher Aufzeichnungen ist bezeichnend, dass der mit 36.19 parallele K-Text ebenfalls Hena und Iwa eingefügt hat' Hans Wildberger, *Jesaja. 3. Jesaja 28-39* (BKAT X/3; Neukirchen–Vluyn: Neukirchener Verlag, 1982), p. 1424.

author undoubtedly had knowledge of some kind or another, but nothing suggests that he had at his disposal particular information about the history of the relations between the majority of the towns he mentions and Assyria'.[21]

Ehud Ben Zvi suggested that v. 12 refers to places where deportees from the Northern Kingdom were settled, and v. 13 refers to places from which came the deportees who were settled in Samaria.[22] However, only one name (Gozan) is common to v. 12 and the list of Israelite deportees settled in Assyria (2 Kgs 17.6), and only two names (Sepharvaim and Ivvah/Avva) appear in v. 13 and the list of deportees to Samaria (2 Kgs 17.24).[23] The assumption that the author of Account B$_2$ was better acquainted with the Assyrian deportations of the time of Sargon II than the Deuteronomist (the author of 2 Kgs 17.6, 24) is unconvincing. Moreover, the text of vv. 12-13 refers to conquests rather than deportations, although deportees could have arrived from/at these places.

Steven W. Holloway suggested that Harran must be treated separately from all the other places mentioned in vv. 12-13.[24] He discussed at length the history and cult of Harran in the Neo-Assyrian period, and concluded that it is unlikely that an Assyrian referred to the cult centre of Harran as a city destroyed by his forefathers. Harran was conquered by the Babylonians in 610–609 BCE, and this is the background for its inclusion in the list of conquered places.[25] Adopting Christoph Hardmeier's suggestion that

21. 'son auteur en avait sans doute connaissance d'une façon ou d'une autre, mais rien n'indique qu'il disposait de renseignements particuliers au sujet de l'histoire des rapports entre la plupart des villes qu'il mentionne et l'Assyrie' Gonçalves, *L'expédition de Sennachérib*, p. 462.

22. Ehud Ben Zvi, 'Who Wrote the Speech of the Rabshakeh and when?', *JBL* 109 (1990), pp. 79-92 (89-91).

23. The city of Hamath mentioned in 2 Kgs 17.24, is located in eastern Babylonia (Zadok, 'Notes', pp. 117-20), whereas the Hamath of 2 Kgs 19.13 is located in central Syria.

24. Steven W. Holloway, 'Harran: Cultic Geography in the Neo-Assyrian Empire and its Implications for Sennacherib's "Letter to Hezekiah" in 2 Kings', in S.W. Holloway and L.K. Handy (eds.), *The Pitcher Is Broken. Memorial Essays for Gösta W. Ahlström* (JSOTSup, 190; Sheffield: Sheffield Academic Press, 1995), pp. 276-314 (311-12).

25. Holloway, 'Harran', pp. 276-314 (312-14). For an extensive discussion of the moon god Sin and his temple at Harran, see Paul-Alain Beaulieu, *The Reign of Nabonidus, King of Babylonia, 556–539 B.C.* (YNER, 10; New Haven and London: Yale University Press, 1989).

the description of Sennacherib's blockade of Jerusalem was patterned on the Babylonian siege of Jerusalem in 588 BCE,[26] Holloway suggested that the inclusion of Harran's name in Rabshakeh's speech should be interpreted in the context of the 588 BCE war against the Babylonians.[27]

As for the other places, Holloway adopted the widely held view that Sennacherib boasted of the victories of his forefathers over them. He offered no explanation for excluding Harran from the list of places. Nevertheless, I believe that he was on the right track in suggesting that the conquest of Harran reflects the Babylonian campaigns of the years 610–609 BCE. It seems to me that the list of cities in vv. 12-13 reflects the conquests of Nabopolassar and Nebuchadrezzar in the late seventh century BCE, and that some of these conquests are mentioned in the Babylonian chronicles, the only source that we have for the emergence of the Babylonian Empire.

Following is a discussion of the list of towns in light of this suggestion.

1.   Harran held an important place in the late Assyrian empire. Sargon, Esarhaddon and Ashurbanipal built the city and its temple, and Ashurbanipal (668–631) nominated his younger brother as high priest (*šešgallu*) in the temple of Sin of Harran.[28] Ashur-uballiṭ, the last king of Assyria, ascended the throne in Harran in 611 BCE.[29] In the following year (610), the Babylonian army under Nabopolassar and the Median troops besieged Harran and captured it, and 'carried off the vast booty of the city and the temple'. In the next year (609), the Babylonian garrison stationed in Harran was attacked by Assyrian-Egyptian troops, but fought back until the withdrawal of the attacking force.[30]

According to the inscriptions of Nabonidus (556–539), the city of Harran suffered heavy damage and declined for many years, until he restored it to its former glory. The temple of Sin was plundered during the Babylonian

26.   Hardmeier, *Prophetie im Streit*, pp. 392-408.

27.   For criticism of the thesis of Hardmeier, see Arie van der Kooij, 'The Story of Hezekiah and Sennacherib (2 Kings 18–19): A Sample of Ancient Historiography', in J.C. de Moor and H.F. van Rooy (eds.), *Past, Present, Future. The Deuteronomistic History and the Prophets* (OTS, 44; Leiden: E.J. Brill, 2000), pp. 107-19.

28.   Maximilian Streck, *Assurbanipal und die letzten assyrischen Könige bis zum Untergange Niniveh's*, II (Leipzig: J.C. Hinrichs, 1916), p. 250, l. 17-18.

29.   Albert K. Grayson, *Assyrian and Babylonian Chronicles* (TCS, 5; Locust Valley: J.J. Augustin, 1975), pp. 94-95, ll. 49-50.

30.   Grayson, *Chronicles*, pp. 95-96, ll. 58-70; Stefan Zawadzki, *The Fall of Assyria and the Median-Babylonian Relations in Light of the Nabopolassar Chronicle* (Poznan: Adam Mickiewicz University Press; Delft: Eburon, 1988), pp. 121-26.

conquest and the city was partly destroyed because of its prominent place in the late Assyrian Empire. The words 'did the gods of the nations save them whom my ancestors destroyed' in 2 Kgs 19.12 may allude to the destruction of Harran and the despoliation of its temples by the Babylonians.[31]

2. After the conquest of Nineveh in 612 BCE, the Babylonian troops advanced westward, and their offensive is described as follows.[32]

> The king of Akkad [dispatched his army, and] they marched to Naṣibin. A he[avy] (*ka-[bit-tu]*) booty and exiles they brought to the king of Akkad at Nineveh [from the lands of GN] and Ruṣapu.

Ruṣapu-Raṣappu is located in the Sindjar plain of Upper Mesopotamia and was the capital of an Assyrian province.[33] Its identification with biblical Rezeph (*Reṣep*) is self-evident.

3. In the following year (611) Nabopolassar marched against the city of Ruggulitu, captured it and killed its inhabitants.[34] Ruggulitu is mentioned in the annals of Shalmaneser III as an important city of the kingdom of Bīt Adini, which he captured and annexed to Assyria (856 BCE).[35] In 611 BCE, about 250 years later, it was conquered and annexed by the Babylonians.

In the following years Nabopolassar conquered all the Assyrian territories up to the Euphrates, so that in 607 he was able to cross the Euphrates and conquer the city of Kimuḫu (modern Samsat).[36]

---

31. Dieter Baltzer, 'Harran nach 610 "medisch"? Kritische Überprüfung einer Hypothese', *WO* 7 (1973), pp. 68-95; Beaulieu, *The Reign of Nabonidus,* pp. 58-61, 104-15; Thomas G. Lee, 'The Jasper Cylinder Seal of Aššurbanipal and Nabonidus' Making of Sîn's Statue', *RA* 87 (1993), pp. 131-36; Walter Mayer, 'Nabonidus Herkunft', in M. Dietrich and O. Loretz (eds.), *DUBSAR ANTA-MEN, Studien zur Altorientalistik. Festschrift für Willem H.Ph. Römer* (AOAT, 253; Munich: Ugarit Verlag, 1998), pp. 245-61.

32. Grayson, *Chronicles*, p. 94, ll. 47-49.

33. Emil Forrer, *Die Provinzeinteilung des assyrischen Reiches* (Leipzig: J.C. Hinrichs, 1920), p. 12; Stephanie Dalley, 'A Stela of Adad-nirari III and Nergal-ereš from Tell al Rimah', *Iraq* 30 (1968), pp. 139-53 (150-51); Cogan and Tadmor, *II Kings*, p. 235; Mario Liverani, 'Raṣappu and Hatallu', *SAAB* 6 (1992), pp. 35-40; Frederick M. Fales, 'Mari: An Additional Note on "Raṣappu and Hatallu"', pp. 105-107.

34. Grayson, *Chronicles*, p. 95, ll. 56-57.

35. Forrer, *Die Provinzeinteilung*, p. 25; Shigeo Yamada, *The Construction of the Assyrian Empire. A Historical Study of the Inscriptions of Shalmaneser III (859–824 BC) Relating to his Campaigns to the West* (CHANE, 3; Leiden: E.J. Brill, 2000), pp. 124, 126.

36. Grayson, *Chronicles*, pp. 97-98, ll. 12-15.

We may conclude that Nabopolassar conquered the cities of Gozan, Harran, Raṣappu and the land of Bīt Adini in the course of his conquest of Upper Mesopotamian in the years 612–610 BCE. Captives were taken from the conquered areas and settled in Babylonia. Among them were probably the Edenites, whom the Babylonians settled at Telassar-Til Aššuri.

4.   Til Aššuri is located on the Diyala River, near the border between Babylonia and Media.[37] Shilḫazi, a place near Til Aššuri, is called by Tiglath-Pileser III 'fortress of the Babylonians', and was probably a Babylonian fort on the border with Media. Babylonians apparently lived in Til Aššuri in the time of Tiglath-Pileser III and worshiped Marduk, their national god, in the local temple. When the Babylonians regained their territories, they established their border with Media along the same line. Deportees from Bīt Adini were probably brought to this place, which must have been the central Babylonian city in this area, and these deportees are mentioned by the author of Account B$_2$.

5.   The district (pīḫatu) of Hamath was conquered by Nebuchadrezzar after he defeated the Egyptian troops in Carchemish (605 BCE).[38] Arpad was captured in the course of this campaign. The combination of Hamath and Arpad is influenced by the references to the cities in Account B$_1$ (2 Kgs. 18.34) and Isa. 10.9. However, for the readers of B$_2$, the reference to the gods of Hamath points to its recent capture by Nebuchadrezzar, rather than to its conquest by the Assyrians long time before (as correctly noted by Hardmeier).[39]

6.   Telassar, Lair, Sepharvaim and Ivvah are located in eastern Babylonia.[40] The place of Hena is unknown, but it may possibly be sought in the same area.[41] Sepharvaim and Ivvah (Avva) are included in the list of

37.   Zadok, 'Notes', pp. 123-124; Hayim Tadmor, *The Inscriptions of Tiglath-Pileser III King of Assyria* (Jerusalem: Israel Academy of Sciences and Humanities, 1994), pp. 72-73.

38.   Grayson, *Chronicles*, p. 99, ll. 6-10.

39.   Hardmeier, *Prophetie im Streit*, p. 404.

40.   For Sepharvaim and Avva/Ivvah, see Zadok, 'Notes', pp. 115, 120-23.

41.   Some scholars suggested transposing the letters of Hena (*Hēna'*) and reading it 'Anah, i.e., the city of 'Anat (modern 'Āna) located on the middle Euphrates. See Šanda, *Die Bücher der Könige*, p. 260; Samuel E. Loewenstamm, 'Hena', *Encyclopaedia Biblica* 2 (Jerusalem: Bialik Institute, 1954), p. 852 (Hebrew); Wildberger, *Jesaja*, p. 1424. The city of 'Anat was conquered by Nabopolassar when he subdued a rebellion that broke out in 613 BCE. See Grayson, *Chronicles*, pp. 93-94, ll. 35-36. However, there is no textual evidence for this suggestion, and we had better follow the MT and versions and assume that Hena is an unknown place in eastern Babylonia.

peoples settled by Sargon in the province of Samerina (2 Kgs 17.24), and Sepharvaim is mentioned in Account B_1 (18.34) (see note 12 above). Lair is identical with Laḫiru, a city located in northeastern Babylonia. It was an Assyrian province under the Sargonids, and is mentioned in numerous Neo- and Late-Babylonian texts.[42]

The late date in which Account B_2 was written and the author's poor knowledge of the policy of Assyria is also revealed in 2 Kgs 19.17-18: 'It is true, O YHWH, that the kings of Assyria have laid waste the nations and their lands, and put their gods to fire...'

In their commentary on 2 Kings, Cogan and Tadmor wrote the following comment.[43]

> Assyrian practice was in fact more tolerant than allowed by this polemic. Usually the gods of the conquered nations were treated with respect, for the Assyrians held that the gods abandoned their followers, thus handing them over to the conqueror. Often the divine statues were brought to Assyria, where they were installed in chapels until sent home. Seldom were the statues actually destroyed...

Did this passage reflect the Babylonian practice of destroying cult statues during their conquest of Assyria, and did the author again select an example familiar to his audience in order to illustrate his theology? In light of the long bitter enmity between Assyria and Babylonia, and the utter destruction of the royal cities of Assyria (e.g. Nineveh, Assur, Calah, Dur-sharrukin, Arbela) by the Babylonian-Median armies, the suggestion is certainly possible. Unfortunately, we do not know enough about the Babylonian cultic policy towards the gods of Assyria. The main source we have is the Babylonian chronicle series, and although the chronicles appear objective, in reality their pro-Babylonian bias is revealed throughout their text.[44] Even if the Babylonians destroyed Assyrian cult statues, the author would avoid mentioning it in his work.

42. John A. Brinkman, *A Political History of Post-Kassite Babylonia 1158–722 B.C.* (AnOr, 43; Rome: Pontificium Institutum Biblicum, 1968) p. 178 n. 1093; Ran Zadok, *Geographical Names according to New- and Late-Babylonian Texts* (Répertoire Géographique des Textes Cunéiformes, Band 8; Beihefte zum Tübinger Atlas des Vorderen Orients, Reihe B Nr. 7/8; Wiesbaden: Ludwig Reichert, 1985), p. 208.

43. Cogan and Tadmor, *II Kings*, p. 236. See also Morton Cogan, *Imperialism and Religion: Assyria, Judah and Israel in the Eighth and Seventh Centuries B.C.E.* (SBLMS, 19; Missoula, MT: Scholars Press, 1974), pp. 9-41; Paul-Alain Beaulieu, 'An Episode in the Fall of Babylonia to the Persians', *JNES* 52 (1993), pp. 243-61.

44. Zawadzki, *The Fall of Assyria*, pp. 114-43; Nadav Na'aman, 'Chronology and History in the Late Assyrian Empire (631–619 B.C.)', *ZA* 81 (1991), pp. 243-67 (260-61).

The statue of Sin of Harran that was fashioned by Nabonidus may indicate that Assyrian statues were indeed destroyed during the Babylonian conquest. Thomas G. Lee demonstrated that the lost statue of the moon god was reconstructed by the image that was engraved on Ashurbanipal's cylinder seal, which he dedicated to the god Sin.[45] The scope of destruction of cult statues is unknown, but the fact that the kings of Babylonia never mentioned the fate of captured Assyrian statues may indicate that the author of Account B_2 referred to events that happened not long before his time.

The Date, Place and Messages of Accounts B_1 and B_2

An analysis of the place names mentioned in Account B_2 indicates that its author knew some details of the Babylonian campaigns to northern Mesopotamia and Syria in the years 612–605 BCE. Moreover, he had specific knowledge of certain places in eastern Babylonia, such as the settlement of the Edenites in Telassar-Til Aššuri and the sites of Laḫiru and Hena. The attachment of Ivvah and Sepharvaim—the origin of the settlers in the province of Samerina—to Laḫiru and Hena may suggest that he was aware of their location in eastern Babylonia. We may safely assume that the author of Account B_2 lived in eastern Babylonia, where some other deportees from the places he mentioned lived, and they must have been his sources for the Babylonian campaigns to northern Mesopotamia.

We may further note the reference to the gods of the nations 'whom my ancestors destroyed (*šiḫātû*)' (v. 12). Ostensibly, the author is referring to Sennacherib's predecessors, the kings of Assyria. Assuming that, in reality, the text refers to the kings of Babylonia who conquered these places, the term 'my ancestors' indicates that Account B_2 was written after the time of Nabopolassar and Nebuchadrezzar, that is, after 562 BCE. We may conclude that the author of the second prophetic story was a descendant of a Judean deportee living in Babylonia. He must have written his story after the death of Nebuchadrezzar, either in the time of the late Babylonian Empire or in the early Persian period. A date after the sixth century BCE is unlikely, since the author would then have drawn the historical episodes from more recent events, and the details of the Babylonian conquests in the late seventh century BCE would not have been memorized so accurately.

The author of Account B_2 expanded and elaborated the early story of Sennacherib's campaign and the 'miraculous deliverance' of Jerusalem (2 Kgs 18.13–19.9a, 36-37) in accordance with his experience in the new

---

45. Lee, 'Jasper Cylinder Seal', pp. 131-36.

place and the message he was trying to convey to his audience, the Judean deportees in Babylonia. The updating of the list of conquered cities is part of his revision. He did not know much about the Assyrian conquests, which happened long before his time, apart from what he had read in the Deuteronomistic history. He therefore wrote a new list of places that were conquered not long before his time and were better known to his audience than the list of places that appears in Account B_1 (18.33-34). The exact historical background of the conquests and deportations was less important to him than the theological conclusions drawn from these events. The updated list of places suited his theological lesson of the helplessness of the foreign gods and the need to trust in YHWH in times of crisis and danger.

The attribution of an exilic date for Account B_2 is commonly accepted among scholars,[46] but my suggestions for the location of the author and a possible date for his composition are new elements in the discussion. The marked difference between the authors of Accounts B_1 and B_2 is worth noting: the former selected his examples of the Assyrian conquests from Sargon II's campaigns, whereas the latter selected his examples from the Babylonian campaigns of the late seventh century BCE. In what follows, I will discuss three other obvious differences between Accounts B_1 and B_2, in order to demonstrate the enormous gap between their respective messages. The comparison may help us to establish the chronological framework in which Account B_1 was written.

1.   The second speech of the Rabshakeh in Account B_1 (2 Kgs. 18.29-35) underlines the difference between YHWH of Jerusalem and the gods of Samaria. E. Ben Zvi noted the close relations between Isa. 10.5-15 and 2 Kgs. 18.32b-35: they both emphasize that Jerusalem is unlike Samaria, and that YHWH of Jerusalem is unlike the gods in whom the people of

---

46.   In addition to the commentaries, see e.g., Childs, *Assyrian Crisis*, pp. 94-103; Ernst Vogt, *Der Aufstand Hiskias und die Belagerung Jerusalems 701 v.Chr* (AnBib, 106; Rome: Pontificium Institutum Biblicum, 1986), pp. 50-58; Alexander Rofé, *The Prophetical Stories. The Narratives about the Prophets in the Hebrew Bible: Their Literary Types and History* (Jerusalem: Magnes Press, 1988), pp. 88-95; Gonçalves, *L'expédition de Sennachérib*, pp. 445-87; Hardmeier, *Prophetie im Streit*, pp. 8-17, 157-59; Steven L. McKenzie, *The Trouble with Kings. The Composition of the Book of Kings in the Deuteronomistic History* (Leiden: E.J. Brill, 1991), pp. 105-106; Dominic Rudman, 'Is the Rabshakeh also among the Prophets? A Rhetorical Study of 2 Kings XVIII 17-35', *VT* 50 (2000), 100-10; Peter Machinist, 'The *Rab Šāqēh* at the Wall of Jerusalem: Israelite Identity in the Face of the Assyrian "Other"', *Hebrew Studies* 41 (2000), pp. 151-68. For criticism of the Stade-Childs hypothesis, see above, n. 5.

Samaria put their trust.[47] These texts could have been written only in the pre-exilic time, when Jerusalem and the temple were still intact and the memory of the destruction of the Northern Kingdom was very much alive. The author of Account B_1 drew conclusions from the 'miraculous deliverance' of Jerusalem in 701 BCE and conveyed the message that Jerusalem was different from all recently conquered places, including Samaria, since YHWH guarantees its safety.

The comparison between the fate of Samaria and Jerusalem is missing in Account B_2, having lost its validity after the destruction of Jerusalem in 587/6 BCE. Instead, the later author expanded the list of conquered places and contrasted the inability of their gods to protect their citizens with the power of YHWH to protect his people and their city.

2.   A second point of comparison is the emphasis on Assyria's power and impending threat in Account B_1, as against an abstract depiction of the enemy in B_2. Reading Account B_1, it is clear that the story was written when the memory of Assyria's enormous military power and its threat to the existence of the Kingdom of Judah was still very much alive. The two speeches of the Rabshakeh in Account B_1 convey the message of an imminent threat of destruction and deportation for the inhabitants of Jerusalem. In Account B_2, on the other hand, Assyria appears as an abstract power, representing more the concept of a strong military power than a concrete historical entity. The story will remain the same if we replace the name Assyria with the name of another power (e.g. Babylonia, Persia). Here only the theological messages are considered important, hence the arena for the scene and details of the situation are described in the shortest and schematic manner.

3.   A third point is the remarkable change in the role of Hezekiah in the two stories. In Account B_1, Hezekiah first made a rite of mourning by tearing his garments, putting on sackcloth and entering the temple (19.1). He then selected distinguished officials and priests and sent them to the prophet to request his intercession in face of the severe crisis. Hezekiah's conduct in the crisis is closely related to Josiah's conduct in 2 Kgs 22.11-12: like Hezekiah, Josiah tore his clothes and sent officials and priests to the prophetess Huldah. The sending of a delegation, and the request for prayer which is followed by a prophecy, are paralleled in Jer. 37.3, 6-8. In Account B_1, Isaiah appears as an intercessor between the king and the God, and only he is capable of addressing YHWH in prayer, while Hezekiah is

---

47. Ben Zvi, 'Who Wrote', pp. 88-92.

acting piously and showing his trust in YHWH and his prophet, but has no power to address the God directly.

The description of Hezekiah and Isaiah in Account B₂ is entirely different. Let me cite the observation of B.S. Childs on the way that the author presented the king and the prophet in this story.[48]

> In B₂ Hezekiah does not even inform Isaiah, but enters the temple, approaches the very presence of God, and offers as a royal priest the prayer of his people. Here the parallel with David (2 Sam. 8.18), and Solomon (1 Kings 8.14-61) is striking. Hezekiah has become the type of the righteous king whose heart is perfect before God. The writer is already far removed from the Hezekiah of 2 Kings 18.13–19.9a. The message of the prophet with its immediate fulfilment is closely attached to the preceding prayer. The prophet plays no independent role nor is his person significant. He is merely a bearer of the divine message. The emphasis falls fully on the power of God in his word which then effects its task. The larger form is, therefore, not the prophetic legend which centers in the prophet's role, but a similar genre which focuses on a picture of the pious king.

Peter R. Ackroyd has demonstrated the growth of the figure of Hezekiah from a king of absolute faith and trust in YHWH in the face of the Assyrian onslaught (in Account B₁), to an ideal figure, a kind of a new David and a new Solomon, in the book of Chronicles, and finally, a figure that gave rise to messianic speculations and hopes in rabbinical literature.[49] Hezekiah's figure in Account B₂ is closer to that of the book of Chronicles than to that of Account B₁. The new elevation of his figure is the outcome of the destruction of Jerusalem and the exile, a catastrophe that gave rise to a new evaluation of the course of the history of Israel. Following the destruction and exile, Hezekiah's conduct in face of the Assyrian threat as described in the early story (B₁) was contrasted with the failure of the last kings of Judah to counter the Babylonian threat. The first stage in the process of the growth of Hezekiah's figure after the exile appears in Account B₂. Its author attributed to the king the kind of power that in Account B₁ (and in other prophetic stories as well) was attributed only to prophets and great kings (David and Solomon). The marked difference in the portrayal of Hezekiah in Accounts B₁ and B₂ is best explained by the assumption

48. Childs, *Assyrian Crisis*, pp. 100-101.

49. Ackroyd, *Studies*, pp. 105-20, 151-71, 172-80 and 181-92; see Hugh G.M. Williamson, *Israel in the Books of Chronicles* (Cambridge: Cambridge University Press, 1977), pp. 119-31; Mark A. Thronveit, *When Kings Speak: Royal Speech and Royal Prayer in Chronicles* (SBLDS, 93; Atlanta: Scholars Press, 1987), pp. 121-24.

that they were composed with different perspectives in different historical circumstances.

In light of this discussion, it is clear that Account B$_1$ was composed in the pre-exilic period. It seems to me that the author of 2 Kgs 18.13–19.9a; 36-37 (the Deuteronomist) combined two early sources that were available to him: a chronistic text (the source of Account A), and a prophetic story of the 'miraculous deliverance' of Jerusalem (Account B$_1$). The chronistic text was written shortly after the conclusion of the Assyrian campaign, which is why its contents so accurately match the text of Sennacherib's inscriptions.[50] It may have been included in the so-called 'chronicles of the kings of Judah'. The story was probably transmitted orally for some time, but was composed in writing at a time when the memory of the power and impending threat of Assyria to the very existence of Judah was still very much alive. The vivid memory of the murder of Sennacherib by his sons (2 Kgs 19.37), including the names of the murderers, the circumstances of the murder, the place where they found shelter, and the name of Sennacherib's successor, all point to a relatively early date of composition.[51] The reference to Tirhakah (Taharqa) 'king of Egypt' in connection with the Assyrian withdrawal from Judah (18.9a; 19.36) is probably an anachronism,[52] but indicates that when the story was written, Tirhaka's name was

50. For a good summary, see Paul E. Dion, 'Sennacherib's Expedition to Palestine', *Bulletin of the Canadian Society of Biblical Studies* 48 (1988), pp. 3-25.

51. This was noted by Rofé, *Prophetical Stories*, 93; Cogan and Tadmor, *II Kings*, pp. 242-43; Seitz, *Zion's Final Destiny*, pp. 99-100. For the murder of Sennacherib, see Simo Parpola, 'The Murderer of Sennacherib', in B. Alster (ed.), *Death in Mesopotamia* (XXVI Rencontre Assyriologique Internationale; Copenhagen: Akademisk Forlag, 1980), pp. 171-82; cf. the literature cited by Gonçalves, *L'expédition de Sennachérib*, p. 444 n. 296; Kenneth S. Langbell, *Solving the Murder of Sennacherib* (Las Vegas, 1989) (brochure).

52. Jurgen von Beckerath suggested that Tirhakah could not have take place in the 701 BCE campaign since he arrived in Palestine no earlier than 700 BCE, and possibly only in 696 BCE. See 'Ägypten und der Feldzug Sanheribs im Jahre 701 v.Chr.', *UF* 24 (1992), pp. 3-8; idem, 'Die Nilstandsinschrift vom 3. Jahr Schebiktus am Kai von Karnak', *GM* 136 (1993), pp. 7-9. However, the Egyptian chronology of the 25th Dynasty is still uncertain, as indicated by the new inscription of Sargon II discovered in Iranian Kurdistan. See Grant Frame, 'The Inscription of Sargon II at Tang-i Var', *Or* 68 (1999), pp. 31-57 (52-54); Donald B. Redford, 'A Note on the Chronology of Dynasty 25 and the Inscription of Sargon II at Tang-i Var', *Or* 68 (1999), pp. 58-60. For the latest discussion of Tirhakah's participation in the 701 BCE campaign, see Robert D. Bates, 'Assyria and Rebellion in the Annals of Sennacherib: An Analysis of Sennacherib's Treatment of Hezekiah', *NEASB* 44 (1999), pp. 39-61 (52-56).

memorized in connection with the Assyrian-Egyptian struggle over the domination of Palestine.[53]

Recently R.E. Clements suggested that 'the earliest that it [the story] could reasonably be thought to have arisen is during Josiah's reign, when the weakness and crumbling authority of Assyrian control had become evident in Jerusalem'.[54] In this conclusion he was relying on the well-known thesis of R. Barth that the anti-Assyrian ideology so characteristic of the book of Isaiah was written in Josiah's time and reflects the flourishing of that ideology when the end of the Assyrian imperialism was in sight.[55] However, not only is Barth's thesis of the date of the anti-Assyrian prophecies in the book of Isaiah a hypothesis (though reasonable), but the argument that an anti-Assyrian ideology emerged only when Assyria withdrew from Palestine is unlikely. Anti-Assyrian sentiments developed ever since Assyria conquered and annexed Israelite territories in the time of Tiglath-pileser III and subjugated all the other kingdoms in the area (733/32). These sentiments must have been particularly strong after the conquest and annexation of Samaria by Sargon in 720, and following the havoc wreaked by Sennacherib on Judah in 701 BCE. The murder of Sennacherib (681) and the struggle of Tirhaka with Assyria (690–664) are the earliest possible dates for the composition of Account B$_1$, which could have been written at any time after these dates. The accurate details of the circumstances of the murder of Sennacherib may support the assumption that the story was written in the late years of Manasseh, although a date in Josiah's early years cannot be ruled out.

Dating the composition of the Deuteronomistic history is problematic, and this is not the place to enter the discussion.[56] I have already suggested

53. For the long struggle between Tirhaka (Taharqa) and the Assyrians, see Anthony Spalinger, 'The Foreign Policy of Egypt Preceding the Assyrian Conquest', *Chronique d'Égypte* 53 (1978), pp. 22-47; Donald B. Redford, *Egypt, Canaan, and Israel in Ancient Times* (Princeton: Princeton University Press, 1992), pp. 351-64; *idem*, 'Tirhakah', *The Anchor Bible Dictionary* 6 (New York: Doubleday, 1992), pp. 572-73, with earlier literature.

54. Clements, 'The Politics of Blasphemy', p. 244.

55. Hermann Barth, *Die Jesaja-Worte in der Josiazeit: Israel und Assur als Thema einer produktiven Neuinterpretation der Jesajaüberlieferung* (WMANT, 48; Neukirchen–Vluyn: Neukirchener Verlag, 1977).

56. For short surveys of the different schools of thought, see Erik Eynikel, *The Reform of King Josiah and the Composition of the Deuteronomistic History* (OTS, 33; Leiden: E.J. Brill, 1996), pp. 7-31; Percy S.F. van Keulen, *Manasseh through the Eyes of the Deuteronomists. The Manasseh Account (2 Kings 21:1-18) and the Final Chapters of the Deuteronomistic History* (OTS, 38; Leiden: E.J. Brill, 1996), pp. 3-52.

some arguments in support of a Josianic date of composition, and will restate here my conviction that the early comprehensive history of Israel was written in the time of Josiah.[57]

The Deuteronomist combined the chronistic and narrative texts (Accounts A and B_1) into a continuous history and integrated them into his composition of the history of Israel. He worked the chronistic source and fitted it into the pattern of other closely related texts that described the campaigns of foreign kings and the payment of tribute (e.g. 1 Kgs 14.25-26; 2 Kgs 12.18-19; 15.19-20; 16.5, 7-9). He copied almost verbatim the prophetic story, as he did with many other prophetic stories that were available to him.[58] His main contribution to Account B_1 is the insertion of 2 Kgs 18.22, which he wrote in order to support and corroborate his description of Hezekiah's cultic reform (18.4).[59] The secondary nature of v. 22 is evident from the way in which it departs from the inner structure of the first speech of the Rabshakeh (18.19-25).[60]

- All the passages open with the time adverb 'now' ('attāh) except for v. 22.
- All other passages address Hezekiah whereas v. 22 addresses the delegation in the second person plural.
- Whereas the other passages address Hezekiah in the second person singular, this passage refers to him in the third person.

E. Ben Zvi concluded his discussion of the Rabshakeh's speech by stating that 'the language of the speech does not resemble Deuteronomistic language. On the contrary, it shows some similarities with some features of

57. Nadav Na'aman, 'Historiography, the Fashioning of the Collective Memory, and the Establishment of Historical Consciousness in Israel in the Late Monarchial Period', *Zion* 60 (1995), pp. 449-72 (Hebrew); 'Sources and Composition in the History of David', in V. Fritz and P.R. Davies (eds.), *The Origins of the Ancient Israelite States* (JSOTSup, 228; Sheffield: Sheffield Academic Press, 1996), pp. 170-86 (180-83); 'Sources and Composition in the History of Solomon', in L.K. Handy (ed.), *The Age of Solomon—Scholarship at the Turn of the Millennium* (Leiden: E.J. Brill, 1997), pp. 57-80 (76-80); 'Royal Inscriptions and the Histories of Joash and Ahaz, Kings of Judah', *VT* 48 (1998), pp. 333-49.

58. Nadav Na'aman, 'Prophetic Stories as Sources for the Histories of Jehoshaphat and the Omrides', *Biblica* 78 (1997), pp. 153-73.

59. Nadav Na'aman, 'The Debated Historicity of Hezekiah's Reform in the Light of Historical and Archaeological Research', *ZAW* 107 (1995), pp. 179-95 (183).

60. For verse 22, see the literature cited by Gonçalves, *L'expédition de Sennachérib*, p. 74 nn. 84-86; Ben Zvi, 'Who Wrote', pp. 85-86.

the Isaianic tradition (including the use of wisdom tradition)'.[61] The note on Hezekiah's cultic reform is the only place where a clear Deuteronomic/ Deuteronomistic feature appears in the speech, and Ben Zvi noted that the verse is probably a Deuteronomic addition to a previous stage of the speech (see n. 60). His observations support my suggestion that Account B₁ is a pre-Deuteronomistic prophetic story and that—like many other prophetic stories—it was integrated by the Deuteronomist into his work on the history of Israel.

The Deuteronomist omitted any reference to Assyria after the end of Account B₁, thereby shaping the figure of Hezekiah in the collective Israelite memory for all generations to come. Anyone reading the Hezekiah-Josiah pericope in the book of Kings would have to conclude that Judah was subjugated in the reign of Ahaz and was freed during the reign of Hezekiah.[62] By attaching Account B₁ after Account A, and omitting any reference to the subjugation of Judah to Assyria from 701 BCE to the Assyrian retreat from Palestine in the 620s,[63] the Deuteronomist depicted Hezekiah's revolt against Assyria as an unqualified success. He was thus able to describe the reign of Josiah without mentioning his subjugation to Assyria. It goes without saying that ideological considerations played an important role in his description of the history of Israel, and that the lesson learned from Hezekiah's conduct at time of dire threat was far more important to him than historical accuracy. This is an exemplary case of the decisive role of the Deuteronomist in shaping the history of Judah according to ideological and theological considerations, although he cited his two sources almost verbatim and added very little to the early texts.

Account B₂ was written in Babylonia, either in the late years of the Babylonian Empire or the early Persian period, and in many ways is a revised theological version of the first account. The prophetic story of the 'miraculous deliverance' of Jerusalem had a prominent place in the theology of the Deuteronomistic history. However, the Deuteronomist left many parts of the Rabshakeh address virtually unanswered. As Peter Machinist observed, there is no critique like the Rabshakeh's letter-address in the rest of the Deuteronomistic History. 'Every one of its points has echoes in or provides a sharp counter to activities and theological positions elsewhere

61. Ben Zvi, 'Who Wrote', pp. 91-92.
62. Nadav Na'aman, 'The Kingdom of Judah under Josiah', *TA* 18 (1991), pp. 3-71 (55-56).
63. For the date of the Assyrian retreat from Palestine, see Na'aman, 'The Kingdom of Josiah', pp. 33-41, with earlier literature.

recorded in the Bible of Judah.'[64] The author of Account B_2 found it necessary to update the early prophetic story, to counter the critique and respond to the Rabshakeh's political and theological claims, and to fit the messages of the story to the new experience of the Jewish community in Babylonia in the second half of the sixth century BCE.

64. Machinist, 'The *Rab Šāqēh* at the Wall of Jerusalem', pp. 156-58.

CLIO IN A WORLD OF PICTURES—ANOTHER LOOK AT THE LACHISH RELIEFS FROM SENNACHERIB'S SOUTHWEST PALACE AT NINEVEH[*]

Christoph Uehlinger

> So, when we look at these Assyrian sculptures, we have to see them not merely as products of one age and place, but as the results of a process which began when they were being manufactured, continued through thousands of years, and is still continuing... Nearly all these things, moreover, are now fragmentary or decontextualized. In interpreting them, we have to allow not only for assumptions that may colour our own image of what they meant and mean, but also for physical changes not directly related to their original appearance and function.[1]

Introduction

The so-called 'Lachish reliefs' from room XXXVI of Sennacherib's 'Palace without Rival' in Nineveh[2] were discovered by A.H. Layard during his

---

* I am grateful to Lester Grabbe for inviting me to contribute a piece to the present volume, and for editorial improvements. This article is based on observations made years ago when I assisted Othmar Keel in the preparation of a monograph on the history of interpretation of ancient Near Eastern iconography and the Bible; see provisionally the entry, 'Iconography and the Bible', in *ABD* III, pp. 358-74 (359-60 for comments on the Lachish reliefs). My own interest in Assyrian palace reliefs goes back to 1983–84, when I was able to study them in London under the guidance of Julian Reade, to whom I owe essential insights in Assyrian monumental art. A few years before, in 1981, I had been lucky to participate in the Lachish excavations directed by David Ussishkin, who was then fully engaged in the interpretation of Sennacherib's room XXXVI reliefs on the basis of his stratum III findings. My critical discussion of his theory should not obliterate the lasting gratitude I owe to this admirable field director, perspicuous interpreter and stimulating writer.

1. J. Reade, 'Restructuring the Assyrian sculptures', in R. Dittmann *et al.* (ed.), *Variatio Delectat: Iran und der Westen* (Gedenkschrift für Peter Calmeyer; AOAT 272; Münster: Ugarit-Verlag, 2000), pp. 607-25 (625).

2. A. Paterson, *Assyrian Sculptures: Palace of Sinacherib. Plates and Ground-Plan of the Palace* (The Hague: Martinus Nijhoff, n.d. [several printings 1912–15]), Pls. 68-78; D. Ussishkin, *The Conquest of Lachish by Sennacherib* (Tel Aviv Publi-

second expedition to Nineveh (October 1849 to April 1851). In contrast to most other Assyrian reliefs, except the Black Obelisk,[3] these slabs could be related to a precise historical event a few months only after their discovery.[4] On display in the British Museum since c. 1856,[5] they figure since then among the best-known and most celebrated pictorial references to Israelite and Judahite history and illustrate almost any account on the Bible and the ancient Near East.[6] Moreover, modern archaeological research has definitely established the identification of Lachish with Tell ed-Duweir in the Judean Shephelah. As a result of substantial excavations on behalf of three major expeditions, the British Wellcome-Marston expedition led by

cations of the Institute of Archaeology, 6; Tel Aviv: Tel Aviv University, 1982), pp. 76-93; R.D. Barnett, Erika Bleibtreu and G. Turner, *Sculptures from the Southwest Palace of Sennacherib at Nineveh*, II (London: The British Museum, 1998), I, pp. 101-105, II, Pls. 322-52.

3.   See O. Keel and Ch. Uehlinger, 'Der Assyrerkönig Salmanassar III. und Jehu von Israel auf dem Schwarzen Obelisken', *ZKT* 116 (4, 1994; A. Gamper Festschrift), pp. 391-420; Ch. Uehlinger, 'Bildquellen und ,Geschichte Israels': grundsätzliche Überlegungen und Fallbeispiele', in C. Hardmeier (ed.), *Steine—Bilder—Texte. Historische Evidenz außerbiblischer und biblischer Quellen* (Arbeiten zur Bibel und ihrer Geschichte, 5; Leipzig Evangelische Verlagsanstalt, 2001), pp. 25-77.

4.   As early as 1851, the Irish reverend E. Hincks identified the names of Sennacherib and Lachish on the caption which accompanies the reliefs, thus allowing Layard to relate the pictures to events and people well-known from the Bible. See below and particularly Layard's *Discoveries in Nineveh and Babylon; with Travels in Armenia, Kurdistan and the Desert: Being the Result of a Second Expedition undertaken for the Trustees of the British Museum* (London: John Murray, 1853), pp. 152-53 with n. * recording Col. Rawlinson's reluctance to accept Hincks' identification.

5.   Their early inventory numbers show that they were registered in the British Museum in 1856 (56–9–9, 13–14 according to Gadd, 14–15 according to Barnett *et al.*, *Sculptures*), where they were then reassembled and restored. The present inventory numbers are WAA 124904–124915, running from restored slabs 5 to 16. See C.J. Gadd, *The Stones of Assyria: The Surviving Remains of Assyrian Sculpture, their Recovery and their Original Position* (London: Chatto and Windus, 1936), p. 174; Barnett *et al.*, *Sculptures*, I, pp. 101-105. A helpful concordance for the numbering systems employed by various authors is found Barnett *et al.*, *Sculptures*, I., p. 105. In the present article, we shall follow the numbering of Barnett *et al.*, which counts the 12 slabs preserved in the British Museum as nos. 5-16.

6.   E.g. R.D. Barnett, *Illustrations of Old Testament History* (London: The Trustees of the British Museum, 1966), pp. 60-65; J.B. Pritchard, *The Ancient Near East in Pictures Relating to the Old Testament*, Second Edition with Supplement (Princeton, NJ: Princeton University Press, 1969), nos. 371-74; T.C. Mitchell, *The Bible in the British Museum* (London: The British Museum, 1988), pp. 60-64 document 27; and cf. below, n. 54.

J.L. Starkey from 1932 to 1938 and two Tel Aviv expeditions headed by Y. Aharoni in 1966/68 and D. Ussishkin from 1973 to 1994, the city attacked by Sennacherib's army can today be identified beyond reasonable doubt with the remains of Lachish stratum III. The last-mentioned project has paid particular attention to the investigation of remains related to the Assyrian attack and to the restoration of major stratum III structures.[7] In the words of David Ussishkin,

> There is no other case in biblical archaeology in which a detailed Assyrian relief depicting a city under attack can be compared to the actual remains of that city and that battle uncovered by the archaeologist's spade, while the same events are corroborated by the Old Testament as well as the Assyrian sources.[8]

Definitely, here is more than 'virtual history'[9], and a pictorial source seems for once to be able to play a major role in historical reconstruction. It comes as no surprise that the 'European Seminar on Historical Methodology' should move beyond its generally text-and-archaeology-focused approach and consider the potential of this apparently unique pictorial source when addressing problems related to Sennacherib's campaign against Judah.[10]

7. See below, nn. 76-80 for references; final reports are in press.
8. Ussishkin, *Conquest*, p. 11.
9. Cf. Diana Edelman, 'What If We Had No Accounts of Sennacherib's Third Campaign or the Palace Reliefs Depicting His Capture of Lachish?', in J. Cheryl Exum (ed.), *Virtual History and the Bible* (Leiden: E.J. Brill, 2000), pp. 88-103, whose article opens with the startling invitation: 'Suppose no accounts of Sennacherib's third campaign in 701 BCE or the palace reliefs from room 36 of the palace of Nineveh, depicting the conquest of Lachish with the accompanying epigraph identifying the scene as Lachish, had survived'. Edelman then concentrates on the virtual absence of verbal accounts, which according to her would not change much of the outlines of the regional history which should be based on archaeology. As far as the reliefs are concerned, she does not consider them for their own sake as independent historical sources but only in an indirect way: 'Without the drawings (*sic*) of the siege of Lachish from the palace of Nineveh, archaeologists would lose a primary anchoring pin for their dating system' (p. 94), namely the dating of the destruction of stratum III and associated Judahite material culture to 701 BCE. The argument implies that what the reliefs depict can be identified on the ground but ignores what the sculptures actually mean. On the Lachish Reliefs see Russell's article 'Sennacherib's Lachish Narratives', in P.J. Holliday (ed.), *Narrative and Event in Ancient Art* (Cambridge Studies in New Art History and Criticism; Cambridge: Cambridge University Press, 1993), pp. 55-73.
10. Note, however, that a recent monograph on the 701 campaign does not expect much new insight from the Lachish reliefs: W.R. Gallagher, *Sennacherib's Campaign to Judah: New Studies* (SHCANE, 18; Leiden: E.J. Brill, 1999), pp. 13-14. By Gallagher's explicitly stated criterion ('Because much has already been written on the

The present article will not provide a comprehensive commentary on the Lachish reliefs. Its aim is a more limited one and may be summarized in two questions: Granted first that the Lachish reliefs may indeed be considered as historical primary sources, how should historians deal with these pictures? To put it another way, how should they approach the reliefs' particular quality as *pictorial* records of an historical event? Second, how should the different categories of information we have concerning the conquest of Lachish (topography, geography, archaeology, pictures, texts and literature) be related one to another in the process of historical reasoning and reconstruction? This paper will argue that while most commentators have indeed tried to follow an integrated or 'holistic' approach, including all or many different types of evidence, text- and archaeology-based preconceptions have often led them to wrong or deficient interpretations of the reliefs and have failed to address the pictorial record as a distinct, partly independent and complementary source of historical information and ancient historiography in its own right. We shall posit that in order to correctly use and evaluate a pictorial source in historical terms, the modern interpreter not only has to learn the particular 'language' of images, in this instance, Assyrian[11] and particularly Sennacherib's palace reliefs,[12] but

Lachish reliefs, they are...not investigated here', p. 13), scholars should first stop investigating the biblical tradition about Sennacherib and Hezekiah, then put an embargo on the study of Sennacherib's inscriptions, and concentrate instead on the analysis of the sculptures which have attracted much less critical scholarly attention than the textual record.

11. Much preliminary work in this respect has been accomplished by J.E. Reade in his 1965 dissertation, published later in a series of articles: 'Assyrian Architectural Decoration: Techniques and Subject-Matter', and 'Narrative Composition in Assyrian Sculpture', *Baghdader Mitteilungen* 10 (1979), pp. 17-49 and 52-110; *idem*, 'Space, Scale and Significance in Assyrian Art' and 'The Architectural Context of Assyrian Sculpture', *Baghdader Mitteilungen* 11 (1980), pp. 71-74 and 75-87. See further by the same author: 'Ideology and Propaganda in Assyrian Art', in M.T. Larsen (ed.), *Power and Propaganda: A Symposium on Ancient Empires* (Mesopotamia, 7; Copenhagen: Akademisk Forlag, 1979), pp. 329-43; 'Neo-Assyrian Monuments in their Historical Context', in F.M. Fales (ed.), *Neo-Assyrian Royal Inscriptions: New Horizons in Literary, Ideological and Historical Analysis* (Orientis Antiqui Collectio, 17; Rome: Istituto per l'Oriente, 1981), pp. 143-68; and finally, *Assyrian Sculpture* (London: British Museum Press, 2nd edn, 1998 [1983]). See also above n. 1. A major recent synthesis is P. Matthiae, *L'arte degli Assiri: Cultura e forma del rilievo storico* (Storia e società; Rome: Laterza, 1996).

12. Sennacherib's reliefs have been thoroughly investigated by J.M. Russell in three major monographs: *Sennacherib's Palace without Rival at Nineveh* (Chicago and London: University of Chicago Press, 1991); *The Final Sack of Nineveh: The Discov-*

also to inquire into the rules which governed their commissioning, production and display in antiquity.

The Lachish Reliefs and their Scholarly Interpretation

Discovery and Documentation

To judge from published information, the Lachish reliefs were discovered by A.H. Layard during the latter part of his second expedition,[13] probably in August 1850.[14] The relevant entries on this phase of work are absent from Layard's original fieldnotes, presumably because he was not at Kuyunjik at the time when room XXXVI was first touched upon by his workers.[15] The earliest statement known to me is contained in a manu-

ery, Documentation, and Destruction of Sennacherib's Throne Room at Nineveh, Iraq (New Haven and London: Yale University Press, 1998); *The Writing on the Wall: Studies in the Architectural Context of Late Assyrian Palace Inscriptions* (Mesopotamian Civilizations, 9; Winona Lake, IN: Eisenbrauns, 1999). On the Lachish Reliefs, see Russell's article 'Sennacherib's Lachish Narratives', in P.J. Holliday (ed.), *Narrative and Event in Ancient Art* (Cambridge Studies in New Art History and Criticism; Cambridge: Cambridge University Press, 1993), pp. 55-73.

13. See Layard, *Discoveries*, p. 148. Although ch. VI starts with December 1849 and ch. VII continues with Layard's visit to Nimrud where he spent Christmas, the very unprecise indication 'During the latter part of residence at Mosul' for the discovery of the Lachish reliefs cannot refer to early December 1849. Since Layard's earlier numbering system followed an alphabetic order, the discovery of room XXXVI, earlier named OO, must indeed be placed in the latter part of the second expedition as a whole. Note that Layard was frequently absent from Nineveh, be it for work at Nimrud or further travels; for a summary, see R.D. Barnett, 'The Palace and its Excavation', ch. I in Barnett *et al.*, *Sculptures*, I, pp. 3-7.

14. See Russell, *Palace*, 39, according to whom the room XXXVI reliefs were found by Layard's foreman Toma Shishman, in contrast to what Layard himself has written in publication.

15. On extant fieldnotes and other manuscripts, see R.D. Barnett, 'Sources for the Study of the Palace', in Barnett *et al.*, *Sculptures*, I, pp. 8-19. The relevant part of the fieldnotes is British Library, Add.MS. 39089E, which contains notes on a few rooms excavated before OO, notably GG and JJ to MM, but more information on later discoveries. According to the inventories published by Barnett *et al.* (*Sculptures*, I, p. 9), rooms NN to RR are not recorded in extant fieldnotes. These would have concerned precisely the suite of adjoining rooms XXXVII, XXXVI and XXXV and—less interesting for our purpose, because unconnected—the two rooms LV and LVI situated at their back. Of all these, XXXVI is to my knowledge the only one where Layard recorded sculptures. We may suspect then that he took no fieldnotes at all on these rooms and decided instead, for lack of time and given the relatively good state of preservation and the complexity of the Lachish reliefs, to concentrate on their drawings. (This judgment may need revision in

script compiled by Layard after the close of the excavations.[16] Ironically, however, although this statement might be considered a true 'primary source' drafted by a major eyewitness,[17] it is not very helpful in every respect since its description of the room XXXVI reliefs is clearly wrong for several major features.[18] Unfortunate as this may be, we cannot know

light of the announced publication of further primary documentation, see G. Turner, 'Sennacherib's Palace at Nineveh: The drawings of H.A. Churchill and the discoveries of H.J. Ross', *Iraq* 63 [2001], pp. 107-138 [107].)

16. British Library, Add.MS. 39077, fol. 75r-79v published by J.M. Russell, 'Layard's Descriptions of Rooms on the Southwest Palace at Nineveh', *Iraq* 57 (1995), pp. 71-85.

17. J.M. Russell, 'Sennacherib's Palace without a Rival Revisited: Excavations at Nineveh and in the British Museum Archives', in S. Parpola and R.M. Whiting (eds.), *Assyria 1995: Proceedings of the 10th Anniversary Symposium of the Neo-Assyrian Text Corpus Project* (Helsinki: The Neo-Assyrian Text Corpus Project, 1997), pp. 295-306, calls the manuscript mentioned in n. 16 'the first and most complete eyewitness description of Sennacherib's palace since antiquity' (p. 295).

18. According to Russell ('Layard's descriptions', p. 92), the relevant entry on fol. 78v reads: 'OO. All drawn except south side and from SE corner to lion, on which apparently King in chariot receiving prisoners, and warriors leading horses'. The exceptions must refer to the first four (or actually five) greatly damaged slabs which were not sent to London. Note that Layard's published description does not mention the king in his chariot anymore but refers instead to 'large bodies of horsemen and charioteers' (*Discoveries*, p. 149). There are rare instances in Sennacherib's palace where the king may appear twice or more on the sculptures of a single room, e.g. in the throneroom or in room V-8, V-11, V-32, [V-42 and] V-48 (see Russell, *Final Sack*, Pls. 118-19, 124-25, 157-59, 176-77, 188-89 which greatly improves the presentation of Barnett *et al.*, *Sculptures*, II, Pls. 50-76). However, these rooms either cover several events of one campaign or several campaigns; the king in his chariot receiving prisoners always closes an episode, with the camp serving as divider between several episodes. Room XXXVI presents a completely different situation. A depiction of the king in his chariot receiving prisoners on one of the first slabs would have been in blatant tension with the composition of the room's pictorial narrative. Room XXXVI concentrates on a single episode and consequently had the king appear only once, receiving booty and subdued people (see below). Layard's mistake is explicable: When describing slabs '1-4' (perhaps from memory, since he had not drawn them), he probably assumed that the OO (= XXXVI) series should start with a review of chariots and horses similar to V-10-12 (discovered already at the end of his first campaign in late spring 1847). On second thought (rather than control of the evidence, which he did not have at hand), he later dropped the reference to the king.

The manuscript statements on rooms OO (XXXVI) and MM (XXXIV) are remarkable for another feature: in striking contrast to Layard's published description which has human-headed winged bull colossi flanking the entrance that led into room XXXVI

anymore what Layard exactly saw in September 1850 and thus shall ever depend on his published account of 1853 (see below) and his drawings.

Concerning the latter, the *original drawings* which Layard drafted from 6 to 11 October 1850 on site[19] have apparently not survived, even though two series of 'Original drawings' are preserved in the famous elephant folio at the British Museum: the first series includes rough, unsigned key sketches made on site, most probably by Layard's draftsman C.I. Hodder (fig. 1). The main purpose of this series was to register and number the many fragments on the wall in order to allow their subsequent dismantling, identification and later reassembling.[20] As a matter of fact, these sketches are not always very accurate, particularly in the marginal and bottom areas of the slabs. The other series consists of drawings made and signed by Layard himself (fig. 2).[21]

(8, b) and which compares them with the biblical cherubim (see *Discoveries*, p. 445), the manuscript mentions a pair of *lions*, as pointed out by Russell ('Layard's descriptions', p. 82; *idem*, in *Assyria 1995*, p. 296). It would seem that in this instance we should favour this earlier record (and thus correct Ussishkin's reconstruction in *Conquest*, p. 70 fig. 60).

19. Barnett *et al.*, *Sculptures*, I, p. 6. On Layard drawing the reliefs, see Barnett *et al.*, *Sculptures*, II, Pls. 200 (no. 278b) and 369 (no. 463b). The latter, however, is clearly an idealized picture, the seated Arab of S.C. Malan's watercolour (Pl. 368 no. 463a) having been replaced by Layard himself on the lithograph of N. Chevalier published in Layard's *Discoveries*, opp. p. 345!

20. Or.Dr. II 7-15; Barnett *et al.*, *Sculptures*, nos. 428b-436b. Layard did not like the work of Hodder, who incidentally lost his health under the burden of his charge. Although Hodder's drawings certainly fulfilled their primary function, they are not always accurate, being the work of a nineteenth-century artist (and as such somehow reminiscent of E. Flandin's drawings from Khorsabad). Our fig. 1 combines two separate drawings. The straight edges, continuous drawings of cracks, siege planes and other devices wrongly suggest that slabs 6 and 7 joined neatly on-site when copied by Hodder. However, when mounted together the two drawings obviously do not fit. As a matter of fact, the artist has overlooked numerous details in the most destroyed marginal areas.

21. Or.Dr. I 58-62; Barnett *et al.*, *Sculptures*, nos. 428a-439a; note Layard's handwritten instructions for the printers on Pls. 324 and 336. Comparison of figs. 1 and 2 show considerable differences along the join of slabs 6 and 7. One of Layard's most blatant errors concerns the bottom of slab 7 (where Hodder's sketch had been more than cursory). Two pairs of slingers at the right bottom of slab 7 may serve to appreciate Layard's drawing: the pair turned right is turned backwards as if moving up the siege ramp, while the pair turned left is considerably enlarged and placed on the plinth, i.e. much too low. It comes as no surprise that neither Hodder nor Layard recorded the Judahite captives marching along the plinth from beneath the gate tower towards the Assyrian king (see below, fig. 7).

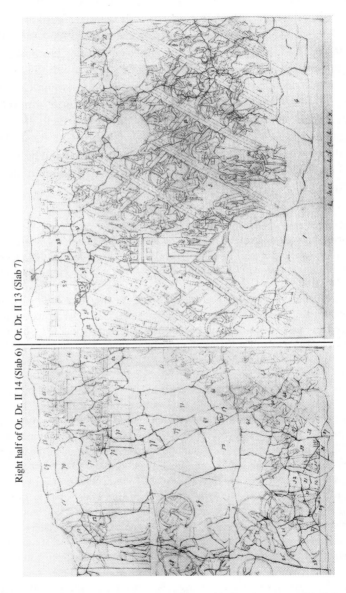

Right half of Or. Dr. II 14 (Slab 6) | Or. Dr. II 13 (Slab 7)

Fig. 1. Section of C. I. Hodder's revised field sketches, assembled from
two separate folios; note the individual numbering of fragments
and the somewhat idealized join between slabs 6 and 7.

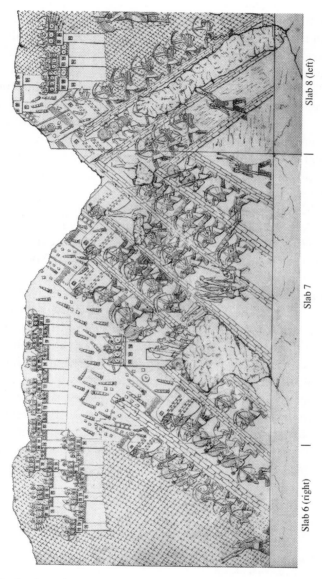

Fig. 2. Section of A.H. Layard's drawings prepared in London. Note that the left margin does not correspond to the left edge of slab 6. The gaps between slabs 6-7 and 7-8 are not recorded on the drawing, and restorations not marked as such. The bottom of slab 7 is severely misinterpreted.

These are sometimes considered to be most reliable since drawn at Nineveh, but Layard actually drew them in England in preparation of his Second Series of *Monuments of Nineveh*,[22] without direct access to the originals which still remained in Nineveh at that time. The precise relationship of these drawings to Layard's on-site sketches is unclear to me. The merits of the drawings produced in London notwithstanding, close comparison with extant reliefs demonstrates that Layard normalized or omitted numerous details probably under the pressure of time, restored others where only fragments of the originals had been preserved, and at times added conjectured features where no material basis of the original reliefs remains. Consequently, both Hodder's and his own drawings (and of course the *published plates* based on the latter, fig. 3)[23] have as a rule to be checked against the originals wherever preserved.

As for the *original slabs* themselves, they were finally dismantled and packed in April and May 1853 by H. Rassam, following a visit to Kuyunjik by Col. Rawlinson. They then travelled in twelve cases (together with a total of 118) to Baghdad (June 1853), Basrah (January to March 1854) and Bombay, from where they left later during the year to arrive in England in late February or March 1855.[24] It follows from this chain of events that neither Layard's London drawings nor the plates in the *Second Series* of his *Monuments of Nineveh* could be checked against the originals before going to the printers. Both depend exclusively on Layard's field drawings, not on the original slabs, a fact which is rarely recognized by scholars. Since the plates became standard reference once they were published, one may reasonably surmise that together with Hodder's sketches they must have guided the people engaged in the difficult task of reassembling and restoring the fragments in the British Museum. Still, certain details restored in plaster on the reliefs presently on display cannot be documented in any early drawing or print.

22. A.H. Layard, *A Second Series of Monuments of Nineveh; including Bas-Reliefs from the Palace of Sennacherib and Bronzes from the Ruins of Nimroud. From Drawings made on the Spot, during a Second Expedition to Assyria* (London: John Murray, 1853), Pls. 20-24.

23. Note that on fig. 3 = *Monuments*, II, Pl. 21, the vertical join of slabs 7 and 8 has totally disappeared, except below the fourth tower from left of the lower wall.

24. See Gadd, *Stones*, pp. 105-107, 174, and cf. supra, n. 5.

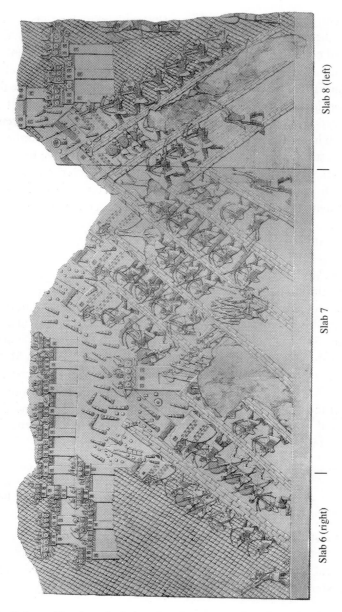

Fig. 3. Layard's plate depicting the siege scene, based on the drawing reproduced in fig. 2 and published as *Second Series*, Pl. 21. Note that the straight line dividing slabs 6 and 7 has disappeared; the straight margin on the left and the wavy margin at the right end of the published section are *ad hoc* devices with no basis in reality.

Just as any exegesis of a text should start with textual criticism, that is to ascertain the material basis of one or several manuscripts, a pictorial analysis should consider the material quality of its primary document before attempting an interpretation, be it iconographical and/or historical. In the particular case of the present study, the complicated history of the discovery, recording, dismantling, reassembling and restoration of the Lachish reliefs needed to be briefly retold, since it may serve as a patent reminder how much in the realm of history depends on processes of recording, storage and restitution of data. Moreover, this history will have to be kept in mind when we come to the discussion of scholarly interpretations, some of which heavily rely on particular drawings or on a particular physical arrangement of the original slabs. (For the sake of convenience, the reader is invited to refer to our fig. 8, which provides an overview on the series together with relevant slab numbers.)

Layard's Published Commentary
But let us turn to Layard's *verbal description* of his discovery. The most ample commentary, partly based upon his fieldnotes, was published in chap. VI of his *Discoveries in Nineveh and Babylon*. It first recalls the discovery in 1848, just before Layard first returned to Europe, of a monumental human-headed bull on the east side of the Kunyunjik palace. More such bulls flanking various entrances to courts and rooms of the palace were unearthed when Layard returned to the site in 1849. The inscriptions running over these bulls allowed Revd Hincks to identify Sennacherib as the builder of this palace in a memoir read at the Royal Irish Academy in June 1849. According to Layard,

> Subsequent discoveries confirmed this identification, but it was not until August, 1851, that the mention of any actual event recorded in the Bible, and in ancient profane history, was detected on the monuments, thus removing all further doubts as to the king who had raised them.[25]

Layard must refer here to Sennacherib's campaign against Judah, which is the only 'actual event' of this king's reign recorded both by biblical texts and ancient profane history (Herodotus and, as far as Phoenicia is concerned, Menander viz. Josephus). He then offers a lengthy paraphrase,

25. Layard, *Discoveries*, p. 139. On the relationship of Layard and Hincks and the latter's rivalry with Col. Rawlinson, see K.J. Cathcart, 'Edward Hincks (1792–1866): A Biographical Essay', in K.J. Cathcart (ed.), *The Edward Hincks Bicentenary Lectures* (Dublin: The Department of Near Eastern Languages, University College, 1994), pp. 1-29.

based on Hincks' analysis and interpretation, of the Bull and two prism inscriptions, the so-called Bellino and Taylor cylinders. Hincks had already recognized place names such as Ashkelon, Ekron, Gaza and Jerusalem in the final paragraph of Sennacherib's account of his third campaign, and identified the names of Padi(ya) and Hezekiah, but did not adopt Rawlinson's suggestion to read the name of Lachish in another, badly preserved passage of the account. Noting that the Assyrian and biblical records agreed 'with considerable accuracy', Layard did not deny 'some chronological discrepancies' but insisted on what he considered an equally interesting task: he had related the details of Sennacherib's inscriptions 'in order that we may endeavour to identify the sculptured representations of these events on the walls of the chambers and halls of that magnificent building'.[26] However,

> Unfortunately the upper parts of nearly all the bas-reliefs at Kouyounjik having been destroyed the epigraphs are wanting; and we are unable, as yet, to identify with certainty the subjects represented with any known event in the reign of Sennacherib. *There is, however, one remarkable exception.*[27]

The exception is of course Lachish, but Layard would not release his 'scoop' too easily. His account now switches to a long description of an exceptionally promising chamber, as yet unnamed,

> in which the sculptures were in better preservation than any before found at Kouyounjik. Some of the slabs, indeed, were almost entire, though cracked and otherwise injured by fire; and the epigraph, which fortunately explained the event portrayed, was complete. These bas-reliefs represented the siege and capture by the Assyrians, of a city evidently of great extent and importance.[28]

Although Layard's account makes it clear from the outset that the decisive 'explanation' of the picture would come from the epigraph, he discloses the city's name only after a three-page description of the reliefs,[29] thus nourishing a growing sentiment of tension and expectation in his readers' minds as in a rhetorically well-organized oral exposition.[30] The account

26. Layard, *Discoveries*, pp. 146-47.
27. Layard, *Discoveries*, p. 148 (emphasis added).
28. Layard, *Discoveries*, p. 149.
29. Layard, *Discoveries*, pp. 149-51; quoted extensively in Barnett *et al.*, *Sculptures*, I, pp. 101-104.
30. One is reminded of Ezekiel's *mise en scène* of the siege of a city drawn on a brick (Ezek. 4–5), developing considerable performance before the city's identity is disclosed by a divine statement (5.5: 'this is Jerusalem'); see Ch. Uehlinger, '"Zeichne

progresses along the extant slabs from left to right, transforming the pictures into a continuous narrative in a way that may come quite close to what the Assyrian designers had originally intended.

Layard's often-quoted narrative ingeniously intermingles four categories of information. First, it identifies particular motifs in a general or more specific sense: double walls, battlements and towers, fig and wine in the hilly and wooded country around, kneeling archers, spearmen, slingers, siege ramps and engines, defenders etc. Particular attention is given to details of dress:

> The vanquished people were distinguished from the conquerors by their dress, those who defended the battlements wore a pointed helmet, differing from that of the Assyrian warriors in having a fringed lappet falling over the ears. Some of the captives had a kind of turban with one end hanging down to the shoulder, not unlike that worn by the modern Arabs of the Hedjaz. Others had no head-dress, and short hair and beards. Their garments consisted either of a robe reaching to the ankles, or of a tunic scarcely falling lower than the thigh, and confined at the waist by a girdle. The latter appeared to be the dress of the fighting-men. The women wore long shirts, with an outer cloak thrown, like the veil of modern Eastern ladies, over the back of the head and falling to the feet.

It is remarkable that Layard already distinguished very clearly two categories of men among the vanquished, which he understood as fighters vs. chiefs, a distinction which O. Tufnell, R.D. Barnett and others would later elaborate upon.[31]

Second, Layard brings in a dramatic, emotional tone when he perceives the footsoldiers on the left as 'a compact and organised phalanx' or when he states that 'the besieged defended themselves with great determination'. Third, his verbal narrative aptly mirrors the structuring of the pictorial representation: while the approaching army on the left is described in orderly separated ranks,[32] the account of the central panels showing the battle at its

---

eine Stadt...und belagere sie!" Bild und Wort in einer Zeichenhandlung Ezechiels gegen Jerusalem', in M. Küchler and Ch. Uehlinger (eds.), *Jerusalem. Texte—Steine— Bilder* (Othmar and Hildi Keel-Leu Festschrift; Novum Testamentum et Orbis Antiquus, 6; Fribourg: University Press and Göttingen: Vandenhoeck & Ruprecht, 1987), pp. 109-200.

31. See below, pp. 283-89.

32. As a matter of fact, Layard does not go into great detail but idealizes the picture according to his own expectations of a well-organized phalanx when he mentions three organized ranks of archers, the first kneeling, the second bending forward and the third standing upright. On the actual reliefs, bowmen and slingers to the left of the city are

height combines attackers and defenders in single sentences, creating a vivid impression of excitement and confrontation:

> Spearmen, archers, and slingers thronged the battlements and towers, showering arrows, javelins, stones, and blazing torches upon the assailants. On the battering-rams were bowmen discharging their arrows, and men with large ladles pouring water upon the flaming brands, which, hurled from above, threatened to destroy the engines. Ladders, probably used for escalade, were falling from the walls upon the soldiers who mounted the inclined ways to the assault.

The description then suddenly returns to calm with a statement announcing capitulation:

> Part of the city had, however, been taken.

Fourth, Layard analyses particular features on the slabs in comparison with reliefs from other rooms and once even from Khorsabad. This comparative procedure allows him to address prominent specificities of the present series, to identify particular personages such as the Assyrian king and to give meaning to some particular scenes with the help of parallels. To quote but two examples, the observation 'In no other sculptures were so many armed warriors seen drawn up in array before a besieged city' justifies the interpretative statement that 'The whole power of the great king seems to have been called forth to take this stronghold'. When describing the Assyrian king sitting on his throne (compare our fig. 9b), Layard notes that 'In his right hand he raised two arrows, and his left rested upon a bow; an attitude, probably denoting triumph over his enemies, and in which he is usually portrayed when receiving prisoners after a victory'.[33]

One may notice that Layard's description remains largely within the limits of iconography, with only a few comments of an iconological order

---

generally shown in pairs standing upright; only occasionally is there a single kneeling archer inserted, more often than not dividing different contingents among the attackers. This feature breaks down the standard order which might otherwise have looked too mass-produced and distracted an onlooker's attention (cf., e.g., the Assyrian overseers along the rows of foreign working teams in court VI and room XLIX). Moreover, it could well have served to delimit or bind together sections which had been executed by different sculptors.

33. The description of the 'ten banks or mounts, compactly built of stones, bricks, earth, and branches of trees' is not only based on the evidence of the Lachish reliefs but rather on more detailed representations such as preserved in room XII (Barnett *et al.*, *Sculptures*, II, Pls. 150-53) and on the unique slabs showing the actual construction of a siege ramp in room XLIII (*Ibid.*, Pls. 374-75).

and minimal recourse to textual information derived from Assyrian inscriptions or the Bible.[34] This is remarkable in the light of his prior discussion of Sennacherib's inscriptions and of his just-announced programme according to which the cities represented on the reliefs should be identified on the basis of the inscriptions.[35] However, we should probably not understand Layard's restriction to iconographical description as reflecting an intentional methodology. Rather, we must remember that he had worked on Assyrian reliefs years before the first cuneiform inscriptions were read and that he was therefore used to close iconographical observation unhindered by texts. The descriptions of the reliefs draw heavily on his fieldnotes which he had written down months before the city was actually identified by Revd Hincks. Still, his account is rhetorically built up to finally lead readers towards the inscription which held the power to disclose at once the identity of the mysterious city:

> Above the head of the king was the following inscription, [follows the cuneiform text] which may be translated, 'Sennacherib, the mighty king, king of the country of Assyria, sitting on the throne of judgment, before (or at the entrance of) the city of Lachish (Lakhisha). I give permission for its slaughter.'[36]

This statement represents a real climax and turning-point in Layard's account, since from now on the Bible leads the pen, producing a whole series of interpretative short-circuits between unrelated sources. As a result, his interpretation from now on loses most of its critical potential:

---

34. The major exception is the—erroneous—identification of the Assyrian official facing the king as 'the Tartan of the Assyrian forces, probably the Rabshakeh himself' (Layard, *Discoveries*, p. 150). As J. Reade has shown, this figure should on 8th- and 7th-century sculptures be identified with the crown-prince; see J.E. Reade, 'Two slabs from Sennacherib's palace', *Iraq* 29 (1967), pp. 42-48 (45-47); *idem*, 'The Neo-Assyrian Court and Army: Evidence from Sculptures', Iraq 34 (1972), pp. 87-112 (93); *idem*, 'Kronprinz', *RLA* VI/3-4 (1982), pp. 249-50; Michelle I. Marcus, *A Study of Types of Officials in Neo-Assyrian Reliefs: Their Identifying Attributes and their Possible Relationships to a Bureaucratic Hierachy* (unpublished PhD thesis, Colombia University, 1981), pp. 69-73, 79-81.

35. See above, nn. 25-26.

36. Layard, *Discoveries*, p. 152. Hincks' translation is itself an interesting testimony to the early interpretation of the scene represented on the reliefs in terms of *judgment* and *slaughter*, both terms with obvious biblical overtones. See below for our current understanding of the caption.

Here, therefore, was *the actual picture* of the taking of Lachish, the city, *as we know from the Bible*, besieged by Sennacherib, when he sent his generals to demand tribute of Hezekiah, and which he had captured before their return [footnote *: 2 Kings, xviii. 14. Isaiah, xxxvi. 2. From 2 Kings, xix. 8., and Isaiah, xxxvii. 8., we may infer that the city soon yielded.]; evidence of the most remarkable character *to confirm the interpretation of the inscriptions*, and *to identify* the king who caused them to be engraved with *the Sennacherib of Scripture*. This highly interesting series of bas-reliefs contained, moreover, an undoubted representation of a king, a city, and a people, *with whose names we were acquainted*, and of *an event described in Holy Writ*. They furnish us, therefore, with *illustrations of the Bible* of very great importance.[37] The captives were *undoubtedly Jews, their physiognomy was strikingly indicated in the sculptures*, but they had been stripped of their ornaments and their fine raiment, and were left barefooted and half-clothed. From the women, too, had been removed 'the splendor of the foot-ornaments and the caps of network, and the crescents; the ear-pendents, and the bracelets, and the thin veils; the head-dress, and the ornaments of the legs and the girdles, and the perfume-boxes and the amulets; the rings and the jewels of the nose; the embroidered robes and the tunics, and the cloaks and the satchels; the transparent garments, and the fine linen vests, and the turbans and the mantles, 'for they wore instead of a girdle, a rope; and instead of a stomacher, a girdling of sackcloth'. [footnote †: Isaiah, iii. 18–24. &c. (…)][38]

This is the language of faith, of prophecy and fulfilment, not of a critical nineteenth-century historian. All of a sudden, the sculptures cease to deliver their own, particular message and become mute under the steamroller-like emphasis with which the Bible is used to interpret the pictures. It is not what the pictures show that is important to this commentary, but rather what they definitely do not show, for example Jewish physiognomy or jewellery of Jewish (rather Judahite) ladies. What could be considered an incredibly rich source of information on how Assyrian artists perceived Judahite Lachish, its environment and its population submitted and exiled dries up and vanishes in the face of biblical, or, to be more precise, biblicist nineteenth-century anti-Jewish rhetoric.

A Methodological Parenthesis
The main methodological lesson to be learnt from this account resembles the well-known conclusions of the debate on the Bible and archaeology

---

37. Footnote * inserted here responds to Col. Rawlinson who had 'denied that this is the Lachish mentioned in Scripture'.

38. Layard, *Discoveries*, pp. 152-53 (emphasis added).

held fifty years ago between W.F. Albright, M. Noth and R. de Vaux, namely that each category of information, each source should be analyzed independently in line with its own particular potential and according to the specific methodology required by the subject. Only when this primary analysis has been accomplished and the limits of each source's information potential have been explored should different sources be brought together.

Moreover, the major fallacy of many comparative studies combining different sets of evidence into a single account is their often unspoken tendency to look for mutual confirmation and agreement between sources instead of different, possibly contradictory testimonies. With regard to pictorial analysis, it appears plainly from Layard's account that textual information should in principle only be imposed on the 'reading' of images when all other interpretative strategies, descriptive and iconological, have been exhausted. One could of course argue against this principle that it represents a purely theoretical construct, since interpretation is practised by scholars who generally have prior knowledge of texts and who cannot at any time blend off this parallel information. Still, the minimal requirement for a methodologically acceptable historical analysis of a pictorial representation is that the interpreter should try to analyze an image according to the possibilities, rules and conventions of figurative representation, not of texts, and that he or she should have a self-critical attitude and check at any stage of analysis whether a particular description or interpretation of a total image or of a particular feature relies on internal iconographical arguments or on external information, whether iconographical or textual.

Once external information is brought into the argument, one should always measure the relative distance, so to speak, between different sources. Parallel information derived from the same medium, for example images, should be privileged wherever available. Within a certain medium, information derived from the same genre, for example Assyrian palace reliefs, and, if possible, the same time or context, for example, the palace of Sennacherib, should also be privileged. This is precisely what Layard had done in the pre-inscriptional phase of his work. Once we bring in texts, inscriptions derived from identical or close contexts will have to take priority over texts of further removed origin. For this reason, the captions or epigraphs on Assyrian reliefs certainly have a major role to play in the process of historical analysis of the reliefs (incidentally, in room XXXVI the king's right hand holding the arrows is raised as if pointing towards the major epigraph, see below, fig. 9a). However, even the epigraphs have to be put in their proper place and should not be misunderstood as condensed summaries of the reliefs.

The Epigraphs

Epigraphs on Assyrian palace reliefs are physically linked to the pictures and must have been drafted more or less at the same time, if not by the same individuals, as the reliefs themselves. A study of the relation between Sennacherib's reliefs and epigraphs is beyond our present topic,[39] but I should briefly comment on the epigraphs in room XXXVI since, as we have seen, they take a prominent role in Layard's and in many later accounts. Two epigraphs are preserved, one above the Assyrian crown-prince and senior officers facing the king (below, fig. 9b) and the other above the royal tent (fig. 9c); my suspicion—which I cannot however substantiate— is that a third epigraph might have identified the city on the now lost upper part of slabs 6-8 (cf. fig. 8).[40] The epigraph above the royal tent simply tells that this is 'the tent (*zaratum*) of Sennacherib, king of Assyria'.[41] One wonders at first sight why this statement was deemed necessary, since the royal tent appears on many other occasions without any such label. Looking for parallels, we may recognize that the camp epigraphs in rooms I, V and X come closest to the unique tent epigraph of room XXXVI. The reason for this particular inscription may well be that only here is the royal tent shown outside the protection of a fortified camp.

J.M. Russell, an expert on Southwest palace sculptures, has rightly noted that Sennacherib's epigraphs take over, to some extent, the role played by bands of annalistic inscriptions in earlier Assyrian palaces. In contrast to earlier epigraphs, they not only identify foreign places and people but often accompany the Assyrian king himself. According to Russell, they thus 'serve a more active role in the interpretation of the images, identifying the participants on both sides and giving a descriptive summary, thereby

39. Note the important contributions by P. Gerardi, 'Epigraphs and Assyrian Palace Reliefs: The Development of the Epigraphic Text', *JCS* 40 (1988), pp. 1-35; Russell, *Palace*, pp. 24-31, 269-78; E. Frahm, *Einleitung in die Sanherib-Inschriften* (AfO Beiheft 26; Horn: Institut für Orientalistik der Universität Wien, 1997), pp. 123-28; Russell, *Writing*, esp. pp. 134-42, 283-92.

40. Note however that Sennacherib's extant epigraphs do not include simple place names in contrast to those from the palaces of Tiglath-Pileser III and Sargon II.

41. Russell, *Palace*, p. 277; Frahm, *Einleitung*, p. 127 T 51; Russell, *Writing*, p. 288.fi

focusing attention on the significant features of the action'.[42] I strongly disagree with this characterization of Sennacherib epigraphs as summaries. In the case of room XXXVI, no sensible onlooker can maintain that the main epigraph summarizes the pictorial narrative, nor even its most significant features, since it simply reads:

1   ^{Id}XXX-PAP^{meš}-SU (*Sîn-aḫḫē-erība*) MAN (*šar*) ŠÚ (*kiššati*) MAN (*šar*) KUR (*māt*) *Aššur*

2   ina ^{giš}GU.ZA (*kussî*) *né-me-di ú-šib-ma*

3   *šal-la-at* ^{uru}*La-ki-su*

4   *ma-ḫa-ar-šu e-ti-iq*

1   Sennacherib, king of the world, king of Assyria,

2   took place on/in[43] a/the *nēmedu* throne,[44] and

3   the booty of Lachish

4   passed before him.[45]

This statement merely characterizes the particular sub-scene to which it is physically related, adding four elements to our understanding of the details: first, it identifies the king by name, whereas the image simply shows *the* Assyrian king in his full attire. But who among ancient onlookers would ever have doubted that this is Sennacherib? One wonders whether the epigraph's main purpose in this respect was not after all to state that the king had been there *himself*.[46] At the same time, we should be aware that identifying the king by name on an epigraph is not really an isolated phenomenon since the royal name was applied to almost any inscription in the palace. The label's second line then puts emphasis on a particular act of royal authority. This feature of the epigraph is unique, so we should attach particular importance to it. The king's sitting down in the *nēmedu* chair probably had a ceremonial function, either at the end[47] or already during

42. Russell, 'Sennacherib's Lachish Narratives', p. 68; *idem, Writing*, p. 140.

43. Not 'set up a throne', as translated in Barnett *et al., Sculptures*, I, p. 104.

44. See Russell, *Final Sack*, p. 223 for the suggestion that the hitherto unclear *nēmedu* may refer to a movable throne, an interpretation that would be consistent with other textual attestations of the term. Other scholars have taken *nēmedu* as a reference to a throne with armrests.

45. Russell, *Palace*, p. 276; Frahm, *Einleitung*, p. 127 T 50; Russell, *Writing*, pp. 287-88.

46. Note that in contrast to the testimony of inscriptions, Sennacherib never plays an active role in battles depicted on the reliefs, but is generally shown receiving homage in his chariot or within his fortified camp (see next footnote for references).

47. The scene is known already on Tiglath-Pileser's reliefs from Nimrud and wall paintings from Til Barsip. It features on several of Sennacherib's reliefs, although

the battle. Third, the epigraph identifies the conquered town (Lachish), which is again a specifically verbal, indexical function. Fourth and final, the epigraph mentions the review of booty. While features 1 and 3 have an identifying function, 1 being generic and 3 more particular, 2 and 4 closely parallel parts of the pictorial scenario. Features 1, 3 and 4 occur on six other Sennacherib epigraphs and define what E. Frahm has called 'Beute-Beischriften'.[48] One may note that these follow a standard formula always put in 3rd pers. masc. sing., whereas the 'Eroberungs-Beischriften' use either 3rd or 1st pers. sing. Clearly, the purpose of these epigraphs is not to summarize the content of the room XXXVI reliefs, but to identify major places and people and to answer implicit questions such as 'what did the king do on that day of victory?' or 'what about this peculiar tent outside the camp?', helping to secure the correct interpretation of *significant details* only which did not simply follow standard pictorial conventions.

Interestingly enough, we know of two cuneiform tablets with epigraphlike notations. Frahm, who has studied these tablets anew, was inclined to consider them as drafts for epigraphs but hesitated because of some formal and linguistic peculiarities.[49] Commenting on one of the tablets, Russell noticed the mixture of campaigns, a feature which would not be consistent with a basic rule of Sennacherib's palace decoration except the throne room. He therefore suggested that the tablet was a later compilation, rather than a preliminary draft of epigraphs.[50] I cannot avoid thinking of some kind of *aide-mémoire* designed for courtiers who would guide visitors through the palace or lead them to particular rooms and explain the meaning of the sculptures. True, this palace certainly was not conceived for tourists visiting a museum,[51] but Sennacherib himself claims to have conceived the palace and 'filled it with splendor for the astonishment of all people'.[52] Visitors must have been numerous, both among courtiers and foreigners, who would have needed and appreciated some basic explanations when looking at these highly complex pictorial compositions.

---

always set inside the camp except for room XXXVI (cf. Barnett, *Sculptures*, II, Pls. 35, 412, 504; other examples are lost, e.g. slab VII-6, *Ibid.*, Pls. 128-29).

48. Frahm, *Einleitung*, p. 124.

49. Frahm, *Einleitung*, pp. 211-13.

50. Russell, *Writing*, p. 139.

51. See Russell, *Palace*, pp. 222-40, 251-52 on intended and actual audience of the palace reliefs.

52. Russell, *Palace*, p. 252.

Studies since Layard, Mainly on Realia

This is not the place to review in detail the numerous studies, paraphrases or spurious remarks that scholars, most of them more at home with the Bible than with Assyria, have devoted to the Lachish reliefs between 1853 and 1980.[53] I suspect that a research history would have to struggle with a considerable bibliography just to conclude that major insights for the over-all understanding of the series as a whole were rarely produced during more than a century, or if produced went unnoticed. As a matter of fact, most commentators confined themselves to repeating what Layard had already seen, elaborating sometimes on one or another particular feature of Juda-hite or 'biblical' realia[54], the 'ethnic' attribution of dress, weapons, a throne and other furniture, carts and sometimes even cattle to ancient Judahite culture having been established on the basis of the main *epigraph*'s testi-mony. The Lachish reliefs have also regularly supplied shorthand informa-tion for research on Judahite fruit economy and silviculture during the Iron Age.[55] In the field of ancient Near Eastern studies concerned with Assyrian

53. 1980 witnessed the publication of a summary article by Pauline Albenda, 'Syrian-Palestinian Cities on Stone', *BA* 43 (1980), pp. 222-29, adding nothing sub-stantial to previous knowledge, and of an article in which D. Ussishkin first outlined his new theory which reads the reliefs on the basis of new archaeological evidence (see below).

54. See, e.g., A. Legendre, 'Lachis', *Dictionnaire de la Bible, Supplément*, IV (Paris: Letouzey et Ané, 1908), pp. 15-16, 23-26 with figs. 4, 11-12; H. Gressmann, *Altorientalische Bilder zum Alten Testament* (Berlin and Leipzig: W. de Gruyter, 1926), figs. 138-41; K. Galling, *Biblisches Reallexikon* (Handbuch zum Alten Testa-ment I, 1; Tübingen: J.C.B. Mohr [Paul Siebeck], 1937): 'Die Reliefs von der Eroberung durch Sanherib...zeigen uns interessante Einzelheiten vom Leben der Bewohner (Kleidung, Wagen, Viehwirtschaft) und die Ausrüstung des judäischen Residenten (Schwert, Thron u. a. m.)' (pp. 347-48).

55. Z. Amar and M. Kislev have recently argued that the Lachish reliefs show sycamores (*Ficus sycomorus*) among the tree species represented. According to Kislev, most trees (79 out of 108, i.e. 73 per cent) are sycamore trees, i.e. he simply suggests an alternative identification for the most commonly figured, fruitless tree type, which is usually held to represent olive trees. See M. Kislev, 'Sycamores in the Lachish Reliefs', in J. Schwartz, Z. Amar and I. Ziffer (eds.), *Jerusalem and Eretz Israel* (Arie Kindler Volume; Bar-Ilan: The Ingeborg Rennert Center for Jerusalem Studies and Tel Aviv: Eretz Israel Museum, 2000), pp. 23-30 (hebr., engl. summary 100*). There are meth-odological problems in Kislev's approach, who does not consider the question on the background of artistic conventions and the overall picture of Sennacherib's reliefs but seems more interested in confirming a biblical description (1 Kgs 10.27 mentioning plenty of sycamores in the Shephelah). Note however his argument that sycamores were grown for logs in antiquity, and that they could be conveniently used for the

monumental art in general, the Lachish reliefs were of course regularly touched upon, but rarely to advance the interpretation of the series as a whole. Here too, scholars used pictorial evidence from room XXXVI mainly because it provided an undisputed historical and geographical anchor for particular details of geography, vegetation,[56] warfare,[57] dress[58] and other realia.[59] While all these studies are obviously important and essential to any 'holistic' approach to history, one cannot escape the conclusion that their scope remains somewhat limited and that they have failed to tell us the better part of the story. Only more recently, scholars have

construction of tracks for the battering-rams. In contrast, Amar distinguishes four instead of three commonly held species among the tree types represented, taking a variant of the fig tree with rounded instead of split leaves as a depiction of the sycamore. See Z. Amar, 'Agricultural Products in the Lachish Reliefs', *Beit Mikra* 159 (1999), pp. 350-56; *idem*, 'Agricultural Realia in the Lachish Reliefs', *UF* 31 (1999), pp. 1-12. This fourth type appears only once on the extant reliefs, namely on the join of slabs 9-10 (see Barnett *et al.*, *Sculptures*, II, Pl. 323 for a close photograph). Note Bleibtreu's opinion that this tree had remained unfinished (*Flora* [below, n. 56], p. 143), but the actual relief does not support her assumption. We should however recall Bleibtreu's distinction between 'Laubbäumen mit unverzweigten Ästen und kugeliger Krone' (*ibid.*, pp. 160-68) and 'Laubbäumen mit unverzweigten fast senkrecht stehenden Ästen' (*ibid.*, pp. 168-70). The former type shows considerable morphological variation, which would fit olive trees, while the latter is much more standardized and could imply, according to Bleibtreu, frequent cutting back.

In any case, it seems to me that the Lachish reliefs call for a distinction of *five* different tree types, which may be numbered from secure to unsecure identification: (I) grapevine (12 extant examples); (II) fig (10); (III) sycamore (1); (IV) leaf tree with relatively thin trunk and irregularly spread branches (olive tree?; 52+); (V) leaf tree with relatively thick trunk and regular, almost vertical branches (18+). Since small fruit such as olives, almonds or the like were never represented on the sculptures, it may be doubted that types IV and V represent one single species. In some rooms of Sennacherib's palace, type IV conventions were used to represent pomegranate trees, the fruit being the only feature allowing for precise identification.

56. Erika Bleibtreu, *Die Flora der neuassyrischen Palastreliefs: Eine Untersuchung zu den Orthostatenreliefs des 9.–7. Jahrhunderts v. Chr.* (WZKM Sonderband 1; Vienna: Institut für Orientalistik der Universität Wien, 1980).

57. See Y. Yadin, *The Art of Warfare in Biblical Lands: In the Light of Archaeological Study* (2 vols.; New York: McGraw-Hill, 1963).

58. See M. Wäfler, *Nicht-Assyrer neuassyrischer Darstellungen* (AOAT, 26; Kevelaer: Butzon & Bercker; Neukirchen–Vluyn: Neukirchener, 1975), pp. 42-55.

59. Note especially the inventories by B. Hrouda, *Die Kulturgeschichte des assyrischen Flachbildes* (Saarbrücker Beiträge zur Altertumskunde, 2; Bonn: Rudolf Habelt, 1965) and T. Madhloom, *The Chronology of Neo-Assyrian Art* (London: Athlone Press, 1970).

begun to address the ideological implications of the particular attention paid by Sennacherib's sculptors to matters of geographical and ethnographical diversity.[60]

What are the reasons for the scholarly reluctance to move beyond an exclusively environmental and artifactual approach? One reason may be that it is always easier for the interpreter to stay with putative 'facts' and 'realia' in a positivist manner. Second, both biblical scholars and Near Eastern historians have recognized that in contrast to what Layard and other nineteenth-century scholars had anticipated, the three major sources for Sennacherib's campaign against Judah (his inscriptions, his sculptures, and the biblical texts) actually tell quite different stories which may ultimately relate to the same history but cannot so easily be related one to another. As we have seen, each story needs to be 'read' and interpreted for itself. However, neither biblical scholars nor historians of the ancient Near East, all essentially involved in philology, are usually trained in iconographical and iconological analysis. Moreover, the artifactual approach has inevitably fragmented the room XXXVI reliefs into a kind of quarry where scholars pick out isolated features here and there without caring for the overall design and rhetorical programme of the series as a whole. As a result, the Lachish reliefs are generally regarded just in the way we look at photographs when reading a newspaper: as convenient illustrations but not as truly independent, and complementary, historical sources.

The Lachish Reliefs, Topography and Archaeology

Layard's discoveries preceded controlled archaeological excavations in Palestine by some forty years. It was to be expected that these would open up another dimension for the interpretation of the Lachish reliefs. Three stages may be distinguished in the development of a topography-and archaeology-based discourse on the reliefs. They coincide with three

60. See Stefania Mazzoni, 'Significato e ruolo del paesaggio nei rilievi di Sennacherib', *Contributi et Materiali di Archeologia Orientale* 4 (1992), pp. 151-66 (note that the article's headline erroneously refers to vol. 3, 1989); Michelle I. Marcus, 'Geography as Visual Ideology: Landscape, Knowledge, and Power in Neo-Assyrian Art', in M. Liverani (ed.), *Neo-Assyrian Geography* (Quaderni di Geografia Storica, 5; Rome: Università di Roma 'La Sapienza', 1995), pp. 193-202; P. Villard, 'La représentation des paysages de montagne à l'époque néo-assyrienne', in A. Serandour (ed.), *Des Sumériens aux Romains d'Orient: La perception géographique du monde* (Antiquités Sémitiques, II; Paris: J. Maisonneuve, 1997), pp. 41-58.

major excavation projects that were meant to bring to light the city known to have been destroyed by Sennacherib.

W.M.F. Petrie: 'the Truth of Geography'

> Everyone who knows the Assyrian sculptures in the British Museum is familiar with one of the largest compositions there—the Siege of Lachish, by Sennacherib. On looking at this, *the truth of geography is seen at once, when the site is known.* The city stands, on the sculpture, with a gentle slope up to it on the left hand, a steeper slope in front, and a vertical cliff directly down from the base of the wall on the right. This corresponds to the view from the south. The left side is the west, the only side on which the ground rises gently; the steep front is the south side; and the cliff on the right is the east side, which was always worn away steeply by the stream. The gateway in front of the town *must be* that of which the steps were found on the south, leading up the glacis. Thence the captives are led away to the king at his camp on the right; this was therefore on the tongue of land between the Wady Muleihah and Wady Jizair… The valley with palms, on the right, must be the Wady Muleihah. This *testing of a sculpture* executed in Assyria, hundreds of miles distant from the place, is of great interest, as it shows that some sketches and notes were actually made, probably by a royal designer attached to the court, one of the secretaries. The essential points of the relative steepness of the three contiguous sides, the gateway, and the likely position for the camp, all show that the view is not a mere fancy piece.[61]

When read 110 years after its redaction, this paragraph written by W.M.F. Petrie, the founding father of the archaeology of Palestine, sounds somewhat pathetic since nobody today is prepared to believe a single word of it. To begin with, Tell el-Hesi is no more identified as the site of Lachish. Based on an improper reading of the topographical details depicted on the reliefs—Petrie simply overlooked the steep, almost vertical slope on the city's left side, and considerably misinterpreted the area to the right of the city as a 'valley of palms'—all of Petrie's 'truth of geography' appears like vanity destined to go down the Wadi Jisair.

Why then should we bother to recall such an accident of scholarship? Two reasons have led me to remember the episode: First, we should be aware that Petrie's arguments were found convincing at the time, as demonstrated, for example, by a 1908 entry in the renowned French *Dictionnaire de la Bible.*[62] Second, in the context of a discussion on meth-

---

61. W.M.F. Petrie, *Tell el Hesy (Lachish)* (London: Palestine Exploration Fund, 1891), p. 38 (emphasis added).

62. Legendre, 'Lachis', p. 27: 'L'image est d'une parfaite exactitude au point de vue topographique et correspond à la vue de la cité prise de sud'.

odology, we must stress the fact that Petrie's demonstration procedes along similar lines as D. Ussishkin's ninety years later (see below): it combines topographical and archaeological observations with a topographical interpretation of the reliefs, which are read in terms of visual perspective that allows a precise positioning of the onlooker; it moves on to locate the Assyrian camp and concludes with remarks on the quality of an eyewitness record taken on site by an Assyrian designer. An interpretative circle is thus construed in which the reliefs, topography and archaeology all play their role supporting one another's testimony. Ussishkin's theory is certainly much more refined and elaborated and based upon a much better informed 'reading' of the reliefs; obviously it will have to be evaluated on its own grounds. However, the structural analogy of his and Petrie's argument is striking and may help to sharpen our critical mind.

Olga Tufnell: Two Walls and a Bastion
A full century after Layard's publication of the Sennacherib reliefs, Olga Tufnell, who was in charge of the publication of the Wellcome-Marston excavations that had been directed during the 1930s by J.L. Starkey, presented another attempt at combining archaeological data with the pictorial record of the Lachish reliefs (viz., slabs 6-8 depicting the city proper; see fig. 4 for a new drawing published in her report).[63]

Tufnell limited herself to an extensive quote of Layard and a few sober, but very acute remarks on major agreements and differences between the city's portrayal on the sculptures and archaeological evidence. Against Starkey's earlier opinion and those of other authorities, Tufnell defended the main thesis that the city attacked and destroyed by Sennacherib should be identified with Lachish stratum III. This was in her opinion the necessary prerequisite for any comparison of the pictorial record and the archaeological findings (in contrast to more recent discussions, where the argument has sometimes been turned the other way round). Tantamount to her demonstration was the recognition of two walls both in the reliefs and on the ground. The excavations had indeed unearthed an upper wall of brick, which followed the edge of the escarpment, and a lower wall or revetment of stone

63. O. Tufnell, *Lachish III: The Iron Age* (Text and Plates) (London: Oxford University Press, 1953), frontispiece of text volume; see pp. 55-56, 62 for Tufnell's discussion of the reliefs. Note that this drawing is the first to show traces of Judahite captives at the bottom of slab 7. Accordingly, the two pairs of slingers mentioned above in n. 21 have been put back to their correct location. On the other hand, many missing parts are left blank in this drawing, a procedure which makes it impossible to appreciate the actual limits of extant slabs.

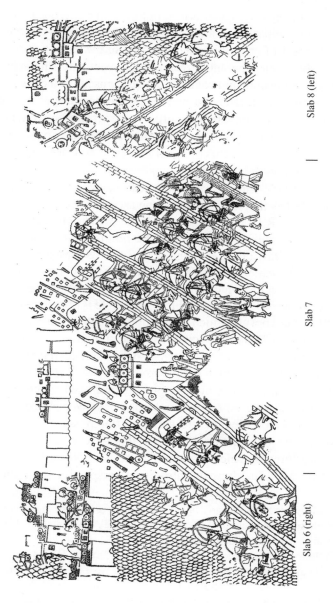

Fig. 4. New drawing of the siege scene published in *Lachish III* (1953); note that gaps are partly restored (particularly siege-planes and engines), partly left blank.

which ran some 16+ metres down around the slope. Both walls had recessed panels and projecting rectangular offsets or towers. Tufnell noted that on the reliefs, these are regularly spaced while on the ground they were set according to the contours of underlying bedrock. As for the bastion at the southwest corner, she saw it apparently freestanding, speculating that it had been unattached to the lower revetment in its earliest phase.[64] Since the details of these constructions were later clarified by the Tel Aviv expedition and are well-known, they need not retain us here any longer. Suffice it to note that Tufnell recognized basic points of agreement as well as considerable disagreements between the archaeological evidence and the sculptures, on which she would however not systematically comment. Of course, she also refered to arrowheads, slingstones, a spearhead, part of a bronze crest mount and the thick destruction layer covering the ascent to the city gate.

Five years later, R.D. Barnett, keeper at the British Museum and longtime the almost exclusive custodian of the reliefs (and of Layard's and others' 'Original drawings'), came back to Tufnell's presentation in order to 'consider the appearance of the city and attempt to reconstruct the events of the siege, a subject to which surprisingly little attention seems to have been devoted hitherto'.[65] Although his short article is often cited in secondary literature it did not add much to the subject beyond a number of questionable statements.[66] Barnett considered the sculptures to 'represent a gallant but confusing attempt by the artist, in the absence of perspective, to show several events happening at the same time which in fact succeeded one another'.[67] While he may be right on both points when they are taken separately, one cannot easily grasp his argument since perspective would not have solved the problem of telescoping different stages in time into a single, two-dimensional picture. Ironically, this is clearly demonstrated by a well-known drawing which a modern artist, Alan Sorrell, executed on Barnett's request.[68] The drawing introduced perspective but maintained

64. Since the bastion was clearly linked to the outer revetment in stratum III, this *ad hoc* hypothesis would certainly not explain why the Assyrian artist should have represented the bastion as a freestanding tower.

65. R.D. Barnett, 'The Siege of Lachish', *IEJ* 8 (1958), pp. 161-64 (162).

66. Ussishkin's understatement that his own studies were 'basically an elaboration of Barnett's work' ('The "Lachish Reliefs" and the City of Lachish', *IEJ* 30 [1980], 174-95 [175]) reads more like a *captatio benevolentiae*. As a matter of fact, the better part of Barnett's insights had been anticipated by Tufnell.

67. Barnett, 'Siege', p. 162.

68. Barnett, 'Siege', Pl. 30.B; see Yadin, *Art of Warfare*, II, pp. 436-37; Reade, *Assyrian Sculpture*, p. 65 fig. 69.

the temporal telescoping of successive events and thus appears even more surrealistic than the ancient original.[69] Barnett opined that the city appeared on the relief as if viewed from the southwest, where the British excavators had indeed found remains of the battle. He wondered 'whether any trace of this great siege-mound was found in the course of excavation',[70] suggesting that a glacis of red earth rising against the west wall of the bastion could represent all that was left of it, but he rightly stated that this hypothesis could 'only be confirmed or refuted by new excavation'.[71]

D. Ussishkin: The Siege-Ramp, the Palace-Fort and 'A Certain Perspective'

Luckily, this task was taken up by D. Ussishkin, whose excavations and restoration work between 1973 and 1994 on behalf of Tel Aviv University and the Israel Exploration Society have managed to resolve numerous problems raised by earlier excavations and subsequent scholarly discussions. Today, Lachish stratum III (see plan fig. 5a) is firmly and definitely identified as the city destroyed by Sennacherib and has become the major chronological cornerstone for the archaeology of Iron Age Judah.[72] The nature of its fortifications has been clarified, Barnett's just-mentioned hypothesis refuted and the Assyrian siege ramp precisely located at the southwest corner of the city, where the ascent to the bastion and city gate together with a natural saddle allowed the Assyrians to launch their attacks closest to the walls and gate but also to retreat with maximum facility.[73]

69.   Judahites leaving for exile calmly descend from gateway to bastion while soldiers of both parties are shooting arrows or throwing stones above their heads. Defenders on the inner wall are much too far removed from the battle that their actions would have any influence on the course of events. As for the the Judahite chariot and weapons which must represent spoils taken from the city, most probably the palace-fort compound, they seem to come out of nowhere or even worse, from the midst of the Assyrian attacking force.

Another modern artist's reconstruction, prepared by H. J. Soulen under the guidance of G.E. Wright, was not available to me: H.W.F. Saggs, 'The March of Empires', in *Everyday Life in Bible Times* (Washington, DC: National Geographic Society, 1967), pp. 258-59 (quoted after Ussishkin, 'Lachish Reliefs', p. 182 n. 23).

70.   Barnett, 'Siege', p. 162.

71.   Barnett, 'Siege', p. 163.

72.   See L.L. Grabbe's introduction to this volume, above pp. 3-20 ('Archaeology and Sennacherib', esp. the section on Lachish and the intermediate conclusions).

73.   According to Ussishkin, it was Yigael Yadin who first suggested this location of the siege-ramp in 1973 (see '[First] Preliminary Report' [below, n. 76]; *idem*, 'Assyrian Attack' [below, n. 79]). See further I. Eph'al, 'The Assyrian Siege Ramp at Lachish: Military and Lexical Aspects', *TA* 11 (1984), pp. 60-70.

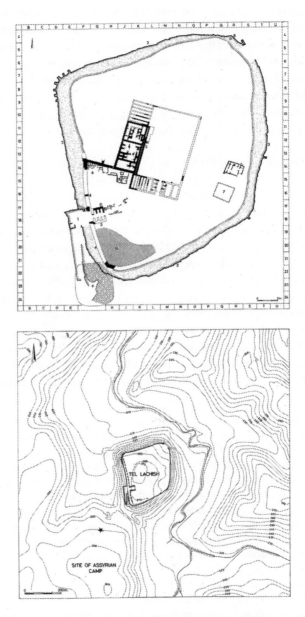

Fig. 5. Plan of Lachish stratum III according to D. Ussishkin's excavations (a) and general plan of the Lachish surroundings (b); the asterisk indicates the putative spot from where Sennacherib is thought to have followed the battle.

That this corner is the highest point of the city's defences partly results from the fact that the Judahite defenders had thrown up a huge interior counter-rampart against the city wall in order to protect it from the assault of the Assyrian battering-rams. All this and many more details surrounding the Assyrian attack and Judahite defence have been clearly expounded by Ussishkin in a number of preliminary publications, which hopefully will soon be superseded by the forthcoming final report.

In the course of his archaeological work and in line with his long-standing acquaintance with North-Syrian and Assyrian architecture and monumental decoration, Ussishkin took growing interest in Sennacherib's Lachish reliefs and, as a result, has published more extensively than anyone else on this particular series of sculptures. His studies go far beyond the simple juxtaposition of archaeological evidence and iconographical analysis. They include a completely new edition of the room XXXVI reliefs together with new drawings by Judith Dekel (see below, figs. 9a-c for some sections) in a monograph that remains the essential reference on the subject. Ussishkin also presented the history of the sculptures discovery and the architectural context in which they had been found[74], to some extent paving the way for the systematic study of the whole palace by J.M. Russell.[75] The following paragraphs summarize Ussishkin's interpretation of the Lachish siege scene as first published in two seminal articles in 1978[76] and 1980,[77] then expanded and slightly adapted in his lavishly illustrated 1982 book,[78] and finally supported with additional observations in another two articles published in 1990[79] and 1996.[80] When reading these

74. On this issue, which cannot be pursued further in the present article, see the basic study by G. Turner, 'The State Appartments of Late Assyrian Palaces', *Iraq* 32 (1970), pp. 177-213 (200-202); *idem*, 'The Architecture of the Palace', in Barnett *et al.*, *Sculptures*, I, pp. 20-39 (27-30). That Hezekiah's tribute and the spoil of Lachish should have been stored in this room, as hypothesized by Ussishkin (*Conquest*, pp. 69/71), is pure speculation. We know enough of Assyrian palaces, magazines and administrative practices to infer that weapons, furniture and other useful items among foreign booty were concentrated in central magazines and partly redistributed to courtiers, officials and other favourites.

75. See references quoted above, n. 12.

76. Ussishkin, 'Excavations at Tel Lachish, 1973–1977. [First] Preliminary Report', *TA* 5 (1978), pp. 1-97 (67-74).

77. Ussishkin, 'The "Lachish Reliefs" and the City of Lachish', *IEJ* 30 (1980), pp. 174-95.

78. *The Conquest of Lachish by Sennacherib* (Publications of the Institute of Archaeology, 6; Tel Aviv: Tel Aviv University, 1982).

79. Ussishkin, 'The Assyrian Attack on Lachish: The Archaeological Evidence from

publications in a line, one can follow the evolution of Ussishkin's theory in accordance with the progress of excavations. From one stage to another, he continuously put his own hypotheses to the test of growing archaeological evidence, thus providing us with a model of critical scholarship. On the other hand, it seems that some basic premises of his theory did not change over a period of almost twenty years; some of these will be questioned below.

For the sake of convenience, we shall follow the path of arguments taken in the 1982 book version and supplement observations from articles wherever necessary. Fig. 6, which is based on a montage of the whole series published in the book,[81] may help the reader to follow the details of the argument. The book starts with a brief outline of 'The historical evidence' (i.e. textual information from inscriptions and the Bible: Part I, pp. 13-18), then turns to 'The archaeological evidence' (Part II, pp. 19-58) and finally addresses 'The Lachish reliefs' (Part III, pp. 59-126). The archaeological evidence plays a pivotal role in this development, which is understandable from the point of view of an archaeologist. However, this setting also implies that the reader is already well aware of what he might look for when he comes to the sculptures, a procedure which recalls Layard's account and many later approaches to the reliefs and which is likely to induce methodological fallacies into the iconographical analysis.[82]

the Southwest Corner of the Site', *TA* 17 (1990), pp. 53-86. The original Hebrew version of the latter article was published in the Yadin Memorial Volume, *Eretz-Israel* 20 (1989), pp. 97-114.

80. Ussishkin, 'Excavations and Restoration Work at Tel Lachish 1985–1994: Third Preliminary Report', *TA* 23 (1996), pp. 3-60.

81. Note that Ussishkin's book contains figures which represent various stages in the execution of the drawings. Our fig. 6 is based on the overall montage of the unshaded drawings on p. 77, fig. 65 of the book. Although this montage is certainly wrong (see below, p. 270, on montage C), it has been used here in order to highlight the problems involved in Ussishkin's hypothesis. The composite drawings published in Ussishkin, 'Lachish Reliefs', p. 179 fig. 3, and *idem, Conquest*, p. 121 fig. 93 come closer to target (see discussion below, pp. 271-73). My own montage in fig. 7 is based on Dekel's shaded drawings of the individual slabs (*Conquest*, figs. 67-69), which can easily be checked against the photographs.

82. Note that Ussishkin's 1980 article followed another path, starting with an examination of the Lachish reliefs (pp. 176-81) before turning to a comparison with the archaeological evidence concerning the city and the siege. The first section concentrated on the technical question of the slabs' arrangement. The only interpretative question discussed in this section concerns the relationship between the impalement scene at the bottom of slab 8 and the row of prisoners leading from slab 8 to 11. Ussishkin assumed 'that the three impaled prisoners shown at the bottom of the siege ramp

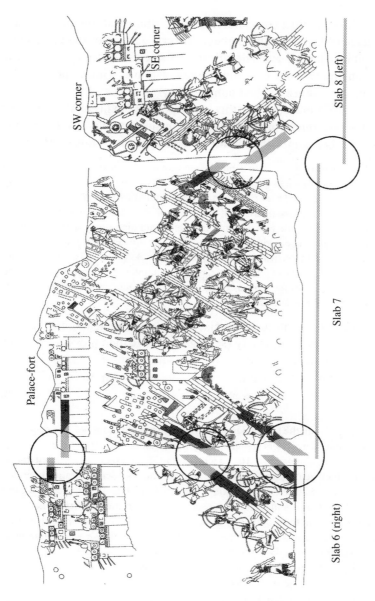

Fig. 6. New drawing of the siege scene by Judith Dekel, assembled as published in *Conquest*, fig. 65. Note that this drawing does not include restorations. Encircled areas highlight errors in the assemblage. Labels identify structures according to D. Ussishkin's theory.

To be fair, we must stress however that after recalling the excavation of
Sennacherib's palace and the architectural context of the Lachish reliefs,
Ussishkin offers a largely descriptive iconographical commentary (pp. 72-
118) which is a mine of insightful observations without precedent in the
scholarly literature on the Lachish reliefs.

Ussishkin's most original thesis is expounded in his final section, entitled
'The Lachish reliefs and the city of Lachish' (pp. 118-26). The main point
of the thesis is announced in the first paragraphs of this section:

> Lachish provides us with a unique opportunity of comparing a Neo-Assyrian
> stone relief depicting in detail an ancient city with the site of the same city
> whose *topography and fortifications* are well known to us... With the data
> of the *renewed excavations* at our disposal, it...becomes apparent that the
> reliefs *portray* the city not only from a certain direction but *from one par-
> ticular spot*. The various features of the city are depicted according to the
> usual rigid and schematic conventions of the Assyrian artists, but they are
> shown *in a certain perspective*, roughly maintaining the proportions and
> relationships of the various elements as they would appear to an onlooker
> standing at one specific point.[83]

Ussishkin even ventures to precisely locate this spot, about 200m from the
southwest corner of the city (see fig. 5b).[84] He then procedes 'to compare
the topographical and archaeological data as observed from our selected
vantage point to the features of the city as shown on the reliefs'.[85] The
gatehouse, which appears as an isolated tower on slab 7,[86] is identified

are associated with the line of deportees rather than with the attack and siege ramp' and
that 'the impaled prisoners are apparently irrelevant to the scene of the storming of the
city' (p. 181; cf. *Conquest*, p. 102). I tend to consider the scene as a kind of double-duty
element, which belongs to both phases of the event. As a demonstrative operation conspicuously placed in the central axis of the city (which is itself the central element of
the reliefs that ties together attack and submission), it is meant to mark the point where
resistance is about to be definitely broken. Moreover, it stresses the contrast of desti-
nies met by those who oppose the Assyrian power and those who acknowledge the
bliss of submission to the Assyrian king.

83. Ussishkin, *Conquest*, pp. 118-19 (emphasis added).
84. On fig. 5b, the spot is marked by an asterisk.
85. Ussishkin, *Conquest*, p. 120.
86. Note however that this impression is based on a wrong interpretation of the
image: since the latter shows Judahites leaving the gate, it clearly implies some connection between the city's habitation quarters and the 'tower'. The Assyrian artist had
no interest in representing this particular connection, since his main emphasis in this
area was to render the heat of the battle. According to Assyrian conventions, the very
peculiar wavy line below the wall segment shown above the 'tower' cannot represent

with Starkey's bastion, or outer gate, which could indeed appear as a massive tower to an ancient onlooker. The path descending from the gate to the right must be the roadway that descends from the outer gate to the southwest corner of the mound, even though the actual roadway does not follow a zig-zag line as the Judahites' procession.[87] Most important for Ussishkin's point is the identification of the large structure above the city gate:

> Apparently this building should be interpreted as the palace-fort, even though its architectural details are rendered exactly like those of the city walls, and soldiers (?) seem to be standing on the battlements. Nevertheless, the structure is clearly placed beyond the scene of the battle, and there are no enemy arrows like those penetrating the city walls stuck into its walls. The battering ram shown below the structure is attacking a feature rendered as a single, angled line, probably representing the city wall. The missiles raining down from it—the flaming torches, square stones, broken ladders and round shields—are all carved below the structure and are clearly dissociated from it. Assuming that the structure represents the formidable palace-fort, we may speculate that it rose to a much higher level in the missing upper part of Slab III [= slab 7].[88]

We shall come back to this latter 'speculation', but cannot avoid quoting here a passage which preceded it in Ussishkin's 1980 article before being excised from the 1982 book version:

> Our suggestion that the palace-fort is shown in the relief is partly based on the assumption that the palace-fort *must* have been represented in the scene. Even today, when only the substructure of the edifice still stands, the palace

the (lower) city wall as maintained by Ussishkin (*Conquest*, p. 121). Rather, it corresponds to the outlined master sketch prepared before the actual carving of the slabs, as may be concluded from a comparison with the similar wave line visible between the city wall and the 'scaley mountain' on slab 6. On slab 7, the space below the wave line was reserved for crumbling bricks and falling torches. This emphasis on the battle prevented the artist from outlining the physical connection between the 'tower' and the (outer) city wall.

87. According to later excavations, it even seems that the level IV-III roadway did not follow the straight line of the present ascent roughly following the stratum II roadway but proceeded closer to the mound, turning into a southeasterly direction at the southwest corner (see Ussishkin, 'Assyrian Attack', p. 65; *idem*, 'Third Preliminary Report', pp. 38-40).

88. Ussishkin, *Conquest*, pp. 120-21, cf. p. 102. On the space between the 'structure' and the 'tower', see the previous footnote. Regarding enemy arrows sticking in walls, note that they only appear at the city's two extremities.

fort is the most impressive structure on the mound, and we can only imagine
its formidable appearance when it was complete.[89]

It is obvious that in this instance Ussishkin followed a *petitio principii*
based on pure imagination in the face of the huge podium preserved on the
tell![90] The omission of the ominous passage from the book demonstrates
that Ussishkin must have been conscious of the argument's relative weakness. It is unfortunate that he did not substantiate his intuition through a
systematic study of Assyrian pictorial conventions for representing heavily
fortified cities with citadels and palace-forts. This would almost certainly
have led him to consider more seriously the now-destroyed upper part of
the relief (see below). Instead he tried, in a mixture of imagination and
positivism, to reconcile his theory with the extant reliefs alone.

Turning then to the siege ramp to the right of the city gate, Ussishkin
reports on new discoveries at the southwest corner of the mound. Again,
he stresses his argument beyond the reasonable, insisting boldly on a
quasi-proportional representation even though he had repeatedly stressed
before that the Assyrian artists who designed the sculptures were not used
to strict perspective:

> *From our vantage point*, located nearly opposite the southwest corner of the
> mound, this ramp appears relatively large in relation to the other features of
> the city; in the relief it gives the same impression. *From our perspective*
> (*sic*), the palace-fort and the outer city-gate appear to the left of the south-
> west corner and the siege ramp, exactly as depicted by the Assyrian artist.
> Furthermore, the left-hand side of the siege ramp reaches the bottom of the
> roadway leading to the outer city gate, and they appear similarly in the
> relief and *from our angle of vision*.[91]

Ussishkin rightly felt that his suggestion would stand or fall to the extent
that it could take into account the 'left' part of the siege ramp depicted on
the reliefs, which he originally thought had been directed against the outer
gate. However, Barnett's hypothesis that the earthen glacis against the
outer gate represented the remains of this ramp had been proven wrong by
the new excavations which established its character as a constructional
fill linked to the bastion. Ussishkin acknowledged in 1982 that 'no other

89. Ussishkin, 'Lachish Reliefs', pp. 188-89 (emphasis added).
90. Note that the 1978 preliminary report on the excavations only referred to the
reliefs when discussing the outer gate or bastion ('[First] Preliminary Report', p. 63)
and the siege ramp (pp. 71-74), not yet in the section on the palace-fort and annexed
buildings (pp. 27-41). These were only later inserted in the argument.
91. Ussishkin, *Conquest*, p. 125 (emphasis added).

remains can be ascribed to such a siege ramp at present, and only future excavations can establish its presence or absence'.[92] Since then, such excavations have indeed taken place around the outer gate, although not exclusively focused on the siege ramp issue, but 'no indications for a second Assyrian siege ramp laid against the city gate have thus far been found'.[93] It is unfortunate that this clear discrepancy between the pictorial and the archaeologial record still did not lead Ussishkin to revise his theory on vantage point and perspective.

Wishful thinking is at work with regard to another feature shown on the reliefs. On the upper left corner of slab 8 as preserved, one can clearly recognize the traces of three chariots flying through the air and possibly burning, presumably being thrown against the Assyrian attackers—most notably a battering ram depicted just below—by Judahite defenders standing on the 'upper' city wall. According to Ussishkin,

> The vehicles are rendered in a schematic though detailed manner, each represented by one wheel with a thick felloe and six spokes, and a yoke with attachments for harnessing two animals... The fact that several identical vehicles are shown here suggests that these were not various carts of the peasants of Lachish but war chariots that may have belonged to the royal Judean garrison stationed at Lachish.[94]

Although respectable evidence for a royal Judahite garrison possibly including chariotry was uncovered after 1982,[95] Ussishkin's iconographical argument cannot be accepted, since the tiny, dismembered chariot depictions simply do not allow for a distinction between horse-driven chariots or oxen-driven carts. One can notice, however, that the relatively primitive wooden stacks visible on the yokes have nothing in common with the elaborate yoke of the Judahite ceremonial chariot which appears on the same slab among the spoil, a chariot conceived to be driven by a team of four horses.

More important from the point of view of the archaeologist, the main difficulty for Ussishkin's theory relates to the city's main fortifications. Slab 8 clearly depicts two walls, even if the 'wall' segment above the gatehouse 'tower' on slab 7 should be identified with the palace-fort. As for slab 6, two walls are evident, although the upper 'wall' could, in a 'reading'

92. Ussishkin, *Conquest*.
93. Ussishkin, 'Third Preliminary Report', p. 46.
94. Ussishkin, *Conquest*, p. 105.
95. Ussishkin, See esp. 'Assyrian Attack', pp. 81-84; 'Third Preliminary Report', pp. 33-37.

sympathetic with Ussishkin's hypothesis, theoretically be regarded as the last segment of the palace-fort.[96] As was mentioned earlier, Tufnell and Barnett had no difficulties with the two walls since Starkey's excavations had apparently discovered remains of such a pair. Ussishkin's excavations established instead that the putative 'outer wall' was 'merely a strong revetment retaining the bottom of a glacis, which in turn supported the base of the city wall itself'.[97] How then should one understand the two walls depicted on the reliefs?

At this point, Ussishkin definitely became prisoner of his own premises and his explanations become particularly convoluted. Considering the city's right end on slab 8, he slips into the mind of the Assyrian artist looking from the presumed vantage point:

> A single tower rising high above the latter wall segment was interpreted as representing an inner city wall, but it seems more likely to have belonged to the now-missing wall segment originally depicted above the siege ramp. This segment of wall was portrayed at a higher elevation than that of the structure to its left, interpreted by us as the palace-fort. From our vantage point the city appears in a similar way. In the southwest corner it rises higher than other parts of the wall, and as the observations of the Assyrian artist were presumably made from a point directly opposite this corner, the fortifications here would have appeared to him to loom even higher. The segment of wall shown in the relief at the right-hand edge of the city must therefore represent the city wall at the south*east* corner, which from our angle of vision—and the Assyrian artist's—would appear roughly level with the palace foundations and the top of the siege ramp, and lower than the fortifications at the southwest corner.[98]

To think that a portion of the city-wall would run higher than the city's citadel and to look at two walls clearly depicted one above the other as two different corners of the mound's fortifications—separated in reality by a horizontal distance of roughly 225m—is to stretch one's imagination and interpretative premises beyond reasonable argument. The apparently ingenious explanation completely ignores the pictorial situation on the city's left hand on slab 6, which shows the two walls one above the other in an almost identical disposition as on slab 8 to the right.

96. Strangely enough, Ussishkin did not prefer this straightforward explanation to his own, which he expressed with much reservation, namely that the Assyrian artist should have taken the buttresses which reinforce the revetment at the northwestern angle of the mound for an outer wall (*Conquest*, p. 126).

97. Ussishkin, *Conquest*, p. 125.

98. Ussishkin, *Conquest* (emphasis added)

Let us sum up: Ussishkin's main thesis (visualized in fig. 6)[99] is that the Lachish relief 'portrays the besieged city as seen from one particular point'[100]. We have mentioned several difficulties of this theory, climaxing in the just-noted, utterly implausible interpretation. Having had the chance to work with Ussishkin in the field at Lachish and having experienced him as an always acute and often very critical scholar, I cannot deny my amazement and wonder about the reasons for his stubborn attachment to such a problematical theory. True, it was somewhat fashionable in the late 70s to locate Assyrian military camps, and Ussishkin had at that time already offered his suggestion concerning the Assyrian camp near Jerusalem.[101] However, his Lachish theory implies more than just a matter of location, and with all due appreciation, I suspect that the motives prompting this interpretation lie somewhere beyond scholarship. The deeper reasons driving Ussishkin's clinging to the very spot from where the Lachish reliefs were designed may be hidden in the answer he gave to his own question, 'Why was this spot chosen by the artist from which to draw the city and immortalize the battle?':

> Our selected vantage point is located just in front of the presumed site of the Assyrian military camp, between it and the city... We should like to offer the suggestion that *this is the very spot where Sennacherib, the supreme commander, sat on his* nimedu-*throne* and conducted the battle. Consequently, we assume that the relief presents the besieged city *as seen through the eyes of the monarch* from his command post.[102]

This is language of commemoration which expresses military fascination and identification with the victor. It comes as no surprise that Ussishkin's

99. See above, n. 81.

100. Ussishkin, *Conquest*, p. 126.

101. D. Ussishkin, 'The 'Camp of the Assyrians' in Jerusalem', *IEJ* 29 (1979), pp. 137-42; cf. *idem*, 'The Water Systems of Jerusalem during Hezekiah's Reign', in M. Weippert and S. Timm (eds.), *Meilenstein* (Herbert Donner Festschrift; Ägypten und Altes Testament, 30; Wiesbaden: Harrassowitz, 1995), pp. 289-307 (290-92). A. Zertal, who acted as area supervisor in the Lachish excavations, claims to have discovered an Assyrian camp at el-Qa'adeh in the neighbourhood of Samaria during his Manasseh survey. See his 'The Heart of the Monarchy: Patterns of Settlement and Historical Considerations of the Israelite Kingdom of Samaria', in A. Mazar (ed.), *Studies in the Archaeology of the Iron Age in Israel and Jordan* (JSOTSup, 331; Sheffield: Sheffield Academic Press, 2001), pp. 38-64 (57-58).

102. Ussishkin, *Conquest* (emphasis added), continuing with an observation on Sennacherib himself depicted on the right wall of room XXXVI of his palace, as if he were looking across towards the siege scene on the broad wall.

latest preliminary report should announce the erection, by the National Parks Authority, of a visitors' centre 'opposite the southwest corner of the mound', designed to receive a copy of the Lachish reliefs and to become the future starting point of guided tours to the site.[103] The procedure recalls some major achievements of Yigael Yadin, 'soldier, scholar, and myth-maker of modern Israel'[104] and one of Ussishkin's most influential teachers, of whom the latter had been a close collaborator at Hazor, Megiddo, in the Cave of the Letters and at Masada[105] and whom Ussishkin repeatedly challenged in later years. We cannot overlook the parallels drawn between the siege ramp of Masada and Lachish in some of Ussishkin's writings,[106] still less his early-stated opinion that

> our siege ramp is (a) the most ancient siege ramp so far discovered in the Near East; (b) the only archaeologically attested Assyrian siege ramp and (c) the only such ramp to have been 'photographed' in detail by a contemporary artist.[107]

Much has been written about the modern Israeli 'Masada complex', and we must certainly be careful not to project this concept into too many issues.[108] Still, one cannot but be struck by the fact that Ussishkin's theory, incidentally grown out of some basic intuitions of Yadin, should materialize over the years in an achievement comparable to Yadin's at Masada, but related to heroic events which preceded Masada's putative mass suicide by centuries.

Intermediate Conclusion: Agreements and Disagreements Between Reliefs, Topography and Archaeological Record
For the sake of convenience, let us briefly summarize the major agreements and disagreements between the city's depiction on the room XXXVI sculptures, the topography of Tell ed-Duweir, and the archaeological record of its stratum III: The topography of Lachish undoubtedly fits the picture

103. Ussishkin, 'Third Intermediate Report', p. 53.
104. Cf. N. A. Silberman, *A Prophet from Amongst You: The Life of Yigael Yadin: Soldier, Scholar, and Mythmaker of Modern Israel* (Reading, MA: Addison-Wesley Publishing Co., 1993).
105. On Yadin and Ussishkin, note Silberman, *Prophet*, pp. 232, 248, 251-54, 265-67.
106. E.g., Ussishkin, '[First] Preliminary Report', p. 73; *idem*, 'Assyrian Attack', p. 77. Note also Ussishkin's involvement at Beitar, where a famous siege took place towards the end of the Bar Kokhba revolt.
107. Ussishkin, '[First] Preliminary Report', pp. 73-74.
108. See R. Alter, 'The Masada Complex', *Commentary* 56 (July 1973), pp. 19-24; B.R. Shargel, 'The Evolution of the Masada Myth', *Judaism* 28 (1979), pp. 357-71.

much better than the one of Tell el-Hesi. As a matter of fact, image and topography concord with regard to an impressively high and well-fortified tell with very steep slopes. Because of this peculiar topographical situation, simultaneous multiple attacks against different sections of the city would have been almost impossible. Interestingly enough, the seven siege planes running against the city from the left and the three from the right form a kind of triangular 'rammer' field which opens one large breach into the lower and upper walls of the city; in contrast, the gate tower shows no sign of destruction. This seems to indicate that only one single siege ramp is actually depicted, as was first suggested by Ruth Jacoby (see below). Her interpretation would concord with the archaeological evidence and make an end to any speculation concerning a second siege ramp laid against the outer gate bastion. Moreover, the pointed top of the siege planes' imagined triangle would lie in a now destroyed segment above the right half of slab 7. I shall argue below that the original reliefs probably showed the citadel or palace-fort of Lachish at that very spot; if correct, this assumption would allow to register another concordance between image and archaeologically recorded reality. (Note, however, that the agreement would be limited to the mere existence or depiction of a citadel; in contrast to Ussishkin's theory, the citadel would not be positioned according to a quasi-perspectival view from a particular spot opposite the siege ramp, but roughly in the centre of the town or slightly off-centre to the right, which heightens the visual impact of the massive attack brought against it mainly from the left.)

As for the *disagreements* between the image and the archaeological record, they are at least as important and numerous as the positive correlations. The most conspicuous disagreement concerns the number of walls—as long as the two walls depicted on the reliefs are regarded as two different fortified city walls, probably thought to run parallel around the mound with apparently no physical connection between them. True, as a result of the just-mentioned breaches, neither the 'lower' nor the 'upper' wall run straight over the whole breadth of the figured city. Still, it seems most reasonable to consider the relative position of the two walls at the two extremities as an almost symmetrical arrangement, which should be and has been understood since Layard's harmonizing drawing as two parallel walls. Whether the wall-like structure on the upper left of slab 7 represents a segment of the city-wall or the palace-fort (as supposed by Ussishkin), the representation of straight wall segments and regularly spaced towers in any case does not reflect the archaeologically recorded evidence but merely follows an ancient Near Eastern pictorial convention. A further disagree-

ment exists between the zig-zag roadway leading downwards from the
gate tower to the bottom of slab 7 and the actual roadway leading to the
gate of Iron Age Lachish which followed the mound without any unnec-
essary bend in a south-southeasterly direction, roughly parallel to the outer
revetment wall.[109]

Taken together, these observations seem to indicate that while the Assyrian artists probably had some knowledge or information concerning the
topography and architecture of 701-BCE Lachish, they did not aim at a quasi-
photographic portrayal of the city. Their particular rendering of 'Lachish'
on the reliefs is apparently determined by standard pictorial conventions and
constraints of compositional balance and does not support Ussishkin's
theory of a quasi-perspectivic portrayal from one particular viewpoint.

A Formal Critique of Ussishkin's Theory

R. Jacoby: Identification Markers and Pictorial Conventions
Surprisingly, Ussishkin's theory that the Lachish reliefs provide an architectural portrait of the city in a quasi-perspectival manner as seen from a
particular spot has not been challenged in any detail except for a short but
important article by R. Jacoby, a younger student of Yadin's, entitled 'The
Representation and Identification of Cities on Assyrian Reliefs'.[110] Following a detailed examination of 108 cities appearing on Assyrian reliefs in her
MA thesis, Jacoby states that as a rule the depictions of cities should be
regarded as 'simplified, generalized portrayals with no pretensions to accuracy'.[111] She cites interesting cases where one and the same city appears in
several depictions on Assyrian monuments but is never represented in the
same way. We should not therefore expect topographical and architectural
accuracy from Assyrian artists in general.[112] On the other hand, Jacoby

---

109. See Ussishkin, 'Attack', p. 65.

110. See *IEJ* 41 (1991), pp. 112-31; the Hebrew version of the article, grown out of
Jacoby's M.A. thesis, was published in *Eretz-Israel* 20 (1989), pp. 188-97. Note also
the cautious remarks by Russell, *Palace*, p. 207 ('I am not sure this hypothesis
is defensible'). According to Russell, 'Ussishkin's recent excavations at Tell ed-
Duweir...have provided convincing evidence that Sennacherib was concerned with
spatial verisimilitude not for its own sake, but rather as a means of constructing the
image of a very particular place' (*Palace*, p. 205).

111. Jacoby, 'Representation', p. 112.

112. Even depictions of Nineveh and some outstanding buildings of the capital may
be inaccurate; see J. Reade, 'Assyrian Illustrations of Nineveh', *Iranica Antiqua* 33
(1998; David Stronach Festschrift), pp. 81-94.

rightly holds that 'the scenes were meant to be recognized'[113]—not least, we may add, because specificity helped to validate the veracity of the pictorial narrative and the king's effective claim for authority.[114] How then would ancient onlookers have identified the cities represented? According to Jacoby, identification was achieved by the following means:

(1)   an epigraph
(2)   physical characteristics of the city's inhabitants (e.g. hairstyle, beards, headdress and clothing)
(3)   the type of booty carried by the vanquished citizens
(4)   topographical and vegetative details
(5)   outstanding structures, such as a palace, a temple or a monument.[115]

Jacoby cites examples for all these categories which demonstrate that the various means each had a different potential for precise identification. In my opinion, the last-mentioned category should be divided into two sub-categories, depending on whether a relief shows a unique feature or whether particular structures (such as shields hung up on the parapets of city walls and towers) serve to specify regional characteristics. Moreover, topographical details can be very specific (e.g. when a town is situated on an island or divided into several settlement units) or more generic (e.g. scaling for the depiction of hills and mountains). Finally, Assyrian reliefs sometimes show singular details of the battle course which probably allude to very specific events. We might thus establish a kind of hierarchy of features and organize them according to their identifying potential:

feature	identifies
(1) singular detail of battle depiction	specific event
(2) epigraph	specific event or location
(3) singular architectural features or a monument	city (*ālu*)
(4) characteristic topographical features (e.g. island)	city or region
(5) type of booty carried by the vanquished	city, region or country (*mātu*)
(6) characteristic features of the city's inhabitants	country or area (e.g. Hatti)[116]
(7) typical architectural features	country, area or 'cardinal quarter' (*kibru*)
(8) topographical and vegetative details	area or 'cardinal quarter'

113. Jacoby, 'Representation', p. 122.
114. On the relation between growing geographical specificity and royal ideology, see the studies mentioned above, n. 60.
115. Jacoby, 'Representation', pp. 114-16.
116. Except the epigraphs, this is the best-studied category which has, however, its particular tricks: one has to bear in mind that the development of Assyrian palace art shows progressive precision over time with regard to the distinction of dress,

Turning to the room XXXVI reliefs, Jacoby asks whether it would be possible 'to identify the city portrayed on the relief as Lachish in the absence of the inscription'[117] and discusses three major features of the depiction, namely the two city walls, the gate, and the siege ramp, none of which according to her analysis would allow for a definite identification. In her opinion, 'It appears that one should not expect the details of the fortification depicted on the relief to correspond to the results of the archaeological excavation', and

> Since Lachish was not mentioned in the annals and was not incorporated in a general description of the field campaign, and since its relief occupied a separate room in Sennacherib's palace, we would not have been able to determine its identity were it not for the inscription.[118]

I generally agree with Jacoby, although her argument would have to be refined, taking into account the chronological development of Assyrian monumental art which arrived at increasing differentiation over the decades from the reigns of Tiglath-Pileser III to Ashurbanipal. The basic problem is how to distinguish between specific and generic markers, an operation which necessitates comparison of a given scene with the total corpus of siege scenes and leaves considerable uncertainty due to the fragmentary state of the corpus. In contrast, Ussishkin's too narrow correlation of iconography and archaeology rests upon his arbitrary isolation of two different sets of data, the room XXXVI reliefs and the results of the Lachish excavations. In the preceding section, we have already formulated a number of critical arguments against his interpretation of the reliefs on internal, iconographical grounds, limiting our discussion to a critique of his own argument. Opening up the iconographic horizon along the lines of Jacoby's study leads to the inevitable conclusion that Ussishkin's interpretation cannot be upheld.[119]

---

particularly in the case of Western peoples, while inhabitants of various regions in the Zagros mountains and beyond remain depicted in the same, more stereotyped manner.

117. Jacoby, 'Representation', p. 122.

118. Jacoby, 'Representation', pp. 130-31.

119. I intentionally leave open the issue of quasi-perspective and deep space in Assyrian art, which is not addressed by Jacoby but would necessitate a lengthy discussion. Dismissing the capacity of Assyrian artists to approach the problem of directional view altogether would be too easy a way to dispense oneself of critical argument. As a matter of fact, Sennacherib's reliefs show nascent tendencies towards quasi-perspective, as has been stressed by a number of scholars. See Russell, *Palace*, ch. 9; *idem*, 'Sennacherib's Lachish Narratives', pp. 57-65, for a recent assessment.

To my knowledge, Jacoby is the first scholar to have remarked that the ten siege planes 'opened up like a fan' should be understood as *one single siege ramp*.[120] On the other hand, my impression is that she somewhat shot beyond target when considering the depiction of the room XXXVI city to be just a generic and conventional one. Comparison with other city depictions clearly shows that the 'Lachish' picture has conspicuous peculiarities, some of which are likely to relate to a particular topographical and architectural reality.[121] In my opinion, this holds true for the gate tower projecting out of the city's fortifications, and probably also for the two walls although, as we have seen, these do not exactly fit the archaeological evidence on the site. Moreover, it seems most probable to me that the palace-fort, which was such an important structure in the stratum-III town, was indeed represented in the now lost upper third of slab 7. Such correlations hint at the strong probability that the depiction of 'Lachish' is more than a purely conventional one but implies definite knowledge about particular features of the 701 BCE town's fortifications and monumental architecture.

A major question is of course from what kind of 'sources' such knowledge derived. Since we do not have any evidence for Assyrian artists working in the field during military campaigns, the most likely explanation seems to be that the artists who designed the reliefs had access to textual information, probably contained in field diaries and syntheses such as must have been used for the redaction of 'letters to the gods' and related reports.[122] Such primarily text-based data processing may explain the depic-

---

However, I think that the main issue is not one of perspective, but one of data processing, namely whether pictorial sketches were taken in the field (let alone from a single spot) or not and whether the artists relied on pictorial or on textual sourcees when designing the reliefs.

120. 'The artist's intention was not to reproduce in the relief an exact replica of reality, but rather to portray in great detail the Assyrian siege technique in all its variations' (Jacoby, 'Representation', p. 130).

121. Cf. Russell, *Palace*, 209: 'it is clear that the Lachish shown in the relief is intended to be recognizable'; *idem*, Sennacherib's Lachish Narratives', p. 72: 'The visual record of this success was presented in a way that would ensure *maximum recognizability*, through highly specific costumes and scenery; and *verisimilitude*, through exploitation of perspective effects in a unified field' (emphasis added).

122. Cf. Russell, *Palace*, pp. 28-30 and pp. 208-209. It is well-known that Lachish is not mentioned in Sennacherib's annals, which rather insist on the destruction of a great number of towns and Hezekiah's having been caught up in Jerusalem (see below, pp. 293-303. The same holds true for at least five other towns represented on Sennacherib's reliefs. Consequently, Sennacherib's reliefs cannot derive directly from annals and other preserved monumental inscriptions.

tion of 'Lachish' with two walls: in verbal terms even a strong revetment wall for a glacis still is a *wall*, which would be represented by the artists according to their standard pictorial conventions for a wall typical of Levantine cities, namely with shields hung up on the parapets and—obviously—defenders, particularly so if the artists had not been eyewitnesses of the actual siege on site.[123]

We should keep in mind that the issue of identification, which is at the heart of Jacoby's critique, is neither the only nor always the major problem involved in the historical interpretation of the reliefs. The room XXXVI sculptures would yield important information on Assyrian and Judahite history even if we did not know that the city depicted is meant to represent Lachish. Let us therefore leave now the matter of archaeology and identification and return to the reliefs themselves. Before having a closer look at their composition and some peculiar features depicted, we must start once more with the basics: a series of heavily fragmented slabs.

123.   The same conclusion was already reached independently by Russell, *Palace*, p. 208; *idem*, 'Sennacherib's Lachish Narratives', p. 64: 'This is the sort of discrepancy one would hardly expect to find in a drawing made on the spot, but which might occur in a written description being translated into visual terms. In this latter scenario, it is easy to imagine "wall" in a written description being translated in its most familiar (and formidable) visual form, that is, a towered fortification, even if this convention does not in fact correspond to the appearence of the original'. Note the doubts expressed by J.E. Reade, review of Russell, *Palace*, ZA 84 (1994), pp. 303-304, who refers to an information from S. Parpola concerning 'an Assyrian letter that mentions a drawing of a fortress made on leather' without, however, specifying its purpose. The letter has since been edited by A. Fuchs and S. Parpola, *The Correspondence of Sargon II*. III. *Letters from Babylonia and the Eastern Provinces* (SAA, 15; Helsinki: Helsinki University Press, 2001), p. 95 no. 136. The reason why the 'fortress' in question, located in the province of Lahiru in Babylonia, was sketched is unclear, but it may well be connected with the letter-writer's plan to establish an Assyrian garrison in it. There is really no hint that his sketch would serve for artists concerned with the design of palace reliefs. Note, however, that Reade has repeatedly stated his sympathy for a hypothesis expressed long ago by T. Madhloom with regard to the pair of Assyrian scribes often depicted on sculptures and wall paintings. One of the two regularly holds a scroll instead of a tablet; according to Madhloom (*Chronology*, p. 122), this figure could represent a draughtsman, on whose copies the sculptors would have relied. As against this interpretation, the man with the scroll is never shown standing in front of a city but he exclusively registers booty and captives; moreover, the pair of scribes may occasionally consist of only tablet-writers. The traditional interpretation of the man with the scroll as a scribe writing in Aramaic provides a better explanation for the pictorial evidence.

Heavily Fragmented Slabs

It is well-known that the reliefs of room XXXVI consisted originally of a series of at least 17 slabs of various dimensions, all measuring c. 264–274 cm[124] in full height but ranging from c. 61 cm (slab '16') to 239 cm (slab '5') in width depending on space restrictions and the raw material which the Assyrian sculptors had at their disposal.[125] The original slabs joined very neatly, and numerous details show an overlap from one slab to another. However, when going through Hodder's sketches which may be considered the most problem-orientated, and thus relatively critical record of the reliefs' state of preservation at the time of their discovery (fig. 1),[126] one is struck by the great number of individually registered fragments (556 items), which does not include a considerable number of smaller pieces that apparently went unrecorded. More intriguing is the fact that whereas the upper ends of extant reliefs and drawings follow a very irregular course, as one would of course expect given the vicissitudes of time, the lateral margins of the slabs were always drawn by Hodder with a ruler, which conveys the impression that at the time of their discovery, the joins between the slabs were all perfectly neat. This impression is certainly wrong; there is no reason why the joins would have been better preserved than the actual slab surfaces at places where the latter are worn or even destroyed. Comparison of Hodder's drawings with extant slabs (and to some extent also with Layard's drawings, e.g. fig. 2) show that in some instances his straight edges do not reflect the real boundaries of the sculptures at all.[127] Published photographs of the original slabs demonstrate that physical joins between the slabs are occasionally preserved; however, they do not always conform to Hodder's sketches. Numerous gaps remain, many of which have been plastered during restoration since 1856. This situation is particularly vexing in the most sensitive case of slabs 6-7 and 7-8. Whether the edges were already damaged at the time of the discovery or only later when the slabs were dismantled, or both, it is obvious that the correct horizontal

124. Compare Barnett *et al.*, *Sculptures*, I, p. 104 no. 437b: 264.1 cm, to Ussishkin, *Conquest*, pp. 72 and 76: 'Height of left side (original height of relief): 2.74 m… Height of right side: 2.63m.' I have not checked the original.

125. Barnett *et al.*, *Sculptures*, I, pp. 101-105, II Pl. 322 count 16 slabs, 12 of which are extant, but the sketch shows actually 17 slabs. The difference goes back to Layard's early plans. Layard's slabs 5-13 actually comprise 12 instead of 9 slabs, see synopsis in Barnett *et al.*, *Sculptures*, I, p. 105. Ussishkin (*Conquest*, p. 71 fig. 61) leaves open the number of slabs preceding the ones actually preserved.

126. But see above, n. 20.

127. Ussishkin, *Conquest*, figs. 62, 64 and 65 allow a convenient comparison.

positioning of adjoining slabs represents a major preliminary issue that must be addressed before attempting any plausible 'narrative reading' of the overall composition, and particularly of the siege scene. As a matter of fact, most studies on the Lachish reliefs have ignored this problem, taking for granted the restoration displayed in the British Museum or, worse, the plates published by Layard (fig. 3) and later copies thereof.[128]

Moreover, earlier studies have not always recognized the fact that the central siege scene running over slabs 6-8, and particularly slab 7, is only preserved to roughly two-thirds of its original height, with minimals on both edges of slab 7 rising to c. 52-56 per cent of the original height (compare fig. 8). However difficult, a cogent interpretation of the series has to take into account the now-missing upper portions. As mentioned above, Ussishkin speculated that the palace-fort, which he erroneously identified with an upper wall feature on the left of slab 7, could have extended into this now-lost part of the relief. Jacoby seems to be the first scholar to have explicitly remarked that the ten siege planes 'all point to one spot no longer visible on the relief'.[129] If we consider comparable siege scenes where citadels rise to almost the total height of sculptured slabs in rooms XII, XIV and XLIII,[130] it is reasonable to surmise that at least the upper third of slab 7 originally showed the Lachish citadel, i.e. the palace-fort of stratum III. Fig. 7 is an attempt to visualize this hypothesis, which will be supported by the following discussion.

Reassembling the Slabs
Ussishkin has rightly stressed that any plausible interpretation of the pictorial narrative requires the correct assembling of the slabs, and particularly of slabs 6-8. His own attempt, however, presents two major difficulties: first, it is intimately linked to his theory of quasi-perspectival view, particularly to an identification of the palace-fort on the upper edge on the left hand of slab 7 which cannot be upheld; second, despite a detailed account of the reliefs' present state of preservation and the difficulties involved in reassembling the slabs,[131] it is startling that he has published no less than five slightly divergent montages of slabs 6-8, four of them appearing in one and the same book:

128. Ussishkin (esp. *Conquest*, p. 72) is a notable exception.
129. Jacoby, 'Representation', pp. 126-27. I shall elaborate below on this observation, which I also made independently when studying the reliefs in London in 1983.
130. See Barnett *et al.*, *Sculptures*, II, Pls. 151, 168-69, 374-75.
131. See particularly Ussishkin, *Conquest*, p. 72.

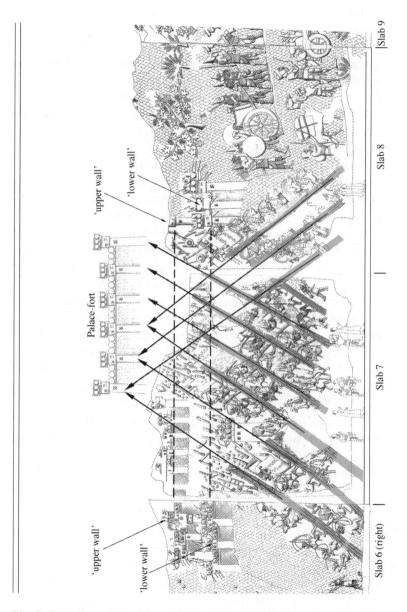

Fig. 7. Tentative reassemblage of slabs 6-9, with selective restorations including the now-missing citadel (Ch. Uehlinger, assisted by J. Eggler).

(A) 'Lachish Reliefs', p. 179 fig. 3 is a much reduced montage of Judith Dekel's shaded drawings of slabs 6-8. It restores some missing details but leaves considerable gaps between the three slabs, which are shown without any physical connection. The assemblage is essentially based on connecting siege planes (cf. our own fig. 7).

(B) *Conquest*, p. 73 fig. 62 (drawings) shows only the relevant margins and fills in missing details by clearly marked hypothetical restorations. The latter do not always correspond to those suggested on the more detailed drawings of individual slabs, *ibid.* pp. 80-84 figs. 67-69. The assemblage is again based on connecting siege planes, which are now drawn out.

(C) *Conquest*, p. 77 fig. 65 above (drawing) shows the whole series of slabs without restorations. For the sake of clear argument, a portion of this montage was used as a starting-point for our fig. 6 (see p. 253), although the montage is obviously wrong: the siege planes between slabs 6-7 and 7-8 do not connect, and the plinth of slabs 5-6 runs more than a centimetre above the one of slabs 9-10 etc. (when calculated for the actual reliefs, this would make a difference in level of almost 20 cm!).

(D) *Conquest*, p. 77 fig. 65 below presents a photo-montage of the extant reliefs in the British Museum. This montage is even more problematic since it inevitably includes the BM plaster restorations. I also wonder whether the photographs actually follow a single scale (slab 7 appears to be slightly too small). While the siege planes connect between slabs 6-7, they do not follow between 7-8, and the whole series of slabs 8 etc. is positioned far too low when compared to slabs 5-7.

(E) *Conquest*, p. 121 fig. 93 is yet another drawing with discrete restorations, running from slab 6 right to slab 8 left; this drawing is similar but not identical to (A).

The point here is not to quibble over this or that restored detail or erroneous assemblage nor to put slander on Ussishkin's and Dekel's generally admirable work. Putting together drawings and photographs such as to allow a continuous 'reading' on one single foldout plate had never been done before and must have been a headache for the two authors, who certainly spent considerable time in moving up and down their photographs and drawings of individual slabs. Moreover, minor distortions are inevitable for optical reasons as long as a montage is based on conventional photography. Finally, the differences involved generally measure a few centimetres; still, since slabs 6-8 include very tiny details these differences inevitably matter. It is noteworthy that both Ussishkin's theory and his location of the palace-fort would be impossible on the basis of his own montages C (fig. 6) and D, since on these the putative palace-fort to the left of slab 7 appears on a lower level than the 'upper wall' on slab 6.[132]

An improved reassemblage of the slabs should ideally be based on a new, independent recording with the help of electronic devices that could avoid or compensate optical distortions. Within the limits of this article, I can but outline the principles which would then determine the reassemblage of slabs 6-8 (compare figs. 6 and 7). The starting point is the well-preserved join of slabs 8 and 9, where two ground-lines and several overlapping details (a soldier carrying a stand, a Judahite cart) allow for a precise relative positioning of slab 8. Since the plinth of slabs 9 etc. must have been roughly on a level with the one visible at the bottom of slabs 5-6, the major difficulty is then to determine the correct position of slab 7, which has no physical join at any point with its neighbours. The most reliable criterion is provided by the course of the first and second siege plane on the left, which runs across slabs 6-7; to this we may add the first of the right-hand siege planes visible on slab 7, which is the implied ground-line for two pairs of kneeling archers approaching left on slab 8. Since the connecting siege-planes on both sides run diagonally, the *vertical* position of slab 7 will depend on how much *horizontal* space we allow for the gaps between the slabs. The answer will have to be determined on the following premises: first, the restoration and insertion of battering rams, soldiers etc. in the gaps must start from preserved traces and accord in proportions with comparable, fully preserved examples mainly on slab 7. Of course it must also fit the overall composition. To judge from fig. 2, this principle already guided Layard's drawing (note, e.g. the restored battering-ram and archers appearing in figs. 2 and 3 on siege-planes 1 and 2 from the left); as we have seen, his restorations must have relied on his field drawings, but he could not check them against the originals. Second, in order not to prejudice the question of whether the fortification segment on slab 7 should be regarded as part of the 'upper wall' or as an independent structure, our reassemblage should provisionally ignore the

132. One wonders whether montages C and D are based on the assumption (of some independant assistant?) that the wall segment on slab 7 should be the straight extension of the 'upper wall' segment on slab 6. Note that this assumption had already led Hodder's attempt at producing a satisfactory join between the two slabs (see above, fig. 1).

problem whether or how the horizontal wall segments of slabs 6 and 7 fit together. Third, it should allow for sufficient space at the bottom of slab 7 in order to accommodate the procession of Judahites leaving the town through the gate tower, descending to the bottom of slab 7, then turning right and proceding in a continuous flow along the plinth of slab 7 before joining the lower register of slabs 8 etc. Of course, our reassemblage should also take into account the probable presence, at the bottom of slab 7, of a plain plinth similar to the ones preserved on slabs 5-6 and 9-13. Finally, although the individual slabs slightly varied in height, an upper edge and plinth of slab 7 may be tentatively restored in order to visualize the extent of once sculptured surface which is missing today.

Fig. 7 presents the hypothetical and provisional result of such a reassemblage based on the manipulation—*faute de mieux*—of Dekel's remarkable drawings of the individual slabs. The restoration was executed on the computer by a member of our Department, Dr Jürg Eggler, working under my supervision and according to the just-mentioned principles. For the sake of convenience, the main features defining the reassembled composition have been marked on the figure; hypothetical restorations are drawn out in lighter tone so as to allow their distinction from features preserved on the extant reliefs. The resulting picture confirms earlier observations about the quasi-symmetrical status of the walls visible on either side of the city; both sides show a 'lower' and an 'upper wall', with corresponding wall segments placed at about the same height. Moreover, although the fortification segment preserved on slab 7 (Ussishkin's 'palace-fort') does not extend in a straight line the 'upper wall' segment of slab 6 (as erroneously suggested by figs. 1 and 4), it may still be regarded as part of the 'upper wall'. Layard had already noted (see his drawing and plate in figs. 2 and 3) that on the left side of the city the two walls do not run horizontally but slightly raise their course towards the centre of the mound. Consequently, tower 3 of the 'lower wall' on slab 6 rises higher than towers 1 and 2, the difference corresponding roughly to the height of a balcony. The same situation prevails for the 'upper wall'. It therefore comes as no surprise that the wall segment on slab 7 should be placed somewhat higher than the one on slab 6. The situation does neither require nor allow Ussishkin's thesis that the segment preserved on slab 7 should represent an independent structure. Instead, the gradual rise of wall segments serves to stress the overall height of the city fortifications. As for the highest point of the besieged town (the expected citadel), it must obviously be looked for somewhere else, more to the right. Our restoration takes into account— for the first time, as far as I can see—that the ultimate target of the attack along the siege ramp, visualized in our figure by diagonal arrows extending from the siege planes, must have been a fortified citadel located in the upper right part of slab 7.[133] This restoration may look daring, but it seems obvious that the bricks, torches, ladders, carts and men visible on the extant slabs must be thrown or fall from some place above. Moreover, it would have been pointless to represent no less than four (perhaps even five) battering-rams running straight into the open breach of the city's fortifications if their ultimate target were not such a massive structure situated somewhere beyond the city walls.

As we have seen, the ten siege-planes running against, through and over the city's fortifications may be understood as parts of one single siege ramp. Their fan-like appearance together with the extension of the 'upper wall' may help to secure the restoration of the missing citadel. The latter's location was not determined by a quasi-perspective view of an artist working on-site, but resulted instead from the general layout of the siege scene along the wall, which in turn depended on a number of formal constraints (see below). We should not deduce from the fact that some of the siege-planes run against the hypothetical citadel that the palace-fort of stratum III and the fortified enclosure on the mound had been assaulted in the actual battle course by Sennacherib's battering-rams. Incidentally, no remains of a siege ramp built against the palace-fort or the enclosure have been located on the mound, although it is of course probable that the enclosure and palace-fort may have served as a kind of ultimate bastion for the town's last defenders. The depiction of battering-rams running across two parallel city walls against the citadel rather stresses the intensity of the Assyrian onslaught against the massive enemy fortifications, whose importance in turn serves to celebrate the heroic character of the Assyrian onslaught.[134]

In conclusion, the overall picture obtained by our restoration and hypothesis strongly favours Jacoby's opinion according to which the Assyrian artists who designed the Lachish series did not represent the actual attack as seen from a certain spot but according to their own, well-established compositional rules and pictorial conventions.

133. For comparison, see n. 130 and a citadel appearing on top of another (Palestinian?) city on slab 23 (respectively 28) of throne-hall I, Barnett *et al.*, *Sculptures*, II, Pls. 46-47; Russell, *Final Sack*, pp. 110-12 Pls. 72-74 (= below, fig. 12).

134. The closest parallels from Sennacherib's palace are again Barnett *et al.*, *Sculptures*, II, Pls. 151, 374-75; contrast Pl. 471.

From Battle to Monument: Building up a Pictorial Discourse
Traditional historical research usually moves backwards from sources to
events and asks for factual substance behind the sources. Not surprisingly,
the Lachish reliefs have generally been addressed in this traditional perspective, which uses archaeological, textual and pictorial sources like windows to the past. In the case of pictorial narrative such as the Assyrian
palace reliefs, relating particular events (Braudel's *histoire événementielle*),
it is naturally tempting for historians to look at them as if they were precisely such windows that allow for an almost photographic restitution of
past reality.

More recent insights in historical hermeneutics and refined studies on
ancient historiography have considerably modified historical methodology,
taking into account the problems of data processing faced by ancient
authors, whether scribes or artists. In order to understand the meaning and
function of ancient documents, we need to consider the way information
was registered, stored, transmitted and eventually rendered in a particular
document, which could claim more or less authority. In the case of Assyrian palace reliefs, the issue of data processing is particularly vexed by the
probable intersection of verbal and visual information and media. When
analyzing pictures such as the room XXXVI sculptures, historians have
to consider the procedures of data processing and social communication
involved in the commissioning of the task, namely to represent an historical event and its significance on the walls of a major palace suite. True,
much of what we can know of these procedures derives from indirect
evidence and argument. Still, a hypothetical account of how the Lachish
reliefs came into existence may prevent us from too naive and historistic
readings of their subject matter.[135]

As argued above with reference to the two fortified walls depicted on the
reliefs, the primary recording of data by Assyrian expedition members was
probably limited to textual media (field diaries and memos which were
then elaborated into synthetical, more or less embellished presentations
leading up to the 'letters of the gods'). Occasionally, missing but required
data may have been supplemented through active memory by officials who
had participated in a campaign. At some point of the redactional process

135. Note the suggestion by Russell, 'Sennacherib's Lachish Narratives', p. 72 that
the prominent placement and reatment of the Lachish episode may be explained by the
fact that the room XXXVI reliefs were executed from c. 700 onwards, i.e. shortly after
what Sennacherib must have perceived as the last great triumph achieved during his
most recently completed campaign.

leading from diaries to the 'letters of the gods', but apparently before the data processing entered the subsequent stage of annalistic redaction, information was handed over to officials responsible for the choice of subjects to be selected for the reliefs. The king himself most probably was involved on several stages of the procedures, acting himself as the definite authorizing instance. Once the general topic and the space to be devoted for it were selected, senior designers must have conceived the way in which the particular event would be rendered on the walls. For that purpose, they had to transpose the verbal (textual and possibly oral) record into another medium, namely pictorial narrative.

Before even addressing issues of subject matter, the designers faced formal constraints, most notably architectural context, which conditioned the space available for the reliefs, and sometimes they would have to take into account the future function of a particular room. Further constraints were put on their design when they considered the problem of layout and macro-syntax.[136] While clearly to be 'read' from left to right, the programme of room XXXVI's pictorial narrative (see fig. 8) obviously aims at a certain symmetry, starting and ending with static processions of horsemen and chariotry[137] and focusing on the intense, almost ecstatic attack of the city in the centre of the room. Ussishkin and Russell have rightly stressed that slab 7 is placed in the centre of the room's southwest (main long) wall. The actual siege scene could probably be seen across the preceding room(s) and doorway(s). On this wall, emphasis is on reversal, with slabs 5-6 showing orderly placed Assyrian attackers while on slabs 8-9 booty and captives are led away. The city itself shows an almost symmetrical disposition, slightly off-centre towards the right in accordance with the general movement of the scenario. While the walls on the left side (slab 6) are manned with defenders, those on the right (slab 8) show Judahites raising their arms in a gesture of surrender (and praise?). The compositional axis is stressed by the people leaving the gate tower following a zig-zag line alongside a famous detail, which shows three naked enemies being impaled by a pair of Assyrian soldiers.[138] Once a visitor had entered the room and considered the 'film' of attack, onslaught and submission, he

136. For the arrangement of slabs along the walls of room XXXVI, compare the sketch provided by Russell, *Palace*, pp. 200-201, fig. 108.

137. See above, n. 18, on the subject matter of slabs 1-4. For the general principles governing narrative composition in Sennacherib's palace, see Reade, 'Narrative Composition', pp. 86-95; Russell, *Palace*, ch. 9 ('space and time').

138. See above, n. 82.

would follow the trail of captives and booty that would lead him towards the Assyrian king, conspicuously enthroned in the centre of the northwest (main short) wall and conveniently placed on eye-level.

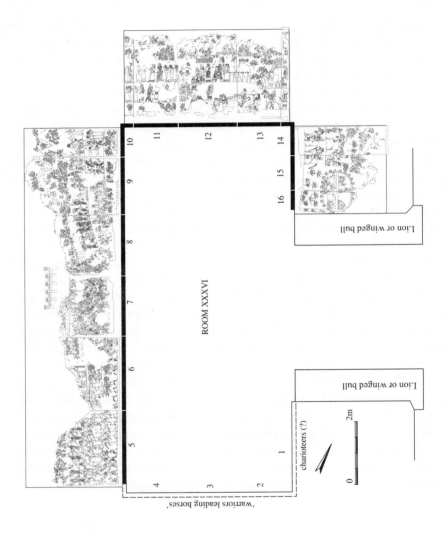

Fig. 8. The Lachish series in its architectural context (room XXXVI).

It should be evident from this brief sketch alone that the layout of the whole scene owes much more to the intentional *mise en scène* trying to make the best of the architectural context than to the knowledge gathered from putative eyewitnesses on real topography around 701-BCE Lachish. The next stage in the shaping of the series would then be to define the details. On this level, scaling does not seem to have been considered a major problem since the scale of people is simply defined according to the requirements of compositional complexity. As for pictorial micro-syntax and 'vocabulary', they were conditioned by pictorial conventions more than anything else. Assyrian soldiers usually operate in pairs, who may be replicated in order to emphasize discipline and coordination; too stereo-typed rows may occasionally be broken up by slightly irregular features (e.g. individual kneeling archers on the central row of attackers on slabs 5 etc.). The main purpose of the composition was now to display the whole spectrum of weaponry and stratagems that the Assyrian army could employ in order to overwhelm its opponents. Movement and onslaught could be translated by the sequential juxtaposition of marching, descending, kneel-ing (slabs 5-6), or kneeling, rising and running (along the siege planes on slabs 6-8). Finally, some stock material could be used to fill in composi-tional blanks (e.g. the pair of stone slingers turned right on the right-hand bottom of slab 7, who do not even have a recognizable target). In conclu-sion, it is clear from this very brief exercise that the input of historical and artistic imagination within the constraints of pictorial conventions was considerable. Hence we should thus definitely abandon any naive approach to these reliefs as 'windows' to an ancient event.

'Reading' and Decoding the Pictorial Discourse

What then, can the historian gain from these sculptures? The most elemen-tary insight, in my opinion, is that they represent an ancient Assyrian *interpretation* of the events at least as authoritative as annals and other monumental inscriptions. As such, they deserve the same serious interest and study as the texts. Their pictorial discourse may be subjected to a similar kind of rhetorical and ideological analysis as the inscriptions.[139]

139. See Irene J. Winter, 'Royal Rhetoric and the Development of Historical Narra-tive in Neo-Assyrian Reliefs', *Studies in Visual Communication* 7/2 (1981), pp. 2-38; R. Lamprichs, *Die Westexpansion des neuassyrischen Reiches: Eine Strukturanalyse* (AOAT, 239; Kevelaer: Butzon & Bercker/Neukirchen–Vluyn: Neukirchener Verlag, 1995).

The historical information contained in and retrievable from the reliefs may concern all three of Braudel's levels of history, including events, social history (*histoire conjoncturelle*) and *longue durée* (much of which is actually geography),[140] although they certainly operate best on the first and second levels. With regard to the first level, history of particular events, it should be noted that not everything on the reliefs is determined by convention and stereotype. As a matter of fact, the *variety* of scenes and situations depicted on Sennacherib's sculptures as well as the variety of individually characterized cities are amazing when compared to the reliefs of his predecessors or even Ashurbanipal and even more so when compared to Egyptian examples of pictorial historical narrative.[141] It is highly improbable that such variety could be arbitrarily handled in antiquity. Rather, one must recognize that Sennacherib's sculptures more than any others[142] conceal (or try to restitute) aspects of 'individual', specific historical events and situations. The basic task for the historian who aims at learning about the *histoire événementielle* is thus to identify and to distinguish such particular details from the more conventional and stock motifs, keeping in mind that the clear distinction between these categories is sometimes hampered by the fragmentary nature of the evidence, since major parts of the sculptures have not been preserved or excavated.

Limits of space do not allow to develop this task much further here. However, I should like to point out a few features on slabs 8-12, depicting the procession of spoils and captives towards Sennacherib and the Assyrian camp (fig. 9a-c), which I consider particularly interesting in this respect. All have already been discussed by other scholars, but some details apparently went unnoticed in earlier studies.

Distinctions among Captives and Defenders
Following early observations by Layard, Tufnell drew attention in 1953 to the different 'sections of the population' represented on the Lachish reliefs among both defenders and captives:

140.   Compare Uehlinger, 'Bildquellen' (above, n. 3).

141.   On the latter, see now Susanna C. Heinz, *Die Feldzugsdarstellungen des Neuen Reiches: Eine Bildanalyse* (Österreichische Akademie der Wissenschaften, Denkschriften der Gesamtakademie, 18; Untersuchungen der Zweigstelle Kairo des Österreichischen Archäologischen Instituts, 17; Wien: Verlag der Österreichischen Akademie der Wissenschaften, 2001).

142.   Except perhaps the different versions of Ashurbanipal's famous, almost cartoon-like Ulai battle series.

The artist has differentiated between the leaders of the city and the rank and file, a distinction which would be accounted for if the governor and his military and civil staff were appointed from Jerusalem. That the civil population joined the troops in defence of the city is shown by the presence on the battlements of men with turbans...[143]

In his 1958 article, Barnett again distinguished two groups among the Judahites advancing towards Sennacherib (fig. 9a-b): some men are bare-headed and wear long tunics, while others have the peculiar Judahite scarf and a short garment. The latter seem to go free; the former, according to Barnett,

are singled out for particular displeasure and are beheaded or flayed alive. Why this difference of dress and treatment? Surely the men in the long dresses with curly hair who have so incensed Sennacherib must be Hezekiah's men, the Jews who influenced the city to resist, while the men with the peculiar head-dresses are native inhabitants of Lachish.[144]

Barnett then refers to the exiled Judahites' destiny in Assyria, recalling the depiction of Judahite workmen in court VI and corridor XLIX[145] and of Judahite elite soldiers along the so-called ramp to the Ishtar temple.[146]

Although Barnett's distinction and interpretation have been followed by a number of scholars, a close look at the sculptures shows that the matter is not quite as straightforward as it seemed. True, the two major categories of Judahite men can easily been distinguished (although we should not overlook cases of overlap and slight irregularity[147]). But the differences

143. Tufnell, *Lachish III*, p. 62.

144. Tufnell, *Lachish III*, p. 163; Barnett is followed by Wäfler, *Nicht-Assyrer*, pp. 52-53.

145. See now Barnett *et al.*, *Sculptures*, II, Pls. 96-97, 101, 104, 106, 112, 114, 122, 414, 418-422; on their identification as Judahites, see Wäfler, *Nicht-Assyrer*, pp. 57-60. Had these Judahites been 'evidently reckoned by the Assyrians amongst the Philistines', as maintained by Barnett ('Siege', p. 164), they would have been represented otherwise!

146. See now Barnett *et al.*, *Sculptures*, II, Pls. 473, 485-89. For recent commentaries on the contrasting careers of Judahite exiles, see S. Stohlmann, 'The Judean Exile after 701 B.C.E', in W.W. Hallo, J.C. Moyer and L.G. Perdue (eds.), *Scripture in Context II. More Essays on the Comparative Method* (Winona Lake, IN: Eisenbrauns, 1983), pp. 147-75 (162-66); Uehlinger, 'Bildquellen', pp. 57-61.

147. As noted by Ussishkin, *Conquest*, p. 109, the man leading the bullock cart on slab 10 wears the short garment but no headdress; instead, his beard and hair are rendered in exactly the same way as for the men in the long tunic. Since he is the first in the row of people departing to exile, and all men preceding him are bare-headed, this may well be an error of execution limited to this slab. Among minor irregularities, one may note differences in the execution of hair and beard among both categories of Judahite men: perfectly curled finish, simple straight hatching, or beard only outlined (note also the just grown-up, beardless youngster leading the camel).

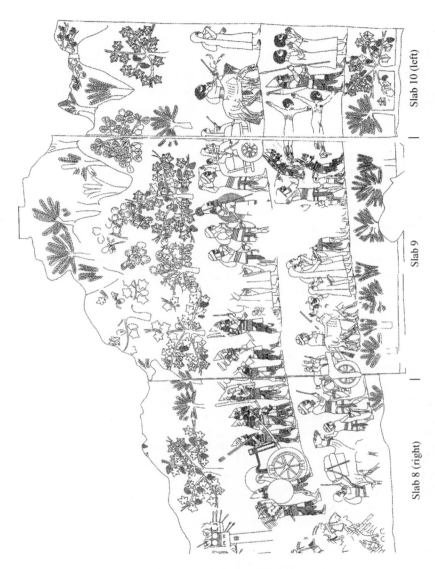

Fig. 9a. Booty taken from the city, Judahite captives leaving for exile, Assyrian soldiers flaying two men.

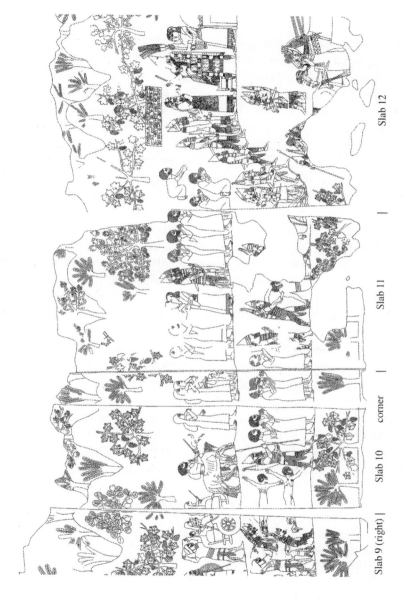

Fig. 9b. Judahite captives leaving for exile, Assyrian soldiers putting to death Judahite prisoners, Judahite leaders advancing towards Sennacherib.

in treatment do not really follow the lines of this major distinction, since the two men who are being stabbed on the lower register of slab 11 undoubtedly wear the short garment (but no scarf). Two other Judahites who are being flayed on the overlap of slabs 9 and 10 are naked and may have belonged to either of the two groups.[148] On the other hand, none of the men clad in long garments are actually being tortured. Nevertheless, they should not be considered a completely homogenous group since they proceed in several sub-units: (1) a group of six, probably leaders, three of whom prostrate themselves in front of the king while three others are still approaching with hands raised in a gesture of supplication; (2) a pair of two, approaching the two scribes who register the booty together with three women and a child—these may be understood as heading the procession leaving for exile; and (3) a group of five is shown between two scenes of torture on the lower register. While groups 1 and 2 are clearly meant to remain alive, the latters' destiny may seem to be undecided; still, the message of the three groups considered together and of the bottom sequence is quite clear: the right to survive of group 3 will also depend on loyal cooperation with Assyria. As for Barnett's suggestion that all these men represent the 'men of Hezekiah'[149] from Jerusalem, it cannot be substantiated from the sculptures, which only point to a higher status of these people who probably represent senior officials of the Judahite administration based at Lachish. Whether they came from Jerusalem or elsewhere[150] cannot be told from the sculptures but only from text-related, general considerations about the composition and organization of Judahite state officials. In my opinion, the three sub-groups rather exemplify three types of possible 'careers' for foreign leaders in captivity: (1) transfer from former service to loyal submission to the Assyrian king, which may even have allowed the pursuit of a career at home; (2) exile together with other people of the land; or (3?) punishment in the case of definite refusal to submit.

148. Note, however, an observation by Pauline Albenda that flaying was a punishment often reserved for important people; see her 'An Assyrian Relief Depicting a Nude Captive in Wellesley College', *JNES* 29 (1970), pp. 145-50 (149, 150 n. 27).

149. The term is taken from Prov. 25.1.

150. *If* the physiognomy of these men should contain negroid features this would pertain for all male Lachishites. One cannot accept therefore Albenda's identification of the men wearing long tunics with Egyptian/Kushite foes, even less with captured charioteers, *pace* Albenda, 'Egyptians in Assyrian Art', *Bulletin of the Egyptological Seminar* 4 (1982), pp. 5-23 (10); also Reade, *Assyrian Sculpture*, p. 66. Note that the Egyptian forces who were instrumental in the battle at Eltekeh are conspicuously absent from the room XXXVI reliefs.

Who then is slayed and put to death by the Assyrian soldiers? The answer to this question has to consider a peculiar distinction made by the artists among the city's defenders. Tufnell correctly noted the presence of Judahite 'civilians' or militia (auxiliaries?) alongside helmeted soldiers among the defenders of Lachish. Interestingly enough, both groups wear the characteristic Judahite scarf, but in the case of the soldiers the latter is partly covered by a pointed helmet.[151] This detail together with the depiction of unarmed natives leaving the town indicates that the Assyrians correctly perceived the double status of Lachish as a civilian city and a major, well-armed Judahite military garrison. The proportion of soldiers and militia/ auxiliaries on the walls is roughly one of 2:3. As far as I can recognize, the sculptures imply a kind of labour division between helmetted soldiers and auxiliaries: while almost all of the former have bows (only one helmetted Judahite standing on the gate tower uses a sling), the latter are slingers or simply throw stones by hand (but one auxiliary posted on the 'lower' wall exceptionally draws a bow). The extant reliefs do not allow recognition of which group is throwing the torches, wheels and carts. Still, they make it very clear to the onlooker that the Assyrians intentionally distinguished among various categories of Judahite defenders. The helmets of regular soldiers and the swords and spears among the spoils taken from the city imply the recognition that Judahite weaponry was quite developed and posed a serious threat to Assyria.

Once we turn to the outcome of the battle, we recognize again soldiers and civilians among the people standing on the city wall and raising their arms in a gesture of surrender. However, the long row of people leaving the city through the gate tower down to the very bottom of slab 10 and then moving right towards the king (or the pair of scribes) does not comprise a single Judahite soldier, but is exclusively formed by civilians, men, women and children. I have already pointed out that their leaving the gate tower and the impalement scene lie on the axis of the whole composition.[152] The juxtaposition expresses a clear alternative: to live or to die— the former actually meaning surrender and exile. One cannot but be struck by the structural parallelism between this rhetoric and the one deployed by

---

151. Incidentally, the Judahite helmet seems to conform quite well to the standard helmet of Assyrian soldiers, although the small dimensions of the figures representing defenders do not allow to be more specific on this point.

152. See above, n. 82.

Rabshakeh's speech in 2 Kgs 18.31-32a, according to which the king of Assyria will bring submissive Judahites into another land that they may live.[153] Note that the whole row of people leaving for exile (originally more than fifty adult individuals) includes only three Assyrian soldiers, all of them on slab 9 (fig. 9a). Two appear in the upper register of the booty procession; one holds his mace upside down[154] so as to minimize the coercitive aspect of this exodus. Another Assyrian soldier appears in the lower register, where the row of calmly walking captives somehow clashes with the flaying scene. In strong contrast to most depictions of departing captives on Sennacherib's sculptures, where Assyrian soldiers regularly inflict various kinds of bad treatment to captives, the Lachish exodus shows neither pushing nor beating, no tearing of hair or beards and not even a menacing attitude from Assyrians who accompany the captives. In contrast to the heavy siege and battle scenes, the row of exiles stresses nonviolence and almost voluntary submission. For this reason, the flaying and stabbing of two pairs of Judahites on slabs 10 and 11 (fig. 9b) cannot relate directly to the submissive captives leaving for exile. We may hypothesize instead that the tortured belong to the vanquished military defenders of Lachish. Consequently, we should better distinguish three rather than two groups among the Judahites: high officials, soldiers and auxiliaries, and civilians.

Spoils from the Citadel
To the right of the surrendered city, eight Assyrian footsoldiers carry away a number of weapons and prestige objects which are certainly meant to come from conquered Lachish (fig. 9a): from left to right, a bundle of six swords,[155] two relatively large, bossed shields, three spears, a light eight-

---

153.   I do not think that there is any direct connection between the sculptures and the biblical text, which plays on inner-biblical topoi and must be understood in terms of Judahite authorship and audience. Still, the text may sharpen our understanding of the reliefs' rhetoric which promises life in the lap of families to civilians who choose life. Compare W.R. Gallagher, 'Assyrian Deportation Propaganda', *SAAB* 8 (1994), pp. 57-65.

154.   The soldier does certainly not hold 'a short sword, its sharpened end threatening the captives who walk before him' as maintained by N. Na'aman, 'The Debated Historicity of Hezekiah's Reform in the Light of Historical and Archaeological Research', *ZAW* 107 (1995), pp. 179-95 (192).

155.   See most recently A. Maeir, 'The "Judahite" Swords from the "Lachish" Reliefs of Sennacherib', *Eretz-Israel* 25 (1996), pp. 210-14 (hebr., engl. summary p. 96*).

spoked chariot with yokes for a team of four horses,[156] a throne with arm-rests, and two large incense-burners. I shall concentrate on the significance of the latter. To my knowledge, it was Y. Aharoni who first suggested that these stands were cult vessels from a local shrine.[157] His proposal has been taken up by N. Na'aman who used this interpretation of the pictorial evidence to question the historical reliability of Hezekiah's cultic reform mentioned in 2 Kgs 18.4, 22.[158] According to Na'aman, the reliefs depict 'three kinds of objects which are mentioned many times in Assyrian royal inscription booty lists: cult vessels, the treasures of the palace and weapons';[159] consequently, the two incense burners should have belonged to a sanctuary.

I agree with Na'aman that the two stands were probably made of bronze. However, I doubt that the relatively small selection of objects should really represent three different predefined categories chosen according to established conventions. Why should these spoils not represent a single, coherent group of objects taken from the governor's main offices in the palace-fort? Since no other objects of clearly cultic use appear among the spoils, the stands may well have belonged to the same 'civil' ceremonial context as the armchair, the chariots and the weapons. On the other hand, one can certainly not exclude the possibility that the stands might indeed have belonged to a 'chapel' within the palace-fort.

More recently, Na'aman has used the same group in an attempt to substantiate biblical information on the aniconic character of Judahite Yahwism.[160] According to Na'aman,

> The cult vessels on the Lachish reliefs must have come from a cult place that was built in Lachish and functioned until 701 BCE, when the Assyrians destroyed the city and despoiled its treasures. Why did the artist omit the cult statue(s) from the booty? Cult images, symbolyzing (*sic*) the surrender of the city's god(s) to the gods of Assyria, were more important and pictorial than bronze incense burners. If such graven image(s) had been taken

156. Barnett *et al.*, *Sculptures*, II, Pl. 341 provides a good close-up.

157. See Y. Aharoni, *Investigations at Lachish. The Sanctuary and the Residency* (Lachish V; Tel Aviv: University of Tel Aviv, 1975), pp. 42-43.

158. In Na'aman, 'Debated Historicity', pp. 191-93.

159. Na'aman, 'Debated Historicity', p. 193.

160. Na'aman, 'No Anthropomorphic Graven Image. Notes on the Assumed Anthropomorphic Cult Statues in the Temples of YHWH in the Pre-Exilic Period', *UF* 31 (1999), pp. 391-415.

from Lachish's cult place, they would have been shown at the head of the booty procession, as in some other reliefs of Sennacherib. It seems that no graven cult image was found in the sacred site, and the artist depicted the most impressive booty taken: a pair of bronze incense burners similar to the depiction of the menorah and cult vessels on the Arch of Titus.[161]

One should be well aware that this argument essentially procedes *e silentio* and must therefore be considered with great caution. Na'aman's answer to his question why the artist should not have shown one or several cult statues as part of the booty allows only one definite answer: because the Assyrians apparently did not capture figurative divine statues from conquered Lachish. We cannot infer however the precise reason for this. It may of course have been the case that no actual cult statue was found in the sacred site, as speculated by Na'aman. However, we should remember that while dozens of spoil processions are recorded on Assyrian reliefs, only a relatively small number of them shows the deportation of cult statuary. The same situation prevails in the textual record: cult statues are rarely mentioned in the virtually hundreds of Assyrian booty lists, because deportation of cult statues was a peculiar method of subjugation which the Assyrian conquerors did not systematically engage. Leading captive foreign gods is not a stock motif in the Assyrian royal inscriptions, and we may be virtually certain that whenever this motif is used in texts or images, it relates to an actual historical event. That no cult statuary is shown among the spoils depicted on the Lachish reliefs thus follows the rule and is not an exception for Sennacherib's or other Assyrian palace reliefs. We cannot therefore conclude from this absence to the general absence of anthropomorphic cultic statuary from Lachish or from the town's sanctuary or *bamah*, which may or may not have been plundered by the Assyrians in 701 BCE.

Sennacherib's Throne and Chariots
The epigraph on slab 12 mentions Sennacherib's taking place in/on a *nēmedu* chair, and while we do not know exactly the lexical meaning of the term *nēmedu*[162], we may be virtually certain that the throne depicted on slab 12 (fig. 9b and c) is just the *nēmedu* chair referred to.

161. Na'aman, 'No Anthropomorphic Graven Image', pp. 404-405.
162. See above, n. 44.

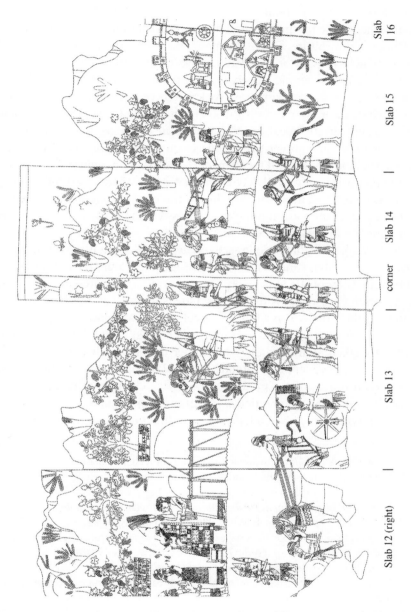

Fig. 9c. Sennacherib enthroned, his tent and chariots, horsemen and Assyrian camp.

This is not the place to study in depth the development of Assyrian royal furniture,[163] but one should note that some royal thrones represented on Sennacherib's sculptures show significant peculiarities when compared to earlier royal furniture. To put the matter squarely, Sennacherib's *nēmedu* chair, which is characterized by three rows of supporting anthropomorphic genies[164] compares more closely to some parts of divine Mulissu's throne, represented on the contemporary rock reliefs of Maltai and Faida,[165] than to the royal thrones of Tiglath-Pileser III or Sargon II. Although Sennacherib's is not strictly speaking a divine throne, it seems that his sitting on the *nēmedu* chair could be perceived as a quasi-divine, and certainly ever-protected manifestation of the royal persona, to which Sennacherib and his contemporaries may well have attached some kind of battle-winning significance.[166] Be this as it may, his sitting on the *nēmedu* throne represents the most obvious 'numinous' feature depicted outside the Assyrian camp on the Lachish series.

It is well-known that in contrast to earlier reliefs, no deity (Ashurnasirpal II), divine symbol (Shalmaneser III to Tiglath-Pileser III) and no divine standards (Sargon II) appear on Sennacherib's sculptures in immediate connection with actual battle scenes. One is tempted at first-hand to consider this development as a kind of 'secularizing' tendency. The gods' role in war is only hinted at on Sennacherib's reliefs,[167] and the major role is certainly taken by the king himself rather than the gods. However, Sennacherib too never appears directly engaged in battle as had been the case for certain reliefs of his predecessors. These changes in representation probably reflect actual practice *and* a different image attached to the royal persona, which must be understood as a direct consequence of the fatal

163. See Hrouda, *Kulturgeschichte*, pp. 67-69 for technical matters.

164. Good close-ups may be found, e.g., in Paterson, *Palace*, Pl. 78; Barnett *et al.*, *Sculptures*, II, Pl. 335; Reade, *Assyrian Sculpture*, Fig. 77 (colour).

165. See J. Börker-Klähn, *Altvorderasiatische Bildstelen und vergleichbare Felsreliefs* (Baghdader Forschungen, 4; Mainz: Philipp von Zabern, 1982), nos. 207-10.

166. Note the remarkable picture on slab I-7 of the king enthroned being carried on a platform over mountainous terrain: Russell, *Final Sack*, p. 86, Pls. 41-42 and discussion on p. 223 with reference to an inscription.

167. Note the consistent depiction of the chariots carrying the standards of Adad and Ninurta, used for divination in the camp. See Erika Bleibtreu, 'Kulthandlungen im Zeltlager Sanheribs', in I. Seybold (ed.), *Meqor Hajjim* (Georg Molin Festschrift; Graz: Styria, 1983), pp. 43-48; Beate Pongratz-Leisten, K. Deller and E. Bleibtreu, 'Götterstreitwagen und Götterstandarten: Götter auf dem Feldzug und ihr Kult im Feldlager', *Baghdader Mitteilungen* 23 (1992), pp. 291-356.

destiny met by Sennacherib's predecessor. Sargon had lost his life in battle, and the Assyrians had been unable to recover his body. In response to this curse-like event and its theological interpretation, the royal persona would never again be so openly exposed to physical danger during war. As a consequence, since the Assyrian artists could no more show the king actively engaged in the course of events, they now concentrated on another traditional scheme of royal iconography, namely the king's ceremonial appearances in his chariot or on his throne.

In order to properly assess this development, we should also consider the curious fact that Sennacherib's retenue on the Lachish reliefs comprises not only one, but two chariots (fig. 9c). The usual royal chariot followed by a man carrying the royal umbrella is shown immediately below the royal tent on slabs 12-13. This chariot is void of any particular figurative decoration. In contrast, another chariot, which appears to the left of the Assyrian camp on slabs 14-15 where it already attracted Layard's particular attention,[168] is richly adorned with figurative decorum (see fig. 10a-b). The fan-like so-called *Deichselzier*, left blank on the drawing of fig. 10b, may have shown the goddess Ishtar in frontal pose, flanked on both sides by the king in adoration;[169] another adoration scene appears in the center of the elliptical object extending from the yoke to the chariot-box, while the segment to the left shows a warrior-god drawing his bow in a nimbus, presumably Ninurta.[170] The horses' harness is more elaborate than any other on these slabs: the bites are stylized as miniature running horses (fig. 10b), and, confirmed by personal inspection, only these two chariot-horses have protective frontlets covering their forehead. The latter feature recalls a ninth-century fashion as does the archaizing chariot itself with its elliptical feature[171] and

168. See Layard, *Discoveries*, p. 151: 'One [of the royal chariots] had a peculiar semicircular ornament of considerable size, rising from the pole between the horses, and spreading over their heads. It may originally have contained the figure of a deity, or some mythic symbol'.

169. Layard's original drawing is fuzzy on this spot, but see the preceding note. Ishtar in frontal stance appears several times on the *Deichselzier* of Ashurbanipal's ceremonial chariot, which is a kind of synthesis of Sennacherib's *two* chariots depicted at Lachish.

170. See Barnett *et al.*, *Sculptures*, II, Pl. 346 for the drawing (= fig. 10a) and Pl. 348 for a close-up photograph; the drawing in Madhloom, *Chronology*, Pl. VI.2(= fig. 10b) is confirmed by personal inspection.

171. This is also attached to the two chariots carrying the standards of Adad and Ninurta which are stationed in the camp for the purpose of divination; note, however, that these chariots have eight-spoked wheels.

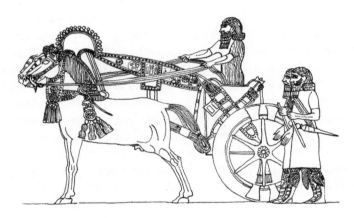

Fig. 10. Sennacherib's second chariot as drawn by A.H. Layard (top) and
T. Madhloom (bottom).

six-spoked wheels.[172] In contrast to the other chariot, this one is fully
furnished with weapons, only some of which (bow and arrows, but not the
double-axe and the mace) would have been helpful in battle for any potential warrior using the vehicle.

The clearly archaizing and non-functional features make Ussishkin's
suggestion that this second vehicle may be Sennacherib's battle chariot
very doubtful.[173] Clearly, it must have fulfilled some ceremonial rather than

---

172. See Hrouda, *Kulturgeschichte*, pp. 95, 147.
173. See Ussishkin, *Conquest*, p. 118. Interestingly enough, Dekel's drawing of this

a practical function.[174] P. Calmeyer once hypothesized that the (empty) chariot represented the god Ashur,[175] and his intuition probably points in the right direction. Ashur does indeed seem to be the only possible candidate as divine owner of a chariot which combines features referring to several deities (Ishtar, Ninurta); moreover, he is the one who during Sennacherib's reign took over the old tradition of the heroic champion among the gods, originally related to Ninurta and then to Marduk and other gods, a tradition which since the third millennium had been consistently connected to a battle chariot carrying weapons and trophies.[176] Ashur's chariot is mentioned in ritual and theological texts from Assur and Nineveh,[177] and in a royal inscription from Nineveh (K 1356) describing a heroic scene applied on bronze bands on the doors of Sennacherib's Akitu festival house.[178] The latter must have shown a very unusual and unprecedented scene most typical of Sennacherib's reign, cultic policy and theology, namely the god Ashur drawing his bow against Tiamat, standing in his chariot led by Amurru. Line 26 of the inscription has given rise to contradicting interpretations:

chariot (cf. the enlarged detail p. 116) is very unprecise and misses any detail beyond rosettes.

174. Hrouda once opined that the chariot had been copied from earlier models of the time of Ashurnasirpal in an attempt at an almost scientific study of chariotry techniques (*Kulturgeschichte*, p. 147: 'um sich Klarheit über die Technik des Fahrwesens zu verschaffen')—an idiosyncratic hypothesis which could possibly work if such a chariot had been excavated among others in a workshop but which does certainly not explain its presence on a sculpture reporting the conquest of a distant Judahite town.

175. P. Calmeyer, 'Zur Genese altiranischer Motive. II: Der leere Wagen', *AMI* 7 (1974), pp. 49-77 (59-61).

176. See Ch. Uehlinger, 'Drachen und Drachenkämpfe im alten Vorderen Orient und in der Bibel', in B. Schmelz and R. Vossen (eds.), *Auf Drachenspuren. Ein Buch zum Drachenprojekt des Hamburgischen Museums für Völkerkunde* (Bonn: Holos, 1995), pp. 55-101.

177. See G. van Driel, *The Cult of Aššur* (Studia Semitica Neerlandica, 13; Assen: Van Gorcum, 1969), pp. 70, 74-75, 86-87; W. Farber, review of van Driel, *BiOr* 30 (1973), pp. 433-36 (435); B. Menzel, *Assyrische Tempel* (Studia Pohl, Series Maior, 10; Rome: Biblical Institute Press, 1981), I, pp. 55-57, II, nos. 662-676, T 59, pp. 69-70.

178. The text is conveniently edited by Beate Pongratz-Leisten, *ina šulmi īrub. Die kulttopographische und ideologische Programmatik der akītu-Prozession in Babylonien und Assyrien im 1. Jahrtausend v. Chr.* (Baghdader Forschungen, 16; Mainz: Philipp von Zabern, 1994), pp. 207-208.

ṣalam Aššur (AN.ŠÁR) *ša ana libbi* (ŠÀ) *Tiāmat ṣalti illiku* (DU-*ku*)
ṣalam Sîn-aḫḫē-eriba (ᴵᵈXXX-PAP.MEŠ-SU) *šar* (MAN) *māt* (KUR) *Aš+šur*

The image of Ashur who goes into the midst of Tiamat for battle,
the image of Sennacherib, king of Assyria.

Earlier readers had erroneously taken this line to indicate that the king had himself depicted standing in Ashur's chariot alongside the supreme god or even that he identified himself with the god, but such interpretations may today be safely laid to rest. Beate Pongratz-Leisten takes the line as a nominal sentence ('the image of Ashur *is* the image of [i.e. a work commissioned by] Sennacherib').[179] One wonders however why this note of authorship should appear precisely at that place, since the tablet mentions numerous other images commissioned by the king. Frahm therefore suggests that the two *ṣalam*-X clauses refer to two different images, an image of Ashur and another one, probably close by, of the king.[180] The latter would have appeared in the attitude of a worshipper similar to what we know from Bavian, Maltai and Faida or, for that matter, the furnishings of the archaizing chariot on the Lachish relief. We know that no other Assyrian king ever associated himself so closely with the god Ashur on public pictorial monuments as Sennacherib did so consistently.

In conclusion, the archaizing chariot on slab 12 probably represents the chariot of Ashur. Sennacherib apparently did not content himself when going to war (at least to the Western campaign of 701 BCE) with the chariots of Adad and Ninurta as his predecessors had done,[181] but took the risk of taking with him the chariot of the supreme god in order to symbolize and secure maximum divine support for his campaign.[182] Note, however, that the Lachish series is the only one which depicts this particular chariot. Together with Sennacherib's *nēmedu* throne, this feature contributes to highlighting the particular numinous significance of the situation and stresses the royal persona's numinous aura. We have already noted that the conspicuous architectural setting of room XXXVI demonstrates that the king regarded the conquest of Lachish as one of the most important victories of his reign, and certainly of the third campaign. The apparently

179. See her commentary, *šulmi īrub*, p. 209.
180. *Einleitung*, p. 224.
181. See above, n. 167.
182. Judging from the reliefs of Ashurbanipal, the latter did not continue this questionable practice but limited himself to his own royal chariot, which he embellished and magnified with a *Deichselzier* depicting his main tutelary goddess Ishtar.

singular depiction of Ashur's chariot in this room confirms this assessment. According to the sculptures' message, not only was this victory the climax of the third campaign, but it seems that the king owed it to his intimate relationship to Ashur.

Lachish and Jerusalem

Having thus outlined but a few clues for a historical-critical understanding of the Lachish reliefs, let us conclude this article by considering an often-raised dilemma: If the victorious conquest of Lachish really did matter that much to Sennacherib, why are his inscriptions absolutely silent about this crucial event, concentrating instead on Hezekiah's surrender at Jerusalem? And since the latter episode is presented by the annals as the ultimate climax of Sennacherib's Western campaign, why should the subjugation of Jerusalem be absent from the pictorial record of Sennacherib's palace sculptures?

A Depiction of Jerusalem in Sennacherib's Palace?

Before offering some tentative suggestions, we should dismiss a number of all too simplistic solutions to the dilemma which represent desperate attempts at cutting through the Gordian knot rather than reasonable hypotheses. Probably the most daring, and unacceptable, thesis has recently been formulated by B. Oded, according to whom

> the city in the 'Lachish Relief' is in fact Jerusalem with its double wall (see 2 Kings xxv 4; Isa. xxii 11; Jer. xxxix 4, lii 7), as it was sketched by the artist on the spot before the besieged capital. But since Jerusalem was not captured, the artist at Nineveh who carved the relief according to the drawing added some conventional features (such as deportees departing through the gate and captives being led from the city into the presence of the king), and on the epigraph...applied to the relief he wrote *Lakisu* (which had actually been conquered) instead of *Ursalimmu*.[183]

Ironically, this thesis rests on the assumption that Assyrian artists drew sketches of conquered cities in the field, a premise essentially developed by Ussishkin on the basis of his detailed comparison of the Lachish reliefs with the specific topographical and archaeological data of Lachish. We have argued above that this assumption cannot be upheld. Oded thinks of the planning and execution of the palace reliefs as quite an arbitrary

---

183. B. Oded, 'History vis-à-vis propaganda in the Assyrian Royal Inscriptions', *VT* 48 (1998), pp. 423-25 (423).

operation, which is highly doubtful once we take a close look at the care invested in the execution of the reliefs on all levels, from general planning to layout and detail. Moreover, Oded's thesis creates more problems than it resolves. According to Sennacherib's annals, Hezekiah did not submit as a result of an Assyrian attack against Jerusalem. Had the siege of Jerusalem been of the kind and intensity of that represented on the Lachish reliefs, Sennacherib and his scribes would not have contented themselves with the relatively pale description known from the annals. On the other hand, it is hard to imagine an Assyrian sculpture celebrating a heroic military victory if such an event had never actually taken place. Oded's hypothesis ignores the relative factual constraints imposed on the design of the palace reliefs, conventions and stereotypes notwithstanding. There is not a single positive argument which would allow us to identify the city portrayed in room XXXVI with Jerusalem.

Other scholars have looked elsewhere in Sennacherib's palace for a depiction of Jerusalem. One suggestion which has at times found some followers is E.A.W. Budge's identification of a besieged city called]-*al-am-mu* depicted on slab 10 of room XIV[184] with Jerusalem on the basis of a restored reading [^{uru}*Ur-sa*]-*al-am-mu*.[185] Although publicized for years by the relevant label in the British Museum and gladly taken up, for example, by Z. Vilnay in his search for pictures of Jerusalem through the ages,[186] the hypothesis has never been accepted in critical scholarship.[187] Grapevines, leaf trees and mountainous environment notwithstanding, iconography does not fit a location of that town in Palestine, since neither the architecture nor the besieged enemies' costume conform to the pictorial conventions that would have to be expected for the Judahite capital. Nor does the orthography of the label fit Jerusalem.[188] Today, most scholars identify the city of XIV-10 with a town called ^{uru}*Alam(m)u* located somewhere near Urartean Muṣaṣir.

184. See Barnett *et al.*, *Sculptures*, II Pls. 168-69; for the epigraph, see also Russell, *Palace*, pp. 56, 158-59, 275; Frahm, *Einleitung*, p. 127 T 49; Russell, *Writing*, p. 287.

185. E.A.W. Budge, *A Guide to the Babylonian and Assyrian Antiquities, British Museum* (London: The Trustees of the British Museum, 1922), pp. 53-54.

186. Z. Vilnay, 'Pictures of Jerusalem and its Holy Places', *Eretz-Israel* 6 (1960), pp. 149-61 (149, 137).

187. See Wäfler, *Nicht-Assyrer*, pp. 281-82; Barnett *et al.*, *Sculptures*, I, p. 78 n. 2.

188. Assyro-Babylonian texts mentioning Jerusalem always spell the toponym with a short second vowel and an *i* as third vowel (*Ursalimmu*).

Many commentators think that the siege of Jerusalem was not represented on sculptures of Sennacherib's Southwest palace because that siege
did not result in an ultimate conquest, and they speculate that the particular
emphasis expressed in the Lachish series should in some way compensate
for the absence of Jerusalem from the pictorial narrative because of Sennacherib's near-failure to subdue Judah's king and capital. We should be
aware, however, that this *communis opinio* rests almost entirely on a partial interpretation of the events along the lines of later biblical tradition,
which negate Sennacherib's ultimate victory and minimize the definitely
humiliating aspects of Hezekiah's surrender to the Assyrian king.[189] To let
biblical tradition condition so much our perception of the event and our
interpretation of the primary evidence is problematic on methodological
grounds. As long as our task is to understand the Assyrian side of the evidence, namely the design of Sennacherib's palace reliefs with a particular
focus on the Lachish series as far as this article is concerned, we should
better look for an explanation which builds upon the rules and conventions
governing the planning and execution of the palace reliefs rather than
follow the track of biblical tradition. A comparative study of all extant
sculptures shows that in order to render a multiplicity of different events
and situations that occurred in war, Sennacherib's artists developed an
even greater spectrum of iconographical schemes than their predecessors.
Massive onslaught and violent attack as depicted, for example, in the
Lachish series, was but one possible scheme among others, which include
long-distance siege, surrender without defence or battle, ranged battle or
pursuit in open countryside, and other situations.

In the absence of field diaries or a 'letter to the gods' relating the event,
we should take as our starting-point the peculiar report on the Jerusalem
operation in Sennacherib's annals. Although scholars discuss the precise
extent of the relevant passage:

> As for Hezekiah the Judahite...I shut him up within Jerusalem, his royal
> city, like a bird in a cage, I surrounded him with earthworks, and made it
> unthinkable for him to exit by the city gate,[190]

it is quite obvious that when looking for possible depictions of this operation we should in no case expect a visual scenario of the Lachish type,

189. Only 2 Kgs 18.13-16 (the so-called A report) does not share this tendency.
190. Translation by M. Cogan, in W.W. Hallo and L.K. Younger (eds.), *The Context
of Scripture*. II. *Monumental Inscriptions from the Biblical World* (Leiden: E.J. Brill,
2000), p. 303; compare W. Mayer's translation in the present volume.

which would rather correspond to Sennacherib's statement on how he besieged 46 other walled cities of Hezekiah. Instead, we have to look for a scenario depicting measures of prolonged siege and cutting off of communication routes as a prelude to a booty procession, but no actual battle.

It is interesting to note in this respect that a number of sculptures from the palace of Sennacherib show low fortified siege walls which are conspicuously built at considerable distance from enemy towns. They are generally manned by Assyrian guards and seem to serve a cut-off function rather than being instrumental for an attack, which may or may not be depicted depending on the actual course of events. Examples of such remote siege-walls include slabs IV-3-4,[191] IV-10 (no guards),[192] V-45-46,[193] X-11,[194] XII-12-13 (heavy siege and attack),[195] and LXVII-1[196] of the Southwest palace. Although not a total novelty, this scheme clearly was a particular favourite of Sennacherib's artists, as probably was the actual stratagem in the field.

Most of these slabs were already heavily damaged at the time of their discovery. Nevertheless, a number of them relate to Sennacherib's campaign to the west. For our purpose, the following examples from rooms IV and X are particularly interesting.

(A) Room IV. Although this was actually the first room discovered during Layard's initial expedition to Nineveh (1847),[197] Layard did not draw the sculptures which he considered to be too badly preserved. The room—a bathroom adjoining the throne-hall—was re-excavated by T. Madhloom in 1965 but had to await full documentation in J.M. Russell's monograph devoted to 'The Final Sack of Nineveh' in the wake of the 1991 war.[198] According to Russell, 'Room IV was decorated with two relief sequences that were apparently similar to one another. Both showed processions of people carrying things, but because of the loss or poor state of preservation of the upper parts of the slabs, it was not clear whether the subject was

191. Russell, *Final Sack*, Pls. 82-84, 258.
192. Russell, *Final Sack*, Pls. 94-95.
193. Russell, *Final Sack*, Pls. 182-85.
194. Barnett *et al.*, *Sculptures*, II, Pl. 143.
195. Barnett *et al.*, *Sculptures*, II, Pls. 144, 150-51.
196. Barnett *et al.*, *Sculptures*, II, Pl. 456.
197. See conveniently Barnett *et al.*, *Sculptures*, I, p. 55 for references; preliminary description in Russell, *Palace*, pp. 50-51.
198. See particularly Pls. 79-104 for photographs and drawings and pp. 227-29 for a catalogue of the room IV sculptures.

tribute or booty. Since no fighting was shown, and none of the figures appeared to be bound, tribute seems more likely'.[199]

Sequence I shows traces of a row of people including Assyrian soldiers above a distant-siege wall (erroneously described by Russell as a city wall). Judging from parallels, the row of people was leaving a besieged city which must have been depicted in the lost upper part of slabs 3-4. The row doubles on slab 4, and on slab 5 one can recognize men, women and children among the people who submit. On slab 6, the row leads up to the two Assyrian scribes who register booty and tribute, followed by officials and finally the king, who was probably depicted standing in his chariot on slab 7, followed by standing cavalry on slabs 8-9. According to the few preserved details which allow an identification of the enemies' dress, the latter cannot be identified as Judahites.

Sequence II shows two rows of men on a distant-siege wall (again misinterpreted by Russell as a city wall). They carry loads of tribute or booty towards a balance installed upon a tripod, where two scribes again register the income. Since some of the carriers are armed with swords, they must belong to the Assyrian army although they are at the same time controlled by more heavily armed senior soldiers. Apparently, they are foreigners taken into the Assyrian army who had perhaps to be prevented from looting. Their dress is occasionally reminiscent of the Judahite short garment and scarf,[200] but it more closely fits non-Judahite soldiers as depicted among the attacking bowmen on the Lachish series.

The representation of topography and vegetation points to some location in thickly wooded mountains. Room IV therefore related events of Sennacherib's second (southeastern mountains, Urartu) or fifth (Judi Dagh) campaign. There is no direct link with the third campaign to the West. Still, when imagining a depiction of the Jerusalem events, the room IV reliefs may inform our expectations regarding a possible pictorial scenario (remote siege and tribute).

(B) Room X. The sculptures of this room have been related by R.D. Barnett and others[201] to the subjugation of Ṣidqa of Ashkelon during Sennach-

199. Russell, *Final Sack*, p. 40.
200. Note especially Russell, *Final Sack*, Pls. 96-97, upper row.
201. R.D. Barnett, 'Lachish, Ashkelon and the Camel: a discussion of its use in Southern Palestine', in J.N. Tubb (ed.), *Palestine in the Bronze and Iron Ages: Papers in Honour of Olga Tufnell* (Institute of Archaeology, Occasional Publications, 11; London: Institute of Archaeology, 1985), pp. 15-30 (25-26); Barnett *et al.*, *Sculptures*, I, pp. 73-74.

erib's campaign to the West. Unfortunately, only a few sketches and descriptions by Layard are preserved, and they hardly allow a full understanding of the overall scenario of room X. However, the deportation of Ṣidqa's family gods may well be the subject of the lower register of slab 11 (see fig. 11), and possibly the now-lost adjoining slab 12, showing captives moving towards Assyrian officials [and the king], followed by Assyrian soldiers who carry three small statues of smiting gods.[202] Slab 7 depicted the Assyrian camp, which was identified by an epigraph. The upper register of slab 11 showed a remote-siege wall guarded by Assyrian soldiers and a row of people leaving for exile, coming out of a city which is again not preserved. One peculiar feature of the room X series is its division into two separate registers: the lower register clearly has its own visual horizon formed by hills and trees, which makes it a relatively self-contained narrative unit and somehow disconnects it from the upper register. It is thus unclear how the two registers relate one to another; they could represent two parallel events of a single episode or different episodes of a single campaign.[203] In the latter case, which would however be unusual in Sennacherib's palace, one might hypothesize that the upper register of room X could have represented the siege of Jerusalem, which together with the Ashkelon episode frames the report on Ekron and the battle of Eltekeh in Sennacherib's annals. We must recognize, however, that the few people leaving the town under remote siege on the upper register of slab X-11 do not look like Judahites in Layard's drawing.[204]

202. See Ch. Uehlinger, 'Anthropomorphic Cult Statuary in Iron Age Palestine and the Search for Yahweh's Cult Images', in K. van der Toorn (ed.), *The Image and the Book: Iconic Cults, Aniconism, and the Veneration of the Holy Book in Israel and the Ancient Near East* (Contributions to Biblical Exegesis and Theology, 21; Leuven: Peeters, 1997), pp. 97-156 (126-27); O. Keel and Ch. Uehlinger, *Göttinnen, Götter und Gottessymbole: Neue Erkenntnisse zur Religionsgeschichte Kanaans und Israels aufgrund bislang unerschlossener ikonographischer Quellen* (Quaestiones disputatae, 134; Freiburg i. Br.: Herder, 5th edn, 2001), §257.

203. The persistence in Sennacherib's palace of the two-register layout inherited from earlier tradition in a few rooms was already noted by Reade, 'Narrative Composition', pp. 88-90.

204. At the time of the discovery of room X (former Q), Layard had already discovered court VI (former I) and would probably have been familiar with the characteristics of Judahite costume (although it had not yet been recognized as distinctly Judahite at that time). On the other hand, the people leaving the town of X-11 appear very close to the broken end of the extant slab, and the details of their dress may have been hard to distinguish.

Fig. 11. Remote siege fortifications as depicted on slab X-12 (Ashkelon episode).

In addition to the above-mentioned sculptures showing remote siege-walls, a further relief from the throne-room most probably belongs to a series depicting Sennacherib's campaign against Philistia and Judah and may relate even more closely to the Jerusalem operation.

(C) Room I (throne-room). This major reception-hall of the Southwest palace was lavishly decorated with an unusually elaborate pictorial narrative, which deserves a detailed study of its own and cannot be summarized here. Full documentation has again been provided by J.M. Russell's recent monograph.[205] Within the limits of this article, I can concentrate on one particular panel on the eastern wall which clearly belongs to a sequence related to the 701 campaign.[206] Slab I-28 (fig. 12)[207] shows an impressively

205. Russell, *Final Sack*, see pp. 36-39 for an overview, pp. 219-27 for the catalogue, and Pls. 24-76 for photographs and drawings. More photographs showing particular details appear throughout the book. For comparison and references to earlier studies, see also Barnett *et al.*, *Sculptures*, I, pp. 50-54, II, Pls. 30-47.

206. Frahm has convincingly demonstrated that the western wall shows events of the fifth campaign. Consequently, the sculptures in this hall cannot antedate 693 BCE; moreover, the throne-hall suite may now be understood as a full circle demonstration of Sennacherib's role as 'king of the four quarters'. See Frahm, *Einleitung*, pp. 124-25.

large city with numerous towers and several gates, a large city gate and a considerably smaller gate nearby. The city's fortified walls bear shields not unlike the walls of Lachish, but there is not a single defender standing on the battlements. The city is clearly not under attack; dismounted cavalrymen of the Assyrian army even have their faces turned away from it. They open the depiction of the Assyrian army entering a battle in open field which was the subject of the adjoining slabs to the left. Russell has tentatively suggested that the series could have depicted the battle of Eltekeh, which is indeed the only battle in open field that Sennacherib's annals report for the third campaign.[208]

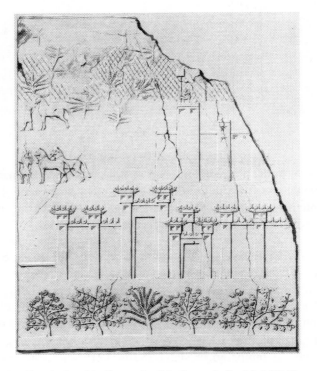

Fig. 12. City depicted in Sennacherib's throne hall, slab I-28 (Jerusalem?).

207. The slab is numbered 23 in Barnett's publication according to earlier plans.

208. *Final Sack*, p. 38. If correct, the still undeciphered epigraph on slab 27 (Layard's and Barnett's 24) would probably have identified Eltekeh. See Frahm, *Einleitung*, p. 125 T 42; Russell, *Writing*, p. 284 for attempts at interpretation.

For our purpose, it is the city that matters most. Above (i.e., inside) the city walls, a monumental building apparently founded on a kind of podium is shown; clearly a citadel, it has towers and walls with windows, but no shields appear on the battlements, and again there is no defender except a somewhat isolated-looking man standing on a tower and holding a standard or *vexillum*. The figure and his gesture are difficult to interpret; clearly a *vexillum* would make more sense in battle rather than here in an apparently deserted city. As for features of topography and vegetation, the city is framed by a horizon of wooded mountains at the upper end and an orchard of grapevines, fig and pomegranate trees at the lower end of the slab.

To my knowledge, no other sculpture among the preserved reliefs of Sennacherib would fit an identification with Jerusalem better than this. According to the annals, the major city involved in the Eltekeh battle was Ekron; however, since Ekron was attacked and severely punished after the battle, our pictorial source does not fit that episode. In contrast, Jerusalem was apparently never attacked. Although we should not link the annals and the sculptures too closely in order not to produce an 'interpretative short-circuit', one wonders whether the lonely man standing on a citadel tower should not be identified with Hezekiah the Judahite, 'shut up like a bird in its cage' in his capital city. There are arguments to question this interpretation—I cannot identify the details of the man's costume on published photographs, and according to W. Boutcher's drawing his head must have been damaged—but for the time being I cannot see any better alternative.[209] Incidentally, the third-campaign events represented in the throne-hall, although only a selection of the sequence known from the annals, would follow the same chronological and geographical order as the annals, namely Sidon![210]—<Ashkelon>—battle of Eltekeh—<Ekron>—Jerusalem? (brack-

---

209. Since the battle of Eltekeh was related to the 'revolt' of Ekron, one should of course first consider Ekron as the most natural candidate to be depicted in this context, but the description of Ekron's destiny in the annals does not fit the picture at all.

210. Not Tyre, as maintained by R.D. Barnett ('Ezekiel and Tyre', *Eretz-Israel* 9 (1969), pp. 6-13 (6-7); *idem, et al., Sculptures*, I, p. 52), nor Jafo as recently argued by W.R. Gallagher ('Room I, Slabs 14-18 of Sennacherib's Palace: Not a Depiction of Tyre', *NABU* 1997/2, pp. 52-53 no. 56; *idem, Sennacherib's Campaign*, p. 128). Jafo was but one of several minor towns conquered along the coastal plain and certainly too small a place to deserve such prominent treatment in Sennacherib's throne-hall. The identification of the city with Sidon is favoured by Matthiae, *L'arte degli Assiri*, p. 170 and fig. 8.17. In my opinion, the Luli and Sidon episodes as known from the annal recensions on the Rassam cylinder and Bulls 2 and 3 clearly fit the pictorial scheme

eted episodes were probably depicted in other rooms, see above on room X).

To sum up, while we have to admit that the available pictorial evidence from Sennacherib's Southwest palace is too poorly preserved as to allow an unquestionable identification of the Jerusalem episode, there are good reasons to suggest that the latter may have been depicted somewhere in the palace, and perhaps even in the throne-hall, the very centre of power. Consequently, we should not give too much weight to the above-mentioned *communis opinio* according to which the Lachish reliefs had to compensate Sennacherib's failure to conquer Jerusalem.

Moreover, regardless of whether the reliefs discussed in this section may directly relate to the Jerusalem operation or not, they can help us to perceive the nuances of Assyrian siege practices and their representation and may thus contribute to a better understanding of the Jerusalem paragraph in Sennacherib's annals. On the other hand, one should be cautious not to enter into a circular argument, since sculptures and annals do rarely run exactly parallel. Our suggestion concerning Jerusalem relies on the annals *faute de mieux*, since they are the only preserved Assyrian textual account of Hezekiah's submission. However, the identification of Jerusalem on slab I-28 cannot as yet be positively proven.

In conclusion, whether or not Sennacherib's army ever laid a siege against Jerusalem and, if yes, to what extent, are questions that will continue to require an answer from the textual rather than the pictorial record.

Reasons Why a Siege against Jerusalem May Not Have Been Depicted in Sennacherib's Palace

Present pictorial evidence can neither prove nor exclude the possibility that the siege of Jerusalem was depicted on one of Sennacherib's palace reliefs. As already mentioned, scholars have generally assumed that a siege of Jerusalem was *not* represented in the palace. To explain this (possible) absence may seem to be an exercise in 'virtual history' to some, and pure speculation to others. However, given the impact of the *communis opinio*

best, although they do not relate a formal siege and conquest of Sidon. Note, however, their distinction of Smaller and Greater Sidon, i. e., the harbour site from where Luli could flee and the town which first came under attack. Only the late source Bull 4, dated seven years after the events, has Luli ultimately flee from Tyre. See discussion in Gallagher, *Sennacherib's Campaign*, pp. 93-104.

that Sennacherib did not represent this event in his palace because it had been a failure, I cannot resist trying to offer a few alternative explanations.

(A)   The siege of Jerusalem and surrender of Hezekiah may have been omitted from the sculptures because the king himself did not participate in the operation.

(B)   The episode may be missing from the sculptures because it was essentially a post-campaign event, thus missing from the field diaries and possibly 'letter to the gods'. Since these were the primary source for the officials and artists who designed the palace decoration, the latter would have had no relevant information concerning Jerusalem at hand.

(C)   Another possible alternative, which is explored in more depth in W. Mayer's contribution to the present volume, is that the siege against Jerusalem was a minor operation in military terms, which made it unfit for inclusion into the heroic schemes of palace reliefs. From a military point of view, the major, even climactic events of the 701 campaign would have been the battle of Eltekeh and the conquest of Lachish.

However, the most important *caveat* against speculating on the reasons for Jerusalem's absence from the sculptures is that we actually do not know whether the episode was depicted somewhere in Sennacherib's palace or not. This is not to say that the *communis opinio* is necessarily wrong, but that it is based on unsufficient evidence and argument.

Conclusion: Towards a Historical-Critical Reading of Pictorial Sources

Within the limited space of this article, I have tried to argue that historical research should take as much interest in a critical analysis of ancient pictures as in the exegesis of textual sources, particularly if the pictures' subject matter is actually 'historical narrative'. As fragmentary as they often are, Assyrian palace reliefs represent an essential, partially independent source for the understanding of past events, and particularly of their perception and interpretation by members of the Assyrian elite. Consequently, historical research should cease to ignore the rich potential of this primary source. At the same time, those historians who recognize the reliefs' potential should move beyond an often-practised positivistic approach which considers the sculptures as a kind of quarry for the search of ancient *realia*. Moreover, we should avoid misreading the sculptures as if they were ancient documentary photographs or cartoons. Instead, these reliefs deserve to be analyzed as just another facet of ancient historiography, based on rules of visual rather than verbal rhetoric and communication.[211]

With regard to historical methodology, I hope to have demonstrated that the only thing which never fits the evidence are simplistic solutions. Problems abound everywhere—to start with the impossibility of getting back to Sennacherib's palace as it stood and to the original authors of texts and images. History-writing is basically a matter of data processing; consequently, historians more than other scholars should be aware of the many difficulties inherent in the recording, storage, transmission and restitution of historical data in ancient sources. In order to interpret ancient documents correctly, we have to consider these difficulties, regardless of whether we are dealing with texts or pictures. The Lachish reliefs even require a twofold historical-critical approach, since in addition to the problems of ancient Assyrian data processing, we have to take into account the fact that data recording and processing was also a major challenge for the nineteenth-century scholars who excavated and restored the series.

Still, if all these problems and necessary premises are taken into account, the historical-critical analysis of ancient pictorial sources may yield important complementary information not contained in any other medium or source category. In this article, I have suggested interpretations of a few features, scenes and episodes that may hopefully refine our perception of Sennacherib's campaign to the West in 701 BCE and its interpretation by contemporary Assyrian court officials and artists. Building up on previous studies by distinguished experts—among whom I would single out the work of A.H. Layard, D. Ussishkin and J.M. Russell—I have tried to evaluate the major problems involved in the study of the Lachish series and

---

211. This conclusion neatly joins Irene J. Winter's comments on the relationship of textual and visual source analysis: 'one simply cannot look at the verbal domains of information and not include the visual in the larger universe of cultural communication; and...one cannot restrict study of the visual to merely establishing chronology and articulating formal properties. Rather, the visual domain contains in it primary information, as well as unique structures of knowledge—oftentimes in parallel or complementary with, occasionally even quite distinct from, the textual record. Consequently, the visual needs to be studied with the full analytical arsenal available to us—art historical, archaeological, anthropological, and textual—and *on its own terms*' ('Art *in* Empire: The Royal Image and the Visual Dimensions of Assyrian Ideology', in S. Parpola and R.M. Whiting [eds.], *Assyria 1995: Proceedings of the 10th Anniversary Symposium of the Neo-Assyrian Text Corpus Project* [Helsinki: The Neo-Assyrian Text Corpus Project, 1997], pp. 359-81 [359]).

have offered some clues for an improved 'reading' of the sculptures from room XXXVI—sculptures which display the conquest of Lachish as one of the most important and perhaps even the major event of the third campaign. In response to a widespread *communis opinio* based on insufficient evidence and argument, I have also considered the possibility that Sennacherib's Jerusalem operation may well have been depicted somewhere in his palace, perhaps even in the throne-hall. While much of this remains in the realm of hypotheses, which will be improved, confirmed or rejected by future scholarship, our iconographical and at times iconological interpretation is not more speculative than any serious study and interpretation of the textual record. Hopefully then, this article may be read by some as an invitation to enter an area of research on the history of the ancient Near East, including the history of ancient Palestine, Israel and Judah, which to the disadvantage of our disciplines has not yet found the forum and attention it deserves.[212]

Sources for Illustrations[213]

1. Assembled and adapted from Barnett *et al.*, *Sculptures*, II, Pls. 327 (no. 429b) and 334 (no. 430b).
2. Assembled from Barnett *et al.*, *Sculptures*, II, Pls. 330 (no. 430a) and 332 (no. 431a).
3. Layard, *Second Series of Monuments of Nineveh*, Pl. 21.
4. Tufnell *et al.*, *Lachish III*, frontispiece of text volume.
5a. Ussishkin, 'Assyrian Attack', p. 55 fig. 2.
5b. Ussishkin, 'Assyrian Attack', p. 54 fig. 1.
6. Adapted from Ussishkin, *Conquest*, fig. 65.
7. Assembled and adapted from Ussishkin, *Conquest*, figs. 67-69.
8. Adapted from Ussishkin, *Conquest*, figs. 61 and 65.
9a-c. Adapted from Ussishkin, *Conquest*, fig. 65.
10a. Barnett *et al.*, *Sculptures*, II, Pl. 346.
10b. Madhloom, *Chronology*, Pl. VI.2.
11. Layard, *Second Series*, Pl. 50.
12. Russell, *Final Sack*, p. 111 Pl. 73.

212.   I should like to thank my colleague Dr Jürg Eggler (Fribourg) for his expert technical assistance in preparing the illustrations, and my assistant René Schurte for his proof-reading, which is reliable as usual.
    213.   Images of the slabs used by permission of the Trustees of the British Museum.

Part III
CONCLUSIONS

REFLECTIONS ON THE DISCUSSION

Lester L. Grabbe

The summary which follows draws both on the papers printed in this volume and on the discussion in the meetings of the Seminar. Participants are indicated by their initials; however, in order to differentiate between points made in the papers and points arising in the discussion, the full surname is given when reference is to the individual papers and responses prepared for the Seminar. Comments in the discussion itself are indicated by the use of only the initials.[1]

We decided that for this meeting we needed to focus our discussion more, and the most appropriate way of doing this might be to concentrate on one specific historical problem. This would make it harder to talk past one another and also clarify to what extent we really agreed or disagreed. We chose the topic of Sennacherib's campaign to Palestine in 701 BCE as one for which there were extensive contemporary data in the form of Assyrian sources and archaeology but also a considerable biblical account (2 Kgs 18–19; Isa. 36–37).

What we found surprising was the extent to which we agreed that there was history in the biblical account. As will become clearer below, everyone seemed to accept that at least 2 Kgs 18.13-16 (usually referred to as

---

1. The following initials are used:
RA   Rainer Albertz
BB   Bob Becking
EBZ   Ehud Ben Zvi
PRD   Philip R. Davies
LLG   Lester L. Grabbe
KJ   Knud Jeppesen
WM   Walter Mayer
HN   Herbert Niehr
NN   Nadav Na'aman
NPL   Niels Peter Lemche
TLT   Thomas L. Thompson

Account A) was an accurate statement of what had happened. There was also a good deal of agreement that little in 2 Kgs 18.17–19.37 (the B$_1$ and B$_2$ accounts) could bear historical scrutiny.

Assyrian Sources

The Seminar was agreed that the Assyrian records should be given primacy in any discussion of Sennacherib. This does not mean that anyone was so naive as to assume that the Assyrian accounts could be taken at face-value, but there were different views on how to interpret and evalute them. The first question was where the information in the Assyrian sources came from and what the aims of the inscriptions were . The 'letter to the god' was seen as quite important because the king had to be faithful to the facts; to do otherwise would be tantamount to lying to the god (WM). The king was the 'viceroy of Ashur' and had to act in a certain way. The oft-made statement that the Assyrians did not admit defeats is a nineteenth-century view (WM). On the other hand, while not lying as such, the inscriptions often contain exaggerations and other devices to exalt and glorify the Assyrian king (Knauf).

A number of participants pointed out that the inscriptions had been misinterpreted as far as Jerusalem is concerned: there was no siege of Jerusalem as such (WM; RA; NN; NPL; Knauf). The action that shut up Hezekiah 'like a bird in a cage' was a blockading of the roads and supply routes (Mayer). There was no besieging army at Jerusalem's gate nor any siege mound cast up around Jerusalem. A parallel example is Ashurbanipal's siege of Tyre which was actually a blockade (NN).

Where did the information come from in the first place? WM pointed out that although no direct evidence is so far known, there must have been a campaign diary that was kept by army scribes. The first stage after this would be the 'letter to the god'. The Shalmaneser III Urartu inscription is a narrative. Some of the details of the 'letter to the god' would be taken out when the information was used to produce the annals. Different versions of the annals were produced, some with the earlier years shortened; nevertheless, the epitomes were taken from the annals. The annals would have been written just after the campaign and certain parts were then abstracted for the epitome. NN noted that in the Egyptian context Thutmosis III mentioned field diaries. Similar diaries, if indeed recorded in the course of the Assyrian campaigns, might have been written on wax tablets. The annals of Tukulti-ninurte II, which are extremely detailed and shift from first to third person, are the closest thing we have to a daily campaign diary.

The question of numbers is a much debated point. However, WM argued that the numbers could be exact. He had pointed out that the 205,000 taken captive by Sennacherib could actually include all living booty, animals as well as humans (Mayer). Thus, rather than the exaggeration it is often alleged to be, it was in fact a number based on records made on the campaign. It was the needs of the army that drove the Assyrian conquests since its maintenance put a burden on resources, and keeping track of booty was very important. EBZ, however, mentioned the comprehensive study of De Odorico on numbers in Assyrian inscriptions.[2] This study would point in a different direction, suggesting that the number of captives was indeed an exaggeration and should not be taken literally. RA mentioned Broshi and Finkelstein's recent article which estimated that the entire population of Judah in the eighth century was about 200,000.[3] Thus, the deportation could have been quite large (RA).

This short discussion of the Assyrian accounts illustrated very well a common failing in biblical studies: when dealing with the Hezekiah and similar biblical episodes, statements are often made about the Assyrian sources, but although these are usually by non-specialists, it does not prevent their becoming a part of the interpretative tradition. On the other hand, investigations of the question by Assyriologists are either scarce or not easily accessible to non-Assyriologists.

It must be admitted that some contributions to our discussion were more positive toward the Assyrian sources than some recent treatments.[4] However, Uehlinger's study not only addressed another important Assyrian source, the reliefs, but also emphasized the need to recognize that the reliefs are as much an interpretation as the texts. That is, they are not an almost photographic representation of the siege of Lachish. They contain both conventional representation from the repertory of Assyrian iconography and unique elements that show a concern to give a true reflection of

---

2. Marco De Odorico, *The Use of Numbers and Quantifications in the Assyrian Royal Inscriptions* (SAAS 3; Helsinki: Neo-Assyrian Text Corpus Project, 1995).

3. Magen Broshi and Israel Finkelstein, 'The Population of Palestine in Iron Age II', *BASOR* 287 (1992), pp. 47-60.

4. E.g., Antti Laato, 'Assyrian Propaganda and the Falsification of History in the Royal Inscriptions of Sennacherib', *VT* 45 (1995), pp. 198-226; Bustenay Oded, 'History vis-à-vis Propaganda in the Assyrian Royal Inscriptions', *VT* 48 (1998), pp. 423-25; Christopher R. Seitz, 'Account A and the Annals of Sennacherib: A Reassessment', *JSOT* 58 (1993), pp. 47-57. See also Knauf, pp. 141-49 above.

the unique siege of Lachish. The reliefs must be used critically as any other historical source, taking account of iconographical conventions just as textual historins take account of literary conventions. Sennacherib's reliefs have often been appealed to as evidence but there is a tendency to be more uncritical than with the texts, as if 'the camera cannot lie'. The reliefs provide valuable information, but they are not photographs. On the other hand, to argue that the artist could have carved a siege of Jerusalem which he then labelled 'Lachish' when Jerusalem did not fall[5] is to ignore the features about the reliefs that are unique to the overthrow of Lachish.

Archaeology

Although none of the participants devoted much space to the questions of archaeology, the archaeology is not only important for Sennacherib's invasion but provides unique information.[6] The excavations at Lachish have allowed the Sennacherib incident to be correlated with the stratigraphy of many sites in Palestine. The *lmlk* jars have now been shown to be confined to the narrow period of Hezekiah's reign and thus provide an important diagnostic tool when found *in situ*. It is therefore possible to say which cities most likely fell to the Assyrians at the time, which provides confirmation both of the Assyrian statements that Sennacherib reduced most of the towns and villages outside Jerusalem and the statement in the biblical text that 'all the fortified towns' were taken (2 Kgs 18.13, though this is a clear exaggeration since not all fortified sites fell to Sennacherib).[7] The *lmlk* jars and their distribution also give support to the textual statements —Assyrian and biblical—about the efforts of Hezekiah to prepare to break free from Assyrian control. Although the present volume has focused on Sennacherib's invasion, the names on the *lmlk* jars and their distribution may assist a reconstruction of the administrative system in Hezekiah's kingdom and even put names to some of the more important officials.

What is not specifically supported by the archaeology are the details of the B$_1$ and B$_2$ accounts. Most importantly, we find no evidence that the

5. Oded, 'History', pp. 423-25.
6. For a survey of the archaeology, including the *lmlk* seal impressions, see pp. 3-20 above.
7. Israel Finkelstein, 'The Archaeology of the Days of Manasseh', in Michael D. Coogan, Cheryl J. Exum, and Lawrence E. Stager (eds), *Scripture and Other Artifacts: Essays on the Bible and Archaeology in Honor of Philip J. King* (Louisville, KY: Westminster/John Knox, 1994), pp. 169-87.

Assyrian army encamped before the walls of Jerusalem. Despite past claims that the archaeology of Arad and Tel Beer-sheba provides evidence for Hezekiah's religious reforms, the archaeology is in fact ambiguous, and this issue is still a moot point.[8]

The Biblical Narrative

No new structural analysis of the parallel biblical accounts in 2 Kgs 18.13–19.37 and Isa. 36–37 had been proposed by any of the contributors, though a number had presupposed the analysis begun by Stade and brought to a widely accepted conclusion by Childs.[9] RA pointed out the recent analysis by C. Hardmeier[10] which proposes some alterations, associating the narrative with the events of the final siege of Jerusalem a century after Sennacherib. BB had been impressed by Hardmeier who had shown how dynamic the text was but the question of sources for the whole narrative is still not settled (e.g. there is a gap in the text between the fall of Samaria and the fourteenth year of Hezekiah). A new analysis is still needed (Becking). Na'aman basically accepts Childs' form-critical analysis of sources and has not attempted a new one, but his contribution to this volume gives a new literary analysis (pp. 201-20 above). He argues that B_1 was probably written in the mid-seventh century. B_2 was modelled on B_1 but was rather later, probably in the late neo-Babylonian period.

EBZ agreed that there is much we do not know about the biblical accounts, even if the conventional analysis is accepted. He puts the final composition of 2 Kgs 18–20 to the postexilic period, the purpose being to contrast Hezekiah's experience with Zedekiah's and explain why Jerusalem was conquered by the Babylonians (Ben Zvi). RA affirmed that Account A (2 Kgs 18.13-16) is definitely a self-contained report, with the following narrative separate. NPL also agree that the present narrative showed a literary process; however, Account A could still be secondary, even though it was not younger than the rest of the narrative.

8. Cf. Nadav Na'aman, 'The Debated Historicity of Hezekiah's Reform in the Light of Historical and Archaeological Research', *ZAW* 107 (1995), pp. 179-95 (184-89); *idem*, 'No Anthropomorphic Graven Image: Notes on the Assumed Anthropomorphic Cult Statues in the Temples of YHWH in the Pre-Exilic Period', *UF* 31 (1999), pp. 405-408.

9. See the survey on pp. 23-26 above.

10. C. Hardmeier, *Prophetie im Streit vor dem Untergang Judas: Erzählkommunikative Studien zur Entstehungssituation der Jesaja- und Jeremiaerzählungen in II Reg 18–20 und Jer 37–40* (BZAW, 187; Berlin: W. De Gruyter, 1989).

Most of the contributors had concentrated their comments on the two parallel accounts in 2 Kings and Isaiah. Ben Zvi was the only one who asked about the Chronicler's account. This caused him to raise some fundamental questions. Accepting that the Chronicler's account was late and drew on the narrative in 2 Kings, he pointed out how this shows how a particular story could be adapted to fit the theological and ideological aims of the redactor. Thus, the Chronicler's version is very much relevant to the discussion, with some historiographical implications (discussed below).

Why Did Hezekiah Remain on the Throne?

For me the fact that Hezekiah remained on the throne—according to both Assyrian and biblical accounts—is a problem. I find it difficult that Sennacherib left him on the throne after his rebellion, yet the Assyrian sources give no reason why this should be. Although NPL also admitted this had bothered him initially, he felt it was not a major issue, and none of the other members saw it as a problem (as noted below, NN and EBZ thought it quite explicable). Nevertheless, I felt another source that has been cited, though often dismissed, might help explain the conundrum. This is the story of Sennacherib in Herodotus which I argue is based on an Egyptian account and is independent of the biblical accounts (Grabbe).

No doubt Herodotus's story in its present form is semi-legendary, but it is not the sort of story to have been made up at a much later time because Sennacherib's name seems to have been forgotten. Yet it appears to be independent of all other known accounts, including the biblical one. Thus, the story is probably rooted in some sort of actual historical incident; on the other hand, the frequent attempt to relate this to 2 Kgs 19.35//Isa. 37.36 by equating the mice of Herodotus's story with a plague ignores its setting. The Greeks (and Egyptians) were well acquainted with plagues. If Herodotus (or his Egyptian informants) had wanted to say that a plague devasted Sennacherib's forces, they would have had no difficulty conveying that clearly. Therefore, the statement that mice chewed up the harness and weapons of the Assyrians does not suggest a plague. If the original account spoke of a plague (which is entirely possible), that datum had become reinterpreted or corrupted by the time it appeared in Herodotus's version.

I have no useful suggestion to make about the exact connotation or origin of this statement about the mice, but it does indicate a military defeat (or considerable setback) of the Assyrians by the Egyptians, for whatever reason. (I do not rule out a plague, but this interpretation cannot be taken from the story in Herodotus.) A major defeat of the Assyrian army by the

Egyptians or even a standoff, perhaps because of some extra-military disaster, would explain why Sennacherib did not pursue his advantage and
remove Hezekiah from the throne: he simply lacked the resources to do so.
Finally, the agreement between both Herodotus and the biblical accounts
that the Assyrian army was in some way incapacitated seems to me to be
significant. It also happens to be an example of Ben Zvi's argument (discussed in the next section) that agreements in the perceptions of quite
different groups may point to a historical event.

Implications for Historiography

A couple of quotations from Lemche served as the jumping off point for
this part of the discussion about historicity.[11]

> The ancient Near Eastern inscriptions that refer to Israel and Judah are
> limited in number but are nevertheless important evidence. They tell us that
> the names of Israel and Judah are not invented—fictitious—names, but
> refer to political structures that really existed. They also mention a selection
> of kings otherwise known from the Old Testament. They show that so far as
> we can control the evidence the succession of these kings as well as the
> synchronisms that can be established between the kings of Israel and Judah
> and Assyrian and Babylonian kings are not totally misleading. Sennacherib
> really attacked Judah in the Days of Hezekiah…

> However, it is my thesis that the authors of ancient literature of the kind
> found in the Old Testament did not care much about the historical exacti-
> tude of their description of the past. The past was not very interesting
> except for the examples of good and bad behaviour it provided for the
> present and future. The past was interesting because it explained the present
> —even sometimes made present arrangements seem legitimate or natural.
> Otherwise let the dead bury the dead!

BB did not disagree with these statements, but he would have put them
differently. PRD also by and large agreed, but his position would be that
even if the Assyrians and Judaeans had agreed exactly on the 'pure facts'
of what had happened, each might disagree on the 'fact' of who had won
or what the episode proved or meant. These things depend on one's view
of the world, the strategic interests of each side, the definition of what
counts as a success and what not. It is mentalities that creat history from
'facts', and no facts by themselves can ever provide a history. RA disagreed with NPL because the latter was writing from a minimalistic stand-

---

11. See pp. 158-62 above.

point. The data can be combined in different ways, depending on the story and the emphasis. The chronological framework is also a part of the data, though the order can be changed. RA rather preferred the approach of Ben Zvi (see below). TLT noted that NPL had implied that the ancient writers had knowledge that they did not care about, but did the ancient writer have knowledge about the past that included a theoretical framework or did he have only some texts which he was using for his own purpose? We assume that the facts are the point of departure, but they could just be the narrator's building blocks which are not important in themselves. NPL replied that the ancient world could and did distinguish between history writing and other sorts of writing.

NN thought the author of Kings was interested in history but not in the way that we understand the term. The historical-critical approach of the kind developed in Greece since the classical period was alien to this author, as it was to all other scribes who worked in the ancient Near East.[12] Source criticism is unknown in the East before the Hellenistic period; the author of Kings must have given equal credibility to all his sources. For this reason we find concrete details and dry accounts side by side with legendary, novelistic and fabulous narratives. Biblical history is founded—with no distinction—on the oral literature as well as the written sources available to the authors. Moreover, biblical historiography was written first of all in order to shape the present and convey religious, ideological and ethical messages to its readers and listeners. The late date at which it was written, its literary and ideological nature and extreme tendentiousness, are serious flaws for its use as a source for writing a history of Israel according to acceptable 'western' standards. Nevertheless, the author of Kings works as a historian, collecting all the sources available to him and making use of these sources in his composition.

NN felt that the writer collected all he could, though he gave it his own interpretation. This is illustrated by the composition of the B_2 account which was written much later (late Neo-Babylonian period) in order to counter the claims made in the Rabshakeh's speech (Na'aman). The Deuteronomist has cited his two sources almost verbatim and added very little, yet the whole is shaped to get across his theological message. Thus, NN preferred to think in terms of sources and composition. The writer was

12. Cf. Grabbe, 'Who Were the First Real Historians? On the Origins of Critical Historiography', in L.L. Grabbe (ed.), *Did Moses Speak Attic? Jewish Historiography and Scripture in the Hellenistic Period* (JSOTSup, 317; ESHM, 3; Sheffield: Sheffield Academic Press, 2001), pp. 156-81.

entirely dependent on his sources but unaware of the necessity to apply historical criticism to them. He did not necessarily make a selection but passed on what he had. However difficult it is, we must make use of what is preserved. And of course there are marked differences between sources: for example, the Deuteronomistic History is entirely different from the books of Chronicles.

TLT suggested that NN was multiplying sources unnecessarily. Why come up with hypothetical sources behind the biblical text? NN replied that in order to account for the many reliable historical details scattered through biblical history we must look for the sources used by the author. This investigation can be made similar to the way that we search for the material used by Berossus and Manetho who wrote the histories of their respective countries hundreds—sometimes even thousands—years after the events they relate. The temple library of Jerusalem must have been available to the author and used as his main source of information. RA pointed out that we must ask what the audience would accept, since even invention must conform to expectation. The compiler can keep or change the facts received, but his product must accord with what is acceptable. BB construed the narrative 1 Kgs 12 to 2 Kgs 25 as an extended example of the genre of a 'letter to the divine', being written during the exilic period for those Yahwists who remained in the land. HN pointed to the importance of asking for whom the texts were written. Were they attempting to establish a new past? He wondered, however, whether the people of the land during the exile would be interested in what had happened in the days of Sennacherib.

Ben Zvi's article had explored the question of the malleability of the tradition. On the one hand, he had noted the different versions of the Sennacherib campaign as they relate to the account in 2 Kings; on the other hand, he shows how they have been shaped to fit a particular literary and/or ideological context. The first account to demonstrate this malleability was the earliest version itself in 2 Kings which was probably the product of a much later age, possibly even the postexilic period. It already evidences a changed and developed interpretation of the original event. Yet this malleability was not limitless. When different groups share a particular perception of an event, it may indicate historicity. A number of the participants found this to resonate with their own views about historicity.

Two contributors explicitly addressed the question of objectivity in writing history (Becking, Davies). Becking focused on chronology as the backbone of history. Chronological study can be considered the most 'objective' of historical methods, but neither chronological data nor any other 'objective datum' has meaning by itself. It is only when it is put into a wider framework, a historical narrative, that meaning emerges. This is adding flesh to the bare bones to create a historical narrative, but this narrative is a subjective picture of the past because one could create other narratives to explain the data. There are two sorts of subjectivity: (1) at the level of values and ideology and (2) at the level of perception. One should try to avoid a biased position (the first sort), but we shall always be subject to the second. Thus, Becking pleads for a moderate position between 'a correspondence theory' and a 'coherence theory' of historical truth.

Davies also emphasizes the narrative nature of historiography. We create the narrative from what we already know: what we know tells us what is history. The Assyrian discourse was of a victorious imperial state. Since this is easy to compare to some modern totalitarian states, we naturally are influenced in our interpretation of ancient Assyria by our knowledge of modern parallels. The Judaean narratives take slightly different forms, but the discourse is of a society whose god has shown his allegience to his chosen city. We could focus on where the two narratives (the Assyrian and the Judaean) agree, but that would produce only a list of data, not history. 'What happened' cannot be represented objectively but only narratively. 'What really happened' is indistinguishable from 'the narrative generated by the modern historian'. But our sources are these ancient discourses, and historians are primarily exegetes. We evaluate them in terms of how far they convey recognizable images of reality. The facts of history cannot be directly observed but show themselves by their effects. We do justice to the ancient narratives by trying to understand what their stories meant to them—what the events they witnessed and recorded meant to them. But the question of reliability matters to us in a way that it did not matter to the ancient Assyrians and Judaeans.

TLT emphasized the importance of literary analysis. I think most of us would agree with him; however, when he went on to assert that this still awaits our attention as a Seminar, I have to disagree. I think various of us have spent a lot of time analysing the literary sources with literary conventions in mind. This literary analysis is a necessary precursor to any historical work using literary sources, but we do not stop there. We must still do a historical analysis and evaluate what historical data might be contained in the source and whether we can make use of them. This brings us to non-literary sources which also require historical analysis.

The survey of the archaeology relevant to the Sennacherib episode illustrated the extent to which archaeological data still depend on narrative to give them meaning. The *lmlk* seal impressions and the pottery assemblage found *in situ* at various sites could be studied in their own right. One could analyse the distribution of *lmlk* jars, and the layers at various Judaean sites could be co-ordinated with those at Lachish. But a great deal still depended on correlating these data with the Assyrian reliefs on the siege of Lachish, the Assyrian inscriptions about Sennacherib's campaign, and the biblical narratives on Hezekiah. The archaeology provided a vital control on and corrective to the narratives,[13] but without the narratives the archaeology would give only a minimal picture. It is not a question of 'either/or' but 'both/and' (though it is axiomatic that each data source must be analysed in its own right before synthesizing its data with those from other sources).

For some time, the 'Fribourg school' has been demonstrating the importance of iconography as a source for the ancient Near East, not only for mythology and religion but also for history. This is particularly applicable here because the reliefs in Sennacherib's palace have often been appealed to in trying to determine what happened in Sennacherib's invasion. The iconography is very important, but it also has to be interpreted (Uehlinger). One must take account of iconographic conventions just as one must take account of literary conventions; yet, as with the textual sources, the existence of stereotypes and conventions does not negate their value for history.

The fact that everyone seemed to agree that there were some reliable historical data in a part of the account (even if for most, it is limited to three or four verses in 2 Kgs 18.13-16) has major implications. The general position that the biblical text contains some early data has been accepted by everyone, including the so-called minimalists. The problem has been to know how to separate out those data and make use of them. The minimalist view has been that this is too difficult to do except where external confirmation exists. But the agreement in the present debate that a particular passage has a genuine historical memory is a significant step: somehow the editor of this passage obtained an account that goes back to a contemporary memory of Sennacherib's invasion and Hezekiah's response to it. The ability to agree on this one particular passage should not be underestimated.

The first question that comes to mind is: What is the source of the narrative with the reliable data? Although a small minority might see the entire Hezekiah narratives as contemporary or nearly contemporary with the

13. Cf. Ernst Axel Knauf, 'History, Archaeology, and the Bible', *TZ* 57 (2001), pp. 262-68.

events described, few find this view at all convincing. A widespread opinion exists among scholars that the text of 2 Kgs 18–19 in its present form (and its parallel in Isa. 36–37) is late.[14] If so, the writer must have obtained his Account A from somewhere other than just late tradition. The bulk of the passage is composed of material of indifferent value for historical purposes. This suggests that little of the material available to the writer was from a reliable source or, to put it another way, his good sources were restricted and provided only a modicum of information. Considering that much of the narrative is made up of diverse legendary material and the creations of the Deuteronomistic writers, the source of reliable historical information was not likely to have been extensive.

So what was his source? We can only speculate, but there are not a lot of choices. It is always possible that he obtained some information from inscriptions.[15] But in light of the observations just made, the Deuteronomistic Historian was not a discriminating historian from a modern perspective. Especially considering that his main purpose was a theological one, he would not have been interested in trying to search out documentary sources as a modern historian would, even if they were available. The one source that seems to fit well the usable data that we can extract from the text would be a type of chronicle, perhaps an official chronicle kept in the palace or the temple. It would provide the data on the names, sequence, and synchronization of the kings, as well as lengths of reign. It would also give short statements about key events, but these would have been minimal in most cases (cf. the Babylonian Chronicles[16]). Most of what can be verified from extra-biblical sources can be explained by use of such a chronicle.

I would argue that this explanation corresponds very well with points I have made in previous studies: where the text of 1 and 2 Kings can be checked against contemporary or near contemporary sources, the writer/

14. The question of how late can be debated but is not essential for our discussion here. As is well known, Martin Noth dated it to the exilic (Neo-Babylonian) period. Some have wanted to put its composition as late as the Hellenistic period (see the discussion in Lester L. Grabbe [ed.], *Did Moses Speak Attic? Jewish Historiography and Scripture in the Hellenistic Period* [JSOTSup, 317; ESHM, 3; Sheffield: Sheffield Academic Press, 2001]).Many would find a dating of the final composition in the Persian period the most congenial.

15. Cf. Nadav Na'aman, 'The Contribution of Royal Inscriptions for a Re-evaluation of the Book of Kings as a Historical Source', *JSOT* 82 (1999), pp. 3-17.

16. A.K. Grayson, *Assyrian and Babylonian Chronicles* (TCS, 5; Locust Valley, NY: J.J. Augustin, 1975).

compiler had reliable information about the names of the Israelite and Judaean kings, their relative order, and the approximate time of their rule.[17] In one sense, this is minimal information, but it is absolutely vital because archaeology and even inscriptions are unlikely ever to provide this sort of information. I should also make it clear that this is not an endorsement or defence of many of the textual details which are often questionable, but this judgment has to be made on a case-by-case basis. In this light, it seems to me that William Hallo has made a good overall point:

> What, then, is the general methodological lesson we can learn from the case of Jerusalem under Hezekiah? The simple test of the minimalists, that the biblical version of events must have extra-biblical, preferably contemporaneous, verification before it can be regarded as historical, is an impossible demand even in the best of circumstances as here, where the events loom so large in Assyrian royal inscriptions and art, but are presented in such a widely divergent manner. However, the maximalist willingness to accept the biblical version until falsified by extra-biblical sources, preferably contemporaneous and bearing on the same matters, also lacks a rational basis, given the randomness of these sources and their accidental discovery. Because Mesopotamian references to Jerusalem by name were confined to the single reign of Sennacherib and his contemporary Hezekiah, we cannot treat the absence of conflicting sources about Jerusalem in other periods as confirmation of every biblical statement about the city. The task of the biblical historian thus remains as before: to weigh the comparative evidence point by point in order to discover, if possible, the nature of its convergence with the biblical data and the reasons for its divergence.[18]

I am not happy with his term 'biblical historian', since we are historians of a place and/or period of time, not of a book. That is, we are historians of ancient Israel, ancient Palestine, the Assyrian empire, the Iron II period, or the like. Just as most now eschew the term 'biblical archaeologist', we should no longer speak of 'biblical historian'. But Hallo's basic point is

17. See Grabbe, 'Are Historians of Ancient Palestine Fellow Creatures—Or Different Animals?' in Lester L. Grabbe (ed.), *Can a 'History of Israel' Be Written?* (JSOTSup, 245; ESHM, 1; Sheffield: Sheffield Academic Press, 1997), pp. 19-36; '"The Exile" under the Theodolite: Historiography as Triangulation', in Lester L. Grabbe (ed.), *Leading Captivity Captive: 'The Exile' as History and Ideology* (JSOTSup, 278; ESHM, 2; Sheffield Academic Press, 1998), pp. 80-100; see also Lemche's comment on p. 314 above.

18. William W. Hallo, 'Jerusalem under Hezekiah: an Assyriological Perspective', in Lee I. Levine (ed.), *Jerusalem: Its Sanctity and Centrality to Judaism, Christianity, and Islam* (New York: Continuum; London: Cassell, Petter, Galpin & Co., 1999), pp. 36-50.

well taken. In the actual execution of reconstructing history, we might well evaluate the specific details rather differently, but I believe a number of us in the Seminar would agree with the general sentiment of his summary statements.

What Sort of History Would You Write?

At the end of the discussion, partcipants were asked what sort of history of Sennacherib's invasion they would write in light of the discussion:

LLG: Would follow the basic account in the Assyrian sources and would be sceptical of much in accounts B_1 and B_2. However, the fact that Hezekiah remained on the throne despite his rebellion is a problem. This makes one wonder whether something significant happened (which is the essence of the message in B_2 that the 'angel of the Lord' destroyed the Assyrian army). Herodotus's account provides an independent story of a defeat of Sennacherib's army while they confronted the Egyptians. Sennacherib's inscriptions also mention an engagement with the Egyptians, but Sennacherib claims to have defeated them. Can we take this at face value? Although clearly legendary in its present form, Herodotus's story should be set alongside other sources and critically evaluated as suggesting that something happened to give significant problems to the Assyrian army, even if the precise nature of that event can no longer be extracted from the narrative.

RA: Would reconstruct using the sources. There is no need for an explanation of why Hezekiah was left on the throne beyond his submitting; on the other hand, why did the biblical author present the story as he did? In any case, an author filled out the gaps with new stories at a later time to support Jerusalem and encourage it to trust in Yhwh.

BB: Would not write a history because it would be too tiny for the publishers. It simply would not make sense to write a history only of Sennacherib's invasion; however, it would make sense to write a hisory of the encounter of Judah with Assyria in its wider ancient Near Eastern context. In that, all the evidence available would need to be used.

EBZ: The Assyrian invasion was successful. True, Hezekiah remained in power, but he was not the first nor the last leader of a local elite who retained his power after an unsuccessful rebellion against Assyria. The goal of Assyria was not to dethrone kings *per se*, but to establish a stable 'agreement' between the Assyrian king (and his elite) and the local elite. It worked. Neither Hezekiah nor any Judahite king after him rebelled against Assyria after 701. The story of Jerusalem being spared destruction developed a life of its own and was later used in a number of ways and raised a number of issues, among them why Jerusalem was not spared destruction in 586 BCE.

PRD: Quoted Morton Smith that the 'big guys always win' (see his study, pp. 106-18 above, for a further explication of this quote from Morton Smith). The modern historian can perhaps confine oneself to simply establishing the 'facts', but this will mean little unless these 'facts' are put into a narrative. We can, of course, interpret the incident as a whole in terms of our own assessment of what they add up to, but why should this assessment be of any particular use? A postmodern historian such as himself should seek not to be blinkered to the 'facts' but open to the worldview that frames the presentations of these facts and determines what they do in fact add up to in terms of history. Put simply, it is mentalities that create history from 'facts' (whether or not the 'facts' are actually true) and no facts by themselves can ever provide a history. He would like the Seminar to focus on what the episode meant for Assyrians and what for Judaeans, in their respective worldviews. It is these, as much as (or more than?) the 'fact' itself, that have determined the shape and substance of the narratives that we now have and which we treat as sources.

KJ: Would start with the few data agreed on, and then tell a story. No knowing where the 'scientific' account ends and the story begins.

NPL: Would describe Sennacherib as in his annals but not in isolation from his other campaigns. How was the Judah campaign any different? It is only that Sennacherib became the boogeyman in the later Jewish sources. It is a mystery as to why Hezekiah was left on the throne, but this can probably be explained by the difficulty of taking Jerusalem. The relationship between the A and the B_1/B_2 narratives needs to be taken into account.

NN: As for Sennacherib's campaign, it is important to note that he changed the policy of his father Sargon II: he relinquished some ground in Asia Minor and had a different policy toward Babylon. Whereas Sargon, like Tiglath-pileser III before him, was a great conqueror, Sennacherib kept to the established borders. Hezekiah was lucky to rebel against Sennacherib rather than Sargon. Sennacherib endeavoured only to break Judah's power, not annex it. He destroyed and deported a good deal and also removed territory from Judaean control. He strengthened Ekron which became a major power in the Shephelah. There are some other examples where the vassal king remained on the throne after rebellion (e.g., Hanunu of Gaza, Necho I of Egypt, Ba'al of Tyre), the fate of the king depending on the Assyrian strength and policy in the region at that time. Sennacherib achieved everything he wanted on his campaign, so he did not make an effort to conquer Jerusalem and replace its king. The B_1 account might have originated from the memory of negotiations and an Assyrian request of total surrender, which suddenly ended with an Assyrian retreat. It came as a total surprise to the inhabitants of Jerusalem and gave rise to the narrative of the miraculous delivery of the city by Yhwh.

HN: Would (1) evaluate the Assyrian sources, taking account of what was known about general Assyrian policy; (2) look at the archaeological data; (3) finally, analyze the biblical texts.

TLT: Would take his position as the resident minimalist. God gave Hezekiah 15 years of life: this is not history. What we have is mainly a series of annotated dates. A thorough literary analysis is needed.

The Next Seminar Session

It was agreed that focusing on a specific historical period or problem with a range of sources had been useful. Thus, it was decided that the sixth meeting (2001) would be devoted to the 'rise and fall of the Omride dynasty' including, where appropriate, the Jehu dynasty which was closely associated with it.

BIBLIOGRAPHY

Abraham, W.J., *Divine Revelation and the Limits of Historical Criticism* (Oxford: Oxford University Press, 1982).

Abush, T, 'Marduk', *DDD*, II, pp. 543-49.

Ackroyd, P.R., 'The Biblical Interpretation of the Reigns of Ahaz and Zedekiah', in W.B. Barrick and J.R. Spencer (eds.), *In the Shelter of Elyon: Essays on Ancient Palestinian Life and Literature in Honor of G.W. Ahlström* (JSOTSup, 31; Sheffield: JSOT Press, 1984), pp. 247-59.

Ackroyd, Peter A., *Studies in the Religious Tradition of the Old Testament* (London: SCM Press, 1987).

Aharoni, Miriam, 'Arad the Israelite Citadels', *NEAEHL*, I, pp. 82-87.

Aharoni, Miriam and Yohanan Aharoni, 'The Stratification of Judahite Sites in the 8th and 7th Centuries B.C.E'., *BASOR* 224 (1976), pp. 73-90.

Aharoni, Yohanan, 'Excavations at Tel Arad: Preliminary Report on the Second Season, 1963', *IEJ* 17 (1967), pp. 233-49.

—*The Land of the Bible, A Historical Geography* (trans. A.F. Rainey; London: Burns and Oates, 1967).

—'The Israelite Sanctuary at Arad', in D.N. Freedman and J.C. Greenfield (eds.), *New Directions in Biblical Arachaeology* (Garden City, NY: Doubleday, 1971), pp. 28-44.

—*Investigations at Lachish: The Sanctuary and the Residency (Lachish V*; Tel Aviv: Tel Aviv University, 1975).

—*The Archaeology of the Land of Israel* (trans. Anson F. Rainey; Philadelphia: Westminster Press, 1982).

—'Ramat Raḥel', *NEAEHL*, IV, pp. 1261-67.

Ahlström, Gösta W., 'Is Tell ed-Duweir Ancient Lachish?' *PEQ* 112 [1980], pp. 7-9

—*The History of Ancient Palestine from the Paleolithic Period to Alexander's Conquest* (ed. D. Edelman; Minneapolis: Fortress Press; Sheffield: Sheffield Academic Press, 1993).

Akenson, D.H., *Surpassing Wonder: The Invention of the Bible and the Talmuds* (New York: Harcourt, Brace & Company; Montreal/Kingston: McGill-Queen's University Press, 1998).

Albenda, Pauline, 'An Assyrian Relief Depicting a Nude Captive in Wellesley College', *JNES* 29 (1970), pp. 145-50.

—'Syrian-Palestinian Cities on Stone', *BA* 43 (1980), pp. 222-29.

—'Egyptians in Assyrian Art', *Bulletin of the Egyptological Seminar* 4 (1982), pp. 5-23.

Albertini, L., *The Origins of the War of 1914* (3 vols.; London: Oxford University Press, 1965–67).

Albright, William F., 'The History of Palestine and Syria', *JQR* 24 (1934), pp. 363-76.

—'New Light from Egypt on the Chronology and the History of Israel and Judah', *BASOR* 130 (1953), pp. 4-11.

—*From the Stone Age to Christianity: Monotheism and the Historical Process* (Garden City, NY: Doubleday, 2nd edn, 1957).

—'Recent Progress in Palestinian Archaeology: Samaria-Sebaste III and Hazor I', *BASOR* 150 (1958), pp. 21-25.

—'Beit Mirsim, Tell', *NEAEHL*, I, pp. 177-80.

Alt, Albrecht, *Der Gott der Väter: Ein Beitrag zur Vorgeschichte der israelitischen Religion* (BWANT, 48; Stuttgart: Kohlhammer, 1929); ET 'The God of the Fathers', in Albrecht Alt, *Essays on Old Testament History and Religion* (Oxford: Basil Blackwell, 1966), pp. 1-77.

Alter, Robert, 'The Masada Complex', *Commentary* 56 (July 1973), pp. 19-24.

Amar, Z., 'Agricultural Products in the Lachish Reliefs', *Beit Mikra* 159 (1999), pp. 350-56.

—'Agricultural Realia in the Lachish Reliefs', *UF* 31 (1999), pp. 1-12.

Amit, Y., 'The Role of Prophecy and the Prophets in the Teaching of Chronicles', *Beth Mikra* 28 (1982-83), pp. 113-33 (Heb.).

Anbar, Moshe, "'*Kai pou eisin oi theoi tēs choras Samareias* 'et où sont les dieux du pays de Samarie?'", *BN* 51 (1990), pp. 7-8.

Anderson, Graham, *Ancient Fiction: The Novel in the Graeco-Roman World* (London/Sydney: Croom Helm; Totowa, NJ: Barnes & Noble, 1984).

Ankersmit, F.R., *Narrative Logic: A Semantical Analysis of the Historian's Language* (Den Haag: Mouton, 1983).

Avi-Yonah, Michael and Amos Kloner, 'Mareshah (Marisa)', *NEAEHL*, III, pp. 948-52.

Avi-Yonah, Michael and Ephraim Stern (eds.), *Encyclopedia of Archaeological Excavations in the Holy Land* (Oxford: Oxford University Press, 1975–78).

Ayalon, Etan, 'Trial Excavation of Two Iron Age Strata at Tel 'Eton', *TA* 12 (1985), pp. 54-62.

Balcer, J.M., *Herodotus and Bisitun: Problems in Ancient Persian Historiography* (Historia Einzelschriften, 49; Stuttgart: Steiner, 1987).

Baltzer, Dieter, 'Harran nach 610 "medisch"? Kritische Überprüfung einer Hypothese', *WO* 7 (1973), pp. 68-95.

Barkay, Gabriel, 'The Iron Age II–III', in Ben-Tor (ed.), *The Archaeology of Ancient Israel*, pp. 302-73.

Barkay, Gabriel and Andrew G. Vaughn, '*Lmlk* and Official Seal Impressions from Tel Lachish', *TA* 23 (1996), pp. 61-74.

Barnett, R.D., 'The Siege of Lachish', *IEJ* 8 (1958), pp. 161-64.

—*Illustrations of Old Testament History* (London: British Museum, 1966).

—'Ezekiel and Tyre', *Eretz-Israel* 9 (1969), pp. 6-13.

—'Lachish, Ashkelon and the Camel: a disscussion of its use in Southern Palestine', in J.N. Tubb (ed.), *Palestine in the Bronze and Iron Ages. Papers in Honour of Olga Tufnell* (Institute of Archaeology, Occational Publications, 11; London: Institute of Archaeology, 1985), pp. 15-30.

Barnett, R.D., Erika Bleibtreu and G. Turner, *Sculptures from the Southwest Palace of Sennacherib at Nineveh* (2 vols.; London: British Museum, 1998).

Barstad, Hans M., *The Myth of the Empty Land: A Study in the History and Archaeology of Judah during the 'Exilic' Period* (Symbolae Osloenses, 28; Oslo/Cambridge, MA: Scandinavian University Press, 1996).

Barth, Hermann, *Die Jesaja-Worte in der Josiazeit* (WMANT, 48; Neukirchen–Vluyn: Neukirchen Verlag, 1977).

Barthélemy, Dominique, *Critique textuelle de l'Ancien Testament. 1. Josué, Juges, Ruth, Samuel, Rois, Chroniques, Esdras, Néhémie, Esther* (OBO 50/1; Fribourg: Éditions Universitaires; Göttingen: Vanderhoeck & Ruprecht, 1982).

Bates, Robert D., 'Assyria and Rebellion in the Annals of Sennacherib: An Analysis of Sennacherib's Treatment of Hezekiah', *NEASB* 44 (1999), pp. 39-61.

Baumgartner, Walter, 'Herodots babylonische und assyrische Nachrichten', in *idem, Zum Alten Testament und seiner Umwelt: Ausgewählte Aufsätze* (Leiden: E.J. Brill, 1959), pp. 282-331, originally published in *Archiv Orientalní* 18 (1950), pp. 69-106.

Beaulieu, Paul-Alain, *The Reign of Nabonidus, King of Babylon 556–539 B.C.* (YNER, 10; New Haven, CT: Yale University Press, 1989).

—'An Episode in the Fall of Babylonia to the Persians', *JNES* 52 (1993), pp. 243-61.

Becker, U. *Jesaja—von der Botschaft zum Buch* (FRLANT, 178; Göttingen: Vandenhoeck & Ruprecht, 1997).

Beckerath, J. von, 'Ägypten und der Feldzug Sanheribs im Jahre 701 v.Chr.', *UF* 24 (1992), pp. 3-8.

—'Die Nilstandsinschrift von 3. Jahr Schebikhus am Kai von Kamat', *GM* 136 (1993), pp. 7-9.

Becking, Bob, *The Fall of Samaria: An Historical and Archaeological Study* (SHANE, 2; Leiden: E.J. Brill, 1992), pp. 51-56; (ET and updating of ch. 2 of the doctoral thesis, *De ondergang van Samaria: Historische, exegetischee en theologische opmerkingen bij II Koningen 17* [ThD, Utrecht Fakulteit de Godgeleerheit, 1985]).

—'Ezra's Re-enactment of the Exile,' in Lester L. Grabbe (ed.), *Leading Captivity Captive: 'The Exile' as History and Ideology* (JSOTSup, 278; ESHM, 2; Sheffield: Sheffield Academic Press, 1998), pp. 40-61.

—'Babylonisches Exil', in H.D. Betz *et al.* (eds.), *Religion in Geschichte und Gegenwart: Handwörterbuch für Theologie und Religionswissenschaft* (Tübingen: J.C.B. Mohr [Paul Siebeck] Verlag, 1998).

—'No More Grapes from the Vineyard? A Plea for a Historical-Critical Approach in the Study of the Old Testament', in André Lemaire and Magne Saebø (ed.), *Congress Volume: Oslo, 1998* (VTSup, 80; Leiden: E.J. Brill, 2000), pp. 123-41.

Ben-Tor, Amnon (ed.), *The Archaeology of Ancient Israel* (trans. R. Greenberg; New Haven, CT: Yale University Press, 1992).

Ben Zvi, Ehud, 'Who Wrote the Speech of Rabshakeh and When?' *JBL* 109 (1990), pp. 79-92.

—'A Sense of Proportion: An Aspect of the Theology of the Chronicler', *SJOT* 9 (1995), pp. 37-51.

—'Inclusion in and Exclusion from Israel as Conveyed by the Use of the Term "Israel" in Post-monarchic Biblical Texts', in S.W. Hollaway and Lowell K. Handy (eds.), *The Pitcher is Broken: Memorial Essays for Gösta W. Ahlström* (JSOTSup, 190; Sheffield: Sheffield Academic Press, 1995), pp. 95-149.

—'The Chronicler as a Historian: Building Texts', in Patrick M. Graham, Kenneth G. Hoglund and Steven L. McKenzie (eds.), *The Chronicler as Historian* (JSOTSup, 238; Sheffield: Sheffield Academic Press, 1997).

—*Micah* (FOTL, 21b; Grand Rapids, MI: Eerdmans, 2000).

—'About Time: Observations about the Construction of Time in the Book of Chronicles', *HBT* 22 (2000), pp. 17-31.

—'Shifting the Gaze: Historiographic Constraints in Chronicles and their Implications', in J.A. Dearman and M.P. Graham (eds.), *The Land that I Will Show You: Essays on the History and Archaeology of the Ancient Near East in Honor of J. Maxwell Miller* (JSOTSup, 343; Sheffield: Sheffield Academic Press, 2001), pp. 38-60.

Biran, Avraham and Joseph Naveh, 'An Aramaic Stele Fragment from Tel Dan', *IEJ* 43 (1993), pp. 81-98.

—'The Tel Dan Inscription: A New Fragment', *IEJ* 45 (1995), pp. 1-18.

Black, J. 'The New Year Ceremonies in Ancient Babylon: "Taking Bel by the Hand" and a Cultic Picnic', *Religion* 11 (1981), pp. 39-59.

Bleibtreu, Erika, *Die Flora der neuassyrischen Palastreliefs: Eine Üntersuchung zu den Orthostatenreliefs des 9.-7. Jahrhunderts v. Chr.* (WZKM Sonderband, 1; Vienna: Institut für Orientalistik der Universität Wien, 1980).

—'Kulthandlungen im Zeitlager Sanheribs', in I. Seybold (ed.), *Meqor Hajjim* (Georg Molin Festschrift; Graz: Styria, 1983), pp. 43-48.

Blenkinsopp, Joseph, *Isaiah 1–39: A New Translation with Introduction and Commentary* (AB, 19; New York: Doubleday, 2000).

Borger, Rykle, *Die Inschriften Esarhaddons Königs von Assyrien* (AfO Beiheft, 9; Osnabrück: Biblio Verlag, 2nd edn, 1967).

—*Babylonisch-assyrische Lesestücke* (Rome: Pontificium Institutum Biblicum; 2nd edn, 1979).

—*Beiträge zum Inschriftenwerk Assurbanipals: Die Prismenklassen A, B, C = K, D, E, F, G, H, J und T sowie andere Inschriften* (mit einem Beitrag von Andreas Fuchs; Wiesbaden: Otto Harrassowitz, 1996).

Borger, Rykle and Hayim Tadmor, 'Zwei Beiträge zur alttestamentliche Wissenschaft aufgrund der Inschriften Tiglathpileser III', *ZAW* 94 (1984), pp. 244-51.

Börker-Klähn, J., *Altvorderasiatische Bildstelen und vergleichbare Felsreliefs* (Baghdader Forschungen, 4; Mainz: Philipp von Zabern, 1982).

Borowski, Oded, 'The Biblical Identity of Tel Halif', *BA* (1988), pp. 21-27.

Bowra, C.M., *Homer* (Classical Life and Letters; New York: Charles Scribner's Sons; London: Routledge, 1972).

Brandl, Baruch, ''Erani, Tell', in Meyers (ed.), *The Oxford Encyclopedia of Archaeology in the Near East*, pp. 256-58.

Braudel, F., *La Méditeraneé et le Monde Méditerranéen à l'époque de Philippe II* (Paris: Collin, 1949).

Braun, M., *History and Romance in Greco-Oriental Literature* (Oxford: Basil Blackwell, 1938).

Bright, John, *A History of Israel* (Philadelphia: Westminster Press, 1959).

Brinkman, John A., 'Merodach-Baladan II' in Robert D. Briggs and John A. Brinkman (eds.), *Studies Presented to A. Leo Oppenheim* (Chicago: The Oriental Institute of the University of Chicago, 1964), pp. 6-53.

—*A Political History of Post-Kassite Babylonia 1158–722 B.C.* (AnOr, 43; Rome: Pontifical Biblical Institute, 1968).

—'The Babylonian Chronicle Revisited', in Tzvi Abusch, John Huehnergard and Piotr Steinkeller (eds.), *Lingering over Words: Studies in Ancient Near Eastern Literature in Honor of William L. Moran* (HSS, 37; Atlanta: Scholars Press, 1990), pp. 73-104.

Broshi, Magen, 'Judeideh, Tell', *NEAEHL*, III, pp. 837-38.

Broshi, M. and Israel Finkelstein, 'The Population of Palestine in Iron Age II', *BASOR* 287 (1992), pp. 47-60.

Brown, Truesdell S., *The Greek Historians* (Civilization and Society; Lexington, MA: D.C. Heath, 1973).

Budge, E.A.W., *A Guide to the Babylonian and Assyrian Antiquities, British Museum* (London: The Trustees of the British Museum, 1922).

Bunimovitz, S. and Zvi Lederman, 'Beth-Shemesh', *NEAEHL*, I, pp. 249-53.

Burney, Charles F., *Notes on the Hebrew Text of the Books of Kings with an Introduction and Appendix* (Oxford: Clarendon Press, 1903; repr. New York: Ktav, 1970).

Burstein, Stanley Mayer, *The Babyloniaca of Berossus* (Sources and Monographs on the

Ancient Near East: Sources from the Ancient Near East 1.5; Malibu, CA: Undena Publications, 1978).

Calmeyer, P., 'Zur Genese altiranischer Motive. II: Der leere Wagen', *AMI* 7 (1974), pp. 49-77.

Camp, L., *Hiskija und Hiskijabild: Analyse und Interpretation von 2 Kön 18-20* (MTA, 9; Altenberge: Telos Verlag, 1990).

Campbell, A.F., 'Homer and Ugaritic Literature', *AbrN* 5 (1964–65), pp. 29-56.

Cathcart, K.J., 'Edward Hincks (1792–1866): A Biographical Essay', in K.J. Cathcart (ed.), *The Edward Hincks Bicentenary Lectures* (Dublin: The Department of Near Eastern Languages, University College, 1994), pp. 1-29.

Cazelles, Henri, 'La guerre Syro-Ephraïmite dans le contexte de la politique internationale', in D. Garrone and F. Israel (eds.), *Storia e tradizione di Israele: Scritti in onore di J. Alberto Soggin* (Brescia: Paideia Editrice, 1991), pp. 31-48.

Childs, Brevard S., *Isaiah and the Assyrian Crisis* (SBT, Second Series 3; London: SCM Press, 1967).

Clements, Ronald E., *Isaiah and the Deliverance of Jerusalem: A Study of the Interpretation of Prophecy in the Old Testament* (JSOTSup, 13; Sheffield: JSOT Press, 1980).

—'The Politics of Blasphemy: Zion's God and the Threat of Imperialism', in Ingo Kottsieper, Jürgen van Oorschot, Diethard Römheld and Harald Martin Wahl (eds.), *'Wer ist wie du, HERR, unter den Göttern?' Studien zur Theologie und Religionsgeschichte Israels für Otto Kaiser zum 70. Geburtstag* (Göttingen: Vandenhoeck & Ruprecht, 1994), pp. 231-46.

Cogan, Mordechai, *Imperialism and Religion: Assyria, Judah and Israel in the Eighth and Seventh Centuries B.C.E.* (SBLMS, 19; Missoula, MT: Scholars Press, 1974).

—'Sennacherib', in W.W. Hallo (ed.), *The Context of Scripture*. II. *Monumental Inscriptions from the Biblical World* (Leiden: E.J. Brill, 2000), pp. 304-305.

—'Sennacherib's Siege of Jerusalem, Once or Twice?', *BARev* 27/1 (January/February 2001), pp. 40-45, 69.

Cogan, Mordechai and Hayim Tadmor, *II Kings: A New Translation with Introduction and Commentary* (AB, 11; Garden City, NY: Doubleday, 1988).

Coles, R.A. and M.W. Haslam (eds.), *The Oxyrhynchus Papyri, Part XLVII* (London: Egypt Exploration Society, 1980).

Cross, Frank M., Jr, 'Judean Stamps', *Eretz-Israel* 9 (1969), pp. 20-27.

Dalley, Stephanie, 'A Stela of Adad-nirari III and Nergal-ereš from Tell al Rimah', *Iraq* 30 (1968), pp. 139-53.

Davies, G.I., 'Tell ed-Duweir = Ancient Lachish: A Response to G.W. Ahlström', *PEQ* 114 (1982), pp. 25-28.

De Odorico, M., *The Use of Numbers and Quantifications in the Assyrian Royal Inscriptions* (SAAS 3; Helsinki: The Neo-Assyrian Text Corpus Project, 1995).

Dearman, Andrew (ed.), *Studies in the Mesha Inscription and Moab* (ASOR/SBL Archaeology and Biblical Studies 2; Atlanta: Scholars Press, 1989).

Dever, William G., 'Archaeology, Material Culture and the Early Monarchical Period in Israel', in D.V. Edelman (ed.), *The Fabric of History: Text, Artifact and Israel's Past* (JSOTSup, 127; Sheffield: Sheffield Academic Press, 1991), pp. 103-15.

—'Social Structure in Palestine in the Iron II Period on the Eve of Destruction', in Thomas E. Levy (ed.), *The Archaeology of Society in the Holy Land* (New Approaches in Anthropological Archaeology; London: Leicester University Press, 2nd edn, 1998), pp. 416-31.

—'Gezer', *NEAEHL*, II, pp. 496-506.

—'Gezer', in Meyer (ed.), *The Oxford Encyclopedia of Archaeology in the Near East*, pp. 396-400.

—'Beth-Shemesh', in Meyer (ed.), *The Oxford Encyclopedia of Archaeology in the Near East*, pp. 311-12.

—'Beit Mirsim, Tell', *ABD*, I, pp. 648-49.

Dijkstra, M., 'Chronological Problems of the Eighth Century BCE: A New Proposal for Dating the Samaria Ostraca', in J.C. de Moor and H.F. van Rooy (eds.), *Past, Present, Future: The Deuteronomistic History and the Prophets* (OTS, 45: Leiden: E.J. Brill, 2000), pp. 76-87.

Dion, P.E., 'Sennacherib's Expedition to Palestine', *Bulletin of the Canadian Society of Biblical Studies* 48 (1988), pp. 3-25.

Donner, Herbert, *Israel unter den Völkern* (VTSup, 11; Leiden: E.J. Brill, 1964).

—*Geschichte des Volkes Israel und seiner Nachbarn in Grundzügen, Teil 2: Von der Königszeit bis zu Alexander dem Großen, mit einem Ausblick auf die Geschichte des Judentums bis Bar Kochba* (Grundrisse zum Alten Testament, Das Alte Testament Deutsch Ergänzungreihe 8/2, Göttingen: Vandenhoeck & Ruprecht, 1995).

Dougherty, Raymond P., 'Sennacherib and the Walled Cities of Judah', *JBL* 49 (1930), pp. 160-71.

Driel, G. van, *The Cult of Aššur* (Studia Semitica Neerlandica, 13; Assen: Van Gorcum, 1969).

Driver, Godfrey R., 'Geographical Problems', *Eretz-Israel* 5 (1958), pp. 16-20.

Dyck, Jonathan E., *The Theocratic Ideology of the Chronicler* (Biblical Interpretation Series, 33; Leiden: E.J. Brill, 1998).

Eddy, Samuel K., *The King Is Dead: Studies in the Near Eastern Resistance to Hellenism 334–31 B.C.* (Lincoln, NB: University of Nebraska, 1961).

Edelman, Diana V., 'What if We Had No Accounts of Sennacherib's Third Campaign or the Palace Reliefs Depicting the Capture of Lachish?', in J. Cheryl Exum (ed.), *Virtual History and the Bible* (Leiden: E.J. Brill, 2000), pp. 88-103.

Eilers, Wilhelm, *Semiramis: Entstehung und Nachhall einer altorientalischen Sage* (Sitzungsberichte der Österreichische Akademie der Wissenschaften, Phil.-hist. Klasse 274; 2. Abhandlung; Vienna: Kommissionsverlag der Österreichischen Akademie der Wissenschaften, 1971).

Elayi, Josette, 'Les relations entre les cites phéniciennes et l'empire assyrien sous le règne de Sennachérib', *Semitica* 35 (1985), pp. 19-26.

Eph'al, Israel, 'The Assyrian Siege Ramp at Lachish: Military and Lexical Aspects', *TA* 11 (1984), pp. 60-70.

Eshel, Hanan, 'A *lmlk* Stamp from Beth-El', *IEJ* 39 (1989), pp. 60-62.

Evans, C.D., 'Judah's Foreign Policy from Hezekiel to Josiah', in *Scripture in Context: Essays on the Comparative Method* (PTMS, 34; Pittsburgh: The Pickwick Press, 1980), pp. 165-66.

Evans, Richard J., *In Defence of History* (London: Granta Books, 1997).

Eynikel, Erik, *The Reform of King Josaiah and the Composition of the Deuteronomistic History* (OTS, 33; Leiden: E.J. Brill, 1996).

Fales, Frederico M. (ed.), *Assyrian Royal Inscriptions: New Horizons in Literary, Ideological, and Historical Analysis (Papers of a Symposium Held in Centona [Siena] June 26-28, 1980)* (OAC, 17; Rome: Istituto per l'Oriente, 1981).

—'Mari: An Additional Note on "Raṣappu and Hatallu"', *SAAB* 6 (1992), pp. 105-107.

Faust, Avraham, 'A Note on Hezekiah's Tunnel and the Siloam Inscription', *JSOT* 90 (2000), pp. 3-11.

Feldman, Louis H., 'Josephus's Portrait of Hezekiah', *JBL* 111 (1992), pp. 597-610.

Finkelstein, Israel, 'Penelope's Shroud Unravelled: Iron II Date of Gezer's Outer Wall Established', *TA* 21 (1994), pp. 276-82.

—'The Rise of Jerusalem and Judah: The Missing Link', in Michael D. Coogan, J. Cheryl Exum and Lawrence E. Stager (eds.), *Scripture and Other Artifacts: Essays on the Bible and Archaeology in Honor of Philip J. King* (Louisville, KY: Westminster/John Knox Press, 1994), pp. 169-87.

—'The Rise of Jerusalem and Judah: The Missing Link', *Levant* 32 (2001), pp. 105-15.

Finkelstein, Israel and Nadav Na'aman (eds.), *From Nomadism to Monarchy: Archaeological and Historical Aspects of Early Israel* (Jerusalem: Israel Exploration Society, 1994).

Finkelstein, Israel and Neil Asher Silberman, *The Bible Unearthed: Archaeology's New Vision of Ancient Israel and the Origin of the Sacred Texts* (New York: Free Press, 2001).

Finkelstein, J.J., 'Mesopotamian Historiography', *PAPS* 107 (1963), pp. 461-72.

Forrer, Emil, *Die Provinzeinteilung des assyrischen Reiches* (Leipzig: Hinrichs, 1920).

Frahm, E., *Einleitung in die Sanherib-Inschriften* (AfO Beiheft, 26; Horn: Selbstverlag des Instituts für Orientalistik der Universität Wien, Druck F. Berger & Söhne, 1997).

Frame, G., 'The Inscription of Sargon II at Tang-i Var', *Or* 68 (1999), pp. 31-57.

Fritz, Volkmar and Philip R. Davies (eds.), *The Origins of the Ancient Israelite States* (JSOTSup, 228; Sheffield: Sheffield Academic Press, 1996).

Fuchs, Andreas, *Die Inschriften Sargons II. aus Khorsabad* (Göttingen: Cuvillier Verlag, 1994).

Fuchs, Andreas (ed.), *Die Annalen des Jahres 711 v. Chr. nach Prismenfragmenten aus Ninive und Assur* (SAAS, 8; Helsinki: Neo-Assyrian Text Corpus Project, 1998).

Fuchs, A. and S. Parpola, *The Correspondence of Sargon II. III. Letters from Babylonia and the Eastern Provinces* (SAA, 15; Helsinki: Helsinki University Press, 2001).

Gadd, C.J. *The Stones of Assyria: The Surviving Remains of Assyrian Sculpture, their Recovery and their Original Position* (London: Chatto and Windus, 1936).

—'Inscribed Prisms of Sargon II from Nimrud', *Iraq* 16 (1954), pp. 173-201.

Galil, Gershon, 'Judah and Assyria in the Sargonic Period', *Zion* 57 (1992), pp. 111-33 (Heb.).

—'Conflicts between Assyrian Vassals', *SAAB* 6 (1992), pp. 55-63.

—*The Chronology of the Kings of Israel and Judah* (SHCANE, 9; Leiden: E.J. Brill, 1996).

Gallagher, W.R., *Sennacherib's Campaign to Judah* (SHCANE, 18; Leiden: E.J. Brill, 1999).

—'Assyrian Deportation Propaganda', *SAAB* 8 (1994), pp. 57-65.

—'Room I, Slabs 14-18 of Sennacherib's Palace: Not a Depiction of Tyre', *NABU* 1997/2, pp. 52-53.

Galling, K., *Biblisches Reallexikon* (HAT 1/1; Tübingen: J.C.B. Mohr [Paul Siebeck], 1937).

Garfinkel, Yosef, '2 Chronicles 11.5-10 Fortified Cities List and the *lmlk* Stamps—Reply to Nadav Na'aman', *BASOR* 271 (1988), pp. 69-73.

—'The *Eliakim Na'ar Yokan* Seal Impressions: Sixty Years of Confusion in Biblical Archaeological Research', *BA* 53 (1990), pp. 74-79.

Gaselee S., (transl.), *The Love Romances of Parthenius and Other Fragments* (LCL; Cambridge, MA: Harvard; London: Heinemann, 1916).

Gelb, I.J., 'Two Assyrian King Lists', *JNES* 13 (1954), pp. 209-30.

Gerardi, P., 'Epigraphs and Assyrian Palace Reliefs: the Development of the Epigraphic Text', *JCS* 40 (1988), pp. 1-35.

Gibson, John C.L., *Textbook of Syrian Semitic Inscriptions* (3 vols.; Oxford: Clarendon Press, 1975–82).

Gibson, Shimon, 'The Tell ej-Judeideh (Tel Goded) Excavations: A Re-appraisal Based on Archival Records in the Palestine Exploration Fund', *TA* 21 (1994), pp. 194-234.

Gill, Dan, 'How They Met: Geology Solves Mystery of Hezekiah's Tunnelers', *BARev* 20/4 (July/August 1994), pp. 20-33, 64.

Goldberg, Jeremy, 'Two Assyrian Campaigns against Hezekiah and Later Eighth Century Biblical Chronology', *Bib* 80 (1999), pp. 360-90.

Gonçalves, Francolino J., *L'expédition de Sennachérib en Palestine dans la littérature hébraïque ancienne* (EBib, 7; Louvain la-Neuve: Institut Orientaliste de l'Université Catholique de Louvain; Paris: Galbalda, 1986).

—'Senaquerib na Palestina et a tradiçao biblica. Da grande derrota de Judá à maravilhosa salvaçao de Jerusalén', *Didaskalia* 20 (1990), pp. 5-32.

Gould, John, *Herodotus* (London: Weidenfeld & Nicolson, 1989).

Grabbe, Lester L., *Leading Captivity Captive: 'The Exile' as History and Ideology* (JSOTSup, 278; ESHM, 2; Sheffield: Sheffield Academic Press, 1998).

—*Did Moses Speak Attic? Jewish Historiography and Scripture in the Hellenistic Period* (JSOTSup, 317; ESHM, 3; Sheffield: Sheffield Academic Press, 2001).

Grabbe, Lester L. (ed.), *Can a 'History of Israel' Be Written?* (JSOTSup, 245; ESHM, 1; Sheffield: Sheffield Academic Press, 1997).

Gray, John, *I and II Kings* (OTL; Philadelphia: Westminster, 2nd edn, 1970).

Grayson, A.K., 'Problematic Battles in Mesopotamian History', in H. G. Gütersbock and Th. Jacobsen (eds.), *Studies in Honor of Benno Landsberger on his Seventy-Fifth Birday, April 25, 1965* (Oriental Institute, Assyriological Studies, 16; Chicago: University of Chicago Press, 1965) 337-42.

—*Assyrian and Babylonian Chronicles* (TCS, 5; Locust Valley, NY: J.J. Augustin, 1975).

—'Königslisten und Chroniken', *RlA* 6, pp. 86-89.

Greenberg, Raphael, 'Beit Mirsim, Tell', *NEAEHL*, I, p. 180.

—'Beit Mirsim, Tell', in Meyers (ed.), *The Oxford Encyclopedia of Archaeology in the Near East*, I, pp. 295-97.

Greenfield, J.C. and B. Porten, *The Bisitun Inscription of Darius the Great: Aramaic Version* (Corpus Inscriptionum Iranicarum, Part I: Inscriptions of Ancient Iran. V. The Aramaic Versions of the Achaemenian Inscriptions, Texts I; London: Humphries, 1982).

Gressmann, H., *Altorientalische Bilder zum Alten Testament* (Berlin: W. de Gruyter, 1926).

Griffith, S.B., *Sun Tzu: The Art of Warfare* (Oxford: Clarendon Press, 3rd edn, 1971).

Gunneweg, A.H.J., *Geschichte Israels bis Bar Kochba* (ThW, 2; Stuttgart/Berlin/Köln: W. Kohlhammer, 3rd edn, 1979).

Hackett, Jo Ann, *et al.* 'Defusing Pseudo-Scholarship: The Siloam Inscription Ain't Hasmonean', *BARev* 23/2 (March/April 1997), pp. 41-50, 68.

Hägg, Tomas, *The Novel in Antiquity* (Oxford: Basil Blackwell, 1983); ET of *Den Antika Romanen* (Uppsala: Carmina, 1980).

Hallo, William W. (ed.), *The Context of Scripture: Volume I Canonical Compositions from the Biblical World* (Leiden: E.J. Brill, 1997).

—'Jerusalem under Hezekiah: an Assyriological Perspective', in Lee I. Levine (ed.), *Jerusalem: Its Sanctity and Centrality to Judaism, Christianity, and Islam* (New York: Continuum; London: Cassell, Petter, Galpin, 1999), pp. 36-50.

—*The Context of Scripture: Volume II Monumental Inscriptions from the Biblical World* (Leiden: E.J. Brill, 2000).

Halpern, Baruch, *David's Secret Demons: Messiah, Murderer, Traitor, King* (Grand Rapids, MI: Eerdmans, 2001).

Handlin, O., *Truth in History* (Cambridge, MA/London: Belknap Press, 1979).

Hardmeier, Christoph, *Prophetie im Streit vor dem Untergang Judas: Erzählkommunikative*

Studien zur Entstehungssituation der Jesaja- und Jeremiaerzählungen in II Reg 18–20 und Jer 37–40 (BZAW, 187; Berlin: W. De Gruyter, 1990).

Heinz, Susanna C., *Die Feldzugsdarstellungen des Neuen Reiches. Eine Bildanalyse* (Österreichische Akademie der Wissenschaften, Denkschriften der Gesamtakademie, 18; Untersuchungen der Zweigstelle Kairo des Österreichischen Archäologischen Instituts, 17; Wien: Verlag der Österreichische Akademie der Wissenschaften, 2001).

Hendel, Ronald S., 'The Date of the Siloam Inscription: A Rejoinder to Rogerson and Davies', *BA* 59 (1996), pp. 233-47.

Herzog, Ze'ev, *Archaeology of the City: Urban Planning in Ancient Israel and its Social Implications* (Tel Aviv University Monograph Series, 13; Tel Aviv: Tel Aviv University, 1997).

—'Beersheba', *NEAEHL*, I, pp. 167-73.

—'Beersheba', in Meyers (ed.), *The Oxford Encyclopedia of Archaeology in the Near East*, I, pp. 287-91.

—'Arad: Iron Age Period', in Meyers (ed.), *The Oxford Encyclopedia of Archaeology in the Near East*, I, pp. 174-76.

Herzog, Ze'ev, Miriam Aharoni, Anson F. Rainey and S. Moshkovitz, 'The Israelite Fortress at Arad', *BASOR* 254 (1984), pp. 1-34.

Hobbs, T.R., 'The "Fortresses of Rehoboam": Another Look', in Lewis M. Hopfe (ed.), *Uncovering Ancient Stones: Essays in Memory of H. Neil Richardson* (Winona Lake, IN: Eisenbrauns, 1994), pp. 41-64.

Holladay, Carl A., *Fragments from Hellenistic Jewish Authors. I. Historians* (SBLTT, 20; Pseudepigrapha Series, 10; Atlanta: Scholars Press, 1983).

Holladay, J.S., Jr, 'Of Sherds and Strata: Contributions toward an Understanding of the Archaeology of the Divided Monarchy', in Frank M. Cross, Werner E. Lemke and Patrick D. Miller (eds.), *Magnalia Dei, The Mighty Acts of God: Essays on the Bible and Archaeology in Memory of G. Ernest Wright* (Garden City, NY: Doubleday, 1976), pp. 253-93.

Holloway, Steven W., 'Harran: Cultic Geography in the Neo-Assyrian Empire and its Implications for Sennacherib's "Letter to Hezekiah" in 2 Kings', in Steven W. Holloway and Lowell K. Handy (eds.), *The Pitcher Is Broken: Memorial Essays for Gösta W. Ahlström* (JSOTSup, 190; Sheffield: Sheffield Academic Press, 1995), pp. 276-314.

Hölscher, L., 'The New Annalistic: A Sketch of a Theory of History', *History and Theory* 36 (1997), pp. 317-35.

Honor, Leo Lazarus, *Sennacherib's Invasion Palestine: A Critical Source Study* (Contributions to Oriental History and Philology, 12; New York: Columbia, 1926).

Hooker, P.K., *The Kingdom of Hezekiah: Judah in the Geo-Political Context of the Late Eighth Century BCE* (Ann Arbor, MI: University Microfilm, 1993).

Horn, Siefried H., 'Did Sennacherib Campaign Once or Twice against Hezekiah?' *AUSS*, 4 (1966), pp. 1-28.

Hrouda, B., *Die Kulturgeschichte des assyrischen Flachbildes* (Saarbrücker Beiträge zur Altertumskunde, 2; Bonn: Rudolf Habelt, 1965).

Irvine, Stuart A., *Isaiah, Ahaz and the Syro-Ephraimite Crisis* (SBLDS, 123; Atlanta: Scholars Press, 1990).

Jacoby, Felix, *Fragmente der griechischen Historiker: Dritter Teil Geschichte von Städten und Völkern (Horographie und Ethnographie), C Autoren über Einzelne Länder Nr. 608a-856* (Leiden: E.J. Brill, 1958).

Jacoby, R., 'The Representation and Identification of Cities on Assyrian Reliefs', *IEJ* 41 (1991), pp. 112-31.

Janssen, J.M.A., 'Que sait-on actuellement du Pharaon Taharqa?', *Bib* 34 (1953), pp. 23-43.

Japhet, Sara, *I and II Chronicles: A Commentary* (OTL; London: SCM; Louisville, KY: Westminster/John Knox Press, 1993).

Jenkins, A.K., 'Hezekiah's Fourteenth Year: A New Interpretation of 2 Kings xviii 13-xix 37', *VT* 26 (1976), pp. 284-98.

Jenkins, K., 'A Postmodern Reply to Perez Zagoria', *History and Theory*, 39 (2000), pp. 81-200.

Jeremias, Alfred, *The Old Testament in the Light of the Ancient East: Manual of Biblical Archaeology* (2 vols.; Theological Translation Library; London: Williams & Norgate, 1911); (revised edition of *Das Alte Testament im Lichte des Alten Orients: Handbuch zur biblisch-orientalischen Altertumskunde* [Leipzig: J.C. Hinrichs, 2nd edn, 1906]).

Jones, G.W. *1 and 2 Kings* (NCB; Grand Rapids, MI: Eerdmans, 1984).

Kalimi, Isaac, *The Book of Chronicles: Historical Writing and Literary Devices* (Jersualem: Mosad Bialik, 2000) (Heb.).

—'History of Interpretation: The Book of Chronicles in Jewish Tradition from Daniel to Spinoza', *RB* 105 (1998), pp. 5-51.

Kapera, Zdzisłav, *The Rebellion of Yamani in Ashdod* (Kraków: Enigma Press, 1978).

Kautsky, K., *Die deutschen Dokumente zum Kriegsausbruch: Van Attentat in Serajevo bis zum Eintreffen der serbischen Antwortnote in Berlin* (Berlin: Deutsche Verlagsgesellschaft für Politik und Geschichte, 1927).

Keel, Othmar and Christoph Uehlinger, 'Der Assyrerkönig Salmanassar III. und Jehu von Israel auf dem Schwarzen Obelisken', *ZKT* 116 (1994), pp. 391-420.

—*Göttinnen, Götter und Gottessymbole. Neue Erkenntnisse zur Religionsgeschichte Kanaans und Israels aufgrund bis lang unerschlossener ikonographischer Quellen* (Quaestiones disputatae, 134; Freiburg i. Br.: Herder, 5th edn, 2001).

Kees, Hermann, 'Sesostris', in Georg Wissowa and Wilhelm Kroll (eds.), *Paulys Real-Encyclopädie der classischen Altertumswissenschaft* (Stuttgart: J.B. Metzlersche Verlagbuchhandlung, 1923), 2ter Reihe (R-Z), II, cols. 1862-76.

Kelm, George L., 'Timnah—A City of Conflict within the Traditional Buffer Zone of the Shephelah', *BAIAS* (1984–85), pp. 54-61.

Kelm, George L. and Amihai Mazar, 'Three Seasons of Excavations at Tel Batash—Biblical Timnah: Preliminary Report', *BASOR* 248 (1982), pp. 1-36.

—'Tel Batash (Timnah) Excavations: Second Preliminary Report (1981–1983)', BASORSup 23 (1985), pp. 93-120.

—'Tel Batash (Timnah) Excavations: Third Preliminary Report, 1984–1989', BASORSup 27 (1991), pp. 47-67.

—*Timnah: A Biblical City in the Sorek Valley* (Winona Lake, IN: Eisenbrauns, 1995).

Kent, Roland G., *Old Persian* (AOS, 33; New Haven: American Oriental Society, 2nd edn, 1953).

Kenyon, Kathleen M., 'The Date of the Destruction of Iron Age Beer-Sheba', *PEQ* 108 (1976), pp. 63-64.

Keulen, Percy S.F. van, *Manasseh through the Eyes of the Deuteronomists: The Manasseh Account (2 Kings 21:1-18) and the Final Chapters of the Deuteronomistic History* (OTS, 38; Leiden: E.J. Brill, 1996).

Kislev, M., 'Sycamores in the Lachish Reliefs', in J. Schwartz, Z. Amar and I. Ziffer (eds.), *Jerusalem and Eretz Israel* (Arie Kindler Volume; Bar-Ilan: The Ingeborg Rennert Center for Jerusalem Studies and Tel Aviv: Eretz Israel Museum, 2000), pp. 23-30.

Kitchen, Kenneth A., 'Egypt, the Levant and Assyria in 701 BC', in Manfred Görg (ed.), *Fontes atque Pontes: Eine Festgabe für Hellmut Brunner* (Ägypten und Altes Testament, 5; Wiesbaden: Harrassowitz, 1983), pp. 243-53.

—*The Third Intermediate Period in Egypt (1100–650 BC)* (Warminster, Wilts.: Aris & Philips, 2nd edn, 1986).

Kloner, Amos, 'Masesha', in Meyers (ed.), *The Oxford Encyclopedia of Archaeology in the Near East*, III, pp. 412-13.

Knauf, E. Axel, 'From History to Interpretation', in Diana V. Edelman (ed.), *The Fabric of History: Text, Artifact and Israel's Past* (JSOTSup, 127; Sheffield: Sheffield Academic Press, 1991), pp. 26-64.

—'The "Low Chronology" and How Not to Deal with It', *BN* 101 (2000), pp. 56-63.

—'Who Destroyed Megiddo VIA?' *BN* 103 (2000), pp. 30-35.

—'Hezekiah or Manasseh? A Reconsideration of the Siloam Tunnel and Inscription', *TA* 28 (2001), pp. 281-87.

—'History, Archaeology, and the Bible', *TZ* 57 (2001), pp. 262-68.

—'Who Destroyed Beersheba II?', in Ulrich Hubner and E.A. Knauf (eds.), *Kein Land für sich allein: Studien zum Kulturkontakt in Kanaan, Israel/Palästina und Ebirnâri für Manfred Weippert zum 65. Geburtstag* (OBO, 186; Freiburg: Universitatsverlag, 2002), pp. 181-95.

Knoppers, G.N., 'History and Historiography: The Royal Reforms', in M.P. Graham *et al.* (eds.), *The Chronicler as Historian* (JSOTSup, 238; Sheffield: Sheffield Academic Press, 1997).

Knudtzon, J.A., *Die El-Amarna Tafeln* (2 vols; VAB 2; Berlin: J.C. Hinrichs, 1908–15).

Kochavi, Moshe, 'Khirbet Rabûd = Debir', *TA* 1 (1974), pp. 2-33.

—'Rabud, Khirbet', in Meyer (ed.), *The Oxford Encyclopedia of Archaeology in the Near East*, IV, p. 401.

—'Rabud, Khirbet', *NEAEHL*, IV, p. 1252.

Konkel, August H., 'The Sources of the Story of Hezekiah in the Book of Isaiah', *VT* 43 (1993), pp. 462-82.

König, Friedrich Wilhelm, *Die Persika des Ktesias von Knidos* (Archiv für Orientforschung Beiheft, 18; Graz: Archiv für Orientforschung, 1972).

Kooij, Arie van der, 'Das assyrische Heer vor den Mauern Jerusalems im Jahr 701 v. Chr.', *ZDPV* 102 (1986), pp. 93-109.

—'The Story of Hezekiah and Sennacherib (2 Kings 18–19): A Sample of Ancient Historiography', in J.C. de Moor and H.F. van Rooy (eds.), *Past, Present, Future: The Deuteronomistic History and the Prophets* (OTS, 44; Leiden: E.J. Brill, 2000), pp. 107-19.

Kuan, Jeffrey Kah-jin, *Neo-Assyrian Historical Inscriptions and Syria-Palestine: Israelite/ Judean-Tyrian-Damascene Political and Commercial Relations in the Ninth-Eighth Centuries BCE* (JDD Series, 1; Bible and Literature, 1; Hong Kong: Alliance Bible Seminary, 1995).

Kuhrt, Amélie, 'Berossus *Babyloniaka* and Seleucid Rule in Babylonia', in Amélie Kuhrt and Susan Sherwin-White (eds.), *Hellenism in the East* (London: Gerald Duckworth, 1987), pp. 32-56.

Kuhrt, Amélie and Susan Sherwin-White (eds.), *Hellenism in the East* (London: Gerald Duckworth, 1987).

Kwasman, T. *Neo-Assyrian Legal Documents in the Kouyunjik Collection of the British Museum* (Studia Pohl, Series maior; Rome: Pontifical Biblical Institute, 1988).

Laato, Antti, 'Hezekiah and the Assyrian Crisis in 701 B.C.', *SJOT* 2 (1987), pp. 49-68.

—'Assyrian Propaganda and the Falsification of History in the Royal Inscriptions of Sennacherib', *VT* 45 (1995), pp. 198-226.

Lamprichs, R., *Die Westexpansion des neuassyrischen Reiches: Eine Strukturanalyse* (AOAT, 239; Neukirchen–Vluyn: Neukirchener Verlag; Kevelaer: Butzon & Bercker, 1995).

Lance, H.D., 'The Royal Stamps and the Kingdom of Judah', *HTR* 64 (1971), pp. 315-32.

Lange, Kurt, *Sesostris: ein ägyptischer König in Mythos, Geschichte und Kunst* (Munich: Hirmer Verlag, 1954).

Laqueur, R., 'Manethon', in Georg Wissowa and Wilhelm Kroll (eds.), *Paulys Real-Encyclopädie der classischen Altertumswissenschaft* (Neue Bearbeitung; Stuttgart: J.B. Metzlersche Verlagbuchhandlung, 1930), XIV, cols. 1060-1101.

Lateiner, Donald, *The Historical Method of Herodotus* (Phoenix Supplement, 23; University of Toronto Press, 1989).

Lawrence, A., *Greek Aims of Fortification* (Oxford: Clarendon Press, 1979).

Layard, Austen Henry, *The Inscriptions in the Cuneiform Character from Assyrian Monuments* (London, 1851).

—*Discoveries among the Ruins of Nineveh and Babylon; with Travels in Armenia, Kurdistan and the Desert: Being the Result of a Second Expedition undertaken for the Trustees of the British Museum* (London: John Murray, 1853).

—*A Second Series of the Monuments of Nineveh; including Bas-Reliefs from the Palace of Sennacherib and Bronzes from the Ruins of Nimroud from Drawings made on the Spot, during a Second Expedition to Assyria* (London: J. Murray, 1853).

Lee, Thomas G., 'The Jasper Cylinder Seal of Aššurbanipal and Nabonidus' Making of Sîn's Statue', *RA* 87 (1993), pp. 131-36.

Leeuwen, C. van, 'Sanchérib devant Jérusalem', *OTS* 14 (1965), pp. 245-72.

Legendre, A., 'Lachis', *Dictionnaire de la Bible, Supplément*, IV (Paris: Letouzey et Ané, 1908), pp. 15-16, 23-26.

Lehmann-Haupt, C.F., 'Semiramis', in W.H. Roscher (ed.), *Ausführliches Lexikon der griechischen und römischen Mythologie* (Leipzig: Teubner, 1909–15), IV, cols. 678-702.

Lemche, Niels Peter, *Israel i dommertiden: En oversigt over diskussionen om Martin Noths 'Das System der Zwölf Stämme Israels'* (Tetst og Tolkning, 4; Copenhagen: C.E.G. Gad, 1972).

—*Early Israel: Anthropological and Historical Studies on the Israelite Society before the Monarchy* (VTSup, 37; Leiden: E.J. Brill, 1985).

—*Ancient Israel: A New History of Israelite Society* (The Biblical Seminar, 5; Sheffield: JSOT Press, 1988).

—'From Patronage Society to Patonage Society', in Volkmar Fritz and Philip R. Davies (ed.), *The Origins of the Ancient Israelite States* (JSOTSup, 228; Sheffield: Sheffield Academic Press, 1996), pp. 106-20.

—*The Israelites in History and Tradition* (Library of Ancient Israel; Louisville, KY: Westminster/John Knox Press, 1998).

—'Good and Bad in History: The Greek Connection', in Steven McKenzie and Thomas Römer (eds.), *Rethinking the Foundations: Historiography in the Ancient World and in the Bible: Essays in Honor of John Van Seters* (BZAW, 294; Berlin: W. de Gruyter, 2000), pp. 127-40.

Levine, Louis D., 'Sennacherib's Southern Front: 704–689 B.C.', *JCS* 34 (1982), pp. 28-55.

—'Preliminary Remarks on the Historical Inscriptions of Sennacherib', in H. Tadmor and M. Weinfeld (eds.), *History, Historiography and Interpretation: Studies in Biblical and Cuneiform Literatures* (The Hebrew University of Jerusalem, The Institute for Advanced Studies; Jerusalem: Magnes Press; Leiden: E.J. Brill, 1983), pp. 58-75.

Levy, Thomas E., 'Preface', in Levy (ed.), *The Archaeology of Society in the Holy Land* (New Approaches in Anthropological Archaeology; London: Leicester University Press, 2nd edn, 1998), pp. x-xvi.

Lewy, Hildegard, 'Nitokris-Naqî'a', *JNES* 11 (1952), pp. 264-86.

Lichtheim, Miriam, *Ancient Egyptian Literature* (3 vols.; Berkeley and Los Angeles: University of California, 1973-80).

Liverani, Mario, 'The Ideology of the Assyrian Empire', in Mogens Trolle Larsen (ed.), *Power and Propaganda: A Symposium on Ancient Empires* (Mesopotamia, 7: Copenhagen: Akademisk Forlag, 1979), pp. 297-317.

—'Critique of Variants and the Titulary of Sennacherib', in F.M. Fales (ed.), *Assyrian Royal Inscriptions: New Horizons in Literary, Ideological, and Historical Analysis, Papers of a Symposium Held in Cetona (Siena), June 26-28, 1980* (Orientis antiqui collectio, 17; Rome: Istituto per l'Oriente, 1981), pp. 253-57.

—'Raṣappu and Hatallu', *SAAB* 6 (1992), pp. 35-40.

Lloyd, Alan B. *Herodotus Book II: Commentary 99-182* (Etudes préliminaires aux religions orientales dan l'Empire romain, 43; Leiden: E.J. Brill, 1988).

Loewenstamm, Samuel E., 'Hena', *Encyclopaedia Biblica* 2 (Jerusalem: Bialik Institute, 1954), p. 852.

Loftus, E.R. and K. Ketcham, *The Myth of Repressed Memory* (New York: St. Martin's Griffin, 1994).

Long, Burke O., *2 Kings* (FOTL, 10; Grand Rapids, MI: Eerdmans, 1991).

Luce, A.A. and T.E. Jessop (eds.), *The Works of George Berkeley, Bishop of Cloyne* (Oxford: Clarendon Press, 1948-1957).

Luckenbill, D.D., *The Annals of Sennacherib* (OIP, 2; Chicago: University of Chicago Press, 1924).

Macadam, Miles Frederick Laming, *The Temples of Kawa: Oxford University Excavations in Nubia* (2 vols.; Oxford University Press, 1949).

Machinist, Peter, 'The *Rab Šāqēh* at the Wall of Jerusalem: Israelite Identity in the Face of the Assyrian "Other"', *Hebrew Studies* 41 (2000), pp. 151-68.

Madhloom, T., *The Chronology of Neo-Assyrian Art* (London: Athlone Press, 1970).

Maeir, A., 'The "Judahite" Swords from the "Lachish" Reliefs of Sennacherib', *Eretz-Israel* 25 (1996), pp. 210-14.

Manar, Dale W. and Gary A. Herion, 'Arad', *ABD*, I, pp. 331-36.

Mannheim, K., *Wissenssoziologie: Auswahl aus dem Werk* (Neuwied: Luchterhand, 1970).

Marcus, Michelle I., A Study of Types of Officials in Neo-Assyrian Reliefs: Their Identifying Attributes and their Possible Relationship to a Bureaucratic Hierarchy (unpublished PhD thesis, Columbia University, 1981).

—'Geography as Visual Ideology: Landscape, Knowledge, and Power in Neo-Assyrian Art', in M. Liverani (ed.), *Neo-Assyrian Geography* (Quaderni di Geografia Storica 5; Rome: Università di Roma 'La Sapienza', 1995), pp. 193-202.

Margalith, Othniel, 'Where Did the Philistines Come From?' *ZAW* 107 (1995), pp. 101-109.

Martin, R., 'Progress in Historical Studies', *History and Theory* 38 (1998), pp. 14-39.

Matthiae, P., *L'arte degli Assiri: Cultura e forma del rilievo storico* (Storia e società; Rome: Laterza, 1996).

Mayer, Walter, *Politik und Kriegskunst der Assyrer* (ALASPM, 9; Munich: Ugarit-Verlag, 1995).

—'Zypern und Ägäis aus der Sicht der Staaten Vorderasiens in der 1. Hälfte des 1. Jahrtausends', *UF* 28 (1996), pp. 463-84.

—'Nabonidus Herkunft', in M. Dietrich and O. Loretz (eds.), *DUBSAR ANTA-MEN: Studien zur Altorientalistik: Festschrift für Willem H. Ph. Römer* (AOAT, 253; Munich: Ugarit-Verlag, 1998), pp. 245-61.

Mazar, Amihai, *Archaeology of the Land of the Bible 10,000–586 B.C.E.* (New York: Doubleday; Cambridge: Lutterworth Press, 1993).

—'Batash, Tel', in Meyers (ed.), *The Oxford Encyclopedia of Archaeology in the Near East*, I, pp. 281-83.

—'Batash, Tel', *NEAEHL*, I, pp. 152-57.

—'Batash, Tell-el', *ABD* I, pp. 625-26.

Mazzoni, Stefania, 'Significato e ruolo del paesaggio nei rilievi di Sennacherib', *Contributi et Materiali di Archeologia Orientale* 4 (1992), pp. 151-66.

McKenzie, Steven L., *The Trouble with Kings: The Composition of the Book of Kings in the Deuteronomistic History* (VTSup, 42; Leiden: E.J. Brill, 1991).

Melville, Sarah C., *The Role of Naqia/Zakutu in Sargonid Politics* (SAAS, 9; Helsinki: The Neo-Assyrian Text Corpus Project, 1999).

Menzel. B., *Assyrische Tempel* (Studia Pohl, Series Maior, 10; Rome: Biblical Institute Press, 1981).

Meyers, Eric M. (editor-in-chief), *The Oxford Encyclopedia of Archaeology in the Near East* (5 vols.; Oxford: Oxford University Press, 1997).

Millard, A.R., 'Assyrian Royal Names in Biblical Hebrew', *JSS* 21 (1976), pp. 1-14.

—*The Eponyms of the Assyrian Empire 910–612 BC* (SAAS, 2; Helsinki: Neo-Assyrian Text Corpus Project, 1994).

—'Babylonian King Lists', in W.W. Hallo (ed.), *The Context of Scripture I* (Leiden: E.J. Brill, 1997).

Mitchell, T.C., *The Bible in the British Museum* (London: British Museum, 1988).

Mittmann, S., 'Hiskia und die Philister', *JNSL* 16 (1990), pp. 91-106.

Mommsen, H., I. Perlman and J. Yellin, 'The Provenience of the *lmlk* Jars', *IEJ* 34 (1984), pp. 89-113.

Montgomery, James A., *A Critical and Exegetical Commentary on the Books of Kings* (ed. H.S. Gehman; ICC; Edinburgh: T. & T. Clark, 1951).

—'Archival Data in the Books of Kings', *JBL* 53 (1934), pp. 46-52.

Na'aman, Nadav, 'Sennacherib's "Letter to God" on his Campaign to Judah', *BASOR* 214 (1974), pp. 25-39.

—'Sennacherib's Campaign to Judah and the Date of the *LMLK* Stamps', *VT* 29 (1979), pp. 60-86.

—'The Brook of Egypt and the Assyrian Policy on the Border of Egypt', *TA* 6 (1979), pp. 68-90.

—'The Inheritance of the Sons of Simeon', *ZDPV* 96 (1980), pp. 136-52

—'Hezekiah's Fortified Cities and the *LMLK* Stamps', *BASOR* 261 (1986), pp. 5-21.

—'Historical and Chronological Notes on the Kingdoms of Israel and Judah in the Eighth Century BC', *VT* 36 (1986), pp. 71-92.

—'The Date of 2 Chronicles 11.5-10—A Reply to Y. Garfinkel', *BASOR* 271 (1988), pp. 74-77.

—'The Kingdom of Judah under Josiah', *TA* 18 (1991), pp. 3-71.

—'Chronology and History in the Late Assyrian Empire (631–619 B.C.)', *ZA* 81 (1991), pp. 243-67.

—'Forced Participation in Alliances in the Course of the Assyrian Campaigns to the West', in M. Cogan and I. Eph'al (eds.), *Ah, Assyria! Studies in Assyrian History and Ancient Near Eastern Historiography Presented to Hayim Tadmor* (ScrH, 33; Jerusalem: Magnes Press, 1991), pp. 80-98.

—'The Historical Portion of Sargon II's Nimrud Inscription', *SAAB* 8 (1994), pp. 17-20.

—'Hezekiah and the Kings of Assyria', *TA* 21 (1994), pp. 235-54.

—'The Deuteronomist and Voluntary Servitude to Foreign Powers', *JSOT* 65 (1995), pp. 37-53.

—'The Debated Historicity of Hezekiah's Reform in the Light of Historical and Archaeological Research', *ZAW* 107 (1995), pp. 179-95.

—'Historiography, the Fashioning of the Collective Memory, and the Establishment of Historical Consciousness in Israel in the Late Monarchical Period', *Zion* 60 (1995), pp. 449-72.

—'Sources and Composition in the History of David', in V. Fritz and P.R. Davies (eds.), *The Origins of the Ancient Israelite States* (JSOTSup, 228; Sheffield: Sheffield Academic Press, 1996), pp. 170-86.

—'Sources and Composition in the History of Solomon', in L.K. Handy (ed.), *The Age of Solomon—Scholarship at the Turn of the Millennium* (Leiden: E.J. Brill, 1997), pp. 57-80.

—'Prophetic Stories as Sources for the Histories of Jehoshaphat and the Omrides', *Biblica* 78 (1997), pp. 153-73.

—'Sargon II and the Rebellion of the Cypriote Kings against Shilta of Tyre', *Or* 67 (1998), pp. 239-47.

—'Royal Inscriptions and the Histories of Joash and Ahaz, Kings of Judah', *VT* 48 (1998), pp. 333-49.

—'No Anthropomorphic Graven Image. Notes on the Assumed Anthropomorphic Cult Statues in the Temples of YHWH in the Pre-Exilic Period', *UF* 31 (1999), pp. 391-415.

—'The Contribution of Royal Inscriptions for a Re-evaluation of the Book of Kings as a Historical Source', *JSOT* 82 (1999), pp. 3-17.

—'New Light on Hezekiah's Second Prophetic Story (2 Kgs 19.9b-35)', *Biblica* 81 (2000), pp. 393-402.

Na'aman, Nadav and Ran Zadok, 'Sargon II's Deportations to Israel and Philistia (716–708 B.C.)', *JCS* 40 (1988), pp. 36-46.

—'Assyrian Deportations to the Province of Samerina in the Light of Two Cuneiform Tablets from Tel Hadid', *Tel Aviv* 27 (2000), pp. 159-88.

Nilsson, Martin P., *Homer and Mycenae* (Philadelphia: University of Pennsylvania, repr. 1972).

Noort, Ed, *Die Seevölker in Palästina* (Palaestina Antiqua, 8; Kampen: Kok Pharos, 1994).

Norin, Stig, 'The Age of the Siloam Inscription and Hezekiah's Tunnel', *VT* 48 (1998), pp. 37-48.

Noth, Martin, *The History of Israel* (revised trans.; London: A. & C. Black; New York: Harper and Row, 1960), pp. 266-69; (ET of *Geschichte Israels* [Göttingen: Vandenhoeck & Ruprecht, 1950]).

Oded, Bustenay, *War, Peace and Empire: Justification for War in Assyrian Royal Inscriptions* (Wiesbaden: Dr Ludwig Reichert Verlag, 1992).

—'History vis-à-vis Propaganda in the Assyrian Royal Inscriptions', *VT* 48 (1998), pp. 423-25.

Oppenheim, A.L., '"Siege-Documents" from Nippur', *Iraq* 17 (1955), pp. 69-89.

Orlinsky, Harry M., 'The Kings-Isaiah Recensions of the Hezekiah Story', *JGR* 30 (1930), pp. 33-49.

Page, Denys L., *History and the Homeric Iliad* (Berkeley and Los Angeles: University of California, 1959).

Parker, S.B., 'Did the Authors of the Book of Kings make use of Royal Inscriptions?', *VT* 50 (2000), pp. 74-76.

Parpola, Simo, 'The Murderer of Sennacherib', in B. Alster (ed.), *Death in Mesopotamia: Papers Read at the XXVIe Rencontre assyriologique international* (Mesopotamia: Copenhagen Studies in Assyriology, 8; Copenhagen: Akademisk Forlag, 1980), pp. 161-70.

Parrot, André, *Nineveh and the Old Testament* (Studies in Biblical Archaeology, 3; London: SCM Press, 1955), p. 55 (ET of *Ninive et l'Ancien Testament* [Neuchâtel: Delachaux et Niestlé, 2nd edn, 1955]).

Paterson, A., *Assyrian Sculptures: Palace of Sinacherib: Plates and Ground-Plan of the Palace* (Den Haag: Martinus Nijhoff, n.d. [1912–15]).

Perry, Ben Edwin, *The Ancient Romances: A Literary-Historical Account of their Origins* (Berkeley: University of California Press, 1967).

Person, Raymond E., *The Kings-Isaiah and Kings-Jeremiah Recensions* (BZAW, 252; Berlin: W. de Gruyter, 1997).

—'II Kings 18–20 and Isaiah 36–39: A Text Critical Case Study in the Redaction History of the Book of Isaiah', *ZAW* 111 (1999), pp. 373-79.

Petrie, W.M.F., *Tell el Hesy (Lachish)* (London: Palestine Exploration Fund, 1891).

Pongratz-Leisten, Beate, K. Deller and E. Bleibtreu, 'Götterstreitwagen und Götterstandarten: Götter auf dem Feldzug und ihr Kult im Feldlager', *Baghdader Mitteilungen* 23 (1992), pp. 291-356.

Pongratz-Leisten, Beate, *ina šulmi īrub. Die kulttopographische und ideologische Programmatik der akītu-Prozession in Babylonien und Assyrien im 1. Jahrtausend v. Chr.* (Baghdader Forschungen, 16; Mainz: Philipp von Zabern, 1994).

Pritchard, James B., *Ancient Near East in Pictures* (Princeton: Princeton University Press, 1954).

Pritchard, James B. (ed.), *Ancient Near Eastern Texts relating to the Old Testament* (with Supplement; Princeton: Princeton University Press, 3rd edn, 1969).

Provan, Iain W., *Hezekiah and the Books of Kings: A Contribution to the Debate about the Composition of the Deuteronomistic History* (BZAW, 172; Berlin/New York: W. de Gruyter, 1988).

—'In the Stable with the Dwarves: Testimony, Interpretation, Faith and the History of Israel', in André Lemaire and Magne Saebø (ed.), *Congress Volume: Oslo 1998* (VTSup, 80; Leiden: E.J. Brill, 2000), pp. 281-319.

Rainey, Anson F., 'Taharqa and Syntax', *TA* 3 (1976), pp. 38-41.

—'Hezekiah's Reform and the Altars at Beer-sheba and Arad', in Michael D. Coogan, Cheryl J. Exum and Lawrence E. Stager (eds.), *Scripture and Other Artifacts: Essays on the Bible and Archaeology in Honor of Philip J. King* (Louisville, KY: Westminster/John Knox Press, 1994), pp. 333-54.

Rawlinson, George, *The History of Herodotus: A New English Edition* (London: John Murray, 1858–60).

—*The Five Great Monarchies of the Ancient Eastern World: The Second Monarchy: Assyria* (4 vols.; London: John Murray, 1864).

Rawlinson, Henry C., *A Commentary on the Cuneiform Inscriptions of Babylonia and Assyria* (London: J.W. Parker, 1850).

—'Outlines of Assyrian History, Collected from the Cuneiform Inscriptions; *XXIVth Annual Report of the Royal Asiatic Society (1852)*, pp. XV-XLVI.

Reade, J.E., 'Two Slabs from Sennacherib's Palace', *Iraq* 29 (1967), pp. 42-48.

—'The Neo-Assyrian Court and Army: Evidence from the Sculptures', *Iraq* 34 (1972), pp. 87-122.

—'Assyrian Architectural Decoration: Techniques and Subject-Matter', *Baghdader Mitteilungen* 10 (1979), pp. 17-49.

—'Narrative Composition in Assyrian Sculpture', *Baghdader Mitteilungen* 10 (1979), pp. 52-110.

—'Ideology and Propaganda in Assyrian Art', in Mogens Trolle Larsen (ed.), *Power and Propaganda: A Symposium on Ancient Empires* (Mesopotamia, 7: Copenhagen: Akademisk Forlag, 1979), pp. 329-43.

—'Space, Scale and Significance in Assyrian Art', *Baghdader Mitteilungen* 11 (1980), pp. 71-74.

—'The Architectural Context of Assyrian Sculpture', *Baghdader Mitteilungen* 11 (1980), pp. 75-87.

—'Neo-Assyrian Monuments in their Historical Context', in F.M. Fales (ed.), *Neo-Assyrian Royal Inscriptions: New Horizons in Literary, Ideological, and Historical Analysis (Papers of a Symposium Held in Cetona [Siena] June 26-28, 1980)* (Rome: Istituto per l'Oriente, 1981), pp. 143-68.

—'Kronprinz', RlA VI/3-4 (1982), pp. 249-50.

—Review of *Sennacherib's Palace without Rival at Nineveh* (Chicago: Chicago University Press, 1991), by J.M. Russell, *ZA* 84 (1994), pp. 303-304.

—*Assyrian Sculpture* (London: British Museum, 2nd edn, 1998 [1983]).

—'Assyrian Illustrations of Nineveh', *Iranica Antiqua* 33 (1998; David Stronach Festschrift), pp. 81-94.

—'Restructuring the Assyrian Sculptures', in R. Dittmann, *et al.* (eds.), *Variatio Delectat: Iran und der Westen* (Gedenkschrift für Peter Calmeyer; AOAT, 272; Münster: Ugarit-Verlag, 2000), pp. 607-25.

Redford, Donald B., *Pharaonic King-Lists, Annals and Day-Books: A Contribution to the Study of the Egyptian Sense of History* (Society for the Study of Egyptian Antiquities Publication 4; Mississauga, Ontario: Benben Publications, 1986).

—*Egypt, Canaan, and Israel in Ancient Times* (Princeton, NJ: Princeton University Press, 1992).

—'Taharqa in Western Asia and Libya', *Eretz-Israel* 24 [1993], pp. 188*-91*.

—'A Note on the Chronology of Dynasty 25 and the Inscription of Sargon II at Tang-i Var', *Or* 68 (1999), pp. 58-60.

Regan, G., *Geoffrey Regan's Book of Military Blunders* (London: Deutsch, 2001).

Reich, Ronny and Baruch Brandl, 'Gezer under Assyrian Rule', *PEQ* 117 (January–June 1985), pp. 41-54.

Rescher, N., *The Coherence Theory of Truth* (Oxford: Clarendon Press, 1973).

Roberts, J.J.M., review of *Isaiah and the Deliverance of Jerusalem* (JSOTSup, 13; Sheffield: Sheffield Academic Press, 1980), by R. Clements, in *JBL* 101 (1982), pp. 442-44.

Rofé, Alexander, *The Prophetical Stories: The Narratives about the Prophets in the Hebrew Bible: Their Literary Types and History* (Jerusalem: Magnes Press, 1988).

Rogers, Robert William, 'Sennacherib and Judah', in Karl Marti (ed.), *Studien zur semitischen Philologie und Religionsgeschichte: Julius Wellhausen zum siebzigsten Geburtstag* (BZAW, 27; Giessen: Alfred Töpelmann, 1914), pp. 317-28.

—*Cuneiform Parallels to the Old Testament* (New York: Eaton & Mains, 1912).

Rogerson, John and Philip R. Davies, 'Was the Siloam Tunnel Built by Hezekiah?', *BA* 59 (1996), pp. 138-49.

Röllig, Wolfgang, 'Nitokris von Babylon', in Ruth Stiehl and Hans Erich Stier (eds.), *Beiträge zur alten Geschichte und deren Nachleben: Festschrift für Franz Altheim* (Berlin: W. de Gruyter, 1969), I, pp. 127-35.

—'Zur Typologie und Entstehung der babylonischen und assyrischen Königslisten', in M. Dietrich and W. Röllig (eds.), *lišan mithurti* (Festschrift W. von Soden: AOAT, 1; Neukirchen–Vluyn: Neukirchener Verlag, 1969), pp. 265-77.

Rosenberg, Stephen, 'The Siloam Tunnel Revisited', *TA* 25 (1998), pp. 116-30.

Rowley, H.H., 'Hezekiah's Reform and Rebellion', in *Men of God: Studies in Old Testament History and Prophecy* (London: Thomas Nelson and Sons, 1963), pp. 98-132 (earlier published in *BJRL* 44 [1961–62], pp. 395-461).

Rudman, Dominic, 'Is the Rabshakeh also among the Prophets? A Rhetorical Study of 2 Kings xviii 17-35', *VT* 50 (2000), pp. 100-10.

Ruprecht, Eberhard, 'Die ursprüngliche Komposition der Hiskia-Jesaja Erzählungen und ihre Umstrukturierung durch den Verfasser des deuteronomistischen Geschichtswerkes', *ZTK* 87 (1990), pp. 33-66.

Russell, John Malcolm, *Sennacherib's Palace without Rival at Nineveh* (Chicago: University of Chicago Press, 1991).

—'Sennacherib's Lachish Narratives', in P.J. Holliday (ed.), *Narrative and Event in Ancient Art* (Cambridge Studies in New Art History and Criticism; Cambridge: Cambridge University Press, 1993), pp. 55-73.

—'Layard's Descriptions of Rooms on the Southwest Palace at Nineveh', *Iraq* 57 (1995), pp. 71-85.

—'Sennacherib's Palace without a Rival Revisited: Excavations at Nineveh and in the British Museum Archieves', in Simo Parpola and R.M. Whiting (eds.), *Assyria 1995: Proceedings of the 10th Anniversary Symposium of the Neo-Assyrian Text Corpus Project* (Helsinki: The Neo-Assyrian Text Corpus Project, 1997), pp. 295-306.

—*The Final Sack of Nineveh: The Discovery, Documentation, and Destruction of Sennacherib's Throne Room at Nineveh, Iraq* (New Haven, CT: Yale University Press, 1998).

—*The Writing on the Wall: Studies in the Architectural Context of Late Assyrian Palace Inscriptions* (Mesopotamian Civilizations, 9; Winona Lake, IN: Eisenbrauns, 1999).

Saggs, H.W.F., 'The Nimrud Letters, 1952—Part I', *Iraq* 17 (1955), pp. 21-56.

—'The Nimrud Letters, 1952—Part II', *Iraq* 17 (1955), pp. 126-60.

—'The Nimrud Letters, 1952—Part III', *Iraq* 18 (1956), pp. 40-56 + plates 9-12.

—'Historical Texts and Fragments of Sargon II of Assyria', *Iraq* 37 (1975), pp. 11-20.

Šanda, Albert, *Die Bücher der Könige übersetzt und erklärt* 2 (EHAT, 9; Münster: Aschendorf, 1912).

Schipper, B.U., *Israel und Ägypten in der Königszeit: Die kulturellen Kontakte von Salomo bis zum Fall Jerusalems* (OBO, 170: Freiburg: Universitätsverlag; Göttingen: Vandenhoeck & Ruprecht, 1999).

Schnabel, Paul, *Berossos und die babylonisch-hellenistische Literatur* (Leipzig: Teubner, 1923).

Schrader, Eberhard, *The Cuneiform Inscriptions and the Old Testament* (trans. O.C. Whitehouse; 2 vols.; London: Williams and Norgate, 1885–88); (ET of *Die Keilinschriften und das Alte Testament* [Giessen: J. Ricker, 2nd edn, 1883]).

Schramm, Wolfgang, 'War Semiramis assyrische Regentin?' *Historia* 21 (1972), pp. 513-21.

—*Einleitung in die assyrischen Königsinschriften* (HdO I, V, I/2; Leiden: E.J. Brill, 1973).

Seger, Joe, E. and Oded Borowski, 'Ḥalif, Tel', *NEAEHL*, II, pp. 553-60.

Seitz, Christopher R., *Zion's Final Destiny: The Developments of the Book of Isaiah, A Reassessment of Isaiah 36–38* (Philadelphia: Fortress Press, 1991).

—'Account A and the Annals of Sennacherib: A Reassessment', *JSOT* 58 (1993), pp. 47-57.

Sethe, Kurt, *Sesostris* (Untersuchungen zur Geschichte und Altertumskunde Aegyptens 2/1; Leipzig: Hinrichs, 1900).

Shargel, B.R., 'The Evolution of the Masada Myth', *Judaism* 28 (1979), pp. 357-71.

Shea, William H., 'Sennacherib's Second Palestinian Campaign', *JBL* 104 (1985), pp. 410-18.

—'The New Tirhakah Text and Sennacherib's Second Palestinian Campaign', *AUSS* 35 (1997), pp. 181-87.

—'Jerusalem under Siege: Did Sennacherib Attack Twice?', *BARev* 26/6 (Nov/Dec 1999), pp. 36-44, 64.

Sherwin-White, Susan and Amélie Kuhrt, *From Samarkhand to Sardis: A New Approach to the Seleucid Empire* (London: Gerald Duckworth, 1993).

Silberman, N.A., *A Prophet from Amongst You. The Life of Yigael Yadin: Soldier, Scholar, and Mythmaker of Modern Israel* (Reading, MA: Addison-Wesley Publishing Co., 1993).

Smelik, Klaas A.D., 'King Hezekiah Advocates True Prophecy: Remarks on Isaiah xxxvi and xxxvii//II Kings xviii and xix', in K.A.D. Smelik, *Converting the Past: Studies in Ancient Israelite and Moabite Historiography* (OTS, 28; Leiden: Brill, 1992), pp. 93-128.

Soggin, J.A., *An Introduction to the History of Israel and Judah: Second, Completely Revised and Updated Edition* (London: SCM Press, 1993).

Spalinger, A., 'The Year 712 B.C. and its Implications for Egyptian History', *JARCE* 10 (1973), pp. 95-101.

—'The Foreign Policy of Egypt Preceding the Assyrian Conquest', *Chronique d'Égypte* 53 (1978), pp. 22-47.

Spieckermann, H., *Juda unter Assur in der Sargonidenzeit* (FRLANT, 129; Göttingen: Vandenhoeck & Ruprecht, 1982).

Stade, Bernhard, 'Miscellen. 16. Anmerkungen zu 2 Kö. 15-21', *ZAW* 6 (1886), pp. 156-89.

Stager, Lawrence E., 'The Impact of the Sea Peoples in Canaan (1185–1050 BCE)', in Levy (ed.), *The Archaeology of Society in the Holy Land*, pp. 332-48.

Starkey, J.L., 'Excavations at Tell ed Duweir', *PEQ* 69 (1937), pp. 228-41.

—'Lachish as Illustrating Bible History', *PEQ* 69 (1937), pp 171-79.

Stern, Ephraim, *Archaeology of the Land of the Bible. II. The Assyrian, Babylonian, and Persian Periods (732–332 B.C.E.)* (The Anchor Bible Reference Library; New York: Doubleday, 2001).

—'Zafit, Tel', *NEAEHL*, IV, pp. 1522-24.

—'Azekah', *NEAEHL*, I, pp. 123-24.

—'Azekah', in Meyers (ed.), *The Oxford Encyclopedia of Archaeology in the Near East*, p. 243.

Stern, Ephraim (ed.), *The New Encyclopedia of Archaeological Excavations in the Holy Land* (4 vols.; New York: Simon & Schuster; Jerusalem: Israel Exploration Society, 1992).

Stern, M., *Greek and Latin Authors on Jews and Judaism* (Jerusalem: The Israel Academy of Sciences and Humanities, 1976).

Stohlmann, S., 'The Judean Exile after 701 B.C.E'., in W.W. Hallo, J.C. Moyer and L.G. Perdue (eds.), *Scripture in Context. II. More Essays on the Comparative Method* (Winona Lake, IN: Eisenbrauns, 1983), pp. 147-75.

Streck, Maximilian, *Assurbanipal und die letzten assyrischen Könige bis zum Untergange Nineveh's* (Leipzig: Hinrichs, 1916).

Stuhlmueller, Carroll, Review of Clements, *Isaiah and the Deliverance of Jerusalem*, *CBQ* 43 (1981), pp. 273-75.

Sweeney, Marvin A. *Isaiah 1–39 with an Introduction to Prophetic Literature* (FOTL, 16; Grand Rapids, MI: Eerdmans, 1996).

Tadmor, Hayim, 'The Campaigns of Sargon II of Assur: A Chronological-Historical Study', *JCS* 12 (1958), pp. 22-40, 77-100.

—*Introductory Remarks to a New Edition of the Annals of Tiglath-Pileser III* (PIASH 2,9: Jerusalem: Israel Academy of Sciences and Humanities, 1969).

—'Rab-saris and Rab-shakeh in 2 Kings 18', in Carol L. Meyers and M. O'Connor (eds.), *The Word of the Lord Shall Go Forth: Essays in Honor of David Noel Freedman in Celebration of his Sixtieth Birthday* (Winona Lake, IN: Eisenbrauns, 1983), pp. 279-86.

—'Sennacherib's Campaign to Judah: Historical and Historiographical Considerations', *Zion* 50 (Jubilee volume) (1985), pp. 65-80 (Heb.).

—*The Inscriptions of Tiglath-Pileser III King of Assyria: Critical Edition, with Introductions, Translations and Commentary* (Jerusalem: Israel Academy of Sciences and Humanities, 1994).

—'History and Ideology in the Assyrian Royal Inscriptions', in F.M. Fales (ed.), *Assyrian 'Royal Inscriptions: New Horizons* (OAC, 17; Rome, 1981).

—'World Dominion: The Expansion Horizon of the Assyrian Empire', in L. Martino, S. de Martino, F.M. Faeds and G.B. Laufrauchi (eds.), *Landscapes, Territories Frontiers amd Horizons in the Ancient Near East* (Part I, History of the Ancient Near East/Monographs III/1; Padova: Sargon srl, 1999), pp. 54-62.

Tadmor, Hayim and M. Cogan, מאירועי שנת ארבע־עשרה לחזקיהו: מחלת המלך וביקור המשלחת הבבלית ('Hezekiah's Fourteenth Year: The King's Illness and the Babylonian Embassy'), *Eretz-Israel* 16 (1982), pp. 198-201 (Eng. abstract 258*-59*).

Tertel, H.J., *Text and Transmission: An Empirical Model for the Literary Development of Old Testament Narratives* (Berlin: W. de Gruyter, 1994).

Thompson, R.C. 'A Selection from the Cuneiform Historical Texts from Nineveh', *Iraq* 7 (1940), pp. 85-131.

Thompson, Thomas L., *The Historicity of the Patriarchal Narratives: The Quest for the Historical Abraham* (BZAW, 133: Berlin/New York: W. de Gruyter, 1974).

Thornley, George (transl.), revised and augmented by J.M. Edmonds, *Daphnis and Chloe by Longus*.

Thronveit, Mark A., *When Kings Speak: Royal Speech and Royal Prayer in Chronicles* (SBLDS, 93; Atlanta: Scholars Press, 1987).

Timm, Stefan, *Moab zwischen den Mächten: Studien zu historischen Denkmälern und Texten* (ÄAT, 17; Wiesbaden: Harrosowitz, 1989).

Toorn, Karel van der, 'The Babylonian New Year Festival: New Insights from the Cuneiform Texts and their Bearing on Old Testament Study', in John A. Emerton (ed.), *Congress Volume: Leuven 1989* (VTSup, 43; Leiden: E.J. Brill, 1991), pp. 331-39.

Tufnell, Olga, *et al.* (eds.), *Lachish III: The Iron Age* (Oxford: Oxford University Press, 1953).

Turner, E.G., *et al.* (eds.), *The Oxyrhynchus Papyri, Part XXVII* (London: Egypt Exploration Society, 1962).

Turner, G., 'The State Appartments of Late Assyrian Palaces', *Iraq* 32 (1970), pp. 177-213.

Tushingham, A.D., 'New Evidence Bearing on the Two-Winged *LMLK* Stamp', *BASOR* 287 (1992), pp. 61-65.

Uehlinger, Christoph, ' "Zeichne eine Stadt...und belagere sie!" Bild und Wort in einer Zeichenhandlung Ezechiels gegen Jerusalem', in M. Küchler and Christoph Uehlinger (eds.), *Jerusalem: Texte—Steine—Bilder* (Othmar and Hildi Keel-Leu Festschrift; Novum Testamentum et Orbis Antiquus, 6; Fribourg: University Press; Göttingen: Vandenhoeck & Ruprecht, 1987), pp. 109-200.

—'Drachen und Drachenkämpfe im alten Vorderen Orient und in der Bibel', in B. Schmelz and R. Vossen (eds.), *Auf Drachenspuren. Ein Buch zum Drachenprojekt des*

Hamburgischen Museums für Völkerkunde (Bonn: Holos, 1995), pp. 55-101.

—'Anthropomorphic Cult Statuary in Iron Age Palestine and the Search for Yahweh's Cult Images', in K. van der Toorn (ed.), *The Image and the Book: Iconic Cults, Aniconism, and the Veneration of the Holy Book in Israel and the Ancient Near East* (Contributions to Biblical Exegesis and Theology, 21; Leuven: Peeters, 1997), pp. 97-156.

—'Bildquellen und "Geschichte Israels": grundsätzliche Überlegungen und Fallbeispiele', in Christoph Hardnneier (ed.), *Steine—Bilder—Texte: Historische Evidenz außerbiblischer und biblischer Quellen* (Arbeiten zur Bibel und ihrer Geschichte, 5; Leipzig: Evangelische Verlagsanstalt, 2001), pp. 25-77.

Ungnad, A., 'Die Zahl der von Sanherib deportierten Judäer', *ZAW* 59 (1943), pp. 199-202.

Ussishkin, David, 'Royal Judean Storage Jars and Private Seal Impressions', *BASOR* 223 (1976), pp. 6-11.

—'The Destruction of Lachish by Sennacherib and the Dating of the Royal Judean Storage Jars', *TA* 4 (1977), pp. 28-60.

—'The Excavations at Tel Lachish—1973–1977, Preliminary Report', *TA* 5 (1978), pp. 1-97.

—'The "Camp of the Assyrians" in Jerusalem', *IEJ* 29 (1979), pp. 137-42.

—'The "Lachish Reliefs" and the City of Lachish', *IEJ* 30 (1980), pp. 174-95.

—*The Conquest of Lachish by Sennacherib* (Publications of the Institute of Archaeology, 6; Tel Aviv: Tel Aviv University, 1982).

—'Excavations at Tel Lachish—1978–1983, Second Preliminary Report', *TA* 10 (1983), pp. 97-175.

—'The Assyrian Attack on Lachish: The Archaeological Evidence from the Southwest Corner of the Site', *TA* 17 (1990), pp. 53-86.

—'The Water Systems of Jerusalem during Hezekiah's Reign', in Manfred Weippert and Stefan Timm (eds.), *Meilenstein* (Herbert Donner Festschrift; Ägypten und Altes Testament, 30; Wiesbaden: Harrassowitz, 1995), pp. 289-307.

—'Excavations and Restoration Work at Tel Lachish 1985–1994: Third Preliminary Report', *TA* 23 (1996), pp. 3-60.

—'Lachish', *ABD* IV, pp. 114-26.

—'Lachish', *NEAEHL* III, pp. 897-911.

Van Ruiten, J. and M. Vervenne (eds.), *Studies in the Books of Isaiah: Festschrift William A.M. Beuken* (BETL, 132 Leuevn: Leuven University Press, 1997).

Van Seters, John, *Abraham in History and Tradition* (New Haven: Yale, 1975).

—*In Search of History: Historiography in the Ancient World and the Origins of Biblical History* (New Haven/London: Yale University Press, 1983).

—'Creative Imitation in the Hebrew Bible', *SR* 29 (2000), pp. 395-409.

Vaughn, Andrew G., *Theology, History, and Archaeology in the Chronicler's Account of Hezekiah* (ABS 4; Atlanta: Scholars Press, 1999).

Vermeylen, J., 'Hypothèses sur l'origine d'Isaïe 36–39', in J. van Ruiten and M. Vervenne (eds.), *Studies in the Book of Isaiah: Festschrift Willem A.M. Beuken* (Bibliotheca Ephemeridum Theologicarum Lovaniensium, 132; Leuven: Peeters/University Press, 1997), pp. 95-118.

Villard, P., 'La représentation des paysages de montagne à l'époque néo-assyrienne', in A. Serandour (ed.), *Des Sumériens aux Romains d'Orient. La perception géographique du monde* (Antiquités Sémitiques, II; Paris: J. Maisonneuve, 1997), pp. 41-58.

Vilnay, Z., 'Pictures of Jerusalem and its Holy Places', *Eretz-Israel* 6 (1960), pp. 149-61.

Vogt, E., *Der Aufstand Hiskias und der Belagerung Jerusalems 701 v. Chr.* (AnBib, 106: Rome: Biblical Institute Press, 1986).

Voigtlander, E.N. von, *The Behistun Inscription of Darius the Great: Babylonian Version*

(Corpus Inscriptionum Iranicarum, Part I: Inscriptions of Ancient Iran, Vol. II: The Babylonian Versions of the Achaemenian Inscriptions, Texts I; London: Humphries, 1978).

Waddell, W.G., *Manetho* (LCL; London: Heinemann; Cambridge, MA: Harvard University Press, 1940).

Wäfler, M., *Nicht-Assyrer neuassyrischer Darstellung* (AOAT, 26; Neukirchen–Vluyn: Neukirchener Verlag, 1975).

Walcot, Peter, 'The Comparative Study of Ugaritic and Greek Literatures', *UF* 1 (1969), pp. 111-18; 2 (1970), pp. 273-75; 4 (1972), pp. 129-32.

Weidner, E.F., 'Šwawilkan(ha)ni, König von Mus??ri, ein Zeitgenosse Sargons II', *AfO* 14 (1941/44) **.

Weinfeld, Moshe, 'Cult Centralization in Israel in the Light of a Neo-Babylonian Analogy', *JNES* 23 (1964), pp. 202-12.

Weippert, Helga, *Palästina in vorhellenistischer Zeit* (HdA, Vorderasien 2, Band 1; Munich: Beck, 1988).

Weissbach, F.H., *Die Keilinschriften der Achämeniden* (VAB, 3; Leipzig: Hinrichs, 1911; reprinted Leipzig: Zentral-Antiquariat der DDR, 1968).

—'Sardanapal', in Georg Wissowa and Wilhelm Kroll (eds.), *Paulys Real-Encyclopädie der classischen Altertumswissenschaft* (Stuttgart: J.B. Metzlersche Verlagbuchhandlung, 1920), 2ter Reihe (R-Z), I, cols. 2436-75.

Wellhausen, Julius, *Prolegomena to the History of Israel* (trans. J. S. Black and A. Menzies, with a preface by W. Robertson Smith; Edinburgh: Adam and Charles Black, 1885); (ET of *Prolegomena zur Geschichte Israels* [2 vols.; Berlin: G. Reimer, 1878]).

Welten, Peter, *Die Königs-Stempel: Ein Beitrag zum Militärpolitik Judas unter Hiskia und Josia* (Abhandlungen der Deutschen Pälastina-Vereins; Wiesbaden: Harrassowitz, 1969).

—*Geschichte und Geschichtsdarstellung in den Chronikbüchern* (WMANT 42; Neukirchen–Vluyn: Neukirchener Verlag, 1973).

West, M.L., *Early Greek Philosophy and the Orient* (Oxford: Clarendon Press, 1971).

—*The East Face of Helicon: West Asiatic Elements in Greek Poetry and Myth* (Oxford: Clarendon Press, 1997).

Wightman, G.J., 'The Date of Bethshemesh Stratum II', *AbrN* 28 (1990), pp. 96-126.

Wildberger, Hans, *Jesaja. 3. Jesaja 28-39* (BKAT X/3; Neukirchen–Vluyn: Neukirchener Verlag, 1982).

Williamson, Hugh G.M., *Israel in the Books of Chronicles* (Cambridge: Cambridge University Press, 1977).

—*The Book Called Isaiah: Deutero-Isaiah's Role in Composition and Redaction* (Oxford: Oxford University Press, 1995).

—'Hezekiah and the Temple', in Michael V. Fox, *et al.* (eds.), *Texts, Temples, and Traditions: A Tribute to Menahem Haran* (Winona Lake, IN: Eisenbrauns, 1996), pp. 47-52.

Winter, Irene J., 'Royal Rhetoric and the Development of Historical Narrative in Neo-Assyrian Reliefs', *Studies in Visual Communication* 7/2 (1981), pp. 2-38.

—'Art in Empire: The Royal Image and the Visual Dimensions of Assyrian Ideology', in S. Parpola and R.M. Whiting (eds.), *Assyria 1995: Proceedings of the 10th Anniversary Symposium of the Neo-Assyrian Text Corpus Project* (Helsinki: The Neo-Assyrian Text Corpus Project, 1997), pp. 359-81.

Wood, Michael, *In Search of the Trojan War* (London: Guild Publishing, 1985).

Wright, G. Ernest, review of *Lachish III: The Iron Age* (Oxford: Oxford University Press, 1953) by O. Tufnell, in *JNES* 14 (1955), pp. 188-89.

—Review of *Lachish III: The Iron Age* (Oxford: Oxford University Press, 1953) by O. Tufnell, in *VT* 5 (1955), pp. 97-105.

Wright, G.R.H., *Ancient Buildings in South Syria and Palestine* (HdO, 7 Abt., Bd. 1/2 Abschnitt B, Lfg 3; Leiden: E.J. Brill, 1985).

Yadin, Yigael, *The Art of Warfare in Biblical Lands, in Light of Archaeological Study* (2 vols.; New York: McGraw-Hill, 1963).

Yamada, Shigeo, *The Construction of the Assyrian Empire: A Historical Study of the Inscriptions of Shalmaneser III (859–824 BC) Relating to his Campaigns to the West* (CHANE 3; Leiden: E.J. Brill, 2000).

Yanai, Eli, 'A Late Bronze Age Gate at Gezer?' *TA* 21 (1994), pp. 283-87.

Yanker, R.W., 'Ramat Rahel', *ABD*, V, pp. 615-16.

Yeivin, Shmuel, ''Erani, Tel', *NEAEHL*, II, pp. 417-19.

Younger, K.L., 'Sargon's Campaign against Jerusalem—A Further Note', *Bib* 77 (1996), pp. 108-10.

—'The Deportations of the Israelites', *JBL* 117 (1998), pp. 201-27.

—'Sargon II', in W.W. Hallo (ed.), *The Context of Scripture*. II. *Monumental Inscriptions from the Biblical World* (Leiden: E.J. Brill, 2000).

Yurco, Frank J., 'Sennacherib's Third Campaign and the Coregency of Shabaka and Shebitku', *Serapis* 6 (1980), pp. 221-40.

—'The Shabaka-Shebitku Coregency and the Supposed Second Campaign of Sennacherib against Judah: A Critical Assessment', *JBL* 110 (1991), pp. 35-45.

Zadok, Ran, 'Geographical and Onomastic Notes', *JANES* 8 (1976), pp. 113-26.

—*Geographical Names according to New- and Late-Babylonian Texts* (Répertoire Géographique des Textes Cunéiformes, Band 8; Beihefte zum Tübinger Atlas des Vorderen Orients, Reihe B Nr. 7/8; Wiesbaden: Reichert, 1985).

Zagorin, Perez, 'History, the Referent, and the Narrative: Reflectons on Postmodernism Now', *History and Theory* 38 (1999), pp. 1-24.

—'Rejoinder to a Postmodernist', *History and Theory* 39 (2000), pp. 201-209.

Zawadzki, Stefan, *The Fall of Assyria and the Median-Babylonian Relations in Light of the Nabopolassar Chronicle* (Poznan: Adam Mickiewicz University Press; Delft: Eburon, 1988).

Zertal, A., 'The Heart of the Monarchy: Patterns of Settlement and Historical Considerations of the Israelite Kingdom of Samaria', in Amihai Mazar (ed.), *Studies in the Archaeology of the Iron Age in Israel and Jordan* (JSOTSup, 331; Sheffield: Sheffield Academic Press, 2001), pp. 38-64.

Zimhoni, Orna, 'The Iron Age Pottery of Tel 'Eton and its Relation to the Lachish, Tell Beit Mirsim and Arad Assemblages', *TA* 12 (1985), pp. 63-90.

Zorn, Jeffrey R., 'The Badè Institute of Biblical Archaeology', *BA* (1988), pp. 36-45.

—'William Frederic Badè', *BA* 51 (1988), pp. 28-35.

—'Estimating the Population Size of Ancient Settlements: Methods, Problems, Solutions, and a Case Study', *BASOR* 295 (1994), pp. 31-48.

—'Nasbeh, Tell en-', *NEAEHL*, III, pp. 1098-1102.

—'Nasbeh, Tell en-', in Meyers (ed.), *The Oxford Encyclopedia of Archaeology in the Near East*, IV, pp. 101-103.

INDEXES

INDEX OF REFERENCES

BIBLE

Old Testament

Joshua

7	110

Judges

1	163
10.10	81

1 Samuel

31	167

2 Samuel

8.18	215
24.17	81

1 Kings

8.14-61	215
10.27	242
12	316
14.25-26	203, 218
16	162
16.27	162

2 Kings

3	39, 153-55
12.18-19	203, 218
14.19	145
15.6-11	159
15.19-20	203, 218
15.21-26	159
15.29-30	158
15.31-36	159
16.5	203, 218
16.7-9	203, 218
17	83, 87
17.1	55
17.6	207
17.24	205-207, 211
18–20	24, 62-65, 312
18–19	28, 38, 39, 63, 85, 137, 151, 152, 203, 308, 319
18	55, 56, 59
18.1	29, 55
18.3	53
18.4	137, 218, 285
18.7-8	172
18.7	81, 84
18.8	70, 176
18.9-12	81, 83
18.9-10	31
18.9	216
18.10	55
18.13–19.37	20, 23, 34, 80, 168, 203, 312
18.13–19.9	212, 215, 216
18.13-16	20, 24, 25, 30, 33, 35, 40, 42, 55, 67, 80, 145, 151, 170, 172, 201, 203, 295, 308, 312, 318
18.13	20, 23, 24, 29, 52, 55, 58, 68, 69, 81, 202, 311
18.14-16	22, 23, 33, 36, 65, 68, 202, 203
18.14-15	85
18.14	67, 68, 182, 237
18.15-16	81
18.16-19	25
18.17–20.19	146
18.17–19.37	21, 24, 25, 35, 36, 39, 65, 69, 80, 82, 309, 312
18.17–19.36	170
18.17–19.9	23, 35, 42, 80, 201
18.17–19.8	23
18.17–19.7	24
18.17-37	202
18.19-25	218

2 Kings (cont.)

18.22	137, 218, 285
18.29-35	213
18.31-32	284
18.32-35	213
18.33-34	204-206, 213
18.34	204, 210, 211
18.36	82
19	137
19.1	214
19.4	82
19.6	82
19.7	80
19.8-37	24
19.8	237
19.9-37	23
19.9-35	35, 41, 201, 202, 204
19.9-20	201
19.9	23, 34-36, 59, 64, 99, 137, 146, 177
19.12-13	41, 204, 206-208
19.12	207, 209, 212
19.13	204, 207
19.16	82
19.17-18	41, 211
19.19-35	80
19.19	80
19.22	82
19.23	82
19.28	82
19.30-37	201
19.34	83
19.35-36	65
19.35	8, 34, 38, 69, 70, 82, 86, 136, 169, 181, 313
19.36-37	35, 80, 201, 212, 216
19.36	42, 99, 216
19.37	29, 82, 94, 201, 216
20.12-19	183
20.20	10
22.4	165
22.11-12	214
23.22	88
24.3	83
24.12	84
24.20	81
25	316
25.4	293
25.18	165
25.27-30	84
36.19	206

2 Chronicles

11.5-10	19
15.1-7	87
29–32	86-88
29–31	86
30.1-12	173
31.20	86
32	62
32.1-23	76, 85, 87, 168, 170
32.1	86-88
32.2-8	173
32.7-8	87
32.10	86
32.13	87
32.20	87
32.21	86
32.23	81
35.18	88
35.20	88
38.1-12	184

Ezra

7.1	165

Isaiah

1.7-9	149
3.18-24	237
10.5-19	29, 34
10.5-15	213
10.9	205, 210
14.4-21	34
20	30
21.1–22.14	34
22.11	293
36–39	34, 62, 146
36–37	38, 80, 81, 168, 170, 308, 312, 319
36	33
36.1-37.38	80
36.2-37.38	202
36.2	203, 237
36.19	204
37	137
37.8	237
37.9	146
37.36	38, 136, 313

Jeremiah

34.4	293
37–40	28
37–39	137
37.3	214
37.6-8	214
38.17-23	84
52.3	81

Ezekiel

4–5	233
5.5	233
17.11-21	84
17.16	81

Micah

1	83
1.14	14

Haggai

2.7-9	81

Talmuds
b. Pes.
119a   82

b. Sanh.
94a   88

Josephus
Ant.
8.10.3   132
10.1-23   76, 89
10.18-23   89

Apion
1.14   121
1.19   120
1.20   120

War
5.7.3   8
5.12.2   8
5.303   171
5.386-388 76, 89
5.387   171
5.404-408 76, 85, 89
5.404-407 171
5.405   82

Classical
Cicero
De oratore
2.9.36   161

Diodorus Siculus
2.1-20   122
2.2.2   122
2.7.1   122
2.7.3-4   122
2.7.3   122
2.15.2   122
2.17.1.2.20.3 122
2.24-28   123
14   180

48–52   180

Herodotus
The Histories
1.105   165
1.110   133
1.184   123
1.185   123
2.102-111 129
2.104   165
2.137-139 135
2.141   20, 119,
           134
2.150   123
3   126
3.5.91   165
3.30   126
3.61   126
3.62-63   126
3.64   126
3.65-66   127
3.67   127
3.68-69   127
3.70-75   127
3.76-79   127
3.80-88   127
3.141   171
3.150-159 127
4.39   165
7.89   165

Tacitus
Annals
2.60   134

Thucydides
1.64.1.3   180
2.70.1   180

Inscriptions
Rassam-cylinder
.32-58   65
.32-35   66

.39-41   66
.42-48   66
.42   66
.55-58   67
.56   68

Annals of Sennacherib II
15   182
37-III49   141
37-60   142
37-41   145
60-68   142
68-72   142
73-III17   144
82-III5   147
83   147

Annals of Sennacherib III
1   147
2   147
3   147
4   147
5   147
6   145
8   148
19-23   145
19   144
20   146
21   146
22   146
23   146
27-30   145
28   145
29   145
30   145
31-34   148
31   148
41-49   148
79-81   149

INDEX OF AUTHORS

Abraham, W.J. 61
Abush, T. 49
Ackroyd, P.R. 88, 203, 215
Aharoni, M. 13, 15, 18
Aharoni, Y. 6, 7, 9, 13, 15, 18, 223, 285
Ahlström, G.W. 6, 54, 57, 58, 68, 69, 160
Akenson, D.H. 105
Albenda, P. 242, 282
Albertini, L. 62
Albertz, R. 309, 310, 312, 314-16, 321
Albright, W.F. 7, 15, 24, 25, 31, 238
Alt, A. 163
Alter, R. 260
Amar, Z. 242, 243
Amit, Y. 87
Anbar, M. 204
Anderson, G. 125
Ankersmit, F.R. 61
Arnold, M. 106
Avi-Yonah, M. 4, 15
Ayalon, E. 15

Balcer, J.M. 126-28
Baltzer, D. 209
Barkay, G. 4, 5, 9
Barnett, R.D. 222, 225-27, 233-35, 240,
        243, 248, 249, 251, 256, 258, 267,
        268, 273, 279, 282, 285, 288, 289,
        294, 296, 297, 299-301, 305
Barstad, H.M. 165
Barth, H. 27, 217
Barthélemy, D. 204
Bates, R.D. 216
Baumgartner, W. 123, 135, 136, 171
Beaulieu, P.-A. 207, 209, 211
Becker, U. 146
Beckerath, J. von 171, 216
Becking, B. 30, 36, 46, 53, 54, 56, 58, 63,

        74, 124, 312, 314, 316, 317, 321
Ben Zvi, E. 19, 29, 36, 62, 79, 81-83,
        100, 113, 165, 207, 214, 218, 219,
        310, 312-16, 321
Berkeley, G. 71
Biran, A. 158
Black, J. 49
Bleibtreu, E. 222, 233, 235, 240, 243,
        251, 285, 288, 294, 296, 297, 299,
        301, 305
Blenkinsopp, J. 146
Borger, R. 35, 54, 59, 78, 186, 190, 194,
        197, 198
Börker-Klähn, J. 288
Borowski, O. 16
Bowra, C.M. 120
Brandl, B. 12, 14, 15
Braudel, F. 61, 274, 278
Braun, M. 132
Bright, J. 25, 31, 59
Brinkman, J.A. 48, 205, 211
Broshi, M. 14, 310
Brown, T.S. 121
Budge, E.A.W. 294
Bunimovitz, S. 13, 164
Burney, C.F. 204
Burstein, S.M. 120, 123

Calmeyer, P. 291
Camp, L. 53, 68, 70
Campbell, A.F. 120
Cathcart, K.J. 232
Cazelles, H. 54
Childs, B.S. 26-28, 62, 64, 68, 80, 119,
        153, 201, 202, 213, 215, 312
Clements, R.E. 26-28, 60, 64, 68, 80,
        136, 202, 217
Cogan, M. 30, 32, 56, 57, 60, 62, 65, 68,

70, 135, 136, 138, 143, 153, 206,
209, 211, 216, 295
Coles, R.A. 125
Cross, F.M. Jr. 5

Dalley, S. 209
Davies, G.I. 6
Davies, P.R. 10, 37, 104, 314, 316, 317,
322
De Odorico, M. 24, 33, 95, 182, 310
Dearman, A. 154
Deller, K. 288
Dessel, J.P. 9
Dever, W.G. 4, 11-13, 15, 60, 67
Dijkstra, M. 54, 56
Dion, P.E. 31, 36, 80, 216
Donner, H. 56, 148
Dougherty, R.P. 24
Driel, G. van 291
Driver, G.R. 206
Dyck, J.E. 89

Eddy, S.K. 122, 123
Edelman, D.V. 53, 75, 76, 223
Eilers, W. 124
Elayi, J. 92-94
Eph'al, I. 249
Eshel, H. 12
Evans, C.D. 59, 60
Evans, R.J. 61, 72
Eynikel, E. 217

Fales, F.M. 209
Farber, W. 291
Feldman, L.H. 89
Finkelstein, I. 3, 10-12, 145, 146, 164,
310, 311
Finkelstein, J.J. 47
Forrer, E. 209
Frahm, E. 35, 51, 52, 56, 59, 60, 65, 66,
70, 78, 93, 94, 144, 145, 148, 149,
169, 170, 186, 190, 192-94, 197,
198, 239-41, 294, 299, 300
Frame, G. 58, 74, 216
Fuchs, A. 56, 58, 59, 74, 205, 266

Gadd, C.J. 222, 230
Galil, G. 53-57, 70, 170

Gallagher, W.R. 29, 33, 34, 55, 57, 60,
63, 66, 68, 70, 78, 93, 94, 202, 223,
284, 301, 302
Galling, K. 242
Garfinkel, Y. 15, 19
Gaselee, S. 125
Gelb, I.J. 51
Gerardi, P. 239
Gibson, J.C.L. 154
Gibson, S. 14
Gill, D. 10
Goldberg, J. 30, 54, 57, 65, 67
Gonçalves, F.J. 28, 80, 201-203, 206,
207, 213, 216, 218
Gould, J. 126
Grabbe, L.L. 2, 38, 63, 116, 165, 171,
249, 313, 315, 319-21
Gray, J. 25, 26, 30, 206
Grayson, A.K. 48-51, 70, 85, 96, 124,
208-10, 319
Greenfield, J.C. 127
Gressmann, H. 242
Griffith, S.B. 182
Gunnewig, A.H.J. 70

Hackett, J.A. 10
Hägg, T. 125
Hallo, W.W. 34, 35, 320
Halpern, B. 141
Handlin, O. 61
Hardmeier, C. 27, 60, 62-64, 80, 146,
203, 207, 208, 210, 213, 312
Haslam, M.W. 125
Hayes, W.C. 130
Heinz, S.C. 278
Hendel, R.S. 10
Herion, G.A. 17
Herzog, Z. 3, 16-18
Hobbs, T.R. 19
Hodder, C.I. 227, 228, 230, 267, 271
Holladay, C.A. 125
Holladay, J.S. Jr 7
Holloway, S.W. 207, 208
Hölscher, L. 90, 102, 104
Honor, L.L. 24, 59
Hooker, P.K. 46
Horn, S.H. 31
Hrouda, B. 243, 288, 290, 291

Hulin, P. 53

Irvine, S.A. 54, 57

Jacoby, F. 120, 131
Jacoby, R. 261-65, 268, 273
Janssen, J.M.A. 25
Japhet, S. 86
Jenkins, A.K. 30, 57-59, 65, 74
Jenkins, K. 73
Jeppeson, K. 322
Jeremias, A. 23
Jones, G.W. 54

Kalimi, I. 88, 100
Kapera, Z. 58
Kautsky, K. 62
Keel, O. 222, 298
Kees, H. 129
Kelm, G.L. 12
Kent, R.G. 127
Kenyon, K.M. 7
Ketcham, K. 46
Keulen, P.S.F. van 217
Kislev, M. 242
Kitchen, K.A. 31, 32, 60, 137, 138
Kloner, A. 15
Knauf, E.A. 10, 14, 16, 18, 38, 46, 53, 61, 145, 309, 310, 318
Knoppers, G.N. 62
Kochavi, M. 17
König, F.W. 121, 124
Konkel, A.H. 201
Kooij, A. van der 9, 62, 63, 208
Kuan, J.K. 47, 54
Kuhrt, A. 120, 140
Kwasman, T. 185

Laato, A. 33, 48, 51, 57, 62, 63, 69, 70, 80, 119, 137, 139, 310
Lamprichs, R. 68, 70, 71, 142, 277
Lance, H.D. 6, 12
Langbell, K.S. 216
Lange, K. 129
Laqueur, R. 131
Lateiner, D. 126
Lawrence, A. 180
Layard, A.H. 8, 42, 57, 193, 194, 222,

225-27, 229-39, 244, 248, 252, 261, 267, 268, 271, 272, 278, 289, 290, 296, 298, 300, 304, 305
Lederman, Z. 13
Lee, T.G. 209, 212
Leeuwen, C. van 59, 62
Legendre, A. 242, 245
Lehmann-Haupt, C.F. 124
Lemche, N.P. 39, 150, 155, 157, 161, 167, 309, 312-15, 320, 322
Levine, L.D. 34, 74, 78
Levy, T.E. 4
Lewy, H. 124, 125
Lichtheim, M. 130
Liverani, M. 74, 90, 209
Lloyd, A.B. 129, 135
Loewenstamm, S.E. 210
Loftus, E.R. 46
Long, B.O. 202
Luckenbill, D.D. 34, 78, 98, 137, 141, 144, 148, 186, 190, 192-94, 197

Macadam, M.F.L. 25
Machinist, P. 213, 219, 220
Madhloom, T. 243, 266, 289, 290, 296, 305
Maeir, A. 284
Mannheim, K. 72
Manor, D.W. 17
Marcus, M.I. 236, 244
Margalith, O. 120
Martin, R. 76, 90
Matthiae, P. 224, 301
Mayer, W. 9, 35, 40, 57, 68, 146, 169, 170, 173, 175, 182, 209, 303, 309, 310
Mazar, A. 3, 4, 12, 19
Mazzoni, S. 244
McGovern, P.E. 167
McKenzie, S.L. 62, 213
Melville, S.C. 124
Menzel, B. 291
Meyers, E.M. 3
Millard, A.R. 47-49, 85, 169
Mitchell, T.C. 222
Mittmann, S. 13, 69
Mommsen, H. 5
Montgomery, J.A. 24, 160, 204

Moshkovitz, S. 18

Na'aman, N. 5, 6, 12-14, 16, 19, 28, 30,
    35, 41, 54, 56-58, 60, 62, 68-70, 74,
    84, 93, 137, 144, 173, 198, 205,
    211, 218, 219, 284-86, 309, 312,
    313, 315, 316, 319, 322
Naveh, J. 158
Niehr, H. 316, 323
Nilsson, M.P. 120
Noort, E. 56, 57, 68, 70
Norin, S. 10
Noth, M. 25, 238, 319

Oded, B. 33, 91, 139, 293, 294, 310, 311
Oppenheim, A.L. 28, 50
Orlinsky, H.M. 204

Page, D.L. 120
Parker, S.B. 53
Parpola, S. 29, 216, 266
Parrot, A. 25
Paterson, A. 179, 194, 197, 221, 288
Perlman, I. 5
Perry, B.E. 125
Person, R.E. 201-204
Petrie, W.M.F. 245, 246
Pongratz-Leisten, B. 288, 291, 292
Porten, B. 127
Pritchard, J.B. 34, 222
Provan, I.W. 27, 62, 80

Rainey, A.F. 16, 18, 31, 32
Rawlinson, G. 20-22, 169
Rawlinson, H.C. 21, 59, 169
Reade, J.E. 221, 224, 236, 248, 262, 266,
    275, 282, 288, 298
Redford, D.B. 32, 60, 68, 74, 131, 132,
    138, 144, 147, 163, 216, 217
Regan, G. 147
Reich, R. 12
Rescher, N. 61
Roberts, J.J.M. 27, 136
Rofé, A. 135, 213, 216
Rogers, R.W. 21, 23
Rogerson, J. 10, 23
Röllig, W. 49, 124
Rosenberg, S. 10

Rowley, H.H. 26, 30, 68
Rudman, D. 29, 81, 85, 213
Ruprecht, E. 62, 202
Russell, J.M. 94, 95, 98, 179, 223-27,
    239-41, 251, 262, 264-66, 273-75,
    288, 294, 296, 297, 299, 300, 304,
    305

Saggs, H.W.F. 26, 205, 249
Šanda, A. 201, 204, 206, 210
Schipper, B.U. 142, 143, 146
Schnabel, P. 121
Schrader, E. 21-23
Schramm, W. 54, 124
Seger, J.E. 16
Seitz, C.R. 32, 67, 80, 83, 202, 216, 310
Seters, J. van 47-49, 51, 55, 63, 68, 78,
    90, 163
Sethe, K. 129
Shargel, B.R. 260
Shea, W.H. 31, 32, 59, 62, 74, 138
Sherwin-White, S. 140
Silberman, N.A. 3, 260
Smelik, K.A.D. 29, 33, 55, 60, 63, 64, 68,
    202
Smith, M. 37, 106-10, 116, 322
Soden, W. von 183
Soggin, J.A. 55, 68, 70
Spalinger, A. 56, 217
Spieckermann, H. 60
Stade, B. 23, 24, 201, 312
Stager, L.E. 13
Starkey, J.L. 6, 7, 246, 255
Stern, E. 3, 4, 11, 13, 14, 19, 69
Stern, M. 104
Stohlmann, S. 62, 279
Streck, M. 208
Stuhlmueller, C. 27
Sweeney, M.A. 80, 201

Tadmor, H. 9, 30, 51, 53, 54, 56-58, 60,
    62, 68, 70, 79, 80, 91, 95, 135, 136,
    143, 153, 179, 205, 206, 209-11,
    216
Tertel, H.J. 60, 62, 66, 86
Thompson, R.C. 193
Thompson, T.L. 163, 315-18, 323
Thornley, G. 125

Thronveit, M.A. 215
Timm, S. 56, 58
Toorn, K. van der 49
Tufnell, O. 6, 7, 234, 246, 248, 258, 305
Turner, E.G. 125
Turner, G. 222, 226, 233, 235, 240, 243,
      251, 285, 288, 294, 296, 297, 299,
      301, 305
Tushingham, A.D. 5, 9

Uehlinger, C. 42, 222, 233, 269, 278,
      279, 291, 298, 310, 318
Ungnad, A. 24
Ussishkin, D. 5-8, 15, 17, 35, 42, 94, 176,
      178, 179, 221-23, 227, 242, 246,
      248-62, 264, 267, 268, 270-72, 275,
      279, 290, 293, 304, 305

Vaughn, A.G. 5, 6, 9, 19, 62
Vaux, R. de 238
Vermeylen, J. 80
Villard, P. 244
Vilnay, Z. 294
Von Rad, G. 108
Vogt, E. 55, 56, 58, 60, 62, 68, 69, 213
Voigtlander, E.N. von 127

Waddell, W.G. 121, 131, 132
Wäfler, M. 58, 62, 243, 279, 294
Walcot, P. 120

Weinfeld, M. 28
Weippert, H. 3, 4, 69, 180
Weissbach, F.H. 123, 127
Wellhausen, J. 22
Welten, P. 5, 160
West, M.L. 120
Wightman, G.J. 13
Wildberger, H. 206, 210
Williamson, H.G.M. 63, 88, 201, 215
Winckler, H. 57, 58
Winter, I.J. 277, 304
Wood, M. 120
Wright, G.E. 7
Wright, G.R.H. 180

Yadin, Y. 243, 248, 249, 252, 260, 262
Yamada, S. 209
Yanai, E. 12
Yeivin, S. 14
Yellin, J. 5
Younger, K.L. 54, 57, 58, 65
Younker, R.W. 9
Yurco, F.J. 31, 32, 74, 138

Zadok, R. 58, 205-207, 210, 211
Zagorin, P. 73, 76
Zawadzki, S. 208, 211
Zertal, A. 259
Zimhoni, O. 15, 18
Zorn, J.R. 11